LANGUAGE INSTRUCTION FOR STUDENTS WITH DISABILITIES

SECOND EDITION

EDWARD A. POLLOWAY
Lynchburg College, Virginia

TOM E. C. SMITH
University of Arkansas at Little Rock

LOVE PUBLISHING COMPANY®
Denver • London • Sydney

We dedicate this book to

James E. Smith, Jr.,

remembered as talented special educator,
professional colleague,
and
special friend.

Revised Printing, 2000
©Copyright 1992 Love Publishing Company
Printed in the U.S.A.
ISBN 0-89108-269-7
Library of Congress Catalog Card Number 99-73507

Contents

Preface   vii

PART ONE   LANGUAGE AND STUDENTS WITH DISABILITIES

1 The Development of Language   1

The Nature of Language, Communication, and Speech 2
Functions of Language 4
Major Elements of Language 4
The Rules of Language 7
Language Acquisition: Theoretical Perspectives 14
Developmental Milestones 24

2 Disabilities in Language Functioning   33

An Orientation 34
Classification of Language Disabilities 35
Severe Language Disabilities 38
Mild-Moderate Language Disabilities 51
Language Intervention Strategies 60

3 Cultural Diversity and Language Differences   67

Variables Affecting Special Education for Children from Minority Groups 68
Diversity in Society 68
Difference or Deficit? 70
Bilingualism 80
Teaching Implications 82
Instructional Approaches 88
Bilingual Education Materials 91
Guidelines and Teaching Strategies 91

PART TWO INSTRUCTIONAL PROGRAMMING

4   Principles of Assessment and Instruction   95
Edward A. Polloway and Loretta C. Jones

Assessment for Teaching   96
Purposes and Processes of Assessment   97
Cautions Relative to Assessment   99
Contemporary Assessment Models   101
Assessment Tools and Procedures   102
Individualized Education Programs   109
Developing Instructional Programs   114

5   Initial Language Skills: Verbal   133
Nikki L. Murdick

An Orientation to Instruction   135
Theories of Acquisition   137
Assessment Strategies   139
Programming   151
Instructional Approaches and Programs   160
Program Selection   164

6   Initial Language Skills: Nonverbal   171
Nikki L. Murdick

Definitions   172
Perspective on Acquisition   173
Assessment Strategies   176
Programming for Communication Development   180

7   Oral Language Skills   201

Nature of Oral Language   204
Assessing Oral Language Skills   205
Consequences of Oral Language Problems   216
Developing Oral Language Programs   218
Developing Instructional Activities   222
Developing a Language-Enriching Environment   232
Specific Intervention Activities   232
Personnel Involved in Language Intervention   234

8 | Reading: Nature and Assessment   239

Reading and Reading Difficulties   241
General Instructional Goals   243
Development of Reading   247
Assessment   261
Developing a Reading Program   274

9 | Reading: Instruction   283

Readiness   286
Word Recognition   288
Comprehension   318

10 | Handwriting Instruction   342

Trends   344
Nature of Handwriting   346
Sequence of Skills   347
Assessment of Handwriting   347
Remediating and Teaching Handwriting Skills   355

11 | Spelling Instruction   372
Mary Beirne-Smith and Beverly H. Thompson

English Orthography   373
Differences in Spellers   374
Development of Spelling Skills   375
Assessment   376
Instructional Approaches   386
Specific Instructional Strategies   398

12 | Written Expression   404

A Model for Written Language   406
Assessment   410
Instructional Strategies   422
Special Considerations   434

13 Adolescents and Language Disabilities 447

Nature of Adolescence 448
Characteristics of Adolescents with Disabilities 453
General Problems Facing Adolescents 455
School Demands Placed on Adolescents 458
Language Problems and Intervention with Adolescents 459
General Instructional Considerations with Adolescents 468
Specific Instructional Approaches 469
General School Survival Skills 472

Author Index 477
Subject Index 484

Preface

L anguage development and language skills have become increasingly recognized as critical concerns in the education of all children, and certainly those who experience disabilities. The substantial amount of research and programming in recent years reflects this growing emphasis. Exciting new developments have typified the work being done in the areas of oral language, reading, and written language. The second edition of this book reflects these new developments.

To present key concepts within the complex subject of language development and instruction for learners with special needs, we have divided this book into two major parts. The first, Language and Students with Disabilities, examines language in general terms, and the problems children have in developing language skills. Chapter 1 reviews language and language development, providing a foundation for the ensuing discussions of language characteristics and needs of learners with special needs. Chapter 2 presents a noncategorical survey of specific problems experienced by children identified as disabled, and Chapter 3 discusses the influences that cultural differences can have on language development and their implications for educators.

Part Two, Instructional Programming, examines teaching methodology and curriculum appropriate to various language skills. Chapter 4 focuses on principles of assessment and instruction. Chapters 5 and 6 concentrate on training strategies that are particularly useful for young children with disabilities or for individuals who have severe disabilities and may not have spontaneously developed early language skills; those chapters cover verbal and nonverbal approaches, respectively. Chapter 7 discusses the further development of oral language skills. Chapters 8 and 9 are devoted to reading, both word analysis and comprehension; the former chapter focuses on the nature of reading and its assessment, and the latter describes instructional approaches. Chapters 10 through 12 look at the three component skills of written language: handwriting, spelling, and compositional skills. Finally, chapter 13 outlines special instructional considerations for adolescents with disabilities.

The primary purpose of this book is to examine language and its components and to suggest instructional strategies for conquering language difficulties. Our target population is composed of children and adolescents who have been identified in school settings as disabled and who have experienced problems within language domains.

ACKNOWLEDGMENTS

We wish to thank those persons in our private and professional lives who have encouraged and supported our efforts in writing this book. While trying to be good teachers, we have found a great need to be good learners as well. Therefore, we would like to acknowledge the students and colleagues whose knowledge, projects, and ideas contributed to our work on this book in one way or another. We reiterate our appreciation for Lynne Cucco, Meg Richards, Ed Paris, Connie Kramer, Phyllis Lane, and Phyllis Smith for their efforts on the first edition of the text. We particularly thank Anne Pingstock, Betty Shelton, Karen Canfield, Tess Roderique, and Donna Donovan for significant assistance with the preparation of this edition. The book has been enhanced tremendously by the special contributions of Nikki Murdick of the University of Arkansas, Mary Beirne-Smith and Beverly Thompson of the University of Alabama, and Loretta Jones-Wilson of Lynchburg College to individual chapters within the book.

Finally, we remember the contribution of James E. Smith. Smitty was co-author of the first edition of the book and a close friend. His death left a significant personal void that has yet to be filled. In memory of his talents, knowledge, good will, humor, and commitment to friends and colleagues and especially to individuals with disabilities, we dedicate this book to James E. Smith, Jr.

The Development Of Language

F|ew areas of human development have generated as much theoretical and empir-
ical interest as the study of language acquisition and its various sub-domains.
Language has been referred to as a uniquely human trait, the essence of human-
ity, and the highest human achievement.

Although all such claims warrant qualification, it is certainly a valid statement
that developing competence in language is one of the most critical processes in anyone's life. No other area of development is more frequently associated with handicapping conditions and with placement in special education. Language-related problems
are frequently among the greatest hurdles individuals must overcome to be fully integrated into society.

This chapter provides a foundation for succeeding discussions of language problems in children and various corrective approaches. In particular, this chapter focuses on
the nature and function of language, elements of language, the rule systems of language,
theoretical perspectives on its origin and development, and developmental milestones.

THE NATURE OF LANGUAGE, COMMUNICATION, AND SPEECH

An understanding of language must begin with some agreement on its meaning. A cen-
tury and a half ago, the American lexicographer Noah Webster (1962) defined *language* as follows:

> Language, in its more limited sense, is the expression of ideas by articulate sounds. In a
> more general sense, the word denotes all sounds by which animals express their feelings,
> in such a manner as to be understood by their own species. (p.19)

Webster's definition captures the essence of language, which is reflected in the definition used throughout this book.

> *Language is a system of verbal and nonverbal symbols and sequences of symbols devel-
> oped for the purpose of communication about experiential events.*

This definition illustrates the fact that language is actually a subset of *communication*; it is a formal communication system. Communication, as the broader construct, can
be defined as the exchange of ideas or information that involves the encoding of an intended message by the sender and the decoding of the message by the receiver (Mc-
Cormick & Schiefelbusch, 1984). Communication also can occur on other levels that are
seen more accurately as nonlanguage, such as gestures or eye contact, or as *paralanguage* (literally, "beside language"), such as crying, whining, or laughing. Thus, communication clearly can take place without the use of language or speech (James, 1990).

By considering the above definition of communication, it clearly would encompass a variety of signals conveyed within the animal kingdom (such as a bee indicating a
source of nectar). Similarly, the cited definition of language raises the question of
whether language is a uniquely human trait. Research conducted with animals, especially with nonhuman primates (Gardner & Gardner, 1969; Gleason, 1989; Premack,
1970), indicates that the capability of intelligent communication in the form of language

systems is most definitely not restricted to human beings. A distinction between human beings and other primates becomes apparent, however, when speech is stipulated.

Speech can be defined as a verbal code developed as a vehicle for expressive language. Speech, therefore, refers to the use of spoken symbols for communication purposes. Instead of being considered the equivalent of language, speech should be viewed as a vehicle for its expression. Speech can be described more accurately as uniquely human, because only human beings express language with spoken symbols. As Whorf (1956, p. 249) suggested, "Speech is the best show that man puts on." *a vehicles of language*

Speech is only one of the possible vehicles for language. Others include systematic gestural communication, signing, communication boards, pictures, and diagrams. As McCormick and Schiefelbusch (1989, p. 4) noted, however, it is the most difficult because it requires the precise coordination of: *Speech requires precise coordination of:*

respiration: the act of breathing
phonation: the production of sound by the larynx and vocal cords
resonance: the vibratory response that controls the quality of the sound
    wave
articulation: the use of lips, tongue, teeth, palates to form speech sounds.

Figure 1.1 presents a schematic illustrating the relationship between communication, language, and speech. It underscores the prior discussion in emphasizing that these three terms should not be used synonymously.

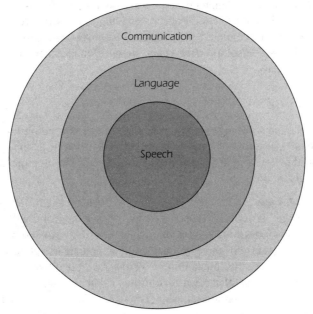

Figure 1.1
The Relationship of Communication, Language, and Speech

FUNCTIONS OF LANGUAGE

The importance of language becomes clear when you investigate its basic functions. Lerner (1985) suggested three functions of language. Most obviously, language is the vehicle for *interpersonal communication*. Through written or spoken words, individuals convey information, feelings, and thoughts about the world and about one another. Language is the primary agent for defining oneself, identifying relationships with others, and influencing or controlling the thoughts or actions of others.

Second, language serves as the *vehicle for many thought processes*. Although many theorists (e.g., Piaget, 1971) have argued persuasively that thought precedes language development, there is little question that linguistic competence influences the continued development of cognitive processes (see Harris-Schmidt, 1983, for a full discussion of this relationship).

The influence of language on thought is illustrated by the concept of *verbal mediation*, which facilitates learning, retention, and understanding. Mediational strategies can include the simple verbal labeling of objects, classification and categorization techniques, the application of previously learned information to facilitate problem solving, and a variety of related tools (Stevenson, 1972). These strategies enable the learner to build a mental bridge between the information or tasks to be learned and the cognitive processes needed for success in learning. One example is the embedding of paired associates in sentences for the purpose of learning and retention (e.g., "The *duck* is a kind of *animal*."). It thus follows that learning and the development of specific cognitive processes are intertwined with the development of language.

A third function of language is the *transmission of culture*. Our understanding of countless scientific and behavioral phenomena hinges on past investigations. Language enables people to accumulate learned knowledge over generations. Human history is characterized by a compelling desire to pass on to future generations insights gathered yesterday and today.

MAJOR ELEMENTS OF LANGUAGE

The major elements of language serve as a key to understanding how language develops specifically in terms of various language skills as well as the so-called language arts. These three elements provide a blueprint for the developmental milestones that lead to linguistic competence:

1. *Inner language* often has been referred to as the language of thought. The term "inner language" is probably best viewed as a hypothetical construct that subsumes various cognitive activities related to the child's ability to assimilate environmental experiences. Its origins in very young children predate receptive and expressive language and, hence, the acquisition of words. As a cognitive process, it enables the child to make sense of the world and thus enhances the development of concepts about the nature of the environment. Throughout later development, inner language provides a central processing or integrative component, which is necessary for the acquisition of other language skills.

2. *Receptive language* is an individual's ability to understand spoken and written symbols. It often is referred to as *decoding*, suggesting that the receiver must understand linguistic symbols in order to perform specific mental operations on them. Receptive language is the vehicle for comprehension, and it also enhances the development of inner language. It is a prerequisite for the development of expressive language skills.

3. *Expressive language,* by contrast, is the ability to *encode*, or transform thoughts and ideas into verbal or written symbols. As the visible or audible products of language, expressive skills often have been inappropriately equated with the term "language." Because these skills rely on input, they can show how well a child comprehends language.

One may logically assume that receptive, or decoding, skills precede expressive language throughout development. This basic interrelationship is suggested by Figure 1.2, which shows that decoding and cognitive processes directly influence encoding processes. The figure presents a simple framework for viewing the major elements of language.

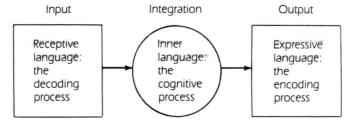

Figure 1.2
Major Elements of Language

One must accept this view of language development cautiously, however, since some theoreticians have questioned whether these three elements necessarily relate in a "comprehension-precedes-production" fashion (Bloom, 1974; Ingram, 1974). As Bloom indicated:

> It is by no means clear that the emergence of speech and understanding shadow each other. . . . Another hypothesis [would be] that the two represent mutually dependent, but different underlying processes with a resulting shifting of influence between them in the course of language development. (p. 286)

From this perspective, the acquisition of language becomes an ongoing, complementary progression between decoding and encoding processes.

Following the above discussion, language learning can be seen as the development of successive receptive and expressive skills. During the first two years of life, experiences combined with biological maturation form the foundation for the initial acquisition of language. With this foundation a young child begins to comprehend other people in his or her environment and to develop *listening skills.* Initial cries, babbles, and gestures lead to the development of true *speaking skills* as a child learns vocabulary and comes to understand the rules of grammar. The bases for these processes are the child's abilities to comprehend and produce verbal symbols, associated with personal needs and desires.

Further language skills develop as a child learns to convert verbal symbols to visual ones. *Reading* represents a twofold decoding process—first transforming the written symbol to a verbal symbol (often seen as word recognition and analysis) and then drawing meaning from it (i.e., reading comprehension). *Writing* is the expressive counterpart of reading; it requires the child to communicate by encoding thoughts into visual symbols. To succeed at written communication, an individual must become skilled in *handwriting, spelling,* and *written expression.* These skill areas also frame the organization of this book.

Figure 1.3 outlines the developmental progression of the language skills discussed. The figure is drawn to convey that no one skill within the hierarchy is necessarily mastered before acquisition of another skill is begun. Rather, the development of various language skills is interdependent. The following section elaborates on the development of language by discussing the systems of rules that constitute the structure of language.

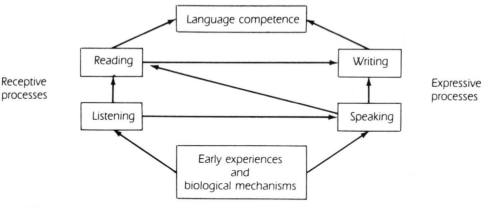

Figure 1.3
The Development of Language Skills

Effective communication requires an individual to develop skill in each of the major elements of language, as discussed. Wiig (1990, p. 129) further specified the nature of fluent and flexible oral and written communication by noting that the mature individual must:

— be able to isolate the features and dimensions of a given communicative task.
— recognize patterns that are implicit in these isolated dimensions.

— develop hypotheses about the significance of these dimensions and patterns as they relate to the communicative task itself, the context of the communication, and the communicator's objective.
— select a plan of action for communication, and then organize it.
— monitor his or her own communication vis-a-vis its effectiveness and the outcome achieved.

Given these assumptions about successful communication, it should be apparent how critical the cognitive component is in language usage.

THE RULES OF LANGUAGE

Hundreds of languages are used throughout the world. All have in common their reliance on a complex and formal set of rules that govern an individual's ability to understand (language comprehension) and formulate (language production) their communicative messages (Bernstein, 1989). The implicit knowledge that an individual may have about a particular system of rules is typically referred to as *linguistic competence,* and the actual demonstration of this competence is referred to as *linguistic performance.* In considering the rules of language, these two concepts have to be differentiated, particularly if we each consider how our performance (either in an expressive or a receptive sense) may occasionally embarrass us and be perceived by others as a negative reflection on our competence.

All languages generally contain rules in these areas: form, content, and use. These essentially constitute a language's framework, and every language, dialects included, follows them. Although rules across languages may differ—sometimes drastically—all languages share the same basic structure. Each language therefore contains rules for dealing with *form*, including a system of sounds, a system of building meaning into words, and a system of forming grammatical sentences; *content*, including a system for deriving meaning from words and sentences; and *use*, essentially a system governing communication with other people.

FORM

The three systems of rules that comprise the form of any language are phonology, morphology, and syntax.

Phonology The system of sounds in a language is called phonology, the set number of pronounceable sounds that any language uses for communication. The smallest units of sound that have linguistic meaning, and thus are relevant, in any language are called *phonemes*. Relevance indicates that substituting one phoneme for another creates a new word with a separate meaning (James, 1990). For example, substituting the phoneme /d/ for /t/ changes the meaning of "duck" to "tuck." On the other hand, substituting a slightly varied phoneme does not change the meaning of a word. Such is the case with many dialectical differences.

Far more speech sounds are available to the human speaker than any given language makes use of. For this reason, the phonological framework for languages can differ considerably. To master a language, a person must learn to discriminate and produce the phonemes used in that language. This might be difficult. A person of Japanese descent, for example, could have a problem using the English phonemes /l/ and /r/ because these phonemes are not used in their native language (deVilliers & deVilliers, 1978). For similar reasons, English-speaking people have difficulty pronouncing the Welsh blend /ll/ as in "llyn" (lake). This phoneme is most similar to an English blend of /hl/, which emanates from the back of the mouth but is nonfunctional in a number of other languages.

Classifying Phonemes Phonemes can be described in various ways by using phonemic classification systems. One system that has relevance for later discussions of reading instruction characterizes phonemes according to their distinctive articulatory and acoustic properties—that is, by the way they are produced and by their soundwave patterns (Chomsky & Halle, 1968; Jakobson, Fant, & Halle, 1963). More than a dozen features have been identified. Each phoneme is described by the presence or absence of each of these features, called *binary contrasts.*

Binary distinctions provide a basis for analyzing speech sounds into major classes, such as vocalic versus consonantal and voiced versus unvoiced sounds. They also make it possible to specify the involvement or noninvolvement of a certain speech mechanism to produce a given sound (e.g., constriction, obstruction, strident features). Table 1.1 briefly describes 10 of the more important distinctive features.

Table 1.1
Distinctive Features of Speech Sounds

Feature	Description
Consonantal	Sound production involves an obstruction in the vocal tract.
Voice	Sound production involves vibration of vocal cords.
Coronal	Tip of tongue is raised from neutral position. "Neutral position" is the position of articulators during production of /e/ as in bed.
Nasal	Mouth resonator is supplemented by resonation of nasal cavity in production of sound.
Back	Sound production involves retraction of the body of the tongue from neutral position.
Round	Constriction of lips during sound production.
Continuant	No constriction in vocal tract during sound production is extreme enough to block air flow.
Strident	Sound production involves rapid rate of air flow over rough surface at sharp angle, resulting in "noisy" sounds.
Vocalic	No obstruction of vocal tract by articulators during production of sound.
Tense	Sound production involves extreme deviation of articulators from neutral position and great muscular effort.

Source: From "Psychological Issues in Language Development in the Mentally Retarded Child" (p. 564) by D. H. Bricker and W. H. Bricker in *The Psychology of Mental Retardation*, edited by I. Bialer and M. Sternlicht, 1977, New York: Psychological Dimensions. Reprinted by permission.

The English language contains an estimated 44 phonemes. These are listed in Table 1.2, along with key words for each. The following paragraphs discuss some basic phonemic discriminations, such as differences between consonants and vowels, voiced and voiceless consonants, and oral and nasal consonants.

On a simple level, consonant sounds can be distinguished from vowels by the specific constriction or obstruction of the vocal tract to produce their sounds. Consonant phonemes consist of sounds that are (a) obstructed and stop (e.g., /b/, /p/, /d/); (b) constricted while produced (e.g., /s/, /z/); (c) obstructed and then constricted (e.g., /ch/, /j/); and (d) constricted so slightly that a sense of "gliding" is produced (e.g., /h/, /y/, /w/). Vowel phonemes, on the other hand, are produced without constriction and pass without obstruction through the mouth (e.g., /ă/, /ĕ/).

Consonant sounds can be further differentiated as *voiced* or *voiceless*. Some sounds are "given voice"; and others are not. Thus, a series of *phoneme pairs* is created. These pairs are produced by similar movements of the tongue, lips, and teeth, but they have different origins in either the mouth or the vocal cords. Distinctions between two consonants in a pair can easily be made by feeling for the vibrations from the larynx that occur with voiced sounds. For example, the /f/ in "fat" is a voiceless consonant, whereas its pair, the /v/ in "vat," is voiced. Nine pairs are listed in Table 1.3.

Table 1.2
Phonemes of the English Language

I. Consonantal (25)		II. Vocalic (19)	
/b/	ball	/ă/	cat
/ch/	chip	/ā/	cake
/d/	dog	/â/	air
/f/	farm	/ä/	art
/g/	goat	/ĕ/	leg
/h/	home	/ē/	meal
/j/	jump	/ĭ/	pin
/k/	kite	/ī/	ice
/l/	lamp	/ŏ/	log
/m/	moon	/ō/	road
/n/	nut	/ô/	stork, ball
/ng/	song	/oi/	boy
/p/	pig	/oo/	book
/r/	rug	/ōō/	moon
/s/	sun	/ou/	cow
/sh/	ship	/ū/	cube
/t/	top	/ŭ/	duck
/th/	thumb	/û/	fur, fern
/th/	that	/ə/	sofa, circl
/v/	vine		
/w/	witch		
/wh/	white		
/y/	yo-yo		
/z/	zipper		
/zh/	pleasure		

Table 1.3
Voiced and Voiceless Consonant Pairs

Voiced consonants		Voiceless consonants	
1. /z/	zebra	/s/	sat
2. /p/	put	/b/	bag
3. /t/	take	/d/	dog
4. /g/	give	/k/	kite
5. /j/	jump	/ch/	chip
6. /v/	vat	/f/	fat
7. /wh/	wheel	/w/	wind
8. /zh/	pleasure	/sh/	shout
9. /th/	that	/th/	think

Another distinction among consonants is based on the *nasality* of certain phonemes. The sounds of /m/, /n/, and /ng/ are produced by forcing air through the nasal passage. To appreciate the nasal quality of these sounds, simply hold your nose and try to pronounce "now" or "sing." Some nasal sounds are related to oral voiced and voiceless phonemes. For example, /m/ differs from /b/ and /p/ on the basis of nasality while otherwise containing similar features. The same is true for /n/ with /d/ and /t/ and for /ng/ with /k/ and /g/, respectively. To develop receptive and expressive oral language skills, children must make distinctions among phonemes by developing auditory discrimination skills.

Phonemes and Graphemes   A related skill—albeit one that comes later in development—is the ability to establish phoneme-grapheme relationships, often referred to as *sound-symbol correspondence.* Because English is relatively complex in an orthographic sense, children may have difficulty associating phonemes with their written equivalents, called *graphemes.*

The English language presents the user with two major difficulties: (a) the representation of more than one phoneme by a single grapheme, and (b) the use of more than one grapheme to indicate a given phoneme. An example of the first case is the grapheme "e," which can stand for a variety of sounds in words such as *eat, edge, tear, ear,* and *error.* An example of the second difficulty is illustrated by the phoneme /f/, which can be represented by a variety of graphemes in words such as *fall, rough,* and *phone.*

The first case presents a key problem because English has only 26 graphemes to represent the 44 phonemes, and three of the 26 (c, q, and x) duplicate sounds attributed to other graphemes. For example, the various sounds associated with the grapheme /c/ could be produced be "s" (as in city) or "k" (as in *cat*). The problem of sound-symbol correspondence is particularly apparent with vowels: Five graphemes must be used for a combined 19 phonemes. These problems are illustrated by the word list in Table 1.4.

Prosodic Features   In addition to phonemes and phonological rules, phonology also includes the study of *prosodic features* in speech. Included within this area are: *stress,* the relative emphasis or loudness placed on specific syllables or words; *juncture,* where pauses occur within a sentence; and *intonation,* referring to the rise and fall of the pitch of voice, which indicates, for example, the type of sentence (e.g., declarative versus exclamatory) (James, 1990).

Table 1.4
Grapheme-Phoneme Correspondence Problems

Word	Graphemes	Phonemes
1. tough	5	3 (/t/, /ŭ/, /f/)
2. flax	4	5 (/f/, /l/, /ă/, /k/, /s/)
3. express	7	7 (/ĕ/, /k/, /s/, /p/, /r/, /ĕ/, /s/)
4. read	4	3 (/r/, /ē/, /d/)
5. chick	5	3 (/ch/, /ĭ/, /k/)
6. yearn	5	4 (/y/, /û/, /r/, /n/)

Morphology   The system for building meaning in words is called *morphology*. This system includes rules for indicating tense, person, and number in verbs and for forming adjectives and adverbs from root words. The basic unit of meaning is a *morpheme*. Parker (1986) defined a morpheme as "a minimal unit having more or less constant meaning associated with more or less constant form" (p. 66). Subdividing a morpheme into phonemes or graphemes results in a loss in meaning. For example, dividing the morpheme *labor* into "la" and "bor" destroys the original meaning of the word, whereas subdividing *walking* into "walk" and "ing" does not.

Morphemes are categorized as *free* or *bound*. Free morphemes, such as the words *house* and *chair*, are basically vocabulary words, which stand alone and represent a unit of meaning. Bound morphemes include prefixes and suffixes, such as -s, -er, and re-, which denote specific meanings but must be attached to a root word. For example, in combination with a free morpheme, -s designates plurality, and re- means again. Table 1.5 provides a list of words divided into free and bound morphemes.

Table 1.5
Free and Bound Morphemes

Word	Free morphemes	Bound morphemes
1. fragmented	fragment	–ed
2. irresistible	resist	ir–, –ible
3. certificate	certify	–cate
4. re-election	elect	re–, –tion
5. dentistry	dent	–ist, –ry
6. hiccup	hiccup	——
7. incurable	cure	in–, –able
8. butterfly	butter, fly	——
9. deinstitutionalization	institute	de–, –tion, –al, –ize, –ation

The rules of morphology bridge an understanding of speech sounds and an understanding of grammar or syntax. They provide a key for drawing meaning from unknown words and for generating new words. Competence in morphology can be illustrated through a classic approach originated by Berko (1958). This method requires children to respond with nonsense words to exercises such as:

I have one botch. I have two _____. (botches)
One who blips is a _____. (blipper)
Today I will need to lim the hook. Tomorrow I may need to _____ it. (relim)

Because morphology concerns units of meaning, it can be used to measure a child's level of expressive language development. Individual morphemes in a child's responses are counted and converted into a *mean length of utterance* (MLU). This is done by averaging the number of morphemes per speech utterance. In the following example, four speech utterances contain 11 morphemes:

My book (2)   Picked up milk (4)
He jumping (3)   No more (2)

The MLU is 11 divided by 4, or 2.75. Although the MLU is an oversimplified concept, it is useful for comparing the level of linguistic development in children and for measuring increases in their mastery of spoken English.

Syntax   Ultimately, linguistic competence is the ability to combine words into meaningful phrases and sentences. The system used to form these linguistic units is called *syntax*. Syntax dictates rules for the arrangement of word sequences. It also governs the morphological adjustments caused by changes in word order.

For a child, developing competence in syntax opens up a world of communication possibilities. With syntax, a child can speak and understand an infinite number of sentences. Using the same skills, a child also can transform statements from declarative to interrogative or exclamatory expressions, and from active to passive forms.

Because grammar is so complex, scholars have proposed varying theories to explain the development of syntax. O'Malley and Tikofsky (1972) suggested that superficially plausible postulates could include viewing the acquisition of syntactical competence as developing a catalogue of possible words, phrases, or simple sentences as responses, or expanding simple utterances by using a set of substitution words or word patterns.

Transformational grammar theory, however, associated with Noam Chomsky (1965, 1967, 1972), is the most widely accepted view of this process. Chomsky (1972) claimed that every sentence has two levels of meaning. The obvious meaning, called the *surface structure,* consists of the written or spoken words that form a sentence. The second level of meaning, called *deep structure,* refers to the underlying meaning of a sentence. The rules of generative transformational grammar tie the surface structure to the deep structure, or intended meaning. For example, the surface structures of the two sentences below are different, even though the meaning is the same.

The boy ran the race.
The race was run by the boy.

Chomsky postulated that the presence of two sentences such as these—with structural differences but equivalent meaning—reveals the existence of two levels of language.

In a parallel situation, some sentences can have more than one plausible meaning with no change in surface structure (Hallahan & Kauffman, 1986). This situation is illustrated by the classic sentences:

The shooting of the hunters was terrible.
Visiting faculty can be incredibly boring.

According to Chomsky, intuition would account for recognizing and understanding two possible deep meanings in these sentences.

According to transformational grammar, the meaning of a sentence depends on the deep structure, which in turn determines the syntactical arrangement and the specific word meanings at the surface level. Thus, grammar is viewed as a reflection of the abstract thought of deep structure rather than as a set pattern of expansions. In the following example, the first four sentences represent the deep meaning expressed more concisely in the fifth sentence:

1. Jim went to the beach today.
2. Jim rode his bicycle today.
3. Joy went to the beach today.
4. Joy rode her bicycle today.
5. Jim and Joy rode their bicycles to the beach today.

Transformational grammar is offered as an explanation for the deletion of unnecessary elements in sentence 5.

CONTENT

The study of content in language is an investigation of meaning. *Semantics* is the system that conveys a language's rules in terms of meanings; it deals with the process of extracting meaning from linguistic units. Development of semantic competence reflects a child's progress from understanding simple concrete utterances, such as "Pick up that book" to comprehending more complex sentences that have multiple meanings and rely on the deep structure of language, such as "Your qualities defy description."

Semantics provides a clear focus on the relationship between language and knowledge. As McCormick and Schiefelbusch (1984) noted, semantic knowledge can be considered to be a subset of cognitive knowledge. Therefore, as concepts within our cognitive knowledge become translated into language, they become part of our semantic knowledge.

Because of the influential work of Chomsky, for years an emphasis on syntax overshadowed the importance of semantics as a primary determinant of language structure in children (McLean & Snyder-McLean, 1978). Research in the 1970s, however, resulted in a shift in this emphasis (e.g., Bloom, 1972; Bowerman, 1973; Schlesinger, 1974). As Bloom (1972) noted:

> The development of language necessarily involves more than an increase in numbers of words and their possible correlations . . . Children learn to talk because they have something to say, and a model for language acquisition that [only] describes the accumulation of words and word combinations presents only part of the story. (pp. 19, 27)

The importance of semantics in structuring language is closely related to the role that cognitive processes play in providing a foundation for language.

The nature of semantics requires attention to meaning on a variety of levels by both a speaker or writer and a listener or reader. O'Malley and Tikofsky (1972) provided an apt example of this phenomenon with the sentence "He is a pig." On a *literal* level the meaning is apparent: The referent has four legs, a squiggly tail, and makes "oink" noises.

On a *figurative* level, however, the meaning may be quite different. The person spoken of may be one who is sloppy, eats heartily, emits a series of gruntlike sounds, belongs to the police force, or makes frequent sexist remarks. If the image the sentence conjures is particularly repulsive to the listener, it also may be interpreted on an *emotive* level.

USE

Although an emphasis on semantic knowledge, and thus meaning, greatly broadened the perspective of theoreticians and practitioners in the area of language development and training, at the same time the increasing attention of linguists to the basic function of language in communication underscored the fact that rules for language can be understood only within its social context (Feldman, 1977). Thus, attention shifted to an exploration of language use and the study of *pragmatics*. Pragmatics refers to the system of rules that emphasize the use of language in social contexts. This rule system governs the reasons for communicating as well as the choice of codes used when communicating (Bernstein, 1989). Gleason (1989) defined pragmatics as "the use of language to express one's intentions and get things done in the world" (p. 22). General functions such as understanding a situation, making judgments, and participating appropriately typify pragmatic demands (Bryan, 1983). Specific acts stemming from those functions, such as thanking, promising, answering questions, greeting another person, asking for assistance or clarification, and ingratiating oneself for some purpose, all fall within the generic concept of pragmatics.

Language use requires an understanding of how to tie in to the implicit rules of conversation. In a given social setting an individual must know how to enter the conversation, initiate speaking on a topic, maintain involvement, drop back when needed, take turns, and exit in appropriate fashion (Bernstein, 1989). An apt example is in the college classroom in a lecture-discourse type of class session (see Eble, 1988). Some students may be unable to enter and initiate at all, and others fail to observe the implicit rules of the discourse and thus deliberately or inadvertently dominate discussion.

Gleason (1989) cited Grice (1975) in identifying the cooperative principles that govern such interchanges. These include attention to:

- *quantity*—being informative but not overly dominant
- *quality*—being truthful and accurate
- *relevance*—maintaining connection with the topic
- *manner*—understanding and complying with patterns of turn taking and presenting ideas in a logical order.

LANGUAGE ACQUISITION:
THEORETICAL PERSPECTIVES

Given the complexity of language, it is amazing that so large a percentage of people develop language skills with minor difficulties and with minimal conscious guidance. It is also incredible that young children acquire language in such a short time with surprisingly little effort. As Gleason (1989) aptly noted, "Language development has been a part of human development for so long that it is exceptionally robust; . . . it is, under most circumstances, almost impossible to suppress" (p. 6). The mystery associated with this phenomenal development has led many linguists to speculate on the primary determinants of the acquisition of language.

Legend suggests that Charles I[1] of England was interested in discovering the origins of language as well as the "natural" language of the world, which he believed to be Hebrew. He hoped to answer this question by placing a newborn boy and girl on a deserted island cared for by a "deaf-mute nursemaid." In this way he could control experiential influences on language development and observe the results.

Although ethically questionable, Charles's experimental design might have shed some interesting light on the origins of language for early language researchers. As the legend goes, however, he was beheaded before he could implement his plan. A variety of other attempts followed this inauspicious beginning.

In recent years a series of preeminent theoretical perspectives of language acquisition has been posited. These perspectives are of interest not only for their contribution to an understanding of language acquisition in general but also for their relationship to respective systems of rules in language. Thus, the *learned theory*, associated with B. F. Skinner and his followers, emphasized language as verbal behavior learned through operant conditioning. It came under significant challenge from a *psycholinguistic* viewpoint, often also referred to as the *innate hypothesis*. Most often associated with Noam Chomsky, this perspective stressed the human's inborn biological ability to generate complex systems of linguistic rules; hence its focus was on syntactical structure.

The "revolution in perspectives" (Gleason, 1989) continued with the ascendancy of semantics and the importance of *cognitive bases* of meaning, influenced by the work of Jean Piaget. Finally, the shift in emphasis to the *social bases* of language, influenced by Halliday (1975) and others, ushered in increased attention to pragmatics.

The discussion below initially highlights the contributions of the learned and the psycholinguistic theoretical perspectives. It continues with attention to several interactionist perspectives that represent central ground among these alternatives. In their excellent discussion on this topic, McCormick and Schiefelbusch (1984) noted that most theorists and practitioners would see themselves as interactionists. The reader also is referred to excellent discussions on this topic in Bohannon and Warren-Leubecker (1989) and Bernstein and Tiegerman (1989).

Although the rationales for constructing and adopting theories of language are many, two points are especially relevant to the succeeding discussion (Payne, 1974):

1. A valid and functional theory can provide a means for understanding an issue or topic.
2. A useful theory can help practitioners determine the proper mode of intervention.

---

[1]Some sources point to James VI of Scotland as the specific monarch involved (see Wood, 1976).

Update

The Impact of Family Experience During the First Three Years

Language development is obviously impacted by a variety of factors. However, the impact of the family on early language development appears to be very critical. Hart and Risley (1995) conducted a longitudinal study of young children from 42 different families to determine some of the factors associated with language development. The families were very heterogeneous, representing all levels of socio-economic status and educational backgrounds. Some of the findings related to the importance of the first three years of family experience included the following:

- Through casual socialization, families give children enormous amounts of experience with quality features of language.
- Almost everything children learn, until they turn to their peers in later childhood, comes from family members.
- Children are very similar to their parents in language style.
- Children are very similar to their parents in vocabulary resources.
- 86% to 98% of words used by children are also used by their parents.
- The size of children's vocabularies is similar to the size of their parents' vocabularies, given expected differences due to age.
- The first years of life form a basis for vocabulary development; everything said and done by parents expands the foundation for young children.
- Nearly everything that children experience during the early years of life is directly related to the wishes of their parents.

While the first three years of a child's life are not the only critical years relative to language development, they are indeed very important years because they form the basis for future language expansion. Since the family plays such an important part in the child's development for several years, the role of family members in language development during the first three years is substantial.

Source: Hart, B. & Risley, R. R. (1995). *Meaningful differences in the everyday experience of young American children.* Baltimore: Brookes.

LEARNED THEORY

In *Verbal Behavior* Skinner (1957) argued that language, like all behavior, is learned through associations made among stimulus, response, and consequence (S-R-C). In Skinner's view, language does not exist as an entity but, rather, is behavior learned through operant conditioning and therefore is controlled by reinforcement. Following the principles of operant conditioning, Skinner posited that verbal behavior consists of sounds an individual emits; consequently, language performance clearly would be of far greater concern than competence (Bohannon & Warren-Leubecker, 1989). If reinforced positively with rewards, the making of sounds increases. Conversely, if the verbal behavior is followed by punishment, it decreases and eventually disappears from a child's repertoire.

The first sounds a child produces are called *operants*, spontaneous sounds or imitations of sounds previously heard. These sounds then are reinforced differentially by adults. In the classic example, a child says "da," and his or her parents become excited. This parental response serves as reinforcement and causes the child to repeat the sound. As the child matures, reinforcement typically occurs only with closer approximations (i.e., shaping) to the correct pronunciation. Eventually, "da" is not enough to elicit parental praise, and the child begins to approximate "daddy" more closely by saying "dada." Over time, the utterance becomes significantly closer to the correct pronunciation. Thus, speech is developed through the shaping of successive verbal approximations by parents or primary caregivers (Staats & Staats, 1963).

After acquiring basic speech responses, a child learns to tell when he or she is appropriately using a given word. By forming associations based on the relevant features of the stimulus, a child learns to differentiate as well as to generalize. At the same time, adults reinforce appropriate usage. In the case of a child who can say "daddy," discrimination allows the child to say "daddy" only when referring to the father. This behavior is reinforced by adults who no longer reward the child for saying "daddy" if the child is not referring to the father. Eventually the child learns to generalize, using "daddy" to refer to all men who have children (Staats & Staats, 1963).

Skinner (1957) stipulated that verbal behavior further develops through discrimination training, which results in the learning of words and the joining of words into sentences. From his perspective, overt acts are emphasized while the speaker's internal state is not a key factor in developing verbal behavior.

PSYCHOLINGUISTIC/SYNTACTIC PERSPECTIVE

Many students of linguistics or psycholinguistics (the study of language and psychology) have questioned the behavioral views and have offered alternative explanations for language acquisition. Because virtually all children speak reasonably well by age 4, Chomsky (1959) contended that a stimulus-response theory could never adequately explain how children so rapidly acquire a complex language system and master its grammatical rules. He contended that the hypothesis that every sentence a child utters must be based on a previous experience puts an unrealistic burden on memory. In reviewing Skinner's *Verbal Behavior,* Chomsky (1959) stated:

It is simply not true that children can learn language only through "meticulous care" on the part of adults who shape their verbal repertoire through careful differential reinforcement. . . . There must be fundamental processes at work quite independent of "feedback" from the environment. . . . (p. 52)

Chomsky (1967) focused on the ability of human beings to process and produce language innately; hence the frequent referral to this perspective as the "innate hypothesis." He postulated that people have a built-in structure that he called the *language acquisition device* (LAD). Chomsky contended that the LAD enables a child to interpret language, construct grammatical rules, and then generate a vast number of utterances. A child processed the language he or she heard. The premise of Chomsky's generative transformational grammar model is that the rules of grammar must enable a person to understand and generate an infinite variety of sentences.

According to Chomsky, every human being has an intuitive knowledge of grammar. Therefore, all children know the rules of language, and thus language acquisition simply becomes the discovery of regularities within one's own language (Bohannon & Warren-Leubecker, 1989). Smith (1973) posited that a child cannot learn rules by imitation or rote because sentence meaning is not directly represented in the sounds. The sentence can be understood only by applying syntactical rules, and these rules are not formally or systematically taught to a child.

Chomsky's work set the stage for the *nativist theory* of language acquisition. This stance is defined by Dale (1972), who postulated that the innate hypothesis is not a statement about how children learn language but, rather, a statement about the aspects of language that do not have to be learned or taught in the usual fashion. In a similar vein, Miller (1964) pointed out that:

. . . the magnitude of the learning task and the speed with which children accomplish it seem . . . to be impressive arguments that children must be naturally endowed with a remarkable predisposition for language learning. (pp. 98–99)

Thus, children can be viewed as creative agents who search the language they hear for meaningful patterns.

Smith (1973) contended that although syntactical rules may never be formally taught to a child, it would be improper to assume that every baby is born with the rules of language neurologically imprinted. Rather, nativist theorists purport that children are born with the capacity to learn language and that the environment plays a significant role in that process by supplying the child with raw data, which is used to discover patterns and generate rules. According to Lee (1968), the parent's role is:

. . . not so much a reinforcement and shaping instrument in the child's language learning as it is the providing of a continuous language model from which the child can abstract meaningful fragments of linguistic information. (p. 24)

Several arguments have been used to support the innate view. The most common arguments concern the similarity of language development in children, the existence of linguistic universals, and the relationship of speech development to physio-logical conditions.

Lenneberg (1966) developed a universal schedule for speech acquisition, which children seem to follow regardless of learning experiences. This timetable given in Table 1.6 shows that children from 18 to 21 months old form two-word sentences, such as "Daddy go." At this stage, two-word phrases are free of transformations and resemble the deep structure of language. This phenomenon, combined with the fact that all typical children learn to talk in similar ways and in the same sequences, suggests that communication can be linked with biological maturation.

Table 1.6
Developmental Milestones

Age (months)	Linguistic skills
12–18	Small number of words; follows simple commands; responds to "no"
18–21	From 20 words at 18 months to 200 words at 21 months; comprehends simple questions; forms two-word phrases; points to many objects
24–27	300 to 400 word vocabulary; forms two- to three-word phrases; uses prepositions and pronouns
30–33	Fastest increase in vocabulary; frequently forms three- to four-word sentences; word order, phrase structure, and grammatical agreement approximate language of surroundings, although many utterances differ from adult grammar
36–39	Vocabulary of 1,000 words or more; well-formed sentences of approximately 10 words; uses complex grammatical rules, although certain rules have not been fully mastered; grammatical errors relatively infrequent
48–60	Most sounds produced accurately; has mastered use of adult grammar and inflections; developments noted in receptive and expressive written language

Source: From "The Natural History of Language" by E. Lenneberg in *The Genesis of Language*, edited by F. Smith and G. Miller, 1966, Cambridge, MA: MIT Press. Copyright 1966 by the Massachusetts Institute of Technology. Reprinted by permission.

On the surface all languages look and sound quite different. But closer examination reveals the superficiality of those differences. Chomsky (1967) maintained that transformational grammar may be used to describe all languages because all have surface and deep levels of meaning. Lenneberg (1967) and McNeill (1970) posited additional linguistic universals. First, all languages have certain phonic elements in common, such as the recognition of differences between vowels and consonants and the use of syllables. And, although phonemes are not the same, they can be classified according to their method of articulation and their acoustic patterns. All children have the capacity to produce the sounds of any language and in fact produce similar sounds as their earliest expressions. Lenneberg (1964) posited:

It is an axiom in linguistics that any human can learn any language in the world. Thus, even though there are differences in physical structure, the basic skills for the acquisition of language are as universal as bipedal gait. (p. 68)

Lenneberg (1964) argued that language development is such an innate part of human development that children generally will learn to communicate even when they have serious disabilities. To prove this point, he cited the case of children who are congenitally deaf and are able to acquire language only through graphic means. He also used the example of children from homes where no language is spoken but who develop their communication abilities with minimal delay after being exposed to language. He asserted that language acquisition occurs even when physiological or environmental deterrents impede its development.

The idea that children are biologically predisposed to acquire language has been strongly supported by many linguists, and this hypothesis is a useful explanation of language development in nonhandicapped children. As noted by Hopper and Naremore (1973), the implication of this theory is clear:

> There is no need to teach a child to talk; his biological inheritance ensures that he will grow up talking. Our job as teachers and parents is to teach children to talk effectively, in ways that benefit the individual and society alike. (p. 17)

But, an important question remains, which will be addressed later throughout this text: How can we teach language to those who have not learned on their own or who are having difficulty progressing in typical fashion? For those who are in this category, the innate theory has dire consequences; it provides limited encouragement for intervention, whereas the learned hypothesis has an altogether different implication, because the principles of operant conditioning can and have been translated into sound pedagogical practice. For this reason, many educators and other professionals have rejected the innate hypothesis. Bricker and Bricker (1977) summarized this perspective when they stated:

> The assumption of a "language acquisition device" would seem to indicate that a child who did not learn this complex system quickly and in the absence of formal instruction is not able to do so under the best instructional conditions. Fortunately this conception has operated as a challenge rather than as an epitaph for many of those who are investigating language training models to be used with developmentally retarded children. (p. 552)

INTERACTIONIST PERSPECTIVES

Debates over the learned and innate theories and attempts to resolve the differences between them dominated the study of language acquisition during the 1950s and 1960s. Since the early 1970s, however, theorists have tried to develop alternative models for understanding language acquisition. Much of the impetus for these new developments has come from the work of Piaget. Initially called *mixture theories* (O'Malley & Tikofsky 1972), these alternative explanations since have evolved into more complete theoretical models of language acquisition.

In pursuing this discussion, we follow the broad concept of "interactionist theories" as defined by Bohannon and Warren-Leubecker (1989) to include those perspectives that seek middle ground between the more radical perspectives represented by the learned and the psycholinguistic perspectives, respectively. The discussion focuses on two such models, the cognitive and social viewpoints.

Cognitive/Semantic Perspective   The cognitive basis for language development is founded on the fact that thought precedes language, and that language develops as a function of cognitive readiness. Flavell (1977) illustrated this relationship as a THOUGHT (language) position as opposed to the reverse LANGUAGE (thought) view, with the capital letters indicating the predominant process. Language is viewed not as an innate characteristic but, rather, as one of several abilities that develop through cognitive maturation (Bohannon & Warren-Leubecker, 1989).

Following Piaget's theory, language is expected to develop during the last substage of sensorimotor intelligence, when the child is able to deal cognitively with symbolic representations (Edmonds, 1976; Flavell, 1977). Specifically, the child first must achieve *object permanence* as a necessary precursor to language acquisition. Reaching that developmental substage signals that the child is beginning to use symbols to represent objects that are no longer physically present (Bohannon & Warren-Leubecker, 1989).

Lucas (1980) provides a useful picture of the development of language, and specifically semantics, as an outgrowth of cognition:

> Each child brings an innate, genetic endowment to an environment that is unique and perpetually changing. At birth the infant is quickly incorporated into the environment as a manipulator as well as a receiver of others' actions and objects. As the child becomes actively incorporated into a unique and individualized environment, an assimilation of the endless changes ensues. Consequently the child shares, through association bonds, these experiences with the significant people [in his or her environment].
>
> The sharing of experiences, by necessity, provides an overlap of common people, objects, and actions that are considered to be joint experiences between the child and the significant others. During personal experience, the objects, actions, and events are linguistically specified by the adults. For example, "Let's take a bath" specifies the action and event for the child in conventional *markers* or *lexicon* (vocabulary). The event of bathing becomes associated with the linguistic markers used by the adult so that the experience becomes a joint reference with the child. (pp. 1-2)

The major contribution of cognitive concerns toward building a theory of language acquisition is that the development of thought processes can serve as guideposts for the pattern of language acquisition. McLean and Snyder-McLean (1978) suggested that language "maps out" or encodes a child's existing knowledge and thus acts as a manifestation of cognitive skills. In summarizing the implications of a cognitive conceptual model developed by Nelson (1973), McLean and Snyder-McLean (1978) suggested that:

> . . . Instead of looking for the elusive "deep structure" link between a child's knowledge and the form and structure by which it is realized in language, theorists may now begin with the assumption that children talk the way they do because that's the way they think. (p. 30)

The cognitive-based model clearly expands our understanding of how language is acquired. In addition, with its focus on sensorimotor experience as a basis for thought (i.e., cognitive development), it naturally leads to an emphasis on semantics in language because, through this emphasis, attention could be given to the way the individual expresses meaning through language.

Social/Pragmatic Approach The social, or pragmatic, perspective emphasizes the central role in language acquisition of the desire to socialize with, and direct, the behavior of others—that is, to develop a degree of social control. The social view underscores the importance of interactions with parents or other caregivers as a key variable in development. Clearly, the social base for acquisition is well illustrated by the young child's desire to communicate to and with his or her parents (McLean & Snyder-McLean, 1978).

The social interactionist perspective seems particularly persuasive when viewing the initial acquisition of language. Bernstein (1989) provides the flavor of this interaction in noting that, "As caretakers respond to infants' early reflexive behaviors and then gestures, the infant learns to communicate intentions. Infants refine these communication skills through repeated communicative interactions with caretakers" (p. 14).

Children's active involvement in seeking this interaction with adults is central to this perspective. Bohannon and Warren-Leubecker (1989) noted that this approach would argue that:

> Children cue their parents into supplying the appropriate language experience that the child requires for language advancement. . . . Children and their language environment [are] a dynamic system, each requiring the other for efficient social communication at any point in development and for improvement in the child's linguistic skill. (p. 187)

The five basic tenets of a social perspective as illustrated by the above discussion were aptly stated by McLean and Snyder-McLean (1978, p. 78):

1. Language is acquired because, and only if, the child has a reason to talk. This, in turn, assumes that he has become "socialized" . . . and has learned that he can affect his environments through the process of communication.
2. Language is first acquired as a means of achieving already existing communicative functions. These preverbal communicative functions seem to be directly related to the functional or pragmatic aspect of later language.
3. Linguistic structure is initially acquired through the process of decoding and comprehending incoming linguistic stimuli. At later stages of development, the processes of imitation and expansion may serve to help the child refine his emerging language system.
4. Language is learned in dynamic social interactions involving the child and the mature language users in his environment. The mature language users facilitate this process through their tendency to segment and mark the components of the interaction and to provide appropriate linguistic models.
5. The child is an active participant in this transactional process and must contribute to it a set of behaviors which allow him to benefit from the adult's facilitating behaviors.

Although the social perspective may be unable to represent by itself a comprehensive view of language acquisition, it clearly does represent an important aspect of this process. Without the social arena, it could be argued that learning language would be quite problematic, if not unnecessary for the child. Efforts to promote development in children from a pragmatic perspective have clear advantages because they derive from the child's natural language-learning abilities and because they promote child selection of activities and guidance of interaction (Virginia Department of Education, 1990).

A Summary of Interactionist Approaches A broad view of language development must accommodate the importance of cognitive and social factors. As Edmonds (1976) stated:

> A multi-disciplinary approach which makes use of perspectives such as cognitive theory and developing mother-child interaction patterns—as well as of linguistic theory—should help provide a more satisfactory account of how a child acquires language. (p. 195)

In using the term "interactionist" in a much narrower sense than we have in this discussion, McCormick and Schiefelbusch (1984) provide an apt summary picture. They indicate that this perspective includes an assumption of an innate preparation to talk followed by environmental experiences that teach the developing child about talking, and, it should be added, develop in that child the desire to communicate.

A PERSPECTIVE ON THEORETICAL APPROACHES

As noted earlier, many theoreticians, researchers, and practitioners have gravitated to interactionist positions in recent decades. At the same time, new models continue to be developed and investigated (see MacWhinney, 1991). Elements of the four models discussed can be observed in the writings, research, and curriculum developmental efforts for children following both typical and atypical developmental patterns. The primary benefits for the educational professional come from deriving a conceptual basis for viewing language acquisition prior to implementing programs for children who have had difficulty with language-related tasks.

We hope that an analogy developed by Bohannon and Warren-Leubecker (1989) will not only bring some further clarity to these variant theoretical perspectives but also will assist practitioners in developing their own eclectic perspective in their quest to help children on their language journey:

> As children begin the developmental journey from birth to fully functional language users, we can examine the initial state of the child and the nature of the trip itself. Within the behavioral approach, children start out naked and helplessly lost. Behaviorists insist that children remain in this sorry state until an adult grabs the child's hand and drags him all the way to the appropriate destination—language. Behaviorists might state, "Children can't be trusted to go anywhere by themselves—leave the driving to us."
>
> According to the linguistic approach, children are not helpless but simply initially ignorant of their destination. Therefore, linguists equip the diminutive travelers with a great deal of durable luggage and maps. This allows children to recognize all of the significant routes to their native language and, moreover, to arrive with little or no help from passers-

by. Using their extensive maps and baggage, children eventually recognize when they have made wrong turns, and they can get back on course without delay or assistance. Linguists might say, "We've packed everything you need. Follow your maps and don't talk to strangers along the way. You're on your own, kid."

In the cognitive approaches, children are equipped with a minimum of baggage, and the maps are fairly global. After all, the main routes are the paths of least resistance, defined by the cognitive topology. When routes diverge, there are easily read street signs in the environment to guide the child to the home language. They ask, "Why burden the child with the excessive baggage when such may be purchased at little cost from the environment along the way?"

In a social interactionist approach, children require even less baggage. Such encumbrances are unnecessary because adult guides are readily available throughout the trip. The adults gladly point out both the main routes and the shortcuts that they themselves have learned through experience. The child need not worry about wrong turns either, for any adult will provide assistance to return the child to the correct path. Social interactionists ask, "Why weigh children down when we will give them what they need during the trip?" (pp. 210–211)

This description of the basic tenets of variant models of language development within a travel analogy provides an apt illustration of the basic concepts underlying the respective models. The teacher's role is to draw from the models in framing a personal professional view of language acquisition that will offer guidance to intervention efforts. Theories or models should not be seen as placing limitations on our expectations for children and adolescents with disabilities but, rather, as aids in providing effective instructional programs.

DEVELOPMENTAL MILESTONES

Regardless of their theoretical stances on language acquisition, most linguists agree on the sequence of language development during the first five years of life. Although interpretations of various milestones may differ, a relatively clear picture can be drawn of this developmental progression. Familiarity with these events furthers understanding of developmental delays in children who have learning difficulties. The reader is referred to Wood (1976), McCormick (1984), Lenneberg (1966), deVilliers and deVilliers (1978), and James (1990) for a more detailed discussion of developmental milestones.

FIRST YEAR

The newborn's cries soon after birth usually are viewed as the initial precursor to language. Within several months, the child's repertoire of sounds increases rapidly. Sachs (1989) referred to this period through 8 weeks after birth as the stage of reflexive crying and vegetative sounds. The initial cries quickly shift from random vocalizations to signals of needs, such as hunger or discomfort (Bzoch & League 1972), as the child learns that language is the vehicle for controlling the environment.

Children's ability to receive language on a primitive level also is established at an extremely early age. Researchers have documented the neonate's ability to discriminate between speech and nonspeech sounds within the first few weeks of life. Eimas (1974), in reporting on his research in this area, cited changes in the rate of sucking as proof that the very young child can detect differences among sounds. To test this assumption, Eimas and his colleagues altered the auditory input to children and were able to demonstrate changes in sucking rate. Naturally, one type of sound that newborns are likely to be most responsive to is their mother's voice, perhaps because they heard it in utero (James, 1990). DeVilliers and deVilliers (1978) emphasized speech sensitivity when they posited that children possess:

> . . . special responsiveness [which] may activate analyzers for the extraction of structure from speech, segmenting it into speech sounds, words, or even larger units; or it may simply enhance the process. Infants are also predisposed to distinguish between certain important speech sounds, apparently because language capitalizes on innate regions of auditory sensitivity. (p. 35)

From these simple beginnings, the remainder of the first year is characterized by an increase in both receptive and expressive skills. *Cooing* represents early efforts at sound production and consists of the repetition of vowel sounds (oooo, ahhhh) for possibly as long as 15 to 20 sounds. Eventually, *babbling* develops, and the child begins to add consonants to his repertoire, thus producing reduplicated utterances such as "goo-goo-goo," "ba-ba-ba," and "ma-ma-ma" (James, 1990). These interrelated events initially are a function of maturation but eventually are influenced by the reactions elicited from others. In a receptive sense, a year-old child has become much more responsive to others and is able to recognize familiar speech sounds and the meanings of voice inflections.

The combination of receptive and expressive skills surfaces most dramatically when a child begins to imitate the sounds of others, a phenomenon called *echolalia*. Throughout these early stages, the child profits from having an interested listener, experiencing visual and auditory stimulation, and learning that "talking" can bring pleasure. By approximately the end of the first year, children are able to comprehend conventional words and thus are able to respond to simple commands (e.g., "point to the tree") and in many cases also are able to produce their first word.

SECOND YEAR

From 12 to 24 months the growth of language skills continues to accelerate. True speech—using conventional linguistic symbols to express a specific thing (e.g., food, mother)—usually appears early in the second year. Initially the words may not match exactly the adult form of the word, but they typically will be similar phonetically (James, 1990).

A child's initial words have to serve multiple functions such as asking for help, labeling, giving orders, and stating facts. Halliday (1975) classified four early pragmatic functions, which include *instrumental* (satisfaction of needs), *regulatory* (controlling others), *interactional* (i.e., with others), and *personal* (expressing feelings), and two *mathetic* (i.e., using language to assist knowing and learning) functions, *heuristic* (investigating the environment), and *imaginative* (creating an environment). These six functions have been observed during 10–24 months of age (Nelson, 1991).

Because words serve multiple functions, a child's first words have been considered extremely versatile utterances and have been termed sentence-like words, or *holophrases*, suggesting that they serve as one-word sentences. This assumption taps the concept of the child "knowing more than he or she is saying." Even though these single-word utterances can serve many communicative purposes, it is questionable whether they indicate true linguistic competence beyond the actual performance level (Bloom 1972, 1973).

The second year also is characterized by extensive growth in vocabulary. Logically, the words that the child first understands and produces include labels for important persons (mommy and daddy), animals (doggie, kitty), objects (doll, ball), body parts (nose, finger), and words referring to eating and drinking (cookie, Coke). As noted earlier (Table 1.6), Lenneberg (1966) suggested that the typical child will achieve an expressive vocabulary of 300 to 400 words at the age of 24 months or shortly thereafter.

Year two also serves as a transitional stage into syntactical competence. Development beyond single-word utterances into two-and three-word constructions shows that the child is beginning to string together modified phrases in grammatically appropriate form. This has been referred to as *telegraphic speech* (Wood, 1976) because it communicates a message with a minimum of excess verbiage. For example:

give milk   me cookie
throw ball   sit chair

THIRD AND FOURTH YEARS

Between ages 2 and 4, children refine their oral language abilities. A central focus of this stage is the increasing mastery of sentence structure. Simple, grammatically accurate sentences are likely to increase at this time. The child has thus developed an understanding of the basic subject-verb-object sentence arrangement (i.e., I love mommy). By the fourth year, according to Wood (1976), a 4-year-old child will be able to convert a simple declarative sentence into a question or statement of demand, using short demand sentences, such as:

Can I have candy?
Give me some candy.

The production of longer utterances reflects gains both in structure and in vocabulary. The dramatic nature of this growth is apparent late in the third year, when a child uses a vocabulary of more than 500 words; during the fourth year a child's vocabulary includes 1,000 words (Lenneberg, 1966).

Update

Facilitating Language Development

Most children do not require special attention from teachers to facilitate their language development. Language development occurs naturally in a variety of environments, including the school, home, and community. However, there are some students who may require assistance in their language development. Bos and Vaughn (1994) suggest the following guidelines in facilitating the language development of students who may require some assistance:

- Make sure that language is taught in the situations that are practical and realistic. Teaching language skills in situations where they are not used is a less effective method of facilitating language development.
- Focus your attention on both receptive skills, such as listening, and expressive skills, including talking.
- Make sure that effective teaching strategies are always used when teaching any new concept or skill.
- Point out to students the relationships and connections to the different things that they are learning.
- Conversation should be the primary mode of instruction, as opposed to questions and drill and practice activities.
- Make sure that students have ample time to respond to questions and situations where their use of language can be encouraged.
- Make sure that instruction is individually tailored to students' needs by adjusting the pace of instruction and the amount of material taught.
- Model the use of self-talk to students as you are teaching to demonstrate how such a strategy can be used effectively and to explain to students what you are doing.
- Include the use of parallel talk to describe to students what other individuals may be doing or learning.
- Always use modeling to help students experience appropriate language usage and specific language skills.
- Show students how information and ideas can be presented in a variety of manners.
- Use language as an intrinsic way of motivating students.

Source: Bos, C. S., & Vaughn, S. (1994). *Teaching students with learning and behavior problems.* (3rd ed.). Boston: Allyn & Bacon.

During this period a child's increased comprehension reveals a strengthening of receptive language skills. Understanding of simple prepositions (on, under) becomes evident (Bzoch & League, 1972). Children often identify primary colors at this time. Personal identities also are shaped during this period, as the child learns his or her family name and age.

LATER CHILDHOOD YEARS

Language development during the fifth and sixth years becomes increasingly synonymous with readiness and academic skills. By age 5 years, a child has mastered the basic rules of grammar—an amazing accomplishment given the complexity of English. Initial reading skills appear as the child recognizes his or her written name and letters of the alphabet. At this time 5- and 6-year-olds also show an increased interest in books and being read to, and early printing skills begin to take shape.

Several important cognitive processes now can be detected through language expression. These include increased memory span, rudimentary verbal problem-solving skills, early classification and categorization skills (e.g., a car is a vehicle), and an understanding of abstract words (e.g., and, or, but).

A child's expressive vocabulary now is likely to include more than 2,500 words, with a receptive vocabulary perhaps in excess of 15,000 words (Webber, 1981). Children use these words in true conversation as they attempt to label and explain all manner of environmental phenomena. Both fantasy and reality become interesting topics for children at this age.

ADOLESCENCE

Discussion of developmental milestones for the adolescent years becomes somewhat problematic as the complexity of oral language, reading, and writing skills increases. Thus, developmental concerns generally parallel the sequence of oral language, reading, and written skills taught in school. Because of the hierarchical nature of language, however, it can be asserted that more advanced skills will be greatly influenced by the foundation developed during the first five or six years. The close relationship between receptive and expressive skills and cognitive processing remains evident throughout the developmental period.

The importance of continued concern for language development is well illustrated by a working list developed by Mandell and Gold (1984, p. 219) of adolescents' linguistic needs beyond academic skills. Specific sample demands made on older children include:

- How to order from a menu
- How to use the phone for local and long-distance calls
- How to make both formal and informal introductions   MR child
- How-to courtesies needed for specific social occasions, such as parties or school open houses (thank you)

- How to set up job interviews
- How to ask for help or clarification of tasks while on the job
- Appropriate demonstrations of positive feelings for family, friends, and acquaintances
- Socially acceptable methods for expressing personal opinions or offering suggestions
- Giving directions, making announcements, and providing simple explanations
- Reporting relevant and interesting information
- Using appropriate gestures, intonations, and inflections (e.g. loudness of voice, body language) to color meaning
- Sharing personal interests, hobbies, and experiences with adults and peers.

Certainly a good deal of the oral language demands made on adolescents comes in the school environment. In her review of the literature on teachers' classroom usage, Robinson (1989) concluded that more than half of the elementary school day required students to listen, whereas the junior and senior levels teachers' talk encompassed 80 percent of the verbal interactions, with three fourths of teachers' time spent lecturing and one fourth engaged in questioning. Thus, although the important emphasis on reading and writing might, of course, be assumed, oral language also continues to be of great importance.

SUMMARY

This chapter introduces the book's focus on examining language and suggesting ways to overcome language difficulties in children with disabilities. Language serves as a vehicle for communication and thought, and to transmit culture. Inner, receptive, and expressive elements are developed sequentially and are related to the domains of speaking, listening, reading, and writing.

Linguistic performance must be distinguished from competence when examining a language's rules of form, content, and use. *Form* is comprised of three areas: phonology, morphology, and syntax. Rules of content and use encompass semantics and pragmatics.

The Learned Theory of Language Acquisition associated with B.F. Skinner stresses operant conditioning. The psycholinguistic view of Chomsky posits the existence of a language acquisition device that, when supported with environmental cues, enables language acquisition to occur. Interactionist perspectives are more useful in children with language difficulties. Cognitive/semantic thought holds that language manifests a child's cognition; social/pragmatic approaches stress the active role of the child in developing social control through communication. In reality, practitioners develop their own eclectic strategies using theory to enable and assist, not to limit, performance expectations.

Language acquisition begins immediately after birth. It accelerates in the second year in function and vocabulary, and is refined and expanded at ages three and four. Language development continues through adolescence, when more complex skills are needed for social purposes.

REFERENCES

Berko, J. (1958). The child's learning of English morphology. *Word, 14,* 150–177.

Bernstein, D. K. (1989). The nature of language and its disorders. In D.K. Bernstein & E. Tiegerman (Eds.), *Language and communication disorders in children* (2nd ed.) (pp. 1-24), Columbus, OH: Charles E. Merrill Publishing.

Bernstein, D.K., & Tiegerman, E. (1989). Language and communication disorders in children (2nd ed.). Columbus, OH: Charles E. Merrill Publishing.

Bloom, L. (1972). Semantic features in language development. In R.L. Schiefelbusch (Ed.), *Language of the mentally retarded.* Baltimore: University Park Press.

Bloom, L. (1973). *One word at a time: The use of single-word utterances before syntax.* The Hague; Netherlands: Mouton.

Bloom, L. (1974). Talking, understanding, and thinking. In R. L. Schiefelbusch & L. L. Lloyd (eds.), *Language perspectives: Acquisition, retardation, and intervention.* Baltimore: University Park Press.

Bohannon, J. N., & Warren-Leubecker, A. (1989). Theoretical approaches to language acquisition. In J. Gleason (Ed.), *The development of language* (2nd ed.) (pp. 167–224). Columbus, OH: Charles E. Merrill Publishing.

Bos, C. S., & Vaughn, S. (1994). *Teaching students with learning and behavior problems.* (3rd ed.). Boston: Allyn & Bacon.

Bowerman, M. F. (1973). Structural relationships in children's utterances: Syntactic or semantic? In T. E. Moore (Ed.), *Cognitive development and the acquisition of language.* New York: Academic Press.

Bricker, D. A., & Bricker, W. A. (1977). Psychological issues in language development in the mentally retarded child. In I. Bialer & M. Sternlicht (Eds.), *The psychology of mental retardation.* New York: Psychological Dimensions.

Bryan, T. (1983). *The hidden curriculum: Social and communication skills.* Lynchburg, VA: Lynchburg College.

Bzoch, K. R., & League, R. (1972). *Assessing language skills in infancy.* Gainesville, FL: Tree of Life Press.

Chomsky, N. (1959). *Review of Verbal Behavior,* by B. F. Skinner, *Language, 35,* 26–58.

Chomsky, N. (1965). *Syntactic structures.* The Hague, Netherlands: Mouton.

Chomsky, N. (1967). The formal nature of language. In E. Lenneberg (Ed.), *Biological foundations of language.* New York: John Wiley.

Chomsky, N. (1972). *Studies on semantics in generative grammar.* The Hague, Netherlands: Mouton.

Chomsky, N., & Halle, M. (1968). *The sound pattern of English.* New York: Harper & Row.

Dale, P. S. (1972). *Language and development.* Hinsdale, IL: Dryden Press.

deVilliers, J. G., & deVilliers, P. A. (1978). *Language acquisition.* Cambridge, MA: Harvard University Press.

Eble, K. E. (1988). *The craft of teaching* (2nd ed.). San Francisco: Jossey-Bass.

Edmonds, M. H. (1976). New directions in theories of language acquisition. *Harvard Educational Review, 46,* 175–198.

Eimas, P.D. (1974). Linguistic processing of speech by young children. In R. L. Schiefelbusch & L. L. Lloyd (Eds.), *Language perspectives: Acquisition, retardation, and intervention.* Baltimore: University Park Press.

Feldman, C. F. (1977). Two functions of language. *Harvard Educational Review, 47,* 282–293.

Flavell, J. H. (1977). *Cognitive development.* Englewood Cliffs, NJ: Prentice Hall.

Gardner, R. A., & Gardner, B. T. (1969). Teaching sign language to a chimpanzee. *Science, 165,* 664–672.

Gleason, J. B. (1989). *The development of language* (2nd ed.). Columbus, OH: Charles E. Merrill Publishing.

Hallahan, D. P., & Kauffman, J. M. (1986). *Introduction to special education* (3rd ed.). Englewood Cliffs, NJ.: Prentice Hall.

Halliday, M. A. K. (1975). *Learning how to mean: Explorations in the development of language.* London: Edward Arnold.

Harris-Schmidt, G. P. (1983). Conceptualization. In C. T. Wren (Ed.), *Language learning disabilities* (pp.217–241). Rockville, MD: Aspen.

Hart, B. & Risley, R. R. (1995). *Meaningful differences in the everyday experience of young American children.* Baltimore: Brookes.

Hopper, R., & Naremore, R. C. (1973). *Children's speech: A practical introduction to communication development.* New York: Harper & Row.

Ingram, D. (1974). The relationship between comprehension and production. In R. L. Schiefelbusch & L. L. Lloyd (Eds.), *Language perspectives: Acquisition, retardation, and intervention.* Baltimore: University Park Press.

Jakobson, R., Fant, C. G., & Halle, M. (1963). *Preliminaries to speech analysis: The distinctive features and their correlates* (2nd ed.). Cambridge, MA: MIT Press.

James, S. L. (1990). *Normal language acquisition.* Austin, TX: Pro-Ed.

Lee, L. L. (1968, November). *Recent studies in language acquisition.* Paper presented to 49th annual convention of American Speech and Hearing Association, Denver.

Lenneberg, E. H. (Ed.). (1964). *New directions in the study of language.* Cambridge, MA: MIT Press.

Lenneberg, E. H. (1966). The natural history of language. In F. Smith, & G. Miller (Eds.), *The genesis of language.* Cambridge, MA: MIT Press.

Lenneberg, E. H. (1967). *Biological foundations of language.* New York: John Wiley & Sons.

Lerner, J. W. (1985). *Children with learning disabilities: Theories, diagnosis, and teaching strategies* (4th ed.). Boston: Houghton-Mifflin.

Lucas, E. V. (1980). *Semantic and pragmatic language disorders.* Rockville, MD: Aspen.

MacWhinney, B. (1991). Connectionism as a framework for language acquisition theory. In J. Miller (Ed.), *Research on child language disorders: A decade of progress* (pp. 73-103). Austin, TX: Pro-Ed.

Mandell, C. J., & Gold, V. (1984). *Teaching handicapped students.* St. Paul: West Publishing.

McCormick, L. (1984). Review of normal language acquisition. In L. McCormick & R. L. Schiefelbusch (Eds.), *Early language intervention* (pp. 35–88). Columbus, OH: Charles E. Merrill Publishing.

McCormick, L., & Schiefelbusch, R. L. (1984). *Early language intervention.* Columbus, OH: Charles E. Merrill Publishing.

McLean, J. E., & Snyder-McLean, L. K. (1978). *A transactional approach to early language training.* Columbus, OH: Charles E. Merrill Publishing.

McNeill, D. (1970). *The acquisition of language.* New York: Harper & Row.

Miller, G. A. (1964). Language and psychology. In E. Lenneberg (Ed.), *New directions in the study of language.* Cambridge, MA: MIT Press.

Nelson, K. (1973). Structure and strategy in learning to talk. *Monographs of the Society for Research in Child Development, 38* (No. 149).

Nelson, K. (1991). Event knowledge and the development of language functions. In J. Miller (Ed.), *Research on child language disorders: A decade of progress* (pp. 125–141). Austin, TX: Pro-Ed.

O'Malley, M. H., & Tikofsky, R. (1972). The structure of language. In J. V. Irwin & M. Marge (Eds.), *Principles of childhood language disabilities.* Englewood Cliffs, NJ: Prentice Hall.

Parker, F. (1986). *Linguistics for non-linguists.* Austin, TX: Pro-Ed.

Payne, J. S. (1974). Psychoeducational diagnosis. In W. M. Cruickshank & D. P. Hallahan (Eds.), *Perceptual and learning disabilities in children* (Vol. 1). Syracuse, NY: Syracuse University Press.

Piaget, J. (1971). Piaget's theory. In P. H. Mussen (Ed.), *Carmichael's manual of child psychology* (Vol. 1). New York: John Wiley.

Premack, D. (1970). A functional analysis of language. *Journal of Experimental Analysis of Behavior, 14,* 107–125.

Robinson, S. M. (1989). Oral language: Developing pragmatic skills and communicative competence. In G. Robinson, J. R. Patton, E. A. Polloway, & L. Sargent (Eds.), *Best practices in mental disabilities* (pp. 133–153). Reston, VA: CEC-MR.

Sachs, J. (1989). Communication development in infancy. In J. B. Gleason (Ed.), *The development of language* (2nd ed.) (pp. 35–58). Columbus, OH: Charles E. Merrill Publishing.

Schlesinger, L. M. (1974). Relationship concepts underlying language. In R. L. Schiefelbusch & L. L. Lloyd (Eds.), *Language perspectives: Acquisition, retardation and intervention.* Baltimore: University Park Press.

Skinner, B. F. (1957). *Verbal behavior.* New York: Appleton-Century-Crofts.

Smith, F. (1973). *Psycholinguistics and reading.* New York: Holt, Rinehart & Winston.

Staats, A. W., & Staats, C. K. (1963). *Complex human behavior*. New York: Holt, Rinehart & Winston.

Stevenson, H. W. (1972). *Children's learning*. Englewood Cliffs, NJ: Prentice Hall.

Virginia Department of Education. (1990, Winter/Spring). Advantages of a pragmatic approach to teaching first words, *DLI Facilitator, 2* (3), 11.

Webber, M. S. (1981). *Communication skills for exceptional learners*. Rockville, MD: Aspen.

Webster, N. (1962). The American spelling book containing the rudiments of the English language for the use of schools in the United States (236th version). In *Noah Webster's American spelling book*. New York: Teacher's College Press, Bureau of Publications.

Whorf, B. L. (1956). *Language, thought, and reality*. Cambridge, MA: MIT—Wiley.

Wiig, E. H. (1990). Linguistic transitions and learning disabilities: A strategic learning perspective. *Learning Disability Quarterly, 13,* 128–140.

Wood, B. S. (1976). *Children and communication*. Englewood Cliffs, NJ: Prentice Hall.

2

Disabilities in Language Functioning

A general timetable for language development was presented in chapter 1. Because of the extreme complexity of language, however, many potential problems can cause children to vary significantly from the language development norm. As a result, it is not surprising that many children with disabilities are also likely to develop problems related to learning (Patton, Bierne-Smith, & Payne 1990; Polloway, Patton, Payne, & Payne, 1989).

People have the ability to express themselves in oral and written language, as well as to receive information auditorially and through reading printed materials. In fact, this sophisticated ability to communicate is one of the important skills that sets the human race apart from other members of the animal kingdom (Smith, Graves, & Aldridge, in press). Deficiencies in any of these areas can result in major problems. If students are in public school programs, disabilities in language can result in significant communication problems. Likewise, adults with deficiencies in language might have problems in social relationships or on the job.

This chapter provides a foundation for understanding language problems. Both general and specific language disorders are discussed, with the intent of providing a sound basis for the discussion in subsequent chapters concerning appropriate assessment and instructional approaches.

AN ORIENTATION

Problems in language vary significantly in scope. A young child making primitive gestures to communicate and an adolescent struggling with noun/verb agreement in written composition could both be experiencing language disabilities. Similarly, a child with a severe speech problem and one with fluent speech but a total inability in written expression are both exhibiting language problems.

Although language disabilities range across a broad spectrum, several distinct types can be determined. Most problems related to language fall within the context of two general areas: (a) those related to the acquisition rate or timing of language development, and (b) those that involve the qualitative aspects of language, such as problems with syntax, semantics, and pragmatics (Peterson, 1987).

Classifying language disabilities presents a task as complex as trying to categorize and group all children with disabilities (Allen, 1989). One common method of classification focuses on etiology or cause. Such a system has several inherent problems, however. Clinical labels such as aphasia, dyslexia, or minimal brain dysfunction imply neurological damage, which can be proven only in rare cases. In addition, focusing attention on causes and their labels may inadvertently direct attention away from linguistic behavior. Finally, the way in which the terms are defined and used varies significantly, particularly across disciplines involved in providing services for children with language problems (Bloom & Lahey, 1978; Hixon, Shriberg, & Saxman 1980).

A second classification system uses the traditional medical, clinical, special education framework, with designations encompassing children who have mental retardation, learning disabilities, and emotional disturbance. This system presents problems similar to those noted for the first classification system, and it offers little information that can be used for intervention. For example, the term "mental retardation" carries no specific picture of language disability and provides no relevant information about the strengths and weaknesses an individual child may have even though children with this disability are likely to have language problems. Although the traditional special education system does not offer much assistance in classifying language disabilities, any framework or model adopted must relate to this system in some fashion to be functional in current educational practices and procedures.

CLASSIFICATION OF LANGUAGE DISABILITIES

As stated, classifying the various types of language disabilities can be complicated. Leonard (1990) categorized language problems by: (a) relationship to normal developmental schedule and sequence, (b) features of language creating problems, and (c) presumed etiology or correlates.

RELATIONSHIP TO NORMAL DEVELOPMENTAL SCHEDULE AND SEQUENCE

One way to discuss and describe language disorders is to compare the development of language in children with problems to those whose language development is considered "normal." When making these comparisons, four different patterns can be observed. First, children might simply be experiencing language delay. In this case, the child develops language in the same sequence as a typical child but is delayed or behind schedule. In the second pattern the child develops language in the expected sequence but never catches up to normal development (Leonard, 1990). Table 2.1 compares the language development patterns of a language-disordered child and a normally developing child.

The final two patterns, although infrequent, do occur occasionally. In the first case, children use language totally different than expected. An example would be a child who puts the *s* sound at the end of each word that actually begins with the *s* sound and thus would say "kees" for "ski," "tops" for "stop," and "tamps" for "stamp." This form of usage is called *metathesis*. The final pattern is when a language-disordered child uses some language feature never reported in nonlanguage-impaired children. An example is when sounds are made by drawing air into the lungs rather than expelling air. This pattern occurs very rarely (Leonard, 1990). Because these last two patterns are so rare, educators' major efforts are focused on the first two patterns of language described.

FEATURES OF LANGUAGE

Another way of organizing types of language disorders is to focus on the specific language components that represent problem areas. For example, students may have trouble with semantics, phonology, syntax, morphology, or pragmatics (the language systems introduced in chapter 1). These types of difficulties are frequently interrelated; children with problems in one area are likely to have problems in several areas. But

Table 2.1
Patterns of Development

Language-Disordered Child			Normally Developing Child		
Age	Attainment	Examples	Age	Attainment	Examples
27 months	First words	this, mama, bye-bye, doggie	13 months	First words	here, mama, bye-bye, kitty
38 months	50-word vocabulary		17 months	50-word vocabulary	
40 months	First two-word combinations	this doggie more apple this mama more play	18 months	First two-word combinations	more juice here ball more TV here kitty
48 months	Later two-word combinations	Mimi purse Daddy coat block chair dolly table	22 months	Later two-word combinations	Andy shoe Mommy ring cup floor keys chair
52 months	Mean sentence length of 2.00 words		24 months	Mean sentence length of 2.00 words	
55 months	First appearance of **-ing**	Mommy eating		First appearance of **-ing**	Andy sleeping
63 months	Mean sentence length of 3.10 words		30 months	Mean sentence length of 3.10 words	
66 months	First appearance of **'s**	The doggie's mad		First appearance of **'s**	My car's gone!
73 months	Mean sentence length of 4.10 words		37 months	Mean sentence length of 4.10 words	
79 months	Mean sentence length of 4.50 words			First appearance of indirect requests	Can I have some cookies?
	First appearance of indirect requests	Can I get the ball?	40 months	Mean sentence length of 4.50 words	

Source: From "Language Disorders in Preschool Children" (p. 163) by L. Leonard in *Human Communication Disorders* by G. H. Shames and E. H. Wiig, 1990, Columbus, OH: Charles E. Merrill Publishing. Reprinted with permission of Merrill, an imprint of Macmillan Publishing Company. Copyright 1990 by Macmillan Publishing Company.

each child will exhibit strengths and weaknesses in all language components (Leonard, 1990). In children experiencing these kinds of problems, a primary objective of intervention programs is to help them understand their strengths and weaknesses.

LANGUAGE DISORDERS BASED ON ETIOLOGY OR CORRELATES

Although many language specialists consider the first two approaches to classifying children with language disorders as the most helpful (see Leonard, 1990) because they have direct links to intervention, some professionals continue to see some merit in relating language problems to specific etiological categories or correlates. In identifying and serving children, the field of special education has been undergoing a transition from a categorical system to a noncategorical system. The idea of focusing on relevant characteristics of students rather than on clinical labels has a great deal of support (Smith, 1990; Smith, Dowdy, & Finn, in press; Smith, Price, & Marsh, 1986). In opposition to this trend, some professionals continue to support the practice of identifying and serving children based on categorical labels. Classifying children with language problems based on etiology or specific characteristics is similar to the categorical special education model. Although the language problems of children may have some unique differences, the uniqueness based on etiology or correlates is limited.

Classifying children according to their unique needs facilitates appropriate intervention services. Student needs based on their strengths and weaknesses are directly related to the development of individualized education programs (IEPs). This is not the case when children are classified using a categorical model. Children grouped for instructional purposes based on their clinical labels or major characteristics may not need the same intervention programs.

OTHER CLASSIFICATION SYSTEMS

Peterson (1987) dichotomized language disorders into (a) deviations in the acquisition or the timing of language learning, and (b) deviations in the qualitative aspects of language. The first category, deviations in acquisition, coincides with Leonard's (1990) first category, which relates problems to normal developmental sequence. Peterson's second category also is the same as Leonard's category addressing features of language. Therefore, although various models are used to classify children with language problems, most of the classification systems are more similar than different.

The classification model presented here is a modified version of those described thus far. Although it is based to some extent on the first two approaches, it also takes into account the system of categorization in special education and the educational strategies presented in subsequent chapters. As the field of special education continues to move toward crosscategorical services (if not noncategorical eligibility guidelines), the emphasis is on functioning ability rather than on clinical label. Dichotomizing groups along the lines of severity of the disability is a growing method for developing services for students who have various disabilities.

The model outlined in Table 2.2 focuses on two levels of language problems: severe and mild-moderate. Although these two groups do overlap, the dichotomy does provide a frame of reference for determining the characteristics and needs of students who fit into these two general groups.

Level I encompasses children whose language disorders result in severe problems. It includes the failure to spontaneously acquire language or speech, and severe delay or distortion in language. Persistent problems at this level require intensive intervention. *Level II* language disabilities are found in individuals who have acquired the ability to communicate but who demonstrate significant developmental delay when

Table 2.2

A General Model for Classification of Language Disabilities

Level I:	Severe Language Disabilities	
	A. Absence of language	
	B. Nonspontaneous acquisition	
	C. Severe language delay or distortion	
Level II:	Mild-Moderate Language Disabilities	
	A. Oral language delay	
	B. Oral language disorders	
	C. Written language disorders	
		1. Reading disabilities
		2. Graphic disabilities
		3. Expressive disabilities

compared to their chronological age peers or who have specific disorders in oral or written language.

These groupings do not imply an assumption of a discrete or static nature; rather, the contrary is intended. Instructors who teach children classified under Level I language problems should seek to expand those children's educational horizons to include goals implicit in Level II. Likewise, specific instruction and opportunities for students in Level II should provide the basis for growth into more advanced linguistic levels and, it is hoped, successful integration into school and society. Organizing language disabilities into groups should not result in the assumption that individuals do not differ significantly within and across groups, or that individual strengths and weaknesses should not be the focal point in intervention plans. Grouping categories of language disabilities merely provides an organizational framework for presenting information.

SEVERE LANGUAGE DISABILITIES

Level I language disabilities are defined in Table 2.2 as problems reflected in an absence of language, a significant delay in spontaneous, initial language acquisition, or severe distortions of language. The question of severity in Level I language disabilities is undebatable; the implications for socialization, learning, and even cognition are obvious. Even though children with these types of language disabilities have severe problems, any suggestion that Level I disabilities are the result of the child's failure must be defused immediately. Educators must presume that individuals who have not learned have not been taught through effective methods. This assumption of parent/teacher responsibility for language development actually has significantly improved the prognosis for those with severe disabilities.

Where, then, should the educational process begin? A good starting point is to review the definition of language. As stated in the first chapter, language is a system of symbols developed for the purpose of communication. Language also can be defined as "a set of spoken and often written symbols and rules for combining them in meaningful ways" (Scarr, Weinberg, & Levine, 1986, p. 263). Because language serves the many and varied purposes of communication, it is subsumed within the global concept of communication (MacDonald, 1979).

The implications of the relationship between language and communication are simple, yet extremely significant. Even if some people do not have verbal skills, all humans have the capacity for communication. A person with profound mental retardation may not be able to speak, but communication may occur through gestures, sign language, or behavioral outbursts. Infants who have not developed speech have little difficulty expressing their needs for food, cuddling, or having their diapers changed; their communication is usually through crying.

In addition to gestures and various sounds, individuals may be able to communicate using a variety of aided augmentative devices such as picture or word boards, notebooks, or computerized aids. Computerized aids include computers with speech, computers with different kinds of switches, and computerized boards. A key factor in computerized aids is that they can be visual or auditory, or both, thereby facilitating the communication of people with a variety of disabilities (Snell, 1987). Therefore, failure to acquire oral or written language does not imply a failure to communicate.

Etiologically, individuals with Level I disabilities include those with severe or profound cognitive, emotional, behavioral, or auditory impairments. Traditional special education labels for these problems vary greatly but, as noted, rarely have significance for intervention. Using a specific label such as mental retardation, for example, to explain rather than describe language deficits is a questionable practice. Frequently, language dysfunction may have been the original diagnostic basis for the label. The dangers of such circular reasoning are real, as many educators have well stated.

CORRELATES OF DISABILITIES

The term *correlate* has been chosen for this section because it offers a more accurate representation of present knowledge than does etiology. The variables discussed here include factors that often have been associated with language disabilities, regardless of whether a specific etiological pattern can be discerned. Several of the factors discussed also have relevance for their relationship to mild-moderate disabilities, dealt with later in the chapter.

Brain Pathology   Several handicapping conditions have been attributed to the primary effects of pathological disorders in the central nervous system (CNS). Serious emotional disturbances, for example, frequently have been associated with physiological factors, although theories on etiology continue to offer alternative views of the mechanics of these variables (Hardman, Drew, Egan, & Wolf, 1990; Kauffman, 1989). Severe mental retardation, in many cases, can be documented as the result of single overwhelming pathological processes (Polloway & Patton, 1989). Also, cerebral palsy, which may result in speech and language problems, is attributed directly to brain injury (McCormick, 1984b).

Pathology in the same sense of damage to the CNS that interferes with normal development or activity is an important correlate of severe language disabilities. Because much of the information gathered on the effects of brain damage has emerged from the study of adults, however, these phenomena may not always be directly applicable to the study of language disorders in children (Rosenberger, 1978). The exact relationship between brain pathology and language disorders remains inconclusive (Aram, 1991). It is helpful to remember that language disability is only one possible deficiency that could result from brain damage. Mental retardation, emotional problems, sensory deficits, learning disabilities, cerebral palsy, and a variety of other problems also can result from brain pathology.

One disability area that has spawned a great deal of interest in the relationship between the brain and learning problems is learning disabilities. Attention has focused on the cerebrum, the part of the brain primarily responsible for conscious functions, including speech and language. The cerebrum has two halves, which are basically identical in composition but perform distinctively different functions. Most authorities in the area of language development and functioning believe that the left cerebral hemisphere is responsible for language (Gearheart & Gearheart, 1989).

The effects of brain damage are determined specifically by the site of the lesion (Menyuk, 1987). Therefore, an injury to the left hemisphere may induce some language impairment. This is often the case with adult stroke victims. But to conclude that brain damage is the cause of language or learning problems is frequently difficult because direct evidence may not be available in some cases (Coles, 1987; Hardman et al., 1990). In fact, one of the most controversial areas in defining learning disabilities is the role that damage to the central nervous system plays (Hallahan & Kauffman, 1991).

Lenneberg (1967) clearly defined the potential effects of serious brain injury on the language of the developing individual. To summarize, he indicated the following potential linguistic consequences of brain pathology, based on developmentally relative, equivalent degrees of damage to specific language centers at relative developmental levels. At various ages of occurrence, these effects may include:

1. *Ages 0–20 months:* Effects during this period are generally not as serious as later damage because nondamaged areas can assume responsibility for damaged ones. Delayed language acquisition is likely, however.
2. *Ages 21–36 months:* Damage probably will produce language delay and possible loss of language function, but recovery is expected, as the right hemisphere is able to compensate.
3. *Ages 3–10 years:* Recovery of oral language abilities is likely but the probability of difficulties with reading and writing increases.
4. *Ages 11–14 years:* Some effects of damage during this period may be irreversible. The brain may no longer be able to compensate for damaged portions. Residual problems in both oral and written language can be expected with some frequency.

Pathological factors demand close attention as an initial correlate of language disabilities, but other factors also are related to language disabilities. These include hearing loss, cognitive factors, social factors, effects of institutionalization and environment, attention deficits, and various competing behaviors. After reviewing studies investigating the relationship between brain damage and language, Aram (1991) concluded:

1. Rarely does a unilateral brain lesion in the right or left hemisphere result in a severe language disorder.
2. When a unilateral brain lesion is present and the child experiences a severe language disorder, there is usually a family history for language problems.
3. Children with lesions in the left hemisphere may have language disorders, but these are usually mild and can be improved significantly with intervention.

People with neurologic disorders exhibit many characteristics, including depression, anxiety, and conversion disorders, or alterations of physical functions related to psychological problems rather than to physical disorders. The resulting speech and language problems in individuals with these types of disorders should not simply be considered aphasia or some other independent language problem but, rather, a result of the psychiatric problem (Sapir & Aronson, 1990).

Hearing Loss An extremely small group of individuals has severe language disabilities as a result of hearing loss alone. Hearing loss is the most likely reason that some children fail to develop language and speech (Eisenson, 1990). The fact that children with hearing impairments fail to develop age-appropriate language abilities "is the most salient finding of literature focusing on language comprehension skills of the hearing impaired" (Robbins, 1986, p. 12).

The critical role that hearing acuity plays in language development has been recognized for centuries. Itard (1962) observed the following during his work with Victor, the "wild boy":

> As, of all the senses, hearing is the one which contributes most particularly to the development of intellectual faculties, I put all imaginable resources into play in order to awaken the ears of our savage from their long torpor. (p. 55)

Children with significant auditory losses also have the most severe language disabilities. Those with profound hearing losses (the equivalent of 90 decibels or greater) have problems with oral language, even with the assistance of hearing aids (Hallahan & Kauffman, 1991). These children have much more difficulty acquiring language than do children with mild hearing losses. The *severity of the loss* interferes with acquisition of phonological constructions and consequently results in syntactical and semantic deficiencies.

The *time of onset* of the hearing loss is also a factor in developing language. Children whose hearing becomes impaired before they acquire expressive language skills have long-term problems with speech and language (Oller, 1991). These children, classified as prelingual, may acquire language, but at a much slower rate and with frequent problems in semantics and pragmatics.

A traditional theory holds that children with hearing losses utter the same sounds as children with hearing. Recent research has altered this theory. Oller (1991) stated that even "the babbling vocalizations that provide the clearest indications of a developing speech capacity are clearly different in deaf and hearing infants during the first year of life, and other differences may also be obtained." (p. 277).

Update

IDEA Reauthorization: General Provisions

In addition to attention to the IEP and minority concerns (both discussed later), the reauthorization of IDEA in 1997 and final regulations in 1999 also addressed a number of areas including several which are directly relevant to teachers concerned with language instruction. These include:

- Existing IDEA language was retained requiring the highest qualified standards for service providers. For example, paraprofessionals must be "appropriately trained and supervised" and the law specifies the circumstances under which they may be used.
- In terms of discipline, the reauthorized law retains the previous language allowing no cessation of services to students with disabilities. However, it does authorize the placement of students in alternative settings for a period of time up to 45 days for certain offenses (i.e., weapons and drugs). If the student's behavior was determined not to be a manifestation of his/her disability, discipline may be handled in the same manner as for any other child. In instances where the student is determined to be a danger to him/herself or others, hearing officers can order emergency changes in placement when parents disagree with the new placement,
- In cases of serious disciplinary problems (e.g., drugs, guns at school), a functional behavioral assessment must be done and a behavioral intervention plan must be developed.
- A new provision adds clarity to the fact that schools must insure that parents are members of any group that is charged with making decisions about the placement of their child.

Sources: Council for Exceptional Children (June, 1997). IDEA sails through Congress! *CEC Today, 3*(10), 1, 9, 15.
Fad, K., Patton, J. R., & Polloway, E. A. (2000). *Behavioral intervention planning* (2nd ed.). Austin, TX: Pro-Ed.

Individuals whose hearing losses are less severe have a much better prognosis for linguistic development. Their ability to benefit from oral language, with or without auditory aids, gives them an advantage in language skills (McCormick, 1984b). Effects of mild and moderate hearing losses on language will be discussed later in the chapter.

Other Disabilities   Individuals classified as having multiple disabilities also are likely to suffer severe language problems. Children with a combination of hearing and visual problems (classified as deaf-blind) and those with hearing, visual, and cognitive problems (deaf-blind and mentally retarded) have received the most attention. These individuals will likely have severe language problems in addition to problems in most areas (Hardman et al., 1990).

Some studies have determined that children and adolescents with emotional and behavior disorders have significant language problems (Prizant et al., 1990). Other studies have linked problems such as spina bifida and hydrocephalus (Byrne, Abbeduto, & Brooks, 1990) and Prader-Willi syndrome (Kleppe, Katayama, Shipley, & Foushee, 1990) with speech and language disorders. As a general conclusion, individuals with disabilities are more likely to have language problems than are nondisabled persons.

Intellectual and Cognitive Factors   One of the most common psychological correlates related to language disorders is the level of intellectual and cognitive functioning. *Cognition* can be defined as "the mental processes (perceiving, remembering, using symbols, reasoning, and imagining) that human beings use to acquire knowledge of the world" (Scarr et al., 1986, p. 133). It, therefore, is more than knowledge; it includes the way information is used and manipulated (Johnston, 1991).

Although the prevalence of language disorders in the population of individuals with mental retardation has been difficult to establish because of problems in definition, classification, diagnosis, and assessment procedures, a high rate can be predicted. Similarly, the "precise relationship of cognitive deficits with communication competence is not clear because there has been little research on the development of pragmatic skills by retarded children" (McCormick & Schiefelbusch, 1984, p. 102).

Several authors have concluded that people with mental retardation have a tendency to exhibit language disorders (Carter & Capabianco, 1976; Gentry & Olson, 1985; Menyuk, 1987; Mire & Chisholm, 1990; Schiefelbusch, 1972). In fact, Yoder and Calculator (1981) reported that communication was the most critical area of need for individuals in this category. Although a positive relationship between mental retardation and language problems seems to be present, the similarity of test items in language and intelligence tests could be one of the main reasons for the high correlation. Much of the research concluding that people with mental retardation have language problems cites information-processing deficits as the primary reason (Menyuk, 1987).

The literature dealing with language and cognition organizes theories into three groups:

1. Language is dependent on cognition.
2. Cognition and language are interdependent.
3. Cognition is dependent on language.

Jean Piaget's position was that cognition and language both result from the development of logical thinking. Heinz Werner associated language and cognitive development with perception. The third view, supported by Lev Vygotsky, emphasizes the relationship between language and thought processes. These three positions are complex; general conclusions about the relationship between language and cognition are difficult to establish (Menyuk, 1987).

A valuable area of study in cognition and language focuses on the relationship between specific cognitive abilities and language skills and deficits. As noted in chapter 1, the THOUGHT (language) position, as illustrated by Flavell (1977), implies that cognitive functioning serves as readiness for language development. Using Flavell's approach, the problems of a child with severe language disabilities can be traced to cognitive-developmental delays.

Studies comparing the cognitive development of children with disabilities and children without disabilities have supported this position. Kahn (1975) compared two groups of children with mental retardation who differed according to Piagetian developmental levels as measured by the Uzgiris and Hunt (1975) scales. One group had reached the final substage (Stage 6) of the sensorimotor period; the other had not. Kahn reported that the Stage 6 group, as predicted by developmental theory, generally exhibited meaningful expressive language, whereas the pre-Stage 6 group did not show this competence. The implications are that a child at Stage 6, severely handicapped or normal, "acquires the ability to represent to himself objects and events which he is not directly perceiving . . . He has developed the necessary cognitive structures for representation and, therefore, is capable of acquiring meaningful language" (Kahn, 1975, p. 642).

A subsequent study further clarified the importance of cognitive readiness to language acquisition (Kahn, 1978). Kahn focused on the establishment of object permanence, which, according to Piagetian theory, indicates the transition from prelingual to lingual stages. For example, a child has achieved object permanence when he or she understands that a doll hidden from view still exists and thus can be found. Kahn demonstrated that training in object permanence improved cognitive functioning. As a result, he stated that it might be a beneficial step in developing readiness for the efficient learning of expressive language. In describing the relationship between cognition and language, Finch-Williams (1984) summarized much of this research. Table 2.3 reports these findings.

The basic rationale for the role of cognition in language acquisition has been well stated by McLean and Snyder-McLean (1978, p. 22):

1. Perception and understanding of environment relationships must be viewed as products of cognition.
2. The products of cognition can be seen as the child's knowledge of his or her world.
3. Therefore, a child's language must reflect and thus encode his or her knowledge.

Social Factors   The social bases of language were mentioned in chapter 1; certainly the need or desire to speak is a major force in language acquisition. Initial social skills and language skills are vitally linked and deficiencies therefore can result in problems.

Table 2.3

Comparison of the Relationship Between Cognitive and Communication Development in Children With and Without Mental Retardation

Cognitive Level and Content	Communication Development	
	Normal	Mentally Retarded
Sensorimotor Stage 4		
Object permanence	Minimal comprehension in routines within context; comprehension of names for present objects and people	No comprehension
Means-end relations, causality, schemes in relation to objects	Few protodeclaratives and protoimperatives; no use of words	Few prodeclaratives; gestural protoimperatives; no use of words
Sensorimotor Stage 5		
Object permanence, schemes in relation to objects, means-end relations	Comprehension within context; comprehension of names for absent objects and persons; comprehension of action words	Limited comprehension found in only a few children
Means-end relations, causality, schemes in relation to objects, symbolic play	Protoimperatives and proto-declaratives; nonreferential speech	Primarily gestural protoimpera-tives and protodeclaratives; jargon with some meaningful single words
Sensorimotor Stage 6		
Causality, means-end relations, symbolic play	Comprehension out of context; comprehension of agent + action sequences	Comprehension of language mainly in concrete situations
Means-end relations, symbolic play, causality, imitation	Referential speech reflecting a variety of semantic relationships	Single-word vocabulary of 10 or more words
Symbolic play	First word combinations	Few word combinations
Concrete Operational Stage		
Reversibility thinking	Production of passive sentences; use of temporal subordinate clauses; comprehension and production of a variety of comparative terms	More ambiguous responses in justification of conservation judgments; comprehension of quantifiers and comparative terms with production equivalent to a much younger normal child

Source: Adapted from "The Developmental Relationship Between Cognition and Communication: Implications for Assessment" by A. Finch-Williams, 1984, *Topics in Language Disorders,* 5(1), p. 9. Reprinted with permission of Aspen Publishers, Inc., © 1984.

Mismatches between a child and his or her environment can be the result of the child's temperament affecting responses of adults in his or her environment, or the environment of the child negatively impacting on language development (Hoff-Ginsberg, 1990; Owens, McNerney, Bigler-Burke, & Lepre-Clark, 1987).

Reciprocity between parent and child is the basis for the transactional model of communication. Several studies have demonstrated the nature of the relationship between children's speech and their role models in the home environment (Hoff-Ginsberg, 1990; McCormick 1984b; Tomasello & Farrar, 1984). This basic communicative match between environment and language development demonstrates that language is closely tied to social motivation. Numerous studies have investigated the effects of social variables in the human development of language in children with disabilities. Much of this research has focused on the interactions between mothers and their children with hearing impairments and mothers and their Down syndrome children. Research has shown that linguistic transactions between mothers and children with hearing impairments and children with Down syndrome are directly related to the children's later language development (deVilliers & deVilliers, 1978). Studies focusing on mothers and their children with Down syndrome have revealed the qualitatively different language interactions that occur as compared with mothers and their children without Down syndrome (e.g., Buium, Rynders, & Turnure, 1974; Gutman & Rondal, 1979; Peterson & Sherrod, 1979).

Although maternal expectations could be a significant factor in language development, it is uncertain whether maternal expectations can be considered an etiological factor in language delays. Also, the relationship of other home environment factors on the development of language in children with disabilities remains to be investigated. This research potentially could reveal relationships impacting on family intervention models.

The role of social variables in language deficits is an area requiring additional research. Of particular interest will be studies of direct intervention with parents of language-delayed children, with the goal of helping parents "read" their child's comprehension signals so they can communicate on a level fitting the child's abilities and skills (Cheseldine & McConkey, 1979; Snyder & McLean, 1977).

Institutionalization   Traditionally, many individuals with severe disabilities have been served in institutions, and the social environments created in these facilities present an excellent setting for research. Most of the studies have tried to determine the potential effects of this type of living environment on residents (Seltzer & Krauss, 1987). In addition to studies on the learning, physical development, and social development of individuals residing in institutions, studies of language development have tried to determine whether specific language deficits result from this restricted form of residential placement.

After an extensive review of research data, Owens et al. (1987) concluded that "significant numbers of adults today, having been reared in an institutional life style, have not had the opportunity to develop pragmatic uses of language" (p. 49). Seltzer and Krauss (1987) found that more than approximately 20 percent of elderly persons with mental retardation living in an institutional setting were nonverbal.

Generalizations about research conclusions developed from studies in institutional settings must be made cautiously, as no two institutions are identical (Zigler &

Balla, 1977); any conclusions from this research must remain tentative. These limitations are even more significant in light of the fact that a great deal of the negative data concerning institutions was accumulated before institutional reform movements in the late 1960s and early 1970s (Robinson & Robinson, 1976). Although intensive training programs developed at some institutions over the past decade may create an environment conducive to language development (McNutt & Leri, 1979), the sheer number of people with mental retardation living together and the nature of the institutional environment result in routine and conformity that makes individual language development abnormal (Owens et al., 1987). Therefore, despite significant improvements in institutional services over the past several years, the institutional environment remains less than optimal for language development. This realization is one of the many reasons why the deinstitutionalization movement has proceeded dramatically through the 1970s and 1980s (Smith & Polloway, 1991).

An interactive model for facilitating language development and usage among people with mental retardation residing in institutions—a model utilizing involvement by all caregivers in the institutional setting—could greatly facilitate language in this population (Owens et al., 1987). One key point in institutional research of any kind is that few absolutes exist. As previously noted, generalizations resulting from research in institutional environments must be developed cautiously.

Several research studies illustrate the potential effects of institutionalization on language. McNutt and Leri (1979) evaluated the performance of institutionalized people with mental retardation on several measures of linguistic competence. The conclusion was that some aspects of language are more susceptible to the effects of institutionalization than others are: Semantic and auditory elements were the most sensitive; grammatical structure seemed to be less affected. In another study on this topic, Phillips and Balthazar (1979) found that prolonged institutionalization could result in language deterioration in individuals who are severely and profoundly mentally retarded. In light of the fact that the deinstitutionalization movement has altered the population of individuals living in institutions, more research is needed to clarify the effects of institutional living on language development.

Attentional Deficits   Attention is a complex, multifaceted phenomenon that impacts many aspects of learning and skill development. Attentional problems have even generated the terms, *attention deficit disorder* (ADD), and *attention deficit hyperactivity disorder* (ADHD). This label was proposed as a new disability category during reauthorization of Public Law 94-142, Individuals with Disabilities Education Act (IDEA), during 1990. While the final revision did not include ADD/ADHD as a separate category, these students can be served as other health impaired and must be provided services under Section 504 of the Rehabilitation Act.

Attention is a prerequisite skill for learning. Primitive attentional problems can be caused by cognitive, physiological, social, or environmental factors. Individuals who cannot focus their attention on a learning task for a specific time may not be able to learn that task. Attention problems have been found to be a significant factor in learning and language problems (Shames & Wiig, 1990). Attending is composed of a variety of behaviors and skills, including focusing the eyes, turning the head, and orienting the body. Without these skills, attending is difficult and can result in significant reduction in learning (Patton et al., 1990). Attentional deficits are a common characteristic in individuals with severe disabilities. In light of the social impact on language development, lack of attention indirectly results in a reduction of stimulation from significant others. This reduction also can adversely affect language acquisition.

Evidence also reveals that gaze and gaze aversion may be linked to personality variables such as aggressiveness and submission (Rago, 1977). Regardless of cause, teachers who work with students on language acquisition must deal with these problems. In fact, many programs begin with approaches to attentional training as prerequisites for verbal language instruction.

Competing Behaviors   Competing behaviors can be defined as various activities with which the individual becomes involved that result in distractions from other activities. Like attention deficits, these behaviors interfere with the speech and language acquisition of individuals who have severe disabilities. The rationale for their high incidence is clear in many cases, as behavioral clusters often develop in the absence of socially acceptable forms of communication. In any case, a successful program of intervention must deal with these behaviors.

Crying and *tantrums* are easily considered as immature behavior. Both represent developmentally normal occurrences, but children with severe language delay may use these behaviors to substitute for appropriate communication and therefore satisfy the need to exercise social control. As early as 1939, Dollard, Doob, Miller, Mowrer, and Sears noted that *aggressive behaviors* might be viewed as individuals' responses to frustration in making their feelings known. Aggressive behaviors also could be used as a primitive means of communication (Talkington, Hall, & Altman, 1971).

To reduce competing behaviors, these have to be understood on at least a basic level. Hopper and Helmick (1977) cautioned teachers against a strategy that "ignores or misreads such attempts to communicate and even programs to eradicate 'annoying' or 'socially inappropriate' behaviors. Such programming may result in a more tolerable environment for the teacher, but ultimately does little to foster effective communication in the child" (p. 112). The challenge, therefore, is to expand these primitive efforts at communication into preferred language forms.

Self-stimulation, or self-stimulatory behaviors, comprise a second class of competing behaviors. Recently, the term *stereotypy* is coming to replace the term *self-stimulation* "because it is descriptive and does not imply that the child is stimulating herself" (Snell, 1987, p. 318). Stereotypy is a way of providing self-reinforcing or self-perpetuating sensory feedback (Kauffman, 1989). The behaviors take many forms, including hand flapping, rocking, spinning, head movements, finger flapping, bizarre motor movements, and eye blinking (Knoblock, 1982). This class of behaviors is highly resistant to modification, perhaps because self-stimulation is a natural substitute for those who are unable to perform more appropriate behaviors. It is logical to assume that self-stimulation occurs when interactive behavior is not rewarded. When this happens, individuals with disabilities fill the void with substitutive tactile or kinesthetic reinforcement (Azrin, Kaplan, & Foxx, 1973). The prevalence of self-stimulation among individuals with severe disabilities has been commonly reported as very high.

Although many behaviors this group of children exhibits may be disturbing, probably the most disturbing are *self-abusive and injurious behaviors.* Not only do these negatively affect observers but they also interfere significantly with training efforts. Examples of these behaviors include hitting oneself on the head or face; banging the head into walls or floors; biting fingers, hands, and arms; and scratching, eye gouging, or poking (Snell, 1987). Self-abusive behaviors, though not as common as self-stimulating activities, must be eliminated or brought under control before effective instruction can begin.

Bizarre language patterns often are found in children with severe disabilities such as severe mental retardation and autism. One of these, mutism, can be defined as "without speech." Approximately half of the children with autism have no functional speech (Kauffman, 1989). Some children are selectively mute; they talk, but only to certain people or in specific circumstances (Kauffman, 1985). Mutism is the most unusual language pattern and, along with self-abuse, is one of the few behaviors considered abnormal in virtually all societies (Kauffman, 1977). Children with severe handicaps who are not mute may use language that is bizarre enough to attract attention. Most individuals with severe disabilities who have primitive language skills show evidence of significant deviation in the form, content, and use of language. With some individuals language becomes almost a game, albeit an often meaningless one to others. Patterns of speech tend to be inappropriate to a given situation and counterproductive to true communication. On the optimistic side, of course, these utterances are speech and, as such, offer an encouraging prognosis compared to mutism, in which no speech is produced.

The repetitious use of language forms is another bizarre linguistic pattern. Some children with severe disabilities, especially those diagnosed as having autism, use such repetitions as most of their verbal repertoire. This type of speech pattern, called *echolalia,* can appear in two forms: immediate and delayed. Echolalia can be defined as "the parroting repetition of words or phrases either immediately after they are heard or later; usually observed only in psychotic, schizophrenic, or autistic children" (Kauffman, 1989, p. 410). Some authorities actually differentiate between echolalia and delayed echolalia (McCormick & Schiefelbusch, 1984). In immediate echolalic speech a child repeats conversational words or phrases without signs of processing or conceptual and linguistic transformation. A typical discourse might proceed as follows:

> Adult: How are you?
> Child: How are you?
> Adult: Well, I'm fine.
> Child: I'm fine.
> Adult: Are you Joey?
> Child: Are you Joey?
> Adult: No, you're Joey.
> Child: No, you're Joey.

Immediate echolalia may be a form of self-stimulation achieved with language (Lovaas, 1977). Some research also suggests that immediate echolalia be considered from its social or transactional foundation. This research has shown that echolalic speech most often occurs when discourse is face-to-face and eye contact is maintained (Campbell & Grove, 1978).

Several behavioral approaches and linguistic considerations have been employed in attempting to eliminate echolalic speech. Children who suffer from echolalic speech seem to converse more appropriately if they understand the message spoken and if the message requires a response within their oral language repertoire (Garber & David, 1975). For this reason, statements or questions presented to echolalic children should be evaluated for their receptive and expressive linguistic demands.

Delayed echolalia can be observed in several forms. For example, children who are severely disturbed or autistic may constantly recite nursery rhymes or television and radio commercials verbatim; in contrast, many normal children paraphrase aspects of commercials (Paluszny, 1979).

Pronominal reversal is a frequent characteristic of children with autism who develop language. Children who have this problem repeat personal pronouns as they hear them. They may refer to themselves as "you" and the person addressed as "I." The possible relationships to echolalia are apparent. The difficulties and speculations this problem creates are certainly unique.

Language, or at least speech, may occur suddenly and unexpectedly in some individuals who are seemingly mute. Cleland (1979) suggested that unexpected speech in individuals with profound mental retardation could be the "confession" of an individual who has been incorrectly diagnosed. He described a situation in which a resident in an institution, who had never been known to utter a word, suddenly told a person in a simulated aggression experiment, "They won't hurt you, honey." Because, by definition and classification (Grossman, 1983), the term *profound mental retardation* should be restricted to those with limited or no speech, the utterance became the basis for more careful assessment of this person, who later was found to have emotional problems that had obscured his actual intellectual potential.

The basic idiosyncratic speech of children with severe disabilities includes some of the characteristics described earlier. For example, children with autistic-like characteristics typically use these linguistic patterns: autoerotic and self-stimulatory vocalizations not intended for interpersonal communications; neologisms (created words); common words with invented meanings; and unusual and varied rhythmic patterns (Paluszny, 1979). If these characteristics appear in severely disturbed children, they may not represent a playful use of language as with many nondisabled children; instead, they often represent a child's effort to pronounce words with seemingly serious meanings (Love, Mainord, & Naylor, 1976).

EFFECTS OF DISABILITY CUES

Specific cues that people with disabilities use may inadvertently affect their language skills. For example, observers who consciously or unconsciously evaluate the abilities or disabilities of other people may develop a prejudiced attitude toward persons with disabilities. As a result, these individuals may unconsciously magnify disabilities by developing a mind-set that leads to negative environmental reactions. This, in turn, may influence the development of a child with a disability.

MILD-MODERATE LANGUAGE DISABILITIES

No clear-cut division exists between Level I and Level II language disabilities. Rather, language functioning occurs on a continuum. Some children fall into the "gray" area between Levels I and II. A specific dichotomy does not exist. The model used here, however, does recognize the different emphases that characterize each level—namely, the initial acquisition of languages skills in Level I and the refinement of language skills in Level II.

Using traditional handicapping categories, children with Level II disabilities would include those classified as having learning disabilities, emotional and behavioral disorders, mild and moderate mental retardation, and hearing impairment. Children with more severe disabilities who have acquired initial language skills also would be included. Some children who have Level II language problems do not have another disability. These children may be labeled as having speech impairment or a communication disorder but may not have any additional learning problems.

Frequently, an arbitrary distinction is made between language delay and specific language disorders. This does not mean that the two are distinct categories. Instead, it identifies them as two possible phenomena, one or both of which may be operative within a person's language abilities. *Language delay* suggests deviations from developmental milestones and would indicate that a child's primary problem is one of lagging behind developmentally typical peers in acquiring more advanced linguistic skills. A *language disorder* indicates that specific areas may be identified as deficiencies in the child's repertoire. Some linguists (Bloom & Lahey, 1978) use the term "disorder" to subsume various language handicaps, including delay. In any case, determining the learner's educational needs will proceed directly from an understanding of specific linguistic strengths and weaknesses.

Children who have Level II language disorders frequently exhibit problems that could be classified as deviations in the qualitative aspects of language (Leonard, 1990) or problems with language features (Peterson, 1987). The most likely problems for children with Level II language disorders focus on various levels of linguistic functioning—phonology, morphology and syntax, semantics, and pragmatics (Allen, 1989); these can interfere with reception, cognitive and integrative processing, and production, or expression. Figure 2.1 organizes these three processes and various components involved with each. Disorders can occur in any area.

Language problems that result in mild-moderate language disabilities can be subgrouped in many different ways. Allen (1989) has identified five clinical subtypes found in expressive and receptive language:

1. Expressive disorders with good comprehension
2. Verbal auditory sensory limitations

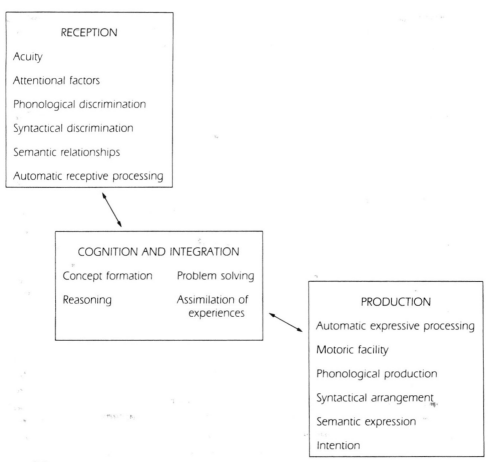

RECEPTION

Acuity

Attentional factors

Phonological discrimination

Syntactical discrimination

Semantic relationships

Automatic receptive processing

COGNITION AND INTEGRATION

Concept formation   Problem solving

Reasoning   Assimilation of
                      experiences

PRODUCTION

Automatic expressive processing

Motoric facility

Phonological production

Syntactical arrangement

Semantic expression

Intention

Figure 2.1
Linguistic Processing Model

3. Phonologic-syntactic disorder
4. Lexical-syntactic disorder
5. Semantic-pragmatic disorder

Table 2.4 lists these subtypes and provides a brief description of each.

ORAL LANGUAGE AS A PROCESS

The relationship between oral and written language disorders seems apparent. Yet the systematic study of oral language as a process underlying the acquisition of reading and written language skills is a fairly recent phenomenon. The concept of *processing*

Table 2.4
Clinical Subtypes of Language Disabilities

Type	Description
Expressive Disorders with Good Comprehension	• severely delayed onset of expressive language • comprehension usually good • know what you want to say, but cannot say it
Verbal Auditory Agnosia	• commonly called "word deafness" • inability to decode verbal language • children with disorder are likely to remain nonverbal
Phonologic-Syntactic Disorder	• mixed expressive and receptive deficits • expressive language delayed until 3 years or later • substitutions, omissions, and distortions common
Lexical-Syntactic Disorder	• mixed deficits in expressive and receptive language • language acquisition late • after language acquired minimal difficulties in producing and comprehending language
Semantic-Pragmatic Disorder	• Likely to be misdiagnosed • many children speak early or on schedule and may have extensive vocabularies • expressive language superior to receptive • word retrieval problems common

Source: Adapted from "Developmental Language Disorders in Preschool Children: Clinical Subtypes and Syndromes" by D. A. Allen, 1989, *School Psychology Review, 18,* p. 442–451.

deficits generally has been defined and limited to a few traditional areas: visual and auditory perceptual handicaps, perceptual-motor and psycholinguistic deficits, and other problems in related domains. Remedial approaches based on these deficits, however, have not proven successful with students with disabilities (Lerner, 1988; Myers & Hammill, 1990; Polloway et al., 1989), so many researchers have either rejected process conceptualizations or turned to alternative perspectives on processing.

The role of oral language as a precursor to later academic skills suggests the idea of a linguistic processing component rather than a perceptual processing component (Wallach & Goldsmith, 1977). Based on preliminary research, this approach seems to hold great promise (Magee & Newcomer, 1978; Reid & Hresko, 1980). Research indicates an increasing likelihood that one's oral language and basic linguistic knowledge will directly influence later skills such as reading and writing.

If the importance of linguistic processing for later learning is supported, it then will be imperative to determine if these deficits are amenable to intervention, particularly for adolescents with disabilities (Wiig, Lapointe, & Semel, 1977). Research developments in this area demand careful scrutiny over the next several years. The possible implications of this perspective will be further discussed in this chapter and in chapter 6.

RECEPTION

Reception can be defined as all of the components involved in decoding and comprehending language. Listening and reading are the two primary modes for receiving language. Therefore, factors associated with these processes can impact on receptive language.

Acuity   Obviously, if a person cannot properly hear information, the ability to receive and accurately decode that information will be affected. As previously discussed, profound hearing losses can result in an inability to acquire oral language. Most people with hearing loss, however, have mild losses and usually acquire language, but at a delayed rate (Robbins, 1986). Prelingual deaf children—those with congenital hearing loss—present the most acute problem regarding reception. As noted previously, the babbling sounds produced by deaf and by hearing infants are different (Oller, 1991).

Otitis media, an infection in the middle ear, is the largest single cause of hearing loss. Young children commonly have middle-ear infections. Usually these infections are treated through antibiotics and result in no permanent damage. But a mild hearing loss can result from the condition, which could impact on language proficiency (Martin, 1990).

Hearing loss directly affects phonological development. Specific speech disorders, including articulation and voice quality problems, often result from hearing impairments. Also, children who have hearing impairments often have problems mastering language subtleties, such as idiomatic expressions.

Attention Problems   Attention deficits discussed under severe language disabilities have implications for mild and moderate disabilities as well, particularly in the area of language reception. Without the ability to focus attention on a speaker, the spoken message may never be received; without the ability to focus on the printed page, the written message may never be received. Therefore, even though a student may have adequate auditory acuity, attentional problems could result in not properly receiving the oral information.

Phonological Discriminations   Many advances have been made recently in the area of phonological development and phonological disorders (Stoel-Gammon, 1991). Some children have difficulty discriminating sounds even though their hearing and attention are normal. At gross levels they may have problems in discriminating noises such as horns and whistles, or telephone rings and doorbells. These kinds of problems also suggest an inability to focus on relevant auditory stimuli, suggesting auditory figure-ground problems. At a more discrete level, difficulty in differentiating words with similar sounds, such as ball-bat, back-bat, and pen-pin, may be the phonological problem (Eisenson, 1972).

A great deal of research has been done relating phonology and reading problems. Obviously, understanding the sounds associated with various letters, and "sounding out" letters, enables people to read. Good readers are able to do this quickly and efficiently; they do not labor over individual letters and words (Hargis, Terhaar-Yonders, Williams, & Reed, 1988; Samuels, 1988).

Several authors have contended that a distinct relationship exists between phonology, or sound discriminations, and reading disorders (Liberman & Shankweiler, 1985; Myers & Hammill, 1990). Logically, a solid relationship would seem to exist between discriminating different sounds and phonetic analysis and its specific sub-skills, such as sound blending. Although many students with phonological problems are capable of learning to read effectively, auditory discrimination skills clearly are needed to develop effective phonetic analysis and word attack skills (Zigmond, 1969).

Syntactical Discriminations   Most studies dealing with receptive disorders have focused on auditory discrimination problems. Recently, however, interest has been growing in the importance of syntax in language disabilities. Children who have trouble distinguishing the meaning of syntactical structures also will have trouble comprehending spoken and written language.

The connection between syntax and comprehension was described by Wallach and Goldsmith (1977). They concluded that comprehension suffers in children who decode isolated words instead of "chunking" clauses together when necessary. In order to chunk, or group, content together, children must be able to use the structure of sentences, both to understand and to remember the information and concepts presented. To comprehend what they read, students must be able to integrate the information they read with background information each student possesses (Wade, 1990).

Gaining proper syntactical forms is a developmental process. Young children frequently use phrases such as "Dog sleep there" and "Me go store." If these kinds of developmental syntactical forms continue beyond certain chronological ages, a language problem could exist (Peterson, 1987). Syntactical errors later have a negative impact on reading and listening comprehension.

Semantic Variables   Difficulties in semantics, or extracting the meaning from words, can result in basic problems in language comprehension. A basic consideration is the strength of a child's vocabulary. Unlike other components of language, which focus on mastering some rule or skill, development of an individual's vocabulary should continue throughout the person's life (Peterson, 1987).

Vocabulary deficits are a frequent characteristic of language-delayed children. As a result of their having fewer opportunities for language interaction, their opportunities for developing vocabulary are restricted. This may result in difficulty attending to teachers or parents because these children do not understand much of the conversation. In reading, vocabulary deficits may be overlooked inadvertently if a child has developed sufficient word recognition skills to be a proficient word caller. The obvious result will be reduced comprehension skills—the essence of reading (Smith, Graves, & Aldridge, in press).

Children frequently have semantic problems with words that have different meanings in different contexts. A child may understand the word "run" when used as a verb to mean "moving" but may not understand "run" when it is used to describe a "run" in a stocking, or a baseball "run" (Lerner, 1988).

Automatic Receptive Processing   Once specific receptive skills become automatic, the process is called "automatic receptive processing" (Chalfant & Scheffelin, 1969). The concept refers to the point when individuals who do not have a receptive language disorder rely on automatic receptive processing routinely; attention shifts from processing a signal to its total meaning (Faas, 1976).

Students who do not develop automatic receptive processing are burdened with laborious, inefficient decoding of written or spoken words. This has detrimental effects on comprehension because so much time and energy must go into decoding and receiving small parts of the whole. As previously noted, efficient readers do not spend a great deal of time or effort decoding (Hargis et al., 1988; Cooper, Warncke, & Shipman, 1988; Samuels, 1988). This results in better attention to the whole and, therefore, more efficient comprehension. The same process works for individuals receiving oral language.

PRODUCTION

Production means to express or encode language. The two predominant means of production are *speech* and *written expression*. A small number of individuals with hearing impairments accomplish production through sign language. Production is an obvious necessity to be successful in school, and production is equally important for adults. Imagine how difficult it would be to survive without the ability to speak, use sign language, or write. Several different components of production pose potential problems for individuals with language problems: intention, semantic expression, and pragmatics, syntactical arrangements, phonological production, and automatic expressive processing.

Intention   The power of the social base of language is clearly revealed in the area of intention to communicate. MacDonald (1979) noted that children often "know more than they say," indicating that language development often is hindered more by a child's desire and interest in expression than by learning specific forms. Children with language delays in particular must develop the concept of intention because the ability to communicate results from the need to satisfy specific needs and to achieve social control, both of which require increasingly complex language skills. Designing social environments to "force" the use of language is a promising method of intervention (MacDonald, 1979). The key in this approach is to stimulate and motivate the child.

Semantic Expression   The semantic component of production, which stems directly from intention, communicates meaning and therefore is an essential aspect of expression. It includes text organization and vocabulary (Gould, 1991). Vocabulary deficiencies often result in communication disorders. Nonverbal speech, usually in the form of gestures or signs, frequently is substituted when children's vocabularies do not meet their needs for communication. This means of communication can delay the development of adequate language competence.

Using expressive language properly in a variety of situations is *pragmatics*. This includes modifying the words used in conversation based on the sophistication of the audience receiving the information. Examples of improper pragmatics would be asking personal questions of someone you have just met, or using poor grammar and slang while making a formal speech (Gearheart, Weishahn, & Gearheart, 1988). Chapter 1 contains a more detailed discussion of pragmatics.

Update

Learning Disabilities/Communication Disabilities

An important area of concern in the field of language disabilities is the co-occurrence of language disorders and learning disabilities. Schoenbrodt, Kumin, and Sloan (1997) indicated that the rate of co-occurrence may be quite high, and may represent manifestations of the same underlying problem, or may be at times the same problem defined differently at different times during the life span. Given this fact, Schoenbrodt et al (1997) suggested the following emphases for intervention programs:

- Enhance the language environments for students to promote their learning opportunities. Specific emphases should include modifications in the physical setting, increased opportunities for social interaction with peers and the teacher, and insuring high levels of teacher responsiveness.
- Target the development of vocabulary with emphasis on words that are most relevant and functional for the individual student.
- Enhance the learning of content by providing semantic (i.e., meaning) organizers such as webs and the use of mapping.
- Specifically focus on the development of the ability to engage in public speaking by teaching appropriate strategies.
- Enhance students' ability to successfully take part in conversations by teaching awareness of conversational rules and the use of social cues.

Source: Schoenbrodt, L., Kumin, L., & Sloan, J. M. (1997). Learning disabilities existing concomitantly with communication disorder. *Journal of Learning Disabilities, 30,* 264–281.

Difficulty with word finding and retrieval is termed *dysnomia* (Wiig, 1990). A significant subgroup of children with language disabilities seems to have this expressive language problem. Retrieval difficulty often is reflected in the use of gestures and phrases such as "whatchamachallit," "thingamajig," or "you know," as well as the tendency to circumlocute or talk around the intended word or idea they are attempting to express. Naming persons, animals, objects, actions, or attributes is a major problem (Wiig, 1990).

Another indicator of semantic deficiencies is "cocktail party speech," in which children use appropriate syntax and phonological patterns, but have a weak conceptual basis for their language and do not seem to understand what they are saying (Bloom & Lahey, 1978). Socially, this form of speech works well for students; however, its impact on achievement and grades can be negative.

Oral expression and reading comprehension seem to be highly correlated (Bailet, 1991). An assumption can be made that oral language deficits are valid predictors of later writing problems. A prevalent problem, however, is presented by children who are skilled in oral expression but show marked written-language deficiencies, including poor word choice, usage, and conceptualization. Educators must approach each child individually and differentiate between difficulties related to oral deficits and those unique to written composition.

One typical measure of semantic production, verbal expression, seems to be highly susceptible to environmental influences. As noted in the literature investigating the impact of institutionalization on language, discussed earlier in this chapter, expressive skills seem to be restricted in individuals who reside in institutional settings.

Syntactical Arrangements   Children with disabilities obviously have problems with standard English syntax and morphology. In addition, many children who are not disabled but who grow up in minority racial, ethnic, and low socioeconomic environments encounter difficulties (Cole & Taylor, 1990). As a result, teachers must scrupulously discriminate between syntactical disorders and linguistic differences. Chapter 3 explores in some depth the problems minority culture children experience with language.

Some children display difficulties within the structure of their own dialects and make regular and irregular errors when they build words and link them grammatically. Some of the common grammatical errors include choice of incorrect verb endings to indicate tense and number, fragmentary phrasing, and problems with specific parts of speech. Weller (1979) found that children with language disorders have particular trouble with descriptors (adjectives) and functor words (prepositions, connectives, and articles). The speech patterns of these children are characterized by restricted noun and verb combinations.

Children who have expressive grammatical problems often are confused with dysnomic children. Rather than "searching" for a specific word like dysnomic children, however, those with expressive grammatical problems may be looking for the correct phrase or sentence to use. The primary problem for these children may be ungrammatical or omitted words necessary for correct syntax (Eisenson, 1972).

Update

Section 504: Implications for Teachers

In 1973, Section 504 of the Rehabilitation Act was passed. Although it did not receive a great deal of attention, the law has had a significant impact on public schools in recent years. Section 504 is civil rights legislation for persons with disabilities. It prohibits entities that receive federal funds (including public schools) from discriminating against individuals with disabilities. It further requires that schools provide a free appropriate public education (FAPE) to students who are considered to have a disability under Section 504.

The definition of disability in Section 504 is much broader than the one in IDEA. The result is that many students who may not be eligible for special education under IDEA may be eligible for services and protections under Section 504; some of these students are likely to have needs for language intervention programs. Section 504 indicates that a person is considered to have a disability if that person:

- has a physical or mental impairment which substantially limits one or more of such person's major life activities,
- has a record of such an impairment, or
- is regarded as having such an impairment.

Physical or mental impairment includes all of the disabilities covered under IDEA, plus many additional ones, such as asthma, diabetes, AIDS, cardiac problems, or cosmetic disfigurement. If the impairment affects a body system, which includes speech organs, then the person is considered to have a disability under Section 504.

For teachers, Section 504 presents many challenges. Teachers need to be aware of the types of children that might be eligible for services and have a process for referring those children for services. Similar to IDEA, Section 504 requires schools to formally refer students that are suspected of being eligible for services under 504. If, after an appropriate evaluation, the student is deemed eligible, then an individual accommodation plan must be developed and implemented for the student. Although the requirement for the individual accommodation plan is not as extensive as the requirements for IEPs are under IDEA, schools must still develop written plans that are designed to ensure an appropriate education for all students who have a disability under Section 504. Because many students not eligible for services under IDEA are eligible under Section 504, general education teachers are primarily responsible for most of these students. For students who are eligible under Section 504 and need speech interventions, schools are required to provide them. This could include speech and audiological services, even for students who do not need and are not eligible for special education.

Source: Smith, T. E. C., & Patton, J. R. 1998). *Section 504 and the public schools: A practical guide*. Austin, TX: Pro-Ed.

Phonological Production   Disorders related to the production of speech sounds are the most prevalent of all conditions that affect school-age children. In addition, they are the most common disability found in combination with other disabilities. Students with mental retardation, learning disabilities, emotional problems, hearing impairments, and other handicapping conditions frequently exhibit speech disorders (McCormick, 1984b; Patton et al., 1990; Lerner, 1988; Seidenberg & Bernstein, 1986; Gibbs & Cooper, 1989).

Many of these phonological production problems result from physiological disorders. Speech might be impeded by *dysarthria,* a dysfunction of the central nervous system that may result in paralysis of the jaw or tongue. *Apraxia,* in contrast, is the inability to produce voluntary motions even though all speech mechanisms are functional. Although this problem is not an expressive language disorder or a motoric problem as such, the child "cannot order his articulators to do his bidding" (Eisenson, 1972, p. 72). Finally, *dysgraphia* is a written language problem in which the brain sends inadequate messages to the visual-motor integration system. As a result, a child cannot copy and is unable to write legible graphemes as the visual symbols of phonemes (Bain, 1991).

Automatic Expressive Processing   Like its counterpart in reception, the automatic processing of spoken and written language occurs when the student has mastered previous areas. Automatic processing naturally results in the increased speed and accuracy of oral and written expression. Syntactical problems, motor deficiencies, visual-motor integration problems, and other basic expressive language skill deficits could result in impaired ability to speak or write.

Limitations in automatic expressive processing skills have profound repercussions in school. Children who are unable to express themselves orally or in writing are at a major disadvantage in the academic arena. Speech pathologists, special education teachers, and regular classroom teachers have to work together to enhance expressive skills of all students to enable them to maximize their educational achievement levels.

LANGUAGE INTERVENTION STRATEGIES

The above discussion highlights the many different language disorders, oral and written, that can create problems for children in school and for adults in the work force. These disorders involve reception difficulties or problems in production. Regardless of the specific disorder, teachers must develop intervention strategies that facilitate appropriate language development. The predominant approach for some students could be to teach strategies that actually will circumvent the language problem.

One resource both regular classroom and special education teachers have for assistance with children's language disorders is the speech-language pathologist (SLP), a professional specifically trained in dealing with these problems. Speech-language pathologists, found in most school systems, provide intervention services to students with a variety of language difficulties. Miller (1989) noted that the services they provide have evolved a great deal over the past 70 years, currently offering intervention services using five different service models:

1. The specialist teaches a self-contained language class.
2. The specialist team teaches with the regular classroom teacher, special education teacher, or resource teacher.
3. The specialist provides one-to-one classroom-based intervention with selected students.
4. The specialist consults with the classroom teachers or special service providers (regular and special education teachers, reading specialist, learning disability teacher, psychologist, social worker, nurse, etc.).
5. The specialist provides staff development, curriculum development, or program development to the school or district.

Children in some schools do not have regular access to a speech-language pathologist's services. The school may not employ them, or, more likely, there simply are not enough speech-language specialists available to meet the needs of all children. In this latter case, the available speech and language services are provided to the students with the most severe disabilities; students with mild language problems are the ones without services.

Regardless of access to speech-language services from a specialist, regular and special education teachers should enhance language development in their classrooms as much as possible. In fact, a growing model for providing speech-language services to children is to rely on students' caregivers, primarily parents and teachers, to facilitate language development. The trend in many cases is away from pure language training methods to activities that more closely reflect normal language learning (McCormick, 1986). Teachers and caregivers must keep in mind that the goals of language intervention "should focus on increasing the frequency of communicative behaviors, shaping production of increasingly more sophisticated language functions, and encouraging expression of familiar functions with more advanced language forms" (p. 125).

Much of what regular and special education teachers do with children to enhance language development involves enriching the language learning environment. Dudley-Marling and Searle (1988) have listed the following guidelines that should lead to an environment facilitating language development:

1. The physical setting must promote talk.
2. The teacher must provide opportunities for children to interact and use language as they learn.
3. The teacher needs to provide opportunities for children to use language for a variety of purposes, for a variety of audiences.
4. The teacher needs to respond to student talk in ways that encourage continued talk. (pp. 140–141)

SUMMARY

This chapter has focused on disabilities that often occur in language functioning. The first section of the chapter dealt with how language disabilities are classified. One model used to differentiate language problems used three different groupings: (1) the relationship of language to normal language development, (2) specific features of language that cause problems, and (3) language differences based on etiology or correlates. Throughout the chapter, the distinction was made between mild language problems and severe language problems.

The next major section of the chapter presented information about correlates of language disabilities. Topics such as brain pathology, cognitive development, social factors, institutionalization, and attention deficits, as they relate to language disorders, were discussed. It was noted that a wide variety of different factors appear to be correlated with language problems.

The final sections of the chapter focused on the characteristics of students with mild language problems and language intervention strategies. A key in trying to characterize students with language disabilities is the notion that this group of individuals comprise a very heterogeneous group. While there are several different ways to implement intervention strategies, the best ways focus on using natural language interactions in natural environments.

REFERENCES

Allen, D. A. (1989). Developmental language disorders in preschool children: Clinical subtypes and syndromes. *School Psychology Review, 18*, 442–451.

Aram, D. M. (1991). Brain lesions in children: Implications for developmental language disorders. In J. Miller (Ed.), *Research on language disorders*. Austin, TX: Pro-Ed.

Azrin, N. H., Kaplan, S. J., & Foxx, R. M. (1973). Autism reversal: Eliminating stereotyped self-stimulation of retarded individuals. *American Journal on Mental Deficiency, 78*, 241–248.

Bailet, L. L. (1991). Development and disorders of spelling in the beginning school years. In A. M. Bain, L. L. Bailet, & L. C. Moats (Eds.), *Written language disorders*. Austin, TX: Pro-Ed.

Bain, A. M. (1991). Handwriting disorders. In A. M. Bain, L. L. Bailet, & L. C. Moats (Eds.), *Written language disorders*. Austin, TX: Pro-Ed.

Bloom, L., & Lahey, M. (1978). *Language development and language disorders*. New York: John Wiley.

Buium, N., Rynders, J., & Turnure, J. (1974). Early maternal linguistic environment of normal and Down's syndrome language learning children. *American Journal of Mental Deficiency, 79*, 52–57.

Byrne, K., Abbeduto, L., & Brooks, P. (1990). The language of children with spina bifida and hydrocephalus: Meeting task demands and mastering syntax. *Journal of Speech and Hearing Disorders, 55*, 118–123.

Campbell, B., & Grove, R. (1978). Social and attentional aspects of echolalia in highly echolaic mentally retarded persons. *American Journal of Mental Deficiency, 82*, 414–416.

Carter, J. L., & Capabianco, R. F. (1976). A systematic language stimulation program—revisited. *Education and Training in Mental Retardation, 11*, 112–116.

Chalfant, J. C., & Scheffelin, M. A. (1969). *Central processing dysfunction of children*. Bethesda, MD: National Institute of Health.

Cheseldine, S., & McConkey, R. (1979). Paternal speech to young Down's syndrome children: An intervention study. *American Journal of Mental Deficiency, 83*, 612–620.

Cleland, C. C. (1979). *The profoundly mentally retarded*. Englewood Cliffs, NJ: Prentice Hall.

Cole, P. A., & Taylor, O. L. (1990). Performance of working class African-American children on three tests of articulation. *Language, Speech, & Hearing Services in Schools, 21*, 17–21.

Coles, G. (1987). *The learning mystique*. New York: Pantheon Books.

Cooper, J. D., Warncke, E. W., & Shipman, D. A. (1988). *The what and how of reading instruction*. Columbus, OH: Charles E. Merrill Publishing.

deVilliers, J. G., & deVilliers, P. A. (1978). *Language acquisition*. Cambridge, MA: Harvard University Press.

Dollard, J., Doob, L. W., Miller, N. E., Mowrer, O. H., & Sears, R. R. (1939). *Frustration and aggression*. New Haven, CT: Yale University Press.

Dudley-Marling, C., & Searle, D. (1988). Enriching language learning environments for students with learning disabilities. *Journal of Learning Disabilities, 21,* 140–143.

Eisenson, J. (1972). *Aphasia in children.* New York: Harper & Row.

Eisenson, J. (1990). Impairments and delays for spoken and written language in children. *Education, 109,* 419–423.

Faas, L. A. (1976). *Learning disabilities: A competency-based approach.* Boston: Houghton Mifflin.

Finch-Williams, A. (1984). The developmental relationship between cognition and communication: Implications for assessment. *Topics in Language Disorders, 5,* 1–13.

Flavell, J. H. (1977). *Cognitive development.* Englewood Cliffs, NJ: Prentice Hall.

Garber, N. B., & David, L. E. (1975). Semantic considerations in the treatment of echolalia. *Mental Retardation, 13,* 8–11.

Gearheart, B. R., & Gearheart, C. J. (1989). *Learning disabilities: Educational strategies.* Columbus, OH: Charles E. Merrill Publishing.

Gearheart, B. R., Weishahn, M. W., & Gearheart, C. J. (1988). *The exceptional student in the regular classroom* (4th ed.). Columbus, OH: Charles E. Merrill Publishing.

Gentry, D., & Olson, J. (1985). Severely mentally retarded young children. In D. Bricker & J. Filler (Eds.), *Severe mental retardation.* Reston, VA: CEC Division on Mental Retardation.

Gibbs, D. P., & Cooper, E. B. (1989). Prevalence of communication disorders in students with learning disabilities. *Journal of Learning Disabilities, 22,* 60–63.

Gould, B. W. (1991). Curricular strategies for written expression. In A. M. Bain, L. L. Bailet, & L. C. Moats (Eds.), *Written language disorders.* Austin, TX: Pro-Ed.

Grossman, H. J. (1983). *Manual on terminology and classification in mental retardation.* Washington, DC: American Association on Mental Deficiency.

Gutman, A. J., & Rondal, J. A. (1979). Verbal operants in mothers' speech to nonretarded and Down's syndrome children matched for linguistic level. *American Journal of Mental Deficiency, 83,* 446–452.

Hallahan, D. P., & Kauffman, J. M. (1991). *Exceptional children.* Englewood Cliffs, NJ: Prentice Hall.

Hardman, M. L., Drew, C. J., Egan, M. W., & Wolf, B. (1990). *Human exceptionality* (3rd ed.). Boston: Allyn & Bacon.

Hargis, C. H., Terhaar-Yonkers, M., Williams., P. C., & Reed, M. T. (1988). Repetition requirements for word recognition. *Journal of Reading, 31,* 320–327.

Hixon, T. J., Shriberg, L. D., & Saxman, J. H. (1980). *Introduction to communication disorders.* Englewood Cliffs, NJ: Prentice Hall.

Hoff-Ginsberg, E. (1990). Maternal speech and the child's development of syntax: A further look. *Child Language, 17,* 85–99.

Hopper, C., & Helmick, R. (1977). Nonverbal communication and the severely handicapped: Some considerations. *AAESPH Review, 2,* 47–52.

Itard, J. M. G. (1962). *The wild boy of Aveyron.* Englewood Cliffs, NJ: Prentice Hall.

Johnston, J. R. (1991). Questions about cognition in children with specific language impairment. In J. Miller (Ed.), *Research on child language disorders.* Austin, TX: Pro-Ed.

Kahn, J. V. (1975). Relationship of Piaget's sensorimotor period to language acquisition of profoundly retarded children. *American Journal of Mental Deficiency, 79,* 640–643.

Kahn, J. V. (1978). Acceleration of object permanence with severely and profoundly retarded children. *AAESPH Review, 3,* 15–22.

Kauffman, J. M. (1977). *Characteristics of behavior disorders of children and youth.* Columbus, OH: Charles E. Merrill Publishing.

Kauffman, J. M. (1985). *Characteristics of behavior disorders of children and youth* (3rd ed.). Columbus, OH: Charles E. Merrill Publishing.

Kauffman, J. M. (1989). *Characteristics of children's behavior disorders* (4th ed.). Columbus, OH: Charles E. Merrill Publishing.

Kleppe, S. A., Katayama, K. M., Shipley, K. G., & Foushee, D. R. (1990). *Journal of Speech & Hearing Disorders, 55,* 300–309.

Knoblock, P. (1982). *Teaching and mainstreaming autistic children.* Denver: Love Publishing.

Lenneberg, E. H. (1967). *Biological foundations of language.* New York: John Wiley & Sons.

Leonard, L. B. (1978). *Cognitive factors in early linguistic development.* In R. L. Schiefelbusch (Ed.), *Bases for language intervention.* Baltimore: University Park Press.

Leonard, L. (1990). Language disorders in preschool children. In G. H. Shames & E. H. Wiig (Eds.), *Human communication disorders* (3rd ed.). Columbus, OH: Charles E. Merrill Publishing.

Lerner, J. (1988). *Learning disabilities* (5th ed.). Boston: Houghton Mifflin.

Liberman, I. Y., & Shankweiler, D. (1985). Phonology and the problems of learning to read and write. *Remedial and Special Education, 6,* 8–17.

Lovaas, O. I. (1977). *The autistic child: Language development through behavior modification.* New York: Irvington Publishers.

Love, H. D., Mainord, J. C., & Naylor, D. (1976). *Language development of exceptional children.* Springfield, IL: Charles C Thomas.

MacDonald, J. D. (1979). *Parent-child interaction: An environmental approach to language assessment.* Paper presented to 57th annual Council for Exceptional Children convention, Dallas.

Magee, P. A., & Newcomer, P. L. (1978). The relationship between oral language skills and academic achievement of learning disabled children. *Learning Disability Quarterly, 1,* 63–67.

Martin, F. N. (1990). Hearing and hearing disorders. In G. H. Shames & E. H. Wiig (Eds.), *Human communication disorders.* Columbus, OH: Charles E. Merrill Publishing.

McCormick, L. (1984b). Review of normal language acquisition. In L. McCormick & R. L. Schiefelbusch (Eds.), *Early language intervention.* Columbus, OH: Charles E. Merrill Publishing.

McCormick, L. (1986). Keeping up with language intervention trends. *Teaching Exceptional Children, 18,* 123–129.

McCormick, L., & Schiefelbusch, R. L. (Eds.). (1984). *Early language intervention.* Columbus, OH: Charles E. Merrill Publishing.

McLean, J. R., & Snyder-McLean, L. K. (1978). *A transactional approach to early language training.* Columbus, OH: Charles E. Merrill Publishing.

McNutt, J. C., & Leri, S. M. (1979). Language differences between institutionalized and non-institutionalized retarded children. *American Journal of Mental Deficiency, 83,* 339–345.

Menyuk, P. (1987). *Language development.* Glennview, IL: Scott, Foresman.

Miller, L. (1989). Classroom-based language intervention. *Language, Speech, and Hearing Services in Schools, 20,* 149–152.

Mire, S. P., & Chisholm, R. W. (1990). Functional communication goals for adolescents and adults who are severely and moderately mentally handicapped. *Language, Speech, and Hearing Services in Schools, 21,* 57–58.

Myers, P. I., & Hammill, D. D. (1990). *Learning disabilities: Basic concepts, assessment practices, and instructional strategies* (4th ed.). Austin, TX: Pro-Ed.

Oller, D. K. (1991). Similarities and differences in vocalizations of deaf and hearing infants: Future directions for research. In J. Miller (Ed.), *Research on child language disorders.* Austin, TX: Pro-Ed.

Owens, R. W., McNerney, C. D., Bigler-Burke, L., & Lepre-Clark, C. (1987). The use of language facilitators with residential retarded populations. *Topics in Language Disorders, 7,* 47–63.

Paluszny, M. J. (1979). *Autism: A practical guide for parents and professionals.* Syracuse, NY: Syracuse University Press.

Patton, J. R., Bierne-Smith, M., & Payne, J. (1990). *Mental retardation* (2nd ed.). Columbus, OH: Merrill.

Peterson, G. A., & Sherrod, K. B. (1979). *Mothers and their language-delayed children: Speech patterns.* Paper presented at 57th annual Council for Exceptional Children convention, Dallas.

Peterson, N. L. (1987). *Early intervention for handicapped and at-risk children.* Denver: Love Publishing.

Phillips, J. L., & Balthazar, E. E. (1979). Some correlates of language deterioration in severely and profoundly retarded long-term institutionalized residents. *American Journal of Mental Deficiency, 83,* 402–408.

Polloway, E. A., & Patton, J. R. (1989). Biological causes of mental retardation. In J. R. Patton, M. Bierne-Smith, & J. S. Payne (Eds.), *Mental retardation* (3rd ed.). Columbus, OH: Charles E. Merrill.

Polloway, E. A., Patton, J. R., Payne, J. S., & Payne, R. P. (1989). *Strategies for teaching learners with special needs.* Columbus, OH: Charles E. Merrill Publishing.

Prizant, B. M., Audet, L. R., Burke, G. M., Hummel, L. J., Maher, S. R., & Theadore, G. (1990). Communication disorders and emotional/behavioral disorders in children and adolescents. *Journal of Speech and Hearing Disorders, 55,* 179–192.

Rago, W. V. (1977). Eye gaze and dominance hierarchy in profoundly mentally retarded males, *American Journal of Mental Deficiency, 82,* 145–148.

Reid, D. K., & Hresko, W. P. (1980). *Reading and language development in normally achieving and learning disabled children.* Paper presented at 2nd annual conference, Division for Children with Learning Disabilities, Denver.

Robbins, A. M. (1986). Facilitating language comprehension in young hearing-impaired children. *Topics in Language Disorders, 6,* 12–24.

Robinson, N. M., & Robinson, H. B. (1976). *The mentally retarded child* (2nd ed.). New York: McGraw-Hill.

Rosenberger, P. B. (1978). Neurological processes. In R. L. Schiefelbusch (Ed.), *Bases of language intervention.* Baltimore: University Park Press.

Samuels, S. J. (1988). Decoding and automaticity: Helping poor readers become automatic at word recognition. *The Reading Teacher, 41,* 756–760.

Sapir, S., & Aronson, A. E. (1990). The relationship between psychopathology and speech and language disorders in neurologic patients. *Journal of Speech and Hearing Disorders, 55,* 503–509.

Scarr, S., Weinberg, R. A., & Levine, A. (1986). *Understanding development.* New York: Harcourt Brace Jovanovich.

Schiefelbusch, R. (1972). Language disabilities of cognitively involved children. In J. V. Irwin & M. Marge (Eds.), *Principles of childhood language disabilities.* Englewood Cliffs, NJ: Prentice Hall.

Schoenbrodt, L., Kumin, L., & Sloan, J. M. (1997). Learning disabilities existing concomitantly with communication disorder. *Journal of Learning Disabilities, 30,* 264–281.

Seidenberg, P. L., & Bernstein, D. K. (1986). The comprehension of similes and metaphors by learning disabled and nonlearning-disabled children. *Language, Speech, and Hearing Services in the Schools, 17,* 219–229.

Seltzer, M. M., & Krauss, J. W. (1987). *Aging and mental retardation.* Washington, DC: American Association on Mental Retardation.

Shames, G. H., & Wiig, E. H. (1990). *Human communication disorders.* Columbus, OH: Charles E. Merrill.

Smith, J. D., & Polloway, E. A. (1991). *Discharge patterns from a facility serving persons with mental retardation.* Unpublished manuscript.

Smith, T. E. C. (1990). *Introduction to education,* 2nd ed. St. Paul: West Publishing.

Smith, T. E. C., Dowdy, C. A., & Finn, D. F. (in press). *Teaching students with mild disabilities.* Ft. Worth: Holt, Rinehart & Winston.

Smith, T. E. C., Graves, S., & Aldridge, J. (in press). *Teaching reading.* St. Paul: West Publishing.

Smith, T. E. C., Price, B. J., & Marsh, G. E. (1986). *Mildly handicapped children and adults.* St. Paul: West.

Snell, M. E. (1987). *Systematic instruction of persons with handicaps* (3rd ed.). Columbus, OH: Merrill.

Snyder, L. K., & McLean, J. E. (1977). Deficient acquisition strategies: A proposed conceptual framework for analyzing severe language deficiency. *American Journal of Mental Deficiency, 18,* 338–349.

Stoel-Gammon, C. (1991). Issues in phonological development and disorders. In J. Miller (Ed.), *Research on child language disorders.* Austin, TX: Pro-Ed.

Talkington, I. W., Hall, S., & Altman, R. (1971). Communication deficits and aggression in the mentally retarded. *American Journal of Mental Deficiency, 76,* 235–237.

Tomasello, M., & Farrar, M. (1984). Cognitive bases of lexical development: Object permanence and relational words. *Journal of Child Language, 11,* 477–493.

Uzgiris, I. C., & Hunt, J. M. (1975). *Assessment in infancy: Ordinal scales of psychological development.* Urbana: University of Illinois Press.

Wade, S. E. (1990). Using think alouds to assess comprehension. *The Reading Teacher, 43,* 442–451.

Wallach, G. P., & Goldsmith, S. C. (1977). Language-based learning disabilities: Reading is language too! *Journal of Learning Disabilities, 10,* 178–183.

Weller, C. (1979). Improving syntactical skills of language-deviant children. *Journal of Learning Disabilities, 12,* 470–479.

Wiig, E. H. (1990). Language disabilities in school-age children and youth. In G. H. Shames & E. H. Wiig (Eds.), *Human communication disorders.* Columbus, OH: Charles E. Merrill Publishing.

Wiig, E. H., Lapointe, C., & Semel, E. M. (1977). Relationships among language processing and production abilities of learning disabled adolescents. *Journal of Learning Disabilities, 10,* 292–299.

Yoder, D. E., & Calculator, S. (1981). Some perspectives on intervention. *Journal of Autism and Developmental Disorders, 11,* 107–123.

Zigler, E., & Balla, D. A. (1977). Impact of institutional experience on the behavior and development of retarded persons. *American Journal of Mental Deficiency, 28,* 1–11.

Zigmond, N. K. (1969). Auditory processes in children with learning disabilities. In L. Tarnpol (Ed.), *Learning disabilities: Introduction to educational and medical management.* Springfield, IL: Charles C. Thomas.

3

Cultural Diversity and Language Differences

D ifferent subcultures in this society use language of different forms and in some cases in different ways. The uses of language by various cultural groups, the similarities and differences of language among various cultural groups, and the implications for teaching will be explored in this chapter. Cultural differences should not be assumed to be predictive of, or associated with, learning problems. The focus here is on children from minority cultural groups who suffer from the "double whammy" (Chinn, 1979) of having a disability.

Children from a minority cultural group who have a disability challenge teachers more seriously than children who are either from a minority cultural group or who are disabled. The emphasis of this chapter is on the ways in which linguistic and cultural diversity can result in a need for alternative assessment and teaching methods. The overriding assumption is that traditional assessment and teaching methodologies must be modified to facilitate nondiscriminatory assessments and appropriate interventions.

VARIABLES AFFECTING SPECIAL EDUCATION FOR CHILDREN FROM MINORITY GROUPS

Students from minority cultural groups (and those from low socioeconomic populations) frequently are considered candidates for special education services in public schools as a result of their minority status. Podemski, Price, Smith, and Marsh (1984) identified the following factors related to providing appropriate services for these children:

- Lack of skilled assessment personnel for children with atypical linguistic and cultural characteristics.
- Inadequate instruments and procedures for assessment and identification.
- Lack of personnel trained to appropriately serve this population.
- Limited research base regarding special education services to minority children.
- Limited materials specifically designed for minority students with disabilities.
- The need for providing bilingual educational programs for these students.

Although these factors affect the provision of special education, the Individuals with Disabilities Education Act (IDEA) requires that appropriate services be provided. Therefore, school personnel must overcome the special problems associated with including minority students in special education programs.

DIVERSITY IN SOCIETY

The United States population is composed of individuals with many different backgrounds (Adler, 1990). Some of these people are third- or fourth-generation and even more experienced Americans; others are first- or second-generation Americans. In addition, a growing number of individuals immigrate each year but have not acquired citizenship. These groups of people represent a wide range of racial, ethnic, and linguistic backgrounds.

This wide spectrum of characteristics associated with students from different cultures reveals that the melting pot theory has not been totally realized (Emihovich, 1988; First, 1988; Smith, 1990). The result is "cultural pluralism"—the realization that assimilation of many individuals from minority cultural groups has simply not occurred (Emihovich, 1988; Smith, 1990; Tiedt & Tiedt, 1986). The acceptance of cultural pluralism results in viewing individuals with different cultural backgrounds as positive; diversity among the population is considered positive for our society (Podemski et al., 1984). The diversity of our population seems to be getting greater rather than smaller (Kellogg, 1988; Koenig & Biel, 1989). In fact, by the year 2,000, 1/2 of all children in public schools will be from minority groups (Hodgkinson, 1985).

The number and diversity of new immigrants is dramatic. People moving into the United States "represent more than 70 language groups and dozens of nations. They come from such modern, industrialized nations as China, Japan, and Korea, and from such rural and war-devastated nations as Laos and Cambodia. They come from severely depressed rural regions of Mexico and Honduras, and they flee from civil wars in Central America. While the majority of immigrant students speak Spanish, there has been a large increase in immigrants who speak Asian languages" (Olsen, 1988, p. 212). Divoky (1988) reported that Oriental immigrants in public schools speak a variety of native languages, including Cambodian, Cantonese, Hmong, Japanese, Korean, Lao, Mandfarin, Tagalog, Samoan, and Vietnamese.

Despite an earlier trend toward assimilation, more recent immigrants cling to their traditional cultures and language. This chapter focuses on those groups that, at least in a generalized sense, demonstrate significant linguistic variance from the standard English of the majority culture. Generalizing within or between minority groups, however, is difficult, if not impossible, because of regional, cultural, and linguistic differences (Baca, 1980). Similarly, Henderson (1980) has cautioned that using stereotypes based on subcultures can be highly misleading. Variances within groups will most often exceed variance between them, indicating that cultural groups are often more alike than different.

Two factors cause the societal mainstream to notice language differences. First, the allegiance theory (McLaughlin, 1978) postulates that people who speak standard English (or American English) with an obvious accent are in a "suspect class" as far as their natural allegiance is concerned. This orientation suggests that individuals with accents are more loyal to the country of their native language than to the country of their current residence. Although this is obviously a narrow and ethnocentric viewpoint, some people in this country adhere to its principles. During World War II individuals of Japanese descent were incarcerated; many German-Americans were also relocated. In the 1990s this form of discrimination will likely continue, possibly against those with Arabic connections, as well as Orientals. Problems in the early 1990s in the Persian Gulf and the growing economic competition with Korea and Japan have created a climate in which this kind of prejudice can easily occur.

Second, the language patterns of groups that rely on public rather than formal language codes have been scrutinized. *Public language codes* are associated with informal speaking and writing and the language of the "common person." *Formal language codes* are considered part of the language of schools, middle and upper class socioeconomic groups, individuals whose vocations are included in the "professions," and others considered above the masses by various criteria. Some individuals who use the formal language system may decide that the language of the other group is inferior. This practice is unfortunate; many linguists have even challenged its validity on a scientific basis. The idea that some language patterns are inferior to others is simply an academic form of discrimination.

form prejudices against various groups

DIFFERENCE OR DEFICIT?

McLaughlin (1978) hypothesized that linguistic diversity is the norm rather than the exception. With the wide range of cultures and racial groups represented in the United States, and with the obvious regional differences present, language diversity should not be surprising. To the contrary, a lack of significant language diversity in our country would be quite unusual.

The form of English spoken in the United States is different from versions used in other English-speaking countries, such as England, Scotland, and Australia. For example, few Americans would understand the statement, "I must get on the trunk line to my solicitor." Translated into the American form of English, this phrase means, "I must make a long distance call to my lawyer." Other English-speaking countries use many other phrases and language forms that Americans would have difficulty understanding. The following list compares terms used in England and their meaning in the American form of English (Tiedt & Tiedt, 1986, p. 133):

English Form	American Meaning
biscuit	cookie
jelly	jello
tinned meat	canned meat
pud	dessert
tea	light meal, supper
boot	trunk of car
lorry	truck
lift	elevator
underground, tube	subway, metro
chemist	druggist, pharmacist
dustman	garbage collector
vest	undershirt
knickers	underpants
jumper	pullover sweater
fringe	bangs, hair

Even within the United States, wide variability in the form of English dialects can be found in different regions of the country (Tiedt & Tiedt, 1986). For example, in the South the words "you" and "all" are frequently pronounced "y'all." In mountain

English an "a" sound often is added to verbs ending with the "ing" sound, as in, "He was a'waitin at the store"—meaning, "He waited at the store" or "He was waiting at the store." In the northern United States speech varies from the staccato, clipped speech associated with New York City to the elongated speech of northern Maine. Ethnic, racial, and socioeconomic groups also speak varying English dialects. The historical question that has often been posed is whether substantial linguistic variance constitutes a language defect or simply a language difference. The following discussion explores the different points of view on this issue.

THE DEFICIT POSITION

Advocates of the deficit viewpoint have asserted that the language of people from lower social classes represents a deficient code, not just one that is different from the majority culture. Popular during the 1950s, 1960s, and early 1970s, this viewpoint has been replaced primarily by the "difference" position. This discussion on the deficit position is presented to describe a hypothesis that at one time was widely accepted.

The deficit viewpoint was associated with the cultural deprivation theory, which assumed that various detrimental factors produced deprived homes and communities that fostered educational handicaps (Polloway & Patton, 1981). Within these environments at the bottom of the social class structure, several forces resulted in learning problems for children: a lack of structure and organization in the home; authoritarian and inconsistent parenting practices; the absence of strong achievement motivation; parent absenteeism; and practical problems associated with poverty.

The language deprivation viewpoint took this position one step farther. It implied strongly that language used in this environment actually caused and perpetuated many of the above-mentioned conditions. Podemski et al. (1984, p. 120) noted several faulty assumptions and interpretations used in an attempt to develop credibility for the language deficit orientation:

Assumptions	*Interpretations*
Norms or standards of appropriate behavior are those of the white middle class.	The white middle class speaks English.
The minority person's behavior is different when compared with that of the white middle class.	The white middle class speaks English; the other speaks Spanish.
A negative value is attached to differences.	The individual has a language problem.
Differences are considered deficiencies, and a cure for deficiencies is sought.	Bilingual education will remedy the language problem.

Assumptions	*Interpretations*
The ultimate goal is assimilation, the elimination of behaviors that differ from those of the white middle class.	After overcoming language problems, the individual can become a part of the "mainstream."

Some of the early research efforts in this area, notably those of Hess and Shipman (1965) and Bernstein (1961), contributed to the concept of language deficit. In the former study, which researched the parenting practices of Black mothers from various social classes, Hess and Shipman contended that various forms of control influenced later cognitive, linguistic, and social behavior. In general, lower-class mothers used control that was less verbal, thus reducing the child's alternatives for action and thought. For example, researchers found that mothers from lower-class environments were more likely to say "Shut up!" than an alternative such as "Please quiet down. I'm trying to talk to your brother." In time, this form of verbal interaction could restrict development of the child's linguistic structures. Hess and Shipman (1965), concluded that a poverty situation is often associated with a deprived learning environment and thus "produces a child who relates to authority rather than to rationale, who, although often compliant, is not reflective in his behavior, and for whom the consequences of an act are largely considered in terms of immediate punishment or reward rather than future effects and long range goals" (p. 885).

Although this research is important to the deficit position, numerous reports from Bernstein (1961, 1964, 1970) were the most significant source of the deficit position. Bernstein's research focused on the language of working-class people in England, and specifically on the concept of two forms of language: *elaborated* and *restricted* codes. Yet Bernstein (1970) questioned the way his premises were applied to the extremely poor child (particularly within the United States), stating: "The use (or abuse) of this distinction (between the codes) has equated with linguistic deprivation, linguistic deficiency, or being nonverbal" (p. 26). Nevertheless, the hypotheses generated about these two codes became the basis for theories about children in American inner cities and thus warrant attention here.

The elaborated code is associated with a wide range of syntactical options available to the speaker. The verbal channel becomes the basic orientation of communications and allows the speaker the opportunity to explicitly state his or her intentions. Within the elaborated language pattern a greater flexibility in terms of vocabulary would be found to refer to abstract concepts (Bernstein, 1970).

A narrower range of syntactic and vocabulary possibilities characterizes the restricted code. It is more rigid in form and relies more on gestures, voice, and facial expressions. It is "we"-oriented in contrast to the "I"-orientation of the elaborated form. As such, it represents an extensive collection of mutual experiences and expectations, such as those shared by prison inmates or adolescent gangs. In this sense, the code controls and transmits culture. But it also may result in stifling expression. Bernstein (1970) noted, "The use of a restricted code creates social solidarity at the cost of verbal elaboration of individual experience" (p. 32).

This point would be as valid for social groups adopting virtually programmed forms of communication, such as the stereotyped hip slang of the 1960s counterculture (e.g., "far out," "I'm hip," "dig it," "doing my own thing," "ripped off"), or even for husbands and wives. The most important implications, however, apply to developing children who must use this restricted code to receive and express aspects of their environment and mediate cognitive processes. Table 3.1 summarizes the characteristics of elaborated and restricted codes.

Specific aspects of the restricted code, drawn from the Bernstein hypotheses and related to the lower-class child, were noted by Ginsburg (1972, pp. 60–61):

1. Short, simple sentences which are often incomplete and syntactically weak.
2. Simple and repetitive use of conjunctions such as "so," "then," "and" "because."
3. Few subordinate clauses.
4. Limited and repetitive use of adjectives and adverbs.
5. Statements which confuse reasons and conclusions so as to produce a categoric statement.

The following conversation, adapted from Bernstein (1970), gives an example of the use of language controls as illustrated by the way in which two mothers might respond to their children in a given situation. The first example uses the imperative form typical of the restricted code; the other draws on the interpersonal level, which, in this case, is more indicative of the elaborated code.

Mother:	Children kiss your Grandpa.
Child:	I don't want to—why must I kiss him always?

Table 3.1
Characteristics of Elaborated and Restricted Codes

Code	Characteristics
Elaborated	Associated with wide range of syntactical options
	Verbal channel is basic orientation to communication
	Great flexibility in using abstracts
	Oriented to "I"
Restricted	Narrower range of syntactical options
	More rigid in form
	Relies more on gestures, voice, and facial expressions
	Oriented to "we"
	Represents extensive collection of mutual experiences and expectations
	Contains much slang and stereotypic forms

Source: Adapted from "A Sociolinguistic Approach to Socialization: With Some Reference to Educability" by B. Bernstein in *Language and Poverty*, edited by F. Williams, 1970, Chicago: Markham Publishing.

Mother 1:   He's not well—I don't want none of your nonsense.
Mother 2:   I know you don't like kissing Grandpa, but he's unwell and is very fond of you, and it makes him very happy.

School problems, IQ test score deficits, difficulty with abstract concepts, and general language failures were traced by Bernstein (1970) to the restrictive code. Still, he cautioned against regarding it as a defective linguistic form, stating:

> Lest the restricted code be misinterpreted as simply poor language, we must be aware that it contains a vast potential of meanings. It is a form of speech which symbolizes a communally based culture. It carries its own aesthetic. It should not be disvalued. (p. 37)

The implications drawn for the language of inner-city children often have been of a stronger nature.

Professionals best known for prior association with the language-deficit position in the 1960s and 1970s in the U.S. were Carl Bereiter and Siegfried Engelmann, who devised an intervention program for inner-city children in 1966. They based their program on the belief that inner-city children were culturally deprived, and that this deprivation was most significant in the area of language. According to Bereiter and Engelmann (1966):

> The lower class child is not without culture, but he is deprived of that part of culture that can only be acquired through teaching—the knowledge, the meanings, the explanations, the structured beliefs that make up the conceptual furniture of culture. (p. 33)

In developing their hypothesis of language deprivation, Bereiter and Engelmann (1966) never implied that inner-city individuals lacked a communication system for sharing experiences, expressing emotions, or controlling behavior. But they did indict the system's inability to complement the growth of cognitive processes, especially those related to deductive thinking, analysis, hypothesis-building, and inquiry. Herein lay the so-called language deficit or defect.

Bereiter and Engelmann suggested that the language problems inner-city children face often involve their use of *giant word units*, which represent a form of "amalgamated noises." Instead of saying, "That's a red truck," for example, the child might say "Da-reh-truh." "He's a big dog" would be "He-bih-daw."

According to Bereiter and Engelmann, giant word units represent more than faulty pronunciation. Instead, they are considered correlates of a child's inability to handle full sentences as meaningful sequences. Without this ability, a child has difficulty comprehending language, building negative statements, and transforming sentences (e.g., from declarative to interrogative forms). These deficiencies result in a diminished capacity for verbal mediation, or what the authors termed "internal dialogue." One significant result of this is its negative impact on problem-solving skills. Bereiter and Engelmann concluded that young children reared in poverty would profit most from learning skills in language-related areas.

Over the past several years the deficit orientation has been losing popularity (Wallace & Goodman, 1989). Professionals who adopted the deficit view may have developed some erroneous generalizations about children whose language was not standard English. One of the major invalid assumptions in this approach was that, automatically, students who did not speak standard English had a language deficiency (Ortiz, 1984). As our society has moved toward integrating minority racial groups into schools, the work force, and society in general, the notion that a different linguistic system is inherently bad has faded. A broader acceptance of cultural pluralism as a reality in our society has forced some professionals to reconsider the deficit position.

THE DIFFERENCE POSITION

The language difference position differs significantly from the deficit orientation. Proponents of this position believe that all languages have the potential for communicating the full range of human experiences and for meeting all of the purposes for language. Ortiz (1984) described a continuum of language skills found in children who do not proficiently use standard English. Even though the continuum focuses primarily on language systems uniquely different from English, it underscores the idea that language systems may be different but still not deficient. Black dialect, regional dialects, or competence in a language other than English only reflect difference, not an absence of language functionality.

When discussing the difference position, one of the primary areas of focus has been Black dialect or Black English. Black English is probably the foremost dialectical variation of standard English studied in the last 25 years. One reason for this interest is that Blacks comprise one of America's largest minority groups. Another is that many Blacks do not use the language forms that have been assumed to enable one to succeed in school. Most of these forms traditionally have been associated with the middle class.

Still another significant rationale for the interest in Black English is America's failure to assimilate Blacks into the mainstream of life to the extent achieved with other ethnic groups. Despite efforts to integrate Black Americans into the majority culture, they still constitute a distinct group in many areas. One can argue that Black English has contributed to this situation.

Although many Black Americans use Black Dialect, the primary use is by people living in large urban centers, and it is characteristic most often of the language of children and teenagers. In addition, certain aspects of the dialect are found in other low socioeconomic areas (such as the rural Southeast). A significant degree of variance can be identified in the different geographical areas where it is found.

An essential element of the difference position is its use of the term "nonstandard" instead of "substandard" to refer to Black English. This perspective views Black dialect as a complete linguistic system rather than as an inferior and error-ridden deviation from standard English.

Labov's Research   Some of the most important research on the language difference concept and nonstandard English was completed more than 20 years ago by Labov

(1967, 1969). Among the conclusions from this research were: (a) there is no empirical basis for the deprivation concept, and (b) young Black children receive a substantial amount of stimulation, actively participate in varied verbal interchanges, and hear many structurally appropriate sentences on which to model their own speech (Labov, 1970). In addition, he stressed that Black dialect provided a basis for conceptual learning and followed linguistic logic similar to that of standard English.

Labov concluded that uninformed assessment and unwarranted conclusions result in the concept of language deprivation. To illustrate this point, he presented a series of conversations with young inner-city children. In the first example (Labov, 1970, pp. 157–158), a White interviewer gives a child an object to describe.

	12 seconds of silence
Interviewer:	What would you say it looks like?
	8 seconds of silence
Child:	A space ship.
Interviewer:	Hmmmmmm.
	13 seconds of silence
Child:	Like a plane.
	20 seconds of silence
Interviewer:	What color is it?
Child:	Orange (2 seconds) An' wh-ite. (2 seconds) an' green.
	6 seconds of silence
Interviewer:	If you had two of them, what would you do with them?
	10 seconds of silence
Child:	Cla-rence.
Interviewer:	Mm. Where do you think we could get another one of these?
Child:	At a store.
Interviewer:	Oh Ka-ay!

The child's limited speech responses in this example do little to contradict the notion of deprived language. In the next example (Labov, 1970, pp. 159–160), a young child (Leon) is interviewed by a Black man (CR) reared in the same community as the child, but still the verbal interchange is limited.

CR:	You watch—you like to watch television? . . . Hey Leon . . . you like to watch television? (Leon nods) What's your favorite program?
Leon:	Uhhmmmm. . . . I look at cartoons.
CR:	Well, what's your favorite one? What's your favorite program?
Leon:	Superman. . . .
CR:	Yeah? Did you see Superman—ah—yesterday, or day before yesterday? When's the last time you saw Superman?
Leon:	Sa-aturday. . . .

CR: You rem—you saw it Saturday? What was the story all about? You remember the story?
Leon: M-m.
CR: You don't remember the story of what—that you saw of Superman?
Leon: Nope.
CR: You don't remember what happened, huh?
Leon: Hm-m.
CR: I see—ah—what other stories do you like to watch on TV?
Leon: Mmmm? . . . umm. . . . (glottalization)
CR: Hmm? (four seconds)
Leon: Hh?
CR: What's th' other stories that you like to watch?
Leon: Mi-ighty Mouse. . . .
CR: And what else?
Leon: Ummmm . . . ahm. . . .

Finally, in the third example (Labov, 1970, pp. 160–161), the situation is changed to include Leon's friend Gregory, some potato chips, CR sitting on the floor, and some taboo topics. The "deprived" language of the first two samples is quite obviously no longer present.

CR: Is there anybody who says your momma drink pee?
Leon: (rapidly and breathlessly) Yee-ah!
Greg: Yup!
Leon: And your father eat doo-doo for breakfas'!
CR: Ohhh! (laughs)
Leon: And they say your father—your father eat doo-doo for dinner!
Greg: When they sound on me, I say C.B.S.
CR: What that mean?
Leon: Congo booger-snatch! (laughs)
Greg: Congo-booger-snatcher! (laughs)
Greg: And sometimes I'll curse with B.B.
CR: What that?
Greg: Black boy!
Leon: (crunching on potato chips) Oh, that's a M.B.B.
CR: M.B.B. What's that?
Greg: Mexican Black Boy.
CR: Oh yeah?
Greg: Yeah.
CR: What they say about Allah?
Leon: Allah—Allah is God.
Greg: Allah—
CR: And what else?

Leon:　I don't know the res'.
Greg:　Allah i—Allah is God, Allah is the only God, Allah. . .
Leon:　Allah is the son of God.
Greg:　But can he make magic?
Leon:　Nope.
Greg:　I know who can make magic.
CR:　Who can?
Leon:　The God, the real one.
CR:　Who can make magic?
Greg:　The son of po'—
CR:　Hm?
Greg:　I'm sayin' the po'k chop God! He only a po'k chop God! (the traditional God of the Southern Baptists.)
　　　(Leon chuckles)

Without this sort of change in social relationships, researchers and educators would have a distorted picture of a child's linguistic capability (Labov, 1970). Obviously, teachers must carefully consider social variables when they assess their students' language abilities and develop them through instruction.

Elements of Black Dialect　Black dialect or Black English can be defined as speech used by many African-Americans who are from lower socioeconomic environments and who may not have achieved extensive formal education. It is "characterized by differences in phonology, morphology, syntax, prosody, pragmatics, and discourse from the feature of standard English" (Cole & Taylor, 1990, p. 171).

Walton, McCardle, Crowe, and Wilson (1990) identified nine areas in which Black dialect and standard English frequently differ. Examples include the is/are auxiliary absence, final stop devoicing, and copula absence. Table 3.2 summarizes each of these major features. Teachers who are unfamiliar with Black English should keep in mind several generalizations about the dialect (Tiedt & Tiedt, 1986):

1. "It" will often be used for "there" (e.g., "It's a book on the table" instead of "There's a book on the table").
2. The verb will tend to be missing where a contraction is commonly used in standard English, especially in the present tense (e.g., "I here" and "We going").
3. More than a single negative form is acceptable in the Black English vernacular (e.g., "I don't take no stuff from nobody").
4. Two or more consonant sounds appearing at the end of words in standard English tend to be reduced in the Black English vernacular (e.g., "tes" for test and "des" for desk). The reduction of consonant clusters affects words that end in "s" (e.g., plurals, third-person singular forms, and possessives like its and father's). The reduction also affects verbs in the past tense ending in -ed.
5. Words in which a medial or final "th" appears often change pronunciation in the Black English dialect (e.g., "wit" or "wif" for with, and "muver" for mother).
6. There are words in which "r" and "l" appear in medial or final positions in standard English. These sounds are often absent in the Black English dialect.
7. Labels and concepts different from the dominant English dialect are generated from a variety of different experiences (e.g., the use of "bad" to mean good). (p. 137)

Table 3.2
Characteristics of Black English

Characteristic	Description
1. Is/Are Auxiliary Absence	Forms of the verb **be** are often omitted. Example: "The boy running" rather than "The boy is running."
2. Final Stop Devoicing	Final stopped consonants often devoiced; results in similar pronunciations. Example: "pig" and "pick."
3. Distributive Be	Use of distributive or unconjugated **be**. Example: "She be there" for "She will be there."
4. Remote Aspect Been	**Been** used to indicate activity in past. Example: "She been married" means "She has been married for a long time."
5. Noun Plural Morpheme Absence	Absence of plurals. Example: "two dog."
6. Third-Person Singular Present-Tense Morpheme Absence	Deletion of **s** to third-person singular. Example: "It toast bread" for "It toasts bread."
7. Possessive Suffix Absence	Absence of **'s**. Example: "It is the boy ball."
8. Final Consonant Cluster Reduction	Reduction of consonant when followed by vowel. Example: "col' eggs" for "cold eggs."
9. Copula Absence	Deletion of connector for nouns, pronouns, or adjectives. Example: "It blue" for "It is blue."

Source: From "Black English in a Mississippi Prison Population" by J. H. Walton, P. McCardle, T. A. Crowe and B. E. Wilson, 1970, *Journal of Speech & Hearing Disorders, 55*, pp. 206–216. Reprinted by permission.

In conclusion, consider Labov's (1970) analysis of the language deficit hypothesis. To accept or reject this hypothesis, carefully consider these points by relating them to preceding discussions. Williams (1970) has presented a complete discussion of both points of view.

1. The verbal deficit noted in young children most often appears in unnatural and possibly intimidating situations.
2. The presence of a deficit in language then is assumed to be the basis for postschool performance.
3. The higher success rates of middle-class children implies that their language is necessary for school achievement.
4. Differences in language between cultural groups also indicate differences in the ability to use higher cognitive processes.
5. The modeling of standard English forms is the basis for teaching logical thinking to children.
6. Acquisition of formal language patterns predicts subsequent school success.

BILINGUALISM

Bilingual education has been a major topic in public schools for many years (Smith, 1990). Although children speaking Black dialect could technically be considered bilingual, the term usually is reserved for those whose primary language is not a form of English. In the past, the diverse languages that immigrants spoke gradually disappeared within several generations. But in recent years the homogeneity of the early 1900s has given way to a greater cultural pluralism. In fact, over the last 20 years people who speak a foreign language—be they natives or immigrants—have, to a much greater extent, preserved their native languages. This preservation of their original language has resulted in a need for bilingual education.

Bilingualism can be defined as the ability to communicate in two languages. Individuals who are bilingual may not be equally competent in both languages, but they do have the ability to understand and to communicate to others using either language (Ortiz, 1984). Bilingualism includes abilities in the respective two languages in language form, content, and use (Kayser, 1989). Programming designed to meet the needs of children who are bilingual is called *bilingual education*. Bilingual education programs have focused primarily on people of Puerto Rican, Cuban, and Mexican descent, all of whom speak Spanish as their primary language. Other groups include Native Americans and Oriental-Americans, whose bilingualism consists of English and the native language. Children of Arabic origin also may be represented in American schools and may require bilingual education.

Children who are bilingual present an extremely heterogeneous group. As Ortiz (1984) noted, a continuum of language skills is present in this generic group classified as bilingual. Figure 3.1 depicts the continuum of different language varieties that could be present in bilingual children. Although the majority of bilingual children in the past have Hispanic origins, the recent increase in immigration from Oriental countries—particularly Vietnam, Cambodia, and Thailand, and the Middle East—makes bilingual education even more complex.

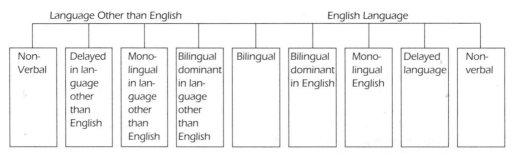

Language Other than English					English Language			
Non-Verbal	Delayed in language other than English	Monolingual in language other than English	Bilingual dominant in language other than English	Bilingual	Bilingual dominant in English	Monolingual English	Delayed language	Non-verbal

Source: From "Choosing the Language of Instruction for Exceptional Bilingual Children" by A. A. Ortiz, 1984, *Teaching Exceptional Children*, p. 208. Copyright 1984 by the Council for Exceptional Children. Reprinted by permission.

Figure 3.1
Continuum of Language Variety Among Minority Students.

A great deal of research on bilingualism and bilingual education has led to the conclusion that children with bilingual skills have certain cognitive and sociocultural advantages over monolingual children (Wallace & Goodman, 1989). Nevertheless, children from minority cultures need to learn English to maximize their success in the dominant English-speaking society (Tiedt & Tiedt, 1986). Their learning English language skills should not be at the expense of maintaining their initial language. "Researchers generally agree that a model of bilingual education which aims to maintain the mother tongue is best for minority children whose dominant language is threatened" (Wallace & Goodman, 1989, p. 545).

Non-English-speaking children suffer if their native tongue is devalued and they do not receive the benefits of bilingual education. Emotionally, children can suffer a tremendous loss of self-esteem when they confront an educational process based on alien cultural and linguistic modes. At the same time, the pressure of learning a new language and using it to acquire new academic skills may overwhelm the child, resulting in serious difficulties and subsequent school failure (John & Horner, 1970).

Continued use of a child's non-majority language may facilitate academic and cognitive development. The mother tongue can serve as a functional vehicle for acquiring memory and problem-solving skills, which in turn may help the child acquire English as a second language. The transition to teaching *through* it might come then when the child is able to learn as well or better in a classroom taught in English (Cohen, 1979). Bilingual education therefore can become a means of both preserving traditional cultures and helping children become functioning members of the English-oriented culture.

A primary theme of bilingual education should be to promote educational success and deter failure in students from minority groups. Unfortunately, bilingual education programs are not successful for all minority-speaking children, and the result is frequent failure. Teachers of these children frequently classify them as language-deficient. This view, which many educators held in the past, may be a cause of high dropout rates among this population; an estimated 30 to 50 percent of Hispanic students, for example, drop out of high school (Commins & Miramontes, 1989).

Numerous groups in the United States can be classified as bilingual. The following brief discussions highlight just two of them—groups who speak varieties of Spanish and those who speak one or several of the many Native American languages.

HISPANIC BILINGUALISM

Generalizing between and within groups of Spanish-speaking persons must naturally be done tentatively. When considering Hispanic children, however, one can assume that many speak solely Spanish, others primarily English without extensive Spanish knowledge, and still others a rudimentary form of English as a second language interspersed with Spanish elements (Naremore, 1980). Therefore, in general, the Spanish bilingual child cannot be equated with a child from Spain who is taught a new and truly foreign tongue (English) in an academic setting.

Just as English is spoken and used in a variety of ways, several varieties of Spanish are spoken in the United States (Tiedt & Tiedt, 1986). Spanish spoken by former Cubans in New York City differs from the Spanish used by individuals who moved from the Dominican Republic to California. Spanish spoken by persons coming across the Mexico/Texas border differs, too. As no group of Spanish-speaking students may have a single Spanish dialect or style, teachers should be aware of the different intralanguage styles. They need to recognize the differences in Spanish and English sounds. Table 3.3 reflects these differences. Specific types of problems of many students moving from predominant communication in Spanish to predominant English include variations in sentences; absence of some endings to indicate plurality, tense, and comparison; and alternative forms for the use of negation (Naremore, 1980).

NATIVE AMERICAN LANGUAGES

A substantial number of non-English-speaking people are Native Americans, or Indians. The "Indian language" is not a basic linguistic structure such as French or Italian; it actually is a generic term that refers to many distinctly separate languages having various degrees of relationship to each other. Because of this complexity, the number of persons who speak one particular language and those who speak several is difficult to specify (Osborn, 1970).

The Native American population is composed of numerous tribes whose languages are different. Also, within each tribe some individuals speak English well; others rely primarily on their native language and use limited English. Tiedt and Tiedt (1986) listed 43 different Indian languages currently being spoken in the United States by a minimum of 1,000 people each. Many words in the English language were "borrowed" from Indian language. Examples include "moose" from "moos," "pecan" from "paccan," and "tomahawk" from "tamahak."

The large number of different languages spoken by Native Americans and the heterogeneity of the population make generalizations about the Indian language difficult. Teachers simply need to be aware that Native American students may bring different linguistic systems to the classroom and then be prepared to research specific languages in greater depth as needed.

TEACHING IMPLICATIONS

Language snobbery can have significant negative effects in the classroom. Unless language bias is drastically reduced or eliminated, many linguistically different children may leave the American public school unprepared to function successfully in the community, partially because of their general frustration and dissatisfaction. Conversely, appreciating linguistic differences can have a productive influence on subsequent adult adjustment. Hilliard (1980) stated: "Respecting cultural diversity is not a benevolent act but a prerequisite for service and a valid professional practice" (p.

Table 3.3
Differences Between Spanish and English Sounds

Consonants	Spanish	English
b	también	rib
	abrir	like v, but with lips almost touching
c	casa	case (before a, o, u)
	nación	cent (before e, i)
ch	chico	church
d	donde	down
	madre	the
f	familia	family
g	gente	like exaggerated h (before e, i)
	gordo	game
h	hacer	silent
j	jugar	like exaggerated h
k	kilómetro	kitchen
l	lástima	little
ll	llena	yellow } (regional variation) million }
m	mañana	morning
n	nada	nothing
n	niño	canyon
p	piña	supper
q	queso	key
r	pero	rich
	rico	trilled r
rr	perro	trilled r
s	sala	sad
t	trabajar	time
v	enviar	like b in también
	la vaca	like b in abrir
w	Wáshington	wash
x	examen	exam
	extranjero	sound
	México	hit
y	yo	yes
z	zapato	save
Vowels		
a	padre	father
e	es	they
i	nida	police
o	poco	poem
u	luna	spoon
	querer	silent after q
ai, ay	traiga	nice
au	auto	mouse
ei, ey	aceituna	tray
eu	deuda	ay plus oo
ia, ya	hacia	yonder
ie, ye	nieve	yes
io, yo	dios	yolk
iu	ciudad	yule
oi, oy	soy	boy
ua	guante	wander
ue	vuelve	weight
y	y	even
ui, uy	muy	we
uo	cuota	woe

588). Even Bernstein (1970), an advocate of the language deficit hypothesis, summed up this matter when he stated:

> That the subculture, or culture, through its forms of social integration, generates a restricted code does not mean that the resultant speech and meaning system is linguistically or culturally deprived, that its children have nothing to offer the school, that their imaginings are not significant. It does not mean that we have to teach these children formal grammar, nor does it mean that we have to interfere with their deficits. There is nothing, but nothing, in dialect as such, which prevents a child from internalizing and learning to use universalistic meanings. But if the contexts of learning, the samples, the reading books, are not contexts which are triggers for the child's imaginings—are not triggers on his curiosity and explorations in his family and community—then the child is not at home in the educational world. If the teacher says continuously, "Say it again, darling; I didn't understand you," then in the end the child may say nothing.
>
> If the culture of the teacher is to become part of the consciousness of the child, then the culture of the child must first be in the consciousness of the teacher. This may mean that the teacher must be able to understand the child's dialect, rather than deliberately attempt to change it. Much of the context of our schools is, unwittingly, drawn from aspects of the symbolic world of the middle class; when such a child steps into school, he is stepping into a symbolic system which does not provide for him a linkage with his life outside. (p. 57)

TEACHER COMPETENCIES

To be effective in the classroom, teachers of bilingual children need a number of competencies. These include general competencies related to effective teaching for all students as well as specific skills necessary to work effectively with bilingual children. In general, teachers of bilingual children need to accept students' diversity and cultural differences and should develop instructional strategies to meet those needs. Because the language skills of bilingual students and students using nonstandard English are so diverse, appropriate education requires individualized instruction.

Koenig and Biel (1989) listed some of the skills necessary for professionals and paraprofessionals who work with bilingual students, including:

- Accepting cultural diversity
- Being familiar with instructional materials
- Providing appropriate contexts for language instruction
- Creating an environment conducive to language learning.

Gonzales and Ortiz (1977) identified several general competencies needed by teachers in a bilingual instructional environment. First, *teachers must be able to communicate effectively in the language of the students.* Teachers and students alike share the task of dealing with language differences, rather than one or the other being totally responsible, but, because a teacher's primary function is to facilitate learning, he or she necessarily will carry more responsibility in this situation.

Second, *teachers must understand the structural differences* between first and second languages. As a result, they can make the transition between languages smoother; their explanations can point out similarities and differences in the first and second languages.

Update

Language Use Plan

The design of instructional programs for students of diverse backgrounds demands that language considerations be given primary importance. Garcia (1995) recommends that a "language use plan" be developed for each student that addresses three important instructional components. These include:

- **the language of instruction:** particular attention should be given to how instruction is provided across the varied of relevant specific academic content areas.
- **responsible parties:** the plan should stipulate the roles being played by bilingual educators, ESL specialists, and general educators or special educators who have ESL training.
- **types of intervention needed:** attention should be given to whether the plan will include language enrichment in either the primary or new language, language development in either language, ESL, or remediation in either language.

Source: Garcia, S. B. (1995, October). Bilingual exceptional students: An assessment and intervention model. Paper presented at the New Mexico Learning Disabilities Association Fall Conference, Albuquerque, NM. (Cited in Nowacek, J. (2001). Spoken language. In E. A. Polloway, & J. R. Patton (Eds.), *Strategies for teaching students with special needs* (7th ed.) Columbus, OH: Merrill).

Third, *teachers must respond positively to crosscultural behavioral diversity*. This will do much to reduce language snobbery and other language-related problems that affect bicultural students today. Just as surface structural differences exist between two languages, behavioral differences should be expected among the individuals who speak these languages.

Fourth, *teachers must recognize similarities and differences between various cultures, particularly as they relate to learning opportunities or conflicts*. Because cultural groups are often locked in by severely restrictive economic factors (e.g., meeting everyday expenses on a too-small budget or paying traveling expenses to and from school), schooling and other activities may assume more or less importance. In situations of this nature, teachers must devise opportunities for the culturally different child to learn. Or differences in cultural groups may simply reflect cultural tradition. For example, in many Oriental cultures eating with chopsticks is the accepted fashion for getting food from a plate to the mouth. Individuals who do this should be accorded the same kind of acceptance as people who eat with forks and knives.

Last, *cultural elements should be incorporated into instructional programs*. This concern is directly related to the previous competency. Again, teachers should recognize cultural similarities and differences and provide opportunities for students to learn more about each other. The verses in Table 3.4 provide an example of one way in which this concern could be included in the classroom.

FAIR ASSESSMENT

One challenge that arises when working with children whose predominant language is other than English is fair, accurate assessment. Many norm-referenced, standardized assessment instruments discriminate against people from minority cultural groups and lower socioeconomic environments (Cummins, 1984; Kayser, 1989; Salvia & Ysseldyke, 1989; Smith, 1990). The traditional overrepresentation of minority groups in special education classes and underrepresentation of the same groups in classes for gifted and talented students underline the need for nondiscriminatory assessment procedures (McCormick, 1990).

Although these problems (e.g., overrepresentation in programs for students with mild mental retardation) continue to be reported (e.g., Epstein, Polloway, Patton, & Foley, 1989; Brady, Manni, & Winnikur, 1983; Polloway et al., 1986), substantial evidence indicates that they are being addressed (MacMillan, 1989; Reschly, 1988). To remedy discrimination in assessment, the Individuals with Disabilities Education Act (IDEA) requires schools to use various methods to reduce discrimination. These include:

- Administering tests in the child's native language.
- Using only tests that have been specifically validated for the purposes they are being used.
- Conducting assessments using a multidisciplinary team.
- Using more than a single instrument to determine the existence of a handicapping condition.

Table 3.4
Sample Verses

BLACK PRIDE

Being born black and free means living in poverty.

It seems like nothing but filth and shame
In front of this proud black name

Not knowing what 3 square meals a day are

But black pride cries on

Not knowing what a decent home is
Black pride cries to be strong.

Not knowing what equal education is

Black pride cries on to be strong but it is still
Taking much too long.

SOUL

I have a feeling that is
As rich as gold
I'm told by blacks it's soul.

It's a good good feeling
You can't mold
I wonder if it's soul.

I dance and swirl
And feel real bold
I think it's soul.

BLACK MOM

I'm hungry and in fear
Wishing for someone to
Hold me near
I shouldn't fear because
My mother is near.

She is a black, beautiful and strong woman
That has held the black family together for many years.

Even when things are wrong
I don't worry because
My mother is strong.

Source: From *Black Treasures* by W. H. Taylor, 1977, Lynchburg, VA: Unpublished manuscript. Reprinted by permission.

Although these requirements will not guarantee nondiscrimination in the assessment process, they should help overcome bias that often results in inappropriate labeling and placement of children from minority cultural groups in special education programs.

Because teachers are the classroom leaders, they must closely evaluate their personal attitudes and expectations of culturally different students. Effectiveness has to begin with tolerance toward, and acceptance of, culturally and linguistically different children.

INSTRUCTIONAL APPROACHES

Children from minority cultural backgrounds who have language problems because English is not their dominant language present a variety of challenges for teachers. Should teachers present all instruction in Standard English and require students to learn the language as quickly as possible or fail? Should teachers be required to teach non-English-speaking students in their dominant language or dialect and hope that English is eventually learned incidentally? Or should teachers take advantage of the child's dominant language but maximize opportunities for helping the child acquire English for later success in school and in the community? Although these may seem to be simple, straightforward questions, they have been the subjects of debate for many years.

CONTINUUM OF APPROACHES

Many instructional approaches have been tried, ranging from almost total reliance on the culturally dominant language to heavy emphasis on maintaining the original language. Cummins (1984) divided these approaches into four major groups: (a) submersion programs, (b) monolingual immersion, (c) majority language bilingual immersion, and (d) minority language bilingual immersion. Whether the area of concern is true bilingualism or language dialectical differences, this discussion has validity.

Submersion Programs   Applying the submersion orientation to bilingual instruction, teachers expect students to develop the majority culture language without the aid of their native language. Students are placed in classrooms where the only language spoken is the majority culture language. Students have limited support with their primary language system. Although this model has been used extensively when teaching a second language to majority-culture students, it has resulted in significant controversy with minority children in the United States. Research has suggested that submersion, or total immersion with limited primary language support, is detrimental to minority students who already are at risk for developing learning and behavior problems (Cummins, 1984).

Monolingual Immersion   One step along the continuum discussed by Cummins (1984) is monolingual immersion. This model allows some linguistic support from the student's original language. Teachers, however, are not required to be bilingual, and initial language literacy is not encouraged. Although apparently inappropriate for many students from minority backgrounds, this model might be useful when schools have classes containing large numbers of students with several different languages. As in the submersion program, minority students at risk for developing problems are likely to experience difficulties with this model.

Majority Language Bilingual Immersion   This model and the monolingual immersion orientation have several primary differences. Three key elements are present in the majority language bilingual immersion model: (a) teachers are bilingual, (b) instructional activities are modified to involve primary language, and (c) literacy in

Update

Minority Concerns and IDEA

The Individuals with Disabilities Education Act has provided careful attention to individuals with diverse backgrounds. In the most recent reauthorization of IDEA (PL 105-17), some additional stipulations were added. These include:

- Revisions to IDEA require that every state monitor school district data to determine if special education placements result in the disproportionate segregation of minority children as well as if a disproportionate number of children have been suspended or expelled. If data indicate such trends, such states must develop appropriate modifications in their policies and practices.
- When programs are requesting support for personnel preparation funds, grant applicants will be asked to demonstrate, in particular, how the specific project will respond to the needs of students with disabilities who come from ethnically and linguistically diverse backgrounds.
- In instances where students have difficulty speaking English (i.e., come from other language backgrounds), schools are required to consider the language needs of the student in the development of the IEP.

Source: Council for Exceptional Children (June, 1997). IDEA sails through Congress! *CEC Today, 3*(10), 1, 9, 15.

the primary language is encouraged and reinforced (Cummins, 1984). Minority students who are at risk for developing problems benefit much more from this model than those previously discussed; the level of support for these students is significantly greater.

Minority Language Bilingual Immersion   The fourth and final model presented by Cummins (1984) "represents a considerably stronger commitment to promoting minority students' first language than (the) majority language" (p. 158). This model allows bilingual students to rely heavily on their primary language. Teachers are bilingual and heavily promote literacy in the initial language. This immersion style allows a familiar language to be the basis for learning for students who are at risk of developing learning and behavior problems. It also does not place a great deal of pressure on the students to learn a new language when they are having major problems achieving success in their own language. Not having to focus on learning a new language allows these students the time to concentrate on academic achievement.

Table 3.5
Characteristics of Program Options

Program	Bilingual Teacher	Modified Input	Literacy Promotion
Submersion	No	No	No
Monolingual Immersion	No	Yes	No
Majority Language	Yes	Yes	Yes
Minority Language	Yes	Yes	Yes

Source: Adapted from *Bilingualism and Special Education: Issues in Assessment and Pedagogy* by J. Cummins, 1984, Clevedon, England: Multilingual Matters.

These four approaches represent steps along a continuum. Schools likely vary from year to year, teacher to teacher, and possibly even child to child in their implementation of bilingual programming. Table 3.5 shows the characteristics of the four models regarding bilingual teachers, modifications in instruction, and emphasis on initial language literacy.

CODE SWITCHING AND MIXING

Regardless of which model is used, two processes may occur. The first is *code switching*, common among young bilingual children as well as adults, and defined as moving from one language to the other. It is often used as a "relief strategy," enabling the individual to rely on the language most familiar to a specific situation (Meisel, 1988). There is a common misconception that students who code switch are not proficient in either language. In fact, students who use code switching abide by appropriate language rules in both languages. Because students who code switch are using both languages properly, they should not be discouraged from the process (Ortiz, 1984).

The other process that frequently occurs among individuals who use two languages is *mixing*, the use of more than one language system indiscriminately. "Mixing is the most likely to occur if (a) one of the two languages is very dominant in the child's competence, and (b) the adults in the child's environment mix or switch quite freely in their own speech" (Meisel, 1988, p. 14). Again, these factors should not be viewed as a lack of language proficiency.

BILINGUAL EDUCATION MATERIALS

Publishing companies are developing a variety of materials for teaching bilingual children, but relatively little is available for students who in addition may have an intellectual or a learning impairment. Because so few Spanish-language materials are available for teaching children with disabilities (Podemski et al., 1984), attempts have been made to translate English materials. But distortions sometimes result from direct translation. Evans and Guevara (1974) illustrated how the English phrase "It is hot" could have multiple meanings when expressed in different ways in Spanish.

Other problems are created by the linguistic variations of Spanish subgroups (e.g., Mexican-American, Puerto Rican), by the effects of cultural experiences on vocabulary, and by Spanish instruction by teachers who may speak Spanish fluently but be unable to read it with ease.

To overcome the scarcity of materials for bilingual students, Evans and Guevara (1974) suggested the following procedures:

1. Have Spanish speakers plan and write activities for instruction to assure an equivalent translation from an English material.
2. Provide instructional guides to teachers in both languages.
3. Include in the classroom a native Spanish speaker who can naturally translate materials while teaching.
4. Use team teaching or trained aides to facilitate the use of native speakers for children who need bilingual instruction.
5. Enlist family members as volunteers, paid assistants, or peer tutors if qualified teachers are not available.

GUIDELINES AND TEACHING STRATEGIES

A number of general guidelines and possible teaching strategies can be gleaned from the discussion in this chapter. These are offered as vehicles to help teachers meet the special classroom needs of language-different students.

1. Avoid negative statements about the child's language or dialect, exercising particular caution in front of large groups. Rather than saying, "I don't understand you" or "You're not saying that right," offer a statement such as, "Could you say that in a different way to help me understand?"
2. Reinforce oral and written language production as it occurs naturally throughout the day. A first goal in working with language-different pupils is to maintain and

subsequently increase their language output. Reinforcing desired productions will help ensure that this goal is reached.

3. During any formal language instruction period, work with five or fewer pupils so each has several chances to make an oral response. Working with a small group allows group members to see each other and permits the teacher to physically prompt and reinforce each student.

4. Set specific goals and objectives for language development just as you would for other instructional areas.

5. Reduce tension during language instruction by moving to a less formal part of the room. Arrange as relaxed an environment as possible so that pupils feel free to make oral and written contributions in the new language they are learning.

6. Encourage the learners to produce longer and more complex utterances. Develop and maintain systematic records showing each pupil's growth in language.

7. During language instruction encourage standard and nonstandard English speakers to talk about language differences and to compare different language forms.

8. Involve people from the linguistically different community in the total school program as much as possible so these persons can share language experiences.

Although this list is by no means exhaustive, it will get an interested teacher started on the right track. Good teachers are present in many classrooms in our public schools. These teachers are effective with minority students with disabilities just as they are effective with nondisabled, majority culture children. With adequate support services, appropriate programs for this group of children can be provided.

SUMMARY

Unlike the first two chapters, which focused on language found in the majority culture, this chapter deals with the issue of cultural diversity and language. It was pointed out that our society is comprised of a wide variety of individuals. Individuals represent Black, Mexican-American, Oriental, and South American cultures. The diversity, which has always been a characteristic of the United States, appears to be increasing rather than disappearing. The "melting pot" theory has not come to fruition.

The next section of the chapter dealt with whether persons from minority cultural groups have different language or deficit language. While there was a time when the deficit theory was widely accepted, currently the majority of professionals believe in the difference approach. That is, the differences found in languages are recognized, but these differences are not considered deficits.

The final sections of the chapter presented information about bilingualism and the teaching implications of students who experience language problems due to cultural differences. Several different intervention approaches were presented. It was noted that the best way to provide instruction for the majority of these children is to take advantage of their native language while helping them develop the majority language.

REFERENCES

Adler, S. (1990). Multicultural clients: Implications for the SLP. *Language, Speech, and Hearing Services in Schools, 21*, 135–139.

Baca, L. (1980). Issues in the education of culturally diverse exceptional children. *Exceptional Children, 46*, 583.

Bereiter, C., & Engelmann, S. (1966). *Teaching disadvantaged children in the preschool.* Englewood Cliffs, NJ: Prentice Hall.

Bernstein, B. (1961). Social class and linguistic development. In A. H. Halsey, J. Floud, & C. A. Anderson (Eds.), *Education economy, and society.* New York: Free Press.

Bernstein, B. (1964). Elaborated and restricted codes: Their social origins and some consequences. *American Anthropologist, 66*, 6.

Bernstein, B. (1970). A sociolinguistic approach to socialization: With some reference to educability. In F. Williams (Ed.), *Language and poverty.* Chicago: Markham Publishing.

Brady, P. M., Manni, J. L., & Winnikur, D. W. (1983). Implications of ethnic disproportion in programs for the educable mentally retarded. *Journal of Social Education, 17*, 295–302.

Chinn, P. C. (1979). The exceptional minority child: Issues and some answers. *Exceptional Children, 45*, 532–537.

Cohen, B. H. (1979). *Models and methods for bilingual education.* Hingham, MA: Teaching Resources Corp.

Cole, P. A., & Taylor, O. L. (1990). Performance of working class African-American children on three tests of articulation. *Language, Speech, and Hearing Services in Schools, 21*, 171–176.

Commins, N. L., & Miramontes, O. B. (1989). Perceived and actual linguistic competence: A descriptive study of four low-achieving Hispanic bilingual students. *American Educational Research Journal, 26*, 443–472.

Cummins, J. (1984). *Bilingualism and special education: Issues in assessment and pedagogy.* Clevedon, England: Multilingual Matters.

Divoky, D. (1988). The model minority goes to school. *Phi Delta Kappan, 70*, 219–222.

Emihovich, C. (1988). Toward cultural pluralism: Redefining integration in American society. *Urban Review, 20*, 3–7.

Epstein, M. H., Polloway, E. A., Patton, J. R., & Foley, R. (1989). Mild retardation: Student characteristics and services. *Education and Training in Mental Retardation, 24*, 7–16.

Evans, J., & Guevara, A. E. (1974). Classroom instruction for young Spanish speakers. *Exceptional Children, 41*, 16–19.

First, J. M. (1988). Immigrant students in U.S. public schools: Challenges with solutions. *Phi Delta Kappan, 70*, 205–207.

Garcia, S. B. (1995, October). Bilingual exceptional students: An assessment and intervention model. Paper presented at the New Mexico Learning Disabilities Association Fall Conference, Albuquerque, NM. (Cited in Nowacek, J. (2001). Spoken language. In E. A. Polloway, & J. R. Patton (Eds.), *Strategies for teaching students with special needs* (7th Ed.) Columbus, OH: Merrill).

Ginsburg, H. (1972). *The myth of the deprived child.* Englewood Cliffs, NJ: Prentice Hall.

Gonzales, E., & Ortiz, L. (1977). Social policy and education related to linguistically and culturally different groups. *Journal of Learning Disabilities, 10*, 331–338.

Henderson, R. W. (1980). Social and emotional needs of culturally diverse children. *Exceptional Children, 46*, 598–607.

Hess, R. D., & Shipman, V. C. (1965). Early experience and the socialization of cognitive modes in children. *Child Development, 36*, 869–888.

Hilliard, A. G. (1980). Cultural diversity of special education. *Exceptional Children, 46*, 584–589.

Hodgkinson, H. L. (1985). *All one system: Demographics of education, kindergarten through graduate school.* Washington: Institute for Educational Leadership.

John, V. P., & Horner, V. M. (1970). Bilingualism and the Spanish-speaking child. In F. Williams (Ed.), *Language and poverty.* Chicago: Markham Publishing.

Kayser, H. (1989). Speech and language assessment of Spanish-English speaking children. *Language, Speech, and Hearing Services in Schools, 20*, 226–244.

Kellogg, J. B. (1988). Forces of change. *Phi Delta Kappan, 70*, 199–204.

Koenig, L. A., & Biel, C. D. (1989). A delivery system of comprehensive language services in a school district. *Language, Speech, and Hearing Services in Schools, 20*, 338–365.

Labov, W. (1967). Some sources of reading problems for Negro speakers of nonstandard English. In A. Frazier (Ed.), *New directions in elementary English.* Champaign, IL: National Council of Teachers of English.

Labov, W. (1969). Contraction, deletion, and inherent variability of English copula. *Language, 45*, 715–762.

Labov, W. (1970). The logic of non-standard English. In F. Williams (Ed.), *Language and poverty.* Chicago: Markham Publishing.

MacMillan, D. L. (1989). Mild mental retardation: Emerging issues. In G. Robinson, J. R. Patton, E. A. Polloway, & L. Sargent (Eds.), *Best practices in mild mental retardation* (pp. 1–20). Reston, VA: CEC-MA.

McCormick, L. (1990). Cultural diversity and exceptionality. In N. G. Haring & L. McCormick (Eds.), *Exceptional Children & Youth*, 5th ed. Columbus, OH: Charles E. Merrill.

McLaughlin, B. (1978). *Second-language acquisition in childhood.* Hillsdale, NJ: Lawrence Erlbaum Associates.

Meisel, J. M. (1988). Early differentiation of languages in bilingual children. In K. Hyltenstam & L. K. Obler (Eds.), *Bilingualism across the lifespan.* New York: Cambridge University Press.

Naremore, R. C. (1980). Language variation in a multicultural society. In T. J. Hixon, L. D. Shriberg, & J. H. Saxman (Eds.), *Introduction to communication disorders.* Englewood Cliffs, NJ: Prentice Hall.

Olsen, L. (1988). Crossing the schoolhouse border: Immigrant children in California. *Phi Delta Kappan, 70*, 211–218.

Ortiz, A. A. (1984). Choosing the language of instruction for exceptional bilingual children. *Teaching Exceptional Children, 16*, 208–212.

Osborn, L. R. (1970). Language, poverty, and the North American Indian. In F. Williams (Ed.), *Language and poverty.* Chicago: Markham Publishing.

Podemski, R. S., Price, B. J., Smith, T. E. C., & Marsh, G. E. (1984). *Comprehensive administration of special education.* Rockville, MD: Aspen Systems.

Polloway, E. A., Epstein, M. H., Patton, J. R., Cullinan, D., & Luebke, J. (1986). Demographic, social, and behavioral characteristics of students with educable mental retardation. *Education and Training of the Mentally Retarded, 21*, 27–34.

Polloway, E. A., & Patton, J. M. (1981). Psychological causes. In J. S. Payne & Y. J. M. Patton, *Introduction to mental retardation.* Columbus, OH: Charles E. Merrill Publishing.

Reschly, D. J. (1988). Assessment issues, placement litigation, and the future of mild mental retardation classification and programming. *Education and Training in Mental Retardation, 23*, 285–301.

Salvia, J., & Ysseldyke, J. E. (1989). *Assessment in Special and Remedial Education* (4th ed.). Boston: Houghton-Mifflin.

Smith, T. E. C. (1990). *Introduction to education* (2nd ed.). St. Paul: West Publishing.

Tiedt, P. L., & Tiedt, I. M. (1986). *Multicultural teaching* (2nd ed.). Boston: Allyn & Bacon.

Wallace, C., & Goodman, Y. (1989). Research currents: Language and literacy development of multilingual learners. *Language Arts, 66*, 542–550.

Walton, J. H., McCardle, P., Crowe, T. A., & Wilson, B. E. (1990). Black English in a Mississippi prison population. *Journal of Speech & Hearing Disorders, 55*, 206–216.

Williams, F. L. (1970). *Language and poverty.* Chicago: Markham Publishing.

4

Principles of Assessment and Instruction

Edward A. Polloway and Loretta C. Jones

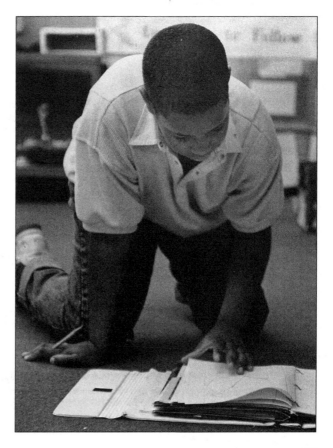

W hat are the purposes and the nature of assessment? How can educators meaningfully bridge the gap between the concept and activities of assessment and the formulative process of teaching? In this chapter we tackle these questions and present contemporary assessment models. We also discuss the development of in structional programs, as well as instructional planning, stages of learning, grouping alternatives in the classroom, and selection of curricular materials.

ASSESSMENT FOR TEACHING

The role of assessment in teaching has long been underestimated. With the emergence of the concept of diagnostic-prescriptive teaching, greater emphasis has been brought to bear on its importance. The assessment model from which the methodology of diagnostic-prescriptive teaching was extracted was a traditional one. Galton and Binet were two prominent proponents of this construct, or attribute model of assessment. It was based on the following assumptions (Swanson & Watson, 1989, p. 10):

1. That individuals can be characterized by attributes that can be placed at some point on a continuum;
2. That children have different amounts or quantities of the same attribute;
3. That there is a true placement (score) on the continuum of attributes that can be approximated by test data.

In a more contemporary vein, the construct model of assessment has given rise to diagnostic-prescriptive procedures. In developing this procedural approach, Swanson and Watson have identified several steps. The first is to select a construct (i.e., language) and then to reduce it into "sequential, quantifiable, measurable categories" (p. 11). For example, oral expressive skills might be initially reduced to: utters sounds, makes one-word utterances, labels simple pictures, and produces two- to three-word combinations. Following the initial process of selecting and developing a sequence, a test composed of these categories/skills is constructed and administered, the performance is evaluated, and an instructional program is developed to guide and determine teaching goals and activities.

Many educators inappropriately use terms such as diagnosis, testing, and assessment interchangeably. These concepts, however, have important distinctions that warrant recognition. Traditionally, *diagnosis* referred to the process of observing symptoms to classify a dysfunction that usually at least suggested a medical context. More recently, the term has been used within a much broader framework, focusing upon the individual child rather than on the condition. It now has a more generic scope encompassing analysis, identification, evaluation, and placement. This accounts for the closer perceived association with the educational realm and with educationally evaluative terms.

Testing specifically refers to the presentation of tasks or questions to an individual within an organized context, to obtain a numerical evaluation, a score. Testing is therefore only one aspect of the assessment, which looks at the global evaluative results and implications of performance.

Assessment is concerned with the qualitative as well as the quantitative components of performance on related tasks, both formally and informally observed within and outside a given testing setting. Assessment seeks to capture a more complete picture by determining the individual's current functioning levels. This is essential to effective educational planning and instruction.

PURPOSES AND PROCESSES OF ASSESSMENT

Enactment of the Education for All Handicapped Children Act without question established the crucial role for assessment in special education. It addresses assessment as required for decision making for eligibility for special services, as well as to encourage its link to educational planning and instructional programming. The procedures set forth in that act have become reasonably standardized across the United States. A comprehensive assessment model for decision making begins with initial screening and proceeds through to the reevaluation phase, which triggers reinitiation of the process. The steps in this general procedure are:

1. Screening
2. Formal assessment procedures
   a. Medical
   b. Educational
   c. Psychological
   d. Sociocultural
3. Eligibility determination
4. Program formulation
   a. Annual goal setting
   b. Development of short-term objectives
   c. Planning of Instructional Strategies
   d. Implementation of Services
5. Evaluation

SCREENING

The primary function of assessment in facilitating decision making is reflected in two distinctive sets of procedures. Screening first attempts to define how well a child functions in the learning environment. The second aim is to determine whether problems exist that warrant more formal testing or more in-depth assessment. Because these screening decisions are so crucial to a child's educational development, they must be based on information about the whole child. For this reason, assessment often explores widely varying aspects of a child's life, including cognitive processes, personal-social factors, and psychomotor development.

Initial screening is conducted at the local school to address concerns that have been voiced, usually by the child's classroom teacher. At this level a group of building personnel reviews available information and attempts to generate recommendations to ameliorate the child's difficulties. If specific areas of difficulty can be identified—for example, in expressive language—evaluative information from screening tests such as the communication domain of the Developmental Indicators in the Assessment of Learning (Mardell-Czudnowski & Goldenberg, 1983) would logically be included as a part of the data to be reviewed for decision making.

FORMAL EVALUATION FOR ELIGIBILITY

If a screening committee recommends more formal evaluation, that is done to prepare for decision making at the next successive level. To prepare for this, evaluative assessments are conducted across disciplines to gather information related to four mandated components, and in many instances a fifth component. These are:

1. A medical assessment, composed of examination and observations from a physician or nurse.
2. A sociocultural assessment, consisting of information obtained from the parent(s) or guardian by a visiting teacher or school social worker.
3. An educational assessment, gaining information from the child's teacher as well as current achievement test results obtained by an educational diagnostician.
4. A psychological evaluation, most often conducted by a school psychologist.
5. In many instances, a specific language assessment, done by a speech/language therapist.

A team of individuals, representing each of the respective disciplines providing data, then reviews each component. Based upon the collective findings, the teams make a decision concerning an individual's eligibility for special education services under the various criteria associated with specific disabilities. Eligibility may be established with a primary disability in mental retardation, for example; or a speech-language impairment and mental retardation may be identified.

INDIVIDUALIZED EDUCATION PROGRAMS

If the consensus of the committee is that special services are warranted, a related but distinctly different set of decision-making procedures is addressed. The focus shifts to development of an appropriate educational plan to match the eligibility determination. Development of the individualized education program (IEP) will be discussed at length later in this chapter. At this point we are briefly establishing its relevance to assessment activities.

Formulation of the IEP should be directly and substantially based on data presented during the prior eligibility decision-making phase. If the IEP is to be consistent with, and effectively address, the concerns of the eligibility decision, it should reflect the evaluative profile that led to that determination of eligibility for services. It stands to reason, therefore, that the assessment results, especially from the educational component, should be utilized in formulating and deciding appropriate IEP annual goals and short-term objectives.

To assure effectiveness and accountability, IEP decision making based on assessment information should be as important as, if not more important than, the eligibility decision. For example, if the eligibility committee decides that learning disabilities (LD) services are warranted in part because of assessed receptive language deficits (among other difficulties), IEP goals and objectives should include important aspects of auditory attention and processing.

The most direct link between assessment and instruction can best be illustrated relative to the specific educational assessment component. Although all decision-making assessment components contribute to instructional planning, the educational component in particular seeks to understand the child's characteristics, abilities, and achievement within the school setting as a basis for developing intervention programs.

Intervention and instructional strategies for home-based programs also should be linked to the assessment process. As initially mandated by Public Law 99-457, an amendment to PL 94-142 focusing specifically on infants and toddlers and transitional services, infant educators are guided by similar steps and characteristics in the decision-making process. The concept of individualized family service plans (IFSPs), comparable in concept to IEPs, should likewise directly reflect instructional goals and objectives based on acquired assessment data. IFSPs, however, have a broader scope, giving more attention to the needs of the entire family as well as the individual child.

CAUTIONS RELATIVE TO ASSESSMENT

Whether assessment instruments are used for decision making or for extracting information on instructional strategies for IEPs or IFSPs, their accuracy and relevance must be determined. Several considerations are warranted.

Technical adequacy. If testing tools do not effectively measure what they purport to measure (i.e., have validity) or show a high level of consistency and stability across time (i.e., have reliability), scores obtained will be of questionable value for any purpose. Sommers (1989) cautioned educators in terms of the technical qualities of tests, specifically in regard to language assessments. Because of the nature and variety of language tests, correlations across instruments may be subject to misinterpretation and subsequently lead to erroneous practices and conclusions. In some instances, selecting an appropriate and comprehensive model of assessment could significantly reduce the likelihood of problems derived from technical inadequacy of the test instruments.

Natural setting. Assessment should take place to the greatest extent possible in the child's natural setting, especially in terms of oral language skills. A teacher who overemphasizes language samples taken from structured classroom situations may inadvertently overlook the child's superior abilities in communicating with parents and peers, and thus make unwarranted assumptions about the child's level of functioning. This point is particularly cogent when evaluating a young child, a student who has a severe disability, or a child from a culturally different background. Teachers who pay close attention to this factor during assessment will be able to help students transfer specific skills beyond the classroom setting. Focusing on the natural setting also reinforces the idea of viewing isolated skills within a whole language perspective. This counteracts the reductionism that can result when test scores are used out of context.

Cultural and experiential backgrounds of learners. When developing diagnostic profiles, the effects of different cultural environments on linguistic patterns must be reviewed so teacher bias does not preclude accurate analysis of a student's abilities, disabilities, and educational needs. Although oral language most obviously reflects variant patterns, reading, spelling, and compositional skills also may be influenced by dialectical differences.

IDEA addressed the question of bias in testing by providing for protection in evaluation procedures to prevent cultural and racial discrimination. Bailey and Harbin (1980) cautioned that nondiscriminatory evaluation is possible only when data are gathered by an interdisciplinary team in a nondiscriminatory fashion, with an awareness of how bias could enter the decision-making process, and with the knowledge of how to control it. Although most efforts have focused on the development of "fair" standardized tests through elimination of bias, the issue is much broader than that. The entire process of collecting and using assessment data to make decisions about pupils has the potential for bias. Ysseldyke and Regan (1980) therefore suggested "...using data on intervention effectiveness, rather than data obtained from norm-referenced tests, to make most psycho-educational decisions" (p. 465).

Given the major concerns that must be considered in assessing students with disabilities, it is useful to review some principles representing a cautious approach to assessment in the schools. These principles, adapted from Grossman (1983), Turnbull and Wheat (1983), and Luckasson (1992), are consistent with the requirements of IDEA and most state regulations:

1. Assessments should be initiated only when sufficient cause has been documented.
2. The child's parent (or guardian) must consent to an assessment and has the right to participate in and appeal any determinations made and any placement and program decisions that follow. Under some circumstances, the parent also may be able to request an external assessment.
3. Assessments are to be undertaken only by fully qualified, certified or licensed professionals under state laws and regulations that govern their particular specialities.
4. Assessment procedures must be adjusted to account for specific deficits in hearing, vision, health, or movement, and modified to accommodate those whose culture or language differs from the general population upon which the specific instruments were standardized.
5. Individuals who conduct assessments should include appropriately trained specialists to assist with any child who has hearing, health, or other problems that warrant special consideration.
6. Conclusions and recommendations should be made on the basis of multiple sources of data, including interviews with people acquainted with the child (the parents and others) and observations of the child's behavior.

7. Periodic reassessments must be made (e.g., triennial review under PL 94-142) not only to confirm or correct previous judgments but also because programming changes may be in order.

Many of the cautions that must be considered in assessment can be crystalized into one key point: Assessment efforts must be undertaken for the expressed purpose of providing information that will lead to effective programming. The utility of the results is ultimately measured by how closely assessment is related to instruction.

CONTEMPORARY ASSESSMENT MODELS

To address issues related to the cautions just cited, we recommend application of assessment models incorporating two facets: (a) a wide array of both formal and informal measures within different environmental confines, and (b) an approach to assessment based on both criterion-referenced and diagnostic-prescriptive data. As defined by Neisworth and Bagnato (1989), an ecological assessment approach would satisfy the initial philosophical model and curriculum-based assessment (CBA) would exemplify the latter. These two approaches are discussed here to provide an overview of their possible merits.

ECOLOGICAL ASSESSMENT

The ecological assessment approach focuses on an interactive model that presupposes that "behavior is a function of personal variables interacting with environmental variables" (Neisworth & Bagnato, 1989, p. 39). It expands the traditional assessment role to include environmental factors as well as evaluation of the child's adaptation to the demands of those environments. Further, it encourages a multidimensional approach that fosters observations of interactive systems across assessment methods, levels of person-group involvement, and specific goals for assessment. Ecological assessment recognizes the importance of addressing issues related to accountability, general and individual needs assessments, strategies for providing instruction, and instructional outcomes (Swanson & Watson, 1989).

In regard to instructional outcomes, Neisworth and Bagnato (1989) reported that researchers such as Brophy (1979) and Flanders (1970) have given greater credence to the ecological assessment model, specifically as it enhances process-product studies of teacher effectiveness. It is increasingly more crucial for our assessments to effectively and reliably link investigative data and findings to instructional planning and outcomes.

Ecological assessment naturally places the process within the individual's natural environment. By doing so, the assessment can take on a *functional* characteristic, emphasizing the assessment of skills as they relate to successful functioning in a given environment. As Henning (1990) noted, those charged with assessment would then:

... observe [individuals] in the natural environment (e.g., home, the corner store, a local craft class) to see where they have needed skills and where they could benefit from some additional instruction or support. If the person is able to talk or to communicate in some way, he/she is asked what skills he/she would like to work on. The focus is on building on strengths and personal interests rather than correcting deficits. (p. 12)

CURRICULUM-BASED ASSESSMENT

Curriculum-based assessment (CBA) further supports and complements an ecological approach to assessment, particularly because CBA measures are likely to be ecologically valid (Fuchs & Fuchs, 1986). CBA, a system of criterion-referenced measures, is utilized in applied settings. These applications reflect a diagnostic/prescriptive orientation. CBA was devised to more closely bridge the gap between assessment and curriculum (Germann & Tindal, 1985) and thus becomes a more viable tool for accountability purposes (Swanson & Watson, 1989). Consequently, CBA has been endorsed by many special educators (e.g., Gickling & Thompson, 1985; Deno, 1985; Deno & Fuchs, 1987).

Curriculum-based assessment provides a measure of a student's specific skills while also providing information relative to overall skill competency levels (Epstein, Polloway, & Patton, 1988); it also can assist with the ongoing monitoring of performance (Bean & Lane, 1990). This orientation, of course, greatly facilitates the formulation of goals and objectives in language domains as well as in other key instructional areas as determined to be appropriate on the IEP. Neisworth and Bagnato (1989) noted that "curriculum-based assessment traces a child's achievement along a continuum of objectives, especially within a...sequenced curriculum" (p. 27).

As CBA relates to the current discussion, its worth in the decision-making process outlined previously in this chapter has been confirmed (Shinn, Rosenfield, & Knutson, 1989). Thus, it is a tool to assist with not only assessment and instructional planning but also with decision making at all levels of the comprehensive assessment model.

ASSESSMENT TOOLS AND PROCEDURES

As mentioned earlier, any assessment must strive to obtain accurate data from evaluative results. We have suggested specific models in addition to the more traditional, norm-referenced techniques (see below) that can be used to enhance the accuracy and value of assessment procedures. Especially with regard to language assessments, the consideration of environmental factors and curriculum-based measures, in addition to traditional methods, could prove most beneficial. More directly, language takes place within a social context to facilitate communicative functions, and success is relative to positive practical outcomes.

ASSESSMENT INSTRUMENTS

Two general categories of assessment instruments provide measures for the assessment process: formal and informal instruments.

Formal Tests   Formal, or standardized, tests are most often norm-referenced. The tests provide quantitative information comparing the performance of one student to that of others in his or her norm group (determined, for example, by age, grade, and gender). Scores usually are reported in the form of test quotients, percentiles, and age or grade equivalents. These tests are especially useful early in an assessment procedure when little is known of a student's abilities, and they can identify problem areas in which informal testing can begin. The ability to compare a student to his or her age and grade peers is also helpful in making eligibility and placement decisions and fulfilling related administrative mandates. Some additional advantages of formal instruments are that they:

— provide a capsule picture of student's overall levels of functioning.
— are ready-made and thus require no time for teacher construction.
— provide a starting point in assessment.
— are objective and generally data-based, with validity and reliability information available.
— allow comparisons of student with peers and with expectancy levels.
— give direction to teachers who may be unsure of informal assessment strategies.
— can serve as group screening instruments in some cases.
— are available in different forms, allowing for reliable evaluations of progress in a test-teach-test sequence.
— meet legal requirements that govern labeling for special education purposes.

Formal instruments also have some distinct limitations and disadvantages, including the propensity to misuse or overgeneralize their results. They may also:

— potentially lack direct relevance for instructional decisions.
— report results influenced by day-to-day fluctuations, and thus may be distorted.
— have inadequate data on reliability and validity and thus may be misleading.
— call for rigid administration procedures that may cloud the tester's ability to gain insight into learner problems.
— be expensive.
— require that administrators be trained.
— require large time commitments for administration.
— be invalid if used with pupils who are not represented within the standardization samples.

Many of these potential disadvantages are actually indictments of test abuse rather than use per se. Within proper bounds, formal tests can be used successfully when combined with other procedures in a total evaluation process.

Although specific tools will be highlighted further within the chapters on the respective language curricular areas, several examples of formal tests used to assess language are briefly mentioned here. The Peabody Picture Vocabulary Test–Revised (PPVT-R) (Dunn, 1980) measures "hearing" vocabulary. The Test for Auditory Comprehension of Language (TACL) (Carrow, 1973) measures comprehension of vocabulary, syntax, and morphology. Other more currently utilized language measures include the Test of Early Language Development (TELD) (Hresko, Reid, & Hammill, 1981); Clinical Evaluation of Language Functions (CELF) (Semel & Wiig, 1980); Test of Adolescent Language–Revised (TOAL-2) (Hammill, Brown, Larsen, & Wiederholt, 1987); and the Test of Written Language-2 (TOWL-2) (Hammill & Larsen, 1988).

Informal Testing   Informal tests must be used when data concerning certain skills is not available from formal measures. Typically, teachers devise these tests to determine what skills or knowledge a child possesses. The major advantage of informal assessment should be the direct application of results to teaching programs. By incorporating informal tests into the teaching program and monitoring student responses each day, teachers can achieve reliable measurements that can even reveal patterns of fluctuation in performance.

Criterion-referenced testing compares a student's performance with a criterion of mastery for a specific task, disregarding his or her relative standing in a group. This form of assessment can be especially useful when documentation of progress is needed for accountability, because the acquisition of skills can be clearly demonstrated. In the past, most criterion-referenced tests have been produced by teachers, but in the last two decades publishers have begun to produce more criterion-referenced assessment tools.

Advantages of informal assessment are that:

— instruments can be readministered frequently, easily, and quickly.
— alternate forms may be developed easily.
— information gathered will often be directly relevant to instruction.
— the validity of criterion-referenced measures can be established relatively easily.
— because of the specific nature of the tests, the results can be kept in perspective more easily.
— they can be used to further explore weak areas pinpointed on diagnostic tests.
— the process of informal assessment is inexpensive in comparison to formal procedures.
— by integrating assessment with instruction, the amount of time spent away from teaching is minimal.

Possible limitations or disadvantages of informal tests are that:

— the tests can be highly specific and limited in scope.
— developing the tests requires substantial time and effort by the teacher.
— subjectivity is often present in the choice and presentation of items and in scoring.
— a lack of awareness of the skills hierarchy could result in a distorted diagnosis and misguided instruction.
— an orientation to isolated skills may take precedence over more general considerations.
— the effective use of informal tests assumes a high level of teacher competence relative to the principles and purposes of assessment.

One can argue the relative merits of formal and informal tests, but it is safe to assume that adequate and inadequate instruments exist for both types and that both formal and informal assessments have a place in the total assessment process. The choice of tests should be determined by the type of information needed and the purpose of the assessment.

PROCEDURES FOR ASSESSMENT

Although formal and informal measures constitute the tools of the assessment process, the most important concern is how data obtained from their administration are used. The following procedures constitute a logical progression, beginning with the identification of language problems and concluding with the selection of prescriptive intervention strategies.

Collect Survey Information   Determining a student's general strengths and weaknesses in language is the first challenge. Two basic considerations figure into the survey-level assessment: (a) identification of a profile of linguistic abilities and disabilities that may be compared to overall expectancy levels (e.g., weaknesses may be noted in reading comprehension and written expression and relative strengths appear in word recognition and spelling), and (b) development of preliminary hypotheses about general language patterns (e.g., weak reading sight vocabulary, difficulty with cursive writing, strong and varied speaking vocabulary).

Several approaches can be used to obtain initial information about a student's general level of language functioning. One approach, *interviewing* with teachers or parents, should be structured so it results in a body of information that pertains to instructionally relevant aspects of the student's problems.

Brief observation of the child also can be a source of information. For example, listening to a child read orally for a few minutes and discussing what has been read reveals many strengths and weaknesses, as well as the student's strategies in dealing with the task of reading. Teachers can tell if a child who reads aloud fluently can recall what is read, and whether a student's oral reading is marred by many errors and unknown words, even though the child may have perfect comprehension of the passage. Brief observation can help form preliminary hypotheses.

Formal testing is the most commonly used approach to obtain survey data. As noted earlier, the instruments available cover a variety of curricular areas and generally report results by age or grade equivalents or in scaled scores that can be used to compare abilities in various language areas. For instance, if a child scores on the fifth-grade level in reading but on the second-grade level in spelling, the general area of disability is clearly pinpointed. And a fourth-grade child who scores on grade level in reading rate, sight vocabulary, and word attack skills but on the second-grade level in reading comprehension obviously requires further assessment in the area of reading.

Formal tests can serve other survey-level functions including the measurement of long-term progress and the initial selection of graded instructional materials. Many formal tools provide only general information, but some diagnostic instruments offer more in-depth analysis of specific skills, depending on the observational skills of the examiner.

Diagnostic tests more easily allow for formulation of preliminary hypotheses about language patterns. As alluded to above, however, the skill of the evaluator who makes observations while administering a test directly affects the amount of information gleaned. Although a written language test score might show that the only weakness a student has is in word usage, a skillful examiner can look at the kinds of errors a student makes and determine, for example, that the child was confused only about verb tense and noun-verb agreement, not about other areas of word usage. Even though formal tests yield information in terms of scores and equivalents, examiners should use the tests to analyze abilities and make hypotheses.

Obtain Data Relative to Curricular Needs   After general information has been obtained, the next step is to determine a student's level of functioning compared to specific skills sequences within various areas of the language curriculum. This assessment goal blends naturally with curriculum-based measurement, as discussed earlier.

Once a teacher understands a student's specific skills, diagnostic information points the way to the appropriate intervention. Certain formal diagnostic tools allow administrators to evaluate more than grade-level equivalents, but even those who are highly skilled at administering formal tests will have to supplement the information and hypotheses gained. *Informal assessment* techniques are used for this purpose. Consider the student who takes a diagnostic reading test. The results lead the examiner to conclude that the student has difficulty using sounds to attack and spell unknown words, and that the child lacks the specific phonic skills of consonant blends and vowel patterns. At this point the assessor does not know which blends or vowel patterns the child can use and which phonic elements are lacking. This highly specific information tied to skill hierarchies has to be obtained prior to intervention. It can be obtained from a variety of informal assessment techniques.

One particularly useful tool for obtaining specific information on an individual is the *language sample*. For example, oral language samples can be gathered and analyzed to provide information relative to a child's mean length of utterance (MLU) and nature of parts of speech used. We evaluate students' speech and language not only on their ability to articulate but also on their ability to expand on these articulated ideas. Expansion includes both length of utterances and nature of words used. The student also should demonstrate the use of a variety of parts of speech consistent with age or assessed cognitive level expectations. Measurement of parts of speech addresses the student's verbal and communicative competence as well as quality of verbal fluency.

In selecting and analyzing language samples as a pertinent assessment technique, we must be cognizant of the limitations of these strategies and the degree to which the observed utterances are representative of the student's general speech/language patterns. According to Amster and Amster (1986), more formalized methods of sample analysis can be utilized; these require at least 50 to 100 utterances as a basis for generating even more valid conclusions about a child's expressive ability. Language samples are discussed again in subsequent chapters.

Often, *skills checklists and sequences* are used to pinpoint exactly what skills have been mastered. In the case described above, administering the consonant blend and vowel pattern portions of a phonics checklist would show precisely which skills the child possesses. Informal tests can reveal the same type of information gathered from a checklist. In this instance, an appropriate informal test might consist of asking the child to pronounce and spell short vowel pattern words. Analysis of errors would indicate whether this is an appropriate place to begin intervention or whether further probing is needed to uncover related weak areas.

Informal assessment based on linguistic skill hierarchies should bridge the gap between formal test information and scores and intervention. Formal testing may allow the teacher to form some hypotheses about specific areas of disability, and informal procedures verify and expand upon these areas to facilitate the selection of appropriate instructional tasks. Informal assessment should be the key to prescriptive teaching tied to the needs of the individual student. The most in-depth diagnostic activities will be useless, however, if teaching is not its direct outcome.

Analyze Instructional Tasks   Once a student's performance level has been established within a skills sequence, appropriate instructional objectives can be selected. The demands the task makes upon the learner can be better understood through *task analysis*, breaking down the overall objectives into a sequence of component steps.

Task analysis clearly serves a dual role of providing (a) a standard sequence against which to analyze learner skills and (b) an outline of specific instructional steps. Wallace and Kauffman (1978) spoke to this dual role by stating: "Task analysis may be viewed as a sequence of evaluative activities which pinpoints the child's learning problem and guides the teacher in planning an effective remedial sequence of instructional tasks" (p. 85).

Motor activities, such as brushing your teeth or tying your shoes, are classic examples of task analysis, because they are easy to break down into sequential steps (e.g., put on shoe, pull up laces, cross laces, and so forth). Task analysis, however, is equally valid for language skills. Table 4.1 provides an analysis of syllabication in reading. Though task analysis often is associated with specific skills (e.g., decoding) such as the reading sample in the table, the technique also has applicability to, for example, reading comprehension (see Bartel, 1990).

Implement Prescriptive Teaching   After identifying the parts of an instructional task, the teaching itself should further contribute to assessment procedures. The term *prescriptive teaching* has been used in various ways, but it refers here to the cyclical nature of instruction: assess, plan, teach, evaluate, and reassess. The basic test-teach-test premise is similar regardless of the discipline in question. This cycle is illustrated by Figure 4.1.

Although initial assessments are done at a specified time during the school year, prescriptive teaching is an ongoing process. Therefore, teachers should be involved continually in reviews of student progress on a weekly, daily, or even moment-by-moment basis. The keys to success in continuous assessment are (a) the construction of

Table 4.1
Task Analysis of a Language Skill

A. Objective:

Given a visually presented list of unknown polysyllabic words in context, the child will correctly pronounce the unknown words with 90 percent accuracy by employing syllabication as a word analysis skill.

B. Prerequisite skills:

1. Possession of basic sight vocabulary (e.g. Dolch lists)
2. Ability to produce sounds of consonants, consonant blends and consonant digraphs
3. Ability to produce sounds of long, short, and variant vowels (r-controlled and dipthongs)
4. Ability to predict vowel sounds in open and closed syllables

C. Component skills:

1. Given a list of orally presented polysyllabic words, the child will orally identify with 100 percent accuracy the number of syllables each word contains.
2. Given a list of orally presented polysyllabic words, the child will orally divide the words into syllables with 100 percent accuracy.
3. Given a visually presented list of unknown polysyllabic words, the child will determine the number of syllables each word contains with 100 percent accuracy by counting the vowels that will be heard.
4. Given a list of visually presented unknown two syllable words containing the vc/cv pattern, the child will correctly divide and phonetically pronounce each word with 90 percent accuracy.
5. Given a list of visually presented unknown three and four syllable words containing only the vc/cv pattern, the child will correctly divide and phonetically pronounce each word with 90 percent accuracy.
6. Given a list of visually presented unknown two syllable words containing the v/cv pattern, the child will correctly divide and phonetically pronounce each word with 90 percent accuracy.
7. Given a list of visually presented unknown three or four syllable words containing only the v/cv pattern, the child will correctly divide and phonetically pronounce each word with 90 percent accuracy.
8. Given a list of visually presented unknown polysyllabic words containing the vc/cv pattern and the v/cv pattern, the child will correctly divide and phonetically pronounce each word with 90 percent accuracy.
9. Given a list of visually presented unknown polysyllabic words containing the vcccv or the vcccv pattern, the child will correctly divide and phonetically pronounce each word with 90 percent accuracy.
10. Given a list of visually presented unknown words ending with –le, the child will correctly divide and phonetically pronounce each word with 90 percent accuracy.
11. Given a list of visually presented unknown polysyllabic words, the child will correctly divide and phonetically pronounce each word with 90 percent accuracy.
12. Given a visually presented passage containing unknown polysyllabic words in context, the child will correctly pronounce the unknown words with 90 percent accuracy.

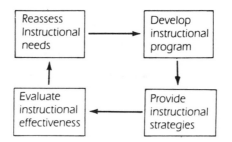

Figure 4.1
Prescriptive Teaching Cycle

diagnostic teaching lessons that provide a clear picture of a student's skills, and (b) refined observation techniques that provide a means of evaluating both the products of learning and the strategy or route the student takes to reach this product.

Analyze Learner Difficulties   The concept of *error* or *miscue analysis* is a basic part of diagnostic teaching. This tool, which has been applied to various language skills, can provide data on the kinds of difficulties a student may experience. The information obtained will be informative for future educational prescriptions.

Consider the following sample uses of error analysis. In spelling, a child writes *cawt* for the word *caught;* a preliminary analysis indicates that the student is overgeneralizing the application of phonic principles. In composition work, an adolescent writes the sentence, "The woman carried her son to the store"; analysis indicates that use of *carried* versus *brought* or *took* reflects a regional variation in language patterns. In reading, a student substitutes the word *house* for *home* in the sentence, "After work on Friday, they drove up to their vacation home in the mountains"; an analysis of this substitution suggests the word *home* should not be classified as an error because of its semantic and syntactic acceptabilities. (See the discussion on miscue analysis in chapter 8.)

Regardless of the assessment tool or procedure utilized, data obtained from this process should be reflected in, and subsequently a reflection of, the intervention goals and strategies inherent in formulation and implementation of the IEP.

INDIVIDUALIZED EDUCATION PROGRAMS

Results of the assessment phase should be transformed and formulated into educational plans for instructional goals. The individualized education program (IEP) is an annual description of services planned for students with disabilities. The IEP is a direct outgrowth of the regulations of the Individuals with Disabilities in Education Act, which mandate that all children with disabilities receive a free and appropriate public education, and which acknowledge that they need both a unique and a specifically designed instructional program.

The IEP mandate formalized procedures and teaching practices that many special educators across the nation were already using. Appropriate services and diagnostic instruction focusing on the needs of the individual child have always been goals in special education programs. At times, however, the emphasis on traditional categorical groups may have obscured the needs of the individual student receiving services. The IEP clearly established the individual child as the focal point by requiring that programs be fitted to the student needs rather than subjugating student needs to existing programs (Harvey, 1978).

JUSTIFICATION FOR IEP

Rationales for IEP development emerge from a variety of educational concerns (Polloway, Patton, Payne, & Payne, 1989). A major justification can be found in the potential *avenues of communication* that can be cultivated during development and implementation of the IEP. Regular classroom teachers have the opportunity to actively participate in planning for and teaching children with disabilities. The IEP also can bridge the gap between the home and school by giving parents a chance to understand the school's goals for their children. Involving parents in IEP planning gives them an active role in their child's education and creates a bond of support and cooperation between the home and school.

A second justification for the IEP is the requirement of annual *evaluation*. Instead of intuition, formal and informal test data are used to plan a child's program and evaluate rate of progress. A third major rationale for the IEP is the *instructional direction* it gives classroom teachers. Conscious written statements of goals and specific objectives enhance the possibilities for diagnostic/prescriptive teaching and clearly define the orientation of the child's educational program. In this respect, IEPs can potentially assist teachers in avoiding extraneous instruction or "cookbook teaching."

IEP COMPONENTS

As outlined in Figure 4.2, the IEP provides a standardized vehicle for the prescriptive process widely used by special education teachers. The IEP is an outgrowth of initial identification (child find) efforts and the collection of assessment data. It specifies the amount and types of services the school will provide and selects services that achieve the most appropriate program within the least restrictive environment. The IEP form also contains an overview of the child's proposed instructional program, with ties to annual evaluation.

IDEA requires that each IEP contain the following major components:

1. Present level of performance
2. Annual instructional goals
3. Short-term objectives
4. Statement of special services to be provided
5. Description of integration into regular programs consistent with least restrictive alternative

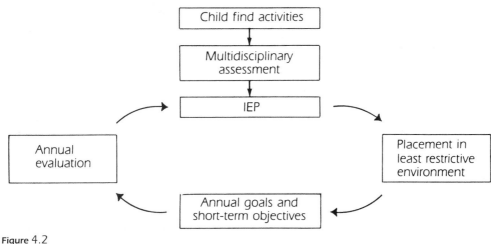

Figure 4.2
Function of the IEP

6. Schedule for initiation of services
7. Schedule for evaluation of objectives
8. Signed consent/documentation

Levels of performance, annual goals, and short-term objectives—the three main instructional requirements of the IEP—are discussed in depth here. The exact form of these components is not spelled out in federal law and thus is open to substantial local latitude in interpretation.

Levels of Performance   This component should summarize a child's current level of functioning and provide a basis for goal setting. Annual goals and short-term objectives should stem logically and directly from information contained in the levels of performance because, in essence, this component justifies the goals selected.

Because goals must be an outgrowth of performance deficits, individual performance levels should be established in each priority area in which instructional services are needed. Consideration might be given to academic skills, vocational talents, overt behavioral patterns, self-help skills, and fine and gross motor skills. The diagnostic skills of professionals who conduct the assessment come into play here, as decisions are made about the aspects of various curricular areas that warrant careful assessment.

Levels of performance can be expressed in various forms including formal and informal test data, behavioral descriptions, and specific abilities delineated by checklists or skill sequences. The most useful summary statement of an individual's strengths and weaknesses draws on information from a variety of sources rather than relying on any one source. Formal test scores in reading, for example, might be combined with a description of how the child performed on a phonics checklist.

Update

IDEA Reauthorization: The IEP

After more than two years of debate and deliberations, the Individuals with Disabilities Education Act (IDEA) was passed by Congress in Spring 1997 and the final regulations were published in 1999. The reauthorization of the Act has implications for all teachers working with students with disabilities. Relevant to IEPs, the reauthorization included the following changes and clarifications:

- IEPs must include a statement of the students' present level of functioning and annual goals that are measurable with the short-term objectives serving as benchmarks. Further, the IEP must indicate how the disability affects the involvement of the student in the general curriculum.
- By the age of fourteen, the IEP must include a statement of the transition needs of the student and how those impact on his/her course of study (i.e., the individual transition plan).
- The IEP must stipulate the extent to which the student will or will not participate in general education classes.
- The IEP must indicate how progress toward annual goals will be measured and how parents will be informed.
- The IEP team was more explicitly defined to include a special education teacher, a general education teacher (as appropriate), the professional to interpret the instructional implications of assessments, parents, an administrator, and other individuals with special expertise (at the discretion of the parents or the school).
- The team should consider the following when developing an IEP: student strengths, parental concerns, recent assessments, the effects of a student's behavior on others, strategies to address that behavior, the implications of English proficiency, the student's communication needs, and the need for assistive technology devices.

Source: Council for Exceptional Children (June, 1997). IDEA sails through Congress! *CEC Today,* 3(10), 1, 9, 15.

Whenever possible, the phrasing used to define levels of performance should be positive and describe things the child *can do*, rather than being negative or even possibly derogatory. The same information is conveyed by the two following statements, but the former demonstrates a more positive approach:

The child can identify 50 percent of the alphabet.
The child does not know how to identify half of the alphabet.

In summation, properly written performance-level statements provide sufficient, specific data that can be used to set goals.

Annual Goals   Once levels of performance have been adequately described, annual goals can be established. To do this, teachers must target deficit areas of performance to work on throughout the forthcoming academic year. Goals serve as long-term predictions of a student's expected gains and provide a focal point for structuring the program. Each child's annual goals should be determined individually to meet his or her unique needs and abilities. Because pinpointing the amount of progress a child will make in a year is not possible, annual goals should be the teacher's best prediction of what the student might accomplish. To have realistic expectations, teachers should consider a number of variables, including the student's chronological age, expected rate of growth based on potential, and past and current learning profiles.

As mentioned in the previous section, annual goals should be a direct outgrowth of information recorded in the levels of performance. The following abbreviated examples illustrate this relationship:

Current Level: Uses initial consonant sounds in attacking and spelling unknown words.

Possible Annual Goals:
1. Uses initial and final consonant blends and digraphs in attacking and spelling unknown words.
2. Uses short and long vowel patterns in attacking and spelling unknown words.

Current Level: Identifies 50 percent of the uppercase letters of the alphabet.

Possible Annual Goals:
1. Identifies all uppercase and lowercase letters.
2. Writes uppercase and lowercase letters.

The choice of wording used to write annual goals should meet, at least, the three basic criteria of being student-oriented, measurable, and stated in positive terminology.

1. *Student-oriented.* A goal must state what the student will be able to do at year's end, rather than what will be taught to the child during the year. An effective measure of a child's progress is skill acquisition rather than a description of curriculum. For example, "will be given verb tense activities" would be better stated, "will use verb tenses correctly in spontaneous speech."

2. *Measurable*. Verbs such as "write," "pronounce," and "identify" should be used in lieu of vague terms such as "appreciate," "understand," and "know." The goal "will know short vowel patterns" becomes measurable and observable only when transformed into "will pronounce short vowel pattern words."

3. *Positive terminology*. For example, the inappropriate goal "will not read so slowly" would be changed to "will read at a rate of 100 words per minute."

Short-Term Objectives   Each annual goal is subsequently broken down into short-term objectives, a logical and sequential series of related skills that coincidentally comprise at least a general teaching plan. Instructional objectives should move a child from the current level of performance through successive objectives toward achievement of the annual goal.

Short-term objectives can be written only after annual goals have been established, and they should be based on a task analysis process. Sequences and skills checklists can provide a foundation for dividing an annual goal into logical major components. The first short-term objective should take the learner a step beyond his or her abilities (as described in the discussion of current levels of performance). Each succeeding short-term objective then would move the child closer to the stated annual goal. The criteria applied to annual goals should be even more stringently applied to short-term objectives. Objectives should be specific, observable, measurable, student-oriented, and positive. Because short-term objectives are more precise, the criterion of being measurable will be enhanced by including a stated criterion for mastery. Some sample goal-objective clusters related to various language skills are given in Table 4.2.

DEVELOPING INSTRUCTIONAL PROGRAMS

The IEP concept introduced in PL 94–142 initially became a symbol of the importance of considering the strengths and weaknesses of the individual student in planning instruction. As Harvey (1978) noted, the IEP concept as initially conceptualized emphasized that the educational program should be "driven" by the child rather than the program driving the child.

For the IEP concept to work, educators immediately noted that the task of IEP writing and implementation must not become overly burdensome and irrelevant but, rather, serve as a catalyst for improving educational services (e.g., Turnbull, Strickland, & Hammer, 1978). In many instances, however, the process indeed has become inoperative and the IEP form itself of somewhat questionable value (e.g., Epstein, Patton, Polloway, & Foley, in press; Smith, 1990a, 1990b). And of particular concern is the relative unimportance IEPs place on oral communication as compared to academic and behavioral domains (Epstein, Polloway, Patton, & Foley, 1989; Smith, 1990a).

If the IEP concept is to become functional, it must transcend forms and paperwork and truly symbolize specially tailored programs in all areas of instructional need. For this to occur, teachers will have to use the plan as a basis for subsequent teaching decisions. Only in this way can annual goals, which should serve as the basis for determining short-term objectives, eventually be reflected in regular instructional planning.

Update

Communicating With Parents

A key element in educational programs is successful collaboration between education personnel and parents. The essence of such collaboration is effective communication. Wilson (1995, pp. 31–32) provided the following outline of principles for effective communication:

- *Accept:* show respect for the parents' knowledge and understanding and convey a language of acceptance.
- *Listen:* actively listen and make an effort to confirm the perceptions of the speaker's intent and meaning.
- *Question:* probe to solicit parents' perspectives. Often questions will generate helpful illustrations.
- *Encourage:* stress students' strengths along with weaknesses. Find positive aspects to share and end meetings or conversations on an encouraging note.
- *Stay directed:* keep the discussions focused on the items being emphasized and direct the parents to resources regarding concerns that lie beyond the teacher's scope.
- *Develop an alliance:* stress that the parents and teachers share a common goal of helping the child.

Source: Wilson, C. L. (1995). Parents and teachers: Can we talk? *LD Forum, 20*(2), 31–33.

Table 4.2
Sample Goal-Objective Clusters

Goal 1   *Student will be able to (SWBAT) use the manual alphabet to correctly sign his/her first name.*

Objective 1: SWBAT identify the correct written form of his/her name with 100% accuracy.

Objective 2: SWBAT sign each letter of his/her name after imitative prompting with 100% accuracy.

Objective 3: SWBAT sign his/her name from memory with 100% accuracy when asked "what is your name."

Goal 2   *SWBAT demonstrate understanding and correct use of common adjectives.*

Objective 1: SWBAT correctly identify all of the primary colors on four of five trials.

Objective 2: SWBAT correctly discriminate between the polar opposites of hot/cold and big/little on four of five trials.

Objective 3: SWBAT correctly identify words referring to common shapes (round, square) on four of five trials.

Objective 4: SWBAT demonstrate correct usage of the words some, any, no, and every on four of five trials.

Goal 3   *SWBAT generate sentences with correct noun-verb agreement.*

Objective 1: SWBAT distinguish between singular/plural nouns with 100% accuracy when given a list of twenty nouns.

Objective 2: SWBAT identify the correct/incorrect production of singular and plural noun-verb agreement in phrases with 90% accuracy.

Objective 3: SWBAT produce phrases that contain correct noun-verb agreement when elicited with related pictures with 90% accuracy.

Goal 4   *SWBAT generate sentences using correct verb tense (present tense).*

Objective 1: SWBAT aurally discriminate present tense verbs from other tense verbs (i.e., walks—walked) with 100% accuracy.

Objective 2: SWBAT aurally discriminate phrases that contain present tense verbs (e.g., Billy plays—Billy will play.) with 90% accuracy.

Objective 3: SWBAT correctly imitate phrases that contain present tense phrases. (i.e., He jumps) with 90% accuracy.

Objective 4: SWBAT produce phrases containing correct present tense verbs with 90% accuracy.

Table 4.2
continued

Goal 5 *SWBAT correctly identify the first 176 of the 220 basic sight vocabulary list.*

Objective 1: SWBAT correctly identify all 88 words on the pre-primer and primer basic sight word list.

Objective 2: SWBAT correctly identify all 44 words on the first grade basic sight word list.

Objective 3: SWBAT correctly identify 90% of the 44 words on the second grade basic sight word list.

Goal 6 *SWBAT write the letters of the alphabet in manuscript form from memory without* error.

Objective 1: SWBAT correctly identify all letter names of the first division of the alphabet (ABC DEFG).

Objective 2: SWBAT write from memory the first division of the alphabet with 100% accuracy.

Objective 3: SWBAT correctly identify all letter names of the second division of the alphabet (HIJK LMNOP).

Objective 4: SWBAT write from memory the first and second divisions of the alphabet with 100% accuracy.

Objective 5: SWBAT correctly identify all the letter names of the third division of the alphabet (QRSTU VWXYZ).

Objective 6: SWBAT write from memory the entire alphabet without error.

Goal 7 *SWBAT copy from a near and far point with 95% accuracy.*

Objective 1: SWBAT copy 10 words from a near point with 95% accuracy.

Objective 2: SWBAT copy five sentences from a near point with 95% accuracy.

Objective 3: SWBAT copy 10 words from a far point with 95% accuracy.

Objective 4: SWBAT copy five sentences from a far point with 95% accuracy.

Goal 8 *By the end of the year, SWBAT spell correctly, both orally and in writing, the first 31* words (a–e) of the Dolch list of common nouns with 100% accuracy.

Objective 1: When the 31 Dolch words are presented one at a time on flashcards, the SWBAT read them correctly with 100% accuracy.

Objective 2: When provided with a a set of four different spellings for each of the 31 Dolch words, the SWBAT circle the correctly spelled version of each word 95% of the time.

Objective 3: When each of the 31 Dolch words is presented with several letters missing, the SWBAT fill in the missing letters to correctly spell each word with 99% accuracy.

Objective 4: When each of the first 31 Dolch words is presented orally, the SWBAT write the correct spelling of each word while at the same time spelling the word correctly aloud with 98% accuracy.

Table 4.2
continued

Goal 9   SWBAT correctly use capitalization and punctuation in sentences with 90% accuracy.

Objective 1: SWBAT begin the first word of each sentence with a capital letter with 90% accuracy.

Objective 2: SWBAT capitalize the pronoun I and the names of other persons with 90% accuracy.

Objective 3: SWBAT capitalize these proper nouns: the name of the school, streets, cities, states, months of the year, and days of the week with 90% accuracy.

Objective 4: SWBAT place a period at the end of all sentences that make a statement with 90% accuracy.

Objective 5: SWBAT place a question mark at the end of sentences that ask a question with 90% accuracy.

Goal 10   SWBAT correctly write a simple sentence using a noun and verb with 100% accuracy.

Objective 1: SWBAT demonstrate comprehension of a noun and verb by listing without error five nouns and five verbs.

Objective 2: SWBAT correctly write the correct verb in a given sentence seven out of ten times.

Objective 3: SWBAT write without error five simple sentences beginning with a noun.

Teachers also should consider how this information base can be translated into weekly and daily instructional planning. As noted earlier, short-term objectives can best be viewed as milestones toward goals that children can realistically achieve within approximately a 1- to 3-month period. Of course, time estimates for objectives are always informed guesses because of the many variables involved. Merbler (1978) suggested that teachers could derive a more systematic estimate by averaging the most optimistic, most likely, and most pessimistic amounts of time required to achieve task success. Whether a formula is or is not used, teachers may find it helpful to predict time from a range bounded by conservative and optimistic estimates.

The steps represented by short-term objectives can become the basis for more specific learning targets. Assume, for example, that the annual goal for a child is the acquisition of 132 new sight words, and the child's first short-term objective is to learn 44 new words from the revised Dolch first-grade list (see chapter 9). A weekly goal therefore, might be to acquire five new words, which are presented in daily lessons in a variety of ways. Figure 4.3 presents a form that could be used to summarize this type of weekly planning. A daily goal might be to identify one or two of the words or to discriminate between the new words. Evaluation of each day's learning becomes the basis for subsequent daily and weekly planning.

Having established basic instructional objectives for an individual student, teachers should select appropriate instructional strategies based on the stage of learning relevant to this objective, to determine what system of grouping, if any, will be used to implement the program and to decide which materials will form the foundation for the overall curriculum. These three areas are discussed below.

LEARNING STAGES

A key first concern is to consider the relevant stage of learning indicated by the instructional objective to be taught. These respective phases are: acquisition, proficiency, generalization, and maintenance. Each of these phases requires the teacher to draw from what Haring and Bateman (1977) called the tools of "hardcore instruction": modeling/demonstration, drill, practice, and application. Each phase also dictates varying demands for supervision, feedback, and reinforcement from the teacher.

Acquisition Learning   In initial or acquisition learning, the child is exposed to new, or at least previously unlearned, material. Within the various areas of language, acquisition might consist of making a manual sign, verbalizing a new word, learning to rhyme words, or writing a complete sentence in grammatically correct fashion.

For acquisition learning to take place, several key elements must be present. First, the teacher must take an active role, *modeling* or *demonstrating* the appropriate skill. Referring to the four examples of acquisition above, these techniques might include, respectively, manual guidance for the specific sign, an imitative prompt for the new word to be spoken, recitation of the reading or rhyming words from word families, or a chalkboard model of an accurately written sentence.

Second, the instruction must be *repetitive* and, when appropriate, *varied*. The most effective way to teach a new vocabulary word, for example, is to present it frequently in a variety of modes and relate it to natural settings. Tying it to its natural usage provides a context for the word and associates it with meaning.

Third, acquisition learning requires *continuous reinforcement* and *feedback*. Children will grasp a new skill or concept faster when practice is followed by feedback and is paired with immediate praise.

Proficiency   At the proficiency stage, the student has learned the skill and now must refine and develop fluency (Hasselbring & Goin, 1989). At this point the student becomes more masterful and adept at exhibiting the newly acquired skill and may demonstrate this mastery through increases in rate or accuracy (Polloway & Patton, in preparation). To maximize both teaching efficiency and learner independence, appropriate timing of the shift from acquisition to proficiency should be carefully determined, based on the teacher's verification that initial learning has taken place (e.g., correct verbal responding to teacher's questions).

At this stage, the teacher's role is less directive, and instruction is based more on activities that provide opportunities for independent drill and practice. To determine when students are ready for maintenance learning activities, the teacher can test them with supervised drills; those who succeed in the drills are ready for independent practice. For example, after initial instruction on consonant blends, the teacher can closely observe how a student locates and pronounces the blends in a series of words. If the student accurately completes this task, the teacher can give the student specific practice assignments.

Child(ren) ___Cathy Stevens___   Dates ___January 10–15___

Weekly Objective: ___Student will be able to spell regular words from the following families: −an,___

___−in, −un.___

	Objective(s)*	Materials/Procedures	Evaluation
Monday	Will correctly spell 6 words from the −an family	Use the following: fan, ban, can, tan, man, van. Have Cathy develop the list through rhyming. Call attention to similar patterns.	Spelling accuracy: 50%. Need additional work on grasping the similar pattern of −an.
Tuesday		Practice rhyming words. Highlight the −an base of each word with red pen. Have her spell them while looking and underline −an.	Spelling accuracy: 100%.
Wednesday	Will correctly spell words from the −in family	Use the following: tin, sin, fin, kin, pin, win. Cue the −in base and practice spelling them.	
Thursday			
Friday			

*Use arrows if objectives or materials/procedures do not change from one day to the next.

Figure 4.3
Sample Weekly Lesson Plan

Tasks that students can complete independently are the key to successful fluency learning. Self-correcting materials are highly useful here. With this type of system, students are led through an entire exercise by a set of simple written or taped directions clearly outlining the task, offering a place to record responses, and providing a vehicle for correction. A list of activities that can be used at the proficiency stage of learning are:

peer tutoring	short compositions on current topics of interest
board work	working with partners
group projects	silent reading assignments
individual seatwork folders	tutoring other students
instructional games	using the Language Master
interest centers	viewing filmstrips
programmed materials	workbook assignments

The most common form of proficiency work in the schools comes through the assignment of homework. With the increased call for rigor in the schools (e.g., National Commission on Excellence in Education, 1983) and the realization that students were being assigned little homework (e.g., Keith, 1982; Strother, 1984; Turvey, 1986), a rush toward its usage ensued. The National Assessment of Educational Progress (NAEP) report (U.S. Department of Education, 1990) found that by 1988 students of all ages were being assigned more homework than they were in 1984. The NAEP report also suggested that those students who spent the additional time on the assigned work and read the most were also found to be the most proficient readers.

While recent reviews have generally revealed a pattern of positive effects on academic achievement for homework (e.g., Cooper, 1989a, 1989b; Turvey, 1986; Walberg, Paschal, & Weinstein, 1985), the question remains whether these effects also obtain with students with disabilities (e.g., Heller, Spooner, Anderson, & Mimms, 1988). However, since homework is a given in the schools of the 1990s, it can present some excellent opportunities for developing proficiency-type assignments. Epstein, Polloway, Foley and Patton (1991) present guidelines for the use of homework with students with mild disabilities that the reader may wish to consult.

Reinforcement at the proficiency stage shifts away from the continuous schedule often needed for acquisition learning. In order to gradually shift a child to self-regulation, the frequency of reinforcement now should reflect an intermittent schedule. This general term refers to a series of schedules in which the desired consequence is tied to the specific number of behavioral occurrences (ratio), to the lapse of time (interval), or the continued performance through a time interval (duration). Such schedules may be provided on a regular, established basis (fixed) or on a predetermined basis that perhaps appears as random to the child (variable). In addition, teachers should consider ways to shift reinforcement away from a teacher-directed emphasis and more to a cognitive behavior modification or self-management strategy (Meichenbaum, 1983; Wallace & Kauffman, 1986). Self-monitoring of attention (e.g., McLaughlin, Krappman, & Welsh, 1985; Rooney, Polloway, & Hallahan, 1985; Hallahan, Lloyd, & Stoller, 1982), and self-reinforcement (see Workman, 1982) are among the many options available.

Generalization Learning   The third stage of learning, generalization, means transferring skills and concepts to other situations. Teachers often have overlooked the critical nature of this stage, basing their evaluation of students primarily on classroom responses. Only when previous skills are applied to new settings, however, can program effectiveness be truly assessed. Generalization opposes a "train and hope" philosophy (Stokes & Baer, 1977).

Given the nature of language and of learners who are disabled, measures clearly are needed to ensure application and generalization. Borkowski and Cavanaugh (1979) concluded their review of research on generalization training by noting, "If training is tied to only one task, the strategy may become 'welded' to that training task. Training on multiple tasks might remedy this problem, producing generalization to new tasks and settings" (p. 160).

To assure generalization, teachers must be aware of several ways to promote it. Specifically, they should train for generalization across settings, persons, time, skills and domains, and reinforcers.

Generalization across settings uses various situations and conditions for learning. If a child has been practicing spelling words in one resource setting the teacher should make sure that these words are used and reinforced in various classroom writing assignments. Or for socialization through spoken language to occur, it must be consistently applied in natural environments.

Generalization across persons is significant because different people impose different conditions on the learner. Thus, including parents in a language training program is important. And if a child has extremely deficient oral language, words and phrases taught in the classroom as the basis for social control (e.g., bathroom trips, meals) also should be produced in the home as well. Generalization of other language/academic skills can be facilitated by involving parents in tutoring programs (e.g., Vinograd-Bausell, Bausell, Proctor, & Chandler, 1986) or other homework assistance (Landers, 1984).

Generalization over time involves ongoing evaluation of response maintenance over designated intervals and students' developing the ability to use a learned skill throughout the day. As Langone and Westling (1979) noted, a structured time schedule offers some distinct advantages to teacher and children alike but inadvertently can leave the child vulnerable to sudden changes in daily routines. For this reason, scheduling reading instruction, for instance, occasionally at different times is suggested to simulate real-life situations.

Generalization across skills and domains focuses on the need to promote the application of skills both within and across domains of language. For example, adopting a *whole language approach* integrates speaking, reading, and writing. Stice and Bertrand (1990) noted that the whole language approach emphasizes the interrelationship of language skills.

Another approach that focuses on these relationships is *unit planning*, in which instructional units on themes or topics of relevance and interest encourage the student to apply language skills to related areas. Unit planning is a particularly beneficial way to facilitate generalization (see Kolstoe, 1976; Polloway et al., 1989). Another option that can be used effectively is the *integrated curriculum*. The reader is encouraged to review Patton and Kataoka (1988) and Kataoka and Patton (1989) for further information.

Generalization across reinforcers relates to the use of various reinforcers and fading strategies. Because behavioral tools are so effective for acquisition learning, many children become hooked on extrinsic reinforcers delivered regularly throughout the school day. Fading strategies gradually move students away from extrinsically oriented and artificial reinforcers and toward self-reinforcement and natural events within the regular class, the home, the residential program, and the community.

Maintenance Learning   This last stage in the learning sequence involves the ability to retain what has been learned over time. Maintenance implies more than simple recall and cannot be equated solely with memory. It takes learners from acquisition/proficiency to solid establishment of a fact, concept, or skill in their response repertoires. The maintenance stage may best be viewed as a combination of remembering and refining learned material (Polloway & Patton, in preparation).

The discussion on reinforcement over time already described the role of response maintenance. In reality, the maintenance stage has elements of both proficiency and generalization in that it focuses on the need for continued fluency in a skill so it can be used or applied in the future. Therefore, the discussion of programming for these respective stages has validity for the maintenance stage as well. Some summary observations about proficiency and maintenance activities derived from Polloway et al. (1989, p. 72) are particularly apt:

1. Assess and ensure that students display acceptable independent working and interpersonal relationship skills.
2. Choose assignments that can be realistically accomplished independently to avoid constant interruptions by students.
3. Be sure directions for completing each task are provided clearly.
4. Build in self-correction methods so that students can receive immediate feedback by checking their own work (as applicable and appropriate).
5. Closely coordinate tasks with teacher-directed instructional lesson.
6. Vary the activities, allowing each student to work on several assignments during a given period.
7. Allow students some freedom to choose their activities.
8. Allow time for students to receive feedback or reinforcement for independent work.
9. If possible, have teacher aides, peer tutors, or volunteers assist in supervising independent work. (See Cooke, Heron, & Heward, 1983, for an excellent discussion of peer tutoring programs.)

INDIVIDUALIZATION AND GROUPING

During a given instructional period, teachers will likely have two general goals for each student: (a) assuring the acquisition of new language skills, and (b) providing for the proficiency, generalization, or maintenance of previously learned skills. Though the emphasis within special education on IEPs may lead some teachers to assume that learning is best achieved on a one-to-one basis, this is often not the case. Therefore, "individual instruction" should first be defined.

Except for short periods of interaction, individual instruction defined as one-to-one teaching is really a physical or temporal impossibility. Often, it is also undesirable because it may limit a child's opportunity to develop independence. Therefore, a more beneficial definition of individual instruction is: *alternative programming designed to meet individual needs and maximize learning success*. Thus, individualization can be seen as instruction appropriate to the individual, whether it is or is not accomplished on a one-to-one basis. It can be accomplished through one-to-one or one-to-two ratios, in small groups, or even occasionally in larger groups (Polloway, Cronin, & Patton, 1986). As Stevens and Rosenshine (1981) stated, "Individualization is considered a characteristic of effective instruction if the term implies helping each student to succeed, to achieve a high percentage of correct responses, and to become confident of his or her competence" (p. 3).

To choose an appropriate grouping arrangement, teachers should determine which strategy demonstrates both *effectiveness* and *efficiency*—that is, the amount of learning progress and the time required for this progress to occur, respectively. In evaluating the benefits of various instructional delivery systems, the group model should not be an inflexible arrangement to which students are assigned for extended periods. Instead, students with similar learning needs should be taught as a group as long as their needs coincide.

A modest literature base exists on the comparison between individual and group instruction as related to the key variables of effectiveness and efficiency. Several studies are briefly reviewed here, and the reader is referred to Polloway et al. (1986) for a more in-depth discussion.

Favell, Favell, and McGimsey (1978) compared the effectiveness of one-to-one and small group approaches in teaching a word recognition task to individuals who had severe retardation. They concluded that children taught in groups of four learned just as rapidly as those taught individually. This, of course, indicates that group instruction is not only as effective but also is four times as efficient in terms of the amount of learning per designated unit of instruction time. Research on motor imitation (Storm & Willis, 1978) and word identification (Fink & Sandall, 1980) also supports the advantages of group training.

Overall, with regard to the variable of effectiveness, results have been mixed, with some research favoring individual instruction (Jenkins, Mayhall, Peschka, & Jenkins, 1974; Matson, DiLorenzo, & Esveldt-Dawson, 1981; Westling, Ferrell, & Swenson, 1982), and studies finding group procedures more effective (Biberdorf & Pear, 1977; Koegel & Rincover, 1974; Oliver, 1983; Orelove, 1982; Rincover & Koegel, 1977; Smith & Meyers, 1979). Frequently, comparable results have been reported (e.g., Elium & McCarver, 1980; Handleman & Harris, 1983; Ranieri, Ford, Vincent, & Brown, 1984). In the critical area of efficiency, however, group instruction has strong support (e.g., Elium & McCarver, 1980; Kazdin & Erickson, 1975; Orelove, 1982; Rincover & Koegel, 1977). Although one should generalize cautiously from these studies conducted on variant populations of students with disabilities, group instruction seems to offer the

Update

What Works in Special Education

There have been numerous efforts to research the effectiveness of specific interventions related to meeting the needs of students with disabilities. Recently, a popularized approach to analyzing this research is through the use of meta-analysis. This type of research "aggregates findings across a particular area of research by converting data in each study to a common 'effect size'" (Forness, Kavale, Blum, & Lloyd, 1997, p. 6). Forness et al (1997) reported a "mega" meta-analysis to highlight interventions that worked. Among the interventions that have been rated most highly are the following:

- The use of mnemonic strategies (i.e., specific interventions to enhance memory and recall)
- strategies to enhance reading comprehension (i.e., interventions which focus on encouraging students to think about what they are reading)
- behavior modification
- direct instruction of specific skills
- cognitive behavior modification (i.e., interventions which teach students to think about their behavior and plan changes)

On the other hand, certain interventions did not receive "high marks" from meta-analysis research. These included:

- modality instruction (i.e., matching apparent student learning styles and preferences; for example, visual and auditory)
- Feingold diet (i.e., restricting the diets of students with certain disabilities to foods absent of additives)
- perceptual training (i.e., attempting to directly strengthen visual, auditory, or perceptual-motor skills with the assumption that these skills, once strengthened, will enhance academic ability, such as in reading).

Source: Forness, S. R., Kavale, K. A., Blum, I. M., Lloyd, J. & Lloyd, J. W. Mega-analysis of meta-analyses: What works in special education and related services. *Teaching Exceptional Children, 29*, 4–9.

most logical and efficient approach when a group of students shares the same instructional need. In addition, it can provide important social benefits (Polloway et al., 1986).

Teachers can apply this information to the demands of varying environments. For teachers in self-contained settings, small groups supplemented by one-to-one instruction are often the most appropriate. For example, within a 1 1/2-hour reading class for 12 children with mild disabilities, four groups of two to four children can receive 15 minutes of direct instruction in acquisition learning tasks, leaving half an hour for organizing ongoing independent proficiency and maintenance activities, switching between activities, correcting the students' work, and providing feedback.

Resource programs generally serve a relatively small number of students at any one time, so the possibilities for one-to-one instruction are greatly enhanced. In addition, given the needs of the students most often served in resource programs, the careful attention to precisely identified learning objectives can lead to corrective action and thus further success within the regular class setting.

Any grouping strategy used with students who have severe disabilities should be evaluated carefully to be certain that it meets the needs of each student. Because individuals often have unique and complex needs, teachers have to balance the presentation of some training on an individual basis with the importance of group instructional activities. The latter are particularly critical for socialization and for practice in applying communication skills.

Finally, the trend toward including students with disabilities in regular classes underscores the need for instruction via group formats. To the extent that the regular education initiative (REI) becomes a reality (Will, 1986; Reynolds, Wang, & Walberg, 1987), the demands on students to be able to function in this environment will increase.

SELECTING CURRICULAR MATERIALS

Even though a curriculum is determined largely by teacher innovation and creativity, the commercial materials and programs proliferating in all areas of language development can be of great assistance to the teacher. Examples of specific materials are given in subsequent chapters. This section outlines some criteria for selecting appropriate instructional materials.

Teachers might begin by considering the curriculum-student-teacher triad (Wilson, 1978; Bartel & Hammill, 1990). This triad is likened to construction projects, following the building-occupant-builder model. Before selecting materials, therefore, teachers should consider:

1. *The nature of the curriculum.* What concepts and skills are to be taught? What methods will have to be used? What theories of curricular development relate to the area of concern?
2. *The student to be taught.* What are the student's unique educational needs? What is his or her level of functioning? What type of grouping strategy will be used? What methods have been used previously with the student? How does the student learn?

#8

3. *The teacher.* What methods does the teacher prefer? How familiar is he or she with the content area? How competent is he or she in delivering his or her own strategies? How much time will be available for teaching within this area? For preparation?

Once these concerns have been addressed, teachers can evaluate the materials under consideration to determine whether they are appropriate. Teachers should consider the following factors, which incorporate suggestions by Wilson (1978), Bartel & Hammill (1990), and Wiederholt and McNutt (1977).

#8

1. Relevance of the material to the student's present or future needs.
2. Level of difficulty of the material (its readability, for example).
3. Scope of the material in relation to the skills and concepts to be taught (scope + sequence).
4. Data available on the efficacy of the material in achieving its stated objectives. (tests)
5. Skill and experiential prerequisites necessary for a student to use the material. (child's experiential background)
6. Type and level of the language used in the program.
7. Degree of motivation that the material is likely to provide for the student.
8. Time required to incorporate the material into the daily instructional periods.
9. Amount of preparation time needed to use the material.
10. Cost of the material in relation to the available budget.
11. Cost of the material relative to its use as a core or supplemental program.
12. Inclusion of manuals, guides, and assessment tools when needed.

Once materials have been selected, the two tasks remaining for the teacher are: (a) acquiring and (b) adapting or modifying them. Patton (in Polloway et al., 1989) aptly described these processes. The *acquisition* of instructional materials can be an involved process for teachers. It requires a knowledge base concerning usefulness, appropriateness, and value. In addition, it demands information about ordering and familiarity with current prices. The ordering and acquiring of materials ideally should precede instruction by several months. Teachers should attempt to remain up-to-date on available materials by requesting current brochures and catalogs from publishers. One effective way to achieve this is by securing literature from exhibitors at professional conferences.

Once materials have been acquired, *adaptation or modification* is often necessary to meet the learning needs of individual or groups of students. Modification of materials usually involves changing the way they look or the way in which they are used. Frequently, materials also must be augmented by other resources. Suggestions for augmentation are offered within the chapters devoted to the respective domains of the language curriculum.

SUMMARY

The emergence of prescriptive/diagnostic teaching has rendered assessment particularly important. The construct model of assessment gave rise to five diagnostic procedures, from selecting and reducing a construct to developing instructional programs. PL 94–142 set standardized assessment procedures: screening, formal eligibility evaluation across several dimensions, and IEP development. Assessment should be approached cautiously, with test limitations, testing environment, examiner bias and one's ultimate goal—effective programming—in mind.

Contemporary assessment models include the ecological and curriculum-based approaches. Tools may be formal or informal; each has benefits and drawbacks to consider. Procedures for assessment include collecting survey information and data relevant to curricular needs, analyzing instructional tasks, implementing prescriptive teaching and analyzing learner difficulties.

Individualized education programs are formulated from assessment results. The three key IEP components are: performance levels (the basis for goal-setting), annual goals and short-term objectives. Concerns exist about IEPs as currently conceptualized and implemented; resolving one important concern involves placing emphasis on translating short-term goals into daily strategies, thus adding functionality to IEPs. When planning instruction, teachers should consider a variety of group formats. Research indicates that grouping often compares favorably to 1 to 1 instruction in terms of effectiveness, and is preferable in efficiency and in the development of social skills.

After IEPs are developed, daily strategies and group arrangements are established. Materials are considered for possible selection based on the nature of the curriculum and upon perceived student/teacher needs. Next, materials are evaluated, acquired, and adapted to the specific needs of teacher and learner.

REFERENCES

Amster, J. B., & Amster, W. M. (1986). Assessment of communication disorders. In P. J. Lazarus & S. Strichart (Eds.), *Psychoeducational evaluation of children and adolescents with low-incidence handicaps.* New York: Grune & Stratton.

Bailey, D. B., & Harbin, G. L. (1980). Nondiscriminatory evaluation. *Exceptional Children, 46,* 590–596.

Bartel, N. R. (1990). Teaching students who have reading problems. In D. D. Hammill & N. R. Bartel (Eds.), *Teaching students with learning and behavior problems* (5th ed.). Austin, TX: Pro-Ed.

Bartel, N. R., & Hammill, D. D. (1990). Important generic practices. In D. D. Hammill & N. R. Bartel (Eds.), *Teaching students with learning and behavior problems* (5th ed.) (pp. 530–546). Austin, TX: Pro-Ed.

Bean, R. M., & Lane, S. (1990). Implementing curriculum-based measures of reading in an adult literacy program. *Remedial and Special Education, 11*(5), 39–46.

Biberdorf, J. R., & Pear, J. J. (1977). Two-to-one versus one-to-one student teacher ratios in the operant verbal training of retarded children. *Journal of Applied Behavior Analysis, 10,* 506.

Borkowski, J. G., & Cavanaugh, J. C. (1979). Maintenance and generalization of skills and strategies by the retarded. In N. R. Ellis (Ed.), *Handbook of mental deficiency: Psychological theory and research.* Hillsdale, NJ: Lawrence Erlbaum Associates.

Carrow, E. (1973). *Test for auditory comprehension of language.* Austin, TX: Urban Research Group.

Cooke, N. L., Heron, T. E., & Heward, W. L. (1983). *Peer tutoring: Implementing classwide programs in the primary grades.* Columbus, OH: Special Press.

Cooper, H. M. (1989a). *Homework.* White Plains, NY: Longman.

Cooper, H. (1989b). Synthesis of research on homework. *Educational Leadership, 47*(3), 85–91.

Deno, S. L. (1985). Curriculum-based measurement: The emerging alternative. *Exceptional Children, 52,* 219–232.

Deno, S. L., & Fuchs, L. S. (1987). Developing curriculum-based measurement systems for data-based special education problem-solving. *Focus on Exceptional Children, 19*(8), 1–16.

Dunn, L. M. (1980). *Peabody picture vocabulary test-revised*. Circle Pines, MN: American Guidance Service.

Elium, M. D., & McCarver, R. B. (1980). *Group vs. individual training on a self-help skill with the profoundly retarded*. (ERIC Document Reproduction Service No. ED 223 060)

Epstein, M. H., Patton, J. R., Polloway, E. A., & Foley, R. (in press). Educational services for students with behavior disorders: A review of individual educational programs. *Teacher Education and Special Education*.

Epstein, M. H., Polloway, E. A., Foley, R., & Patton, J. R. (1991). *Homework: A comparison of the problems experienced by students identified as behaviorally disordered, learning disabled and non-handicapped*. Manuscript submitted for publication.

Epstein, M. H., Polloway, E. A., & Patton, J. R. (1988). Academic achievement for students with mild mental retardation. *Special Services in the Schools, 5*, 23–31.

Epstein, M. H., Polloway, E. A., Patton, J. R., & Foley, R. (1989). Mild retardation: Student characteristics and services. *Education and Training in Mental Retardation, 24*, 7–16.

Favell, J. E., Favell, J. E., & McGimsey, J. F. (1978). Relative effectiveness and efficiency of group vs. individual training of severely retarded persons. *American Journal of Mental Deficiency, 83*, 104–109.

Fink, W. T., & Sandall, S. R. (1980). A comparison of one-to-one and small group instructional strategies with developmentally disabled preschoolers. *Mental Retardation, 18*, 34–35.

Forness, S. R., Kavale, K. A., Blum, I. M., Lloyd, J. & Lloyd, J. W. Mega-analysis of meta-analyses: What works in special education and related services. *Teaching Exceptional Children, 29*, 4–9.

Fuchs, L. S., & Fuchs, D. (1986). Effects of systematic formative evaluation: A meta-analysis. *Exceptional Children, 53*, 199–208.

Germann, G., & Tindal, G. (1985). An application of curriculum-based assessment: The use of direct and repeated measurement. *Exceptional Children, 52*, 244–265.

Gickling, E. E., & Thompson, V. P. (1985). A personal view of curriculum-based assessment. *Exceptional Children, 52*, 205–218.

Grossman, H. J. (1983). *Classification in mental retardation*. Washington, DC: American Association on Mental Deficiency.

Hallahan, D. P., Lloyd, J. W., & Stoller, L. (1982). *Improving attention with self-monitoring: A manual for teachers*. Charlottesville, VA: University of Virginia Learning Disabilities Research Institute.

Hammill, D. D., Brown, V. L., Larsen, S. C., & Wiederholt, J. L. (1987). *Test of adolescent language-2*. Austin, TX: Pro-Ed.

Hammill, D. D., & Larsen, S. C. (1988). *Test of written language-2*. Austin, TX: Pro-Ed.

Handleman, J. S., & Harris, S. L. (1983). A comparison of one-to-one versus couplet instruction with autistic children. *Behavioral Disorders, 9*, 22–26.

Haring, N. C., & Bateman, B. (1977). *Teaching the learning disabled child*. Englewood Cliffs, NJ: Prentice Hall.

Harvey, J. (1978, May). *What's happening in personnel preparation at BEH?* Presentation at 58th annual convention of Council for Exceptional Children, Kansas City.

Hasselbring, T., & Goin, L. (1989). Microcomputer applications. In E. A. Polloway, J. R. Patton, J. S. Payne, & R. A. Payne (Eds.), *Strategies for teaching learners with special needs* (pp. 147–165). Columbus, OH: Charles E. Merrill Publishing.

Heller, H. W., Spooner, F., Anderson, D., & Mimms, A. (1988). Homework: A review of special education practices in the southwest. *Teacher Education and Special Education, 11*, 43–51.

Henning, D. (1990, Fall). Assessment and selection of functional goals. *Aging MRIG Newsletter*, 12–13.

Hresko, W. P., Reid, D. K., & Hammill, D. D. (1981). *The test of early language development*. Austin, TX: Pro-Ed.

Jenkins, J. R., Mayhall, W. F., Peschka, C. M., & Jenkins, J. M. (1974). Comparing small group and tutorial instruction in resource rooms. *Exceptional Children, 40*, 245–251.

Kataoka, J. C., & Patton, J. R. (1989). Teaching exceptional learners: An integrated approach. *Science and Children, 16*, 52–58.

Kazdin, A. E., & Erickson, L. M. (1975). Developing responsiveness to instructions in severely and profoundly retarded residents. *Journal of Behavior Therapy and Experimental Psychiatry, 6*, 17–21.

Keith, T. Z. (1982). Time spent on homework and high school grades: A large-sample path analysis. *Journal of Educational Psychology, 74*, 248–253.

Koegel, R. L., & Rincover, A. (1974). Treatment of psychotic children in a classroom environment: I. Learning in a large group. *Journal of Applied Behavior Analysis, 7*, 45–59.

Kolstoe, O. P. (1976). *Teaching educable mentally retarded children.* New York: Holt, Rinehart and Winston.

Landers, M. F. (1984). Helping the LD child with homework: Ten tips. *Academic Therapy, 20*, 209–215.

Langone, J., & Westling, D. L. (1979). Generalization of prevocational and vocational skills: Some practical tactics. *Education and Training of the Mentally Retarded, 14*, 216–221.

Luckasson, R. (in press) *Classification in mental retardation.* Washington, DC: American Association on Mental Retardation.

Mardell-Czudnowski, C., & Goldenberg, D. (1983). *Developmental indicators for the assessment of learning.* Edison, NJ: Childcraft Education.

Matson, J. L., DiLorenzo, T. M., & Esveldt-Dawson, K. (1981). Independence training as a method of enhancing self-help skills acquisition of the mentally retarded. *Behavior Research and Therapy, 19*, 399–405.

McLaughlin, T. F., Krappman, V. F., & Welsh, J. M. (1985). The effects of self-recording for on-task behavior of behaviorally disordered special education students. *Remedial and Special Education, 6*(4), 42–45.

Meichenbaum, D. (1983). Teaching thinking: A cognitive-behavioral approach. In *Interdisciplinary voices in learning disabilities and remedial education.* Austin, TX: Pro-Ed.

Merbler, J. B., Jr. (1978). A simple method of estimating instructional time. *Education and Training of the Mentally Retarded, 13*, 397–399.

National Commission on Excellence in Education (1983). *A Nation At Risk.* Washington, DC: U.S. Government Printing Office.

Neisworth, J. T., & Bagnato, S. J. (1989). Assessment in early childhood special education: A typology of dependent measures. In M. B. Karnes & S. Odom (Eds.), *Research perspectives in early childhood special education.* Baltimore: Paul H. Brookes.

Oliver, P. R. (1983). Effects of teaching different tasks in group versus individual training formats with severely handicapped individuals. *Journal of the Association for the Severely Handicapped, 8*, 79–91.

Orelove, F. P. (1982). Acquisition of incidental learning in moderately and severely handicapped adults. *Education and Training of the Mentally Retarded, 17*, 131–136.

Patton, J. R., & Kataoka, J. C. (1988). *Integrated programming at the elementary level: Dreams, schemes and themes.* Unpublished manuscript.

Polloway, E. A., Cronin, M. E., & Patton, J. R. (1986). The efficacy of group instruction V. One-to-one instruction: A review. *Remedial and Special Education, 7*(1), 22–30.

Polloway, E. A., & Patton, J. R. (in preparation). *Strategies for teaching learners with special needs* (5th ed.). Columbus, OH: Charles E. Merrill Publishing.

Polloway, E. A., Patton, J. R., Payne, J. S., & Payne, R. A. (1989). *Strategies for teaching learners with special needs* (4th ed.). Columbus, OH: Charles E. Merrill Publishing.

Ranieri, L., Ford, A., Vincent, L., & Brown, L. (1984). 1:1 versus 1:3 instruction of severely multihandicapped students. *Remedial and Special Education, 5*(5), 23–28.

Reynolds, M. C., Wang, M. C., & Walberg, H. J. (1987). The necessary restructuring of special and regular education. *Exceptional Children, 53*, 391–398.

Rincover, A., & Koegel, R. L. (1977). Classroom treatment of autistic children: II. Individualized instruction in a group. *Journal of Abnormal Child Psychology, 5*, 113–126.

Rooney, K., Polloway, E. A., & Hallahan, D. P. (1985). The use of self-monitoring procedures with low-IQ learning disabled students. *Journal of Learning Disabilities, 18*, 384–390.

Semel, E. M., & Wiig, E. H. (1980). *Clinical evaluation of language functions.* Columbus, OH: Charles E. Merrill Publishing.

Shinn, M. R., Rosenfield, S., & Knutson, N. (1989). Curriculum-based assessment: A comparison of models. *School Psychology Review, 18*, 299–316.

Smith, M., & Meyers, A. (1979). Telephone skills training for retarded adults: Group and individual demonstrations with and without verbal instruction. *American Journal of Mental Deficiency, 83*, 581–587.

Smith, S. W. (1990a). Comparison of individualized education programs for students with behavioral disorders and learning disabilities. *Journal of Special Education, 24*, 85–99.

Smith, S. W. (1990b). Individualized education programs (IEPs) in special education: From intent to acquiescence. *Exceptional Children, 57*, 6–14.

Sommers, R. K. (1989). Language assessment: Issues in the use and interpretation of tests and measures. *School Psychology Review, 18*, 452–461.

Stevens, R., & Rosenshine, B. (1981). Advances in research on teaching. *Exceptional Education Quarterly, 2*(1), 1–9.

Stice, C. F., & Bertrand, N. P. (1990). *Whole language and the emergent literacy of at-risk children: A two year cooperative study.* Charleston, VA: Appalachia Educational Laboratory.

Stokes, F., & Baer, D. M. (1977). An implicit technology of generalization. *Journal of Applied Behavioral Analysis, 10*, 349–367.

Storm, R. H., & Willis, J. H. (1978). Small group training as an alternative to individual programs for profoundly retarded persons. *American Journal of Mental Deficiency, 83*, 283–288.

Strother, D. B. (1984). Homework: Too much, just right, or not enough. *Phi Delta Kappan, 28*, 423–426.

Swanson, H. L., & Watson, B. L. (1989). *Educational and psychological assessment of exceptional children* (2nd ed.). Columbus, OH: Charles E. Merrill Publishing.

Turnbull, A. P., Strickland, B., & Hammer, S. E. (1978). I.E.P.s: Presenting guidelines for development and implementation. *Journal of Learning Disabilities, 11*, 40–46.

Turnbull, H. R., & Wheat, M. J. (1983). Legal responses to classification. In J. L. Matson, & J. A. Mulick (Eds.), *Handbook of mental retardation* (pp. 157–169). New York: Pergamon.

Turvey, J. S. (1986). Homework: Its importance to student achievement. *NASSP Bulletin, 70*(487), 27–35.

U.S. Department of Education (1990). Reading and writing proficiency remains low. *Daily Education News,* January 9, pp. 1–7.

Vinograd-Bausell, C. R., Bausell, R. B., Proctor, W., & Chandler, B. (1986). Impact of unsupervised parent tutors on word recognition skills. *Journal of Special Education, 20*, 83–90.

Walberg, H. J., Paschal, R. A., & Weinstein, T. (1985). Homework's powerful effects on learning. *Educational Leadership, 42*(7), 76–79.

Wallace, G., & Kauffman, J. M. (1978). *Teaching children with learning problems* (2nd ed.). Columbus, OH: Charles E. Merrill Publishing.

Wallace, G., & Kauffman, J. M. (1986). *Teaching children with learning problems* (3rd ed.). Columbus, OH: Charles E. Merrill Publishing.

Westling, D. L., Ferrell, K., & Swenson, K. (1982). Intraclassroom comparison of two arrangements for teaching profoundly mentally retarded children. *American Journal of Mental Deficiency, 86*, 601–608.

Wiederholt, J. L., & McNutt, G. (1977). Evaluating materials for handicapped adolescents. *Journal of Learning Disabilities, 10*, 132–140.

Will, M. C. (1986). Educating children with learning problems: A shared responsibility. *Exceptional Children, 52*, 411–415.

Wilson, C. L. (1995). Parents and teachers: Can we talk? *LD Forum, 20*(2), 31–33.

Wilson, J. (1978). Selecting educational materials and resources. In D. D. Hammill & N. R. Bartel (Eds.), *Teaching children with learning and behavior problems.* Boston: Allyn & Bacon.

Workman, A. E. (1982). *Teaching behavioral self-control to students.* Austin, TX: Pro-Ed.

Ysseldyke, J. E., & Regan, R. R. (1980). Nondiscriminatory assessment: A formative model. *Exceptional Children, 46*, 465–466.

5

Initial Language Skills: Verbal

Nikki L. Murdick

F or most children "the primary first-learned language system is oral" (Compton, 1990). But in a small, although educationally significant group of people, language may fail to develop spontaneously (Rittenhouse & Myers, 1985) or may be characterized by extreme language delay or communication patterns that have been labeled as primitive. This group includes young children experiencing significant delay in language development as well as people of all ages with severe cognitive, emotional, behavioral, auditory, or multiple impairments that may affect language acquisition. Although these individuals may not have an identifiable or complex language system, this does not preclude the possibility that a communication system, either vocal or nonvocal, may be in place.

Prior to the mid-1960s, many educators were distinctly pessimistic about the ability of individuals with severe language delay to develop language competence. As discussed in chapter 1, a general acceptance of the innate hypothesis of language development (Chomsky, 1968) added to the sentiment that individuals have a built-in structure for acquiring and producing language. Based on this hypothesis was the belief that the absence of spontaneous language is a fundamental characteristic for some individuals with severe disabilities. Bricker (1972) noted that linguistic training was thus often viewed as a "well-intentioned but futile gesture" (p. 75) for those with severe handicaps who had not acquired language, because the general assumption was that language instruction was to be built upon whatever language a child had already spontaneously acquired.

The current status of research on the development of language reflects the changes that have taken place in the last three decades. Although some people have cautioned that the optimistic flavor of the times led to the egocentric wishes of trainers taking precedence over the individual's needs (Burton & Hirshoren, 1979; Rago & Cleland, 1978), few would disagree that communication programs for individuals with serious disabilities, developmental delays, or an absence of verbal language are now viewed in a radically different way than in past years.

There are several reasons for these rapid changes in the language acquisition arena. An increased concern for those who have severe disabilities been a central factor. Other major factors that also have had a significant impact are (Stainback, Stainback, & Maurer, 1976):

— litigation supporting the right to treatment (*Wyatt v. Stickney*, 1971) and the right to education (*PARC v. Pennsylvania*, 1971).
— legislation mandating primary attention to individuals with handicaps who are unserved or inadequately served (PL 94–142 and its latest amendments, PL 99–457).
— the Bureau of Education for the Handicapped (now the Office for Special Education and Rehabilitative Services, known as OSERS) designating the area of severe handicaps as a top funding priority.
— the development of a professional organization focused specifically on the needs of persons with severe handicaps (The Association for Persons with Severe Handicaps, formerly The Association for the Severely Handicapped, and prior to that The American Association for the Education of the Severely and Profoundly Handicapped).

— a variety of other commitments by the federal and state governments, professionals, and local school districts.

Substantial changes in understanding and teaching people who have severe disabilities have accompanied this increased commitment. Continued growth in the use of cognitive and behavioral theories of development and learning is especially important. Cognitive theories, based on the work of Paiget, have emphasized optimistic developmental variables, such as cognitive readiness skills, rather than defects or differences. These cognitive theories also have provided a basis for understanding the quality of an individual's specific abilities relative to his or her overall level of functioning. Behaviorists, on the other hand, have generated a variety of tools and technology for the refinement of educational procedures to use with students who are considered difficult to teach (i.e., those who have severe disabilities). A blending of cognitive and behavioral theories is now occurring and will continue throughout the 1990s to challenge educators of individuals who have severe disabilities.

This chapter presents a general orientation to verbal language instruction for persons with severe disabilities. Sections within it discuss assessment tools, programming techniques, and a review of specific programs. Chapter 6 utilizes the same format to provide a description of nonverbal language instruction for persons with severe handicaps. Although these two chapters review the current state of the knowledge base, the language acquisition field is both new and expanding. Professionals, therefore, will have to continue to review the research to stay knowledgeable about concepts and trends as they emerge in the future.

AN ORIENTATION TO INSTRUCTION

To develop a firm foundation for assessing and teaching those who have severe disabilities, this section highlights some of the special problems educators face. This discussion is followed by a review of the major theories of language acquisition that provide the bases for the assessment instruments and training programs discussed at the end of the chapter.

INSTRUCTIONAL PROBLEMS

Teaching language to children who have not acquired it is a unique task with distinct problems (Schiefelbusch, Ruder, & Bricker, 1976), but it is an essential task. As Brimer (1990) says, if people are "to be actively and totally integrated into a community, they must be able to communicate." Because language is the "key to other forms of symbolic learning . . . as well as to an enormous range of complex social behaviors" (Warren & Kaiser, 1988, p. 89), many professionals believe that the learner's apparent lack of language—the base from which normal teaching proceeds—is the main obstacle facing teachers.

Providing instructions and explanations, establishing rapport, and perceiving a learner's difficulties all take on a different meaning with children who are nonverbal, and thus create special demands on the teacher. Nonverbal communication has to substitute for verbal exchanges, and the instruction itself has to be geared to children who may have very limited receptive vocabularies. Nonlingual alternatives must be developed as needed. These alternatives include the use of tangible reinforcement in lieu of praise, and physically guiding learners through motor activities instead of giving verbal directions. A second problem facing the teacher is the student's lack of verbal mediation skills. With no ability to rehearse and code incoming stimuli, the learner will have difficulty acquiring, understanding, and remembering new information.

Contributing to the difficulty teachers face when developing and implementing instruction with children who lack fluent verbal language skills is a group of behaviors known as *extralinguistic behaviors* (e.g., the lack of prelinguistic behavior development and the acquisition of competing behaviors). Brimer (1990) stated that extralinguistic behaviors may actually compete with or interfere with the development of communication in children who have severe handicaps.

Prelinguistic behaviors (e.g., imitation, gestures, verbal turn-taking, means-end behavior, and symbolic play) are important precursors of verbal language development (Bruner, 1975; Bullis, Rowland, Schweigert, & Stremel-Campbell, 1986; Sugarman, 1978; Uzgiris, 1981). As a result of a lag or deficit in the acquisition of these prelinguistic behaviors, subsequent verbal and nonverbal communication may be delayed or may not develop. Instruction based on developing the prelinguistic behaviors would therefore become the focus prior to beginning a verbal language program. Competing behaviors (e.g., aggressive acts, self-stimulatory and/or stereotypic behaviors, random vocalizations, echolalia, distractibility) impede the development of meaningful communication skills in individuals with severe disabilities (Smith, 1990). Many professionals believe that involving children with severe language delay in instructional programs early on will assist in their development of prelinguistic behaviors and at the same time decrease their acquisition of competing behaviors (Alberto, Garrett, Briggs, & Umberger, 1983; Brimer, 1990; Reichle & Karlan, 1985).

GENERAL INSTRUCTIONAL GOALS

Despite the problems, teachers must help people with severe handicaps acquire a method of communication that will be useful in the individual's own environment (Keogh & Reichle, 1985; Owens, 1988). Because verbal communication is the traditional method of communication, oral speech should be encouraged and taught. By whatever means the individual is taught to communicate, Premack (1970) indicated that proficiency in a language requires that the individual understand and make a series of discriminations. These discriminations can be viewed as an analysis of the task confronting the preverbal child, adolescent, or adult.

First, the learner must learn that symbols stand for *referents*, that is, objects, actions, or agents (persons). Once the pupil understands referents, he or she can acquire a host of specific verbal and nonverbal forms. According to Piagetian theory, children initially develop *signifiers*, first consisting of their own symbols and later expanded to include social *signs* representing true language (Bricker & Carlson, 1981; Robinson &

Robinson, 1976). According to Lahey (1988), children should be taught language in terms of action relations (e.g., *catch ball, touch nose*) instead of static labels (e.g., *ball, nose*). Teaching language in this manner more closely approximates normal language development and therefore is more "efficient in terms of both the information selected to code and the forms selected for representing this information" (p. 181).

Next, the child must learn and then discriminate between symbols that are more cognitively and linguistically complex. The child first must make gross distinctions between symbols, then progress to finer ones. Eventually the child will be able to differentiate similar sounds and words that stand for various environmental events. As a child masters this phase of development, he or she will be able to hear the differences between word pairs of increasing similarity, such as *dog/cat, dog/bag, dog/door*.

Finally, the child must learn to organize these symbols into sentences and discriminate between different arrangements of the same words. Syntactical considerations underlie the ability to string words together and then understand their different meanings. For instance, the child must comprehend the difference between *I throw the ball/ the ball throws me*, or *Bill sweeps the floor/the floor sweeps Bill* (Schiefelbusch et al., 1976).

Cognitive discrimination tasks are further circumscribed by the specific components included in any initial language development program. The teacher's ultimate objective is to expand the learner's comprehension and verbal production repertoire so that he or she can make and understand an infinite number of specific utterances in order to control his or her environment. The task is indeed awesome when one realizes that "five-year-olds have acquired virtually the entire language system by their fifth birthday" and "may . . . have an active vocabulary of 3,000 words" (Warren & Kaiser, 1988, p. 89). Although this is an impressive feat for children without severe language disorders (Wagner, 1985), it is an essential accomplishment for any individual who will acquire fluent verbal communication skills.

THEORIES OF ACQUISITION

When selecting a language assessment or instructional program for an individual with both severe handicaps and delayed verbal communication, the theory of language acquisition to which the teacher adheres is important. According to Owens (1988), four theories of language development are presently in use: behavioral, psycholinguistic/syntactic, semantic/cognitive, and sociolinguistic/programmatic. Although these theories were discussed in chapter 1, they are briefly highlighted here as related to specific subsequent discussions in this chapter.

BEHAVIORAL THEORY

The most widely known proponent of behavioral theory is B. F. Skinner. According to Skinner and his compatriots, all behaviors are learned and can be changed based on modifications of any of the three parts of the behavioral schema (*antecedent-behavior-consequence*). These behaviors produce patterns that cause changes in other behaviors and affect the individuals who are involved in the behavioral exchange (Thurman & Widerstrom, 1985). Language, therefore, can be defined as a learned behavior subject to all the rules of operant conditioning (Owens, 1988). Skinner described his theory of language acquisition in his classic text, *Verbal Behavior*, published in 1957. Research continues concerning the behavior-analytic framework for language development, in an attempt to demonstrate the continued usefulness of this theory in explaining the development of word learning and grammatical structure (Stemmer, 1990).

Behavior modification techniques, considered to be applications of the behavioral theory, are presently the most well known and most often used methods in language programs for children with severe language delay (Musselwhite & St. Louis, 1982). But Siegel and Spradlin (1978) have cautioned that "behavior modification is now seen as a form of behavioral engineering rather than a theoretical system" (p. 371) and, as a result, often has been incorporated into programs that have other theoretical bases. In fact, most remedial programs used with children who have delayed language utilize structured behavioral techniques (Owens, 1988).

PSYCHOLINGUISTIC/SYNTACTIC THEORY

The psycholinguistic/syntactic theory focuses on language form and the underlying mental processes it represents rather than focusing on language as "something we do," as in the behaviorist theory (Lee, 1981). The leading proponent of this theory was Noam Chomsky (1957, 1968) who questioned the behavioral theory of language acquisition. According to Chomsky and his peers, the multitude of rule-based languages humans have developed has a universality, indicating that this language ability has a biological/neurological basis. These early psycholinguists called this innate language ability a *language acquisition device* (LAD) (Chomsky, 1968). Lenneberg (1967), a colleague of Chomsky, asserted that all humans, no matter what their level of ability, do communicate and that these communications follow some type of linguistic rules. Therefore, the problem with communication development among human beings of differing capacities is one of *degree* of communication, not of *ability* to learn to communicate.

SEMANTIC/COGNITIVE THEORY

Fillmore (1968) and Katz and Fodor (1963) were early linguists who questioned Chomsky's model of language acquisition. To these theorists, Chomsky's model was incomplete because it dealt with syntax only and omitted the meaning of the language the individual acquired (i.e., semantics). According to Thurman and Widerstrom (1985), "the move from syntactic to semantic emphasis in language acquisition theory paved the way for researchers to consider language as a correlate of cognitive development" (p. 78). This semantic/cognitive theory was advanced by Bloom's research and subsequent publication in 1970 of *Language Development: Form and Function of Emerging Grammars*. Bloom's research also seemed to advance a biological basis for language acquisition. Later semanticists, such as McLean and Snyder-McLean (1978), assumed that the common rules used by children in their language were related to the level of their cognitive development.

Thus, to the semantic/cognitive psycholinguist, "thought precedes language." The link between an individual's cognitive abilities and his or her propensity for language acquisition is still not adequately explained (Owens, 1988; Rice, 1983). The question of cognitive/language link continues to elicit controversy among researchers (e.g., Newport, 1990; Sinclair, 1969, 1971, 1973; Vygotsky, 1962).

SOCIOLINGUISTIC THEORY

A perspective different from that of either the semantic/cognitive or syntactic linguists is that of the sociolinguists, who view language from the aspect of the communication unit (word, sentence, paragraph) used to convey information. According to Bruner (1975), the *use* of language in communication is the most significant focus of the linguistic process; hence, this model focuses on a concern for pragmatics. To the sociolinguists, motivation and the context in which the linguistic interaction is to occur are also extremely important. This emerging theory is known also as the interactionist perspective (Warren & Kaiser, 1988) or the pragmatic perspective (Carrow-Woolfolk, 1988).

The sociolinguists believe that "language is preceded by, and possibly evolves from, a well integrated nonverbal communication system" (Mahoney & Seely, 1976, p. 94). According to Owens (1988), this theory contrasts with that of the psycholinguists in the focus of adult-child language interaction. Whereas the psycholinguist believes that the adult provides segments of language for the child to interpret in the form of syntax or semantics, the sociolinguist believes that language is acquired through socialization and adult-child shared communication (conversation) (Kysela, Holdgrafer, McCarthy, & Stewart, 1990; MacDonald, 1985; Warren & Rogers-Warren, 1985). This belief is known as the "centrality of communication in social affairs" (Turnure, 1986).

Each language acquisition theory has its proponents as well as antagonists. In preparing to teach students who have severe language delay, teachers should understand and recognize the principles of these theories, because assessment procedures, instructional methods, and communication systems are based on research resulting from these theoretical bases. The trend is toward interactionist models, which provide an attractive alternative for those who design instructional programs.

ASSESSMENT STRATEGIES

The method of diagnosing learners with severe disabilities in language follows the basic assessment process discussed in chapter 4. As such, language assessment requires the use of various instruments to pinpoint a child's communication skills and evaluate progress. According to Stremel-Campbell (1977), a language assessment should be:

1. complete, including all relevant communication behavior and noting both strengths and weaknesses;

2. directly related to training, rather than oriented just to a test score;
3. current, according to a child's present level of functioning; and
4. continuous, so as to provide constant input into programming.

Teachers can use a variety of methods and instruments to meet the multiple needs of assessment. This section outlines approaches that will enable teachers to (a) determine a child's general level of functioning, including an overview of strengths and weaknesses, (b) develop a functional analysis of a child's language behavior, and (c) evaluate the social and cognitive variables that may affect a child's readiness for language acquisition. Teachers also should be alert to possible medical variables (e.g., hearing loss) that can significantly affect a child's ability to acquire verbal language.

Further information on these techniques is available in many resources. Introductory special education texts include *Exceptional Children: Introduction to Special Education,* 5th ed. (Hallahan & Kauffmann, 1991); *Human Exceptionality,* 3rd ed. (Hardman, Drew, Egan, & Wolf, 1990); and *Exceptional Children and Youth* (Haring & McCormick, 1990). Comprehensive methods texts in the area of severe handicaps include *Systematic Instruction of Persons with Severe Handicaps,* 3rd ed. (Snell, 1987); *Students with Severe Disabilities: Current Perspectives and Practices* (Brimer, 1990); and *Educating Students with Severe or Profound Handicaps,* 2nd ed. (Sternberg, 1988).

FORMAL ASSESSMENT

A variety of assessment tools is available commercially to provide survey and diagnostic information on early language skills. The purpose of any oral language assessment is "to gather information for instructional planning" (McLoughlin & Lewis, 1990, p. 408). Several representative tests that can provide a description of the student's level of language functioning are discussed here. For a more extensive list of available assessment tools accompanied by brief descriptions, the reader is referred to Compton (1990), Lahey (1988), McLoughlin and Lewis (1990), and Taylor (1989).

Adaptive Behavior Scales   Most scales that measure adaptive behavior include sections on language. Various adaptive behavior scales are available. One of the most frequently used is briefly described next.

American Association on Mental Deficiency-Adaptive Behavior Scale (AAMD-ABS)   The AAMD-ABS (Nihira, Foster, Shellhaas, & Leland, 1969, 1975) has been adapted and standardized for use in public schools (Lambert & Windmiller, 1981; Lambert, Windmiller, Cole, & Figueroa, 1975; Lambert, Windmiller, Tharinger, & Cole, 1981) and contains a domain devoted to language development. This domain includes three subdomains: Expression, Comprehension, and Social Language Development (McLoughlin & Lewis, 1990; Sternberg, 1988). Items identified in this language development domain give an initial overview of a variety of language skills (e.g., preverbal expression, sentence and word usage) that can be compared to normative data for children in institutions (Nihira et al., 1975) and those in public schools (Lambert et al., 1981).

Screening Instruments   Language development information that can be compared with developmental language milestones can also be obtained from several commonly used screening instruments. A selection of screening instruments that address language and communication is reviewed next.

   Denver Developmental Screening Test-Revised (DDST)   The DDST (Frankenberg, Dodds, Fandal, Kazuk, & Cohrs, 1975) is an individually administered assessment tool for use in screening young children's social, fine motor, gross motor, and language skills. Its purpose is to detect developmental delays in children from birth to age 6 (Compton, 1990; McLoughlin & Lewis, 1990; Walker, Bonner, & Milling, 1984). The language subtest contains 20 items ranging from early receptive and expressive language skills to more advanced receptive and expressive language skills (i.e., recognizing colors to understanding analogies. The DDST can be a useful tool for obtaining a general picture of a child's level of language functioning. In fact, it is "perhaps the most widely used norm-referenced developmental screening test" (Taylor, 1989, p. 113).

   Utah Test of Language Development-3   The Utah Test of Language Development-3 (Mecham, 1989) is a compilation of 51 items tied to linguistic developmental milestones for ages 3 to 12 years. A variety of specific items is provided at each age level, including digit repetition, color naming, simple responding, and vocabulary. This test is used primarily to measure expressive and receptive language skills, thus providing an objective appraisal of language competence.

Assessment Instruments   Several assessment instruments now available reflect both survey information and specific assessment information within the area of initial language development. These assessment instruments may provide a base of limited normative data for deriving standard scores, but their primary purpose is to provide an initial guide to educational programming. Examples of language assessment instruments are described next. A list of other commercially available language assessment instruments is provided in Table 6.1, in chapter 6.

   TARC (Topeka Association for Retarded Citizens) Assessment System   The TARC (Sailor & Mix, 1975) individualized inventory was developed to provide a quick assessment or "snapshot" of observable behaviors in several areas. It serves as a beginning point for goal and objective development of persons with severe handicaps from ages 3 to 16 years. Table 5.1 illustrates the communication skills subtest along with the scoring instructions. Interpretation of results could include conversion to standard scores, general profiling, and, most important for individuals with more severe disabilities, program planning.

   Test of Language Development-2 (TOLD)   The Test of Language Development-2 (Hammill & Newcomer, 1987) measures both expressive and receptive language in children ages 4 years to 13 years of age. The TOLD-2 is an individually administered test that can be used to assess children's language difficulties without requiring reading and writing skills.

   The revised version of the TOLD is actually two tests, the Test of Language Development-Primary (TOLD-P) and the Test of Language Development-Intermediate (TOLD-I). The TOLD-P evaluates receptive and expressive semantics, receptive and ex-

Table 5.1
Communication Skills Assessment

INSTRUCTIONS: In this section items I and II are scaled items: circle the number of the <u>one</u> that best describes child's behavior. Item III is a categorical item: circle the letters of <u>all</u> that apply.

I. UNDERSTANDING SPOKEN (RECEPTIVE) SPEECH (score one)
1. Respond primarily to objects, but not to people
2. Tends to ignore people, little or no eye contact
3. Reacts more to tone of voice than to words
4. Shows a little understanding of spoken speech (e.g. follows some directions)
5. Understands some spoken words and responds
6. Understands and usually responds when talked with

II. USE OF EXPRESSIVE SPEECH (score one)
1. Makes no vocal or speech-like sounds
2. Babbles only
3. Attempts to imitate spoken sounds or words
4. Uses a few understandable words
5. Uses short sentences or phrases to express self (e.g., "I (or me) want milk," "Don't do that," etc.)
6. Can carry on an understandable conversation with an adult

III. PREACADEMIC COMMUNICATION SKILLS (score <u>all</u> that apply)
1. Obeys command "No" or "Stop that"
2. Responds to own name by eye contact
3. Says own name when asked
4. Uses some second person pronouns correctly (you, your)
5. Uses pronouns "me, mine," correctly (you, your)
6. Uses pronoun "I" correctly
7. Points to objects or people when requested
8. Names objects or people when requested
9. Imitates different sounds
10. Responds to and enjoys music
11. Usually follows simple directions
12. Points to colors when named by another
13. Names red, yellow, or blue when asked "What color is that?"
14. Names most colors when shown
15. Names some objects in pictures
16. Names many objects in pictures
17. Counts by rote correctly to 5
18. Counts by rote correctly beyond 10
19. Matches objects in picture with real objects
20. Recognizes own name in print
21. Carries a tune in singing
22. Names days of the week
23. Sings simple songs with recognizable words
24. Understands simple number concepts such as "how many?"
25. Understands these opposite comparisons: big-little, slow-fast, open-shut, hot-cold
26. Understands these relative comparisons: in-out, up-down, over-under, first-last

Source: From *The TARC Assessment System* by W. Sailor and B. J. Mix, 1975, Lawrence, KS: H & H Enterprises. Reprinted courtesy of the publisher.

pressive phonology, and receptive and expressive syntax, in children ages 4 years to 8 years 11 months. The TOLD-I evaluates only receptive and expressive syntax and receptive and expressive semantics, in children ages 8 years 6 months to 12 years 11 months.

Both of these tests provide the instructional planner specific information concerning the testee's strengths and weakness as well as any irregularities in language development at the time of testing. According to Luftig (1989), these tests are effective tools to use in "describing children's language strengths and weaknesses and indicating areas that may benefit from remediational programming" (p. 283).

Environmental Pre-Language Battery (EPB)   The Environmental Pre-Language Battery (EPB) (Horstmeier & MacDonald, 1978a), developed by MacDonald and his colleagues to evaluate linguistic and prelinguistic skills from a transactional perspective, is one of three assessment instruments included in the Environmental Language Intervention Program (ELIP). As the authors, Horstmeier and MacDonald, noted, the EPB "is a series of diagnostic tests assessing and training those prelinguistic skills assumed necessary for a child to develop spoken language" (iii). The EPB was developed as an assessment tool to use with children who have not acquired oral language. The test focuses on prelinguistic skills such as attention and object permanence, motor and verbal imitation, object identification, following directions, and production of single-word responses (Molt & Younginger, 1988). Specific ages are not stipulated for the EPB, but developmental levels clearly are related to skills ranging from about 12 to 30 months.

Environmental Language Inventory (ELI)   The ELI (MacDonald, 1978a), also included in the ELIP, is an individually administered semantic-based assessment instrument for use with children with severe language delays who are at the early stages of acquiring language. It is designed specifically to assess the child whose expressive language is limited to one- or two-word utterances and who engages in few spontaneous verbalizations. The ELI is appropriate to use with individuals ages 2 through adulthood who have disabilities (Luftig, 1989).

This assessment tool concentrates on evaluating the individual's ability to imitate speech, to converse with the examiner, and to communicate during nonstructured situations. Data are gathered on eight semantic-grammatical rules, as well as mean length of utterance and intelligibility of words and phrases (Molt & Younginger, 1988). Luftig (1989) stated that, despite problems with questionable technical adequacy, the ELI "represents virtually the only test of semantics appropriate for this population" (p. 280) (i.e., individuals with severe language delay).

INFORMAL ASSESSMENT

Informal assessment tools are most useful in the ongoing evaluation of early language skills. Their major advantages are their specificity and their relevance to instructional planning. To serve as the crux of the diagnostic activities, however, these informal tools must closely parallel the sequence of skills that compose a curriculum. Table 5.2 is an overview of initial language skills, to illustrate the components of language that must be included in any language acquisition program.

Table 5.2
Initial Language Skills

A. Attention

1. Remains seated for: 15 seconds _____
   30 seconds _____
   60 seconds _____
2. Does not engage in interfering behavior during this time frame.   _____
3. Makes eye contact: "look at me" _____
   name called _____

B. Imitation

1. Motorically imitates clapping _____
   (when told "do this") other movements
   _____
2. Orally imitates: series of vowel sounds
   _____
3. Orally imitates in response to commands:
   "Say this . . . ball (etc.)" for series of labels _____

C. Receptive Skills

1. Responds to series of verbal commands calling for gross motor movements ("stand up") _____
2. Responds to series of verbal commands calling for pointing ("point to ball")
   _____
3. Responds to series of verbal commands pointing to pictures of agents, objects and actions _____

D. Expressive Skills

1. Responds to series of questions asking "What is this?"   object _____
   action _____
2. Responds to series of questions about pictures asking "What is this?" with one word response   object _____
   action _____
3. Responds to series of questions about pictures asking "What is this?" with:
   "This is . . ."   two word phrases _____
   three word phrases _____

E. Expansions

Shows receptive comprehension and expressive usage of:

(a) prepositional forms
   in _____   to _____
   on _____   into _____
   under _____   with _____
   by _____   from _____
   for _____

(b) adjective forms
   big _____   numbers _____
   little _____   other relevant
   colors (list)   forms _____

(c) pronominal forms
   I _____   himself _____
   me _____   his _____
   my _____   she _____
   you _____   her _____
   your _____   herself _____
   he _____   they _____
   him _____   them _____
   other(s) _____ themselves _____

(d) alternative verb forms
   past tense _____   subject-verb
   future tense _____   agreement _____
   to be verbs _____   other(s) _____
   –ing verbs _____

(e) negative forms
   no _____   contractions:
   not _____   won't _____
   none _____   don't _____
                    other(s) _____

(f) interrogative forms
   who _____   reversals:
   what _____   is _____
   when _____   does _____
   where _____   will _____
   why _____   did _____
   how _____   tags _____

As indicated in the table, the sequence of events begins with initial attention and ends with advanced expressive and receptive skills. Once the child's attention is brought under stimulus control ("look at me"), instruction proceeds to the imitation of motor movements and speech. From there, various instructional steps are followed to develop functional language. Each stage has substantial variety in the programs available. Teachers who understand the sequence of language skill development can use several kinds of informal assessment tools. These include informal tests, task analysis, language probes, and the analysis of language samples.

Informal Tests   Informal tests can be defined as assessment procedures used to "sample skills and behaviors relevant to the curriculum with the use of teacher-made and criterion-referenced devices" (Evans, Evans, & Mercer, 1986). According to Gearheart and Gearheart (1990), informal tests include "systematic observation, work sample analysis, task analysis, error analysis, inventories, diagnostic teaching, checklists, interviews, questionnaires, analysis of records, and others" (p. 4). Informal assessment procedures enable teachers to construct methods to analyze a learner's performance in a selected skill area. When structured according to a standard format, the procedure involves identifying the specific skill, specifying the objective for task success, and stating directions for administration. Tables 5.3 and 5.4 illustrate two informal tests of initial language development. Both tests have been organized to elicit information about specific skills, so the results can be used to write educational programs.

Task Analysis   Task analysis can be defined as "the process of isolating, sequencing, and describing all of the essential components of a task" (Howell, Kaplan, & O'Connell, 1979, p. 81). The three phases entail identifying the terminal objective, detailing the specific task step sequence, and stating the prerequisite skill (Alberto & Sharpton, 1988). Because task analysis divides a skill into its component subskills, it can guide curriculum-building as well as assessment. Task analytic procedures are useful because they pinpoint small, precisely defined steps leading to terminal task objectives. Tables 5.5 and 5.6 outline two representative task analyses for receptive and expressive language skills, respectively. Both of these follow a format that specifies the task as a learning objective, provides a list of key prerequisite skills, and delineates major task sub-components, written in terms of the learner rather than the teacher.

In any task analysis, the number of steps identified initially is arbitrary and depends on both the teacher's methodology and the child's ability to learn (Crist, Walls, & Haught, 1984; Gold, 1980). In many cases, the task will have to be divided into additional component steps to meet the individual's instructional needs (Falvey, 1986).

Language Probes   The probe is defined by White and Haring (1980) as "a device, instrument, or period of time used by a teacher to sample a child's behavior" (p. 49). Probes are less structured than informal tests and can be easier to use. Probes generally include a sampling of words, or sounds, that elicit specific information on a receptive or expressive skill. They can be used to test skills that have been, or will be, taught (Schiefelbusch et al., 1976). Table 5.7 illustrates four simple probes for testing initial language of learners, each providing a relatively straightforward measure of the designated skill.

Table 5.3
Informal Assessment of Four-Word Phrases

Informal Assessment of Expressive Language

Specific Skills: Identifying a picture or object with a complete phrase.

Objective: When the child is presented with a picture or object and the verbal question, "What is this?" he will respond by saying, "This is a _____," correctly 90% of the time.

Test Exercise: Test exercise to be administered visually and orally. The materials will consist of 20 pictures or objects familiar to the child.

Each of the twenty pictures or objects will be presented to the child with the verbal question, "What is this?" The child is to respond verbally with the complete phrase, "This is a _____."
A practice session will be held first to make sure the child understands the directions. The child will have two tries. Only limited assistance will be given.

Pictures or Objects			Words said properly and in correct sequence			
	No Response	This	is	a	(Name of object)	Comments:
1. cup	____	____	____	____	____	_____
2. dish	____	____	____	____	____	_____
3. dog	____	____	____	____	____	_____
4. cat	____	____	____	____	____	_____
5. spoon	____	____	____	____	____	_____
6. fork	____	____	____	____	____	_____
7. coat	____	____	____	____	____	_____
8. shoe	____	____	____	____	____	_____
9. ball	____	____	____	____	____	_____
10. truck	____	____	____	____	____	_____

As with other informal tools, probes should be used to assess a child's performance on instructional exercises. To be effective, the materials used during the probe procedure should be selected from a sequence of skills relevant to the child's needs. Probes can provide a baseline level of performance before instruction, a quick evaluative measure of instructional effectiveness during the intervention, and a follow-up assessment to evaluate the extent of skill maintenance over time.

Language Samples   Probes may be the preferred way to informally assess initial language skills, but they will not be sufficient to provide an appropriate assessment of learners who have acquired some language and conversational skills and are, therefore, considered more linguistically advanced. For this purpose, an accurate analysis of strengths and weaknesses may have to rely more on discrete language samples of a child's verbal expression of language.

Table 5.4
Informal Assessment of Two-Word Constructions

Specific Skill: Receptive recognition of two-word constructions.

Objective: The student will successfully identify 80 percent of the following behaviors receptively.

Test to be administered orally.

Directions: Three pictures will be presented to the student. The student should point to the correct picture when told, "Show me . . ."

Scoring: + = correct
         − = incorrect

Behavior	Receptive Recognition	Behavior	Receptive Recognition
1. girl eat	_____	6. girl sleep	_____
2. boy sit	_____	7. girl sit	_____
3. boy eat	_____	8. dog eat	_____
4. boy run	_____	9. dog sleep	_____
5. dog run	_____	10. girl run	_____

Table 5.5
Sample Receptive Language Task Analysis

Task:

The child will be able to correctly respond to simple sentences or phrases containing agent, action, and object constructions by choosing a correct picture or object.

Prerequisites:

1. Maintain eye contact for five seconds.
2. Imitation of variety of motoric activities and vocalizations.
3. Identification of five noun and five verb labels.

Task Component Steps:

1. The child will be able to select correct food picture in response to food name.
2. The child will be able to point to body parts in response to spoken word.
3. The child will be able to select correct item of clothing in response to spoken word.
4. The child will be able to select correct picture or object in response to color word.
5. The child will be able to select correct objects in response to spoken word.
6. The child will be able to select correct action picture in response to spoken word.
7. The child will be able to select correct picture depicting noun and verb combinations in response to noun and verb combinations presented verbally.
8. The child will be able to identify three-word phrases by selecting correct picture in response to phrases presented verbally.
9. The child will be able to identify expanded phrases or sentences containing noun, verb, and adjective combinations by choosing correct picture in response to phrases or sentences presented verbally.

Table 5.6
Sample Expressive Language Task Analysis

Task:

Presented with a picture or object and the verbal question, "What is this?", the child is to respond by saying, "This is a _____ ," correctly 90 percent of the time.

Prerequisites:

1. Eye contact
2. Attending behavior (30 seconds)
3. Imitation of words
4. Identification and repertoire of nouns familiar to the child

Task Component Steps:

1. Child will imitate the last two words of the chain, "This is a _____ ," when a picture or object is presented.
2. Child will imitate the four words of the chain when a picture or object is presented.
3. Child will answer with a one-word verbal response when presented with a picture or object and the verbal question, "What is this?"
4. Child will verbally answer the last two words of the four-word chain, "This is a _____ ," when presented with a picture or object and the words "This is."
5. Child will respond with the last two words of the four-word chain, "a _____ ," when presented with a picture or object and a verbal question, "What is this?"
6. Child will answer verbally the last three words of the four-word chain when presented with a picture or an object and the word, "This . . ."
7. Child will answer with the four-word verbal response, "This is a _____ ," when presented with a picture or object and the verbal question, "What is this?"

Table 5.7
Sample Probes

1. Labeling—Select six common objects. Present each to the child three times and ask, "What is this?" Criteria: 2 of 3 for each object.
2. Imitation—Present a series of vowel sounds to child orally and use the directions, "Say _____ ." Criteria: 2 of 3 for each sound.
3. Receptive Vocabulary—Select six common objects and present each to the child three times with the directions, "Give me _____ ." Criteria: 2 of 3 for each object.
4. Two-Word Phrases—Present a series of pictures to the child and have him/her point to the correct one when given specific directions such as "Show me—boy run." Criteria: 2 of 3 for each item.

Language samples can be defined as transcriptions or recordings of conversations between children or between the child and an adult during structured or nonstructured time. These spontaneous samples of verbal language give a more representative diagnostic picture of the child's language skills. Language samples are useful for assessing advanced syntactical skills, vocabulary variety, semantic intents in communication, and use of inflections as well as other speech and gestural variations that add emphasis to communication. According to Salvia and Ysseldyke (1991), some profes-

Update

Guidelines for Interacting with Children During Assessment

Assessing communication skills of children requires a great deal of patience and time. Often, children simply do not want to communicate with other individuals, especially in situations that are not "typical" or "ordinary" situations. The results may be that the assessment is invalid, or at the very least, does not accurately reflect the true language capacity of the child. Crais and Roberts (1996) suggest several guidelines that professionals should keep in mind during language skills assessment. These include:

- Make sure that materials that are being used by the child during the evaluation are developmentally appropriate. You may want to use play and motor assessment scales in their selection.
- Make sure that you give the child time to do most of the talking. Limit your talking, especially when asking questions of the child, and encourage the child to respond.
- Be alert to any form of communication that the child may be using, including body language such as eye gaze, shrugs, or gesturing.
- Use parallel play and animated play with the child and objects or toys to encourage any form of communication.
- Encourage the child to use language by placing objects that he or she may want slightly out of his or her reach or hidden from his view.
- Allow the child to choose activities and objects to interact with at the beginning of any assessment session.
- Use a parent or other child in the beginning to help the child get used to your presence. You may even need to stay out of the immediate area during the initial observations of the child.
- Begin all activities with those requiring nonverbal interactions, slowing moving toward activities that require more verbal interactions.
- Do not ask questions that are obvious to the child that you know the answer to; ask only questions that you really want answered.
- Keep the child focused on topics that are interesting and motivating to the child.
- Always show your respect and concern for the child through your actions and interactions; don't act as if you don't care about the child or interactions with him or her.

Source: Adapted from E. R. Crais and J. E. Roberts (1996). Assessing communication skills. In M. McLean, D. B. Bailey, & M. Wolery (Eds.). *Assessing infants and preschoolers with special needs.* Englewood Cliffs, NJ: Merrill.

sionals believe that this spontaneous assessment of language is the *only* way to provide a valid measure of a child's language skills.

SOCIAL ASSESSMENT

Although focusing on an individual's ability with language is obviously important, teachers also can profit from understanding the social variables that affect the student. Assessment of the child's use of language and his or her individual social behaviors will help clarify the effects of these variant social patterns on the development of language, as well as provide a means for evaluating the quality and format of these interactions (Lombardino, 1979; Peterson & Sherrod, 1979). McLean and Snyder-McLean (1978) pointed to three social aspects of importance to the teacher: (a) the child's general level of socialization, (b) the preverbal communicative behaviors the child emits, and (c) specific interactive behaviors the child is able to use.

General level of socialization refers to the child's relationships with his or her primary caregivers and involves an understanding of the significant attachments the child has formed. This information reveals whether the individual is isolated from or involved with his or her environment. *Preverbal communicative behaviors* should be evaluated to determine whether the child is attempting to communicate his or her interests and desires to others through sounds, gestures, or other means (Hoffnung, 1989). *Specific interactive behaviors* are the child's specific actions that lead to social interaction within his or her immediate environment. Specific interactive behaviors should be considered in conjunction with the patterns of interactions of individuals who relate to the child.

To provide a basis for evaluating language in its social context, the teacher can use MacDonald's (1978b) Oliver (parent-assisted communication inventory), the third assessment tool developed for use in the ELIP. Parents complete this assessment inventory by organizing information on the social variables related to prelanguage and language skills the child is emitting in the home environment. Two important sections included in this instrument are: (a) analysis of the ways a child communicates, and (b) summary of the parents' recall of the child's specific prelinguistic and linguistic behavior. This inventory also is used as the basis for determining the base level on which to begin assessment when using the EPB or the ELI (both described in a previous section).

COGNITIVE ASSESSMENT

Because of the potential importance of cognitive factors in determining readiness for language acquisition, evaluation in the area of cognition should be an integral part of any assessment. This is particularly true for individuals who are still in the early stages of developing language.

An example of a developmental checklist that teachers can use is Uzgiris and Hunt's (1975) *Assessment in Infancy: Ordinal Scales of Psychological Development*. Probably the most extensively conceived and researched assessment scales, they are based on Piagetian theory. Their purpose is to measure cognitive and perceptual development in children birth to age 2. The scales are based on the assumption that this cognitive and perceptual development can be analyzed according to a consistent, ordered sequence (Gorrell, 1985). These six scales measure the level of the child's development in the areas of (a) visual pursuit and the permanence of objects; (b) means for obtaining desired environmental events; (c) vocal and gestural imitation; (d) operational causality; (e) construction of object relations in space; and (f) schemes for relating to objects.

The manual accompanying the scales discusses their construction, administration, and interpretation, and provides support for the rationale for assessing cognitive variables as a prerequisite to instruction. Although the Uzgiris and Hunt scales were developed for use with young children, Taylor (1989) noted that the scales have been used with older individuals who have severe handicaps. To make the scale more usable for individuals with severe handicaps, Dunst (1980) developed a manual incorporating additional items.

Instructors have a twofold goal in the areas of cognitive and linguistic assessment. In addition to evaluating a child's skills and relating them to linguistic potentials, the teacher must establish beginning points for teaching cognitive, social, and language skills.

PROGRAMMING

Systematic arrangement of the instructional environment is critical to teaching children, especially those who have severe disabilities. Therefore, educators must be knowledgeable about the assessment tools and programs available. Proficiency in using these specific tools and techniques, appropriate to the development of an effective learning situation for children with delays in language development, is essential.

Instructional programming and selection of methodology should incorporate a variety of means of manipulating the natural environment to assist the child in acquiring language. Several methodological approaches critically important to those who teach students with severe delays in language development are highlighted next.

INSTRUCTIONAL ANTECEDENTS

A key instructional goal is to bring the child's behavior and skills under *stimulus control*, also known as *instructional control*. Specifically, the child must learn to discriminate between instructional cues or stimuli so he or she can perform the appropriate actions when confronted with a specific situation. For example, the student must learn to distinguish between a picture of a dog and one of a cat, and then must apply the correct verbal label when he or she sees the picture or hears the direction, "Point to the. . . ."

Prompts   Prompts are an effective way to "prime responses" —to simplify the task so the child makes the correct response (discriminates between stimuli) (Cooper, Heron, & Heward, 1987). The two major types of prompts are known as response prompts and stimulus, or antecedent, prompts.

Update

IFSP Meetings

In addition to the development of IEPs for students of school age, IDEA also requires that Individual Family Service Plans be developed for all preschool children. The IFSP concept was introduced within Public Law 99-457. This legislation focuses services for individuals with disabilities on the entire family, and not just on the child. Given the fact that individuals with more severe disabilities need to be served during the preschool years, the development of IFSPs is an important consideration. The IFSP must contain:

- A statement of the child's present functioning level in key areas (i.e., physical development, cognitive development, language and speech, psychosocial development, self-help skills).
- A statement of the family's strengths and needs.
- Specific outcomes and goals for the family and for the child.
- Means to evaluate goals and outcomes.
- Services required to facilitate goal achievement.
- Identification of the family's case manager to ensure effective programs.

Source: Crais, E. R. and Roberts, J. E. (1996). Assessing communication skills. In M. McLean, D. B. Bailey, & M. Wolery (Eds.). *Assessing infants and preschoolers with special needs.* Englewood Cliffs, NJ: Merrill/Prentice-Hall.

Response Prompts The teacher uses a specific behavior to assist the child in making the correct response to the request or stimulus (Alberto & Sharpton, 1988). The four types of response prompts are: imitative (or models), verbal, gestural, and physical.

1. *Imitative prompts*, or *modeling*, provide the child with a demonstration of the correct behavior to follow. For example, the instructor may say, "Touch your knee," and then perform the action himself or herself. This visual model simplifies the learner's task and helps to prevent errors.

2. *Verbal prompts* are useful when the teacher wishes to highlight the stimuli presented to the child without using physical guidance (Snell, 1987). These prompts make the appropriate response more apparent and thus tend to minimize error. An example of a verbal prompt is the use of voice inflection to help a student select the correct response (e.g., "Is this the *ball*?").

Another form of verbal prompting is the teacher's use of simple, explicit directions. The frequent and consistent pairing of words with objects and events is a good initial strategy. If a child has a restricted vocabulary, it may have to be expanded before communication can be established in less structured settings (Greer, Anderson, & Davis, 1976). As reinforcement for developing language, varied, novel, and interesting objects or activities (e.g., toys, colorful items) or food can be helpful. In any case, the learner's attention should be drawn to the task through verbal means and then reinforced whatever assistance is necessary for success.

Teachers often face what Skinner (1968) termed "the problem of the first instance" (p. 206), the question of what to do when the student does not perform any identifiable behavior. As Snyder, Lovitt, and Smith (1975) noted: "In order for a response to be reinforced, it must first exist in the student's repertoire" (p. 13). Teachers may have to use another type of prompt to generate initial responses. The most common forms of response prompts are gestural prompts or physical prompts.

3. *Gestural prompts* are those in which the teacher uses hand and body movements to direct the child's response, to achieve learning without errors. Examples of gestural prompts are pointing, waving, and nodding.

4. *Physical prompts* require the teacher to assist the child by providing either full or partial manual guidance to successfully complete the activity. Physical prompts can be used to assist in receptive motor activities such as hand-raising or jumping or to elicit a verbal response by helping a child form his or her lips to make a specific speech sound.

Stimulus or Antecedent Prompts   These "alterations of, or additions to, the instructional material focus students' attention on the natural cue(s) for making correct responses" (Alberto & Sharpton, 1988, p. 192). A cue is any procedure used to highlight the correct response within an array of options so that error-free learning can occur. Snell (1987) identified three types of cues: movement, position, and redundancy.

When using a *movement cue*, the teacher taps or touches the correct object while providing a verbal direction to the child. This type of cue is useful when developing a child's receptive language vocabulary. *Position cues* are less directive than movement cues. The teacher places the object to be identified closer to the child than any of the other items in the array so the correct response is more apparent. *Redundancy cues* require a higher level of discrimination by the child. Differences in physical aspects of the object (e.g., size, shape, color) are used to highlight the correct response to the teacher's verbal direction or question.

Guiding Principles Two principles should guide the use of prompts. First, the prompt selected should be the least intrusive—just strong enough to initiate the response. Some researchers believe that providing a prompt of greater strength can create dependence in the learner (Alberto & Sharpton, 1988).

Second, the use of prompts should be considered a temporary measure, only to provide success at the beginning of the learning process. Prompts should be faded as soon as the child learns to respond appropriately. If the teacher continues to use prompts when they are no longer needed, the child may become dependent on the prompt and less likely to react spontaneously and independently. With verbal cues, fading can be accomplished by reducing inflections and volume; with gestural and physical prompts, reduction can occur by lessening the amount of movement or manual guidance; and with nonverbal cues, reduction of the amount of difference between the objects will fade the prompt.

CONTINGENCY MANAGEMENT

Appropriate consequences made contingent on specific behaviors can influence the rate of responding as well as success or failure on the specified task. Successful training frequently depends on the selection and use of effective reinforcement strategies. With individuals who have severe disabilities, the teacher should be aware that unusual reinforcers may be needed and that specific reinforcers may over time lose their reinforcing power; i.e., satiation may occur (Carrier, 1979).

Positive reinforcement is the mainstay of contingency management. Specific reinforcers should be selected from a reinforcer hierarchy determined for each learner (Zigler & deLabry, 1962). Positive reinforcers can be classified into five categories (Kaplan, 1991):

1. *Primary reinforcers*, such as food or drink.
2. *Tangible reinforcers*, such as toys or prizes.
3. *Social reinforcers*, such as smiles and attention.
4. *Activity reinforcers*, such as reading or playing games.
5. *Token reinforcers*, such as points or chips, which can be exchanged for other types of reinforcers.

In a review of research on initial language training, Snyder et al. (1975) noted that tangible rewards have been used extensively and that the advantages of praise and other intangible reinforcers often have been overlooked. Token systems also have been identified as effective in the development of language in some training situations (Stremel & Waryas, 1974). The type of reinforcement that will be the most effective hinges on the student's preferences. The student should be evaluated to determine this. The use of reinforcer preference is especially important when spontaneous verbalizations are the goal. Research has indicated that reinforcers the individual selects elicit spontaneous verbalizations sooner than when others have chosen the reinforcer (Dyer, 1989).

When a child does not spontaneously verbalize on a consistent basis or no verbalizations are identifiable, positive reinforcement can be accompanied by shaping. *Shaping* is a procedure that successively molds the desired behavior through use of specified criteria and reinforcement contingent on eliciting behaviors approximating the desired outcome. Shaping is considered one of the most practical ways to teach new behaviors (Heron, 1987), as well as one of the most efficient methods to gradually develop verbal speech from random vocalizations.

INSTRUCTIONAL SEQUENCES

The preceding discussions presented a series of instructional and reinforcement procedures in isolation, but teachers must combine these elements into effective instructional sequences. Although many language acquisition programs provide detailed guidance for implementation, the program selected will have to be modified to provide for the individual needs of each child.

Table 5.8 provides a model for the development of initial language training sequences. After assessment tools have guided the selection of an appropriate skill to be learned, the teacher can choose alternative ways to teach the identified skill. Teachers can create precise and effective methods by stating the target behavior in observable and measurable terms, in identifying varied antecedent events, and in selecting appropriate reinforcement contingencies. The examples in Table 5.8 represent a variety of specific skills included in the initial language acquisition process.

CAPITALIZING ON THE NATURAL ENVIRONMENT

Although operant techniques are valuable in initial language training, they should be supplemented with approaches that capitalize on the role of the natural environment in language acquisition. This use of the natural environment is known as *milieu language training*. Snell (1987) defined milieu language training as:

> . . . procedures that are brief and positive in nature, carried out in the natural environment as opportunities for teaching functional communication naturally occur, and occasioned by child interest in the topic to which training will relate. (p. 250)

Because children who are language-delayed may have a problem gathering information about their surroundings, the identification and training of strategies that can assist the children in their natural environments is of great importance (Snyder & McLean, 1977). An orientation to the individual's environment can facilitate the teaching of a natural language with multiple communicative uses rather than a routinized and possibly artificial, restrictive language (Paul-Brown, 1979). Also, by encouraging attachment of language to activities the child initiates, the teacher or parent can take advantage of the child's motivation and attention (Seitz & Marcus, 1976).

According to Paul-Brown (1979), responding to the potentials for language development within the natural environment requires a teacher to be attentive to the individual child and his or her communication behaviors rather than "following programs . . . too rigidly, at the expense of creative and natural interactions . . ." (p. 3). Eyde and Altman (1979) acknowledged this in stating, "What is surprising is that so few programs have truly emphasized the essentially social nature of language transactions" (p.

Table 5.8
Sample Instructional Sequences

Language Training: Instructional Sequences

Description of Skill	Sample Target with Criteria	Task Stimuli: Direction & Materials	Possible Prompts	Consequence Appropriate Behavior/ Inappropriate Behavior
Eye Contact	Learner will look at teacher for 5 seconds on command—4 out of 5 times	"Look at me" Toys interesting objects, food	Physical prompts, food held near eye	Praise, hug, food Ignore, prompt correct response, time out
Motoric imitation	Learner will model teacher's specific motor activity 4 out of 5 times	"Do this" Single materials, such as bells, toys, etc.	Physical prompts, exaggerated non-verbal cue	Smile, praise, repeat behavior Select different motoric act, time out, prompt
Expression: Labeling Objects	Give 5 common objects, learner will give correct labels for each 90 percent of time	"What is this?" Familiar object from child's environment, such as ball, doll, etc.	Imitative prompt, verbal cue	Praise, imitation of response, pat Imitative prompt, ignore echolalic response, bring time out for inattention
Reception: Two-word phrases	Given 3 pictures, learner will correctly identify the one designated by a 2-word phrase with 90 percent accuracy	"Point to . . ."—Series of single pictures depicting environmental events such as sweep floor, girl run, man eat, etc.	Physical prompt, verbal cue, non-verbal aid via positioning of correct picture	Smile and praise, repeat of directions Prompt response, simplify task, remove materials, and withhold contact for inattention

131). It might be added that rigid language programs also risk removing the natural flow from the development of the individual child's language.

An orientation to the natural use of language carries with it a much more flexible approach to instruction. The instructor's role shifts from direct teaching to designing the environment in such a way that the child is "forced" to use language in order to participate in various activities. This may involve an "upping of the social ante" (Mac-Donald, 1979) as the teacher steps into the child's activities and then gradually modifies the activities to facilitate achievement of specific linguistic goals. The fundamental nature of instruction of this type evokes what Hunt (1973) referred to in the following quotation as the "problem of the match."

> The nature of the problem is based on the idea that adaptive growth takes place only, or at least chiefly, in situations that contain for any given infant or child information and models just discrepant enough from those already stored and mastered to produce interest or challenge and call for adaptive modifications in the structure of the intellectual coping, in his beliefs about the world, and in the motor patterns that are not beyond his adaptive capacity at the time. (p. 124)

In a similar vein, Kamii (1973, p. 203) stated that "the task of the teacher is to figure out what the learner knows and how he reasons in order to ask the right question at the right time so that the learner can build his own knowledge." Consistent with developmental linguistic guidelines, then, language instruction should constantly move the child slightly ahead of his or her current level of linguistic functioning.

In practice, a variety of specific techniques might be used to tie language instruction more closely to the natural environment. Snell (1987) reviewed four milieu teaching procedures known as the *child-directed model*, the *mand-model*, the *time-delay model*, and *incidental teaching procedures*. Paul-Brown (1979) clearly described ways to achieve the goal of developing language in the natural environment. First, teachers should attempt to interpret a child's utterances and, on the basis of this judgment provide an appropriate response. For example, if the child said "baw," these responses might include: a repetition of the sound or word assumed to be uttered ("ball"); a syntactic expansion ("catch the ball"); or a semantic extension ("yes, the boys are throwing the ball"). The primary goal of this interaction would likely be semantic rather than phonological in nature.

A second technique would be to supplement or replace direct instruction (e.g., "What is this? Cookie") at a given time during the day, with attention to specific words and phrases used throughout the day. According to Paul-Brown (1979):

> The teacher could, for example, point out some children playing outside, and say, "Look. The children are playing. What are they playing with?" If the child does not respond, the teacher might comment, "They're playing with a ball."

A third technique would be to stimulate true conversation whenever possible during instructional sessions. Some techniques encourage rapid shifting from one focus to another. Label training does this by asking questions about diverse objects (e.g., "What is this? Ball. What is this? Dog"). The merits of adhering to related topics should be considered. Teachers may find it advantageous to pursue a new word and concept with a child by presenting it in various phrases ("open the door; shut the door") and having the child act out the procedures (actually opening and shutting a variety of doors, in this example).

GENERALIZATION

Despite a teacher's preference for one methodology or another, the only true test of instructional effectiveness is the generalization of a skill. Often, language instruction procedures have been less than successful because the person's newly developed language skills are not used "spontaneously in the natural environment" (Kaczmarek, 1990, p. 160). Because generalization does not occur automatically, instructional procedures must be chosen and implemented to encourage its development. For discussion purposes, the generic term *generalization* can be broken down into three related parts: stimulus generalization, response generalization, and generalization over time (Lovaas, Schreibman, & Koegel, 1974).

Stimulus or *situation generalization* is the ability to transfer an acquired skill to another setting, to another trainer, or to another form of instruction. This is particularly important in light of recent educational trends spotlighting the need to generalize from school to home, from teacher to direct-care staff in a residential facility, or from residential facility to community for an individual who has been or will be deinstitutionalized.

Response generalization is the transfer of learned skills to related linguistic units and structures. With this type of generalization, the learner spontaneously develops competence in language forms and vocabulary beyond those specifically taught. Response generalization is essential because teaching all of the infinite number of language constructions used in spontaneous conversations is impossible. The use of organizational matrices can provide a starting point for an analysis of the method by which to transfer a specific skill. Using the example of Figure 5.1, several different verbal labels are presented to the child, who is assessed on his or her ability to generate a series of two-word constructions.

Generalization over time, or *response maintenance,* refers to the ability to perform the task again successfully at a given point in time after instruction. Successful generalization indicates that retention and use of language skills previously learned occur and continue to occur.

Skills learned during early language development can be maintained only when teachers, aides, or parents continue to conduct periodic follow-ups. The active involvement of parents is critical to generalization. Salisbury, Walmbold, and Walter (1978) offered five reasons why parents should participate in nonoral language programs, although these reasons are equally valid for any language training program:

1. If the system is functional, the child will be able to use it in all environments and with all people with whom she has contact;

	boy	girl	man	woman	dog
runs					
eats					
sweeps					
jumps					
walks					
throws					
rides					
drinks					
cries					

Figure 5.1
Matrix for Two-Word Constructions

2. Signs used at school are quickly extinguished in the home environment if not re-inforced;
3. Handicapped children generally require a large number of trials to learn new skills and this cannot take place at school alone;
4. Parents have a right to set the program goals for their children; and
5. Parents will more rapidly carry out programs at home if they are convinced that the program is necessary. (p. 395)

Kauffman and Snell (1977, pp. 215–216) found that the following techniques may help students learn to generalize: (a) the gradual fading of reinforcement contingencies; (b) a gradual increase in the reinforcement schedule; (c) a shift from artificial reinforcers (e.g., edibles) to natural reinforcers (e.g., praise); (d) an increase in the use of a variety of trainers and training settings; and (e) an increased emphasis on self-control and self-regulation. Each of these techniques is a critical component of operant technology and affects the maintenance of language skills.

For rather obvious reasons, the concerns over generalization of language skills have generated attention and discussion. Using operant techniques to improve the transfer of skills represents a dramatic leap forward; however, successes in this area should not suggest complacency. DeVilliers and deVilliers (1978) provided a particularly apt statement summarizing the methodological aspects of this section:

> Simply training a given language skill in a variety of situations may not help the transfer of that skill to a natural setting if arbitrary rewards continue to be used. Even if there are linguistic forms that the disordered child can only learn in a strict training procedure with powerful primary rewards, he must still learn what that language is good for when the artificial rewards are no longer provided. In short, to be successful in establishing truly functional speech in the retarded or autistic child, any language training program must at some point create a context in which the child has something to say, in which communicative effectiveness can serve as the reward, and it must make provision for transfer of the acquired language skills to the child's environment. (p. 271)

INSTRUCTIONAL APPROACHES AND PROGRAMS

Even though research and programming in language acquisition are of fairly recent vintage, the phenomenal interest in this area has resulted in a variety of instructional approaches and programs. Of course, no individual program provides the definitive approach to initial language training for individuals with delays in language development. Current and future research within the area will continue to call into question the assumptions, models and procedures upon which these instructional systems are based. Though a number of these programs are discussed in the following pages, this discussion is not intended to be all-inclusive. The programs discussed here simply represent a few of the many approaches available to practitioners. Selected examples of other commercially available language development programs are listed in Table 6.2 in chapter 6.

LANGUAGE ACQUISITION PROGRAM (LAP)

Even though Kent's (1974) Language Acquisition Program (LAP) was designed for 5- to 20-year old nonverbal residents of institutions with severe retardation, it subsequently has been used with a broader population. The LAP is a highly structured, sequential approach based on behavioral principles. It includes continuous assessment and evaluation, flexibility to allow for modifications in accordance with the individual needs of any individual child, and immediate and consistent positive reinforcement using verbal praise and food rewards.

The program curriculum is divided into three major sections (Preverbal, Verbal-Receptive, and Verbal-Expressive). Content ranges from initial attending skills to advanced receptive and expressive training. The emphasis on attention reflects Kent's beliefs that "nothing is more important to learning than good attending behavior" (p. 17). Therefore, the initial sections focus on procedures that teach sitting-still behavior and eye contact, as well as motor imitation and structured play. The curriculum also contains behavior reversal procedures geared to eliminate echolalia, self-stimulation, and other interfering behaviors. Following these prelinguistic concerns, verbal receptive and expressive phases alternate throughout the program.

The *verbal receptive* sections are divided into the basic initial receptive phase, the development of a limited receptive vocabulary, and the receptive expansion phases. The expansion phase has instructions for teaching initial and more complex commands, an expanded noun and verb vocabulary, verb-noun-adverb commands, negation, colors, numbers one through five, and the use of various concepts. The *verbal expressive* section covers vocal imitation; the basic expression of labels such as body parts, objects, and parts of a room; and expressive expansion including responses to questions, two-word phrases, naming nouns from pictures (instead of objects), colors, and numbers.

The LAP provides precise instructions to help teachers assess, teach, and evaluate their students. Detailed data sheets serve as models for the notation and measurement of specific behaviors. The LAP's specific and clear guidance is especially valuable for teachers who have a limited background in linguistics. For those with a more extensive background in language, the commitment to instructional flexibility within the program permits alternative procedures.

INTERVENTION STRATEGY PROGRAM

The Intervention Strategy Program developed by William and Diane Bricker (1974) has been reported and amplified in numerous publications over the past two decades (W. Bricker, 1972; Bricker & Bricker, 1970; D. Bricker & Denison, 1978; D. Bricker, Ruder, & Vincent, 1976). The scope of the program is extremely broad and uses "an integrated training paradigm" (Sternberg & Adams, 1982). According to Sternberg and Adams (1982), the Bricker and Bricker program is based on a language training lattice—a programming decision-making tree. As a result of its gradual and continuous evolution, the program's components are not as specifically delineated as those in the LAP but are basically an outline or instructional paradigm on how to accomplish language training with individuals who have severe disabilities. Nevertheless, this program (or more aptly, programs) provides a sound basis for developing appropriate intervention strategies.

   According to D. Bricker et al. (1976), the development of the agent-action-object (e.g., boy eats cookie) semantic and structural relations of normal language acquisition is the focal point of this program. The first phase teaches the functional classification of objects, the comprehension of object labels, and the production of three-word utterances. The three basic components of the initial phase are verbal imitation, comprehension, and production. Figure 5.2 illustrates the interrelationship of these three components in the first phase. The second phase requires the student to perform operations on the initial learned utterances. Comprehension and production of modifiers, phrases and sentences, pronouns, interrogatives, negation, and auxiliary verbs are covered in this phase.

   This project (Bricker, Ruder, & Vincent, 1976) has been a true effort to combine major behavioral, developmental, cognitive, and transactional processes into a language training program. The emphasis placed on generalization of the learned language skills reflects their concern that:

> Mere knowledge of the form and function of certain linguistic structures is not sufficient. A child may go through an entire language intervention program and not become an effective communicator. Only when the child utilizes his language tools in an appropriate and effective manner can the language intervention process be said to be complete. (p. 340)

PROGRAM FOR THE ACQUISITION OF LANGUAGE WITH THE SEVERELY IMPAIRED (PALS)

The Program for the Acquisition of Language with the Severely Impaired (PALS) was developed to assist teachers, through the use of behavioral techniques, in developing functional communication skills in their students. The program contains assessment tools, training strategies and specific activities targeting both presymbolic and sym-

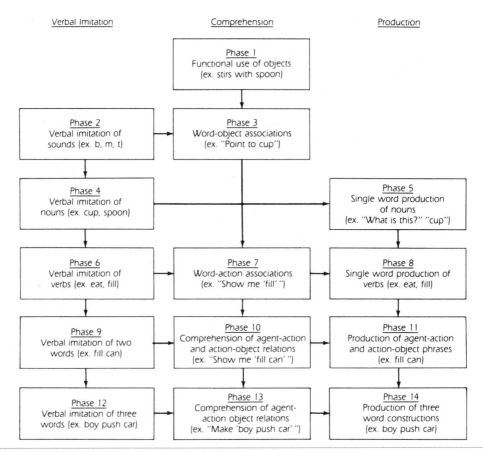

Source: From "An Intervention Strategy for Language Deficient Children" by D. Bricker, K. Ruder, and L. Vincent in *Teaching Special Children* (p. 311), edited by N. Haring and R. Schiefelbusch, 1976, New York: McGraw-Hill. Reprinted by permission of McGraw-Hill.

Figure 5.2
Language Program: Part I

bolic language skills (Owens, 1982). The program provides a three-step assessment of the individual's communication within his or her environmental context, specific communication behaviors critical to development of spontaneous language, and the prerequisites for development of language. Task analyses, stimulation methods and incidental teaching strategies are offered to assist the teacher in strengthening the child's previous language skills, in stabilizing the child's present level of language skills, and in assisting in future language development leading to effective communication.

FUNCTIONAL SPEECH AND LANGUAGE TRAINING PROGRAM

The Functional Speech and Language Training Program developed by Guess, Sailor, and Baer (1974, 1976, 1977, 1978) is a behavioral approach to language development based on the fundamentals of remedial logic. The program emerged after many years of research and field-testing with individuals who have severe disabilities. It is based upon the performance of these individuals, rather than on normal development, for the outline of the training sequence.

The program's specific goal is to develop oral speech in the individual and, therefore, has a prerequisite of verbal imitation ability for entrance into the program. The actual teaching content includes six basic language instructional areas (Sternberg & Adams, 1982): (a) persons and things; (b) actions with persons and things; (c) possession; (d) color; (e) size; and (f) relation and location. The program consists of 60 training steps within five dimensions (reference, control, self-extended control, integration, and reception), representing the major instructional objectives of the program (Guess et al., 1977, p. 365). For each of the 60 steps, a goal, sample items, procedures, instructions, and scoring sheets are provided along with summary sheets and a special section on generalization.

The Guess et al. program is geared to observable variables rather than cognitive factors. From an interactional perspective the program might be considered self-limiting, because it focuses on specific behaviors instead of how language is used interactionally within the environment (McLean & Snyder-McLean, 1978). Nevertheless, the authors do offer substantial evidence of their success with the program (Warren & Rogers-Warren, 1985), as well as continual revision based on use.

READY-SET-GO: TALK TO ME

Ready-Set-Go: Talk To Me is the instructional component of the Environmental Language Intervention Program (Horstmeier & MacDonald, 1978b). Ready-Set-Go was designed as a true transactional approach to language training. Its purposes are to integrate the individual's language into his or her total environment, and it stresses prelanguage and early language skills. Parents and teachers can use this language program to incorporate a child's life experiences into the language teaching situation.

Components are outlined in its accompanying program manual. The manual contains general hints on talking to children, a screening test, and descriptions of instructional phases including preliminary skills, functional play, motor and sound imitation, receptive skills related to actions and objects, following directions, and beginning social conversation. Suggestions within each section give teachers additional flexibility in lesson development. Individual prescriptive training lessons, actually linguistic interactions, help parents or teachers present stimuli, assist with responses, and provide reinforcement to establish prelanguage skills and to initiate oral communication.

Ready-Set-Go is a significant attempt to blend cognitive, semantic, and social concerns into a language training program. It is appropriate for young children who are developmentally delayed, who are living at home, and who have been identified as capable of progress when given appropriate linguistic stimulation. Any application to older persons who are nonverbal, or to individuals in residential settings, would be experimental because the program was not intended for this use.

THE TEACHING RESEARCH INITIAL EXPRESSIVE LANGUAGE PROGRAM (TRIELP)

The Teaching Research Initial Expressive Language Program (Fredricks, McDonnell, & Grove, 1978; McDonnell, Fredricks, & Grove, 1975) was developed for classroom use with individuals who have moderate or severe mental retardation. It has eight phases ranging from establishment of eye contact and word training through imitation. These phases are clearly explained in the teacher's manual, which also includes a placement test, behavioral objectives for each phase, data sheets, and instructional cue cards. The precise nature of instructional materials precludes the need for specialized teacher training.

The program's authors attribute its methodological background to techniques utilized in the DISTAR program. As such, it has a decided behavioral orientation, including an emphasis on the role of systematic procedures for skills progression, reinforcement, and daily formative evaluation. The program was field-tested in 50 classrooms over a 5-year period, so both longitudinal and comparative data are available, and show the program's effectiveness. The TRIELP has merit as a guide to behavioral curricular building in a preschool or primary classroom for children with moderate and severe disabilities.

PROGRAM SELECTION

Obviously, no one program or methodology is suitable for teaching language to all children with severe deficits in language. Instead, the choice of a program will be affected by the number of children to be taught, the instructional time available, the expertise of the teaching staff, and the availability of assistance and support. In addition, the varied needs of learners may best be met by group versus individual instruction, by a behavioral versus a developmental approach, by direct instruction versus instruction integrated into other activities, or by gradations among any of these options. As teachers become familiar with the many alternatives available, they will be better able to design individual prescriptive programs in their classroom for the children with severe delays in verbal language.

SUMMARY

For some individuals with severe disabilities, oral language abilities are not acquired spontaneously. For those individuals, and for others who experience significant delays in language development, intensive training in verbal and/or nonverbal communication is needed.

Language training programs have traditionally been allied with the various conceptual models of language acquisition. Behavioral, psycholinguistic, cognitive-semantic, and socio-linguistic (pragmatic) models have all given rise to implications for language instruction.

A variety of assessment tools are available for use with individuals with minimal verbal skills. Formal tools typically help establish a developmental age and may provide general information about language functioning. Other informal assessment measures including the use of task analysis, probes, language samples, and social and cognitive assessment, however, are necessary to develop a comprehensive picture of instructional needs.

Teachers can select from a range of instructional programs designed to teach verbal communication. While some approaches emphasize behavioral training and may focus on the arrangement of instructional antecedents and consequences, others focus on capitalizing on communicative aspects of the child's natural environment. A key concern is certainly the need for generalization. A number of commercially available programs can also be used to develop an intervention plan.

Obviously, there is no one program or methodology suitable for teaching language to all children with severe disabilities. Instead, the choice of a program will be affected by the number of children to be taught, the instructional time available, the expertise of the teaching staff, and the availability of assistance and support. In addition, the varied needs of learners may best be met by group versus individual instruction, by a behavioral versus a developmental approach, by direct instruction versus instruction integrated into other activities, or by gradations among any of these options. As teachers become familiar with the many alternatives available, they will be better able to design individual prescriptive programs.

REFERENCES

Alberto, P., Garrett, E., Briggs, T., & Umberger, F. (1983). Selection and initiation of a nonverbal communication program for severely handicapped students. *Focus on Exceptional Children, 15*(7), 1–15.

Alberto, P., & Sharpton, W. (1988). Components of instructional technology. In L. Sternberg, *Educating students with severe or profound handicaps* (2nd ed.). Rockville, MD: Aspen.

Bloom, L. (1970). *Language development: Form and function of emerging grammars.* Cambridge: MIT Press.

Bricker, D., & Carlson, L. (1981). Issues in early language intervention. In R. Schiefelbusch, & D. Bricker (Eds.), *Early language: Acquisition and intervention.* Baltimore: University Park Press.

Bricker, D., & Denison, L. (1978). Training prerequisites to verbal behavior. In M. Snell (Ed.), *Systematic instruction of the severely and profoundly handicapped.* Columbus, OH: Charles E. Merrill Publishing.

Bricker, D., Ruder, K., & Vincent, L. (1976). An intervention strategy for language deficient children. In N. Haring & R. Schiefelbusch (Eds.), *Teaching special children.* New York: McGraw-Hill.

Bricker, W. (1972). A systematic approach to language training. In R. Schiefelbusch (Ed.), *Language of the mentally retarded.* Baltimore: University Park Press.

Bricker, W., & Bricker, D. (1970). A program of language training for the severely language handicapped child. *Exceptional Children, 37,* 101–111.

Bricker, W., & Bricker, D. (1974). An early language training strategy. In R. Schiefelbusch & L. Lloyd (Eds.), *Language perspectives: Acquisition, retardation, and intervention.* Baltimore: University Park Press.

Brimer, R. (1990). *Students with severe disabilities: Current perspectives and practices.* Mountain View, CA: Mayfield Publishing.

Bruner, J. (1975). From communication to language: A psychological perspective. *Cognition, 3,* 225–287.

Bullis, M., Rowland, C., Schweigert, P., & Stremel-Campbell, K. (1986). *Communication skills center for young children with deaf-blindness.* Monmouth, OR: Teaching Research Publications.

Burton, T., & Hirshoren, A., (1979). Some further thoughts and clarification on the education of severely and profoundly retarded children, *Exceptional Children, 45*, 618–625.

Carrier, J. (1979). Perspectives on non-speech symbol systems. In R. Schiefelbusch & H. Hollis (Eds.), *Language intervention from ape to child.* Baltimore: University Park Press.

Carrow-Woolfolk, E. (1988). *Theory, assessment and intervention in language disorders: An integrative approach.* Philadelphia: Grune & Stratton.

Chomsky, N. (1957). *Syntactic structures.* The Hague, Netherlands: Mouton.

Chomsky, N. (1968). *Language and mind.* New York: Harcourt, Brace and World.

Compton, C. (1990). *A guide to 85 tests for special education.* Belmont, CA: Fearon Education.

Cooper, J., Heron, T., & Heward, W. (1987). *Applied behavior analysis.* Columbus, OH: Charles E. Merrill Publishing.

Crais, E. R. and Roberts, J. E. (1996). Assessing communication skills. In M. McLean, D. B. Bailey, & M. Wolery (Eds.). *Assessing infants and preschoolers with special needs.* Englewood Cliffs, NJ: Merrill.

Crist, K., Walls, R., & Haught, P. (1984). Degrees of specificity in task analysis. *American Journal of Mental Deficiency, 89*, 67–74.

deVilliers, J., & deVilliers, P. (1978). *Language acquisition.* Cambridge, MA: Harvard University Press.

Dunst, C. (1980). *A clinical and educational manual for use with the Uzgiris-Hunt scales of infant psychological development.* Baltimore: University Park Press.

Dyer, K. (1989). The effects of preference on spontaneous verbal requests in individuals with autism. *The Journal of the Association for Persons With Severe Handicaps, 14*(3), 184–189.

Evans, S., Evans, W., & Mercer, C. (1986). *Assessment for instruction.* Boston: Allyn & Bacon.

Eyde, D., & Altman, R. (1979). Classroom techniques: Communication training in the classroom: A joining of theory. *Education and Training of the Mentally Retarded, 14*, 131–136.

Falvey, M. (1986). *Community-based curriculum.* Baltimore: Paul H. Brookes.

Fillmore, C. (1968). The case for case. In E. Bach & R. Harmas (Eds.), *Universals in linguistic theory.* New York: Holt, Rinehart & Winston.

Frankenberg, W., Dodds, J., Fandal, A., Kazuk, E., & Cohrs, M. (1975). *Denver development screening test.* Denver: Ladoca Publishing Foundation.

Fredricks, H., McDonnell, J., & Grove, D. (1978). Language programming for the moderately and severely handicapped. *Education and Training of the Mentally Retarded, 13*, 316–322.

Gearheart, C., & Gearheart, B. (1990). *Introduction to special education assessment: Principles and practices.* Denver: Love Publishing.

Gold, M. (1980). *Try another way: Training manual.* Champaign, IL: Research Press.

Gorrell, J. (1985). Ordinal scales of psychological development. In D. Keyser, & R. Sweetland (Eds.), *Test critiques* (Vol 2). Kansas City: Test Corporation of America.

Greer, J., Anderson, R., & Davis, T. (1976). Developing functional language in the severely retarded using a standardized vocabulary. In R. Anderson & J. Greer (Eds.), *Educating the severely and profoundly retarded.* Baltimore: University Park Press.

Guess, D., Sailor, W., & Baer, D. (1974). To teach language to retarded children. In R. Schiefelbusch & L. Lloyd (Eds.), *Language perspectives: Acquisition, retardation, and intervention.* Baltimore: University Park Press.

Guess, D., Sailor, W., & Baer, D. (1976). *Functional speech and language training for the severely handicapped.* Lawrence, KS: H & H Enterprises.

Guess, D., Sailor, W., & Baer, D. (1977). A behavioral-remedial approach to language training for the severely handicapped. In E. Sontag, J. Smith, & N. Certo (Eds.), *Educational programming for the severely and profoundly handicapped.* Reston, VA: Council for Exceptional Children, Division on Mental Retardation.

Guess, D., Sailor, W., & Baer, D. (1978). Children with limited language. In R. Schiefelbusch (Ed.), *Language intervention strategies.* Baltimore: University Park Press.

Hallahan, D., & Kauffmann, J. (1991). *Exceptional children: Introduction to special education* (5th ed.). Englewood Cliffs, NJ: Prentice Hall.

Hammill, D., & Newcomer, P. (1987). *Test of language development-2*. Austin, TX: Pro-Ed.

Hardman, M., Drew, C., Egan, W., & Wolf, B. (1990). *Human exceptionality: Society, school, and family*, 3rd ed. Boston: Allyn & Bacon.

Haring, N., & McCormick, L. (1990). *Exceptional children and youth: An introduction to special education* (5th ed.). Columbus, OH: Charles E. Merrill Publishing.

Heron, T. (1987). Behavioral shaping. In J. Cooper, T. Heron, & W. Heward. *Applied behavior analysis*. Columbus, OH: Charles E. Merrill Publishing.

Hoffnung, A. (1989). The development of oral language. In P. Valletutti, M. McKnight-Taylor, & A. Hoffnung (Eds.), *Facilitating communication in young children with handicapping conditions: A guide for special educators*. Boston: Little, Brown.

Horstmeier, D., & MacDonald, J. (1978a). *Environmental pre-language battery*. Columbus, OH: Charles E. Merrill Publishing.

Horstmeier, D., & MacDonald, J. (1978b). *Ready-set-go*. Columbus, OH: Charles E. Merrill Publishing.

Howell, K., Kaplan, J., & O'Connell, C. (1979). *Evaluating exceptional children: A task analysis approach*. Columbus, OH: Charles E. Merrill Publishing.

Hunt, J. (1973). Psychological assessment, developmental plasticity, and heredity, with implications for early education. In R. Allen, A. Cortazzo, & R. Toister (Eds.), *Theories of cognitive development: Implications for the mentally retarded*. Coral Gables, FL: University of Miami Press.

Kaczmarek, L. (1990). Teaching spontaneous language to individuals with severe handicaps: A matrix mode. *The Journal of The Association for Persons With Severe Handicaps, 15*, 160–169.

Kamii, C. (1973). An application of Piaget's theory to the conceptualization of a preschool curriculum. In R. Parker (Ed.), *The preschool in action*. Boston: Allyn & Bacon.

Kaplan, J. (1991). *Beyond behavior modification: A cognitive-behavioral approach to behavior management in the school*. Austin, TX: Pro-Ed.

Katz, J., & Fodor, J. (1963). The structure of a semantic theory. *Language, 39*, 170–210.

Kauffman, J., & Snell, M. (1977). Managing the behavior of severely handicapped persons. In E. Sontag, J. Smith, & N. Certo (Eds.), *Educational programming for the severely and profoundly handicapped*. Reston, VA: Council for Exceptional Children, Division on Mental Retardation.

Kent, L. (1974). *Language acquisition program for the retarded or multiply handicapped*. Champaign, IL: University Park Press.

Keogh, W., & Reichle, J. (1985). Communication intervention for the "difficult-to-teach" severely handicapped. In S. Warren & A. Rogers-Warren (Eds.), *Teaching functional language: Generalization and maintenance for adults with developmental skills*. Baltimore: University Park Press.

Kysela, G., Holdgrafer, G., McCarthy, C., & Stewart, T. (1990). Turntaking and pragmatic language skills of developmentally delayed children: A research note. *Journal of Communication Disorders, 23*, 135–149.

Lahey, M. (1988). *Language disorders and language development*. New York: Macmillan.

Lambert, N., & Windmiller, M. (1981). *AAMD adaptive behavior scale: School edition*. Monterey, CA: Publishers Test Service.

Lambert, N., Windmiller, M., Cole, L., & Figueroa, R. (1975). *Manual: AAMD adaptive behavior scale, Public school version* (1974 rev.). Washington, DC: American Association on Mental Deficiency.

Lambert, N., Windmiller, M., Tharinger, D., & Cole, L. (1981). *Administration and instructional planning manual: AAMD adaptive behavior scale: School edition*. Monterey, CA: Publishers Test Service.

Lee, V. (1981). Terminology and conceptual revision of the experimental analysis of language development: Why? *Behaviorism, 9*, 25–55.

Lenneberg, E. (1967). *Biological foundations of language*. New York: Wiley.

Lombardino, L. (1979, April). *Maternal speech acts in the context of mother-child discourse: A taxonomy and descriptive-comparative study*. Paper presented at 57th Annual Council for Exceptional Children convention, Dallas.

Lovaas, O., Schreibman, L., & Koegel, R. (1974). A behavior modification approach to the treatment of autistic children. *Journal of Autism and Childhood Schizophrenia, 4*, 111–129.

Luftig, R. (1989). *Assessment of learners with special needs*. Boston: Allyn & Bacon.

MacDonald, J. (1978a). *Environmental language inventory*. Columbus, OH: Charles E. Merrill Publishing.

MacDonald, J. (1978b). *Oliver*. Columbus, OH: Charles E. Merrill Publishing.

MacDonald, J. (1979, April). *Parent-child interaction: An environmental approach to language assessment*. Paper presented to 57th Annual Council for Exceptional Children convention, Dallas.

MacDonald, J. (1985). Language through conversation: A model for intervention with language-delayed persons. In S. Warren & A. Rogers-Warren (Eds.), *Teaching functional language: Generalization and maintenance of language skills*. Baltimore: University Park Press.

Mahoney, G., & Seely, P. (1976). The role of the social agent in language acquisition: Implications for language intervention programs. In N. Ellis (Ed.) *International review of research in mental retardation* (Vol. 8). New York: Academic Press.

McDonnell, J., Fredricks, H., & Grove, D. (1975). *The teaching research initial expressive language program*. Monmouth, OR: Teaching Research Publications.

McLean, J., & Snyder-McLean, L. (1978). *A transactional approach to early language training*. Columbus, OH: Charles E. Merrill Publishing.

McLoughlin, J., & Lewis, R. (1990). *Assessing special students* (3rd ed.). Columbus, OH: Charles E. Merrill Publishing.

Mecham, M. (1989). *Utah test of language development-3*. Austin, TX: Pro-Ed.

Molt, L., & Younginger, K. (1988). Language instruction. In L. Sternberg, *Educating students with severe or profound handicaps* (2nd ed.). Rockville, MD: Aspen.

Musselwhite, C., & St. Louis, K. (1982). *Communication programming for the severely handicapped: Vocal and non-vocal strategies*. San Diego: College Hill Press.

Newport, E. (1990). Maturational constraints on language learning. *Cognitive Science, 14,* 11–28.

Nihira, K., Foster, R., Shellhaas, M., & Leland, H. (1969). *Adaptive behavior scales*. Washington, DC: American Association on Mental Deficiency.

Nihira, K., Foster, R., Shellhaas, M., & Leland, H. (1975). *Adaptive behavior scale*. Washington, DC: American Association on Mental Deficiency.

Owens, R. (1982). *Program for the acquisition of language with the severely impaired*. San Antonio, TX: Psychological Corporation.

Owens, R. (1988). *Language development: An introduction* (2nd ed.). Columbus, OH: Charles E. Merrill Publishing.

Paul-Brown, D. (1979, April). *Organizational and conceptual characteristics of language intervention programs for young handicapped children*. Paper presented at 57th Annual Council for Exceptional Children convention, Dallas.

Peterson, G., & Sherrod, K. (1979, April). *Mothers and their language-delayed children: Speech patterns*. Paper presented at 57th Annual Council for Exceptional Children convention, Dallas.

Premack, D. (1970). A functional analysis of language. *Journal of Experimental Analysis of Behavior, 14,* 107–125.

Rago, W., & Cleland, C. (1978). Future directions in the education of the profoundly retarded. *Education and Training of the Mentally Retarded, 13,* 184–186.

Reichle, J., & Karlan, G. (1985). The selection of an augmentative system in communication intervention: A critique of decision rules. *Journal of the Association for Persons with* Severe Handicaps, 10, 146–156.

Rice, M. (1983). Mismatched premises of the communicative competence model and language intervention. In R. Schiefelbusch (Ed.), *Language competence: Assessment and intervention*. San Diego: College Hill Press.

Rittenhouse, R., & Myers, J. (1985). Teaching functional sign language to severely delayed children. *Teaching Exceptional Children,* Fall, 62–67.

Robinson, N., & Robinson, H. (1976). *The mentally retarded child* (2nd ed.). New York: McGraw-Hill.

Sailor, W., & Mix, B. (1975). *TARC assessment system*. Lawrence, KS: H & H Enterprises.

Salisbury, C., Walmbold, C., & Walter, O. (1978). Manual communication for the severely handicapped: An assessment and instructional strategy. *Education and Training of the Mentally Retarded, 13,* 393–397.

Salvia, J., & Ysseldyke, J. (1991). *Assessment* (5th ed.). Boston: Houghton-Mifflin.

Schiefelbusch, R., Ruder, K., & Bricker, W. (1976). Training strategies for language-deficient children: An overview. In N. Haring & R. Schiefelbusch (Eds.), *Teaching special children.* New York: McGraw-Hill.

Seitz, S., & Marcus, S. (1976). Mother-child interactions: A foundation for language development. *Exceptional Children, 42,* 445–449.

Siegel, G., & Spradlin, J. (1978). Programming for language and communication therapy. In R. Schrefelbusch (Ed.), *Language intervention strategies.* Baltimore: University Park Press.

Sinclair, H. (1969). Developmental psycholinguistics. In D. Elkind & J. Flavell (Eds.), *Studies in cognitive development.* New York: Oxford University Press.

Sinclair, H. (1971). Sensorimotor action patterns as a condition for the acquisition of syntax. In R. Huxley & E. Ingram, *Language acquisition: Models and methods.* New York: Academic Press.

Sinclair, H. (1973). Language acquisition and cognitive development. In T. Moore (Ed.), *Cognitive development and the acquisition of language.* New York: Academic Press.

Skinner, B. (1957). *Verbal behavior.* New York: Appleton-Century-Crofts.

Skinner, B. (1968). *The technology of teaching.* New York: Appleton-Century-Crofts.

Smith, M. (1990). *Autism and life in the community: Successful interventions for behavioral challenges.* Baltimore: Paul H. Brookes Publishing Co.

Snell, M. (1987). *Systematic instruction of persons with severe handicaps* (3rd ed.). Columbus, OH: Charles E. Merrill Publishing.

Snyder, L., Lovitt, T., & Smith, J. (1975). Language training for the severely retarded: Five years of behavior analysis research, *Exceptional Children, 42,* 7–15.

Snyder, L., & McLean, J. (1977). Deficient acquisition strategies: A proposed conceptual framework for analyzing severe language deficiency. *American Journal on Mental Deficiency, 81,* 338–349.

Stainback, S., Stainback, W., & Maurer, S. (1976). Training teachers for the severely and profoundly handicapped: A new frontier. *Exceptional Children, 42,* 203–209.

Stemmer, N. (1990). Skinner's *Verbal Behavior,* Chomsky's review, and mentalism. *Journal of the Experimental Analysis of Behavior, 54*(3), 307–315.

Sternberg, L. (Ed.) (1988). *Educating students with severe or profound handicaps* (2nd ed.). Rockville, MD: Aspen.

Sternberg, L., & Adams, G. (1982). *Educating severely and profoundly handicapped students.* Rockville, MD: Aspen.

Stremel, K., & Waryas, C. (1974). A behavioral-psycholinguistic approach to language training. In L. Reynolds (Ed.), *Developing systematic procedures for training children's language* Monograph No. 18. Washington, DC: American Speech and Hearing Association.

Stremel-Campbell, K. (1977). Communication skills. In N. Haring (Ed.), *Developing effective individualized education programs for severely handicapped children and youth.* Washington, DC: Department of Health, Education and Welfare, Bureau of Education for the Handicapped.

Sugarman, S. (1978). Some organization aspects of pre-verbal communication. In I. Markova (Ed.), *Social context of language.* London: John Wiley.

Taylor, R. (1989). *Assessment of exceptional students: Educational and psychological procedures* (2nd ed.). Englewood Cliffs, NJ: Prentice Hall.

Thurman, S., & Widerstrom, A. (1985). *Young children with special needs: A developmental and ecological approach.* Newton, MA: Allyn & Bacon.

Turnure, J. (1986). Instruction and cognitive development: Coordinating communication and cues. *Exceptional Children, 53*(2), 109–117.

Uzgiris, I. (1981). Experience in the social context, imitation, and play. In R. Schiefelbusch & D. Bricker (Eds.), *Early language: Acquisition and intervention.* Baltimore: University Park Press.

Uzgiris, I., & Hunt, J. (1975). *Assessment in infancy: Ordinal scales of psychological development.* Urbana: University of Illinois Press.

Vygotsky, L. (1962). *Thought and language.* New York: Wiley.

Wagner, K. (1985). How much do children say in a day? *Journal of Child Language, 12,* 475–488.

Walker, C., Bonner, G., & Milling, L. (1984). Denver developmental screening tests. In D. Keyser & R. Sweetland (Eds.), *Tests: A comprehensive reference for tests in psychology, education, and business* (Vol. 2.). Kansas City, MO: Test Corporation of America.

Warren, S., & Kaiser, A. (1988). Research in early language intervention. In S. Odom & M. Karnes (Eds.), *Early intervention for infants and children with handicaps: An empirical base.* Baltimore: Paul H. Brookes.

Warren, S., & Rogers-Warren, A. (1985). A longitudinal analysis of language generalization among adolescents with severely handicapping conditions. *The Journal of The Association for Persons With Severe Handicaps, 8*(4), 18–31.

White, O., & Haring, N. (1980). *Exceptional teaching* (2nd ed.). Columbus, OH: Charles E. Merrill Publishing.

Zigler, E., & deLabry, J. (1962). Concept switching in middle-class, lower-class, and retarded children. *Journal of Abnormal and Social Psychology, 65,* 267–273.

6

Initial Language Skills: Nonverbal

Nikki L. Murdick

M ost people achieve communication through verbal language that "develops in a natural, seemingly serendipitous way" (Rittenhouse & Myers, 1985). But the development of communication by means of verbal language is not automatic, and for many individuals with severe disabilities is either significantly delayed or nonexistent. This population has been described by Sailor, Guess, Goetz, Schuler, Utley, and Baldwin (1980) as *prelinguistic*. Educators, parents, and other professionals continue to show concern because these individuals often lack a consistent method of oral communication even after participating in intensive language instruction. Warren and Kaiser (1988) stated that:

> Failure to acquire language normally is a developmental disaster. If unremediated, a language disorder will have pervasive effects on many aspects of a child's life. (p. 89)

According to Siegel-Causey and Guess (1989), when professionals in the past attempted remediation with individuals who had a combination of severe handicaps and a lack of verbal language, the assumption that they *do* communicate was often ignored. When communication *does* occur it "is achieved in a variety of ways that are not readily observed or even acknowledged by many attending adults" (Siegel-Causey and Guess, 1989, p. xi). Today, many educators are adopting the position that *all* people communicate, even though this communication may be sporadic and primitive in its form. A significant problem noted by Mirenda and Iacono (1990) is if teachers do not hold a belief in the communicative ability of individuals with severe disabilities who are nonverbal, they "will continue to disregard communicative behaviors even when they are obvious and will be prevented from persistently looking for them when they are not" (p. 3).

The theoretical bases for language acquisition presented earlier in the text are reviewed in this chapter. Representative approaches to teaching nonverbal language skills to individuals with severe handicaps, assessment procedures, and nonoral language development programs are described. The field of nonverbal language development is a new and rapidly changing field. Thus, professionals must continue to review language concepts and trends as they emerge in the future.

DEFINITIONS

When discussing communicative abilities of individuals with severe disabilities, the terms *communication, language,* and *speech* often are used interchangeably. According to Sternberg and McNerney (1988), this "synonymity of *communication* and *language* is certainly not warranted" (p. 311) and, as a result, their meanings are confused. *Communication* can be defined as the method by which information is exchanged, a process by which feelings, ideas, and perceptions can be exchanged (Barney & Landis, 1988; Moerk, 1977) or as a "signaling behavior that occurs in an interactional process and that provides a means to create shared understanding . . . between persons" (Warren & Kaiser, 1988, p. 89). The term *communication* therefore differs from the term *language*, which usually is defined as a symbol system with specific rules (e.g., grammar) used to transmit something the individual wishes to communicate (Cole & Cole, 1981; Sailor, Wilcox, & Brown, 1980). Thus, as noted in chapter 1, language can be seen as one means of communication.

Most individuals transmit language through a spoken method of communication known as *speech* (Brimer, 1990). But some individuals, especially those with severe handicaps, use a nonspoken (nonverbal) system of communication. The two types of nonverbal or nonvocal systems of communication (Molt & Younginger, 1988) are called:

1. *Nonsymbolic* or *gestural systems*, which include facial expressions, hand gestures such as sign language, body movements, and physical touch (Musselwhite & St. Louis, 1982; Stillman & Siegel-Causey, 1989).
2. *Symbolic communication systems* such as Rebuses and Blissymbols (Musselwhite & St. Louis, 1982).

Descriptions of these nonvocal systems are included in a later section of the chapter.

PERSPECTIVE ON ACQUISITION

Since the debate concerning the behavioral theory of Skinner (1957) and the psycholinguistic theory of Chomsky (1957) began approximately three decades ago (Stemmer, 1990), a variety of other theories (e.g., semantic/cognitive, sociolinguistic) have emerged. A description of these theories is contained in chapters 1 and 5. Two of the major theories of language acquisition currently used in intervention programs are the behavioral and the interactional theories. To develop a firm foundation for communication assessment and program development for children with disabilities, teachers need to understand the implications inherent in these basic theories of language acquisition. A strict emphasis on either theory is unusual (Warren & Kaiser, 1988) because researchers and teachers are advocating programs based on any theory that assists in developing instruction to facilitate communication (Rice, 1983; Schiefelbusch & Lloyd, 1988).

According to the behavioral perspective, language development is an extension of *operant conditioning* (Skinner, 1957). From this perspective, crying, babbling, and other early sounds that children produce are somewhat unpredictable and varied. These primitive utterances eventually are brought under *consequent control* as children imitate adult speech and receive reinforcement. As the child's language develops, *antecedent events* such as the child's imitation of his or her parents begin to assert control. Thus, in the behavioral model of acquisition, a young child first learns to discriminate between symbols and sounds, then makes learned responses to environmental stimuli.

The behavioral model, with its clear linking of theory to practice and its clearly stated objectives, revolutionized language training and "resulted in tremendous progress in teaching the form or structure of language" (Halle, 1987, p. 28). But this model has been criticized for its limited attention to cognitive, social, and semantic variables. One nagging question is whether behaviors (i.e., language competencies) acquired by this method will develop into spontaneous language and then generalize to other sites (Halle, 1987). Not long after the initiation of behavioral approaches, Miller and Yoder (1974) highlighted this concern when they stated that:

> One might ask . . . what we have demonstrated other than the fact that retarded children can learn some topographical language responses. . . . Allowing a child to develop a system to communicate basic needs, wants, and ideas requires more than mere acquisition of linguistic features taught in specified ways and places. (p. 506)

By contrast, the interactional view of language acquisition is more strongly founded in an ecologically oriented perspective. It emphasizes cognitive development in conjunction with the social interactions that shape the child's language. The interactional model stresses the child's natural use of language in lieu of an artificial, stilted training language (Guralnick, 1979). With the social relationship as a basis for language training (MacDonald, 1979; MacDonald & Gillette, 1985), instruction must capitalize on the child's intent to communicate what he or she already knows.

Mahoney's (1975) perspective further emphasized the role of social variables in language development. After evaluating the relative merits of solely a behavioral or a behavioral-linguistic approach, Mahoney encouraged a shift in emphasis to "the principle that language evolves from the social interaction and nonverbal communication system which exists between children and their primary language models" (p. 145). The interactional perspective, according to Warren and Kaiser (1988) "is grounded in the increasing evidence that normal language acquisition is dependent on a variety of environmental processes and properties" (p. 90).

The potential implications of an interactional teaching model obviously are far-reaching. For example, one critical factor is the establishment of a social base for language. In referring to a population of individuals who had been institutionalized, Michaelis (1978) illustrated the point when he stated that:

> Without warm personal exchange with direct care personnel, the profoundly handicapped child has no psychological reason to want to communicate and no core of repeated data to learn. Even a normal child could not learn language under these circumstances. (p. 348)

In keeping with the importance of language for social interaction and to facilitate the development of language, symbols to be taught to the child must match learned concepts drawn from his or her natural environment. As Knox (1983) noted, "Language does not exist as an end in itself, but as a means to achieve a specific communicative function" (p. 185).

Given the variant perspectives offered by the behavioral and the interactional models, individuals responsible for language acquisition programming must make a decision concerning the type of training model. First, the instructor can decide not to intervene, and thus to allow the child to proceed at his or her own rate of language development. This *maturational view*, however, can have disastrous results for children who have severe disabilities, as their failure to acquire oral language has had, and will continue to have, a profound effect on all aspects of their educational and social life.

Second, the instructor could forego the selection of normal developmental guidelines and adopt *remedial logic* (Guess, Sailor, & Baer, 1977) as a curricular basis. Switzky, Rotatori, Miller, and Freagon (1979) supported this rationale and questioned whether the normative developmental model could be appropriate. Lahey (1988) stated that the child with delayed language "is, by definition, not learning language as a normal child would" (p. 180). To Switzky et al. (1979), an awareness of developmental sequences might help bring attention to the key aspects of a skill, but additional sequences must be used to teach the acquisition of the particular skill. Remedial logic dictates an emphasis on the selection of words to teach for practical, rather than ideal, considerations. In the case of individuals with severe disabilities, words to be taught would be selected with an emphasis on a basic functional, workable vocabulary (Greer, Anderson, & Davis, 1976). For example, appropriate initial words might include *eat, drink, ball, more, and toilet.*

Third, the instructor can select developmentally appropriate skills for students to learn. This approach takes into account the linguistic and cognitive priorities inherent in the developmental approach and provides the teacher with indicators of which skills the child needs and is ready to learn. In the developmental approach, the learning environment would be redesigned to enhance development through the encouragement of language usage and the selection of instructional objectives from normal developmental guidelines. According to Lahey (1988) this is the "most reasonable and practical hypothesis" (p. 180) because both linguistic and concept development are dependent on specific stages occurring and providing the basis for the next stage of language development.

Most of the initial language training program models have been developed based on the developmental and the remedial logic models described in the previous paragraph. But accepting a strict dichotomy between these two approaches would be presumptuous, for, as McCormick (1986), stated "A review of language intervention research suggests a trend toward searching for overlapping and complementary principles and strategies in developmental and behavior procedures" (p. 123). Thus, the selection of *eclectic* programs that facilitate "the development of communicative competence" and "the generalization of the child's communication skills across all environments" (Warren & Kaiser, 1988, p. 90) is more appropriate. Teachers, therefore, should consider possible blends of theoretical approaches and heed the advice of McCormick and Elder (1978), who stated that:

> Until more efficacy data is available, the front-line professional must exploit the normative research which is so rapidly accumulating, integrate this knowledge with what they know about operant technology and consider the special learning characteristics of the children for whom they are responsible (p. 34).

The following sections therefore will attempt to integrate these perspectives into an approach for language training. More detailed discussions of the theoretical foundations for language intervention are found in Bryen and Joyce (1985), Carrow-Woolfolk (1988), Kymissis and Poulson (1990), and Warren and Kaiser (1988).

ASSESSMENT STRATEGIES

According to MacDonald and Gillette (1986), "A primary problem in special education is to discover how persons with disabilities can learn to communicate what they know in socially and vocationally acceptable ways" (p. 255). This becomes especially difficult when attempting to plan a program to assist an individual in developing either nonverbal or verbal language or in selecting a communication system for an individual who is nonverbal (Woltosz & Woltosz, 1989). In both of these situations, a comprehensive communication assessment program is required. The purposes of this communication assessment should be to "describe the student's existing language skills and to construct a data base for prescribing a set of treatment goals and strategies for intervention" (Snell, 1987, p. 257). To address these purposes effectively, a careful assessment of three different areas must be completed: (a) the characteristics (e.g., physical, verbal) of each child, (b) the characteristics of each communication system being considered (Woltosz & Woltosz, 1989), and (c) the prerequisite behaviors necessary for the system to be appropriate for the individual (Chapman & Miller, 1980; Harris-Vanderheiden & Vanderheiden, 1977).

STUDENT CHARACTERISTICS

Harris-Vanderheiden and Vanderheiden (1977) have stated that during a language evaluation specific characteristics of each student must be assessed. These characteristics are:

1. The amount of *visual ability* the person has for use in seeing and discriminating between stimuli such as gestures or a visual display of symbols.
2. The amount of *auditory ability* the person has for use in receiving language input, in terms of both acuity and discrimination.
3. The amount of *mobility* the student has, particularly as related to persons who are wheelchair-bound versus persons who are ambulatory.
4. The amount of *positioning and postural variables* the person with a physical disability will require (e.g., amount of head control, ability to maintain seated position) in order to use an alternative communication system.
5. The availability of a *consistent, motoric response mode*, which will be necessary as a substitute for verbal responding (e.g., pointing or head nodding).
6. The amount of *ability to associate, store, and retrieve symbols and their meaning* in relation to the complexity of the alternative system being considered.

Along with the assessment of the characteristics listed, an evaluation of the student's receptive language ability is necessary. Other areas that must be evaluated are the individual's present and future communication needs; educational and vocational needs; motivation to communicate; variables within the environment such as availability of staff and parents for training; and the motivation of other people in the environment to communicate with the person with a severe disability.

Sternberg (1988) developed a screening tool known as *A Communication Programming Inventory*, which can be used to assess the characteristics of the child with language delay. The purpose of this inventory is to "give an indication to the teacher (or other communication facilitator) of the developmental level of functioning of a student in cognition, receptive communication, and expressive communication" (p. 324). Each of these three areas is divided into six separate age levels (birth to 1 month; 1–4 months; 4–8 months; 8–12 months; 12–18 months; 18–24 months), which provide the teacher with a tentative initial instructional placement in a language development program. The information requested in the inventory is to be provided by observation of a person who is familiar with the student being assessed.

A list of instruments that can be used in evaluating a child's language skills is presented in Table 6.1. Other evaluative instruments and formal and informal techniques used in assessing student characteristics were discussed in chapter 5, on verbal skills.

COMMUNICATION SYSTEM CHARACTERISTICS

The characteristics of each alternative communication system being considered for use with the specific child and the prerequisite skills required to master this system also must be addressed. The prerequisites discussed in this section relate to behaviors that must be present, or taught, to the child "in order that language training tasks will be more easily attended to and acquired by the student" (Sternberg, 1982, p. 236). Assessment of the characteristics of the communication system include (a) the physical abilities required to manipulate this alternative communication system; (b) the cognitive level of development required to understand and effectively communicate by means of this system; and (c) the ability or amount of training required of family and friends for effective communication to occur.

During the analysis of possible alternative communication systems, Woltosz and Woltosz (1989) stated that one should consider the "expected changes in the user's physical, cognitive, and language skills, as well as changes which might occur in environmental factors" (p. 7). Other variables to consider are the output mode that can be used during the life of the system, the speed of the device, the ease with which the system can be learned and used, the durability and reliability of the system, and the cost (Woltosz & Woltosz, 1989).

According to Brimer (1990), to increase the effectiveness in selecting an augmentative communication method, the selection process should include not only an evaluation prior to selection but also an evaluation during the selection process, and another after the selection has been finalized. A commercially available checklist that "provides a systematic way to observe electronic and manual augmentative communication aid users" (Bolton & Dashiell, 1989, p. 3), and therefore to assess the interaction between user and augmentative system, is known as *INCH: INteraction CHecklist for Augmentative Communication* (Bolton & Dashiell, 1989).

A thorough analysis of the (a) child's physical characteristics, (b) characteristics of the alternative communication system, and (c) appropriateness of the system will

Table 6.1
Selected Examples of Commercially Available Language Assessment Instruments

Title	Author	Publisher
Adapted Sequenced Inventory of Communication Development for Adolescents and Adults with Severe Handicaps (A-SICD) (1989)	S. McClennen	University of Washington Press Seattle, WA
Assessing Prelinguistic and Early Linguistic Behaviors in Developmentally Young Children (1987)	L. Olswang, C. Stoel-Gammon, T. Coggins & R. Carpenter	University of Washington Press Seattle, WA
Behavior Analysis Language Instrument (BALI)	E. Cipani et al.	Edmark Corp. P.O. Box 3903 Bellevue, WA 98009-3903
Clinical Evaluation of Language Functions (1980)	E. Semel & E. Wiig	The Psychological Corporation Harcourt Brace Jovanovich, Inc. 555 Academic Court San Antonio, TX 78204-2498
Clinical Evaluation of Language Fundamentals, Revised (CELF-R) (1987)	E. Semel, E. Wiig, & W. Secord	The Psychological Corporation Harcourt Brace Jovanovich, Inc. 555 Academic Court San Antonio, TX 78204-2498
CELF-R Screening Test (1989) W. Secord	E. Semel, E. Wiig, &	The Psychological Corporation Harcourt Brace Jovanovich, Inc. 555 Academic Court San Antonio, TX 78204-2498
Evaluating Communicative Competence: A Functional Pragmatic Procedure (Revised Edition) (1986)	C. Simon	Communication Skill Builders, Inc. P.O. Box 42050 Tucson, AZ 85733
Expressive One-Word Picture Vocabulary Test (EOWPVT)	M. Gardner	Slosson Educational Publications, Inc. P.O. Box 280 East Aurora, NY 14052
Let's Talk Inventory for Children (1987)	C. Bray & E. Wiig	The Psychological Corporation Harcourt Brace Jovanovich, Inc. 555 Academic Court San Antonio, TX 78204-2498
NonSpeech Test (1989)	M. Huer	Don Johnston Developmental Equipment, Inc. P.O. Box 639 1000 N. Rand Rd., Bldg. 115 Wauconda, IL 60084
Preschool Language Scale (1979)	I. Zimmerman, V. Steiner, & R. Pond	The Psychological Corporation Harcourt Brace Jovanovich, Inc. 555 Academic Court San Antonio, TX 78204-2498

Table 6.1
continued

Title	Author	Publisher
Preschool Language Assessment Instrument (1978)	M. Blank, S. Rose, & L. Berlin	The Psychological Corporation Harcourt Brace Jovanovich, Inc. 555 Academic Court San Antonio, TX 78204-2498
Receptive One-Word Picture Vocabulary Test (ROWPVT)	M. Gardner	Slosson Educational Publications, Inc. P.O. Box 280 East Aurora, NY 14052
Screening Kit of Language Development (SKOLD)	L. Bliss & D. Allen	Slosson Educational Publications, Inc. P.O. Box 280 East Aurora, NY 14052
Sequenced Inventory of Communication Development (SICD) (Revised) (1984)	D. Hedrick, E. Prather, & A. Tobin	University of Washington Press Seattle, WA
Test of Adolescent Language (TOAL-2) (1987)	D. Hammill, V. Brown, S. Larsen, & L. Wiederholt	Slosson Educational Publications, Inc. P.O. Box 280 East Aurora, NY 14052
Test of Early Language Development (TELD) (1981)	W. Hresko, K. Reid, & D. Hammill	Slosson Educational Publications, Inc. P.O. Box 280 East Aurora, NY 14052
Wiig Criterion Referenced Inventory of Language (1990)	E. Wiig	The Psychological Corporation Harcourt Brace Jovanovich, Inc. 555 Academic Court San Antonio, TX 78204-2498

assist in selecting an effective communication system for a child with severe language delays. Many professionals, as well as parents, are "looking toward nonverbal forms of communication for their students who cannot communicate verbally" (Hamre-Nietupski, Nietupski, & Rathe, 1986, p. 130). Any communication system identified will be effective only if it can provide an affirmative answer to the following question: "Will it let children say what they want to say, to the people they want to talk to, for the reasons they want to talk, now and in the future?" (Chapman & Miller, 1980, p. 190). A communication system that does not answer this question in the affirmative should not be selected as the system of choice, because "language does not exist as an end in itself, but as a means to achieve a specific communicative function" (Knox, 1983, p. 185).

Once a language assessment, including all the areas just described, is completed and the assessment team makes a decision concerning the feasibility of an alternative communication system (Molt & Younginger, 1988; Reichle & Karlan, 1985), program development can begin. Nonoral communicative systems and the development of language programming are discussed next.

PROGRAMMING FOR COMMUNICATION DEVELOPMENT

According to Carr and Kologinsky (1983), "The acquisition of language and communication facility is critical to the social development of young . . . children" (p. 297). This is also essential for those who have the dual condition of severe disabilities and delayed or nonexistent language. The overriding goal of communication programming, as Snell (1987) stated, is "to increase the student's functional communication" (p. 248). This goal will be met only when the communication (i.e., language) behaviors taught to the individual are "functional, spontaneous, generalized and appropriate" (Wulz, Myers, Klein, Hall, & Waldo, 1982, p. 128).

As MacDonald and Gillette (1986) stated, "A useful model for language development may be one that views a child's words as emerging from a larger repertoire of nonverbal communications and from a still larger base of interactive behavior" (p. 259). Any program or method a teacher uses should reflect MacDonald and Gillette's definition of a useful language development model and also the means by which the goal of functional communication can be achieved.

PRELANGUAGE COMMUNICATION SKILLS

Recently, researchers have begun to indicate that *prerequisite language skills*, also known as *prelanguage communication skills, prelinguistic communication skills,* and *precursor language skills* (Sternberg, Pegnatore, & Hill, 1983; Valletutti, 1989), must be addressed prior to beginning any communication training effort. The acquisition of prelanguage communication skills is essential "for the purpose of communication even in the absence of language" (Sternberg, 1982, p. 236).

According to Oller and Seibert (1988), research with infants has shown that the systematic development of sensorimotor, social, and nonverbal communication abilities are related to the future development of verbal skills in children, although the extent of the relationship is still uncertain (Smith & von Tetzchner, 1986). Kaczmarek (1990) described prelanguage communication skills as "listener preparatory behaviors" (p. 162) and separated them into three separate skills: listener selection, listener proximity, and listener attention.

1. *Listener selection* is defined as the ability of the "person wishing to say something to . . . decide whom to approach" (p. 162) in order to effectively communicate.
2. *Listener proximity* is "the form of approach and the socially acceptable distance between oneself" (p. 162) and the one with whom the individual wishes to communicate.
3. *Listener attention* is the ability to obtain "someone's attention before delivering the message" (p. 162) in order to accomplish the communication interaction.

If the individual who is being taught to communicate is not able to perform these listener preparatory behaviors, the chances that he or she will be able to learn to communicate effectively and to generalize that communication throughout the natural environment are lessened.

Prelanguage communication programming is still in its infancy, as most programs do not address the issue of behaviors that must be in the individual's repertoire prior to implementing a language program (Sternberg & McNerney, 1988). In fact, a paucity of research has been noted in the area of program development and effective training techniques for use with individuals who have not acquired prelanguage communication skills (Sternberg, McNerney, & Pegnatore, 1987).

One representative example is the Van Dijk Program (Van Dijk, 1965a, 1965b). This is a prelanguage communication program, which originally was developed for individuals who are deaf/blind but which has been found to be effective with persons who lack communication skills. The program was designed "to develop communicative intentions and communication procedures through conversation, using movement, signals, gestures, objects, pictures, signs, or speech" (Sternberg, 1982, p. 210). An in-depth description of this program and cautions concerning a lack of data-based validation are given in Sternberg (1988).

The Van Dijk approach suggests that prior to developing communication, and to become an effective communicator, the child must master three concepts: (a) an awareness that he or she is an entity separate from the rest of the surrounding environment; (b) an awareness that he or she can communicate; and (c) an awareness that there are things around him or her about which he or she can communicate, as well as people to whom he or she can communicate.

The goal of the Van Dijk Program is to assist the "prelanguage, noncommunicative individual develop communication and eventually language" (Sternberg, 1982, p. 211). To accomplish this, a three-stage procedure is used (Sternberg, Pegnatore, & Hill, 1983). *The Communication Programming Inventory* (Sternberg, 1982), described previously, is useful in pinpointing the child's level of language development so the child can be effectively placed in the correct stage of the Van Dijk Program.

Sternberg (1988) developed a *modified Van Dijk approach* to assist in prelanguage communication development. Modifications to the original program involve control, or simplification, of the instructional elements of communicator distance, interchange time, and program procedures. This modified program "tends to emphasize . . . the various skill developments imbedded in very early prelanguage communication" (Sternberg & McNerney, 1988, p. 320). An in-depth description of this program is included in Sternberg (1988). Table 6.2 contains a list of selected examples of other commercially available early language development programs.

NONORAL COMMUNICATION PROGRAMMING

Nonoral communication programs can provide an auxiliary communication system for children who have a poor prognosis for developing oral language. The terms *nonoral, nonspeech, nonvocal,* and *nonverbal* seem to imply that speech will not be used (Nietupski & Hamre-Nietupski, 1979), but this does not have to be the case. Contrary to the assumption that nonoral communication programming means abandoning speech development, verbal and nonverbal communication systems are complementary

Table 6.2
Selected Examples of Commercially Available Language Development Programs

Title	Author	Publisher
A Transactional Approach to Early Language (1982)	J. McLean, L. Snyder-Mclean, & S. Sack	The Psychological Corporation Harcourt Brace Jovanovich, Inc. 555 Academic Court San Antonio, TX 78204-2498
Behavior Analysis Language Program (BALP)	E. Cipani	Edmark Corp. P.O. Box 3903 Bellevue, WA 98809-3903
Communicative Competence (CC): A Functional-Pragmatic Language Program	C. Simon	Slosson Ecucational Publications, Inc. P.O. Box 280 East Aurora, NY 14052
Clinical Language Intervention Program (1982)	E. Semel & E. Wiig	The Psychological Corporation Harcourt Brace Jovanovich, Inc. 555 Academic Court San Antonio, TX 78204-2498
Developing Expressive Language: A Functional Approach for Children 3–8 (1986)	M. Zegar	Communication Skill Builders, Inc. P.O. Box 42050 Tucson, AZ 85733
Developmental Communication Curriculum (1982)	R. Hanna, E. Lippert, & A. Harris	The Psychological Corporation Harcourt Brace Jovanovich, Inc. 555 Academic Court San Antonio, TX 78204-2498
The Early Vocabulary Development Series	—	Laureate Learning Systems, Inc. 110 East Spring Street Winooski, VT 60084
Great Beginnings for Early Language Learning (1988)	L. Levine	Communication Skill Builders, Inc. P.O. Box 42050 Tucson, AZ 85733
Language Stories (Revised): Teaching Language to Developmentally Disabled Children (1986)	A. McGivern, M. Rieff, & B. Vender	Communication Skill Builders, Inc. P.O. Box 42050 Tucson, AZ 85733
Let's Communicate (1984)	B. Martin & G. Momeier	Communication Skill Builders, Inc. P.O. Box 42050 Tucson, AZ 85733
Let's Talk for Children (1983)	E. Wiig & C. Bray	The Psychological Corporation Harcourt Brace Jovanovich, Inc. 555 Academic Court San Antonio, TX 78204-2498
Let's Talk: Developing Prosocial Communication Skills— Ages 9-Adult	E. Wiig & C. Bray	Charles E. Merrill Publishing Company 1300 Alum Creek Drive Box 508 Columbus, OH 43216-0508

Table 6.2
continued

Title	Author	Publisher
Peabody Language Development Kits (Revised)—Levels P-3 (1981)	L. Dunn, J. Smith, L. Dunn, K. Horton, & D. Smith	American Guidance Corp., Circle Pines, MN
PLA-ACT: A Language Remediation Program (1985)	J. Rosenberg	The Psychological Corporation Harcourt Brace Jovanovich, Inc. 555 Academic Court San Antonio, TX 78204-2498
Sign Language Training for the Developmentally Disabled (1987)	L. Edly & G. Schumacher	Communication Skill Builders, Inc. P.O. Box 42050 Tucson, AZ 85733
TOTAL: Teacher Organized Training for the Acquisition of Language (1986)	B. Witt & J. Boose	Communication Skill Builders, Inc. P.O. Box 42050 Tucson, AZ 85733
Using Computers and Speech Synthesis to Facilitate Communicative Interaction with Young and/or Severely Handicapped Children	L. Burkhart	Don Johnston Developmental Equipment, Inc. P.O. Box 639 1000 N. Rand Rd., Bldg. 115 Wauconda, IL 60084

(Brimer, 1990; Jones, 1980). Even if nonoral systems of communication are selected, efforts should be made to assist the child in developing verbal skills, thus using nonoral communication as "augmentative channels, not substitute channels, of communication" (Brimer, 1990, p. 161).

Development of Alternative Communication Approaches   The pioneering research in development of nonverbal communication methods originally focused on attempting to teach language to the higher primates (i.e., chimpanzees and gorillas). Early work by Yerkes (Yerkes & Nissen, 1939) and the Kelloggs (Kellogg, 1931) was followed years later by that of Gardner and Gardner (1969) and Premack (1970a; 1970b; 1971; 1972; 1986), who reported the development of elaborate communication systems in chimpanzees. Because chimpanzees are incapable of human verbalizations, alternative systems had to be developed to provide a means of communication. Premack's system (1970a, 1970b), for example, allowed the chimp, Sarah, to match specific arrangements of symbols to environmental events. According to Owens (1988), more recent studies with KoKo, the mountain gorilla, have shown that "although primates appear to be capable of creating sentences, they have failed so far to master the more difficult task of conversation" (p. 33).

An anthology edited by Schiefelbusch and Hollis (1979), as well as studies by Carrier and Hollis (1975) and Terrace (1979), discussed in detail some of the important early work with primates. These studies elaborated on the questions and issues this research raises in relation to the definition of language and the amount of time and staff the training methods require to facilitate success.

Results of research with primates have been used in the development of nonoral communication training programs that can be used by individuals with severe disabilities who show profound deficits in the areas of language and communication. For example, in their 1983 research with children labeled as autistic, Carr and Kologinsky stated that "children who would otherwise remain nonverbal can be taught a variety of sign language skills in lieu of speech" (p. 297).

Recipients of Nonoral Programming   Nonoral systems, therefore, have been developed as a means of teaching language to those who cannot acquire, or have difficulty acquiring, oral language (Hamre-Nietupski et al., 1986). Nonoral systems can be used to augment or supplement programs that teach verbal language, to supply children with a method of communication before they learn to speak, or to give children a method of communication as they are acquiring verbal skills. Nonoral systems usually are designed for those who can learn symbols but who have severe problems imitating speech, have severe hearing loss, or have severely impaired speech mechanisms. Many of these individuals are extremely restricted in social interactions because of the magnitude of their language impairment(s). Although nonoral systems have been developed for use with various populations, this section focuses on their use with individuals who have severe disabilities as well as little or no oral language.

NONORAL AUGMENTATIVE SYSTEMS

Various communication techniques and programs have been developed for students who are nonvocal. All of these techniques and programs can be used to augment other language development programs. The factors noted in the communication assessment section should provide an approach to decision making concerning the appropriateness and usefulness of each communication program as it pertains to the individual. These nonoral communication systems, also known as augmentative systems, usually are divided into two categories: (a) symbolic or aided systems and (b) gestural or unaided systems (Molt & Younginger, 1988). Table 6.3 contains selected examples of commercially available augmentative communication aids.

Symbolic or Aided Systems   According to Musselwhite and St. Louis (1982), symbolic systems involve the use of symbols that are external to the individual's body and are located on some type of communication device. The symbols are usually one of three types:

1. *Representational*, such as rebus (Pecyna, 1988) or Blissymbols (Bliss, 1975).
2. *Abstract*, such as lexigrams (Romski, Sevcik, & Pate, 1988).
3. *Language Codes*, such as braille, Morse code, or traditional orthography.

Symbolic systems have been gaining in popularity because of their ease of use by individuals with both a lack of verbal language and severe physical disabilities. An overview of several symbolic systems that have been identified as effective with individuals who are nonverbal follows. For a more in-depth review of available communi-

Table 6.3

Examples of Commercially Available Augmentative Communication Aids

Title	Author	Publisher
ALLTALK	—	Adaptive Communication Systems (ACS) Box 12440, Pittsburgh, PA 15231
AudScan II (1989)	—	Words+ P.O. Box 1229, Suite L 44421 10th St. W, Lancaster, CA 93584
Augmentative Communication Evaluation System	—	Words+ P.O. Box 1229, Suite L 44421 10th St. W Lancaster, CA 93584
Augmentative Communication Series (1989)	H. Shane	The Psychological Corporation Harcourt Brace Jovanovich, Inc. 555 Academic Court San Antonio, TX 78204-2498
Augmentative Communication Training System	—	Words+ P.O. Box 1229, Suite L 44421 10th St. W, Lancaster, CA 93584
E-Z Com, E-Z Keys, & E-Z Talker	—	Words+ P.O. Box 1229, Suite L 44421 10th St. W, Lancaster, CA 93584
FAST Communication System	B. Fox & M. Wilson	Laureate Learning Systems 110 East Spring Street Winooski, VT 05404
Fold-It System: Portable Communication	—	Don Johnston Developmental Equipment, P.O. Box 639 1000 N. Rand Rd., Bldg. 115 Wauconda, IL 60084
Partners in Augmentative Communication Training (PACT) (1988)	D. Culp & M. Carlisle	Communication Skill Builders P.O. Box 42050 Tucson, AZ 85733
PassPorts to Independence	—	Crestwood Co., Communication Aids for Children & Adults 6625 N. Sidney Pl. Milwaukee, WI 53209-3259
Picture Communication	—	ComputAbility 101 Route 46, Pine Brook, NJ 07058
PRC IntroTalker (1990)	—	Prentke Romich Co. 1022 Heyl Rd., Wooster, OH 44691
RealVoice	—	Adaptive Communication Systems (ACS) Box 12440, Pittsburgh, PA 15231
Talking Pictures (1990)	S. Lou & R. Leff	Crestwood Co., Communication Aids for Children & Adults 6625 N. Sidney Pl. Milwaukee, WI 53209-3259

Table 6.3
continued

Title	Author	Publisher
TouchCom	L. Smolin & J. Brink	Don Johnston Developmental Equipment, P.O. Box 639 1000 N. Rand Rd., Bldg. 115 Wauconda, IL 60084
Touch 'n Talk Communication Notebook	—	Don Johnston Developmental Equipment, P.O. Box 639 1000 N. Rand Rd., Bldg. 115 Wauconda, IL 60084
Vocaid (1982)	Texas Instruments	Communication Skill Builders P.O. Box 42050, Tucson, AZ 85733
VOIS 140: Speech Output Communication Systems for Non-speaking People	—	Phonic Ear 250 Camino Alto, Mill Valley, CA 94941
Words+ Talking Board	—	Words+ P.O. Box 1229, Suite L 44421 10th St. W, Lancaster, CA 93584

cation (augmentative) options, the reader is referred to Musselwhite and St. Louis (1988), Silverman (1989), and Woltosz and Woltosz (1989).

Communication board is a generic term referring to a host of tools that require a motoric response for the person to communicate. Communication boards can be used with any of the three types of symbolic language systems—representational, abstract, or language code. Communication boards are particularly valuable for individuals with severe speech disabilities whose ability to hear and process messages may be relatively intact but whose speech is absent or unintelligible (e.g., individuals with cerebral palsy). These children are often deprived of conversations with other people, which some researchers believe may eventually retard the development of cognitive skills.

For conversation to occur, communication boards typically use one of three modes of physical response: direct selection, scanning, and encoding (Snell, 1987; Vanderheiden & Grilley, 1977).

1. *Direct selection.* This type of response, the most common one, requires the user to make a choice by pointing with a hand or finger or, when the student's arm function is impaired, a head-pointing device utilizing a stick or a light (Molt & Younginger, 1988). With the increased use of computers and electronic switches, direct selection (as well as scanning) procedures have been much simplified.

2. *Scanning.* The correct response is selected from a series of options provided by the person with whom the individual with the language delay is attempting to communicate or by an electronic system that presents the symbols on the communication board in a sequential order (Molt & Younginger, 1988). In the simplest sense, the

Update

Considerations in Constructing Communication Boards

Communication boards are a form of augmentative communication that provide nonverbal children a means of communicating with peers and teachers. Symbols or pictures are placed on a board that the student has access to select from, indicating preferences or other communication needs. While communication boards can be computer operated, they can also be a simple piece of cardboard or other sturdy paper with symbols or letters. Teachers can construct their own communication board with information that is specific to a particular child. When constructing communication boards, teachers should always consider the following:

- The different choices that the student can make. The communication board may be the only method of communicating for the student. Therefore, it is very important to include the important choices that the student needs.
- The different methods of representing choices must be considered. If the child is capable of reading, then the choices would be very different from those necessary for a child who is not a reader.
- The method of selecting choices is a consideration. Some students have limited use of their arms or hands, creating unique needs relative to a communication board. If a communication board is computer-based, various electronic switches or other forms of assistive technology will be needed.
- The number of choices and their arrangement should be considered. Young students, or those with cognitive deficits, may be overwhelmed with a large number of choices. Therefore, when constructing communication boards always keep in mind the capabilities of students for dealing with a large number or small number of choices.
- The exact method of construction of the board must be a consideration. If the board will be used by a student who will be rough with the board, the construction must be such that it will not be rendered unusable after a few times.

Communication boards provide excellent opportunities for students to communicate with their peers and teachers. Their construction can be a relatively simple process; however, these factors should be taken into consideration to enable the learner to benefit the most from the end product.

Source: Lewis, R. B. (1993). *Special education technology: Classroom applications.* Pacific Grove, CA: Brookes.

individual stops the scanning when he or she reaches the appropriate item, and then continues the scan if multiple symbols are required to communicate. Examples of commercially available scanning systems are *PRC Light Talker* and *PRC Touch Talker* (1990) and *Opticommunicator* (1990).

3. *Encoding.* This response mode requires the responder to communicate using a patterned or coded system of symbols. For example, a series of number combinations may be used to represent an equivalent series of letters or words. The individual can communicate by pointing or gazing at the appropriate numbers (Molt & Younginger, 1988; Vanderheiden & Grilley, 1977).

An example of a commercially available communication board is *Self-Talk: Communication Boards for Children and Adults* (Johnson, 1986). For any communication board or related tool to be used effectively, it must be adapted specifically for the individual's ability and needs, and the design must relate to the person's level of functional and intellectual ability. For example, Robinett (1977) reported on a program that created individualized systems for three individuals who were nonverbal and living in an institution. Pictures used as stimuli were printed on charts, wallet fold-out cards, and photo album pages so the individuals could communicate their desires to visit, for example, the chapel, library, canteen, dining hall, doctor's office, and gym. Detamore and Lippke (1980) offer further suggestions for individual modifications based on location and availability of the communication boards, their size, and the identification of appropriate pictures.

Figure 6.1 illustrates two relatively simple examples of communication boards that reflect individualized planning based on a specific child's level and needs. In the second example, a keyboard is included as orientation for a learner who later may be taught to use keyboard entry.

Students who function on a more complex level need more sophisticated tools, such as *electronic communication aids*. Electronic aids include computers and commercially available products such as the *Auto-Com* (Wendt, Sprague, & Marquis, 1975) and the *Minspeak* (Baker, 1986). Both of these communication aids were developed for individuals whose primary disability is physical and whose receptive language skills are intact. Electronic aids produce visual output (printed communication on a screen or paper), auditory output (artificial speech), or a combination of visual and auditory output. Electronic aids that use artificial speech, either produced by another human voice or by computer synthesis, are known as VOCAs (voice output communication aids).

Computer technology presently offers the individual without oral speech a myriad of ways to communicate that were not possible in the past. As computer technology is advancing at a rapid pace, professionals must be aware of the varied options available (Blackstone, 1987) so they will be able to provide the nonverbal person with the most viable method of communication augmentation.

Representational Communication Systems A prime example of a representational symbolic system is *Blissymbols*. This system, developed by Charles Bliss (1975), was loosely based on the Chinese method of using characters to bridge the gap between oral communication and traditional English orthography to convey meaning.

Update

Facilitated Communication as an Augmentative System?

Individuals who support the practice of facilitated communication believe that this process serves as an augmentative communication strategy that makes it possible for persons with severe language disorders, such as autism, to communicate effectively. The system utilizes a hand-over-hand and other physical assistance approach to *facilitate* communication. A person without a disability generally provides a physical prompt or stimulus to the arm of the person whose language is being facilitated. The result, supposedly, is communication. Some persons, who were considered to be totally nonverbal and noncommunicative, have purportedly expressed that they have capabilities that significantly exceed what professionals believed them to have.

Support for facilitated communication has primarily come from anecdotal evidence, including case studies and informal testimonials. Recently, more substantive research studies have focused on the efficacy of facilitated communication and have found some questionable results. Some findings and conclusions (Myles, Simpson, & Smith, 1996) include the following:

- Facilitated communication has not resulted in "unexpected, independent literacy when facilitators lack information needed to answer questions posed to individuals being facilitated." (p. 37)
- Facilitated communication may actually result in psychological, emotional, and financial injury to individuals with disabilities and their families because of situations where unsubstantiated reports of abuse have been made.
- False and exaggerated claims about the efficacy of facilitated communication with persons with disabilities have been exposed.
- Facilitated communication has not been shown to have value as an educational tool when attempting to evaluate student learning.

In summarizing their research on the efficacy of using facilitated communication as an educational tool, Myles, Simpson, and Smith (1996) suggest that schools will not likely adopt the use of facilitated communication without assurances that it can be effective. They further note that there has been no demonstration of its worth in educational programs. In summary, they acknowledge facilitated communication "as an interesting phenomenon that has claimed its 15 minutes of fame and they suggest educators move on to more functional and potentially useful tools for improving the lives of individuals with autism." (p. 44)

Source: B. S. Myles, R. L. Simpson, & S. M. Smith. (1996). Impact of facilitated communication combined with direct instruction on academic performance of the individuals with autism. *Focus on Autism and Other Developmental Disabilities, 11*, 37–44.

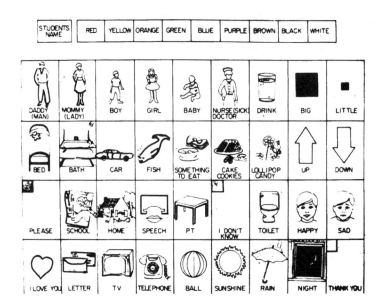

Source: From "Conventional Symbols of English" by E. T. McDonald in *Non-vocal Communication Techniques and Aids for the Severely Physically Handicapped* (pp. 82–83), edited by G. C. Vanderheiden and K. Grilley, 1975, Baltimore: University Park Press. Reprinted by permission of PRO-ED, Inc.

Figure 6.1
Sample Communication Boards

This symbolic system uses pictorial symbols that tap possible meaning cues contained within each picture. About 100 elements form the symbolic "vocabulary" comprising *pictographs*, which look like what they represent, and *ideographs*, which represent various ideas. Figure 6.2 presents several sample Blissymbols. McNaughton (1977) presents a full discussion of the rationale behind the selection of these symbols.

Advocates of the Blissymbol system cite several major advantages: (a) the ease by which children can learn the symbols; (b) the facility by which the symbols promote generalization to other symbols and also to word communication; (c) the amount of active learning and participation involved; and (d) the facilitation of a good transition to later reading for some children (McNaughton, 1977).

One major disadvantage of Blissymbols is that everyone who uses the system must be trained in its use, making it difficult to use in the natural environment. A second disadvantage is that parents are sometimes afraid to adopt such a nonoral system, fearing that they cannot learn the symbols and believing (without real cause) that using the symbols means their child will never learn speech. Finally, individuals who are able to use the system most appropriately are those who are able to understand the meaning on which the symbols are based instead of just learning them by rote (Mc-Naughton & Kates, 1980).

Blissymbolics is an encouraging attempt to meet the needs of nonvocal persons who can advance beyond simple communication boards. Research with Blissymbolics (Clark, 1984; Harris-Vanderheiden, 1977; Vanderheiden, Brown, MacKenzie, Reinen, & Scheibel, 1975) indicated that this system is effective with people who were variously described as severely retarded, physically handicapped, and functioning at a 2-year-old language level.

Rebus symbols, developed as a nonoral communication system by Hurlbut, Iwata, and Green (1982), is another representational system with pictures and symbols representing either entire words or parts of words. The rebuses are of three types: concrete, relational, and abstract. *Concrete* rebuses are pictures of the object (e.g., girl's face to indicate the word *girl*). *Relational* rebuses are pictures identifying the relationship of objects in a concept (e.g., a ball in a square to indicate the word *in*). *Abstract* rebuses are symbols that stand for a word (e.g., = to indicate the word *are*). A set of 800 rebuses has been developed (Clark, Davies, & Woodcock, 1974) along with a reading system known as the Peabody Rebus Reading Program (Woodcock, Clark, & Davies, 1979).

Abstract Communication Systems   Some individuals can use an abstract communication system. Carrier (1974; 1979, Carrier & Peak, 1975) developed a nonspeech communication system known as *Non-SLIP* (Non-Speech Language Initiation Program). Based on Premack's (1970b; 1971; 1972) work with chimpanzees, Carrier's program uses various geometric shapes on tiles marked with colored tape to designate different parts of speech. As in conventional reading and writing, these shapes are placed horizontally in a response board or tray. In the initial stages of the program, the person learns to label by using 10 symbols to represent 10 environmental events. Next comes the rote sequencing program, to teach the child to arrange the geometric shapes sequentially from left to right in the response tray. Subsequent lessons, including sub-

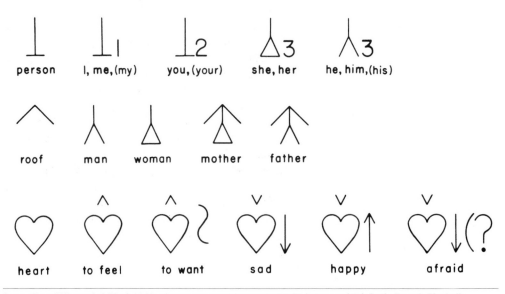

Source: From "Bliss symbols" by S. McNaughton in *Non-vocal Communication Techniques and Aids for the Severely Physically Handicapped* (pp. 95, 97), edited by G. C. Vanderheiden and K. Grilley, 1975, Baltimore: University Park Press. Reprinted by permission of PRO-ED, Inc.

Figure 6.2
Blissymbols

ject and verb selection, teach the child to build a sentence.

Carrier and his colleagues based this communication system on the semantic rules that govern the selection of symbols to represent meanings and the syntactic rules that prescribe the arrangement of symbols in a standard grammatical response. Rules of syntax are particularly significant in this approach.

Carrier (1979) reported that the Non-SLIP system is an efficient and effective approach to nonverbal training. In particular, his research showed that the system facilitates language learning; students were able to generate seven-word responses after a mean time of less than 15 hours of training (Carrier & Peak, 1975). The unique nature of the system, however, restricts the number of people with whom the individual can communicate. Therefore, the program's value ultimately depends on how easily a person can successfully transfer language skills to a more conventional system.

Language Code Systems   The third type of symbolic or aided system, the language code, combines *Morse code* and *traditional orthography*, which use symbols to represent letters in the written language. Morse code usually is used with individuals who have visual impairments as well as severe motor limitations. For these individuals, computerized communication systems that use Morse code are available. A commercially available example is *Morse WSKE II* (1989), which "incorporates a unique set of extended Morse codes . . . to minimize the cognitive load on the user" (Woltosz

& Woltosz, 1989, p. 17).

Traditional orthography, or print, would be most appropriate to use with students who are able to read. When using computers or voice output communication systems, traditional orthography is usually the system of choice (Coon & Lambert, 1985). This system can be the primary method for communication instruction or a replacement for other communication systems that may not be as effective in the natural environment. When used as a replacement system, the nonverbal person learns to communicate through one of the other aided or unaided communication systems and then switches to traditional orthography after obtaining proficiency in communicating with others (Mithaug & Liberty, 1980).

Gestural or Unaided Systems   Systems of communication that are considered gestural necessitate movement of the arms or hands. These systems do not require mechanical devices separate from the person's body. Typically these systems can be divided into natural gestures, sign language systems such as Ameslan, and educational sign systems such as Signing Exact English.

Natural Gestures   Also known as illustrative gestures (Molt & Younginger, 1988), natural gestures are physical gestures that individuals commonly use to accentuate or clarify communication (Topper, 1975). People with and without disabilities use natural gestures. Examples of natural gestures are shaking a fist, pointing, shivering, shrugging, and waving. Hamre-Nietupski et al. (1977) catalogued a list of more than 160 natural gestures often used as a form of communication.

Although the terms *natural gestures* and *sign language* are often confused, they are two different forms of communication (Bryen & Joyce, 1985; Lloyd, 1985). Natural gestures are considered prelinguistic signals without a formal structure, whereas sign language is a complete language system using symbols and rules (Bryen & Joyce, 1985; Hamre-Nietupski et al., 1977; Snell, 1987). An advantage of natural gestures is that they usually require less fine motor coordination than sign language does (Snell, 1987). But natural gestures typically are used only with highly concrete concepts and may limit the individual's expressive vocabulary (Lloyd, 1985; Miller & Allaire, 1987).

Sign Language   The most common form of nonverbal communication taught to individuals with severe impairments is *sign language* (Fristoe & Lloyd, 1978; Goodman, Wilson, & Boorstein, 1978; Mirenda & Iacono, 1990). Although signing traditionally has been associated with people who have hearing impairments, it also has been used effectively with others who have disabilities in verbal language production, such as people who have severe handicaps or autism (Horner & Budd, 1985).

American sign language (Ameslan or ASL) is a structured system of hand gestures that was developed in France. This language system contains an extensive vocabulary and its own rules, which differ from the English language system. Figure 6.3 illustrates signs for some common words and phrases.

Sign language also can be supplemented by *fingerspelling* the letters of the manual alphabet and digits from 1 to 10. Figure 6.4 illustrates the manual alphabet. The reader is referred to O'Rourke (1978) and Riekehof (1963) for information on specific techniques for teaching or learning a variety of signs and the manual alphabet, and to Fristoe and Lloyd (1978) for a compilation of signs arranged according to their frequency of occurrence in various instructional manuals.

The basic advantages of signing include: (a) its potential speed in communication, (b) its obvious portability, and (c) the fact that no skills are required in reading or spelling written symbols. Goodman et al. (1978) noted that signing was most often selected because of its convenience and its basis in an existing natural language.

Potential disadvantages include: (a) the great number of signs needed for fluent communication, (b) the limited audience of people who understand the signs (Molt & Younginger, 1988; Rotholz, Berkowitz, & Burberry, 1989), and (c) the fine motor skills required to make gestural responses (Stremel-Campbell, Cantrell, & Halle, 1977). The last point is particularly true of fingerspelling, which involves complex fine motor skills.

Educational Sign Language   Because Ameslan varies from Standard English syntax, many professionals advocate the use of educational sign systems that conform to standard English language structure. Educational sign systems have evolved as a result of the need to teach children with language impairments in the schools. These educational systems, although drawing their basic signs from ASL, parallel spoken English and therefore are useful in the classroom. According to Lloyd (1985), these systems are called *manually coded English* and include a variety of different systems such as Signed English (Bornstein, Saulnier, & Hamilton, 1983); Seeing Essential English (SEE) (Anthony, 1971); and Signing Exact English (SEE) (Gustason, Pfetzing, & Zawolkow, 1980).

Combination Gestural Systems   Although signing is one of the most versatile and widely used of the nonverbal systems (Kirschner, Algozzine, & Abbott, 1979), we still need to explore combination programs, just as many educators are doing for peo-

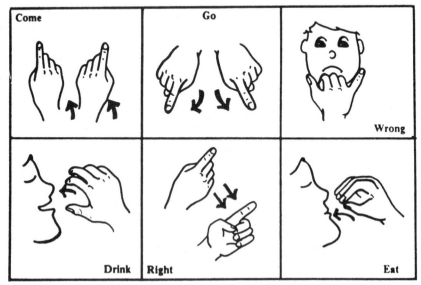

Figure 6.3
Common Signs

Source: Gallaudet College, Division of Public Services, Kendall Green, Washington, DC 20002.

Figure 6.4
Manual Alphabet

ple who are deaf. Despite the *oralist* (speech training) and *manualist* (sign training) advocates, many professionals believe that children who have hearing impairments are best served through *total communication training*, a system that combines oral elements, sign language, and finger spelling (Jago, Jago, & Hart, 1984). According to Gustason, Pfetzing & Zawolkow (1986) "Total Communication is the most used communication mode" (p. 2).

Many people who are both nonverbal and severely disabled can profit from the same type of program (Cohen, 1981; Stremel-Campbell et al., 1977). In fact, Reich (1978) found that a program combining gestures with oral elements was more effective than one solely emphasizing speech. It is also encouraging to note that sign language can result in some spontaneous verbalizations if sign language and verbal language are paired during training (Kahn, 1977). Descriptive reports (Grinnell, Detamore, & Lippke, 1976; Weller & Mahoney, 1983) also offer encouraging data on the effectiveness of using sign language and verbal language together.

SUMMARY

For a small number of children and older individuals, the acquisition of verbal communication skills presents particularly significant hurdles. Often these problems are related to sensory or motor disabilities, which may hinder development of competence and/or production. In these cases, nonverbal communication mechanisms should be entertained either as an alternative to verbal communication or as augmentative efforts. Assessments can assist in determining how best to proceed with nonverbal interventions.

A variety of nonverbal communication systems have been developed for individuals with severe disabilities. Gestural systems range from obvious natural forms of communication to the formal structures of American Sign Language. Communication boards, especially those related to computer control, can be adapted for individuals with differing disabilities and differing communication needs. Representational and abstract symbol systems have been designed for a variety of purposes and at varying levels of complexity.

Selecting the methodology and curriculum, as well as any required augmentative device, which will be most effective in developing communication in students with delayed language is a critical responsibility. Program development for functional communication can not be completed without considering all aspects of the individual's strengths and weaknesses. As Berko (1969) noted, the child with a disability is:

> . . . primarily a child is like all other children and must be approached accordingly. All too often, persons concerned with the habilitation of these children become so involved with the correction of their problems—the ways in which they differ from the average child—that they lose sight of the fact that essentially there are far more similarities than differences between these and other children, and it is these similarities that provide the key to successful habilitation (p. 268).

The teacher, therefore, is responsible for providing initial instruction in language, regardless of the method of communication chosen or whether the goal of this instruction is to develop a verbal or a nonverbal method of communication.

REFERENCES

Anthony, D. (1971). *Seeing essential English.* Anaheim, CA: Educational Services Division, Anaheim Union School District.

Baker, B. (1986, March). Using images to generate speech. *Byte,* 160–168.

Barney, L., & Landis, C. (1988). Developmental differences in communication. In J. Neisworth & S. Bagnato (Eds.), *The young exceptional child: Early development and education.* New York: Macmillan.

Berko, F. (1969). Special education for the cerebral palsied: A group language learning experience. In M. Mecham et al. (Eds.), *Communication training in childhood brain damage.* Springfield, IL: Charles C. Thomas.

Blackstone, E. (Ed.) (1987). *Augmentative communication: An introduction.* Madison, WI: Trace Research & Development.

Bliss, C. (1975). *Semantography.* Sydney, Australia: Semantography Publications.

Bolton, S., & Dashiell, S. (1989). *INCH: INteraction CHecklist for Augmentative Communication.* Wauconda, IL: Don Johnston Developmental Equipment.

Bornstein, H., Saulnier, K., & Hamilton, L. (1983). *The comprehensive signed English dictionary.* Washington, DC: Gallaudet College Press.

Brimer, R. (1990). *Students with severe disabilities: Current perspectives and practices.* Mountain View, CA: Mayfield Publishing.

Bryen, D., & Joyce, D. (1985). Language intervention with the severely handicapped: A decade of research. *Journal of Special Education, 19,* 7–39.

Carr, E., & Kologinsky, E. (1983). Acquisition of sign language by autistic children II: Spontaneity and generalization effects. *Journal of Applied Behavior Analysis, 16*(3), 297–314.

Carrier, J. (1974). Application of functional analysis and a non-speech response mode to teaching language. In L. Reynolds (Ed.), *Developing systematic procedures for training children's language* (Monograph No. 18). Washington, DC: ASHA.

Carrier, J. (1979). Perspectives on non-speech symbol systems. In R. Schiefelbusch & J. Hollis (Eds.), *Language intervention from ape to child*. Baltimore: University Park Press.

Carrier, J., & Hollis, J. (1975). Research implications for communication deficiencies. *Exceptional Children, 41,* 405–412.

Carrier, J., & Peak, T. (1975). *Non-speech language initiation program.* Lawrence, KS: H & H Enterprises.

Carrow-Woolfolk, E. (1988). *Theory, assessment and intervention in language disorders: An integrative approach.* Orlando: Grune & Stratton.

Chapman, R., & Miller, J. (1980). In R. Schiefelbusch (Ed.), *Nonspeech language and communication: Analysis and intervention.* Baltimore: University Park Press.

Chomsky, N. (1957). *Syntactic structures.* The Hague, Netherlands: Mouton.

Clark, C. (1984). A close look at the standard rebus system and Blissymbolics. *Journal of the Association for Persons with Severe Handicaps, 9,* 37–48.

Clark, C., Davies, C., & Woodcock, R. (1974). *Standard rebus glossary.* Circle Pines, MN: American Guidance Service.

Cohen, M. (1981). Development of language behavior in an autistic child using total communication. *Exceptional Children, 47,* 374–379.

Cole, M., & Cole, J. (1981). *Effective intervention with the language impaired child.* Rockville, MD: Aspen.

Coon, C., & Lambert, H. (1985). A communication skills learning and improvement program. *Communication Outlook, 7,* 5–6.

Detamore, K., & Lippke, B. (1980). Handicapped students learn language skills with communication boards. *Teaching Exceptional Children, 12,* 104–106.

Fristoe, M., & Lloyd, L. (1978). A survey of the use of non-speech systems with the severely communication impaired. *Mental Retardation, 16,* 99–103.

Gardner, R., & Gardner, B. (1969). Teaching sign language to a chimp. *Science, 165,* 664–672.

Goodman, L., Wilson, P., & Boorstein, H. (1978). Results of a national survey of sign language programs in special education. *Mental Retardation, 16,* 104–106.

Greer, J., Anderson, R., & Davis, T. (1976). Developing functional language in the severely retarded using a standardized vocabulary. In R. Anderson & J. Greer (Eds.), *Educating the severely and profoundly retarded.* Baltimore: University Park Press.

Grinnell, M., Detamore, K., & Lippke, B. (1976). Sign it successful: Manual English encourages expressive communication. *Teaching Exceptional Children, 8,* 123–124.

Guess, D., Sailor, W., & Baer, D. (1977). A behavioral-remedial approach to language training for the severely handicapped. In E. Sontag, J. Smith, & N. Certo (Eds.), *Educational programming for the severely and profoundly handicapped.* Reston, VA: Council for Exceptional Children, Division on Mental Retardation.

Guralnick, M. (1979, April). *Interdisciplinary basis of effective language intervention programs.* Paper presented at 57th Annual Council for Exceptional Children Convention, Dallas.

Gustason, G., Pfetzing, D., & Zawolkow, E. (1980). *Signing exact English* (3rd ed.). Los Alamitos, CA: Modern Signs Press.

Gustason, G., Pfetzing, D., & Zawolkow, E. (1986). For your information. *Signing exact English: The system that matches signs to English words.* Los Alamitos, CA: Modern Signs Press.

Halle, J. (1987). Teaching language in the natural environment: An analysis of spontaneity. *The Journal of the Association for Persons With Severe Handicaps, 12*(1), 28–37.

Hamre-Nietupski, S., Nietupski, J., & Rathe, T. (1986). Letting the data do the talking: Selecting the appropriate nonverbal communication system for severely handicapped students. *Teaching Exceptional Children,* Winter, 130–134.

Hamre-Nietupski, S., Stoll, A., Holtz, K., Fullerton, P., Ryan-Flottum, M., & Brown, L. (1977). Curricular strategies for teaching selected non-verbal communication skills to non-verbal and verbal severely handicapped students. In L. Brown, J. Nietupski, S. Lyon, S. Hamre-Nietupski, T. Crowner, & L. Gruenewald (Eds.), *Curricular strategies for teaching functional object use, nonverbal communication, problem solving, and mealtime skills to severely handicapped students* (Vol. 7, Part. 1). Madison: University of Wisconsin and Madison Metropolitan School District.

Harris-Vanderheiden, D. (1977). Blissymbols and the mentally retarded. In G. Vanderheiden & K. Grilley (Eds.), *Non-vocal communication techniques and aids for the severely physically handicapped.* Baltimore: University Park Press.

Harris-Vanderheiden, D., & Vanderheiden, G. (1977). Basic considerations in the development of communicative and interactive skills for non-vocal severely handicapped children. In E. Sontag, J. Smith, & N. Certo (Eds.), *Educational programming for the severely and profoundly handicapped.* Reston,

VA: Council for Exceptional Children, Division on Mental Retardation.

Horner, R., & Budd, C. (1985). Acquisition of manual sign use: Collateral reduction of maladaptive behavior, and factors limiting generalization. *Education and Training of the Mentally Retarded, 20,* 39–47.

Hurlbut, B., Iwata, B., & Green, J. (1982). Nonvocal language acquisition in adolescents with severe physical disabilities: Blissymbol versus iconic stimulus formats. *Journal of Applied Behavior Analysis, 15,* 241–258.

Jago, J., Jago, A., & Hart, M. (1984). An evaluation of the total communication approach for teaching language skills to developmentally delayed preschool children. *Education and Training of the Mentally Retarded, 19,* 175–182.

Johnson, J. (1986). *Self-Talk: Communication boards for children and adults.* Tucson, AZ: Communication Skill Builders.

Jones, T. (1980). Is it necessary to decide whether to use a non-oral communication system with retarded children? *Education and Training of the Mentally Retarded, 15,* 157–160.

Kaczmarek, L. (1990). Teaching spontaneous language to individuals with severe handicaps: A matrix model. *The Journal of the Association for Persons With Severe Handicaps, 15,* 160–169.

Kahn, J. (1977). A comparison of manual and oral language training with mute retarded children. *Mental Retardation, 15,* 21–23.

Karlan, G., & Lloyd, L. (1983). Considerations in the planning of communication intervention: Selecting a lexicon. *The Journal of the Association for Persons With Severe Handicaps, 8*(2), 13–25.

Kellogg, W. (1931). Humanizing the ape. *Psychology Review, 38,* 160–176. [Reprinted in R. Schiefelbusch & J. Hollis (Eds.) (1979). *Language intervention from ape to child.* Baltimore: University Park Press.]

Kirschner, A., Algozzine, B., & Abbott, T. (1979). Manual communication systems: A comparison and its implications. *Education and Training of the Mentally Retarded, 14,* 5–10.

Knox, M. (1983). Changes in the frequency of language use by Down's syndrome children interacting with nonretarded peers. *Education and Training of the Mentally Retarded, 18,* 185–190.

Kymissis, E., & Poulson, C. (1990). The history of imitation in learning theory: The language acquisition process. *Journal of the Experimental Analysis of Behavior, 54,* 113–127.

Lahey, M. (1988). *Language disorders and language development.* New York: Macmillan.

Lloyd, L. (1985). Comments on terminology. *Augmentative and Alternative Communication, 1,* 95–97.

MacDonald, J. (1979, April). *Parent-child interaction: An environmental approach to language assessment.* Paper presented to 57th Annual Council for Exceptional Children convention, Dallas.

MacDonald, J., & Gillette, Y. (1985). Taking turns: Teaching communication to your child. *Exceptional Parent, 15,* 49–52.

MacDonald, J., & Gillette, Y. (1986). Communicating with persons with severe handicaps: Roles of parents and professionals. *The Journal of The Association for Persons with Severe Handicaps, 11,* 255–265.

Mahoney, G. (1975). Ethological approach to delayed language acquisition. *American Journal on Mental Deficiency, 80,* 139–148.

McCormick, L. (1986). Keeping up with language intervention trends. *Teaching Exceptional Children,* Winter, 123–129.

McCormick, L., & Elder, P. (1978). Instructional strategies for severely language deficient children. *Education and Training of the Mentally Retarded, 13,* 29–36.

McNaughton, S. (1977). Blissymbols. In G. Vanderheiden & K. Grilley (Eds.), *Non-vocal communication techniques and aids for the severely physically handicapped.* Baltimore: University Park Press.

McNaughton, S., & Kates, B. (1980). The application of Blissymbolics. In R. Schiefelbusch (Ed.), *Nonspeech language and communication: Analysis and interventions.* Baltimore: University Park Press.

Michaelis, C. (1978). Communication with the severely and profoundly handicapped: A psycholinguistic approach. *Mental Retardation, 16,* 346–349.

Miller, J., & Allaire, J. (1987). Augmentative communication. In M. Snell (Ed.), *Systematic instruction of persons with severe handicaps.* Columbus, OH: Charles E. Merrill Publishing.

Miller, J., & Yoder, D. (1974). An ontogenetic language teaching strategy for retarded children. In R. Schiefelbusch & L. Lloyd (Eds.), *Language perspectives: Acquisition, retardation, and intervention.* Baltimore: University Park Press.

Mirenda, P., & Iacono, T. (1990). Communication options for persons with severe and profound disabilities: State of the art and future directions. *The Journal of the Association for Persons with Severe Handicaps, 15,* 3–21.

Mithaug, D., & Liberty, S. (1980). Word discrimination training to improve the communication skills of a severely retarded, non-vocal woman: A case study. *Education and Treatment of Children, 3,* 1–12.

Moerk, E. (1977). Processes and products of imitation: Additional evidence that imitation is progressive. *Journal of Psycholinguistics Research, 6,* 219–230.

Molt, L., & Younginger, K. (1988). Language instruction. In L. Sternberg, *Educating students with severe or profound handicaps* (2nd ed.). Rockville, MD: Aspen.

Morse WSKE II. (1989). Lancaster, CA: Words+.

Musselwhite, C., & St. Louis, K. (1982). *Communication programming for the severely handicapped: Vocal and non-vocal strategies.* San Diego, CA: College Hill Press.

Musselwhite, C., & St. Louis, K. (1988). *Communication programming for persons with severe handicaps: Vocal and augmentative strategies* (2nd ed.). Boston: College Hill Press.

Myles, B. S., Simpson, R. L., & Smith. S. M. (1996). Impact of facilitated communication combined with direct instruction on academic performance of the individuals with autism. *Focus on Autism and Other Developmental Disabilities, 11,* 37–44.

Nietupski, J., & Hamre-Nietupski, S. (1979). Teaching auxiliary communication skills to severely handicapped students. *American Association for the Education of the Severely/Profoundly Handicapped Review, 4,* 107–124.

Oller, D., & Seibert, J. (1988). Babbling of prelinguistic mentally retarded children. *American Journal on Mental Retardation, 92*(4), 369–375.

Opticommunicator. (1990). Milwaukee, WI: Crestwood Co.

O'Rourke, T. (Ed.). (1978). *A basic course in manual communication.* Silver Spring, MD: National Association for the Deaf.

Owens, R. (1988). *Language development: An introduction (2nd ed.).* Columbus, OH: Charles E. Merrill Publishing.

Pecyna, P. (1988). Rebus symbol communication training with a severely handicapped preschool child: A case study. *Language, Speech, and Hearing Services in Schools, 19,* 128–143.

PRC Light Talker. (1990). Wooster, OH: Prentke Romich Co.

PRC Touch Talker. (1990). Wooster, OH: Prentke Romich Co.

Premack, D. (1970a). A functional analysis of language. *Journal of Experimental Analysis of Behavior, 14,* 107–125.

Premack, D. (1970b). The education of Sarah. *Psychology Today, 4,* 54–59.

Premack, D. (1971). Language in chimpanzee? *Science, 172,* 808–822.

Premack, D. (1972). Teaching language to an ape. *Scientific American, 227,* 808–822.

Premack, D. (1986). *Gavagai! or the future of the animal language controversy.* Cambridge, MA: MIT Press.

Reich, R. (1978). Gestural facilitation of expressive language in moderately/severely retarded preschoolers. *Mental Retardation, 16,* 113–117.

Reichle, J., & Karlan, G. (1985). The selection of an augmentative system in communication intervention: A critique of decision rules. *Journal of the Association for Persons With Severe Handicaps, 10,* 146–156.

Rice, M. (1983). Contemporary accounts of the cognition/language relationship: Implications for speech-language clinicians. *Journal of Speech and Hearing Disorders, 48,* 347–359.

Riekehof, L. (1963). *Talk to the deaf.* Springfield, MO: Gospel Publishing House.

Rittenhouse, R., & Myers, J. (1985). Teaching functional sign language to severely delayed children. *Teaching Exceptional Children,* Fall, 62–67.

Robinett, J. (1977). *Communication boards for institutionalized non-verbal mentally retarded.* Unpublished manuscript, Lynchburg College, Lynchburg, VA.

Romski, M., Sevick, R., & Pate, J. (1988). Establishment of symbolic communication in persons with severe retardation. *Journal of Speech and Hearing Disorders, 53,* 94–107.

Rotholz, D., Berkowitz, S., & Burberry, J. (1989). Functionality of two modes of communication in the community by students with developmental disabilities: A comparison of signing and communication book. *The Journal of the Association for Persons with Severe Handicaps, 14,* 227–233.

Sailor, W., Guess, D., Goetz, L., Schuler, A., Utley, B., & Baldwin, M. (1980). Language and severely handicapped persons: Deciding what to teach to whom. In W. Sailor, B. Wilcox, & L. Brown (Eds.), *Methods of instruction for severely handicapped students.* Baltimore: Paul H. Brookes Publishers.

Sailor, W., Wilcox, B., & Brown, L. (Eds.). (1980). *Methods of instruction for severely handicapped students.* Baltimore: Paul H. Brookes Publishers.

Schiefelbusch, R., & Hollis, J. (Eds.). (1979). *Language intervention from ape to child.* Baltimore: University Park Press.

Schiefelbusch, R., & Lloyd, L. (1988). *Language perspectives II: Acquisition, retardation and intervention.* Austin, TX: Pro-Ed.

Siegel-Causey, E., & Guess, D. (1989). *Enhancing nonsymbolic communication interactions among learners with severe disabilities.* Baltimore: Paul H. Brookes Publishers.

Silverman, F. (1989). *Communication for the speechless* (2nd ed.). Englewood Cliffs, NJ: Prentice Hall.

Skinner, B. (1957). *Verbal behavior.* New York: Appleton-Century-Crofts.

Smith, L., & von Tetzchner, S. (1986). Communicative, sensorimotor, and language skills of young children with Down syndrome. *American Journal of Mental Deficiency, 91*, 57–66.

Snell, M. (Ed.). (1987). *Systematic instruction of persons with severe handicaps* (3rd ed.). Columbus, OH: Charles E. Merrill Publishing.

Stemmer, N. (1990). Skinner's verbal behavior, Chomsky's review, and mentalism. *Journal of the Experimental Analysis of Behavior, 54*, 307–315.

Sternberg, L. (1982). Communication instruction. In L. Sternberg & G. Adams. (1982). *Educating severely and profoundly handicapped students.* Rockville, MD: Aspen.

Sternberg, L. (1988). *Educating students with severe or profound handicaps* (2nd ed.). Rockville, MD: Aspen.

Sternberg, L., & McNerney, C. (1988). Prelanguage communication instruction. In L. Sternberg, *Educating students with severe or profound handicaps* (2nd ed.). Rockville, MD: Aspen.

Sternberg, L., McNerney, C., & Pegnatore, L. (1987). Developing primitive signalling behavior of students with profound mental retardation, *Mental Retardation, 25*, 13–20.

Sternberg, L., Pegnatore, L., & Hill, C. (1983). Establishing interactive communication behaviors with profoundly mentally handicapped students. *The Journal of The Association for the Severely Handicapped, 8*(2), 39–46.

Stillman, R., & Siegel-Causey, E. (1989). Introduction to nonsymbolic communication. In E. Siegel-Causey & D. Guess (1989), *Enhancing nonsymbolic communication interactions among learners with severe disabilities.* Baltimore: Paul H. Brookes Publishers.

Stremel-Campbell, K., Cantrell, D., & Halle, J. (1977). Manual signing as a language system and as a speech imitation for the non-verbal severely handicapped student. In E. Sontag, J. Smith, & N. Certo (Eds.), *Educational programming for the severely and profoundly handicapped.* Reston, VA: Council for Exceptional Children, Division on Mental Retardation.

Switzky, H., Rotatori, A., Miller, T., & Freagon, S. (1979). The developmental model and its implications for assessment and instruction for the severely/profoundly handicapped. *Mental Retardation, 17*, 167–170.

Terrace, H. (1979). *Nim.* New York: Alfred A. Knopf.

Topper, S. (1975). Gesture language for a non-verbal severely retarded male. *Mental Retardation, 13*, 30.

Valletutti, P. (1989). The nature and development of nonverbal communication. In P. Valletutti, M. McKnight-Taylor, & A. Hoffnung, *Facilitating communication in young children with handicapping conditions: A guide for special educators.* Boston: Little, Brown.

Van Dijk, J. (1965a). The first steps of the deaf/blind child towards language. *Proceedings of the conference on the deaf/blind, Refsnes, Denmark.* Boston: Perkins School for the Blind.

Van Dijk, J. (1965b). Motor development in the education of deaf/blind children. *Proceedings of the conference on the deaf/blind, Refsnes, Denmark.* Boston: Perkins School for the Blind.

Vanderheiden, D., Brown, W., MacKenzie, P., Reinen, S., & Scheibel, G. (1975). Symbol communication for the mentally handicapped. *Mental Retardation, 18*, 34–37.

Vanderheiden, G., & Grilley, K. (1977). *Non-vocal communication techniques and aids for the severely physically handicapped.* Baltimore: University Park Press.

Warren, S., & Kaiser, A. (1988). Research in early language intervention. In S. Odom & M. Karnes, *Early intervention for infants and children with handicaps: An empirical base.* Baltimore: Paul H. Brookes Publishing.

Weller, E., & Mahoney, G. (1983). A comparison of oral and total communication modalities on the language training of young mentally handicapped children. *Education and Training of the Mentally Retarded, 18*, 103–110.

Wendt, E., Sprague, M., & Marquis, I. (1975). Communication without speech. *Teaching Exceptional Children, 8*, 38–42.

Woodcock, R., Clark, C., & Davies, C. (1979). *Peabody rebus reading program.* Circle Pines, MN: American Guidance Service.

Woltosz, W., & Woltosz, G. (1989). *How to select a communication aid.* Lancaster, CA: Words+.

Wulz, S., Myers, S., Klein, M., Hall, M., & Waldo, L. (1982). Unobtrusive training: A home-centered model for communication training. *Journal of the Association for the Severely Handicapped, 7*, 36–47.

Yerkes, R., & Nissen, H. (1939). Pre-linguistic sign behavior in chimpanzees. *Science, 89*, 585–587.

7

Oral Language Skills

S ome students with severe language problems never develop verbal skills sufficient for adequate communication and must resort to an augmentative communication system. Others, while not requiring augmentative communication, need extensive intervention to develop limited language. For the most part, however, children spontaneously acquire initial language. The language problems these children experience require the refinement of oral language skills..

Regular and special education teachers frequently have overlooked oral language skills, for several reasons.

1. One traditionally cited reason for this oversight is that oral language is difficult to break into manageable presentations (Morley, 1972).
2. A more probable reason is that regular and special education teachers have assumed that children with oral language problems would "outgrow" the problems, or that a speech/language therapist would be available to provide intervention services. This, plus the fact that many teachers, both in regular and special education, do not receive training in how to deal with oral language problems, has often resulted in limited intervention efforts. The challenge for teacher education programs is to include sufficient amounts of content related to oral language development to adequately prepare teachers to provide intervention.
3. Another reason for the limited attention given to oral language is the heavy emphasis placed on academic skill development. Reading, writing, and arithmetic—commonly referred to as the three R's—have received more emphasis than any other instructional areas, including oral language. The educational reform of the 1980s reemphasized the development of these basic skills (Smith, 1990). With so much focus in these curricular areas, teachers may have little time remaining for domains such as oral language.
4. Most children develop oral language spontaneously and to a level that does not cause parental concern.
5. Parents and teachers often overlook children with oral language difficulties, assuming that the children are simply "shy."
6. The absence of a record of oral language can make diagnosis of a student's problems difficult.

Regardless of the reasons for the limited attention given to oral language in schools, programs for oral language refinement seem to be changing. Several trends have highlighted the importance of oral language skills, including the emphasis on electronic media and technology, interpersonal skills, long-distance communications, various teaching and learning situations, and new vocational opportunities.

In addition to these encouraging trends, authorities have begun to recognize the relationships between oral language and academic skills (Wesson, Otis-Wilborn, Hasbrouck, & Tindal, 1989; Santos, 1989; Mann, Cowin, & Schoenheimer, 1989; Rice, Buhr, & Nemeth, 1990). For example, Eisenson (1990) stated, "Children who are significantly delayed in establishing a vocabulary and learning the grammar (syntax) for the production of their oral code are also likely to be at high risk for learning to read" (p. 419). Scarborough and Dobrich (1990) followed four cases of early language delay over a 3-year period. Though the subjects' early problems in syntax, phonology, and lexical semantics gave way to normal or near normal language skills by age 5, all but one of the children developed severe reading disabilities 3 years later. In addition to the negative effect of poor language on reading skills, a relationship may exist between reading and understanding spoken language. Mann et al. (1989) found that problems in phonological processing skills present in students with reading problems correlated with poor comprehension skills.

These research findings and conclusions have not gone unnoticed. Schools have initiated oral language instructional programs and have begun to address the development of oral communication in students. These programs are beneficial to all students but are particularly helpful to students with disabilities who already suffer from other problems.

As discussed in chapter 1, language has several major functions, and oral language is a major component in many of these functions. Halliday (1975) identified the seven functions as:

1. *Instrumental:* to satisfy material (physical) needs.
2. *Regulatory:* to gain control over others' behavior.
3. *Interactional:* to maintain social contact with significant others.
4. *Personal:* to serve as a vehicle of self-awareness and experiences.
5. *Heuristic:* to serve as a basis for exploring the environment.
6. *Imaginative:* to establish an environment in one's own image.
7. *Informative:* to convey specific and varied information.

Because oral language is such an integral component of language, and therefore human functioning, it is amazing that schools often have overlooked or downplayed instruction in this area. If teachers are to remedy this oversight, they must view oral language as a repertoire of specific and identifiable skills, all related to the five linguistic components of phonology, morphology, syntax, semantics, and pragmatics.

While reading this chapter, you should keep in mind that children have very different needs regarding oral language instruction. Children with severe disabilities, for example, often need continued intervention that focuses on initial language development (Kleppe, Katayama, Shipley, & Foushee, 1990; Byrne, Abbeduto, & Brooks, 1990; Snell, 1989). For some of these children, augmentative communication mechanisms must be developed (see chapter 5). Children who are from different cultural backgrounds or who are bilingual need assistance in developing competence in standard English abilities, in concert with, rather than at the expense of, their native language. Therefore, as discussed in chapter 3, they need specific kinds of language intervention programs to increase their proficiency in English.

Children with mild disabilities also frequently experience oral language disorders. In one study, Gibbs and Cooper (1989) found that 90.5 percent of children classified as learning disabled had some sort of language disorder. Language disorders also are a common characteristic of children with mild mental retardation and behavior problems, as well as those with sensory deficits (Epstein, Polloway, Patton, & Foley, 1989; Smith, Price, & Marsh, 1986; Patton, Beirne-Smith, & Payne, 1989). For children with mild disabilities who have developed initial language skills, development and refinement activities are in order. These children need to improve their oral language abilities so they can maximize their opportunities for assimilation in society.

Finally, all students, even those without disabilities, need a certain competence level in oral language in order to achieve success in reading and writing, social interactions, and emotional development. Oral language instructional programs can benefit all students.

NATURE OF ORAL LANGUAGE

Oral language can be divided into two major components: receptive and expressive. Receptive oral language refers to the ability to understand spoken language. The primary skill involved in this receptive process is "listening," or decoding. *Listening* has no single, simple definition (Burns & Richgels, 1988); it is a complex physiological process that goes well beyond simply "hearing" spoken language. Listening begins with sensing sounds, and it involves the process of determining meaning from communication (Hammill & Bartel, 1990).

Listening requires receiving and interpreting spoken language. It has a myriad of components, including auditory acuity, attention to auditory stimulation, sound discrimination, memory, and listening comprehension. Most students have little or no difficulty with their listening skills; they hear what is said, interpret the message accurately, and respond accordingly. But some students have listening deficits, and these students need assistance with auditory acuity, attention, memory, or comprehension.

The primary behavior involved in expressive oral language is *speaking*. Just as in listening, speaking is not a single process; it is more than expressing words orally. Speaking "involves a complex process of identifying ideas or feelings, formulating these into an appropriate and grammatical sequence of words and sentences, and finally coordinating the speech-producing mechanisms of human anatomy to produce speech sounds, intonation, pitch, stress, and juncture" (Hammill & Bartel, 1990, p. 33).

Speaking can be simply defined as the encoding of thoughts into meaningful intelligible utterances, and expressing those thoughts in a manner that *other people* can receive and interpret. The act of speaking is composed of a wide range of expressive processes, from the initial intention to communicate to the organization of specific speech utterances. Think about how you express yourself through spoken language. You know what you want to say, and you say it. Although that may seem like a simple process, it is actually quite complex. First, you develop an intent to speak; you want to express something in words. You formulate what you want to say, encode that into oral language, and move the appropriate muscles to produce specific sounds.

Although the process is indeed complex, many times you speak without even consciously thinking of the exact words you want to say. Routine conversation becomes so automated for many people that it occurs with limited conscious effort. Unfortunately, for others, even simple oral expression proves difficult. If students have these problems, teachers should assess what skills the learners need assistance with and develop interventions to facilitate improvement.

Hammill and Bartel (1990) have schematically depicted the oral language process, and it is shown in Figure 7.1. The figure readily reveals the complex nature of oral language. Although talking and listening are often taken for granted, the whole process requires a high level of cognitive functioning. An analogy illustrating the complexity of oral language is seen in people with mental retardation. Though many people with profound mental retardation are capable of ambulation, few have acceptable oral language skills. Individuals who have less severe levels of mental retardation still commonly have ambulation, but oral language is lacking in a large number. This reveals the higher level of complexity of oral language than ambulation (Smith, Price, & Marsh, 1986).

ASSESSING ORAL LANGUAGE SKILLS

As a result of the complexity of oral language, problems are frequently present in school-age children regardless of whether they have been identified as having disabilities. Although oral language is not as easily measureable as other skills (Wesson et al., 1989) such as reading, writing, math, or spelling, it must be assessed to determine the child's functioning level. When they have assessment data, teachers are better able to determine if students need intervention in listening and speaking skills and, if so, how to provide that intervention. Accurate assessment of oral language requires knowledge of how skills develop and familiarity with both formal and informal approaches to diagnosis. Lack of valid assessment data in the area of oral language could lead to inappropriate language intervention, or no intervention at all. In either case the end result could be children with deficient oral language skills.

Assessment of oral language skills has not received the attention given to assessment of key academic areas. Many tests are available to evaluate a child's functioning level in reading, math, and even spelling, but limited assessment procedures exist for oral language. Reasons for the abundance of assessment materials in academic areas include: (a) the specific content for assessment purposes, (b) general agreement regarding specific skills related to these academic areas, and (c) overall emphasis on programming in these areas.

PURPOSES OF ASSESSING ORAL LANGUAGE

Several steps should be completed prior to specific oral language assessment. Miller (1978) suggested:

— determining why you are assessing the child's language.
— determining what specific areas you are going to assess.
— determining how the assessment will be completed.

Oral language functioning is assessed for several reasons. Schiefelbusch and Mc-Cormick (1984) described three purposes: screening, baseline determination, and detecting changes.

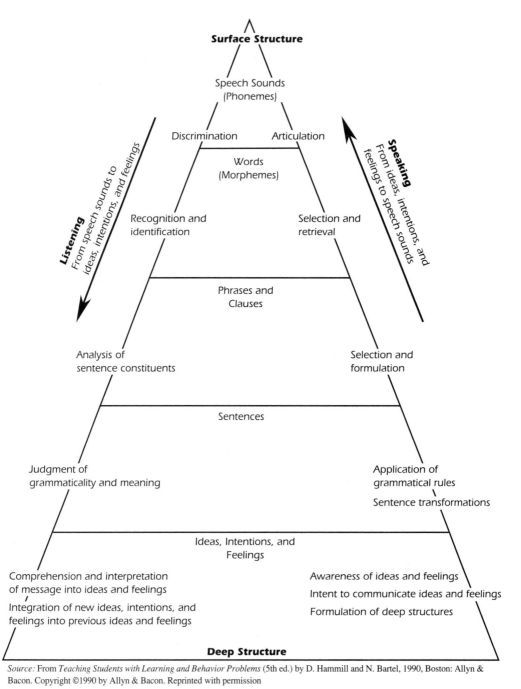

Source: From *Teaching Students with Learning and Behavior Problems* (5th ed.) by D. Hammill and N. Bartel, 1990, Boston: Allyn & Bacon. Copyright ©1990 by Allyn & Bacon. Reprinted with permission

Figure 7.1
Oral Language Process

1. *Screening* is used to determine which children need additional language assessment. Probably the best screening information related to language functioning comes from parents, health care workers, counselors, teachers, and others who interact verbally with the child on a routine basis. Screening enables school personnel to determine which children need additional, more in-depth language assessment. If the screening suggests that additional assessments are necessary, speech therapists and other language specialists may become involved in a more detailed evaluation of the child.

2. *Establishing a baseline functioning level* for children is done to determine the child's current language functioning level, the extent of the language problem, and the specific nature of any existing problem.

3. Assessment is useful in *determining any changes* that result from an intervention program. Without this capacity, school personnel are unable to accurately determine the efficacy of individual intervention programs. This could result in prolonged intervention that is ineffective.

Hammill and Bartel (1990) described three goals of language assessment:

1. To determine if the student has functional communication skills in a variety of contexts. Students need to be able to communicate effectively in a variety of settings. At a minimum, these include school, home, and community. Being able to communicate only in a school setting will not enable the student to be functional in other environments.

2. To determine if the student can communicate functionally with a variety of audiences. Students must interact with peers, teachers, parents, family members, and others in the environment; they must possess the ability to communicate effectively with all groups.

3. To determine if the student's communication skills reveal evidence of metacommunication, or the ability to talk about communication.

ORAL LANGUAGE ASSESSMENT PROCESS

When assessing oral language skills, the first step is to obtain the child's case history. This should include information about the child's language skills, as well as data on academic, social, and emotional functioning. Following the compilation of a case history, reliable, valid assessment information specifically related to language skills should be obtained. An analysis of data from these two sources leads to a determination of language strengths and weaknesses (Wiig, 1990) and, possibly, specific intervention techniques.

Evaluation of language functioning should occur in natural settings (Taenzer, Cermak, & Hanlon, 1981). Evaluating a child's language skills in only a structured testing situation may not yield valid results. Allen (1989) suggested that professionals who conduct language evaluations remember that spontaneous language during play situations may provide extremely valuable information and augment more formal assessment strategies.

FORMAL ASSESSMENT OF ORAL LANGUAGE

Oral language can be assessed using formal and informal procedures. "Formal assessment procedures employ tightly organized test materials, structured test situations, and group-based comparisons" (Guerin & Maier, 1983, p. 7). Standardized, norm-referenced tests are formal tests.

Although not as many formal assessment instruments are available to test oral language as there are in other areas, several measures are in common use. Some of these focus on speech, such as articulation and grammatical morphemes; others assess receptive language, including listening and word meanings. Table 7.1 summarizes some of the commonly used formal tests for speaking and listening.

Formal assessment of listening skills presents several unique problems because of the many different definitions of "listening." Because of this lack of conformity, listening tests measure different skills (Burns & Richgels, 1988). Some listening tests measure vocabulary; others simply assess if the child understands the spoken materials. Therefore, teachers have to be careful to not compare assessment results that have been obtained from different tests, because of the variations of components included in listening tests.

Most tests of listening skills follow one of five approaches (Burns & Richgels, 1988):

1. Total recall.
2. Following directions.
3. Multiple choice.
4. Free recall.
5. Informal reading inventory.

Table 7.2 summarizes each of these different approaches.

INFORMAL ASSESSMENT OF ORAL LANGUAGE

Many teachers use formal assessment instruments to determine the student's initial diagnosis and eligibility. Following the determination that a student is eligible for language intervention programming, teachers collect additional information using informal means. Often, data obtained from informal assessment procedures are more directly linked to programming activities than the scores obtained from formal, norm-referenced testing. This is because informal assessment typically occurs in a natural setting rather than one structured just for the evaluation, and the activities used to generate informal assessment data are flexible rather than structured and ordered (Guerin & Maier, 1983). Information obtained through informal assessment enables teachers to further specify students' strengths and weaknesses and, therefore, provide more germane information for intervention.

Table 7.1
Summary of Formal Tests for Speaking and Listening

Name (Author of Test)	Aspect of Language Measured	Target Population	Purported Purpose	Comments
Bankson Language Screening Test (Bankson, 1990)	Semantic knowledge, morphological and syntactic rules, visual perception, and auditory perception	Ages 4 to 8	To screen aspects of language and visual skill areas	Standardized on representative U.S. sample
Carrow Elicited Language Inventory (Carrow-Woolfolk, 1985)	Expressive language in elicited situation (emphasis on syntax)	Ages 3 to 8	To assess a child's productive control of grammar	52 stimulus sentences and phrases are used to elicit responses; child's responses are taped, requiring phonemic transcription; analysis system covers 12 grammatical categories and 5 error types; provides for in-depth analysis of child's errors on verbs.
Clinical Evaluation of Language Function (CELF) (Wiig & Semel, 1987) (Screening aspect below may be used separately.)	Comprehensive test of language functions	Kindergarten through grade 12	To provide an analysis of student's ability to understand and use language in functional ways	Comprehensive test of receptive and expressive ability in language content, form, and use; includes screening tests and diagnostic battery
Clinical Evaluation of Language Function (CELF) Screening Tests: Elementary Level and Advanced Level (Semel & Wiig, 1980)	Language comprehension and expression	Elementary Level: grades K through 5; Advanced Level: grades 5 through 12	To screen aspects of comprehension and production	Each level has two sections requiring verbal understanding and verbal or motor responses in gamelike format
Goldman-Fristoe Test of Articulation (Goldman & Fristoe, 1972)	Articulation	Above age 2	To assess child's ability to produce speech sounds	Attractively illustrated; well standardized; takes about 30 minutes to administer; measures initial, medial, and final speech sound production in words and sentences
"Let's Talk" Inventory for Adolescents (Wiig, 1982)	Language use: context and function	Age 9 to young adulthood	To probe speech-act formulation ability in relation to communication function and intent and to audience	Measures speech-act formulation and association in ritualizing, informing, controlling, and feeling functions; uses pictorial situational-audience contexts

Table 7.1
continued

Name (Author of Test)	Aspect of Language Measured	Target Population	Purported Purpose	Comments
Peabody Picture Vocabulary Test (Dunn & Dunn, 1981)	Receptive vocabulary of standard English	Mental ages 2 to adult	To derive an IQ score	Test is untimed and well standardized; child points to appropriate picture on plate in response to stimulus word spoken by examiner; may be given by teacher; takes 10–20 minutes
Test for Auditory Comprehension of Language (Carrow-Woolfolk, 1985)	Word meanings, grammatical morphemes, and the understanding of complex sentence constructions	Ages 3 to 10	To evaluate receptive language	Newest revision; well done
Test of Adolescent Language–2 (TOAL–2) (Hammill, V. Brown, Larsen & Wiederholt, 1987)	Receptive and expressive aspects of vocabulary and syntax	Ages 11 to 18½	To give indication of student's overall strengths and weaknesses in each area tapped	Also measures reading and writing abilities; composite scores are reliable mostly in the .90s
Test of Early Language Development (Hresko, Reid & Hammill, 1990)	Content and form in both receptive and expressive modes	Ages 3 to 7	To indicate screening and documenting problem	Short (36 items); uses Stanford-Binet format; has basals and ceilings to facilitate administration
Test of Language Development–2: Intermediate (Hammill & Newcomer, 1988)	Receptive and expressive aspects of vocabulary and syntax	Ages 8 to 13	To give indication of child's overall strengths and weaknesses in each area tapped	Short and easy to administer; 6 principal subtests measure receptive and expressive aspects of vocabulary and grammar; subtests (generally internally consistent and stable) correlate with criterion tests, with r's mostly in .70s
Token Test for Children (DiSimone, 1978)	Teach perceptive research language	Ages 3 to 12	To screen for receptive language dysfunction or rule out language impairment	Uses small geometric shapes; child follows directions given by examiner
Utah Test of Language Development (UTLD) (Mecham, 1989)	Expressive and receptive language, aspects of conceptual development	Ages 2 to 15	To derive overall picture of child's language development as compared with peers	Consists of 2 sections: Production and Comprehension; Language Quotients reported; normative sample representative of U.S. population

Source: From *Teaching Students with Learning and Behavior Problems* (5th ed., pp. 61–63) by D. Hammill and N. Bartel, 1990, Boston: Allyn & Bacon. Copyright ©1990 by Allyn & Bacon. Reprinted with permission.

Update

Approaches to Informal Assessment

In addition to the other informal assessment tools discussed in text, a variety of other informal measures complement the assessment process. These include:

- *Curriculum-Based Assessment:* approaches that are based on observing and recording students' performance within the context of the school curriculum in order to determine the instructional mismatch that may occur.
- *Curriculum-Based Measurement:* assessment that focuses on ongoing evaluation of student progress toward academic goals and modifications made in instructional plans to facilitate reaching the goals.
- *Error Analysis:* assessment focused on the identification of response patterns in student work samples as a basis for designing instructional programs.
- *Academic Probes:* measurement techniques that observe specific academic behaviors within a time sample in order to assess the acquisition, fluency, and maintenance of a specific skill.
- *Portfolio Assessment:* an approach to authentic assessment in which documentation is provided of the experiences and achievements of students as a basis for demonstration of the knowledge they have achieved in a particular area.

Table 7.2
Approaches Used to Assess Listening Skills

Approach	Description
Rote Recall	• Most basic assessment approach • Students recall information presented orally • Requires students to repeat digits, words, or sentences
Following Directions	• Assesses ability to listen and follow a series of verbal directions • Demands more than rote recall • Requires integration of several skills
Multiple Choice	• Uses multiple-choice responses • Frequently used in group assessment
Free Recall	• Examiners read passages orally • Student must retell story • Closely resembles listening activities in classroom
Informal Reading Inventory	• Most commonly used method to assess listening • Examiner reads passages orally, then asks questions

Source: "From "A Critical Evaluation of Listening Tests" by J. M. Burns and D. J. Richgels, 1988, *Academic Therapy, 24,* 153–162. Copyright ©1988 by PRO-ED, Inc. Reprinted by permission.

The informal assessment process should start by collecting information that enables teachers to develop a profile of a student's strengths and weaknesses in language content, form, and usage. This profile provides a transitional stage from formal to informal assessment by clearly identifying areas in which further assessment is needed. This information also provides teachers a base for initial instructional activities.

An example of an informal language assessment profile is given in Figure 7.2. The student's language performance is organized into various linguistic components, with some suggested skills for each area. Using an instrument of this type enables teachers to evaluate each skill to determine if students have a deficit or a strength in a given area. Most of the information needed to complete this type of profile is obtained through observing the child in a natural environment such as the classroom. Observations in classrooms, cafeterias, and hallways, and on the playground provide a better understanding of the child's language functioning than information collected in a testing room (Moran, 1990).

The assessment of language usage complements the evaluation of content and form. It may include brief notations regarding the times, places, situations, and purposes for which oral language is used. This assessment information enables the teacher to observe any interaction between the quality of language content and form and the way it is used (Bloom & Lahey, 1978). The increasing emphasis on pragmatics, which is concerned with the use of language in various social contexts, underscores the importance of assessing language usage.

An illustration of the use of information collected from an informal inventory, such as the oral language assessment profile depicted in Figure 7.2, can be drawn regarding a child whose dialect results in nonstandard syntax. Additional data could be

I. Form and Content

	Weak	Adequate	Strong	Comments

A. Phonology
   1. Gross Discrimination
   2. Phonetic Discrimination
   3. Articulation
   4. Other factors: _____

B. Syntax/Morphology
   1. Syntactical arrangement
   2. Sentence length
   3. Prefixes
   4. Suffixes
   5. Dialectical variations
   6. Negation
   7. Interrogatives
   8. Other word endings
   9. Other factors: _____

C. Semantics
   1. Word choice
   2. Variety of words
   3. Relationships
   4. Basic concepts
   5. Listening comprehension:
      Literal skills
      Inferential skills
      Critical skills
   6. Other factors

II. Usage
   A. Situational context of language usage:

   B. Purposes for use of language:

   C. Typical topics of language:

Figure 7.2
Oral Language Assessment Profile

collected using informal means to identify the specific nonstandard forms the child uses so the teacher can help the child translate from these structures to standard English. By understanding usage, teachers can differentiate between dialogue that occurs in the classroom and that which occurs in the neighborhood. This more comprehensive set of assessment data differs from information obtained strictly from formal assessments, which is unlikely to result in such an understanding.

Although informal assessment procedures can consist simply of collecting information by observing children in natural environments, it most often is structured by some specified procedures. Structured opportunities to collect information are more likely to produce useful assessment data than is time spent in general observation.

Many different informal assessment methods are used to collect information about oral language skills. Observing children in a variety of natural environments, surveying children's parents and others who have language interactions with the child, and analyzing anecdotal information are examples. In addition to the sources of information, a variety of information can be collected. Guerin & Maier (1983) listed a series of skills that could be used as a basis for informally assessing oral language skills. These are given in Table 7.3.

The exact nature of the informal assessment will depend on the skills teachers want to assess. Clary and Edwards (1989) have suggested that teachers answer the following questions when informally assessing general listening skills in students:

- Does the student establish and maintain eye contact with the person speaking?
- Is the student restless in a group activity of varying duration (5, 10, 15 minutes)?
- Is the student's attention easily diverted during a group activity?
- Can the student complete a simple task below the student's ability level? at ability level?
- Can the student repeat simple and complex statements? follow simple and complex commands? (p. 189)

Similar questions could be asked when informally assessing other aspects of oral language.

One example of an informal language assessment procedure is the *language sample*. Unlike highly structured tests, language samples enable teachers to evaluate more varied and representative patterns of children's speech. Pronunciation, fluency, voice, syntax, morphology, and semantics all can be assessed in a natural context (Moran, 1990).

Using the language sample procedure, teachers transcribe a section of spontaneous verbal expression from a child. This transcription becomes a sample of the child's oral language abilities. The sample can be collected by asking students specific questions. Two questions that could be asked to elicit a spontaneous language sample are (Wiig & Semel, 1984):

Will you tell me what you saw on television last night?
Can you tell me the story of the three bears?

Table 7.3
Examples of Skills Used in Assessing Oral Language

Receptive language

1. Nonverbal
   a. Response to gestures: The teacher can make gestures to the child, moving his or her hands to indicate things such as "come here," "stop," "sssh" (finger in front of mouth); or the teacher can show the child pictures of faces and ask him to identify if the person is sad, happy, angry, and so on. The Peabody Language Development Kit (Dunn and Smith, 1966) is a good source of such pictures.
   b. Identification of pictures: The child is asked to identify objects and people in pictures.
   c. Identification of function of objects—The child is able to identify an object's use: broom/to sweep, telephone/to talk, suitcase/to carry clothes.

2. Verbal
   a. Listening
      (1) Auditory closure: The child is able to identify words that are distorted, spoken with a foreign accent, or partially pronounced. This can most often be observed in daily activities, and no formal task need be constructed.
      (2) Vocabulary: The teacher determines if the child understands words spoken by most children his age.
      (3) Prepositions (location): The teacher determines if the child understands location words such as under, next to, over, behind, in front of, and so on.
      (4) Adverbs (sequence): The teacher determines if the child understands words indicating sequence, such as later, then, first, before, after, and so on.
   b. Comprehension
      (1) Words: Similar to vocabulary. Does the child understand the words used in classroom activities at his grade level?
      (2) Sentences: The child's ability to understand the meaning of sentences used in his academic program. Literal comprehension for syntax and information needs to be assessed here.
      (3) Paragraphs: The teacher needs to assess whether the child understands the content of a paragraph, and whether he understands that the sentences within the paragraph all relate to the same general topic.
      (4) Understanding sequence: Ability to comprehend the order of activity or logic presented in classroom activities. The teacher may ask the child to list the sequence in order, or may ask the child specific questions to determine that it was understood.

Source: From *Informal Assessment in Education* (pp. 196–198) by G. R. Guerin and A. S. Maier, 1983, Palo Alto, CA: Mayfield Publishing Co. Reprinted by permission.

With the transcription of the child's response, teachers analyze the sample for various oral language skills. One method of analysis is the *case grammar* approach. This model involves an analysis of the semantic features and a representation of the meaning features. For more information on analysis of language samples, see Wiig and Semel (1984).

When using formal and informal tests to determine language competence, one concern is the relationship of the child's performance on these tests to the child's language performance in a free speech context. Does the child's performance during the structured testing situation reflect the child's day-to-day language abilities as used in natural settings (Blau, Lahey, & Oleksiuk-Velez, 1984)? Data collected during assessments should reflect the child's everyday language competence if appropriate intervention strategies are to be developed (Allen, 1989; Taenzer et al., 1981). Language samples provide an opportunity to do this.

Language samples can be evaluated to determine current levels of language development and to provide a basis for later comparisons. Specific skills resulting from the profile in Table 7.4 can be evaluated through the analysis of samples to yield information leading to intervention strategies. For example, the mean length of utterance (MLU) can provide a useful form of comparative data, and varied clinical tools can be used to assess language more precisely.

When analyzing language samples, teachers must determine the effective use of various syntactic devices. In general, teachers should ask the following questions when surveying the overall language sample (Wesson et al., 1989, p. 6):

1. Does the vocabulary used match the student's intent?
2. Do sentences fit together meaningfully?
3. Are sentences connected by linguistic references to aspects of time and space?

Though effective for assessing language, some professionals question the validity of data obtained from language samples compared to data collected from formal assessment instruments. Blau et al. (1984) studied the results obtained when assessing children's language competence using a standardized test (the Carrow Elicited Language Inventory), and a language sample. The comparison revealed high correlations between the language sample and the standardized test. The researchers concluded that "while a language test, such as the CELI, serves well to identify children in need of language intervention, the CELI cannot replace language sampling techniques for the development of appropriate goals in language intervention" (p. 79).

CONSEQUENCES OF ORAL LANGUAGE PROBLEMS

Several different types of oral language problems can impact negatively on a child's educational and social success. Difficulties in oral expression or in understanding spoken language can severely restrict communication abilities. For school-age children, difficulties in expressive or receptive language can create significant problems related to academic success. For adults, these kinds of deficits can result in vocational and social problems.

PROBLEMS IN SPEAKING

Children experience a variety of problems in speaking that can create difficulties for them in academic work and social interactions. Embarrassment, negative self-concepts, difficulty interacting with peers, and other problems may result from speaking difficulties. In school, teachers expect students to express themselves verbally. Because oral reports, oral reading, and simple oral interactions are part of every school day, children with deficits in oral expression are at a major disadvantage. Their language deficits may actually result in school failure and social problems.

Table 7.4
Profile for Language Sample

Name	Purpose	Age Range	Stimuli	Responses	Scoring
MEAN LENGTH OF UTTER-ANCES (MLU)	Evaluates the average length of the child's spontaneous utterances. Provides an indirect estimate of early syntactic growth.	1 yr. 9 mo. to 9 yr. 5 mo.	Stimulus objects, toys, or illustra-tions of a familiar story are used to elicit a spon-taneous speech sample of 50 consecutive utterances.	The child's spontaneous speech is recorded on audiotape for later transcription and scoring.	The number of words in each utterance are counted, totalled, and divided by 50 to obtain the mean word length.
DEVELOP-MENTAL SENTENCE ANALYSIS	Evaluates the child's knowl-edge and expressive use of selected syntactic struc-tures in spon-taneous speech.	3 yr. 0 mo. to 6 yr. 11 mo.	Stimulus objects, toys, or illustra-tions of a familiar story are used to elicit a spon-taneous speech sample of 50 consecutive utterances.	The child's spontaneous speech in response to the stimuli is recorded on audiotape for later transcription and scoring.	Each utterance is scored to reflect which of eight grammatical form categories are used. Each gram-matical form is given a weighted score. The total weighted score is divided by 50 to obtain a Develop-mental Sentence Score (DSS). The DSS may be converted to a percentile or a mean age level.
14 MORPHEME ANALYSIS	Evaluates the presence and accuracy in using 14 grammatical morphemes related to the early stages of language acquisition.	Stages II-V+	Stimulus objects, toys, or illustra-tions are used to elicit a spon-taneous speech sample of 50 consecutive utterances.	Occurrences of the 14 morphemes are recorded and assigned to stages (II, III, V, or V+).	A percentage is calculated that reflects the num-ber of accurate uses of each morpheme in relation to the number of obligatory contexts.

Source: From *Language Assessment and Intervention for the Learning Disabled* (p. 378) by E. H. Wiig and E. Semel, 1984, Columbus, OH: Charles E. Merrill. Reprinted with permission of Merrill, an imprint of Macmillan Publishing Company. Copyright © 1984, 1980 by Bell & Howell Company.

PROBLEMS IN LISTENING

Difficulties in listening have obvious consequences for students. Research investigating how children's listening skills relate to communication is limited, but investigations into several components of listening, such as attending to specific environmental ac-tions, have revealed that students with disabilities often have significant problems (Robinson, 1989). Teachers expect children to listen to their instructions, lectures, and guidelines. When children have problems with listening, their school success likely will be affected. They may miss important directions required to complete assignments, or they may not hear certain information required on a test.

For adults, listening problems can severely restrict various types of vocational opportunities as well as social relationships. Most jobs and social opportunities require certain kinds of receptive oral language competence. For example, persons who work in jobs where interaction with customers or other workers is required may have problems. Also, simple social interactions require the ability to listen and converse with other people. Deficiencies in these social skills can easily result in rejections.

DEVELOPING ORAL LANGUAGE PROGRAMS

The problems cited can greatly impede the success of children in academic and social settings. Therefore, teachers and other school personnel must be prepared to develop and implement intervention programs that facilitate the development of adequate oral language skills. Without such programming, many students will never develop oral language competence, and this deficit may have a negative impact on academic, social, and later vocational success. Wesson et al. (1989) have suggested that teachers adhere to the following process when designing, implementing, and assessing language intervention programs:

1. Identify discrete language errors, omissions, or delays demonstrated by the child.
2. Develop instructional plans for working on the discrete language errors.
3. Assess general language functioning. Answer the question: Is overall language improving? If not, are the discrete skills selected for instruction appropriate: Or are the choices of instructional strategies inappropriate or ineffective?
4. Revise/make adjustments in the choice of discrete skills targeted for instruction or revise the instructional plan. (p. 3)

Even though this process is recommended for language intervention, it would be an appropriate model for many different types of intervention.

CONSIDERATIONS IN ORAL LANGUAGE PROGRAMS

Professionals who develop and implement oral language programs must take into consideration several factors. McCormick and Goldman (1984) listed four areas for consideration: Who should teach language? Where should language be taught? When should language be taught? What materials should be used to teach language?

1. *Who should teach language?* All people in the child's environment should be involved with language instruction so that it is tied to the natural setting and the skills can be readily generalized. These people include parents, siblings, grandparents, babysitters, and neighbors (McCormick & Goldman, 1984). Although all of these individuals are likely candidates to teach language skills, professionally trained school personnel probably will develop the program and direct its implementation with students who need more intensive intervention. Depending on the severity of the language problem, the special education teacher or the speech/language therapist might be the most significant teacher.

Professional educators provide language intervention through formal instructional programs and informal modeling. They must establish an environment where students feel comfortable and secure in using language. Nonprofessionals in the child's environment (parents, siblings, and others) are involved less formally. They have to provide a supportive environment and opportunities for appropriate language modeling, and reinforce both listening and speaking efforts.

2. *Where should language be taught?* As previously emphasized, assessment of language should occur in natural environments (Allen, 1989; Spinelli & Terrell, 1984). Conducting evaluations in structured environments specifically designed for assessment may not result in an accurate analysis of the child's functional language skills. Likewise, language intervention programs should be implemented in settings where students will be expected to use the skills. If language instruction is provided only in unnatural, highly structured environments such as the speech therapy room, the skills learned may not generalize to natural settings (Rieke & Lewis, 1984). In discussing the generalization of language skills, Fey (1988) cautioned that children who perform well in language in a clinical setting quite possibly will not perform similarly in natural settings.

Language intervention programs, therefore, should be implemented in a variety of settings, including the home, classroom, lunchroom, and playground. If intensive programming in a speech therapist's room is needed, it should be supplemented with instruction in natural settings. At a minimum, the natural setting should provide opportunities for the student to practice appropriate language skills and receive positive reinforcement. Table 7.5 contains a list of child and teacher roles in language instruction in natural settings.

Notwithstanding the extent to which the literature supports language intervention in natural settings, some instructional service delivery models focus on specialized settings. These include a model in which speech language therapists provide intervention in a self-contained language class (Miller, 1989). Although this may not be the ideal site for intervention, some children with severe language problems may require some amount of intensive intervention that can best occur in a self-contained setting. But a more likely intervention model for children who need the services of a language specialist would call for the speech language therapist to work with regular and special education teachers in the child's regular classroom placement (Miller, 1989). This provides the opportunity for intensive intervention by a language specialist, but in a more natural and integrated setting than the therapy room.

3. *When should language be taught?* Language intervention programs should be implemented as early as possible. Programming for children identified as having a language delay or disorder prior to their entering school should be a priority. Children identified after entry into school programs should receive programming as soon as possible after referral and identification.

Early intervention is recommended for several reasons. First, the longer inappropriate language is used, the more habitual it becomes. This makes successful intervention more difficult. Further, inappropriate language may result in negative self-concepts, poor school performance, and limited social interactions. The longer these

Table 7.5
Intervention Roles in Natural Environment

Child	Language Facilitator
▪ Freely explores and investigates play environment in the most meaningful way; language occurs spontaneously	▪ Is responsive to the child and situation where and when language is occurring; facilitates rather than controls responses
▪ Responds to adult as a playful interactor; perceives adult as a peer; child may order, request, question, argue, dialogue	▪ Is a playmate who stimulates verbal interaction by sitting on floor, knocking things down, climbing; assumes other childlike qualities
▪ Demonstrates the attained level of language function without constraint of a specific task, question, game, etc.	▪ Is critically aware of the child's developmental level; interaction is responsive to child's level of emerging language
▪ Explores the many possibilities of interpersonal responses: plays peek-a-boo, hide and seek, or is shy, silly, or angry	▪ Formulates assumptions about the child's language that are continually modified or restructured depending upon nuances of the child's words or interaction
▪ Leads the language interaction and is an active explorer rather than a passive receiver of instruction	▪ Responds as an evocateur; arranges the interaction to respond to the child rather than provoke a specific response; changes style of interaction to meet or polarize the child's style

Source: From "Outside the Therapy Room: A Naturalistic Approach to Language Intervention" by S. F. Taenzer, C. Cermak, and R. C. Hanlon, 1981, *Topics in Learning and Learning Disabilities, 1*, p. 44. Copyright 1981 by PRO-ED, Inc. Reprinted by permission.

negative consequences are allowed to continue, the greater is the risk of permanent damage to the child's psychological status.

4. *What materials should be used?* A variety of materials facilitate language instruction. These include commercial as well as teacher-made materials. Abundant stimuli are present in natural instructional settings for students to manipulate and talk about. Too often, teachers rely on language centers that contain concrete objects and events found only in visual stimuli (McCormick & Goldman, 1984). These kinds of materials may remove the spontaneity from the language activity. Although commercial materials and other materials orchestrated for specific language activities are beneficial and may stimulate language, natural objects in the child's natural environments are preferred.

LANGUAGE INTERVENTION TRENDS

Numerous language intervention trends have begun to impact the delivery of services to children with language disorders. McCormick (1986) described three trends that currently are affecting language services: (a) simulation of natural language learning conditions, (b) attention to communication functions rather than form, and (c) training across activities.

Simulating natural language learning conditions moves away from relying on inflexible, artificial teaching/learning environments. The *incidental model* is based on a simulation of the natural environment to give children sufficient opportunities to use words and to practice new words. Other models that adhere to this trend support training in natural settings that simulate natural language learning (McCormick, 1986).

Some obvious implications derive from this trend. First, the model of programming requires extensive participation by many people including aides, volunteers, parents, and siblings. Second, implementing this model requires continuous programs located in many different settings. Finally, this particular trend calls for natural reinforcers (McCormick, 1986), ones that occur in the natural environment. Students' use of language is rewarded by positive feedback from individuals in their environments. This is in lieu of using artificial reinforcements and later having to phase them out in favor of natural ones.

The second trend in language intervention noted by McCormick (1986) is a focus on communication *function* rather than form. Functionality is the key component. This represents a shift from how well the person uses language to how effectively the person uses language. Major goals relate to frequency and the improvement of language form. Proponents contend that if a person's language is ineffective, it really does not matter if the form is correct or incorrect.

A third trend reported by McCormick (1986) is *training across activities*. Rather than isolating language programming in a single time frame during the day, it occurs throughout the day in most activities. The routine activities of the school day present the opportunities for language training. Learning how to use appropriate language across activities means that generalization is not necessary; the language is learned in the environments where it is to be used. This trend is quite consistent with whole language approaches that focus on the interrelationship between speaking, listening, reading, and writing.

COMMERCIAL LANGUAGE PROGRAMS

Various approaches and programs are available for teachers' use in facilitating the development of oral language skills in their students. Oral language development programs can be based on commercial materials and packaged language programs, as well as teacher-made, individually designed programs. Frequently teachers use a combination of commercial-based programs and teacher-developed intervention strategies. Before teachers choose a commercial-based language program, however, they should consider at least three points:

1. Is the program an entire oral language curriculum for a child?
2. Is the program an entire oral language curriculum for a class?
3. Can the cost and time needed to implement the oral language program be justified?

Table 7.6 provides a brief description of many commercial programs designed to improve speaking and listening skills. When reviewing this list, keep in mind that few programs meet the needs of all students. Commercial programs may be appropriate without modification for some children but not for others. Also, as noted earlier, most children benefit from teacher-made activities that occur spontaneously in natural environments. Therefore, if teachers use commercial programs, they should supplement them with teacher-made activities to facilitate generalization of the language skills.

DEVELOPING INSTRUCTIONAL ACTIVITIES

Commercial programs provide specific suggestions for oral language programming. Still, the teacher is responsible for individualizing language instruction to meet the unique needs of individual students. The specific methods for developing receptive and expressive oral language skills discussed below provide examples of effective methods to facilitate oral language development. Used in conjunction with commercial programs, these instructional activities should prepare creative teachers to match a student's oral language needs with instructional strategies.

GENERAL STRATEGIES

Salend (1990) described several general strategies to promote the development of language skills. These include modeling, role playing, prompting, coaching, and scripting. Modeling provides students with opportunities to observe appropriate social interactions and the language that is involved. Through role playing, teachers are able to facilitate development of basic, interpersonal communication skills. The strategies of prompting, coaching, and scripting require extensive manipulation by the teacher. In these approaches the teacher prompts the use of certain skills, coaches specific skills, or actually scripts (writes) what the learner should say. If managed properly, students are able to improve their oral language skills as a result of these activities.

LANGUAGE STIMULATION

Language stimulation can benefit all children, even those without oral language problems. It can be defined as "facilitative techniques that are designed to increase the frequency of occurrence of language behaviors already within the productive domain of the child, thus expanding the child's performance" (Hedrick & Kemp, 1984, p. 60). Language stimulation differs from language intervention in that intervention programs may focus on developing skills the child does not have. For purposes of this chapter, "language intervention" includes language stimulation along with the development of new language skills.

Many children who experience relatively mild oral language problems routinely have the opportunity to interact orally with adults. This extensive oral interaction precludes the need for later oral language remediation for some of these children. For children who suffer more serious language deficits, a stimulating environment complements the teacher's direct instructional efforts. The reciprocal nature of oral language affords ample opportunity for both receptive and expressive language so children can develop competence in both areas.

Table 7.6
Summary of Commercial Programs to Facilitate Oral Language

Program (Authors/Publishers)	Description
Auditory Memory for Language (language-delayed or disordered children) (K. Stefanakos & R. Prater. Austin, TX: Pro-Ed.)	Sequenced tests and lesson plans to teach auditory memory
Auditory Perception Training (primary, intermediate) (R. Willette, I. Peckins, & B. Galofaro. Allen, TX: DLM Teaching Resources)	Audiocassettes and spirit masters to develop auditory memory, motor, figure-ground discrimination, and imagery skills
Auditory Processing in Action (APA) (K-6) (East Moline, IL: LinguiSystems)	Classroom and individual activities for teaching listening skills
Basic Concept Stories: Spatial Concepts, Comparatives and Opposites (regular and special ed., preschool to primary) (Allen, TX: DLM Teaching Resources)	Pictures accompanied by stories, photos, activities, and questions as basis for program
Clark Early Language Program (language and hearing impaired from CA 2 1/2 to adult) (C. R. Clark & D. F. Moores. Allen, TX: DLM Teaching Resources)	Teaches receptive and expressive language with rebuses, oral language, and an optional sign language component
CLAS: Classroom Listening and Speaking (K-2, 3-4) (L. Plourde. Tucson, AZ: Communication Skill Builders)	Activities for vocabulary, concepts, listening, giving and following directions, memory, describing, etc.
Communication Training Program (CTP) Levels 1, 2, and 3 (preschool) (C. L. Waryas & K. Stremel-Campbell. Allen, TX: DLM Teaching Resources)	Oral communication from prelanguage through development and remediation of three- and four-word utterances
Communication Workshop (LD adolescents) (East Moline, IL: LinguiSystems)	Exercises in workbook and role-playing form
Communicative Competence: A Functional-Pragmatic Approach to Language Therapy (CA 6-adult) (C. S. Simon. Tucson, AZ: Communication Skill Builders)	Includes theoretical monograph, teaching manual, filmstrips, photo-diagram book, stimulus cards, and spinner boards for developing communication skills
Comprehensive Language Program (CLP) (MA 0 months-5 years, handicapped) (Bensenville, IL: Scholastic Testing Service)	Lesson plans for teaching low-functioning students attending, identifying, matching, following directions, etc.
Concepts for Communication (CFC) (elementary) (Allen, TX: DLM Teaching Resources)	Manuals, cassettes, picture books, games for teaching receptive and expressive language
Conversations: Language Intervention for Adolescents (adolescents) (B. Hoskins. Allen, TX: DLM Teaching Resources)	Utilizes natural conversation as a means of language remediation
Developing Understanding of Self and Others (DUSO): Play Kit and Manual (elementary) (D. Dinkmeyer. Circle Pines, MN: American Guidance Service)	Exercises for enhancing success in interpersonal communication; includes filmstrips, puppets, manual
Development of Functional Communication Competencies (K-6, 7-12) (B. S. Wood. Urbana, IL: Clearinghouse on Reading and Communication Skills)	Group-based regular classroom activities for elementary and secondary levels; designed to increase communicative options relative to different participants, settings, topics, and purposes
Developmental Communication Curriculum (DCC) (developmental ages 1-5) (San Antonio, TX: Psychological Corp.)	Activities for developing form, content, and function in prelinguistic, symbolic, and complex symbolic relationships
Developmental Syntax Program (Coughran-Liles Syntax Program) (CA 3-10) (L. Coughran & B. V. Liles. Allen, TX: DLM Teaching Resources)	Exercises for syntactic development and remediation
DISTAR I, II, III (K-8) (S. Engleman & J. Osborn. Chicago: Science Research Associates)	Presentation books, workbooks, behavioral objectives, mastery tests

Table 7.6
continued

| Program
(Authors/Publishers)	Description
Early Learning and Language Activities (ELLA) (birth-3 years) (M. B. Karnes. Bensenville, IL: Scholastic Testing Service)	Activities for early language development in form, content, and use—preverbal, first words, and constructions
FILE (CA 9-16) (East Moline, IL: LinguiSystems)	600 cards of language exercises in semantics, syntax and morphology, pragmatics
Fokes Sentence Builder, Fokes Sentence Builder Expansion (elementary) (J. Fokes. Allen, TX: DLM Teaching Resources)	Grammatical approach to sentence building; expansion permits building of additional sentences
Follow Me (K-3) (East Moline, IL: LinguiSystems)	Worksheets and lessons for teaching following directions and other listening skills
Following Directions Series (FDS) (grades 2–4) (Chatsworth, CA: Opportunities for Learning)	Spirit master activities for teaching listening skills
Functional Speech and Language Training for the Severely Handicapped (severely handicapped children and adults) (D. Guess, W. Sailor, & D. M. Baer. Austin, TX: Pro-Ed)	Behavioral management approach to language training for persons with autism, brain damage, severe impairment
Grammar for Teens (CA 10-18) (East Moline, IL: LinguiSystems)	Workbooks for teaching grammar, syntax
Great Beginnings for Early Language Learning (Language, speech, and developmentally delayed students) (L. Levine. Tucson, AZ: Communication Skill Builders)	Photographs, pictures, and manipulatives for teaching nouns, concept, verbs, prepositions, and associations
Helm Elicited Language Program for Syntax Stimulation (adolescents and adults) (N. Helm-Estabrooks. Austin, TX: Pro-Ed)	Practice provided on 11 sentence types sequenced in order of difficulty
HELP 3 (CA 6-adult) (East Moline, IL: LinguiSystems)	Workbook of exercises for teaching pragmatic skills
Language Big Box (primary) (Allen, TX: DLM Teaching Resources)	Activities for teaching associations, categorizing, auditory discrimination, sequencing, etc.; includes cards, puppet, picture books
Language Facilitation: A Complete Cognitive Therapy Program (preschool, elementary) (J. M. Cimorell Strong. Austin, TX: Pro-Ed)	Piagetian-based language development program for language-impaired children; more than 400 activities to teach syntactic, semantic, and pragmatic aspects of language
Let's Talk for Children (CA 4-9) (E. H. Wiig & C. Bray. Columbus, OH: Charles E. Merrill Publishing)	Communication cards for modeling, role playing, activities with puppets, etc.
Let's Talk: Intermediate Level (CA 10–young adult, handicapped) (E. H. Wiig & C. Bray. Columbus, OH: Charles E. Merrill Publishing)	Communication activities to develop pragmatic functions of ritualizing, informing, controlling, and feeling
Listening to Go (CA 4–8) (East Moline, IL: LinguiSystems)	Worksheet activities for teaching listening skills
Listening to the World (K–2) (Circle Pines, MN: American Guidance Service)	Storybook, games, markers, cards, exercises, etc., to develop awareness of sounds of music, speech, and the environment
Magic of Sentence Sense: Activities of Syntax Practice (CA 7–12, language delayed, learning disabled) (E. B. Krassowski. Tucson, AZ: Communication Skill Builders)	Exercises for analyzing and changing language structures. From simple to complex
Monterey Language Program (Programmed Conditioning for Language) (elementary) (B. B. Gray & B. P. Ryan, Palo Alto, CA: Monterey Learning Systems)	Programmed approach to teaching expressive language

Table 7.6
continued

Program (Authors/Publishers)	Description
PALS: Pragmatic Activities in Language and Speech (adolescents) (B. X. Davis. Austin, TX: Pro-Ed)	Pragmatic language skills developed through pantomiming, role playing, memo writing, telephoning, job interviewing, etc.
Peabody Language Development Kits—Levels P, 1, 2, 3 (CA 4–8) (L. M. Dunn, J. O. Smith, & K. B. Horton. Circle Pines, MN: American Guidance Service)	Lesson cards, teacher's manuals, posters, picture cards, puppets, audiocassettes, etc., for general language development stimulation
PEP: Spoken Language Enhancement Program, Volumes I–IV (elementary, language-delayed) (Austin, TX: Pro-Ed)	34 audiocassettes for teaching speech sound discrimination, following directions, improving listening skills, and chunking words, numbers, and phrases
PLA-ACT (CA 6–12), second-grade reading level) (San Antonio, TX: Psychological Corp.)	12 script adaptations of familiar stories and fairy tales for play acting
Program for the Acquisition of Language with the Severely Impaired (PALS) (all ages) (San Antonio, TX: Psychological Corp.)	Training activities for development of functional language with severely impaired persons at the presymbolic and symbolic levels
Question the Direction (K–6) (East Moline, IL: LinguiSystems)	Exercises for teaching careful listening and questioning of unclear or incomplete directions
Ready, Set, Grammar! (CA 4–10) (East Moline, IL: LinguiSystems)	Picture pages for early language structures
Resource of Activities for Peer Pragmatics (RAPP) (CA 9–18) (East Moline, IL: LinguiSystems)	Activities for developing social language, interpersonal communication, and communicative confidence
Semantic Fitness (CA 13–adult) (East Moline, IL: LinguiSystems)	Vocabulary worksheets
Semantics for Teens (CA 10–18) (East Moline, IL: LinguiSystems)	Workbooks for teaching semantics, vocabulary
Sourcebook Series: A Sourcebook of Pragmatic Activities (K–6); Sourcebook of Adolescent Pragmatic Activities (grades 7–12 and ESL); Sourcebook of Remediating Language (CA 2–14) (A. J. Glaser, E. B. Johnston, & B. D. Weinrich. Tucson, AZ: Communication Skill Builders)	Instructional objectives and activities for improving communication skills through a variety of age-appropriate, pragmatic activities
Syntax Development: A Generative Grammar Approach to Language Development (M. S. Wilson. Cambridge, MA: Educators Publishing Service)	Workbooks and grammar activities
Syntax Flip Books (nonreaders, preschoolers) (D. Phelps-Terasaki & T. Phelps-Gunn. Austin, TX: Pro-Ed)	Stimulus pictures representing basic sentence elements used to elicit key grammatic and semantic structures
Syntax of Kindergarten and Elementary School Children (elementary) (R. C. O'Donnell, W. J. Griffin, & R. C. Morris. Urbana, IL: National Council of Teachers of English)	Workbooks and activity sheets
TOTAL: Teacher Organized Training for the Acquisition of Language (6 months and up, handicapped) (B. Witt & J. Boose)	Games, lesson plans, songbook, art projects, storybooks, photographs, pictures, signed English illustrations, etc., for teaching language skills
WORD KIT (CA 7–12) (East Moline, IL: LinguiSystems)	Workbook, games, pictures for teaching vocabulary
Words, Expressions and Contexts (CA 9–adult) (San Antonio, TX: Psychological Corp.)	Activities for teaching figurative language to adolescents and young adults

Teachers can promote appropriate language interaction among students in several different ways (Hurvitz, Pickert, & Rilla, 1987):

• Give children a variety of leadership activities, such as leading circle time, acting as class messenger, and assigning jobs for the day to other students.
• Facilitate social interactions among students.
• Use dramatic play to encourage language interactions.
• Enable nonverbal children to control the environment without talking.

VOCABULARY DEVELOPMENT

A common measure of oracy is the strength of an individual's receptive and expressive vocabularies. For communication to be truly spontaneous, children must learn to understand and use a vast number of words. This may be particularly difficult for a child with problems in word retrieval. Therefore, a primary goal of language intervention is the development of a strong oral vocabulary.

Students with limited vocabularies have problems dealing with the reception of oral language, as well as expression. Although the best way to learn vocabulary is through natural activities such as reading (DeSerres, 1990), writing, and general conversation, specific vocabulary-building activities are warranted for some students. In these situations teachers should develop vocabulary-building activities as part of the language intervention program.

Many programs and activities can be used for vocabulary development. In a study of six elementary classrooms, Blachowicz (1987) found that approximately 15–20% of reading instruction time was spent on vocabulary activities, and slightly less than half of this instruction occurred in context. Still, numerous programs focus strictly on vocabulary instruction. Some of these are components of reading and language programs; others rely on teacher creativity. Squires and Reetz (1989) use popular board games in teaching vocabulary. Table 7.7 summarizes these suggested activities.

In teaching vocabulary to young children, words for objects familiar to the child are best to start with. Next, the vocabulary instruction should focus on verbs the student can perform. Finally, words that will enable the child to express various functions are taught, such as rejection and location (Ruder, Bunce, & Ruder, 1984). Table 7.8 contains 280 commonly used English words that can be used to guide vocabulary training. Because these are words children should know, teachers could start with this list to determine the basic words the child does not know.

DEVELOPMENT OF LISTENING SKILLS

Understanding what is heard, or auditory perception, incorporates areas previously noted and represents the ultimate measure of receptive language. Without the ability to attend to auditory stimuli, students will not be able to comprehend the information. Teachers and speech/language therapists have at their disposal a wide variety of instructional activities for oral language programming. In the area of listening skills,

Table 7.7
Games for Vocabulary Development

Game	Description
Trivia games	▪ Use teacher-made cards as question cards for use with commercial trivia board. ▪ Relabel categories to correspond with study topics. ▪ Use cloze technique.
Tic-Tac-Toe gameboards	▪ Put flashcards in plastic containers. ▪ If student gets vocabulary correct, place an X or O on gameboard.
Football field	▪ Place cards of vocabulary words on sidelines of board laid out as football field. ▪ Move 5 or 10 yards each time a word is correct.
Jeopardy	▪ Arrange terms in categories. ▪ Divide students into two teams. ▪ Write questions for each term, to earn points.
Checkers gameboard	▪ Give each student a set of flashcards. ▪ Before checker moves, student must define opponent's word.

Source: From "Vocabulary Acquisition Activities" by E. L. Squires and L. J. Reetz, 1989, *Academic Therapy, 24,* pp. 589–592. Copyright 1989 by PRO-ED, Inc. Reprinted by permission.

however, teachers must develop ways to help students maintain their attention to the auditory message. Forster and Doyle (1989) described a program for teaching listening skills to students with attention problems. The 10-step process is:

1. *Prepare materials.* Tape-record a news broadcast; develop an outline of the newscast with blanks for students to complete; make a list of new vocabulary words; develop a test covering the content of the tape.
2. *Establish a purpose.* Tell students they are to listen to a tape recording of a newscast, and remember the main ideas.
3. *Organize prelistening.* Instruct students that they will learn about the organization of a news broadcast; give them an outline; tell them to circle words they do not know.
4. *Present the exercise.* Have the students listen to the recording and make notes on their outlines.
5. *Clarify.* Encourage the student to ask questions about issues they do not understand.
6. *Recapitulate.* With notes put away, ask students to describe the broadcast from memory.
7. *Summarize.* Have students dictate a summary of the broadcast.
8. *Test.* Give students the predeveloped test.
9. *Grade.* Grade orally so students are able to clarify any concepts that are still confusing or unknown to them.
10. *Evaluate.* Compare students' outlines with test performances.

Table 7.8
Basic Oral Vocabulary

a	come	great	may	room	time
about	could	had	me	run	to
afraid	cry	hand	men	said	today
after	cup	happy	money	saw	together
again	cut	hard	more	say	told
all	daddy	has	morning	school	too
along	day	hat	most	see	took
always	dear	have	mother	sew	truck
am	did	heard	much	shall	turn
an	do	help	must	she	under
and	dog	her	my	shoe	until
any	dolly	here	myself	should	up
are	done	him	name	show	upon
arm	door	his	never	sing	us
around	down	held	new	sit	use
as	each	home	next	sleep	very
ask	eat	horse	nice	small	walk
at	enough	hot	night	some	want
away	ever	house	no	something	warm
baby	every	how	not	soon	was
back	eye	I	now	spoon	watch
bad	fall	if	of	stand	water
ball	far	in	off	start	way
be	fat	into	old	stay	we
because	father	is	on	still	week
bed	feet	it	once	summer	well
been	few	jump	only	sure	went
before	find	just	open	table	were
best	fire	keep	or	take	what
big	fish	kind	other	talk	when
black	five	knife	our	teacher	where
blue	floor	know	out	tell	which
book	for	last	over	than	while
both	fork	laugh	own	thank	white
boy	found	left	page	that	who
brother	four	let	people	the	will
brown	friend	letter	place	their	wish
but	from	light	plate	them	with
bye-bye	full	like	play	then	work
call	gave	little	please	there	would
came	get	live	pretty	these	write
can	girl	long	put	they	year
car	give	look	rain	thing	yes
carry	go	made	read	think	you
child	good	make	ready	this	your
children	gone	man	red	those	
cold	got	many	right	thought	

Source: From *Developmental Language Programming for the Retarded* (pp. 112–113) by R. VanHattum, 1979, Boston: Allyn & Bacon. Reprinted by permission.

This particular set of activities is merely a sample of an exercise that can be used to enhance listening skills. Students are taught to concentrate on auditory information, especially information that has been targeted as important. Even though a news broadcast was used in the example, teachers also could target information related to history, science, literature, or some other subject area. By using content from academic subjects, teachers can teach content as well as listening skills in the same activity.

Another way to facilitate attention to auditory stimuli is to use *advanced organizers*. These are statements or questions that help the listener attend to what will be said. Robinson (1989) described how to use advanced organizers to facilitate listening attention. The main components of the process include telling students what they will hear and providing some organization, such as an outline, to the content.

DEVELOPMENT OF LISTENING COMPREHENSION SKILLS

Once the student is attending to the auditory information, teachers can focus their efforts on comprehension, a key skill for successful performance in the regular classroom, especially lecture-type classes. Even though listening comprehension begins to develop at a very young age, improvement in this area should occur throughout life. The academic, social, and economic benefits that result from good listening make its importance obvious.

Students are better able to develop listening comprehension if teachers direct them to the goal of comprehension lessons. In doing this, teachers should clearly establish specific purposes for listening and explain them to students. As students become skilled in listening comprehension, they can move on to more complex levels of comprehension that require literal, interpretive, and critical skills. Literal comprehension simply means recalling the facts heard, whereas interpretive and critical skills require the student to determine relationships and make judgments.

Some of the activities suggested to improve listening attention also are effective in dealing with auditory comprehension problems. Wallace (1977) suggested the following areas in which activities could be developed to facilitate listening comprehension.

1. *Following directions.* Have students play games, such as "Simon Says," draw designs based on oral directions, and trace various routes on maps.
2. *Listening for main ideas.* Read a story to students and have them develop a title, summarize the main ideas, and describe characters.
3. *Vocabulary.* Provide new vocabulary words to students before they encounter the words in a story, and have students listen to oral reports to determine if the words are used correctly.
4. *Interpretation.* Have students interpret what various quotes mean, how characters in a story may feel, and the meaning of a poem.
5. *Listening for sequence.* Have students make something that requires understanding a series of directions, and have them place a series of pictures in proper sequence to depict a story.

Update

Socio-Cultural Strategies

Strategies which emphasize a social-cultural orientation are predicated on the fact that learning develops through interactions with other people. In order to enhance language development through social-cultural approaches, the following strategies can be used:

- **Expansion** is based on a teacher expanding on the utterances of a student in order to shape it toward a more mature and grammatically correct form.
- **Extension** requires the teacher not only to model a more mature utterance tied to the student's response but the "extension" component indicates that the teacher will attempt to move the learner to a more advanced language form such as with different content.
- **Self-Talk** refers to having the teacher provide a model for students of the ways in which competent language-users speak. It can be used to place emphasis on particular aspects of language that are important for the student to learn.
- **Parallel-Talk** refers to communication in which the teacher describes activities in which the student is engaged or which are occurring in the student's environment.

Source: Nowacek, J. (2001). Spoken language. In E. A. Polloway, & J. R. Patton (Eds.) *Strategies for teaching learners with special needs* (7th Ed.) Columbus, OH: Merrill.

6. *Critical listening.* Have students listen to a news broadcast and determine which parts of the story are subjective versus objective.

SYNTACTICAL AND MORPHOLOGICAL SKILL-BUILDING

The comprehension and production of syntactically accurate sentences and the building of morphemes provide the child with structural links between the phonological characteristics of speech and the meaning being expressed. Problems commonly found here include delay in understanding correct grammar, use of negatives and interrogatives, and difficulties presented by the translation to standard structure from dialectical forms.

Complementary visual and verbal activities can enable teachers to help children build syntactical and morphological skills. For example, students can be asked to select the correct picture for a given phrase or sentence or to verbalize the correct word, phrase, or sentence for expressive drill. Verbal lessons can be highlighted by games calling for the identification of correct and incorrect usage by the teacher.

A variety of teaching methods focuses on syntactical structure. Muma (1971) outlined 10 techniques that emphasize syntax and semantics. Among them are:

- *Correction:* involves both identifying and correcting mistakes. It should be used sparingly because it may be ineffective or even detrimental to language use.
- *Expansion:* refers to increasing a short utterance and can help a child learn syntax by supplying omitted structures.
- *Expatiation:* adds semantic features in response to the child's statement. The child says something, then the adult expands the statement.
- *Completion:* provides the child with a stimulus and elicits a syntactically correct form.
- *Combination Model:* presents a series of short sentences the child combines into one.
- *Revision:* requires the child to retell a story, in his or her own words, that has been told by an adult.

PHONOLOGICAL PRODUCTION

Teachers usually work with speech or language therapists to develop and implement appropriate speech patterns. Common problems are (a) articulation difficulties, (b) voice disorders, and (c) speech dysfluencies, such as stuttering. These problems frequently require the services of a speech/language therapist for adequate intervention.

Teachers assist children with phonological problems by referring them for speech/language services, modeling appropriate phonological production, and reinforcing the therapy the speech/language therapist provides. Teachers, in conjunction with speech therapists, form an interdisciplinary team to develop and implement services. Readers interested in further information on speech intervention are encouraged to consult Allen and Brown (1977); Bernthal and Bankston (1988); Case (1984);

Perkins, (1971, 1983); Reich (1986); Shames and Wiig (1990); Wiig (1990); and Wiig and Semel (1984) as well as the numerous applicable issues of *Speech and Hearing Disorders, Journal of Speech and Hearing Research, ASHA,* and the *Journal of Speech Disorders.*

DEVELOPING A LANGUAGE-ENRICHING ENVIRONMENT

What are the characteristics of an environment that facilitates language development? Dudley-Marling and Searle (1988) reviewed research related to language intervention strategies and concluded that children with language deficits "will benefit from rich language learning environments that immerse them in language" (p. 140). They presented four guidelines to facilitate the creation of an environment favorable for language development.

1. *Establish a physical setting that encourages talking.* Teachers can encourage talking by developing group activities for students, arranging the physical environment so groups of students can work together, and bringing to class objects and topics that elicit discussion.
2. *Provide opportunities for students to interact with language.* Teachers are well aware that students like to talk; talking among students does not have to be orchestrated. But teachers have to redirect the simple desire to talk into more formalized learning activities. Reporting on experiences and group learning from each other are ways to enhance learning through talking.
3. *Provide opportunities for students to use language for a variety of purposes and with different audiences.* Older students, peers, and younger students offer various audiences for language activities. Having a variety of audiences mirrors the reality of speaking to many different kinds of people in different situations. This opportunity is important because learning language solely for a specific population will not lead to functional language abilities.
4. *Encourage student speech.* Students need to be reinforced for their behaviors; thus, their use of language should be reinforced. Assuming that students will use their language without appropriate reinforcement is frequently disproven. When experiencing language problems, students likely will avoid language and therefore avoid certain failures. Often, students with oral language problems withdraw from social situations to avoid failure.

SPECIFIC INTERVENTION ACTIVITIES

Teachers can use numerous activities to develop receptive and expressive oral language skills in students. The following two lists give examples of specific activities for improving receptive and expressive oral language skills. They are meant to be examples only. Teachers have to be creative in developing similar activities.

Clary and Edwards (1989, pp. 201–202) listed the following classroom activities designed to improve receptive language.

1. Go for a nature walk, naming trees, flowers, and so forth. Back in the classroom, show pictures of things named outside. Say the name of one, and ask whether that is what the picture is. Require a yes or no answer.

2. Ask one student to find three "rough" items in the room and bring them to you. Send another student to find three "soft" items. Use other concepts that you know the children have studied.

3. Play a tape of various sounds and ask the students to raise their hands each time they hear an animal.

4. Instruct students to stand up each time they hear a certain word in a short story read aloud to them.

5. Play recordings of different sounds in the environment and have several students identify each sound.

6. Say two words that differ only in the initial consonant sound (e.g., hat, mat, or fun, run). Have a pupil say whether the words were the same or different in beginning sounds. Occasionally say the same word twice so the pupil cannot always correctly respond that the words were different. As students become more familiar with this task, have them name initial consonants for each word you say. A similar activity requiring finer discriminations is to say several words with the same beginning consonant sound; include a word with a different initial sound and ask pupils to repeat the word (e.g., fun, fan, four, ball; dad, do, man, doll).

7. Beginning with one simple direction and lengthening the list of directions, have a child perform a simple task in the classroom (e.g., stand up, turn around, close the door).

8. Play "Teacher, may I?" with students. The students stand at the back of the room. The teacher gives an instruction (e.g., "Sam, take three giant steps"), to which the child replies, "Teacher, may I?" The teacher then says yes or no. A child who forgets to say "Teacher, may I?" must go back to the beginning. The first child to reach the front of the room wins. Many kinds of steps may be used (baby steps, leaps, bunny hops, and so on).

9. Place two students at a table, separated by a screen. Place identical objects in front of both students. Have one describe an object; the other must pick the object being described. Later they can tell how the object works or can describe its uses.

10. Orally present a list of three words of which two are related in some way. Ask a student to tell which are related and why (e.g., horse, tree, dog).

11. Divide a sheet of paper into four sections, and label each with a color. Have students draw or cut out objects that are the same colors and attach them to the appropriate sections.

12. Tape-record a 5-minute segment of information—part of a story, a weather report, or a morning news broadcast. Play the tape while you take care of beginning-of-the-day details. Have students respond to prepared questions about the recording (Leverentz & Garman, 1987).

13. Read the description of a physical scene to the class. Encourage students to draw pictures related to what they heard.

14. Label a box "Treasure Chest" and fill it with familiar objects. Designate one student as king or queen. The royal person begins by saying, "Bring me my ____ , my ____ , and my ____ ." A "subject" is then chosen to follow the directions. If the directions are followed correctly, the subject becomes the king or queen (Glazzard, 1982).

Isaacson (1987, p. 287) suggested the following simulational activities to facilitate the functional aspect of oral expression:

1. Make phone calls in response to an ad.
2. Act as a seller of pens and pencils (or other "products" you find in the classroom).
3. Act as a person at home trying politely to get rid of the pencil seller at the door.
4. Give directions to help another find a hidden treasure in the room.
5. Be a TV talk-show host (learn how to maintain a conversation through the use of questions).
6. Make introductions at a party.
7. Build conversations by expanding and elaborating the previous speaker's statement.

PERSONNEL INVOLVED IN LANGUAGE INTERVENTION

As noted previously, oral language intervention should occur in a variety of environments, with an emphasis on natural settings (Allen, 1989; Spinelli & Terrell, 1984). Everybody in the student's environment should be involved in the oral language program. The individuals most obviously providing language programming are parents, teachers, and speech/language therapists.

ROLE OF PARENTS IN LANGUAGE INTERVENTION

Parental involvement in educational programs for their children has long been recognized as beneficial. The Education for All Handicapped Children Act, Public Law 94–142, requires local school districts to involve parents in special educational decisions about their children (Polloway, Patton, Payne, & Payne, 1989; Smith, 1990). The involvement of parents of children with oral language problems is particularly significant. Because language interventions should occur in natural settings and through spontaneous activities, parental participation is even more important (Fitzgerald & Fischer, 1987; McDade & Varnedoe, 1987).

McCormick (1984) suggested that parents participate in all stages of language programming: assessment, planning, and service delivery. In involving parents in language programming, professionals should emphasize the following points (McCormick, 1984, p. 382):

• Unless children are placed in the position of having to understand and use language, language growth will be minimal.
• How consistently parents stimulate and respond to their children's communicative efforts will significantly affect the learning process.

- Whether language and communication skills trained at school generalize to the home and other environments will depend largely upon the parents' ability to make the skills functional for the child in those settings.

Although language intervention can be beneficial to students even without the support of parents, the nature of programming in natural environments makes intervention efforts less than optimal.

ROLE OF TEACHERS IN LANGUAGE INTERVENTION

The teacher of students with language disorders is a vital component in delivering effective intervention programming. Special education and regular classroom teachers must collaborate in developing language programs for students. The exact role these teachers play will depend on the child's placement. For example, regular classroom teachers generally have to take the lead in implementing language programs for students who spend the major portion of the day in their classes, whereas special education teachers should take the lead in language programs for students who spend most of the day in their classes. In either case, collaborative planning and program intervention should be stressed to assure effectiveness of the program.

Teachers participate in providing language programming for their children in several ways. First, they facilitate the generalization of language skills learned; and second, they collect information regarding the progress of the student in a natural setting (Moran, 1990). In addition, special education teachers may provide direct language instruction during time in the resource room or self-contained special education classroom.

ROLE OF SPEECH/LANGUAGE THERAPISTS IN INTERVENTION

The most highly trained specialist providing language intervention programming to students in schools is the speech/language therapist. This professional is highly trained to work with students who have a wide variety of speech and language problems.

Speech/language therapists may offer services in a resource language classroom using group or one-on-one instruction. Adhering to this model, the therapist provides intensive language intervention programming that requires the isolated environment for effectiveness. And speech/language therapists can go into regular and special education classrooms to provide services (Miller, 1989). Use of this model enables the therapists to provide services in a natural environment, reducing the necessity to provide generalization activities following the therapy.

Regardless of the setting where services are provided, speech/language therapists perform several functions (Prizant et al., 1990):

1. Providing direct language intervention.
2. Referring children with language disorders for additional services, if needed.
3. Identifying children early for language problems.
4. Training caregivers and other professionals in ways to provide language training.

The provision of language services to children with problems should be a team effort. Getting the active involvement of parents, other caregivers, and all educational personnel should be a goal for each child who experiences oral language problems.

SUMMARY

The information presented in this chapter dealt with the development and refinement of oral language skills. The first section of the chapter noted that the development of oral language has been neglected in the past by educators. This is due to several reasons, one of which is that most students develop oral language without specific instruction. It was pointed out, however, the importance of oral language and the fact that with deficiencies in this area students as well as adults face significant problems.

The nature of oral language was discussed. It was noted that oral language can be receptive, which involves listening, and expressive, accomplished through talking. For students in school, deficits in listening or speaking result in limitations. Adults who suffer from these kinds of problems will have problems in job settings as well as social situations. Both listening and speaking are very complex skills which require a combination of many different subskills.

Ways to assess oral language were presented. These include formal means, such as standardized tests, as well as informal, teacher-made methods. Assessing oral language informally in natural settings is the best way to obtain valid results.

The final section of the chapter focused on different types of oral language problems and ways to implement intervention strategies to correct these problems. Commercial materials and teacher developed activities were discussed.

REFERENCES

Allen, D. A. (1989). Developmental language disorders in preschool children: Clinical subtypes and syndromes. *School Psychology Review, 18,* 442–451.

Allen, R. R. & Brown, K. L. (1977). *Developing communication competence in children.* Skokie, IL: National Textbook.

Bankson, N. W. (1990). *Bankson Language Screening Test.* Austin, TX: Pro-Ed.

Bernthal, J. E., & Bankston, N. W. (1988). *Articulation disorders* (2nd ed.). Englewood Cliffs, NJ: Prentice-Hall.

Blachowicz, C. L. Z. (1987). Vocabulary instruction: What goes on in the classroom? *Reading Teacher, 41,* 132–137.

Blau, A. F., Lahey, M., & Oleksiuk-Velez, A. (1984). Planning goals for intervention: Language testing or language sampling? *Exceptional Children, 51,* 78–79.

Bloom, L., & Lahey, M. (1978). *Language development and language disorders.* New York: John Wiley.

Burns, J. M., & Richgels, D. J. (1988). A critical evaluation of listening tests. *Academic Therapy, 24,* 153–162.

Byrne, K., Abbeduto, L., & Brooks, P. (1990). The language of children with spina bifida and hydrocephalus: Meeting task demands and mastering syntax. *Journal of Speech and Hearing Disorders, 55,* 118–123.

Carrow-Woolfolk, E. (1985). *Test of Auditory Comprehension of Language.* Allen, TX: DLM-Teaching Resources.

Case, J. L. (1984). *Clinical Management of voice disorders.* Rockville, Maryland: Aspen Systems Corp.

Clary, D. L., & Edwards, S. (1989). Spoken language. In E. A. Polloway, J. R. Patton, J. S. Payne, & R. A. Payne (Eds.), *Strategies for teaching learners with special needs* (4th ed.). Columbus, OH: Charles E. Merrill Publishing.

DeSerres, B. (1990). Putting vocabulary in content. *Reading Teacher, 43,* 612–613.

DiSimone, F. (1978). *Token Test for Children.* Allen, TX: DLM/Teaching Resources.

Dudley-Marling, C., & Searle, D. (1988). Enriching language learning environments for students with learning disabilities. *Journal of Learning Disabilities, 21,* 140–143.

Dunn, L. M., & Dunn, L. M. (1981). *The Peabody Picture Vocabulary Test.* Circle Pines, MN: American Guidance Service.

Dunn, L., & Smith, J. O. (1966). *Peabody development kit.* Circle Pines, MN: American Guidance Service.

Eisenson, J. (1990). Impairments and delays for spoken and written language in children. *Education, 109,* 419–423.

Epstein, M. H., Polloway, E. A., Patton, J. R., & Foley, R. (1989). Mild retardation: Student characteristics and services. *Education and Training in Mental Retardation, 24,* 7-16.

Fey, M. E. (1988). Generalization issues facing language interventionists: An introduction. *Language, Speech, and Hearing Services in Schools, 19,* 272–281.

Fitzgerald, M. T., & Fischer, R. M. (1987). A family involvement model for hearing-impaired infants. *Topics in Language Disorders, 7,* 1–18.

Forster, P., & Doyle, B. A. (1989). Teaching listening skills to students with attention deficit disorders. *Teaching Exceptional Children, 21,* 20–23.

Gibbs, D. P., & Cooper, E. B. (1989). Prevalence of communication disorders in students with learning disabilities. *Journal of Learning Disabilities, 22,* 60–63.

Glazzard, P. (1982). *Learning activities and teaching ideas for the special child in the regular classroom.* Englewood Cliffs, NJ: Prentice-Hall.

Goldman, R., & Fristoe, M. (1972). *Goldman-Fristoe Test of Articulation.* Circle Pines, MN: American Guidance Service.

Guerin, G. R., & Maier, A. S. (1983). *Informal assessment in education.* Palo Alto, CA: Mayfield Publishing.

Halliday, M. (1975). Learning how to mean. In E. Lenneberg & E. Lenneberg (Eds.), *Foundations of language development: A multidisciplinary approach* (Vol. 1). New York: Academic Press.

Hammill, D., Brown, V., Larsen, S., & Wiederholt, J. L. (1987). *The Test of Adolescent Language-2.* Austin, TX: Pro-Ed.

Hammill, D., & Newcomer, P. (1988). *The Test of Language Development-2: Intermediate.* Austin, TX: Pro-Ed.

Hammill, D. D., & Bartel, N. R. (1990). *Teaching students with learning and behavior problems* (5th ed.). Boston: Allyn & Bacon

Hedrick, D. L., & Kemp, J. C. (1984). Guidelines for communicative intervention with younger retarded children. *Topics in Language Disorders, 4,* pp. 58–65.

Hresko, W., Reid, D., & Hammill, D. (1990). *The Test of Early Language Development.* Austin, TX: Pro-Ed.

Hurvitz, J. A., Pickert, S. M., & Rilla, D. C. (1987). Promoting children's language interaction. *Teaching Exceptional Children, 19,* 12–15.

Isaacson, W. (1987). *Pro and con.* New York: G. P. Putnam.

Kleppe, S. A., Katayama, K. M., Shipley, K. G., & Foushee, D. R. (1990). The speech and language characteristics of children with Prader-Willi syndrome. *Journal of Speech and Hearing Disorders, 55,* 330–309.

Leverentz, F., & Garman, D. (1987). What was that you said? *Instruction, 96,* 66–77.

Mann, V. A., Cowin, E., & Schoenheimer, J. (1989). Phonological processing, language comprehension, and reading ability. *Journal of Learning Disabilities, 22,* 76–89.

McCormick, L. (1984). Extracurricular roles and relationships. In L. McCormick & R. L. Schiefelbusch (Eds.), *Early language intervention.* Columbus, OH: Charles E. Merrill Publishing.

McCormick, L. (1986). Keeping up with language intervention trends. *Teaching Exceptional Children, 18,* 123–129.

McCormick, L., & Goldman, R. (1984). Designing an optimal learning program. In L. McCormick & R. L Schiefelbusch (Eds.), *Early language intervention.* Columbus, OH: Charles E. Merrill Publishing.

McDade, H. L., & Varnedoe, D. R. (1987). Training parents to be language facilitators. *Topics in Language Disorders, 7,* 19–30.

Mecham, M. (1989). *Utah Test of Language Development.* Austin, TX: Pro-Ed.

Miller, L. (1978). Pragmatics and early childhood language disorders. *Journal of Speech and Hearing Disorders, 43,* 419–436.

Miller, L. (1989). Classroom-based language intervention. *Language, Speech, and Hearing Services in Schools, 20,* 149–152.

Moran, M. R. (1990). Speech and language disorders. In E. L. Meyen (Ed.), *Exceptional Children.* Denver, CO: Love Publishing.

Morley, J. (1972). *Improving aural comprehension.* Ann Arbor, MI: University of Michigan Press.

Muma, J. R. (1971). Language intervention: Ten techniques. *Language, Speech and Hearing Services in Schools, 2,* 7–17.

Patton, J. R., Beirne-Smith, M., & Payne, J. S. (1989). *Mental Retardation* (3rd ed.). Columbus, OH: Charles E. Merrill Publishing.

Perkins, W. H. (1971). *Speech pathology: An applied behavioral science.* St. Louis, MO: CU Mosby.

Perkins, W. H. (1983). *Current therapy of communication disorders: phonologic-articulatory disorders.* New York: Thieme-Stratton, Inc.

Polloway, E. A., Patton, J. R., Payne, J. S., & Payne, R. A. (1989). *Strategies for teaching learners with special needs.* Columbus, OH: Charles E. Merrill Publishing.

Prizant, B. M., Audet, L. R., Burke, G. M., Hummel, L. J. Maher, S. R., & Theadore, G. (1990). Communication disorders and emotional/behavioral disorders in children and adolescents. *Journal of Speech and Hearing Disorders, 55,* 179–192.

Reich, P. (1986). *Language development.* Englewood Cliffs, NJ: Prentice-Hall.

Rice, M. L., Buhr, J. C., & Nemeth, M. (1990). Fast mapping word-learning abilities of language-delayed preschoolers. *Journal of Speech and Hearing Disorders, 55,* 33–42.

Rieke, J. A., & Lewis, J. (1984). Preschool intervention strategies: The communication base. *Topics in Language Disorders, 5,* 41–57.

Robinson, S. M. (1989). Oral language: Developing pragmatic skills and communicative competence. In G. A. Robinson, J. R. Patton, E. A. Polloway, & L. R. Sargent (Eds.), *Best practices in mental retardation.* Reston, VA: Council for Exceptional Children, Division on Mental Retardation.

Ruder, K. R., Bunce, B. H., & Ruder, C. C. (1984). Language intervention in a preschool/classroom setting. In L. McCormick & R. L. Schiefelbusch (Eds.), *Early language intervention.* Columbus, OH: Charles E. Merrill Publishing.

Salend, S. J. (1990). *Effective mainstreaming.* New York, NY: Macmillan.

Santos, O. B. (1989). Language skills and cognitive processes related to poor reading comprehension performance. *Journal of Learning Disabilities, 22,* 131–133.

Scarborough, H. W., & Dobrich, W. (1990). Development of children with early language delay. *Journal of Speech and Hearing Research, 33,* 70–83.

Schiefelbusch R. L., & McCormick, L. (1984). (Eds.), *Early Language Intervention.* Columbus, OH: Charles E. Merrill Publishing.

Semel, E., & Wiig, E. (1980). *Clinical evaluation of language functions.* Columbus, OH: Merrill.

Shames, G. H., & Wiig, E. H. (Eds.), (1990), *Human communication disorders.* Columbus, OH: Charles E. Merrill Publishing.

Smith, T. E. C. (1990). *Introduction to education.* St. Paul, MN: West Publishing.

Smith, T. E. C., Price, B. J., & Marsh, G. E. (1986). Mildly handicapped children and adults. St. Paul, MN: West Publishing.

Snell, M. (1987). Systematic instruction of persons with severe handicaps, 3rd ed. Columbus, OH: Charles E. Merrill Publishing.

Spinelli, F. M. & Terrell, B. Y. (1984). Remediation in context. *Topics in Language Disorders, 5,* 29–40.

Squires, E. L., & Reetz, L. J. (1989). Vocabulary acquisition activities. *Academic Therapy, 24,* 589–592.

Taenzer, S. F., Cermak, C., & Hanlon, R. C. (1981). Outside the therapy room: A naturalistic approach to language intervention. *Topics in Learning and Learning Disabilities, 1,* 41–46.

Van Hattum, R. J. (1979). *Developmental language for the retarded.* Boston: Allyn & Bacon.

Wallace, T. (1977). *Listening comprehension.* Unpublished manuscript, Lynchburg College, Lynchburg, VA.

Wesson, C., Otis-Wilborn, A., Hasbrouck, J., & Tindal, G. (1989). Linking assessment, curriculum, and instruction of oral and written language. *Focus on Exceptional Children, 22,* 1–12.

Wiig, E. (1982). *Let's Talk Inventory for Adolescents.* San Antonio, TX: The Psychological Corporation.

Wiig, E. H. (1990). Language disabilities in school-age children and youth. In G. H. Shames & E. H. Wiig (Eds.), *Human communication disorders.* Columbus, OH: Charles E. Merrill Publishing.

Wiig, E. H., & Semel, E. (1984). *Language assessment and intervention for the learning disabled,* 2nd ed. Columbus, OH: Charles E. Merrill Publishing.

Wiig, E. H., & Semel, E. (1987). *Clinical Evaluation of Language Function: Revised.* San Antonio, TX: The Psychological Corporation.

8

Reading: Nature and Assessment

R eading is the area of language that most frequently troubles school-age children. For students identified as mildly disabled or remedial, reading is often the first problem area identified by classroom teachers, leading to referral and eventually delivery of special services. For students who are more seriously impaired, it may be the key problem that obstructs independent functioning. For nearly all children who are disabled, reading disabilities are not isolated problems. They may relate to other academic skills, as well as personal, social, and behavioral adjustment. Certainly, the fact that reading is one of several key language domains reinforces this point. For this reason, although reading is discussed herein as a discrete subject area, it should not be perceived as a series of skills isolated from other language, academic, and life skills domains.

To illustrate the pervasiveness of reading problems, government statistics cited by Allen (1969) several decades ago indicated that one in four students had significant reading deficiencies, three million adults were illiterate, three fourths of all juvenile offenders in New York City were two or more years behind in reading, and in large city school systems about half of all students read well below expected levels.

More recently, the federal government has reported comparable data. For example, consider this news release from the U.S. Department of Education (1990):

> The reading and writing skills of American students remain dreadfully inadequate. . . . As a nation, we should be appalled that we have placed our children in such jeopardy. Reading and writing are the basic tools of learning, the crux of the academic enterprise. Without solid literacy skills we can never expect to see improvements in math or science, history or geography. And the costs will be staggering. (p. 1)

To provide a fuller appreciation of these comments, consider the data reported from the National Assessment of Educational Progress (NAEP) (U.S. Department of Education, 1990):

— Since 1980, the percentage of 9-year-olds who possess basic reading skills—the ability to understand specific or sequentially related information—has declined from 68 to 63 percent. Seven percent lack rudimentary skills required to carry out simple . . . tasks.
— Forty-two percent of all 13-year-olds lack the skills needed to read at the next highest level, which calls for the ability to interrelate ideas and make generalizations.
— The percentage of 17-year-olds reading at the intermediate level has increased steadily—from 81 percent in 1980 to 86 percent in 1988.
— Fifty-eight percent of 17-year-olds cannot read at the adept level—which is defined as the ability to find, understand, summarize, and explain relatively complicated information.
— Less than five percent of the nation's 17-year-olds are reading at the advanced level, which includes skills needed to understand scientific materials, literary essays, historical documents, and materials generally found in professional and technical work environments. (p. 5)

A review of literacy in young adults provides a more complete picture on reading ability. The National Assessment of Educational Progress final report (Kirsch & Jungebut, 1986) concluded that "illiteracy is not a *major* problem for the population of 21–25 year olds. It is also clear, however, that 'literacy' (i.e., using printed and written information to function in society, to achieve one's goals, and to develop one's knowledge and potential) *is* a major problem" (p. xii, xvi).

Because reading is one of the keys to school success or failure, it has been researched more thoroughly than any other instructional domain in education. In addition, more assessment instruments and curricular materials have been developed in the area of reading than in any other language domain. To accommodate the vast amount of information available to the practitioner, the topic is addressed in two chapters. This chapter focuses on the concept of reading and reading problems, the scope of this area, approaches to assessing disabilities, and general principles for developing a reading program. Chapter 9 then discusses strategies for reading instruction related to methodology and curriculum.

READING AND READING DIFFICULTIES

Reading is the written receptive language domain that requires students to break down linguistic codes and translate them into meaningful thought, the basis for appropriate response. Most precisely, reading refers to the comprehension of words, sentences, and passages (Wiederholt & Bryant, 1987). To achieve true reading, the learner is confronted with numerous tasks. Thus, the act of reading requires coordination of various abilities. In her classic how-to remedial reading manual, Pope (1967, p. 30) delineated the skills that might be needed to read the simple sentence, "Tom is fat," noting that the successful reader would have to understand:

— that the English language is read from left to right.
— how to sound the consonants *t, m, f.*
— how to sound the short vowels *o, a.*
— how to blend sounds, *f a t* to sound as *fat.*
— how to recognize *is* at sight.
— that "Tom" is a referent for a proper name.
— the meaning of the word *fat.*

Even though this example is somewhat simplistic and overlooks the multifaceted nature of comprehension, it illustrates just how complex the act of reading is.

When evaluating the reading ability of students who have a disability, teachers must be aware that problems can originate in a variety of areas. Some of the most significant ones are:

1. *Readiness* for written language decoding based on oral language development.
2. *Visual skills* that enable discrimination of letters and words.
3. *Auditory skills* that allow discrimination and blending of sounds into words.
4. *Memory* necessary for retaining images of specific words and their meanings, and the meaning of passages or stories.
5. *Other cognitive abilities* related to the ability to comprehend what is read.

Given the intricate nature of reading, and the tremendous inter- and intra-individual differences among students, few easy answers are forthcoming for assessment

Update

Perspectives on Reading Disabilities

In congressional hearings on disability policy, Dr. Reid Lyon addressed the Committee on Labor and Human Resources of the Senate to share perspectives on learning disabilities particularly as related to the area of reading. His introductory remarks capture the challenges that face students in our schools.

> For most individuals with learning disabilities, the primary difficulty is one that involves reading. In fact, at least 80 to 85 percent of children and adults diagnosed with LD have their most severe difficulties in learning to read. This is unfortunate since the major task in the early school grades is to learn to read, and most activities in the early and later grades, as well as in adulthood, involve and rely upon the ability to read. For example, consider being a child in elementary school, who, at the tender age of seven, cannot read — who cannot do what most others are able to do effortlessly — and knows it. Consider the humiliation and embarrassment that this youngster feels when called upon to read aloud in class and can respond only in a labored and inaccurate fashion. Think ahead to the fourth grade and beyond, where the ability to learn about history, the English language, mathematics, current events, and the rich tapestries of literature and science are inaccessible because all of this learning requires the ability to read rapidly, fluently, and accurately. Finally, consider the long-term consequences of these unexpected difficulties in learning that go beyond school and childhood. The eager third graders experiencing reading difficulties become, in turn, the frustrated ninth graders who drop out of school, the barely literate twenty-five year-olds who read at the fourth grade level, the members of the thirtysomething generation who are unemployed, and the defeated adults struggling to raise families and needing to go on public assistance.

Source: Lyon, G. R. (May, 1995) Statement to the Sub-Committee on Disability Policy, Committee on Labor and Human Resources, United States Senate. Unpublished manuscript, p. 3.

and instruction. When one considers not only the skills an individual possesses but also *how* he or she attempts to attack words and comprehend passages, the complexity of the task of reading instruction becomes even more apparent.

One manifestation of the magnitude of the task of learning to read is in the serious difficulties some students experience. Educators and psychologists have struggled for decades to understand and classify these reading problems. Bartel's (1986) discussion of this dilemma is particularly apt:

> Students with reading problems are often labeled as "developmental," "corrective," "retarded," or "remedial." Sometimes more complicated and threatening labels are attached— "strephosymbolic," "dyslexic," "brain injured," and so on. It should be pointed out that these words have no precise (i.e., no generally accepted) meaning among professionals working in the field.
>
> For example, "developmental" may refer to a class (or to a student) taught using regular class methods; sometimes the use of the term is limited to students who are performing at a level commensurate with their ability; sometimes it is used with students who are working far behind their expectancy but are still being taught by regular class methods. A "corrective" class may be one in which the students are functioning below expectancy but do not appear to have any associated learning problems (brain damage, specific learning disabilities, etc.); "corrective" may also refer to any student who is one to two years behind expectancy regardless of the presence or absence of any associated learning problems. To some professionals, "remedial" students have associated learning problems; to others, the term is applied to all students who are more than two years behind expectancy in reading. (p. 32)

We advocate avoiding terms with apparent clinical meanings or other terms that lead to confusion. Bartel (1986) concluded her discussions by recommending that teachers become familiar with terms used in their own school divisions and their corresponding local definitions. Thus, the discussion in these two chapters will not focus on clinical labels and classification systems. The reader may wish to consult Westman (1990) for information on that orientation.

GENERAL INSTRUCTIONAL GOALS

In planning instruction for children with reading difficulties, the ideal goal is to help each student become a competent reader. Realistically, however, this objective is often impossible to reach. As a result, viewing reading for its relevance to the children and adolescents being taught is useful. In his classic book on teaching slow learners to read, Kirk (1940) presented three goals that still have relevance more than 50 years after publication and hence provide a framework for the discussion in this section. These goals are: survival, functional reading, and pleasure and profit.

SURVIVAL

An initial instructional goal is to teach students to read for survival. This objective is based on the child's need to develop a protection vocabulary (e.g., cold, hot, men, women) that facilitates daily living and provides a minimal basis for independent functioning. For individuals with severe reading disabilities, survival reading frequently serves as the primary focus of instruction. For students with mild disabilities, it is one of many important instructional objectives. In any case, the critical concern is that all children achieve this minimal level of functioning. Therefore, it warrants the careful attention of special educators.

A child's ability to function independently is influenced significantly by the survival words and phrases he or she knows (Folk & Campbell, 1978). This is likely to be true for individuals with moderate and severe retardation as well as those who have severe specific reading disabilities. Although a dominant role for survival words in basic reading curricula is not being advocated, these words continue to be a critical part of those programs.

Tables 8.1 and 8.2 present two functional lists of survival words and phrases developed by Polloway and Polloway (1981), based on a survey of teachers working with adolescents with learning problems. The intent of the survey was to determine which words and phrases were most important in developing daily living skills. Given the problems inherent in teaching a large list of words, it was assumed that a rank ordering would produce an outline of vital words. The teachers rated each item from 1 (limited value) to 5 (essential).

From the vocabulary list in these two respective tables, teachers would select the terms of greatest relevance to individual students. As Snell (1978) pointed out, the actual words taught may vary according to a teacher's philosophy, community setting, and the student's vocational preparation program. Within this framework, however, teachers have a substantial choice of words to teach. Because it may be unreasonable for the student to learn all these words—and unwieldy for the instructor to teach all of them—a practical approach would be to first teach the words and phrases that are most functional. Logically, the most relevant words will be the easiest for students to learn and retain because of their meaningful value and potential for use.

The rank-ordered list is a useful basis for beginning to make selections. In the next chapter, two programs designed to teach words from this list (Dyck et al., 1983; Robinson, 1986) are discussed briefly. Reliance on a list of targeted survival words should be considered carefully as a comprehensive strategy for teaching reading to individuals with severe disabilities, however, because students will likely be restricted to the words taught, with minimal generalization (Barudin & Hourcade, 1990).

To maximize the utility of a survival vocabulary, teachers should view the ecology of the individual student. To provide an ecological context to teaching survival words, teachers should analyze current and subsequent environments in which students will function, to ascertain highest priorities for instruction (Browder & Snell, 1987). An ecological inventory can assist in accomplishing this objective (Snell, 1988). Table 8.3, derived from Langone (1990), provides an excellent beginning point for this process. Teachers are encouraged to adopt a "subsequent environments as attitude" view of their work with students who have disabilities—that is, to base current instructional programs on projected environments in which their students will function (Polloway, Patton, Smith, & Roderique, 1991).

Table 8.1
50 Most Essential Survival Vocabulary Words

Word	N*	X̄†	Word	N*	X̄†
1. Poison	52	4.90	26. Ambulance	54	4.02
2. Danger	53	4.87	27. Girls	54	4.00
3. Police	52	4.79	28. Open	53	3.98
4. Emergency	54	4.70	29. Out	53	3.98
5. Stop	53	4.66	30. Combustible	54	3.94
6. Hot	53	4.53	31. Closed	54	3.90
7. Walk	53	4.49	32. Condemned	54	3.90
8. Caution	54	4.46	33. Up	53	3.89
9. Exit	53	4.40	34. Blasting	54	3.87
10. Men	54	4.39	35. Gentlemen	52	3.86
11. Women	53	4.32	36. Pull	53	3.73
12. Warning	53	4.32	37. Down	53	3.72
13. Entrance	53	4.30	38. Detour	53	3.71
14. Help	54	4.26	39. Gasoline	54	3.70
15. Off	52	4.23	40. Inflammable	53	3.70
16. On	53	4.21	41. In	54	3.68
17. Explosives	52	4.21	42. Push	53	3.68
18. Flammable	53	4.21	43. Nurse	52	3.58
19. Doctor	54	4.15	44. Information	54	3.57
20. Go	53	4.13	45. Lifeguard	52	3.52
21. Telephone	53	4.11	46. Listen	54	3.52
22. Boys	54	4.11	47. Private	53	3.51
23. Contaminated	54	4.09	48. Quiet	53	3.51
24. Ladies	53	4.06	49. Look	53	3.49
25 Dynamite	52	4.04	50. Wanted	54	3.46

*The number of participants varies due to omissions or errors by raters.
†Maximum rating of item was 5; minimum was 1.

Source: From "Validation of a Survival Vocabulary List" by C. H. Polloway and E.A. Polloway, 1981, *Academic Therapy, 16,* pp. 443–448. Copyright 1981 by PRO-ED, Inc. Reprinted by permission.

FUNCTIONAL READING

Most students with special needs are able to move far beyond the survival goal. The next step for these students is to achieve a level of truly functional reading—the degree of literacy that will enable them to cope with a variety of additional living situations.

Functional reading should allow the student to use his or her skills to gather information and provide a vehicle for instruction. This degree of achievement is equivalent to partial reading literacy[1], at an estimated level of third- or fourth-grade reading,

---

[1]We use the term "reading literacy" here merely to describe an approximation of the reading skills needed to access printed material. A full definition of literacy (provided earlier) quite properly places reading and writing (and oral language) skills within the social context of an individual's life demands (see Kirsch & Jungebut, 1986).

Table 8.2
50 Most Essential Survival Vocabulary Phrases

Phrase	N	X̄	Phrase	N	X̄
1. Don't walk	53	4.70	26. Wrong way	53	3.96
2. Fire escape	54	4.68	27. No fires	54	3.96
3. Fire extinguisher	54	4.59	28. No swimming	53	3.92
4. Do not enter	53	4.51	29. Watch your step	52	3.92
5. First aid	54	4.46	30. Watch for children	54	3.91
6. Deep water	50	4.38	31. No diving	54	3.91
7. External use only	53	4.38	32. Stop for pedestrians	54	3.89
8. High voltage	54	4.35	33. Post office	52	3.85
9. No trespassing	52	4.35	34. Slippery when wet	53	3.85
10. Railroad crossing	52	4.35	35. Help wanted	54	3.85
11. Rest rooms	52	4.35	36. Slow down	53	3.81
12. Do not touch	52	4.33	37. Smoking prohibited	54	3.80
13. Do not use near open flame	53	4.24	38. No admittance	54	3.78
14. Do not inhale fumes	53	4.24	39. Proceed at your own risk	53	3.77
15. One way	53	4.24	40. Step down	52	3.77
16. Do not cross	53	4.17	41. No parking	52	3.75
17. Do not use near heat	53	4.11	42. Keep closed	54	3.74
18. Keep out	53	4.09	43. No turns	53	3.73
19. Keep off	54	4.07	44. Beware of dog	54	3.72
20. Exit only	53	4.07	45. School zone	53	3.72
21. No right turn	52	4.04	46. Dangerous curve	53	3.71
22. Keep away	52	4.00	47. Hospital zone	54	3.70
23. Thin ice	53	3.98	48. Out of order	53	3.66
24. Bus stop	54	3.98	49. No smoking	53	3.66
25. No passing	52	3.98	50. Go slow	52	3.65

Source: From "Validation of a Survival Vocabulary List" by C. H. Polloway and E.A. Polloway, 1981, *Academic Therapy, 16*, pp. 443–448. Copyright 1981 by PRO-ED, Inc. Reprinted by permission.

which requires skills in word recognition and reading comprehension, and should be a reasonable goal for most adolescents who have mild disabilities as well as some students with more serious disabilities.

Because students who reach this level may be vulnerable to erosion or regression of skills after school, teachers must provide relevant reading experiences for them, especially if they are adolescents. Opportunities to read classified ads, recipes, instructional manuals, and labels on foods and drugs are especially valuable because they facilitate the generalization of reading skills from classroom to community.

PLEASURE AND PROFIT

Once students have refined the basic skills and have moved toward independent reading on a voluntary basis, they should learn to view these skills as a means for deriving pleasure and profit. Profit is meant in its broadest sense, for personal and professional

Table 8.3
Potential Community Environments for Using Reading and Written Expression

Community Environment	Related Reading and Written Expression Skills
Fast-food restaurants	Reading sight words from an over-the-counter menu
Family restaurants	Reading sight words from an individual menu
Grocery stores	Reading sight words on store items Reading sight words on signs Writing checks
Employment agency	Reading job notices Filling out forms Developing a resumé
Public library	Locating and reading books and magazines Listening to and visually following talking books Researching information about various topics and summarizing it in writing
Home	Reading a newspaper Reading directions for assembling items, cooking, and cleaning Writing letters and cards Writing expressively for pleasure

Source: From *Teaching Students with Mild and Moderate Learning Problems* (p. 218) by J. Langone, 1990, Boston: Allyn & Bacon. Copyright ©1990 by Allyn & Bacon. Reprinted with permission.

development. Although this may not be a realistic goal for all students, teachers should help children strive toward it whenever it is feasible.

When students achieve literacy (variant definitions may place it at the fifth- to seventh-grade level), they can be directed toward a wide variety of reading experiences. At this stage, advanced abilities become the focus of instructional programs. These include critical comprehension, specific study skills, and recreational reading.

DEVELOPMENT OF READING

Although establishing absolute stages of development and skill sequences for any student is impossible and any discussion that removes reading from language in general is somewhat reductionistic, this discussion of reading development provides a useful profile to assist teachers in evaluating their students. The stages discussed here have been adapted from the model originally devised in 1925 by the National Committee of Reading and presented by Harris (1970; Harris & Sipay, 1990). They relate reasonably well to other common conceptualizations (e.g., Chall, 1983). Although many specific skills apply across several stages, they are listed here in general developmental sequence.

What is referred to as "reading" is in reality a progression of abilities and skills that change continually throughout a student's academic career. It can be seen as beginning as an effort to learn to read (recognizing letters and words, learning sound-symbol correspondence) to eventually reading to learn (using reading skills as an instrument to acquire content knowledge and skills) (Chall & Snow, 1988). Overriding these skills is the need to consider how the student, at these various stages, struggles to learn to read.

READINESS

The concept of readiness suggests a stage of prereading (Chall, 1983) and has been defined in various ways. In the broad sense it refers to readiness for school learning in general, while more specifically, it refers only to reading. Kirk, Kliebhan, & Lerner, (1978) used the term *reading readiness* to mean "the collection of integrated abilities, traits, and skills that the child needs in order to learn the complex process called reading" (p. 32). Many professionals have argued that the term is a misnomer because young children should instead be viewed as at a stage of *emergent literacy*; thus, all reading-related opportunities prior to formal instruction represent learning-to-read activities (Harris & Sipay, 1990).

Rather than enjoin the debate, readiness as discussed here is simply used as a generic term including the visual, auditory, and linguistic skills needed to read and encompassing "learning-to-read" activities such as listening to stories and responding. It therefore encompasses many specific skills delineated in chapter 7, on oral language, and at the same time cannot be clearly distinguished from reading itself, just as readiness instructional activities cannot be separated from reading activities (Heilman, Blair, & Rupley, 1986).

The determination of a child's readiness to read has been based on a variety of criteria, ranging from specific chronological age (5 or 6 years), measured developmental levels, the instructor's readiness to teach the child to read, or sometimes in practice as the completion of a readiness workbook. At any rate, teachers should focus on skills that relate most closely to the act of reading, and should evaluate readiness on the basis of acquiring those skills. Letter names and sound-symbol correspondences, for example, have been identified as the best predictors of later reading success (Busch, 1980). In addition, fluency in oral language and an interest in books and other printed matter indicate a child's readiness for formal reading instruction.

The following summarizes some key readiness skills. The skills outlined here focus on four interrelated areas of concern. The list is intended to serve an illustrative purpose rather than to function as a checklist.

A. *Visual Discrimination*
1. Identifies likenesses and differences in pictures.
2. Identifies likenesses and differences in geometric forms/designs/patterns.
3. Recognizes various shapes.
4. Recognizes sizes of objects.
5. Notices specific details in pictures.
6. Recognizes primary colors.
7. Demonstrates left-to-right directionality by following a line of print.

8. Finishes incomplete designs and puzzles.
9. Draws reasonably straight lines following dot-to-dot designs.
10. Draws well-rounded and closed circles.
11. Identifies likenesses and differences in letters.
12. Identifies number of words in a printed phrase or sentence.
13. Identifies likenesses and differences in words.
14. Recognizes own name in manuscript form or selects from several choices.

B. *Auditory Discrimination*
1. Locates the source of sounds.
2. Discriminates among sounds in the environment.
3. Reproduces sounds heard.
4. Identifies words that are dissimilar as same or different.
5. Reproduces words that are heard.
6. Identifies initial sounds as same or different.
7. Identifies words with minimal differences as the same or different.
8. Identifies final sounds as same or different.
9. Identifies simple one-syllable words that rhyme.
10. Produces general rhyming words when given a one-syllable stimulus word.

C. *Alphabet Recognition*
1. Matches letter forms that are similar.
2. Identifies letter forms that are dissimilar.
3. Selects letter named from an array of choices.
4. Identifies individual letters when flashed visually.
5. Recognizes the difference between uppercase and lowercase letters.
6. Matches uppercase letters with their lowercase counterparts.

D. *Linguistic Prerequisites*
1. Uses substantial and varied oral vocabulary in verbal expression.
2. Demonstrates listening skills at age-appropriate levels.
3. Demonstrates understanding of letters and words as symbols for oral language.
4. Follows directions presented orally.
5. Demonstrates auditory attention span at level appropriate for instruction.
6. Recalls and relates simple stories.
7. Can sequence past events in logical fashion.
8. Predicts outcomes of simple stories or picture sequences.
9. Comprehends meaning of common vocabulary words used in early reading programs and illustrates by using them in context.
10. Can evaluate subjective variables about stories in terms of characters, emotions displayed, and reality versus fantasy.

INITIAL READING

After acquiring many basic readiness skills, the student can begin formal reading instruction. The child experiencing early reading problems will need to develop a sight vocabulary and acquire basic word-attack skills. Attention to vocabulary and skills acquisition must be augmented by an understanding of reading as the process of gathering meaning from the printed page.

To acquire a *sight vocabulary,* a child must learn words that are frequently used in reading materials and are often phonetically irregular. The Dolch 220 word list, developed in the 1920s and still popular, is the most common source of high-frequency words. Table 8.4 presents a revision of the Dolch list as originally suggested by Johnson (1971) and based on a computer analysis. Kirk et al. (1978) organized these words in a functional fashion for planning and instruction by dividing them into five 44-word lists corresponding to pre-primer through third-grade levels, respectively. Table 8.5 presents a more complete and up-to-date list, which Walker (1979) generated by computer. Though a variety of words is presented here, students will not master many of them until they reach the later stages of reading development.

Word attack skills represent the reader's ability to analyze words not easily identified on sight. Three skills that can benefit a reader are phonetic, structural, and contextual analysis. During the initial stage of reading, the instructional focus frequently is on phonics.

Phonetic analysis uses sound-symbol correspondences to decode unknown words. The successful reader learns to internalize specific phonics generalizations, apply them to new words, and then blend the sounds of phonemes represented by the various graphemes. Phonetic analysis as a reading aid has had a long history of use and criticism in the American educational system since Noah Webster first developed lists of English phonic generalizations such as, "When two vowels go walking, the first one does the talking" (in Crain, 1988).

Although phonetic analysis usually begins during the initial stage of reading, many specific skills are acquired at a later developmental level. For ease in illustration, however, the following is an inclusive list of fundamental skills. The student should be able to:

1. Recognize single initial consonants (e.g., t, d, b, p).
2. Recognize short vowel sounds (e.g., a, e, i).
3. Recognize variant consonant sounds (e.g., hard and soft c, hard and soft g).
4. Recognize single final consonant sounds.
5. Identify consonant-vowel-consonant (cvc) trigrams (e.g., fat, bat, bit, tug).
6. Recognize long vowel sounds and patterns (e.g., ee in seen, a-e in bake, ai in pain).
7. Identify a variety of simple three- and four-letter words (e.g., ate, bite, pine, bone).
8. Recognize initial and final consonant blends (e.g., bl, br, st, tr; -nd, -ld, -ft, -st).
9. Recognize initial and final consonant digraphs (e.g., sh, th, ch, sh; -sh, -th, -ng).
10. Recognize vowel diphthongs and r-controlled vowels (e.g., ou, oi, oy, ar, ir).

Table 8.4
Basic Sight Vocabulary List

The 220 Most-Frequent Words in the Kucera-Frances (1967) Corpus

Rank	Word	Rank	Word	Rank	Word	Rank	Word	Rank	Word
1	the	45	when	89	many	133	know	177	don't
2	of	46	who	90	before	134	while	178	does
3	and	47	will	91	must	135	last	179	got
4	to	48	more	92	through	136	might	180	united
5	a	49	no	93	back	137	us	181	left
6	in	50	if	94	years	138	great	182	number
7	that	51	out	95	where	139	old	183	course
8	is	52	so	96	much	140	year	184	war
9	was	53	said	97	your	141	off	185	until
10	he	54	what	98	may	142	come	186	always
11	for	55	up	99	well	143	since	187	away
12	it	56	its	100	down	144	against	188	something
13	with	57	about	101	should	145	go	189	fact
14	as	58	into	102	because	146	came	190	through
15	his	59	than	103	each	147	right	191	water
16	on	60	them	104	just	148	used	192	less
17	be	61	can	105	those	149	take	193	public
18	at	62	only	106	people	150	three	194	put
19	by	63	other	107	Mr.	151	states	195	thing
20	I	64	new	108	how	152	himself	196	almost
21	this	65	some	109	too	153	few	197	hand
22	had	66	could	110	little	154	house	198	enough
23	not	67	time	111	state	155	use	199	far
24	are	68	these	112	good	156	during	200	took
25	but	69	two	113	very	157	without	201	head
26	from	70	may	114	make	158	again	202	yet
27	or	71	then	115	would*	159	place	203	government
28	have	72	do	116	still	160	American	204	system
29	an	73	first	117	own	161	around	205	better
30	they	74	any	118	see	162	however	206	set
31	which	75	my	119	men	163	home	207	told
32	one	76	now	120	work	164	small	208	nothing
33	you	77	such	121	long	165	found	209	night
34	were	78	like	122	get	166	Mrs.	210	end
35	her	79	our	123	here	167	thought	211	why
36	all	80	over	124	between	168	went	212	called
37	she	81	man	125	both	169	say	213	didn't
38	there	82	me	126	life	170	part	214	eyes
39	would*	83	even	127	being	171	once	215	find
40	their	84	most	128	under	172	general	216	going
41	we	85	made	129	never	173	high	217	look
42	him	86	after	130	day	174	upon	218	asked
43	been	87	also	131	same	175	school	219	later
44	has	88	did	132	another	176	every	220	knew

*The word "would" mistakenly appeared twice in the original list.

Source: From "The Dolch List Reexamined" by D. D. Johnson, 1971, *Reading Teacher, 24*, pp. 455–456. Reprinted with permission of Dale D. Johnson and the International Reading Association.

Table 8.5
Rank Order: 1,000 High-Frequency Base Words

the	your	know	think	high	four
of	how	water	say	such	between
to	said	than	help	follow	state
and	an	call	low (be)	act	keep
in	each	first	line	why	eye
is	she	who	differ (ent)	ask	never
it	which	may	turn	men	last
to	do	down	cause	change	let
you	their	side	much	went	thought
that	time	been	mean	light	city
he	if	now	before	,kind	tree
was	will	find	move	off	cross (a)
for	way	any	right	need	farm
on	about	new	boy	house	hard
are	many	work	old	picture	start
with	then	part	too	try	might
as	them	take	same	us	story
!	write	get	tell	again	saw
his	would	place	does	animal	far
they	like	made	set	point	sea
be	so	live	three	mother	draw
at	these	where	want	world	left
one	her	after	air	near	late
have	long	back	well	build (t)	run
this	make	little	also	self	don't
from	thing	only	play	earth	while
or	see	round	small	father	press
had	him	man	end	head	close
by	two	year	put	stand	night
not	has	came	home	own	real
word	look	show	read	page	life
but	more	every	hand	should	few
what	day	good	deport	country	north
some	could	me	export	found	open
we	go	give	import	answer	seem
can	come	our	report	school	together
out	did	under	large	grow	next
other	number	name	spell	study	white
were	sound	very	add	still	children
all	no	through	even	learn	begin
there	most	just	land	plant	got
when	people	form	here	cover	walk
up	my	sentence	must	food	example
use	over	great	big	sun	ease (y)

Table 8.5
continued

paper	list	during	town	produce	bring
group	though (al)	hundred	fine	fact	yes
always	feel	five	certain	street	distant (ce)
music	talk	remember	fly	inch	fill
those	bird	step	fall	multiply (r)	east
both	soon	early	lead (mis)	nothing	paint
mark	body	hold	cry	course	language
often	dog	west	dark	stay	among
letter	family	ground	machine	wheel	grand
until	direct	interest	note	full	ball
mile	pose	reach	wait	force	yet
river	compose	fast	plan	blue	wave
car	suppose	verb (al)	figure	object	drop
feet	leave	sing	star	decide	heart
care	song	listen	box	surface	am
second	measure	six	noun	deep	present
book	door	table	field	moon	heavy
carry	product	travel	rest	island	dance
took	black	less (un)	correct	foot	engine (er)
science	short	morning	able	system	position
eat	numeral	ten	pound	busy	arm
room	class	simple	done	test	wide
friend	wind	several	beauty	record	sail
began	question	vowel	drive	boat	material
idea (l)	happen	toward	stood	common	size
fish	complete	war	contain	gold	vary
mountain	ship	lay	front	possible	settle
stop	area	against	teach	plane	speak
once	half	pattern	week	stead (in)	weigh (t)
base	rock	slow	final	dry	general
hear	order	center	gave	wonder	ice
horse	fire	love	green	laugh	matter
cut	south	person	oh	thousand	circle
sure	problem	money	quick	ago	pair
watch	piece	serve	develop	ran	include
color	told	appear	ocean	check	divide
face	knew	disappear	warm	game	syllable
wood	pass	road	free	shape	felt
main (re)	since	map	minute	equate	perhaps
enough	top	rain	strong	hot	pick
plain (ex)	whole	rule	special	miss	sudden
girl	king	govern	mind (re)	brought	count
usual	space	pull	behind	heat	square
young	heard	cold	clear	snow	reason
ready (al)	best	notice	tail	tire	length
above	hour	voice	entail	attire	represent
ever	better	unit	detail	entire	art (ist)
red	true	power	retail	retire	subject

Table 8.5
continued

region	weather	sand	design	wire	student
energy	month	soil	poor	cost	corner
hunt	million	roll	lot	lost	party
probable	bear	temperature	experiment	brown	supply
bed	finish	finger	bottom	wear	bone
brother	happy	industry	key	garden	rail (road)
egg	hope	value	iron	equal	imagine
ride	flower	fight	single	sent	provide
cell	clothe	lie (lying)	stick	choose	agree
believe	strange	beat	flat	fell	thus
fraction	gone	excite	twenty	fit	capital
forest	jump	natural	skin	flow	won't
sit	baby	view (re)	smile	fair (y)	chair
race	eight	sense	crease (in)	bank	danger
window	village	ear	hole	collect	fruit
store	meet	else	trade	save	rich
summer	root	quite	melody	control	thick
train	buy	broke	trip	decimal	soldier
sleep	raise	case	office	gentle	process
prove (ap)	solve	middle	receive	woman	operate
lone	metal	kill	row	captain	guess
leg	whether	son	mouth	practice	necessary
exercise	push	lake	exact	separate	sharp
wall	seven	moment	symbol	difficult	wing
catch	paragraph	scale	die	doctor	create
mount (a)	third	loud (a)	least	please	neighbor
wish	shall	spring	trouble	protect	wash
sky	held	observe	shout	noon	bat
board	hair	child	except	whose	rather
joy (en)	describe	straight	wrote	locate	crowd
winter	cook	consonant	seed	ring	corn
sat	floor	nation	tone	character	compare
written	either	dictionary	join	insect	poem
wild	result	milk	suggest	caught	string
instrument	burn	speed	clean	period	bell
kept	hill	method	break	indicate	depend
glass	safe	organ	lady	radio	meat
grass	cat	pay	yard	spoke	rub
cow	century	age	rise (a)	atom	tube
job	consider	section	bad	human	famous
edge	type	dress	blow	history	dollar
sign	law (yer)	cloud	oil	effect	stream
visit	bit	surprise	blood	electric	fear
past	coast	quiet	touch	expect	sight
soft	copy	stone	grew	crop	thin
fun	phrase	tiny	cent	modern	triangle
bright	silent (ce)	climb	mix	element	planet
gas	tall	cool	team	hit	hurry

Table 8.5
continued

chief	particular	wrong	suffix	total	bar
colony	deal	gray	especial	basic	offer
clock (o')	swim	repeat	fig	smell	segment
mine	term	require	afraid	valley	slave
tie	opposite	bread	huge	nor	duck
enter	wife	prepare	sister	double	instant (ce)
major	shoe	salt	steel	seat	market
fresh	shoulder	nose	discuss	arrive	degree
search	spread	plural	forward	master	populate
send	arrange	anger (ry)	similar	track	chick
yellow	camp	claim	guide	parent	dear
gun	invent	exclaim	experience	shore	enemy
allow	cotton	proclaim	score	division	reply
print	born	acclaim	apple	sheet	drink
dead	determine	reclaim	bought	substance	occur
spot	quart	continent	led	favor	support
desert	nine	oxygen	pitch	connect	speech
suit	truck	sugar	coat	post	nature
current	noise	death	mass	spend	range
lift	level	pretty	card	chord	steam
rose (a)	chance	skill	band	fat	motion
continue	gather	women	rope	glad	path
block	shop	season	slip	original	liquid
chart	stretch	solution	win	share	log
hat	throw	magnet	dream	station	meant
sell	shine	silver	evening	dad	quotient
success	property	thank	condition	bread	teeth
company	column	branch	feed	charge	shell
subtract	molecule	match	tool	paper	neck
event	select				

Source: From "High Frequency Word List for Grades 3 through 9" by C. M. Walker, 1979, *Reading Teacher, 32*, pp. 805–812. Reprinted with permission of the International Reading Association.

11. Recognize silent consonants (e.g., k in knight, g in gnome).
12. Apply basic generalizations to all one-syllable (regular) words, demonstrating knowledge of open and closed syllables (e.g., go and got, respectively).

Mastery of these generalizations opens up a new world of words to the reader. Although mature readers may find little need to rely on these skills, to the child with reading disabilities they are an important bridge to subsequent developmental stages.

RAPID SKILL ACQUISITION

After students reach approximately the second-grade reading level, they will be able to learn new words and process messages more quickly. Chall's (1983) stage of "confirmation, fluency, ungluing from print" provides a flavor of this period when the student is not so much gaining new information as confirming what is already known (Harris & Sipay, 1990). When rapid reading is achieved, students have reached a level of automatic decoding (Snider, 1989).

Achieving automaticity is critical to the development of fluency in reading (Samuels, 1981). In addition to increasing their sight vocabularies and mastering specific analysis skills, students now typically make greater use of structural and contextual analysis and expend basic comprehension skills. At this stage of reading, students with learning problems may face specific difficulties because they cannot remember or retrieve word-attack strategies or specific word images. They also may have difficulty comprehending what they read, either because of cognitive deficits or occasionally because of overemphasis on word-calling.

Structural analysis, a tool that focuses on word form, basically requires students to learn the parts of a word that serve as meaning or pronunciation units. Identifying morphemes within words is a key task of structural analysis, because it helps make the unit easier to recognize and understand. Structural analysis subsumes that the student will be able to:

1. Identify common suffixes or inflectional endings for verbs (e.g., -ing, -ed, -s, -es).
2. Identify common plural forms for nouns (e.g., -s, -es, -ies).
3. Identify common suffixes that indicate comparatives or superlatives (e.g., -er, -est) or specific actions or states of being (e.g., -ful, -ness, -tion). Table 8.6 provides further examples.
4. Identify common prefix forms (e.g., re-, dis-, mis-, pre-) (see Table 8.6).
5. Find and identify root words when combined with affixes.
6. Recognize and demonstrate understanding of logical compound words (e.g., baseball, fireplace, cowbell, shoelace). Table 8.7 provides further examples.
7. Recognize and demonstrate understanding of more obscure or illogical compound words (e.g., butterfly, breakfast) (also see Table 8.7).
8. Recognize pronoun-verb contracted forms or words and substitute the equivalents (e.g., I'll, he's, I've, they've). Table 8.8 gives a partial listing.
9. Recognize negative contracted forms of words and substitute the equivalents (e.g., didn't, won't, can't, haven't) (see Table 8.8 for further examples).
10. Identify the number of syllables in a spoken word.
11. Divide and decode unknown words into syllables, using phonetic and related structural analysis generalizations.

Contextual analysis is a word analysis tool that bridges recognition and comprehension. It assists the reader in anticipating words that are likely to occur in a given phrase, sentence, or story, through the use of syntactical and semantic cuing. Used with other word analysis skills, it promotes a smooth and effective reading style by minimizing interference with the process of understanding. For beginning readers, contextual analysis may mean using picture cues that visualize the action occurring in a sentence or short story. At more advanced levels it is based primarily on context cues found in the semantic and syntactic features of a written passage.

Table 8.6
Common Affix Forms

Suffix	Meaning	Examples
–able	capable of being	trainable, breakable
–ance	state of being	attendance, guidance
–ant	one who	servant, informant
–ent	being, one who	excellent, dependent
–er	relating to, like	painter, baker
–ful	full of	careful, wonderful
–fy	to make	purify, simplify
–ish	like	childish, yellowish
–ist	one who	terrorist, machinist
–ive	relating to	attractive, excessive
–less	unable to, without	harmless, homeless
–ly	in a way	slowly, simply
–ment	state of being	judgment, payment
–ness	state of being	goodness, weakness
–ous	full of	joyous, dangerous
–tion	act, state of being	action, election
–ward	turning to	eastward, homeward

Prefix	Meaning	Examples
anti–	against	antiwar, antifreeze
co–	with, together with	coworker, coeducation
de–	down, from, away	deflate, detour
dis–	opposite	dislike, discontinue
en–	in, into, make	enforce, endanger
ex–	former, from	expresident, express
im–	not, in	imperfect, impress
in–	not, into	insane, inland
inter–	between	interstate, interview
ir–	not, into	irregular, irresponsible
mis–	wrong	mistake, misplace
non–	not	nonsmoker, nonsense
pre–	before	prefix, preview
pro–	for, in front of	pro-American, pronoun
re–	back, again	repay, review
semi–	half, partly	semicircle, semisweet
sub–	under, less than	subway, substandard
super–	over, above	supernatural, superhighway
trans–	beyond, across	transplant, transcontinental
un–	not	unhappy, unlock

Source: From *Campbell County (VA) Reading Skills Sequence*, edited by C. H. Polloway, undated, Rustburg, VA: unpublished manuscript.

Table 8.7
Partial Listing of Compound Words

inside	bookcase	something	wherever	snowball
outside	workbook	sometime	become	cowboy
indoors	cookbook	somewhere	maybe	cowgirl
outdoors	handbag	anyone	weekday	raincoat
upstairs	necktie	anywhere	without	rainbow
downstairs	dustpan	anytime	within	railroad
doorbell	popcorn	anybody	forgot	mailman
bedroom	rowboat	anything	himself	mailbox
bathroom	sailboat	nobody	herself	milkman
hallway	somewhat	everyone	myself	sunshine
downtown	sometimes	everywhere	yourself	sunset
homework	somehow	everything	themselves	windmill
notebook	someone	everybody	basketball	weekend
classroom	somebody	whenever	football	

Source: From *Campbell County (VA) Reading Skills Sequence*, edited by C. H. Polloway, undated, Rustburg, VA: unpublished manuscript.

Following a progression of contextual analysis skills, a student will be able to:

1. Complete an unfinished oral sentence meaningfully.
2. Supply a meaningful missing word in a sentence given a picture cue.
3. Supply a meaningful missing word in a sentence given an initial consonant clue.
4. Supply a meaningful missing word in a sentence.
5. Arrange scrambled words into a meaningful sentence.
6. Decode an unknown word in a sentence using phonics skills in conjunction with context clues.
7. Select the correct dictionary definition of a word with multiple meanings based on the context in which it is used in a sentence.
8. Define an unknown word from the context of a sentence or paragraph.

WIDE READING

By about the fourth- or fifth-grade level the student can read voluntarily and with plea-sure. At this stage, students stop "learning to read" and shift to "reading to learn" (Snider, 1989); hence the reference to this period as "reading for learning the new" (Chall, 1983). If the child has a history of reading problems, skills instruction still will likely include attention to the continued development of word analysis skills. The most significant concern, however, will be for comprehension—that is, true reading, the re-ception of language-based information from visual symbols.

Students at this stage face new tasks that challenge their reading ability. As Chall and Snow (1988) reported, this period of time frequently is associated with a slump in the reading developmental patterns of many students, including those identi-fied as being disadvantaged or having learning disabilities, hearing impairments, or language disorders. Those authors attribute the slump to the fact the reading materials

Table 8.8
Commonly Used Contractions

I've	doesn't	they're
we've	can't	we're
you've	hasn't	you've
they've	hadn't	
	didn't	I'm
I'll	wouldn't	it's
they'll	couldn't	who's
we'll	shouldn't	that's
you'll	weren't	he's
he'll	isn't	she's
she'll	aren't	let's
I'd	don't	here's
we'd	haven't	there's
you'd	hasn't	what's
they'd	wasn't	
he'd	won't	
she'd	mustn't	

Source: From *Campbell County (VA) Reading Skills Sequence*, edited by C. H. Polloway, undated, Rustburg, VA: unpublished manuscript.

are more abstract and complex and vocabulary is more specialized. The difficulties are exacerbated because textbooks are increasingly the focus of classroom activities and they may present difficulties to readers beyond simply their readability level (Armbruster & Anderson, 1988). Those researchers suggested that unless texts selected are "user friendly" (clearly structured, coherent, and appropriate for the audience), they will give rise to problems beyond superficial readability (as measured by formulae) concerns.

Although specific aspects of comprehension have not been listed until now, many of those noted in the following list are important from the beginning phases of reading development. By the stage of wide reading, however, comprehension rather than word recognition clearly becomes the emphasis of educational efforts, regardless of the philosophical underpinnings of the reading program selected. A student at this stage should be able to:

1. Identify specific details after oral and silent reading of a passage.
2. Recognize and synthesize the central idea of a given passage.
3. Relate the sequence of events within a story.
4. Demonstrate the ability to draw conclusions and inferences and predict outcomes based on the information implicit in the passage.
5. Follow written directions of increasing complexity.
6. Apply multiple meanings to words.
7. Recognize absurdities in printed material.
8. Ascertain cause-and-effect relationships within passages.
9. Compare and contrast specific features within or between passages and stories.

10. Distinguish between personal biases, fiction, and factual information.
11. Interpret or analyze the underlying themes of material read.
12. Create fresh insights or new ideas based on what has been read.

The list of specific aspects of comprehension is virtually boundless. The key point is that comprehension ability ranges from simple factual recall of explicitly stated information to the interpretive skills involved in literary criticism. Though comprehension is seemingly open-ended and broad, it nevertheless can be defined and attacked instructionally in direct fashion (Gersten & Carnine, 1988). This is significant because the importance of comprehension, particularly in the wide-reading stage, cannot be overstated. During this stage students must acquire much of the knowledge foundation essential for the subsequent development of higher-level concepts (Snider, 1989).

REFINEMENT

Although the acquisition of basic skills may seem to be the penultimate achievement for learners who have disabilities, teachers should encourage virtually all students to read independently. Besides further developing comprehension, the refinement stage also focuses on increasing the rate of reading, enhancing the student's ability to read for a variety of purposes, and helping the student mature in terms of study skills. The interrelationship between reading and various content areas (e.g., mathematics, government, science, history) builds throughout school and reaches its peak during this stage.

The challenge to adolescents with learning problems is significant, because texts frequently are written above the tenth-grade level even though reading skills may be at the upper elementary level (Lenz & Hughes, 1990). Therefore, teachers should evaluate student problems at this time to determine whether deficits in *advanced reading skills* are contributing to the learner's problems. When a student masters advanced skills, he or she will be able to:

1. Adjust reading rate to correspond to purpose (e.g., scanning, skimming, slow rereading).
2. Study material through selective "passes" through content material.
3. Sustain attention to specific reading tasks sufficiently to accomplish the purpose.
4. Read maps to gather relevant information.
5. Use charts, graphs, and diagrams to enhance comprehension.
6. Use a book's table of contents and index.
7. Apply alphabetizing skills to use a dictionary.
8. Interpret dictionary word presentations in terms of derivations, syllabication, accents, and parts of speech.
9. Use encyclopedias and other reference books for suitable purposes.
10. Identify and use various sections of newspapers.
11. Use the telephone directory.
12. Demonstrate the ability to use library facilities.

13. Write an accurate summary of material read.
14. Organize main ideas and supporting details into outline form after reading a passage or story.

With a fundamental understanding of the scope and sequence of reading skills, as outlined, teachers can begin to determine the specific strengths and weaknesses of an individual student. Then teachers can utilize the approaches to reading assessment discussed next.

ASSESSMENT

As in other language areas, reading diagnosis of a student's abilities guides instructional planning and delivery. Because no other educational curricular area can boast the number and variety of assessment tools that have been developed for the reading domain, teachers can draw on a wealth of sources to develop a diagnostic picture and plan instructional programs. The complexity of the process of reading is likely to render any single measure of reading an overly simplistic view of an individual's skill (Valencia & Pearson, 1988). And any judgments derived from assessment activities require continuous, systematic, and ongoing revision as teaching progresses. Most significant, assessment must be matched to instruction (Barclay, 1990).

Before instruction can begin, reading teachers have to determine a student's approximate level of reading and identify specific strengths and weaknesses. With an idea of their students' reading levels, the teacher has a "ballpark" figure with which to make some preliminary decisions about grouping, scheduling, and selecting educational materials. An awareness of reading levels is especially important for teachers who are about to begin work with a new class or who need a general score that serves as a measure for pre/post evaluation. Although practitioners often use the term "reading level" with confidence, the term has no agreed-upon definition and different tests may produce widely variant measures for an individual child (Silberberg & Silberberg, 1977).

After establishing reading levels, teachers have to assess the specific needs of each child so teaching strategies can be devised. Formal tests can be used to determine the level of reading, whereas informal approaches are typically more useful in assessing individual strengths and weaknesses. The key to appropriate assessment is to use varied sources so no one measure or no one aspect of reading dominates the development of an assessment picture (Valencia & Pearson, 1988). An excellent discussion of approaches to reading assessment can be found in Wiederholt and Bryant (1987).

SURVEY TESTS

Numerous and varied formal, standardized instruments have been developed to assess reading abilities. These tools can be divided into survey (general evaluative) and diagnostic instruments. But there is not a perfect dichotomy between the two, and most can serve dual purposes, at least to a limited extent. In the discussion here, the tests are grouped on the basis of their primary function, and the instruments reviewed are ones commonly used in educational settings.

These tests serve mainly to establish estimated levels of performance. Because the tests are used to screen new students and to make global, long-term evaluations of their progress, they have value mainly when used for initial referrals and annual reviews. The benefits of these tests diminish rapidly when they are administered frequently or are used to attempt to make educational decisions beyond the identification process.

Peabody Individual Achievement Test—Revised (PIAT) (Dunn & Markwardt, 1988). The PIAT screens the academic achievement of children from kindergarten to high-school age. It consists of five subtests: mathematics, spelling, reading recognition, reading comprehension, and general information. The reading comprehension subtest follows a four-item multiple-choice format and measures comprehension by having a child read a sentence silently, then select the picture that best illustrates its meaning. Word recognition is assessed by having the student identify a list of letters and words presented in isolation. Results of both the spelling and the reading recognition subtests can be analyzed to provide preliminary, general indicators of difficulties in phonetic analysis and visual discrimination. The general information subtest determines a child's knowledge of the world about him or her and provides additional information about the child's cultural awareness. It therefore may have general implications for content knowledge.

Age- or grade-equivalent scores are given for each subtest, as well as percentile ranks and standard scores. The PIAT is a screening instrument and is not intended for use in the analysis of specific problems.

Wide Range Achievement Test—Revised (WRAT) (Jastak & Wilkinson, 1984). The WRAT, an achievement test widely used by psychologists and educators, provides a quick estimate of a child's spelling, word recognition, and arithmetic skills. The spelling subtest begins with a series of marks for nonreaders to copy. The child then is asked to spell his or her name and an additional 45 words. The reading subtest focuses strictly on letter and word recognition, requiring the examinee to name and match letters and to read a list of 100 words. The test does not assess reading comprehension.

Grade equivalent, standard scores, and percentile grades are provided for each subtest. The WRAT is highly correlated with various group achievement tests of reading. This test often gives inflated scores, particularly at lower-grade levels. The WRAT is not a diagnostic tool and serves primarily as a rapid estimator of academic development.

Slosson Oral Reading Test (SORT) (Slosson, 1981). The SORT is strictly a word recognition test that determines a child's reading level according to the number of words he or she reads correctly. Designed to be administered individually, the test provides lists of 20 words each for primer- to high-school reading levels. Teachers can informally use an error analysis approach on the basis of the responses, even though the test was not designed specifically for that purpose. The SORT has been found to have high reliability, which allows for repeated testing to measure progress throughout a school year. Any judgments about increases in reading achievement, however, must be made cautiously because the test consists only of isolated word lists.

DIAGNOSTIC TESTS

Like the instruments just described, these tests can help teachers elicit general information, but their primary purpose is to provide relevant information for planning educational programs. Diagnostic tests attempt to provide a more comprehensive analysis of specific abilities and disabilities, and thus more precision in determining how a child attempts to read (Mercer & Mercer, 1989). Therefore, they should be viewed as to whether they do or do not offer the types of specific data teachers desire. The descriptions that follow highlight diagnostic features of representative tests.

Durrell Analysis of Reading Difficulty (Durrell & Catterson, 1980). The Durrell was designed to record and analyze the difficulties children experience in reading. The test is divided into eight subtests for children ranging from prereading through junior high/middle school reading skill levels. The subtests measure oral and silent reading, listening comprehension, word recognition, letter identification, sounds, visual memory, spelling, and handwriting. The oral and silent reading subtests give the examiner an opportunity to record specific reading difficulties on detailed checklists and compare recall and comprehension differences between oral and silent reading. Grade norms are determined by the amount of time required to read the passage. The word recognition and sounds subtests allow for an error, or miscue analysis (see page 269) of written and spoken words. The visual memory and letters subtests may be used with nonreaders. Although grade norms are provided for most subtests, the test is more appropriately used for the analysis of errors.

Woodcock Reading Mastery Test—Revised (Woodcock, 1986). The Woodcock provides subtests appropriate for children from grades 1 through 12. These subtests cover letter and word identification, word attack, word comprehension, and passage comprehension. The letter identification subtest begins with Roman letters and moves on to cursive and more elaborate letter types. The word attack subtests can be paired with the word identification subtest to analyze phonetic difficulties. The word comprehension subtest is actually a test of word analogies; it requires the child to provide a word that matches the relationship demonstrated by the stimulus words. The passage comprehension subtest uses a cloze procedure with phrases and pictures at the lower levels and more complex passages at higher levels.

Grade- or age-level scores for three levels of reading accuracy are provided for each subtest. These correspond to the independent, instructional, and frustration levels of reading (discussed further below). The test also gives a percentile score for predicting reading mastery at the child's grade level, percentile ranks for grades, and tables and information to allow for differences between genders and socioeconomic communities. Two forms of the test are available to facilitate retesting.

Diagnostic Reading Scales (Spache, 1981). The Spache scales were designed for children in the first through seventh grades and consist of word recognition, reading passages, and word analysis and phonics subtests. The scales give examiners an independent, instructional, and potential reading level for each child. The word recognition lists establish a starting point for the passages and allow for an analysis of errors according to an enclosed checklist. The reading passages begin at the first-grade level and are scored for time, errors, and comprehension. Oral reading exercises and comprehension tests determine the instructional level of reading. Silent reading comprehension tests determine the independent level, and reading potential is based on listening comprehension. The phonics subtest requires the child to make the sounds of letters, blends, and common syllables outside the context of words. Syllabication skills also can be assessed.

Gray Oral Reading Test—Revised (Wiederholt & Bryant, 1986). The Gray Oral is a classic test of reading skills, which recently has been revised and renormed. It consists of 13 reading passages ranging from pre-primer through college levels of difficulty. It is individually administered and can be used to measure oral reading fluency and to identify specific oral reading difficulties. Comprehension is measured by questions accompanying each passage. The Gray Oral is relatively easy to administer and serves as a transitional evaluation tool because it can serve as both a survey and a diagnostic test. The absence of a silent reading component (as the name indicates) is one of the test's weaknesses.

INFORMAL ASSESSMENT

Although formal instruments can help teachers begin assessment of students, informal tools and teacher evaluation can provide information on the way a child approaches a reading task, specific strengths and weaknesses, other intraindividual variables, and interaction between the reader and the text, itself. Thus, it can assist the teacher in determining how a student learns to read. Informal assessment is fundamental to daily, ongoing assessment. Several informal approaches that may help teachers collect data with direct relevance to instruction are described next.

Informal Reading Inventory (IRI). IRIs represent a prototypical model for informal assessment that uses a series of graded reading paragraphs to generate specific diagnostic information. They generally consist of 50- to 200-word passages from outdated basal readers. Although they are nonstandardized tools, IRIs typically are developed systematically following a set construction pattern. They can be used to determine reading competence levels and to highlight specific skill deficiencies and trends.

Figure 8.1 presents a sample IRI scoresheet based on passages from an outdated Winston Basic Reading Series. Notations list the source of this oral reading passage (book/level/page), the number of words it contains, an error deduction multiplier to use in computing the overall percent of errors, the passage itself, comprehension questions, and a scoring summary section. A system for designating and scoring specific errors is provided in Table 8.9. Similar passages then can be selected for other grade levels and for silent reading exercises as well. After using this tool, the teacher can determine error trends as related to sequence of skills and reading levels as discussed below.

Four reading levels are commonly computed from an IRI. Although they are not rigidly defined, the levels suggest general considerations that subsequently can guide in the selection of appropriate reading materials (see Table 8.10). The *independent* level indicates fluent reading, accurate recall, and thus high comprehension. It determines the difficulty level of materials that would be appropriate for student-directed free reading

Come With Me (Primer Level)

Source: page 92   Passage Length: 55 words   Error Multiplier: 1.82

Oral Reading Passage

"Here, Nancy," said Mother. "This money is for the paper. The paper boy will stop for it." Nancy put the money in her book. "I will sit here," she said. "I have a new book to read. The paper boy can see me here." Mother went down the street to the store.

Type	Comprehension Questions
detail	1. Why did Mother give some money to Nancy? (to pay for the paper)
vocabulary	2. What is a paper boy? (boy who delivers papers)
main idea	3. Why couldn't Mother pay the paper boy herself? (she was going down the street to the store)
detail	4. Where did Nancy put the money? (in her book)
inference	5. What makes you think Nancy and her family like to read? (they get the paper, and Nancy has a new book to read)

Oral Recording	# of Errors	Types of Questions	Correct/Total
Omissions	_____	Main Idea	_____
Substitutions	_____	Vocabulary	_____
Inversions	_____	Inference	_____
Miscalling	_____	Detail	_____
Teacher Assistance	_____		
		Total	_____
Total	_____		

Source: Adapted from *McGuffey Informal Reading Inventory*, undated, Charlottesville, VA, unpublished manuscript.

Figure 8.1
Sample IRI Score Sheet

periods. The *instructional* level implies that passages present some difficulty but that students can be taught to handle them and will profit from information at this level. The *frustration* level represents the point at which fluency breaks down, the child becomes dismayed by the difficulty of the task, and comprehension suffers dramatically. Finally, the *capacity* level indicates the comprehension to expect from each student. It is based on the student's responses to material presented orally, and thus is more accurately viewed as a listening comprehension measure. Therefore, it provides a somewhat crude assessment of reading disability as compared to oral receptive skills.

Informal inventories are relatively easy to construct. Some suggested procedures are outlined in Polloway and Smith (1982). Commercial inventories have been developed by Ekwall (1986) and by Silvaroli (1986); the latter is described briefly below.

Table 8.9
Oral Reading Scoring Systems

1. Mispronunciations: Write the child's pronunciation above the word.

   brought

   (E.g., They bought the bread at the store.)

2. Assistance: Write the letter A above each word pronounced for the child after allowing five seconds to elapse.

   A

   (E.g., Hawkeye performed the delicate operation.)

3. Omissions: Circle each word or portion of word that the student omits.

   (E.g., After the race, the runner was winded.)

4. Letter or Word Inversions: Use the traditional typographical mark to indicate this type of error.

   (E.g., The ball seemed to fly forever—it was a homerun!)

5. Self-correction: Write the letter C above the word if the student corrects an error on his/her own.

   arose

   (E.g., They were late but they arrived just in time to ride the train.)

6. Insertions: Use a carat to indicate additions inserted by the reader.

   old

   (E.g., She was afraid to go into the ^ haunted house.)

7. Hesitations and Repetitions: Though not errors, these can be noted by a check mark and a wavy line, respectively.

   ✓

   (E.g., The dog scratched and itched until they put on his flea collar.)

Table 8.10
IRI Levels of Reading Competence

Level	Word Recognition	Literal Comprehension	inferential Comprehension	Vocabulary
1. Independent	99–100%	90–100%	90–100%	100%
2. Instructional	90–95%	80–90%	70–80%	90%
3. Frustration	<90%	<70%	<60%	<80%
4. Capacity/Expectancy	[not assessed]	80–90%	70–80%	90%

Source: Adapted from *Teaching Elementary Reading* (p. 52) by R. Karlin, 1991, Orlando, FL: Harcourt Brace Jovanovich. Reprinted by permission.

The Classroom Reading Inventory (Silvaroli, 1986) was based on the principles of the IRI and can be used to generate reading-level scores for elementary-level children, adolescents, and adults. It also can serve as a diagnostic tool. The test includes word recognition exercises and graded paragraphs for oral and silent reading. The word recognition test is a list of words graded from pre-primer to sixth grade. The student's performance on this subtest determines where he or she will start on the reading paragraphs;

the results can be used to analyze phonetic difficulties. The oral reading paragraphs are scored for word recognition and comprehension. Independent, instructional, and frustration levels are determined by a combination of word recognition and comprehension scores. Factual, inferential, and vocabulary questions are provided for each reading selection and for a checklist of difficulties that may be discovered during testing.

Informal Tests   Specification of a student's reading strengths and weaknesses can be greatly enhanced through the use of informal tests. Teachers can develop assessment tools for specific problem areas by following the sequence of reading skills presented earlier in the chapter. When used appropriately, informal measures provide for direct conversion of results into remedial activities. The informal tests presented in Table 8.11 illustrate this basic concept by clearly identifying the skill being tested, the indicators of possible difficulties, and the types of measures that can be taken when problems are found.

Informal tests constructed and administered by the teacher are especially useful because they allow teachers to assess specific problems within a student's overall development. Using tools such as those described in Table 8.11, the teacher can probe students' abilities, to determine specific problems on which to focus instruction. Educational plans should emphasize trends in problem areas rather than isolated mistakes.

Cloze Procedure   The cloze procedure can be used as both an assessment tool and an instructional procedure. For assessment purposes, it provides a useful approach for determining a student's ability to use contextual analysis in particular and to ascertain an instructional level in general. Essentially it taps into the individual's syntactic and semantic cuing systems. Wallace and Kauffman (1986, p. 214) described the steps for designing a cloze assessment as follows:

1. Randomly select a minimum of two reading passages of approximately 250 words in length from each graded reading selection to be assessed. Reading passages should begin a new paragraph.
2. Delete every fifth word from the passage, starting with the second sentence, and replace the deleted word with lines of equal length.
3. In individual administration, have pupils simply say the word. In group administration, instruct students to fill in the missing words of duplicated passages.

In chapter 9 further attention is given to the cloze procedure in an instructional sense, and a sample cloze passage is provided in Figure 9.7.

Curriculum-Based Assessment   Curriculum-based assessment (CBA) or measurement (CBM) is a systematic approach to evaluation based on the use of tools that typically are informally constructed and are tied to the actual curriculum as the criterion standard. CBA can serve several purposes: identification, eligibility, program planning, progress monitoring, and program evaluation (Marston & Magnusson, 1985). Consistent with the principles of applied behavior analysis, CBA can assist in focusing attention on changes in academic behavior within the context of the curriculum being used, thus enhancing the relationship between testing and teaching (Deno & Fuchs, 1987).

Because it encourages reliance on methods keyed to the curriculum and administered by classroom teachers, CBA is also more ecologically valid (Fuchs & Fuchs,

Table 8.11
Sample Informal Tests

Sample Informal Test (1)

General Objective:	Sound Blending
Directions:	Here are some nonsense words—they really are not words at all, but I'd like to see if you can read them anyway.

Test Items:							
	fis	hin	lort	bame	nebe	nel	faim
	lote	sut	tam	grue	vin	bute	hife
	gud	jav	sive	nibs	wab	kim	doke
	keat	tope	muts	pad	beed	sult	doam

Analysis:	Listen carefully as the student blends consonant and vowel sounds in order to determine whether the pupil can blend sounds together to attack unfamiliar words.
Sample Remedial Follow-ups:	1. DISTAR—"say it fast" technique. 2. Oral Language Exercises: "I am thinking of a word that begins like dig and ends like log"—dog. 3. Language master exercises.

Sample Informal Test (2)

General Objective:	Use of Contextual Analysis (Cloze Procedure)
Directions:	This story has some words missing. Try to read the story by guessing the missing words. (Can be developed at various reading levels.)
Test Item:	"Dick," xxxx Mother, "Will you go to the store for me?" "Surely, xxxxxx, What shall I get?" "I need a xxxxx of butter, a loaf of xxxxx, and a xxxxx eggs," said xxxxxx. "Hurry." xxxx ran to the xxxxx and was soon back. "That's a good xxx," said xxxxxx. "Thank xxx very much." "You're welcome, Mother," said xxxx, and ran off to xxxx ball with his xxxxxxx.
Analysis:	If the student cannot guess most of the words of these fifteen opportunities, he/she is weak in his/her ability to use context clues as an aid in word identification. Insure the fact that assessment is done at the student's instructional level.
Remedial Follow-up:	1. Controlled practice in using context clues. Explain that many words can be guessed if the pupil is "making sense" while he reads. 2. Prepare other materials of similar nature by using old textbooks of child's grade level, cutting out words and adding blanks in place of letters. May need to provide first letter of first syllable. 3. Tape record scripts with missing words for student to supply.

Table 8.11
continued

Sample Informal Test (3)

General Objective:	Recognition of Common Prefixes
Directions:	Here are some words that don't make sense. Read them as well as you can.

Test Items:	repan	ungate	birate
	conjump	excry	misrow
	inwell	proread	disstud
	delike	prehead	antichank
	disbite	enstand	cospore
	combent	retike	semituff

Analysis:	Carefully listen to the pupil's pronunciation of the prefix units that begin each nonsense word. A failure to recognize these prefixes indicates that the pupil is not familiar with these common units and should have help on the specific difficulties.

What May Be Done:	1. Use flash cards with color coded prefixes.
	2. Use word wheels for root words and prefixes.
	3. Teach common prefixes and suffixes that child exhibits difficulty in.
	4. Select a prefix of the day and have students generate lists of words that can be formed with it.

Source: From unpublished manuscript by Gerald Wallace, University of Virginia, undated.

1986) than norm-referenced testing. The inherent attractiveness of direct, frequently collected measures in curriculum-based assessment has contributed to their widespread endorsement by special education professionals (Deno, 1985; Gickling & Thompson, 1985). But, unlike many norm-referenced tests that have been subjected to validity and reliability evaluations, curriculum-based measures have directed relatively little attention to these concerns (Epstein, Polloway, & Patton, 1988).

Curriculum-based measures can be developed though systematic analysis of the reading curriculum, selection of specific items, and construction of assessment formats (e.g., questions, cloze activities, worksheets). Idol, Nevin, and Paolucci-Whitcomb (1986) suggested that three different forms of the same test be developed to be used on alternate days of testing.

Bean and Lane (1990) reported that curriculum-based measures have proven to be useful even in an adult literacy program, particularly by providing a reliable measure of student progress. As these researchers noted, "CBM appeared to facilitate ongoing monitoring and assessment. In that sense, it enhanced teacher and student interest in and knowledge of progress" (p 46). Although resources for developing curriculum-based instruments exist (e.g., Deno & Fuchs, 1987; Idol et al., 1986), they should serve primarily as guides because the instruments should reflect the reading curricula in a given program that is being assessed.

Miscue Analysis In the 1970s, psycholinguistic researchers developed and promoted the concept of miscue analysis as an alternative approach to assessment and as a model to facilitate a fundamental understanding of the reading process (e.g., K. Goodman, 1969; Y. Goodman & Burke, 1972). Goodman (1973, p. 5) defined a miscue as "an actual observed response in oral reading which does not match the expected response" (e.g., "The boy went into the *horse* and sat by the fire"). Goodman suggested that miscues can serve as windows on the reading process and that the relationship between miscues and expected outcomes provides a basis for investigating the way a student responds to the task of reading.

From the viewpoint of miscue analysis, the term *error* is a misnomer that often stems from inadequate or inappropriate assessment of a child's reading. Hence advocates of miscue analysis would view the typical systems for scoring oral reading (see Figure 8.2) as highlighting mistakes in *word perfect* reading (e.g., repetitions, some substitutions) that may not be critical to the basic reading goal of deriving meaning from printed words. In lieu of concerns for errors of questionable importance, the key focus of miscue analysis is rather on how the student's specific responses affect the meaning of the sentence or passage.

Goodman (1973, p. 10) suggested that a teacher can judge how proficiently a student reads by following these steps:

1. Count the reader's miscues.
2. Subtract all those which are shifts to the reader's own dialect; these are not really miscues since they are what we should expect the reader to say in response to the print.
3. Count all the miscues which result in acceptable meaning (even if changed) before correction.
4. Count all miscues which result in unacceptable meaning but which are successfully corrected.
5. Add the miscues in steps 3 and 4. The result is the total number of miscues semantically acceptable or corrected.

Using this procedure, a comparison can be drawn between the total number of miscues and the number that actually do not affect meaning—those that might be termed "high-quality miscues."

A good example of the application of miscue analysis to reading assessment is provided in the Gray Oral Reading Test—Revised (GORT-R) (Wiederholt & Bryant, 1986). Wiederholt and Bryant (1987) discussed this approach, identifying five types of miscues scored with the GORT-R, four of which are particularly relevant here. Using the sentence, "A blue jay was perched on a limb looking for water" as an illustration, they noted the following types of miscues:

1. *Meaning similarity:* The meaning would not change for the substitutions of *sitting* (for *perched*) and *the* (for *a*), but change would be effected with *at the* (for *for*).
2. *Function similarity:* Each of the three examples of miscues cited in item 1 would result in appropriate grammatical form and, hence, functional similarity.
3. *Graphic/phonemic similarity:* In this focus on the sound-symbol correspondence used, a miscue such as *sitting* for *perched* obviously would not reflect similarity, whereas *moment* for *minute* would, by their definition.

4. *Self-correction:* Student-generated correction strategies are a helpful notation when observing oral reading to further understand a student's strategic reading behaviors.

Miscue analysis offers teachers an alternative perspective, especially for evaluating maturing readers. Many students with learning problems struggle to master initial reading skills. But as the emphasis begins to move more significantly to comprehension and away from word recognition, teacher and student concerns also should shift away from word-for-word accuracy toward passage understanding.

At this juncture, a miscue analysis approach can be extremely beneficial. With miscue analysis, instruction can encourage readers who are less prone to labor over the pronunciation of unknown but possibly semantically unnecessary words (e.g., proper names), less likely to correct miscues that don't affect meaning (e.g., "home" for "house"), and less likely to rely solely on phonetic analysis to predict what a given word is, relying instead on a combination of semantic and syntactical cues complemented by phonetic ones.

ASSESSING COGNITIVE STRATEGIES

An area of assessment that has been receiving increased attention in recent years has been the assessment of a student's metacognitive awareness during the reading act— that is, his or her use of cognitive strategies. Focusing on reading comprehension, Barclay (1990) stressed that "the role of assessment must be to determine the extent to which the reader actively and purposefully selects and utilizes 'while reading' strategies. Such assessment leads to the discovery of additional strategies the reader needs in order to fulfill various reading tasks" (p. 84). Ellis (1989) noted that these strategies could include focusing on critical information, summarizing and paraphrasing the information from text, and self-questioning about comprehension.

The assessment of cognitive strategies enables the teacher to balance *product* assessment (as discussed in much of the preceding material) with *process* assessment focused on how the student reads and how he or she should respond to strategy instruction. Thus, as Ellis (1989) noted, product measures obtained on decoding and comprehension then can be complemented with process measures (i.e., the student's ability to respond strategically to teacher-mediated cues) and with a metacognitive interview (which asks students about their own thought processes, their use of strategies, and their response to the teacher's mediation. Table 8.12 gives one example and Ellis (1989) provides further examples of how this assessment process can be implemented.

USING ASSESSMENT DATA

Given the variety of tools and techniques available to evaluate reading skills, the skilled teacher can develop a detailed profile of the difficulties students face. Naturally, evaluative judgments should emerge from a series of observations rather than a single test administration. Therefore, a logical assessment sequence would first identify the general difficulties observed on survey tests, confirm these problem areas on diagnostic tests, develop informal tools to probe specific aspects of the skills in question rela-

Table 8.12
Sample Questions for Metacognitive Interview

In the reading activity we just did together, we talked about how some readers ask themselves questions or make predictions (substitute appropriate strategies mediated by the teacher) as they read to help them concentrate and remember what they read. I helped you do this a little bit. How did you like reading the way we did together? . . . Do you think it helped you remember what was in the story? . . . Why, or why not?

Do you ever do this sort of thing on your own? . . . If so, how often?

How well do you think you use these tricks or strategies? . . . Do you think they help? . . . Why?

Do you do these tricks or strategies differently from what we did a few minutes ago? What do you do?

Do you know some other reading tricks or strategies that good readers use? . . . Do you use them?

How do you know when it's a good time to use them?

Describe for me the kinds of things you think about or do **just before** you start to read that help you understand and remember the material. . . . **As** you are reading? . . . **After** you have finished reading?

Do you think learning to use these reading tricks or strategies could help you read better?

Which strategies do you think might be best to learn? Why?

Source: From "A Model for Assessing Cognitive Reading Strategies" by E. S. Ellis, 1989, *Academic Therapy, 24*, p. 422. Copyright 1989 by PRO-ED, Inc. Reprinted by permission.

tive to the curriculum being followed and the reading tasks being utilized, design diagnostic teaching lessons that enable collection of further data, and, finally use the results of instructive probes and lessons to modify programs.

The underlying purpose of this procedure is to verify a reader's specific errors or miscues, hypothesize reasons for the difficulties, and then derive implications that can guide instructional planning. Specifically, a teacher may examine reading skills to detect a variety of possible problems: poor attention to words, word details, or sentences; poor recognition of high-frequency words; inability to apply phonetic analysis skills for which competence had been demonstrated in drill exercises; failure to use contextual analysis as indicated by comparable (or superior) levels of accuracy for words presented in isolation versus those encountered in context; overattention to word analysis that may interfere with meaning cues and comprehension; and, significant deviations between recall in oral and silent reading.

Figure 8.2 presents a useful form for summarizing this kind of diagnostic data. Again, however, assessment must not simply result in the reduction of the interactive reading process to the isolated skills of the reader but, rather, place these data within the context of the reading act.

The verification of errors or miscues and the analysis of problems allows the teacher to write learning objectives and then develop and implement educational programs. Chapter 9 explores ways in which teachers can choose reading methods and materials to meet the instructional needs of individual learners.

This chapter concludes with some general suggestions for the overall development of a reading program. Because these suggestions include elements relevant to as-

Student's name: _____   Age: _____
Class placement: _____   Teacher: _____

Key: N = Not acquired   P = Needs practice   M = Mastered

Reading levels: Independent _____   Tests used: IRI _____
                Instructional _____   Survey _____
                Frustration _____   Diagnostic _____
                                                  Other _____

Sight word vocabulary: SORT _____   Dolch list _____   Other _____

Phonics:
  Consonants

b	c	d	f	g	h	j	k	l	m	n	p	q	r	s	t	v	w	x	y	z

Vowels:

	a	e	i	o	u	y
Long sound						
Short sound						

Digraphs

ch	sh	th	wh

Variant vowels

ar	er	ir	or	ur	au	al	on	ow	oi	oy

Blends

bl	cl	fl	gl	pl	sl	br	cr	dr	fr	gr	pr	tr	wn	ap	st

Comprehension: Factual questions _____   Main idea _____
               Inferential questions _____   Sequence of events _____
               Application questions _____   Cause and effect _____

Reading interests: _____
Comments: _____
_____

Source: From "Reading" by R. Schewel in *Strategies for Teaching Learners with Special Needs* (p. 217), edited by E. A. Polloway, J. R. Patton, J. S. Payne, and R. A. Payne, 1989, Columbus, OH: Charles E. Merrill. Reprinted with permission of Merrill, on imprint of Macmillan Publishing Company. Copyright © 1989 by Macmillan Publishing Company.

Figure 8.2
Reading Diagnosis Form for an Individual Student

sessment planning and instruction, it is presented here to serve as a transition between the discussions of this chapter and the next.

DEVELOPING A READING PROGRAM

Building a successful reading program requires more than reliable assessment instruments and appropriate curricular materials. Equally important is to develop instructional strategies that will help the student progress. The following principles, including some adapted from Polloway, Payne, Patton and Payne (1985) and from Schewel (1989), are intended to underlie an effective program.

Reduce anxiety. For students with a history of failure, reading may have become a painful activity that they refer to as hateful, boring, or a waste of time. As a consequence, the teacher is responsible for finding ways of reversing this cycle and making reading more pleasurable. Establishing rapport, selecting assessments and materials not associated with past failures, assigning materials at an appropriate difficulty level (Graham & Johnson, 1989), and removing tension from the actual process of testing or teaching are good ways to begin.

Ensure success. A blend of challenge and success is productive for most learners. If students have failed before, teachers should emphasize success by choosing activities well within the student's abilities, by beginning instruction with success experiences and by concluding individual lessons with a review of skills that the child has learned. Successful experiences are the first step to motivating children to perform. The use of graphing, for example, can help to illustrate skills acquisition and serve as a consistent reminder of progress for the student.

Use appropriate prereading activities. A key predictor of successful reading activities consists of the strategies used prior to beginning the lesson. Graham and Johnson (1989) provided an excellent review of research-validated practices that promote successful reading. Included are goal-setting, making predictions, activating prior knowledge, using advanced organizers, and previewing material. A number of these also help to develop the natural relationships between reading and oral language development. Further information on instructional strategies are discussed in chapter 9.

Provide incentive. Various tools can be used to motivate students who find reading not motivating, uninteresting, or perhaps even repulsive. Some students respond to social recognition for achievement, in the form of praise, achievement certificates, or notes to parents. Other students may require more extrinsically oriented reinforcement. Those who believe that reading should be an intrinsically reinforcing process have questioned the use of reinforcement strategies in reading. In his classic volume on reading disabilities, Ross (1976) succinctly responded to this concern when he stated:

> Ultimately, since the child will be learning to read in the process and to discover that interesting things can be garnered from the page, reading will become "its own reward." Then the child will be at the point where extrinsic reinforcers will no longer be needed. Such a child will now be reading for the same reasons most people read, but to assume that a disabled reader should be reading for the same reasons that motivate most people is to over-

look the fact that the disabled reader is disabled and is thus not like most people. A judicious, temporary use of artificial reinforcers can help make reading its own reward. (p. 165)

Encourage cooperation. Successful programs rely on the active involvement of various individuals. For example, students can be invited to help set goals for themselves on a short-term basis and to select the instructional activities to meet those goals. Collaboration with other teachers who share responsibility for instruction is a key area of cooperation that has increasingly become part of the responsibilities of special education professionals (e.g., Heron & Harris, 1988; Idol, Nevin & Paolucci-Whitcomb, 1986; West & Idol, 1990). Cooperation with parents is also important; it is discussed at greater length in item 12.

Design flexible programs. Teachers who adhere rigidly to a single approach may discover that a student's achievement decelerates. When designing a total reading program, therefore, teachers must consider whether the material under consideration can meet all the needs of one child or a group of children. Adoption of a core program should be followed by close monitoring of student progress to verify the effectiveness of the approach. Teachers should operate under the assumption that every reading approach may be successful with some children and unsuccessful with others (Heilman et al., 1986).

Avoid substitutive programs. The field of learning disabilities has historically produced many reading-related instructional approaches oriented to processes that are purported to be related to reading achievement. Support for these programs has not been impressive. Adopting perceptual training programs, for example, must be questioned, especially because this takes time away from direct teaching of reading skills (see Hammill & Bartel, 1982, for a comprehensive review). Research validates the adage, "The best way for students to learn to read is to teach them to read."

Exercise caution with modalities. Research on preferred modalities has produced similarly discouraging results. For example, efforts to match visual approaches to reading (a look-way approach) with so-called visual learners, and auditory ones (phonics) with auditory learners simply has not been validated in the research literature (Kampwirth & Bates, 1980; Tarver & Dawson, 1978). As with training in related areas, teachers who choose to incorporate modality preferences into instructional plans should do so only on an experimental basis and should commit to evaluating effectiveness on a regular basis.

A special issue of the *Journal of Special Education* highlighted concerns about the relevance of individual differences to instruction. Speece (1990) argued that the concept of aptitude-treatment interactions, which underlies the notion of modality preferences, may have validity but that the complexity of the relationships has hindered the process of verification. Hofmeister (1990) contended that focusing on the instructionally relevant aspects of individual differences (e.g., prerequisite knowledge, guided practice needed on a given skill, feedback required) would result in a more productive perspective. Deno (1990) also stressed the importance of evaluating learning progress as a basis for individual differences in treatment as a preferred alternative to evaluating aptitude variance at the outset of a program.

Update

The Challenges of Homework

During the 1990s, a substantial amount of research has addressed the problems experienced by students with disabilities in the area of homework. In an article by Bryan and Sullivan-Burstein (1997), the difficulties that students experienced in homework were summarized. In research primarily focused on students with learning disabilities, the most common difficulties found by students included the following:

- expressed a higher incidence of negative feelings
- were less likely to complete assignments
- expressed boredom and resistance to assignments
- perceived themselves as less competent than their peers in doing assignments
- reported that they received less help and encouragement and more criticism from parents
- were most likely to procrastinate
- more often needed to be reminded to do the work
- more often needed to have someone in the room
- tended to daydream while doing homework
- were more easily distracted

Source: Bryan, T., & Sullivan-Burstein, K. (1997) Homework how-to's. *Teaching Exceptional Children, 29,* 32–37.

Shift from oral to silent reading. Although initial reading often is done orally to monitor the skills of beginning readers, the teacher should keep in mind that this emphasis may detour students from the ultimate goal of silent reading. Therefore, as children progress beyond this initial stage, the emphasis should shift to silent reading, which eventually will enhance both rate and comprehension, and it will develop self-monitoring abilities. Once this shift has occurred, oral reading can be used primarily for diagnostic purposes or to reinforce specific skills or concepts.

To determine when students are ready to shift from oral to silent reading, Lovitt (1975) suggested two criteria successfully used in the programs run by him and his colleagues. If a child's rate of silent reading is higher than his or her oral reading rate, and if comprehension is at an equal or superior level, the emphasis should be shifted.

Be organized. Effective reading instruction demands careful planning. Because time is at a premium for students who have disabilities, only careful planning can maximize the benefits of a 55-minute or hour instructional period. Although organization does not assure successful programs, their absence is likely to preclude it (Heilman et al., 1986).

Provide sufficient time. A critical variable in reading instruction, as well as in all other curricular areas, is simply *time,* a variable that Simmons' (1990) research indicates is not sufficiently provided. As Graden, Thurlow, and Ysseldyke's (1982) model emphasized, time can be successively broken down as follows: time *in* the school day, time *allocated* to instruction, time *spent* in instruction, time of *active engagement,* and *academic responding* time. Time available—in particular, time of successful active engagement and academic responding—is highly predictive of achievement. This is an especially valid observation for students with learning and behavior problems (Graden et al., 1982; Marzano, Hagerty, Valencia, & DiStefano, 1987). Figure 8.3 provides an illustration of these phenomena, with the emphasis being placed on the limited amount of *academic learning time* often available to the individual student.

Promote home-school cooperation. Developing good working relationships with parents can enhance any reading instructional effect in the classroom. Homework in regular programs often has been demonstrated to have a positive effect on achievement and reading proficiency, especially for adolescents (e.g., Chall & Snow, 1988; Cooper, 1989a, 1989b; U.S. Department of Education, 1990). Even for younger students, where the benefits have not been clearly demonstrated (Cooper, 1989b), homework can help to develop good "habit-formation" in terms of reading practices, study skills, and building of positive attitudes (Epstein, Polloway, Foley, & Patton, 1991).

The limited experimental literature on the efficacy of homework with students who have mild disabilities can be viewed cautiously as indicating that homework has positive effects on their school achievement as well. But clear documentation of a causal or even correlative relationship between homework and achievement has yet to be established (Heller, Spooner, Anderson, & Mimms, 1988). Nevertheless, in research on students with low ability in the regular classroom, Keith (1982) indicated that these students "can achieve grades commensurate with their . . . peers through increased study" (p. 252).

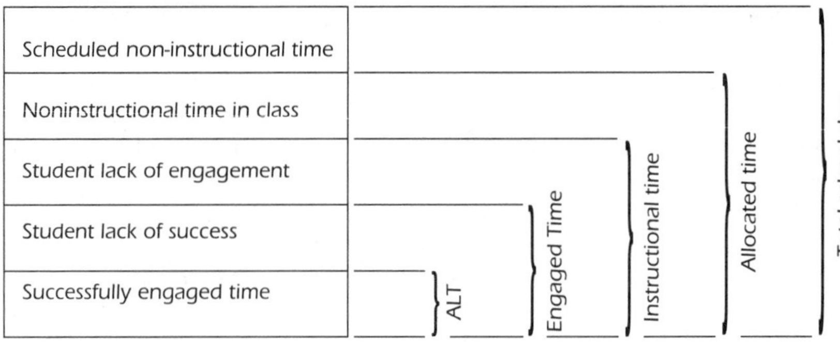

Source: From *Reading Diagnosis and Intervention: Theory into Practice* (p. 250) by R. J. Marzano, P. J. Hagerty, S. W. Valencia, and P. P. DiStefano, 1987, Englewood Cliffs, NJ: Prentice Hall. Reprinted by permission of Allyn & Bacon.

Figure 8.3
Academic Learning Time (ALT)

Teachers should carefully consider programs that involve parents in assisting their students at home. For example, tutoring (Shapero & Forbes, 1981; Vinograd-Bausell, Bausell, Proctor, & Chandler, 1986), establishing a designated study area and set study time (Landers, 1984), providing encouragement, and establishing rewards for completion may all be quite effective in promoting positive attitudes toward achievement in students, when handled appropriately. Based on their research on homework and achievement, Holmes and Croll (1989) encouraged parental involvement, noting that homework, for example, provides in a "practical and symbolic fashion a link between home and school and an opportunity for parents to exert influence" (p. 44). In a critical area such as reading, such a potentially important contribution to student learning should not be overlooked.

SUMMARY

Reading is the most common area of difficulty experienced by students in general and in particular students with disabilities. At the same time, reading competency is critical for a variety of academic tasks and life skill demands. Reading instruction can be considered within the context of stages related to development as well as within the context of varying purposes.

Numerous assessment tools are available within the reading domain. Formal tests can provide both survey and diagnostic information. Criterion-referenced, informal, and curriculum-based measures can offer more specific information that assists in designing instructional programs.

Since reading is a critical area for school and life success, it is helpful to consider overriding principles which govern assessment and instructional practices. These include ways to structure daily lessons, provide motivation, select instructional materials, and promote home-school cooperation.

REFERENCES

Allen, J. E., Jr. (1969). The right to read: Education's new national priority. *American School Board Journal, 157,* 25–27.

Armbruster, B. B., & Anderson, T. H. (1988). On selecting "considerate" content area textbooks. *Remedial and Special Education, 9*(1), 47–52.

Barclay, K. D. (1990). Constructing meaning: An integrated approach to teaching reading. *Interventions in School and Clinic, 26,* 84-91.

Bartel, N. R. (1986). Teaching children with reading problems. In D. D. Hammill & N. R. Bartel (Eds.), *Teaching children with learning and behavior problems* (4th ed.). Boston: Allyn & Bacon.

Barudin, S. I., & Hourcade, J. J. (1990). Relative effectiveness of three methods of reading instruction in developing specific recall and transfer skills in learners with moderate and severe mental retardation. *Education and Training in Mental Retardation, 25,* 286-291.

Bean, R. M., & Lane, S. (1990). Implementing curriculum-based measures of reading in an adult literacy program. *Remedial and Special Education, 11*(5), 39-46.

Browder, D. M., & Snell, M. E. (1987). Functional academics. In M. E. Snell (Ed.), *Systematic instruction of persons with severe handicaps* (pp. 436–468). Columbus, OH: Charles E. Merrill Publishing.

Bryan, T., & Sullivan-Burstein, K. (1997) Homework how-to's. *Teaching Exceptional Children, 29,* 32–37.

Busch, R. (1980). Predicting first grade reading achievement. *Learning Disability Quarterly, 3,* 38–48.

Chall, J. (1983). *Stages of reading development.* New York: McGraw-Hill.

Chall, J. J., & Snow, C. E. (1988). *School influences on the reading development of low-income children.* ERIC Digests On-line Project.

Cooper, H. M. (1989a). *Homework.* White Plains, NY: Longman.

Cooper, H. (1989b). Synthesis of research on homework. *Educational Leadership, 47,* 85–91.

Crain, S. K. (1988). *The role of phonics in reading instruction.* ERIC Digests On-line Project.

Deno, S. L. (1985). Curriculum-based measurement: The emerging alternative. *Exceptional Children, 52,* 219–232.

Deno, S. L. (1990). Individual differences and individual difference: The essential difference in special education. *Journal of Special Education, 24,* 160–173.

Deno, S. L., & Fuchs, L. S. (1987). Developing curriculum-based measurement systems for data-based special education problem solving. *Focus on Exceptional Children, 19*(6), 1–16.

Dunn, L. M., & Markwardt, F. C. (1988). *Peabody individual achievement test—Revised.* Circle Pines, MN: American Guidance Service.

Durrell, D. D., & Catterson, J. (1980). *Durrell analysis of reading difficulty.* New York: Harcourt, Brace.

Dyck, N. J., Sankey, P., & Sundbye, N. W. (1983). *Survival words programs.* Hingham, MA: Teaching Resources.

Ekwall, E. E. (1986). *Ekwall reading inventory.* Boston: Allyn & Bacon.

Ellis, E. S. (1989). A model for assessing cognitive reading strategies. *Academic Therapy, 24,* 407–242.

Epstein, M. H., Polloway, E. A., Foley, R. M., & Patton, J. R. (1991). *Homework: A comparison of the problems experienced by students identified as behaviorally disordered, learning disabled, and nonhandicapped.* Manuscript submitted for publication.

Epstein, M. H., Polloway, E. A., & Patton, J. R. (1988). Academic achievement probes: Reliability of measures for students with mild mental retardation. *Special Services in the Schools, 5*(1/2), 23–31.

Folk, M. C., & Campbell, J. (1978). Teaching functional reading to the TMR. *Education and Training of the Mentally Retarded, 13,* 322–326.

Fuchs, L. S., & Fuchs, D. (1986). Effects of systematic formative evaluation: A meta-analysis. *Exceptional Children, 53,* 199–208.

Gersten, R., & Carnine. D. (1988). Direct instruction in reading comprehension. In E. L. Meyen, G. A. Vergason, & R. J. Whelan (Eds.), *Effective instructional strategies for exceptional children* (pp. 65–79). Denver: Love Publishing.

Gickling, E. E., & Thompson, V. P. (1985). A personal view of curriculum-based assessment. *Exceptional Children, 52,* 205–218.

Goodman, K. S. (1969). Analysis of oral reading miscues: Applied psycholinguistics. *Reading Research Quarterly, 5,* 9–30.

Goodman, K. S. (1973). Miscues: Windows on reading. In K. S. Goodman (Ed.), *Miscue analysis.* Urbana, IL: ERIC.

Goodman, Y., & Burke, C. (1972). *Reading miscue inventory.* New York: Macmillan.

Graden, J., Thurlow, M. L., & Ysseldyke, J. E. (1982). *Academic engaged time and its relationship to learning: A review of the literature.* Minneapolis: University of Minnesota Institute for Research on Learning Disabilities.

Graham, S., & Johnson, L. A. (1989). Teaching reading to learning disabled students: A review of research supported procedures. *Focus on Exceptional Children, 21*(6), 1–12.

Hammill, D. D., & Bartel, N. R. (1982). *Teaching children with learning and behavior problems* (3rd ed.). Boston: Allyn & Bacon.

Harris, A. (1970). *How to increase reading ability* (5th ed.). New York: David McKay Publishing.

Harris, A. J., & Sipay, E. R. (1990). *How to increase reading ability: A guide to developmental and remedial methods.* New York: Longman.

Heilman, A. W., Blair, T. R., & Rupley, W. H. (1986). *Principles and practices of teaching reading.* Columbus, OH: Charles E. Merrill Publishing.

Heller, H. W., Spooner, F., Anderson, D., & Mimms, A. (1988). Homework: A review of special education practices in the southwest. *Teacher Education and Special Education, 11,* 43–51.

Heron, T. E., & Harris, K. C. (1988). *The educational consultant: Helping professionals, parents and mainstreamed students* (2nd Ed.). Austin, TX: Pro-Ed.

Hofmeister, A. M. (1990). Individual differences and the form and function of instruction. *Journal of Special Education, 24,* 150–159.

Holmes, M., & Croll, P. (1989). Time spent on homework and academic achievement. *Educational Research, 31,* 36–45.

Idol, L., Nevin, A., & Paolucci-Whitcomb, P. (1986). *Collaborative consultation.* Rockville, MD: Aspen.

Jastak, J. F., & Wilkinson, F. (1984). *The wide range achievement test—Revised.* Wilmington, DE: Jastak Associates.

Johnson, D. D. (1971). The Dolch list reexamined. *Reading Teacher, 24,* 455–456.

Kampwirth, T. J., & Bates, M. (1980). Modality preference and teaching method: A review of the research. *Academic Therapy, 15,* 597–606.

Karlin, R. (1971). *Teaching elementary reading.* New York: Harcourt, Brace, Jovanovich.

Keith, T. Z. (1982). Time spent on homework and high grades: A large-sample path analysis. *Journal of Educational Psychology, 74,* 248–253.

Kirk, S. A. (1940). *Teaching reading to slow learning children.* Boston: Houghton Mifflin.

Kirk, S. A., Kliebhan, J. M., & Lerner, J. W. (1978). *Teaching reading to slow and disabled learners.* Boston: Houghton Mifflin.

Kirsch, I. S., & Jungebut, A. (1986). *Literacy: Profiles of America's young adults.* Princeton, NJ: National Assessment of Educational Progress.

Landers, M. F. (1984). Helping the LD child with homework: Ten tips. *Academic Therapy, 20,* 209–215.

Langone, J. (1990). *Teaching students with mild and moderate learning problems.* Boston: Allyn & Bacon.

Lenz, B. K., & Hughes, C. A. (1990). A word identification strategy for adolescents with learning disabilities. *Journal of Learning Disabilities, 23,* 149–159.

Lovitt, T. C. (1975). Applied behavior analysis and learning disabilities: Part 2. *Journal of Learning Disabilities, 8,* 504–518.

Marston, D., & Magnusson, D. (1985). Implementing curriculum-based measurement in special and regular education settings. *Exceptional Children, 52,* 266–276.

Marzano, R. J., Hagerty, P. J., Valencia, S. W., & DiStefano, P. P. (1987). *Reading diagnosis and instruction: Theory into practice.* Englewood Cliffs, NJ: Prentice Hall.

McGuffey informal reading inventory. (1960). Unpublished manuscript, McGuffey Reading Center, Charlottesville, VA.

Mercer, C. D., & Mercer, A. P. (1989). *Teaching students with learning problems* (3rd ed.). Columbus, OH: Charles E. Merrill Publishing.

Polloway, C. H. (Ed.) (n. d.). *Campbell County reading skills sequence.* Unpublished manuscript, Campbell County Public Schools, Rustburg, VA.

Polloway, E. A., Patton, J. R., Payne, J. S., and Payne, R. A. (1989). *Strategies for teaching learners with special needs.* Columbus, OH: Charles E. Merrill Publishing.

Polloway, E. A., Patton, J. R., Smith, J. D., & Roderique, T. (1991). Issues in program design for elementary students with mild retardation: Emphasis on curriculum development. *Education and Training in Mental Retardation, 26,* 142–150.

Polloway, E. A., Payne, J. S., Patton, J. R., & Payne, R. A. (1985). *Strategies for teaching the mentally retarded and special needs learners.* Columbus, OH: Charles E. Merrill Publishing.

Polloway, E. A., & Polloway, C. H. (1981). Survival words for disabled readers. *Academic Therapy, 16,* 443–448.

Polloway, E. A., & Smith, J. E. (1982). *Teaching language skllls to exceptional learners.* Denver: Love Publishing.

Pope, L. (1967). *Guidelines to teaching remedial reading to the disadvantaged.* New York: Faculty Press.

Robinson, G. (1986). *Essential vocabulary: Words and phrases found in community settings.* Des Moines, IA: State Department of Education.

Ross, A. D. (1976). *Psychological aspects of learning disabilities and reading disorders.* New York: McGraw-Hill.

Samuels, S. J. (1981). Some essentials of decoding. *Exceptional Education Quarterly, 2*(1), 11–26.

Schewel, R. (1989). Reading. In E. A. Polloway, J. R. Patton, J. S. Payne, & R. A. Payne (Eds.), *Strategies for teaching learners with special needs* (pp. 207–254). Columbus, OH: Charles E. Merrill Publishing.

Shapero, S., & Forbes, C. R. (1981). A review of involvement programs for parents of learning disabled. *Journal of Learning Disabilities, 14,* 499–504.

Silberberg, N. E., & Silberberg, M. C. (1977). A note on reading tests and their role in defining reading difficulties. *Journal of Learning Disabilities, 10,* 100-103.

Silvaroli, N. J. (1986). *Classroom reading inventory* (2nd ed.). Dubuque, IA: Wm. C. Brown.

Simmons, E. (Oct., 1990). *Peer-mediated instruction in reading.* Paper presented at Council for Learning Disabilities annual conference, Austin, TX.

Slosson, R. L. (1981). *Slosson oral reading test.* East Aurora, NY: Slosson Educational Publications.

Snell, M. E. (1978). Functional reading. In M. E. Snell (Ed.), *Systematic instruction of the moderately and severely handicapped.* Columbus, OH: Charles E. Merrill Publishing.

Snell, M. E. (1988). Curriculum and methodology for individuals with severe disabilities. *Education and Training in Mental Retardation, 23,* 302–214.

Snider, V. E. (1989). Reading comprehension performance of adolescents with learning disabilities. *Learning Disability Quarterly, 12,* 87–96.

Spache, G. D. (1981). *Diagnostic reading scales.* Monterey, CA: California Test Bureau/McGraw Hill.

Speece, D. L. (1990). Aptitude-treatment interactions: Bad rap or bad idea? *Journal of Special Education, 24,* 139–149.

Tarver, S. G., & Dawson, M. M. (1978). Modality preference and reading: An assessment of the research and theory. *Journal of Learning Disabilities, 11,* 5–17.

U.S. Department of Education (1990). Reading and writing proficiency remains low. *Daily Education News* (January 9), pp. 1–7.

Valencia, S. W., & Pearson, D. P. (1988). Principles for classroom comprehension assessment. *Remedial and Special Education, 9*(1), 26–35.

Vinograd-Bausell, C. R., Bausell, R. B., Proctor, W., & Chandler, B. (1986). Impact of unsupervised parent tutors on word recognition skills. *Journal of Special Education, 20,* 83–90.

Walker, C. M. (1979). High frequency word list for grades 3 through 9. *Reading Teacher, 32,* 803–812.

Wallace, G., & Kauffman, J. M. (1986). *Teaching students with learning and behavior problems* (3rd ed.). Columbus, OH: Charles E. Merrill Publishing.

West, J. F., & Idol, L. (1990). Collaborative consultation in the education of mildly handicapped and at-risk students. *Remedial and Special Education, 11*(1), 22–31.

Westman, J. C. (1990). *Handbook of learning disabilities: A multisensory approach.* Boston: Allyn & Bacon.

Wiederholt, J. L., & Bryant, B. (1986). *The Gray oral reading test—Revised.* Austin, TX: Pro-Ed.

Wiederholt, J. L., & Bryant, B. (1987). Assessing reading. In D. D. Hammill (Ed.), *Assessing the abilities and instructional needs of students* (pp. 161–340). Austin, TX: Pro-Ed.

Woodcock, R. W. (1986). *Woodcock reading mastery tests—Revised.* Circle Pines, MN: American Guidance Service.

9

Reading Instruction

T he question of how to teach a child to read, particularly a child who has disabilities, has virtually dwarfed other subject areas in terms of research inquiry and programming development. This chapter surveys some of the techniques that practice and empirical data have shown to be the most effective for teaching learners with special needs. Although this wealth of information deals primarily with students who have mild handicaps, the increasing interest in students with moderate to severe disabilities is also reflected here.

Approaches to teaching reading often have been classified as "bottom-up" or "top-down" in orientation. As Bartel (1986) noted, the former are skills-oriented approaches characterized by attention to reading letters, then words and sentences and fully meaningful paragraphs; they often are referred to as decoding approaches. The latter, often termed "holistic" and derived from whole language orientations, emphasize the meaning of what is read and thus focus on the way the reader comprehends the printed word.

Top-down approaches traditionally have received strong support through the theoretical orientations of Smith (1973), Goodman (1973), and others, whereas the decoding emphasis has been bulwarked by empirical data (Carnine & Silbert, 1979; Chall, 1967; Chall & Snow, 1988; Tarver & Ellsworth, 1981). Both pure approaches have inherent limitations that require consideration (O'Shea, 1990) and consequently call for an interactive position. Interactive models "view reading as all levels of processing interacting together. In addition, information is believed to be generated by any level (i.e., the meaning of the text, the structure of the language, or the features of the words or letters)" (Wiederholt & Bryant, 1987, p. 171).

A useful model for understanding reading instruction was presented by Samuels (1981). His perspective accommodates the importance of both decoding and meaning emphases in instruction, but holds that only a limited amount of attention is available (especially to the immature or disabled reader) to accomplish both tasks at the same time. Specifically, his assumptions for the model are as follows (p. 15):

- The reading process can be broken into decoding and comprehending.
- Attention is required in reading.
- Attention may be used simultaneously for decoding and comprehending, as long as the amount of attention these processes demand does not exceed an individual's attention capacity.
- If the combined attention demands of decoding and comprehending exceed attention capacity, the reader can alternately direct attention to decoding and comprehending.

Samuels' developmental model of reading is presented in Figure 9.1. Most important, he illustrates how the beginning reader must devote virtually his or her entire attention first to decoding (rather than to comprehension) and later, at the fluent stage, decoding and comprehension can be handled simultaneously. This model offers a useful perspective on reading instruction that can accommodate varied approaches to instruction.

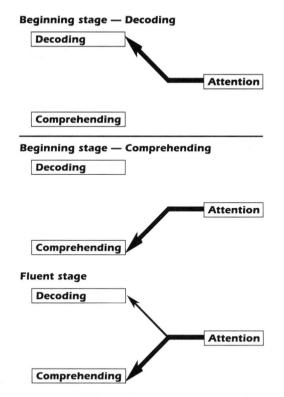

Note: Beginning stage shows attention alternating between decoding and comprehending. Fluent stage shows attention divided between decoding and both processes occurring simultaneously. The thin line indicates that just a small portion of attentional resources is allocated; the thick line indicates that a major portion of attentional resources is on comprehension.

Source: From "Some Essentials of Decoding" by J. Samuels, 1981, *Exceptional Education Quarterly, 2:1*, p. 16. Copyright 1981 by PRO-ED, Inc. Reprinted by permission.

Figure 9.1
A Developmental Model of Reading

Curriculum and methodology are discussed in the areas of readiness, word recognition, and comprehension. Although these areas are addressed separately, practitioners should realize that readers with disabilities require a comprehensive approach to instruction that considers skills within a broad context. Selected general commercial programs for reading instruction are reviewed throughout the chapter. Because we believe that there is *no one correct way* to teach reading, the following discussion surveys many valid approaches that teachers can draw upon to remedy specific problems in individual children and adolescents. Most important to understand is that the teacher virtually determines student success; the instructor's ability to teach so that a student learns to read takes precedence over any approach, material, or program. The reader should remember that the study of reading is so vast that all teachers must continue to be learners. The goal of this chapter is to promote a solid foundation for this continual learning process.

READINESS

As noted in chapter 8, readiness is not an absolute concept and does not suggest an absolute point at which reading should begin. Rather, it reflects emergent literacy as the child successfully engages in reading-related tasks (Harris & Sipay, 1990). Generally, a child is approaching reading readiness when he or she shows an interest in stories and books and in words and visual symbols. At this time, teachers must emphasize the skills that will assist in the transition to formal reading instruction.

Because oral language skills initially precede reading and then develop in parallel fashion with reading, few would disagree that young or developmentally young children need a variety of linguistic opportunities, exercises, and activities to achieve reading readiness. Assuming that a child's physiological needs, such as diet and rest, are met, he or she must possess several interrelated language skills before reading is possible.

1. The child must comprehend language. In the general sense, this means that a child must be familiar with vocabulary and be able to meet the receptive and expressive demands of the environment.
2. The child must have the auditory skills necessary to read, including the ability to make increasingly finer discriminations between environmental noises, dissimilar words, dissimilar and later similar phonemes, initial consonants, final consonants, and vowel sounds. Based on these skills, the child can learn phonetic analysis skills, as noted later in this chapter. In their significant research study on disadvantaged children, Wallach and Wallach (1976) cited the ability to recognize and blend phonemes as one of the essential skills necessary for reading success.
3. The child needs the visual skills that precede successful reading—namely, the ability to discriminate figures of increasing similarity, the ability to recognize consistencies in object forms, and the ability to coordinate eye and motor movements.

LETTER DISCRIMINATION

The ability to identify distinctive features of letters is an important aspect of visual readiness. In her classic research in this area, Gibson (1963) identified the following as developmentally important to emerging readers:

1. Breaks versus closes (e.g., o/c).
2. Rotations (e.g., m/w).
3. Reversals (e.g., b/d).
4. Line to curve (e.g., v/u).
5. Rotation and closure (e.g., A/V).

As the child refines his or her abilities to discriminate these features, errors that are initially common in young children (e.g., line to curve) are distinguished more readily because they are tied closely to the central task of letter discrimination. The area of reversals, however, seems to present special problems for some learners who are handicapped, perhaps because of the demand for spatial orientation skills (Cohn & Stricker, 1979).

LETTER REVERSALS[1]

Although many young children initially may struggle with reversals, this problem becomes more crucial when it persists into the second or third grade. Reversals of the letters b and d warrant special attention because they are popularly (and often inaccurately) viewed as typical of learning disabilities Various approaches have been advocated for reversal difficulties. Smith and Lovitt (1973) outlined three general options that educators have chosen to use with reversals.

1. *No intervention* is rooted in the concept of maturational lag, and assumes that teachers must wait for improvement to take place naturally.
2. *Indirect intervention* implies a belief in reading-related programs (e.g., visual-perceptual training) rather than reading programs to remedy the problem.
3. *Direct intervention* suggests the concept of reversals as a cognitive skill deficit related to the ability to analyze critical features.

The work of Moyer and Newcomer (1977) and Deno and Chiang (1979) has supported the idea that reversals are cognitive skill deficits that respond to training. Both pairs of researchers reported that direct training with incentives resulted in decreased occurrences of reversals. It follows then that the most effective educational techniques would teach a child to determine the distinctive features of letters. This goal can be achieved through fading strategies that begin with comparisons at a gross level of discrimination and gradually progress to finer levels.

The program described by Polloway and Polloway (1980) is based on introducing the lowercase *b* through a fading-out technique from its uppercase counterpart *B*. In this manner, letter directionality could be initially highlighted with a cue so that the *b-d* distinction would be readily apparent, and then the salience of the cues can be gradually reduced. The standard lowercase *d* is held constant throughout the program.

Selection of these instructional stimuli was based on two rationales. First, younger children have relatively less difficulty with uppercase letters and, second, the uppercase *B* highlights the directional feature that can be easily faded to its lowercase counterpart over a prescribed series of steps. Figure 9.2 is an illustration of 14 sequential steps used in this fading procedure. Salience of the prompt is reduced to a final cue "dot" before the student is asked to make the actual *b-d* discrimination in the last step. At this point, the critical features differentiating *b* and *d* should have been internalized.

In concluding their review of the reversals problem, Moyer and Newcomer (1977) noted:

---

[1] This section is adapted from "Remediating Reversals Through Stimulus Fading" by C. H. Polloway and E. A. Polloway, 1980, *Academic Therapy, 15*, pp. 539–543. Reproduced courtesy of the publisher, ATP, 20 Commercial Blvd., Novato, CA 94947.

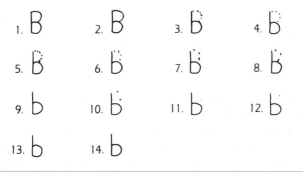

Source: From "Remediating Reversals Through Stimulus Fading" by C. H. Polloway and E. A. Polloway, 1980, *Academic Therapy, 15*, p. 541. Reproduced courtesy of the publisher, ATP, 20 Commercial Blvd., Novato, CA 94947.

Figure 9.2
Gradual Fading of Uppercase B to Lowercase b

> Until children encounter those letters of the alphabet that have mirror image counterparts, they have no occasion to consider spatial orientation when identifying objects in the environment. A chair is recognized and called a chair no matter which way it faces. (p. 428)

Teachers who view reversals as cognitive deficits and design programs accordingly will succeed in helping children overcome this problem. As Polloway and Polloway (1980) concluded:

> Because they are generally aware of their own inability to make the correct discrimination, this deficit is often a source of great frustration for children. However, these difficulties can become the source of strong motivation in a child to learn to understand and overcome the problem. (p. 543)

WORD RECOGNITION

When presented with a passage to read, a child must respond to two demands: (a) identifying the specific words presented, and (b) understanding what he or she has read. The former includes the process of word recognition and analysis, and the latter is concerned with reading comprehension. Methods of teaching four critical elements of word recognition/analysis are discussed next, followed by a discussion of comprehension and its development. By emphasizing both concerns, teachers should be able to build an effective program without stifling student interest.

The four word-recognition approaches discussed here are sight word identification, phonetic analysis, structural analysis, and contextual analysis. The former is associated with *immediate word identification,* and the latter three can be termed *mediated word recognition* strategies, for reasons that will be apparent in the discussion (Marzano, Hagerty, Valencia, & DiStefano, 1987). A fifth approach, *configurational analysis* (focusing on the outline or shape of a word) has been omitted because of equivocal findings, at best, on its efficacy (Ekwall & Shanker, 1988; Harris & Sipay, 1990).

SIGHT VOCABULARY

Sight word recognition implies to some extent the idea of a whole word orientation to reading, which assumes that a child can identify a given word without having to analyze its details or components. Although some advocate the whole-word approach as the primary basis for reading instruction, this chapter emphasizes the development of sight recognition skills as just *one* of several functional word identification tools. Consistent with this philosophy, Wallen (1972) noted three basic reasons for teaching sight words: (a) to expedite reading by minimizing the time spent on word analysis, (b) to provide models for subsequent word analysis instruction, and (c) to teach phonetically irregular words.

The word lists presented in chapter 8 include prime examples of high-frequency words that should be recognized on sight. Lists of this nature should not convey, however, a sequence for presenting these words. To the contrary, Simms and Falcon (1987), for example, made an excellent case for presenting the words in a categorical fashion. The ultimate goal for mature readers, in any case, is to recognize all words quickly on sight.

The goal of sight vocabulary building is *automatic recognition*, the immediate identification of words, to maintain the flow of reading. To achieve automatic recognition, readers must have words firmly in their memories, ready for rapid recall. Therefore, the basis of sight word instruction is to provide a child with repeated exposures to a variety of words. Depending on the learner, teachers should think in terms of 20 or more exposures before a student locks a word into his or her memory store. Obviously, the student's ability, the relevance of the word, and the extrinsic motivation involved will affect the number of exposures needed. Hargis (1982) provided a particularly apt discussion on the importance of multiple exposures to a given word.

Teachers should draw upon various instructional activities to achieve this frequency of exposures. The following approaches represent some beneficial tools for building a strong sight vocabulary. Although these include some activities based on teaching words in isolation (e.g., timed drills), these efforts should be complemented by strategies that teach words in context (e.g., repeated readings).

Word Banks   Sight word building can be oriented toward the use of word banks as an outgrowth of a language experience approach (see discussion later in the chapter) or as a technique in its own right. With this system, each word is written on an index card and filed in a plastic box as a new, instructional, or mastery word. These words can be used for a variety of exercises, including flashcards, timed drilling that requires a child to recognize a specified number of words per minute, and meaning activities in which a child writes definitions, uses the words in sentences, or constructs short stories. The teacher should regularly evaluate activities with word cards to ensure transfer to reading in context.

Multiple Oral Readings   As the Samuels (1981) model (discussed earlier) conveys, the ideal approach to the decoding versus meaning dilemma is to follow a repeated readings approach or a multiple oral reading (MOR) orientation. As described by Moyer (1982), MOR is based on the assumption that limiting the number of possible responses results in an increased probability of accuracy; the greater the problems the child experiences in word recognition, the greater is the need for redundancy.

Moyer (1982) outlined the following steps for MOR:

1. Choose materials at a level that results in limited difficulty in word recognition.
2. Read initially at a comfortable pace.
3. Reread three to four times, increasing the speed with each reading.
4. Use passages of approximately 3-4 paragraphs on the average; vary according to the student's needs.

Although we arbitrarily placed this discussion of MOR in the sight vocabulary section, the technique has far greater utility. Research with students who have learning disabilities, for example, indicates that having students read the same passage three or more times and cuing them to read for meaning resulted in improvement in fluency (words read correctly per minute) and comprehension (retelling story propositions) (O'Shea, Sindelar, & O'Shea, 1987).

Neurological Impress Method (NIM)   NIM is an imitative system of unison reading for teachers and students. With NIM, the teacher calls out words in a passage while a child repeats them after a short (half-second) delay. This system theoretically gives the student both auditory and visual input as he or she progresses through the passage following the instructor.

Although methodology texts commonly advocate NIM, Lorenz and Yockell (1979) reported the technique did not produce direct increases in reading recognition or comprehension among students identified as having learning disabilities. They did indicate that teachers subjectively reported enhanced attitudes, rapport, oral reading patterns, and left-right progression. Therefore, this research suggests that teachers should use the tool on an experimental basis with other techniques and evaluate its effectiveness.

Modeling Strategies   Other specific modeling strategies may provide effective alternatives to NIM. Smith (1979), for example, reported a rather simple and straightforward modeling technique in which the teacher first read a passage aloud to a class of students and they read the stories themselves later. This initial exposure to the passage significantly increased reading rates and decreased error rates.

Hendrickson and Shores (1978) also reported that the systematic use of modeling was effective. These researchers found that word recognition improved significantly when a specific word was presented in a written sentence (This word is _____.) and the child then was asked to repeat the sentence three times in answer to the question: What is this? Teachers could develop other similar strategies to increase the number of word exposures through modeling.

Fernald Approach   Fernald's multisensory method utilizes the visual, auditory, kinesthetic, and tactile (VAKT) modalities to teach reading. Although it is discussed here as a sight word technique, it has functions far beyond this limited sphere. The text containing the program was originally published in 1943, but it was updated by Idol in 1988.

Fernald discussed the four stages of her method at length in her text, identifying the following basic procedures. Initially, the student helps to select the words he or she will learn. These words become the basis for story writing and thus can be used for comprehension as well.

1. *Tracing*. The student traces each new word with the index finger, saying *each* part of the word during the process. This step is repeated until the child can trace the word from memory. After the word is written, the teacher ensures that the word is identified by having it reread to guarantee recognition. In addition, the child must demonstrate use of the word in context.
2. *Writing without tracing*. The student looks at each word, says it several times, then writes it from memory. Teachers should use index cards to file the words during this stage.
3. *Recognition of words in print*. The student at this level should be able to retain words by merely looking at them and saying them aloud several times. Although putting the words on cards is less important during this stage, writing can be used for words that present difficulty.
4. *Transfer to word analysis*. In the final stage, the student transfers word recognition skills to the analysis of new words. Phonetic analysis is not taught as such, but students are encouraged to analyze unknown words by comparing them to words they already know and noting resemblances.

The Fernald method is an intensive instructional program with a decidedly clinical orientation, and even though Fernald (1943) clearly specified the steps to be taken in reading instruction, teachers may want to vary these to meet classroom realities or the needs of individual children. For example, Miccinati (1979) suggested adaptations such as using raised letters, tracing in the air, visual imagery, color coding, and typing the words to be learned. Without modifications, the approach should be best considered as an option for use with students who have severe reading disabilities and taught on an individual basis (Ekwall & Shanker, 1988).

Word Imprinting For students with severe visual memory impairment, Carbo (1978) suggested a multisensory procedure to intensively *imprint* the word using six instructional steps:

1. Seeing and repeating the word following the teacher's model.
2. Establishing the meaning of the word.
3. Tracing around the word to increase awareness of its configuration.
4. Tracing the word itself to provide a tactile experience.
5. Tracing and saying the word.
6. Picturing the word by looking at it, developing a visual image with eyes closed, and writing it in the air.

Regardless of whether Carbo's full sequence is needed for a given child, several of the steps could be used separately, as suggested with the Fernald method.

Behavioral Approach The Staats Motivation Activation Reading Technique (SMART) is an intensive approach based on operant technology. The SMART methodology was based on research by Staats and his colleagues (Staats & Butterfield, 1965; Staats, Finley, Minke, & Wolfe, 1964) and others (Camp, 1973). Their data show that this approach merits consideration when more traditional techniques fail. Although SMART is not designed solely to teach sight word acquisition, it offers an instructional alternative.

As described by Staats and Butterfield (1965), the procedure for implementing the program is:

1. Select the reading material to serve as a source for passages and vocabulary words (that research utilized the kit developed by Science Research Associates, SRA).
2. Develop a running list of new vocabulary words from the stories typed on 3″ x 5″ cards.
3. Type each paragraph from the stories on 5″ x 8″ cards.
4. Type each complete story with comprehension questions on 8½″ x 13″ paper.
5. Present all new vocabulary words individually to the student. Reward correct responses with a mid-value token. For each incorrect response, pronounce the word for the student, have him or her pronounce the word, and return it to the file. Continue until the student has pronounced all words correctly and been rewarded with low-value tokens.
6. Present each paragraph individually to the student. If he or she makes no errors, reward with high-value token. If errors are made, repeat reading at a later time until it is read correctly; then reward with a mid-value token.
7. Present story for silent reading. Reward attentive behavior during reading. Have the student write answers to the questions, and present a high-value token for accurate responses with spelling errors corrected. For inaccurate responses, have the student reread the appropriate paragraphs, and reward accurate responses with mid-value tokens.

In the study by Staats and Butterfield (1965), these techniques were successful with a 14-year-old juvenile delinquent who initially was a nonreader. When problems reach this level of severity, SMART is an effective tool to consider because it provides an intensive program with powerful extrinsic motivation.

Survival Words   The protection or survival words presented in chapter 8 should be taught as sight words because students need to recognize them as they appear in daily life. In essence, the teaching of survival words can be justified for people who are severely disabled if they can learn to respond differentially to the words (e.g., entering the correct room marked MEN or WOMEN), regardless of whether they can actually read them. In addition, the words being taught must be determined to be functional in their environment. Thus, teaching road signs to an individual who will not drive makes little sense (Browder & Snell, 1987). The approaches discussed below have been effective in teaching survival words and could be adapted for use with other sight words.

Dorry and Zeaman (1973, 1975) reported on an instructional program that uses paired associate learning for teaching sight recognition. Survival words were taught by showing children a picture and pairing it conceptually with its meaning. Later, the word was paired with the picture and, finally, the picture was faded out, leaving the association of the meaning paired only with the word. These researchers (Dorry and Zeaman, 1973) reported that the fading technique helped beginning readers both in initial acquisition and in transfer of specific words. The system is successful because the gradually faded picture forces the reader to depend on the salient stimuli, the nonfaded printed word (Dorry & Zeaman, 1975). Figure 9.3 presents several sample pictures that could be paired for teaching survival words.

Two program have been developed that provide an instruction approach to teach the survival words listed in chapter 8. Robinson (1986) developed a brief videotape program to illustrate the essential words and phrases and their matching sign for those who use manual communication. Also, the *Survival Words Program* (Dyck, Sankey, & Sundbye, 1983) is available. This is a kit that includes assessments, worksheets, books, and comprehension exercises. A teacher's manual provides details on use of the program.

Errorless discrimination is another way of teaching survival or other sight words. This system presents a key item along with distractor words, then gradually increases the degree of discrimination difficulty. Figure 9.4 illustrates how teachers can use errorless discrimination to teach the word "danger"; the tasks require students to select the correct choice from options of increasing similarity.

Related activities can be designed to reinforce the learning of survival words. McMullen (1975) suggested a variety of techniques including matching exercises (e.g., word to word, picture to word), classroom obstacle courses, and experiential learning in the community where school-based instruction could be applied. Barudin and Hourcade (1990) compared three approaches to sight recognition (flashcards, fad-

MEN

WOMEN

NO SMOKING

TELEPHONE

FIRE EXTINGUISHER

NO FIRES

Figure 9.3
Paired Associates: Picture and Survival Word

1.	—	DANGER	—
2.	—	—	DANGER
3.	RD	DANGER	—
4.	DANGER	GAX	VC
5.	NGR	AN	DANGER
6.	DANGER	DNG	DGR
7.	DA	DANGER	GER
8.	NGER	DAN	DANGER
9.	ANGE	DANGER	DANG
10.	DANGER	DAGGER	ANGER

Figure 9.4
Errorless Discrimination for Survival Words

ing, and kinesthetic-tactile) and found that all three were effective in teaching the words. They cautioned, however, that the techniques did not lead to generalization.

An important caution about teaching protection words such as those on product warning labels is implicit in the study reported by Fletcher and Abood (1988). They reported on an effort to transcribe the cautionary words on labels of potentially hazardous products and then subject these wordings to a readability analysis. Table 9.1 lists the words that appeared on multiple warning labels, with their frequencies. Because most of the key words on labels are above fourth-grade reading level, they encouraged teachers to determine whether the words could be learned and used before launching an instructional program. Given that partial success only on reading the labels may be dangerous for students and learning to read the labels is improbable, they encouraged instead a focus in identifying common hazardous materials by displaying the actual containers and then teaching appropriate handling of the substances and treatment for exposure.

Of course, not all survival words are associated with hazardous materials. Another example is represented by words and terms associated with entering the workforce. Schilit and Caldwell (1980) derived a list of 100 career/vocational words to prepare students for jobs, presented in Table 9.2.

VOCABULARY BUILDING

This emphasis on recognition of words on sight should not obscure the important concern for development of vocabulary in the sense of word meanings. Although many words initially learned by approximately the third or fourth grade have apparent meanings, students encounter many words whose meanings they do not know (Harris & Sipay, 1990). Building vocabulary is a particularly difficult task for students with disabilities or those identified as disadvantaged (Chall & Snow, 1988; Kameenui, 1990). The assumption of instruction in this area is that increases in vocabulary will have a positive effect on comprehension (Graham & Johnson, 1989b; Rupley & Blair, 1989). Teachers

Update

Phonological Awareness

Throughout the 1990s, there has been an increasing awareness of the importance of phonological awareness to the process of learning to read. Numerous researchers have begun to draw the same conclusion that students experiencing difficulty in reading frequently have in common problems in responding to the sounds which constitute our language. In his statement to the Subcommittee Disability Policy of the Committee Laboring Human Resources of the United States Senate, Lyon (1995) succinctly emphasized the importance of the implications of this point. Specifically, he indicated:

- reading is a reflection of language and the deficit which results in the majority of cases of reading disability occurs at the basic level of the phoneme (i.e., sound-symbol correspondences).
- in order to successfully read, children must learn how to break words down into their individual phonemes.
- successful reading requires automatic recognition and decoding of words in order to avoid slow and inefficient reading approach.
- children that experience slow and inaccurate decoding are frequently ones who will subsequently have problems in reading comprehension.
- phonological awareness therefore becomes a critical area of emphasis for young children.
- approximately 3/4 of children who experience reading disabilities in third grade continue to have related problems in the tenth grade.
- the implication for education is to identify at an early age children who experience difficulty in this area and then provide appropriate interventions.

Source: Adapted from Lyon, G. R. (May 1995). Research in learning disabilities supported by the National Institute of Child Health Human Development. Subcommittee on Disability Policy, Committee on Labor Human Resources, United States Senate. Unpublished manuscript.

Table 9.1
Frequency of Occurrence of Key Words on 169 Product Warning Labels

138	water	29	induce, vomiting, ingested	7	intentional, reuse, deliberately, concentrating, contents, cover, slippery, misuse
117	caution	24	medical, danger, attention		
113	eye(s)	21	contaminate(ion)		
109	avoid	20	causes, container, inhale(tion)		
106	harmful			6	foodstuffs, magnesia
99	contact	17	flammable, vapor spray(ing)	4	human, rinse, seek, treatment, wrap, discard, trash
93	physician				
81	swallowed	16	wash		
75	call	15	flood, burn(s)	3	hazardous, inaccessible, processing, emergency, center, surfaces, doctor, cleaned, dishes
72	irritant	13	breathe(ing)		
68	flush	12	fatal, internally		
46	skin	11	severe, combustible		
44	milk, drink	10	empty, absorbed, injuries, give, flame	2	utensils, domestic, chemicals, acids, chlorine, mist, fluids
36	precaution				
34	warning	9	prompt, membranes, immediate, consult		
31	prolonged			1	edible, dispose, apply, minimize (and 44 other words)
30	quantities	8	poison		

Source: From "An Analysis of the Readability of Product Warning Labels: Implications for Curriculum Development for Persons with Moderate and Severe Mental Retardation" by D. Fletcher and D. Abood, 1988, *Education and Training in Mental Retardation, 23,* p. 226. Copyright 1988 by the Council for Exceptional Children. Reprinted with permission.

should plan to incorporate vocabulary-building activities as appropriate in sight word lessons, as well as in comprehension instruction (discussed further later in the chapter).

PHONETIC ANALYSIS

Many readers who have disabilities cannot automatically recognize words on sight, so word-attack skills will be essential for them to "crack the code" and read the word. *Phonetic analysis* is a decoding skill that requires the student to determine sound-symbol correspondences and then blend the sounds together. As Westman (1990) stated, "The phonic approach gives the child a lawful code with which to reconstruct written words into their already meaningful spoken equivalents. Word recognition thus becomes more of rational problem solving than of random guessing" (p. 335).

The Debate Because the use of phonics is not actual reading, theoreticians who challenge it from a psycholinguistic or holistic perspective have downplayed its importance. From this viewpoint, phonics is questionable because it breaks down units of meaning, may interfere with reading by calling for verbalizations, may demand that the learner recall generalizations or rules, and may be impractical because of the high prevalence of irregular English words. These points have considerable validity, especially for students who can read easily.

Phonics, however, can be justified for learners with exceptional needs. These students may have difficulty recognizing whole words and need a systematic approach for attending to details. Gaskins et al. (1988) noted that, "Unlike skilled readers, poor

Table 9.2
100 Most Essential Career/Vocational Words

1. rules	26. supervisor	51. entrance	76. withholding
2. boss	27. vacation	52. responsibility	77. vote
3. emergency	28. apply	53. hospital	78. break
4. danger	29. fulltime	54. hourly rate	79. cooperation
5. job	30. income	55. schedule	80. dependable
6. social security	31. quit	56. instructions	81. money
7. first-aid	32. check	57. save	82. physical
8. help-wanted	33. careful	58. union	83. hazardous
9. safety	34. dangerous	59. credit	84. net income
10. warning	35. employee	60. elevator	85. strike
11. signature	36. layoff	61. punctuality	86. owner
12. time	37. take-home-pay	62. rights	87. repair
13. attendance	38. unemployed	63. hours	88. alarm
14. absent	39. cost	64. payroll	89. gross income
15. telephone	40. deduction	65. attitude	90. manager
16. bill	41. fired	66. reliable	91. reference
17. hired	42. closed	67. work	92. uniform
18. overtime	43. parttime	68. caution	93. hard-hat
19. punch in	44. correct	69. license	94. authority
20. directions	45. foreman	70. poison	95. training
21. paycheck	46. time-and-a-half	71. office	96. holiday
22. wages	47. worker	72. power	97. late
23. appointment	48. buy	73. qualifications	98. personal
24. income tax	49. raise	74. earn	99. tools
25. interview	50. on-the-job	75. transportation	100. areas

Source: From "A Word List of Essential Career/Vocational Words for Mentally Retarded Students" by J. Schilit and M. L. Caldwell, 1980, *Education and Training of the Mentally Retarded, 75,* p. 115. Copyright 1980 by the Council for Exceptional Children. Reprinted with permission.

readers often do not seem to *discover* clues about relationships; rather they depend on explicit instruction to learn how our language works" (p. 37). The memory demands for a few rules may be significant, but they will be relatively small compared to those required for sight recognition. Although Francis's (1958) estimate that 85 percent of all English words are regular may seem generous, many words confronting the child have a common phonetic base.

As Ross (1976) pointed out, readers who have learned the verbal code will find it easiest to say sounds and words silently or aloud, then derive meaning from them. Adult readers usually skip this verbal stage and get meaning directly form the printed word, but sound-symbol relationships are important for young children or older students who have reading difficulties. Phonics generalizations thus are acting as verbal mediators (see chapter 1), which students with disabilities do not spontaneously produce but which they can be taught to apply.

Little can be gained by arguing the merits of pure phonics versus pure whole word approaches. Rather, it is mostly a question of appropriate emphasis (Crain, 1988; Heilman, Blair, & Rupley, 1986; U.S. Department of Education, 1987). Phonics certainly has an important role. For example, Chall's (1967) extensive review of reading research indicated that within the first two years of school, the phonetic orientation produced significantly greater gains than a sight orientation on a variety of reading success measures (word recognition, oral reading, vocabulary, comprehension).

Chall concluded her review by stating: "The research indicates that a code-emphasis method—i.e., one that views beginning reading as essentially different from mature reading and emphasizes learning of the printed code for the spoken language—produces better results, at least up to the point where sufficient evidence seems to be available, the end of third grade" (p. 307). The point is, however, that phonics and sight approaches can be integrated into a unified system for building word recognition skills.

To use phonics effectively, teachers should:

1. Teach as a way to learn to read, not as reading per se.
2. Begin instruction after the child has acquired a small sight vocabulary (so the student is familiar with common sounds) of about 50 words.
3. Provide structured opportunities to apply skills and ensure transition to reading in context; avoid phonics instruction as isolated skill development.
4. Be certain that comprehension instruction is not neglected while phonics is being taught.
5. Do not emphasize the teaching of high-frequency, irregular words through phonetic analysis.
6. Teach those generalizations that will be the most useful for students.

In reference to the last point, teachers should be aware of the extent to which various rules are functional. Clymer (1963) studied the usefulness of 45 common phonic generalizations, and Table 9.3 presents those most frequently used. Although some of these generalizations had surprisingly low usefulness, several of them are still functional when restricted to a given instructional vocabulary. One rule—"When two vowels go walking, the first one does the talking"—has only 45 percent utility, so students should be given a controlled vocabulary that lets them appropriately apply this generalization. At a later point, teachers can introduce strategies for handling exceptions.

Phonetic analysis instruction can include both analytic and synthetic approaches. *Analytic* phonics derives sounds from known words by having the child break down and analyze known words into their component phonemes (e.g., bat /b/ /a/ /t/); it is most often just a beginning approach. In *synthetic* phonics, the learner blends known sounds into new words (e.g., /b/ /a/ /t/ bat).

Teaching Phonics Skills   When all its generalizations are taught, phonics instruction places great demands on the student. Therefore, a sequential program emphasizing the most critical elements is essential. The child with reading problems usually needs help synthesizing this information into a workable system of word-attack skills and needs repeated opportunities to practice these rules on unknown words.

The approach to teaching phonetic analysis discussed next is based on the following sequence:

1. Initial and final consonants.
2. Consonant digraphs (e.g., *ch, sh, th*).

Table 9.3
Utility of Common Phonic Generalizations

Generalization	No. of words conforming	No. of exceptions	Percent of utility
1. When there are two vowels side by side, the long sound of the first one is heard and the second is usually silent.	309 (bead)	377 (chief)	45
2. When a vowel is in the middle of a one-syllable word, the vowel is short.	408	249	62
Middle letter	191 (dress)	84 (scold)	69
One of the middle two letters in a word of four letters	191 (rest)	135 (told)	59
One vowel <u>within</u> a word of more than four letters	26 (splash)	30 (fight)	46
3. If the only vowel letter is at the end of a word, the letter usually stands for a long sound.	23 (he)	8 (to)	74
4. When there are two vowels, one of which is final <u>e</u>, the first vowel is long and the <u>e</u> is silent.	180 (bone)	108 (done)	63
5. The <u>r</u> gives the preceding vowel a sound that is neither long nor short.	484 (horn)	134 (wire)	78
6. The first vowel is usually long and the second silent in the digraphs <u>ai</u>, <u>ea</u>, <u>oa</u>, and <u>ui</u>.	179	92	66
<u>ai</u>	43 (nail)	24 (said)	64
<u>ea</u>	101 (bead)	51 (head)	66
<u>oa</u>	34 (boat)	1 (cupboard)	97
<u>ui</u>	1 (suit)	16 (build)	6
7. Words having double <u>e</u> usually have the long <u>e</u> sound.	85 (seem)	2 (been)	98
8. When words end with silent <u>e</u>, the preceding <u>a</u> or <u>i</u> is long.	164 (cake)	108 (have)	60
9. When the letter <u>i</u> is followed by the letters <u>gh</u>, the gh is silent and the <u>i</u> is long.	22 (high)	9 (neighbor)	71
10. When <u>y</u> is the final letter in a word, it usually has a vowel sound.	169 (dry)	32 (tray)	84
11. When <u>y</u> is used as a vowel in words, it sometimes has the sound of long <u>i</u>.	29 (fly)	170 (funny)	15
12. When <u>c</u> and <u>h</u> are next to each other, they make only one sound.	103 (peach)	0	100
13. When <u>c</u> is followed by <u>e</u> or <u>i</u>, the sound of <u>s</u> is likely to be heard.	66 (cent)	3 (ocean)	96
14. When the letter <u>c</u> is followed by <u>o</u> or <u>a</u> the sound of <u>k</u> is likely to be heard.	143 (camp)	0	100
15. The letter <u>g</u> often has the sound similar to that of <u>j</u> in jump when it precedes the letter <u>i</u> or <u>e</u>.	49 (engine)	28 (give)	64

Source: Adapted from "The Utility of Phonetic Generalizations in the Primary Grades" by Theodore Clymer, 1963, *Reading Teacher,* *16,* pp. 223–225. Reprinted by permission of Theodore Clymer and the International Reading Association.

3. Short vowels (*vc, cvc* stems).
4. Consonant blends (e.g., *bl, st, tr*).
5. Long vowels (final *e*, double vowel patterns).
6. *r*-influenced vowels.
7. Diphthongs and other vowel sounds (e.g., *aw, ou, ow, eu, ew, oi*).

This approach, based on a modified system of phonics instruction, reduces the number of rules to be learned and relies on context to explain exception. The methods discussed here apply to one-syllable words, whereas the later presentation of a modified phonics approach under the heading of "syllabication" applies a similar strategy to polysyllabic words.

Consonant sounds should be taught first because they are easier than vowels for students to learn; they are most consistently associated with only one sound, often begin words, and relate well to context (Heilman et al., 1986). First, teachers must ensure that students can discriminate between the sound being taught and different consonant sounds at the beginning of a word. In introducing *b*, for example, the child should be able to tell that butter and ball start with the same sound but that butter and fish begin with different sounds. Consonant sounds are best taught with key words and pictures, such as those given in Figure 9.5.

When a student masters an individual sound, he or she can:

1. Identify the symbol from a spoken word (What is the letter that names the first sound you hear in *buttonhole?*)
2. Produce the sound when decoding an unknown printed word (If *ax* is pronounced "ax," what does it become when *b* is added at the beginning, as on this card?). The response is correct if *b* sound is used correctly, even if the "ax" is distorted.
3. Use the sound to spell an unknown word (e.g., "bax"). The response is correct if *b* is in the initial position, even if the *ax* stem is not written correctly.

Individual consonants and digraphs should be introduced one at a time and then reviewed along with all the sounds previously taught. Later, teachers can introduce blends along with short vowel instruction, providing instructional drills that encourage transition from single consonants to blends (e.g., *r + at,* followed by *b + rat*).

Before moving to vowel sounds, students should have mastered consonant sounds in the initial and final positions and should be able to blend teacher-pronounced sounds into words (e.g., *c + at, sn + ail*). Teachers also should determine students' sight vocabulary, especially if they are older. With this information, the teacher can provide new, unknown drill words that require students to practice the skills being taught.

Vowels generally are harder for children to learn, so a sequential presentation is particularly useful.

1. Give the child auditory experiences that demand discrimination between similar sounds (as with consonant sounds). This phase is critical because a student must be able to hear how a sound is different and unique before he or she can reproduce it in a new word or identify it in a word to be spelled. Teachers might use the words

Source: From *Guidelines to Teaching Remedial Reading* by Lillie Pope, 1967, New York: Book-Lab, Inc. Reprinted by permission.

Figure 9.5
Phonetic Analysis: Key Words/Pictures

igloo and *ice cream* to teach short *i,* for example, and ask students to categorize *i* words by vowel sounds. Children should first learn to discriminate between words with *i* in the initial position. When they have mastered this skill, they can move on to words with *i* in the medial position.

2. Teach students to blend a vowel sound to final consonants and blends, and to spell these stems. With short *i,* the child would learn to pronounce and spell stems such as *ick, id,* and *ist.*

3. Teach students to blend initial consonant sounds to these stems. Using short *i* as an example, the child would be asked again to pronounce *ick* and then *t* and *ick,* or *int* and then *h + int.*

4. Present words containing the vowel sound being taught, and have the student rehearse the following procedure: find the vowel; cover all the letters that come before it; pronounce the vowel stem; add the initial consonant or blend; pronounce the whole word.

5. When the child can attach words (which in isolation contain the sound in question), provide guided opportunities that allow the child to use the new sound to decode unknown words in the context of a sentence.

After a child masters an individual phonic element, he or she must integrate it with previously learned sounds. For example, after learning short *a* and short *i,* and before going on to short *o,* the child must be able to discriminate, pronounce, and spell words containing short *a* and short *i.* Although most students have relatively little difficulty learning single phonic elements in isolation, they may have problems when faced with an assortment of words that requires them to integrate new elements with previously learned information.

These procedures for teaching vowel sounds also can be used to teach the two long vowel patterns (*cvvc, cvcv*), *r*-controlled vowels (e.g., *ar, ir*), and the most common diphthong patterns. In this way, students can learn the most important generalizations (see Table 9.3). For variant sounds and exceptions to the rules, teachers can rely on the context to supply meaning, freeing phonics from rigid sound-symbol correspondences. If a child were to decode the word "bread" according to the basic double-vowel rule, he or she would pronounce it "breed." A child who does not know this word may encounter it in the sentence, "There is a loaf of bread on the table," skip past the word to the end of the sentence and possibly pronounce the word correctly because he or she knows its meaning. Contextual analysis is discussed further later in the chapter.

STRUCTURAL ANALYSIS

Structural analysis enables readers to see the forms of words and their subparts. Generally this requires a morphological analysis of words—a focus on morphemes or meaning units. As noted in chapter 8, students should learn to find the morphemes within words, to facilitate both word recognition and word comprehension. McClure, Kalk, and Keenan (1980) noted that beginning reading programs often have whole word or phonetic emphases and exclude structural analysis. Reporting that poor readers had more difficulty than good readers with morphemes, they concluded that more time should be devoted to morphologic analysis in the early stages of reading. (One key structural analysis skill, syllabication, does *not* use morphologic, or meaning-based, cues.)

Attention to structural analysis can improve word recognition ability and both word and passage comprehension skills. As with phonetic and contextual analysis, teachers can initially use drill activities but then must apply these skills in actual reading opportunities.

Compound Words To orient a child to compound words, teachers should design various activities that highlight the two components. Particularly beneficial exercises are:

- Matching drills using two lists of words with pairs that can be combined.
- Adapting the cloze procedures in which one half of each compound word is left blank (e.g., When the winter winds blow, we huddle around the _____ place).
- Giving students ridiculous pictures to label (e.g., a stick of flying butter for butterfly).
- Providing a list of invented words or colloquialisms to be defined (e.g., slamdunk, skyhook).

Affixes Teachers can develop an orientation toward root words, prefixes, and suffixes by devising exercises that highlight the common forms and indicate how they affect word meanings. Emphasis should be placed on having students recognize those parts of words that they have already studied (Heilman et al., 1986). Some appropriate activities are:

- Color coding of the designated affix being taught.
- Word wheels with root words in the center surrounded by prefixes, or a suffix in the center surrounded by root words. Sample word wheels are illustrated in Figure 9.6.
- Speed listing of all the words that begin with a given prefix (e.g., *un-*: undress, untie, uncover, undo).

An excellent source for the development of a training sequence in teaching affixes, and for that matter, structural analysis in general, is Shepherd's (1980) work in this area.

Contractions Many of the activities listed for compound words and affixes can be adapted for teaching contractions, the third structural analysis skill with a morphological basis. With contractions, students have to know which forms are equivalencies for specific words.

Syllabication One of the most practical structural analysis skills is that of syllabication. For this reason, the discussion that follows explains how a variety of word analysis tools can be blended into an instructional sequence based on attacking polysyllabic words.

Many students face a dilemma when they confront polysyllabic words that do not seem to respond to basic phonetic rules. A structured program teaching syllabication can provide a decoding method for generalizing previously learned rules to new, longer words. Polloway and Polloway (1978) proposed a modified phonics approach for teaching syllabication skills to upper elementary and middle school readers with

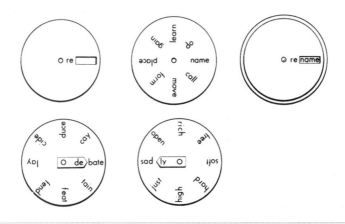

Source: From *Guidelines to Teaching Remedial Reading* by Lillie Pope, 1967, New York: Book-Lab, Inc. Reprinted by permission.

Figure 9.6
Word Wheels for Structural Analysis

disabilities.[2] This system has only two key rules and eliminates the need to teach variations and exceptions. Using the system, a child first decodes irregular words as if they followed the rules, then relies on context clues to clarify slight pronunciation distortions. Students who have been taught to syllabicate using this system divide the unknown word "between" as "bet/ween." When pronounced accordingly, a slight distortion occurs, which becomes readily recognizable when placed in the context of a sentence. Thus, context skills serve as tools in making the transition from phonics to word identification. Because the reader does not have to make exact sound-symbol correspondences, many syllabication rules and their inconsistencies can be discarded.

This program is aimed specifically at older readers with disabilities who already have the prerequisites for basic sight vocabulary, know the sounds of consonants, blends, long, short and variant vowels as well as of diphthongs and digraphs, and are able to predict vowel sounds in open and closed syllables. Many older children with reading difficulties possess these skills in rudimentary form and need practice to develop them. Once that is accomplished, the student is ready to learn the two basic rules of syllabication.

Rule 1: When a word has the pattern of vowel, two consonants, and vowel, divide between the consonants (*vc/cv*).

Rule 2: When a word has the pattern of a vowel, consonant, and vowel, divide between the first vowel and the consonant (*v/cv*).

---

[2]This section is adapted from "Expanding Reading Skills Through Syllabication" by C. H. Polloway and E. A. Polloway, 1978, *Academic Therapy, 13*, pp. 455–462. Reproduced courtesy of the publisher, ATP, 20 Commercial Blvd., Novato, CA 94947.

Polloway and Polloway (1978) subdivided these rules into 11 steps to be taught one at a time and mastered before moving on to the next. The student learns each step using known words, and then practices on unknown words out of context. Surnames, rather than known words, are used so that pronunciation distortions are not critical to meaning and are not readily apparent to the student. When students have mastered this principle, they move on to decoding unknown words, using context clues to correct distortion and provide recognition. The steps are:

A. *Objectives:*
   1. Student will be able to identify how many syllables are heard in a known word.
   2. Student will be able to divide a known word orally.
   Procedure:
   1. Teacher orally explains concept and demonstrates on known words.
   2. Student is given words to divide orally.
   Sample Word List: tomato sunshine toe cucumber peanut

B. *Objective:* Student will recognize that a word has as many syllables as vowels heard.
   Procedure:
   1. Teacher writes known words and student tells how many syllables are heard and how many vowels are seen and heard in each word.
   2. Procedure 1 is continued until student draws conclusion that the number of vowels heard in a word equals the number of syllables.
   Sample Word List: tomato sunshine toe cucumber peanut

C. *Objective:* Student will be able to determine how many syllables an unknown word will have.
   Procedure:
   1. Review silent *e* rule, and rule that when two vowels come together, one sound results.
   2. Teacher writes an unknown word; student determines which vowels will be silent and predicts the number of syllables.
   Sample Word List: domino barbecue stagnate mousse

D. *Objective:* Student will be able to syllabicate words that follow the *vc/cv* pattern (Rule 1).
   Procedure:
   1. Teacher writes and student divides two-syllable known words that fit the pattern.
   2. Student practices dividing and pronouncing two-syllable *vc/cv* words.
   3. Teacher demonstrates process of dividing longer known words:
      a. Determine number of syllables.
      b. To establish first division, start with first vowel and look for *vc/cv* pattern, then divide.
      c. To establish second division, start with second vowel and look for *vc/cv* pattern, then divide.

d. Continue procedure until all syllables are determined.

e. Pronounce word.

4. Student practices dividing and pronouncing unknown words that contain *vc/cv* pattern.

Sample Word List:

1. Teaching words: rabbit bitter pepper mixture

2. Practice words: Volpone Vermeer Bellew Aspic

E. *Objective:* Student will be able to syllabicate words that contain the *v/cv* pattern (Rule 2).

Procedure: Follow instructions for Step D, substituting the *v/cv* pattern.

Sample Word List:

1. Teaching words: labor favor basic demand

2. Practice words: Cahill Zuzo Theimer Tatum

F. *Objective:* Student will be able to syllabicate words that contain both *vc/cv* and *v/cv* patterns.

Procedure:

1. Teacher writes and student divides known words that contain both patterns.

2. Student practices dividing and pronouncing unknown words that contain both patterns.

Sample Word List:

1. Teaching words: envelope cucumber remainder resulting

2. Practice words: Provenzano Tedesco Dannewitz Oberlin

G. *Objective:* Student will be able to syllabicate words that have a *vcccv* or *vccccv* pattern.

Procedure:

1. Teacher writes and student divides known words containing *vcccv* or *vccccv* patterns until student recognizes that the division is based on consonant blends and digraphs.

2. Student practices dividing and pronouncing unknown words containing *vcccv* or *vccccv* pattern.

Sample Word List:

1. Teaching words: concrete pitcher contract merchant

2. Practice words: Omohundro Armentrout Marshall Ostrander

H. *Objective:* Student will be able to syllabicate words that end with *-le*.

Procedure:

1. Teacher writes and student divides known words ending with *-le* until student generalizes that when preceded by *l*, final *e* is not silent but produces a syllable that contains *-le* and the preceding consonant.

2. Student practices dividing and pronouncing unknown words containing the *-le* ending.

Sample Word List:

1. Teaching words: candle rattle dribble staple

2. Practice words: Whipple Biddle Noble Radle

I. *Objective:* Student will recognize the *y* in the medial or final position is a vowel and must be treated as such.
Procedure:
1. Teacher tells student that *y* will be a vowel in the medial or final position.
2. Teacher writes and student divides known words containing *y* in both positions.
3. Student practices dividing and pronouncing unknown words that contain *y* in the medial or final position.
Sample Word List:
1. Teaching words: funny my cranky style
2. Practice words: Snydor Murtry Tyson Gentry

J. *Objective:* Student is able to divide and pronounce unknown words containing any of the patterns taught.
Procedure: Student practices dividing and pronouncing unknown words containing all the patterns taught.
Sample Word List: Hirshoren Shirly Ruckle Espenshade

K. *Objective:* Student will be able to syllabicate and pronounce unknown words met in context.
Procedure:
1. Student silently reads material on instructional level.
2. After reading is completed, teacher checks student's accuracy in decoding unknown words in context.

To reach the final step, teachers should devote one instructional period to presenting the concept for each step, and any additional periods needed for repetition and overlearning to produce mastery. Step K should be actively continued until the teacher feels confident of the student's ability to use syllabication independently. This system is based on the application of various analysis skills to words of two or more syllables. It can help the child cross a major word recognition hurdle encountered at approximately the third- or fourth-grade reading level.

CONTEXTUAL ANALYSIS

Contextual analysis bridges the graphic emphasis of phonetic and structural analysis and the underlying meaning of the sentence. Its obvious value is in providing semantic and syntactic cues that facilitate identification of words that might be more difficult to recognize in isolation.

According to Hargis (1972), contextual analysis has been a deficit area for readers who are retarded, primarily because they cannot produce synonymous, grammatically acceptable words for unknown or omitted ones. To some extent, the remedy is straightforward. Allington (1980) stated that:

> The teacher can reinforce the utilization of contextual information during reading instruction by simply asking "what makes sense" when children are confronted with an unknown word. . . . Emphasizing "making sense" could have a positive effect in producing

readers who see reading as getting the message rather than just getting the sounds right. (p. 120)

Contextual analysis, then, can be seen as a skill that students need to develop. In addition to complementing the use of other word analysis strategies, it has ties to comprehension because the better one comprehends what is being read, the better he or she can use context. It also encourages hypothesis testing because the student is learning how to make predictions (Samuels, 1981). The successful use of context cues, however, presumes that the reader can either recognize or sound out every word in the sentence except for the one that is unknown (Heilman et al., 1986). Thus its effective use for immature readers is inherently problematic.

To help students use contextual analysis, teachers must help them understand that only a few possible words can fill a place in a sentence. Specifically, this process includes teaching children to expect the types of words that may come up in a sentence, to anticipate specific unknown words, and to attach an unknown word based on its position in the sentence and on the known words that surround it. Contextual skills are graphically illustrated by Kameenui and Simmons (1990) in Figure 9.7. Phonetic and structural cues can complement contextual analysis.

Cloze Procedure.   The cloze procedure is the most common skill-building activity used for contextual analysis. This method removes about every fifth word from reading passages at the student's instructional level, and requires students to complete the sentences by filling in the blanks. Figure 9.8 presents a sample cloze procedure exercise based on fourth-grade reading material. An alternative approach to this form of the cloze procedure would be to select words to remove from a passage according to the role they play in the structure or meaning of a sentence.

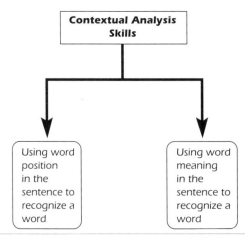

Source: From *Designing Instructional Strategies: The Prevention of Academic Learning Problems* (p. 217) by E. J. Kameenui and D. C. Simmons, 1990, Columbus, OH: Charles E. Merrill Publishing. Copyright © 1990 by Merrill Publishing Company. Reprinted with permission of Merrill, an imprint of Macmillan Publishing Company.

Figure 9.7
Contextual Analysis Skills

Before the excitement of independence passed, Thomas Jefferson began _____ for the future of _____ nation. In his own _____, Virginia, he worked hard _____ get laws that he _____ belonged to a democratic _____. He helped pass a _____ granting freedom of religion _____ the people of Virginia. _____ worked especially hard to _____ free public schools in _____ state. But his work _____ put aside when he _____ chosen President of the _____ States in 1800.

Jefferson _____ with him to the _____ his strong feeling for _____. He tried hard to _____ a leader of all _____ people, not just the _____ people. Jefferson came from _____ important family in Virginia. _____ was used to having _____ to look after him _____. Yet President Jefferson often _____ everyday things in order _____ he might appear as _____ everyday citizen. One thing _____ sometimes did was to _____ grocery shopping.

Source: From *With American Heroes* (p. 65) by H. Bamman and R. Whitehead, 1968, Westchester, IL: Benefic Press. Reprinted by permission.

Figure 9.8
Cloze Procedure

To construct a cloze exercise, these steps can be followed: *1st//last sentence must be intact*

1. Select a reading passage of approximately 250–300 words from a story at the student's instructional level.
2. Do not alter the initial sentence.
3. Beginning with the second sentence, delete every fifth word until reaching a total of 50 deletions. Replace each of these deleted words with a blank.
4. Add one more complete sentence after the sentence containing the last deletion.

Other Techniques A variety of other activities can help students use context clues. Teachers can present beginning readers with pictures such as rebuses, then ask the children to substitute the appropriate words. Riddles can be presented in written form, requiring students to identify the "thing" being described; and nonsense words can be placed within sentences and students asked to define what they mean. Finally, teachers can read stories aloud and periodically leave a word blank or pause so that students can fill in the noun, verb, or modifier that completes the thought.

As with any skill training, the instructional goal for contextual analysis is to transfer into actual reading situations the ability to fill in blanks, answer riddles, or translate nonsense words. Once students understand the nature of contextual analysis and can use context to complete exercises, teachers must encourage and reinforce their use of clues in passage reading. As Hargis (1972) noted, problems often occur when the words do not "jump out" at the reader. Bailey (1975) suggested that students should be carefully prepared for the following cues:

1. A word with similar meaning within the sentence or paragraph.
2. Commas used to set off the explanation or definition of the word (linked synonyms).
3. A descriptive activity that surrounds the word within the sentence.
4. Words or phrases that infer the meaning of the specific target word.

Expanding on this theme, Dulin (1970, pp. 441–444) encouraged teachers to help their students become aware of syntactical and semantic aids in sentences. In addition to some of those noted above, he suggested the following, which can assist not only in word recognition but vocabulary development as well:

1. *Contrast or opposites* (e.g., "Rather than his usual mood of cheerful good humor, today his manner appeared quite *dour"*).
2. *Cause-effect relationships* (e.g., "Strength and size seemed to be the key qualities needed: therefore a *Leviathan* of a man was chosen").
3. *Tone* (e.g., "We assumed that the man was from Texas when we saw the *gargantuan* size of his appetite").
4. *Combined with other word analysis* (e.g., "She was gently lowered into the pool because it was now time for *hydrotherapy"*).
5. *Combined contrast with linked synonyms* (e.g., "Their lives now became regular, routine, and *placid,* a welcome change after the many days of conflict during the campaign").

COMBINED WORD RECOGNITION APPROACHES

Specific systems are recommended for combining word recognition tools to help maturing readers with mild disabilities and children or adolescents with moderate or severe impairments. Again, none of these skills can be effective in isolation.

Students with Mild Disabilities   The syllabication approach discussed earlier is one way of integrating various word analysis skills. Once a student acquires these skills, the teacher should implement a program that promotes an efficient reading style by minimizing interruptions in the flow of the passage. The steps in this approach are:

1. Utilize context clues to figure out which word(s) would fit the meaning and syntax of the sentence (useful for occasional unknown words).
2. Determine if the word is important to meaning when it cannot be defined through context. If pronunciation does not seem crucial to overall meaning (e.g., a proper noun or a foreign phrase), read past it unless it recurs regularly.
3. Combine context clues with a rapid survey of structure and initial phonetic elements to help predict the word.
4. Identify major structural features of the word (e.g., roots, affixes) that may suggest cues as to meaning or pronunciation.
5. Break down the word into syllables and use phonetic analysis to facilitate pronunciation.
6. Use a dictionary to determine a word's pronunciation or meaning if it affects the meaning of the passage.

This approach can be handled by teaching a word attack learning strategy. Table 9.4 outlines steps in a word identification strategy suggested by Polloway, Patton,

Payne, and Payne (1989). Another strategy, reported by Lenz and Hughes (1990) is entitled DISSECT (*D*iscover the context, *I*solate the prefix, *S*eparate the suffix, *S*ay the stem, *E*xamine the stem, *C*heck with someone, *T*ry the dictionary).

Students with Moderate-Severe Disabilities   In past years many researchers questioned the value and relevance of reading instruction for individuals who have moderate or severe retardation. When it was provided, teaching usually focused on the basic survival vocabulary. In light of increasing research data on this topic (Browder & Snell, 1987; Snell, 1978), however, the professional community has challenged these assumptions of limited potential. Folk and Campbell (1978, p. 323) posited that "The question is not whether students are competent enough to acquire basic reading skills but whether we . . . are competent enough to teach them." As a consequence of this attitude shift, researchers have devised various teaching programs to help students with moderate-severe impairments develop stronger reading vocabularies. All of these programs integrate several word recognition strategies because relying solely on the acquisition of a small sight vocabulary is inherently limiting (Barudin & Hourcade, 1990; Browder & Snell, 1987).

Vandever and Stubbs (1977) cautioned that during the first year, children who have moderate retardation may progress slowly as they begin to understand facets of the reading process (e.g., left-right orientation, spaces between words). Nevertheless, those authors indicated that systematic, precise instructional procedures would be ultimately successful. Given the need for precision, teachers should consult the representative programs described next, for specific information.

Entrikin, York, and Brown (1977) reported on a three-phase program emphasizing sight words, phonics, and context clues. The first phase uses pictures and initial consonant sounds to help students decipher unknown words; the second phase relies on pictures and context clues; the third phase integrates all three components (pictures, initial consonants, and context). Table 9.5 summarizes these three phases. Building on basic prerequisites, including a 50-word sight vocabulary, the ability to imitate, left-right eye movements, and speech, these researchers found that students made good progress toward reading simple sentences and identifying newly introduced words.

Table 9.4
Word Identification Strategy

C	Context: Use contextual analysis to anticipate occasional unknown words.
U	Unimportant: Skip over words that are unimportant to meaning.
R	Rapid: Quickly analyze the word (i.e., initial consonant) in conjunction with context.
S	Structural: Analyze specific structural attributes (prefixes, suffixes, compound words).
S	Syllabicate: Apply syllabication strategy and phonetically analyze.
E	External: Ask for external help (teacher, aide).
D	Dictionary: Look up the word.

Source: From *Strategies for Teaching Learners with Special Needs* (p. 174) by E. A. Polloway, J. R. Patton, J. S. Payne, and R. A. Payne, 1989, Columbus, OH: Charles E. Merrill Publishing. Copyright ©1989 by Macmillan Publishing Company. Reprinted with permission of Merrill, an imprint of Macmillan Publishing Company.

Table 9.5
Task Analysis of Reading Program for Students with Moderate Retardation

PHASE 1. The use of pictures and initial consonant sounds to read unknown words.

Part 1. Teaching students to label object pictures and describe action pictures.

Part 2. Teaching students to sound consonants presented on flashcards.

Part 3a. Teaching students to touch the first letter (color-coded) in printed words.

Part 3b. Teaching students to touch the first letter (not color-coded) in printed words.

Part 4. Teaching students to sound initial consonants in selected printed words.

Part 5. Teaching students to label object pictures, to describe action pictures, and to make the initial consonant sounds of the objects and actions represented in the pictures (e.g., Q—"What is this? A—"(ball)"; Q—"What is the first sound in (ball)?" or "What is the (boy) doing?" A—"(running)"; Q—"What is the first sound in (running)?")

Part 6. Teaching students to label object pictures, to describe action pictures, and to make the initial consonant sounds of the objects and action represented in those pictures (e.g., Q—"What is this?" A—"(ball)"; Q—"What is the first sound in that word?" or Q—"What is the (boy) doing?" A—"(running)"; Q—"What is the first sound in that word?")

Part 7. Teaching students to make the initial consonant sounds of objects and actions represented in pictures (e.g., "What is the first sound in this?").

Part 8. Teaching students to touch the appropriate object or action picture in response to a consonant sound stated by the teacher (e.g., "Touch the thing that begins with (bb), as in boy.").

Part 9. When students are presented with a printed word they cannot label and four pictures that represent objects and actions with differing initial consonant sounds, they will determine the label of the unknown word by finding and labeling the picture which represents the object or action with the same initial consonant sound.

PHASE II. The use of pictures and context to read unknown words.

Part 1. Teaching students to label object pictures and describe action pictures.

Part 2. When students are presented with eight sets of two pictures, one component of each set depicting an absurd action (e.g., teacher combing hair with toothbrush) and the other component depicting a logical action (e.g., teacher combing hair with comb) and the question "Does this picture make sense?" they will respond "yes" to pictures of logical actions and "no" to pictures of absurd actions.

Part 3. When students are read sentences which are logical or absurd following the question, "Does this sentence make sense?" they will respond "yes" to logical sentences and "no" to absurd sentences.

Part 4a. When students are presented with a printed sentence read by the teacher with one word missing in the object position (e.g., "the boy hit the _____ ") and three object pictures, they will touch the one picture that represents the object which logically completes the sentence.

Part 4b. When students are presented with a printed sentence read by the teacher with one word missing in the verb position (e.g., "the boy _____ the ball") and three action pictures they will touch the one picture that represents the verb which logically completes the sentence.

Part 4c. When students are presented with a printed sentence read by the teacher with one word missing in the subject position (e.g., "the _____ hit the ball") and three object pictures they will touch the one picture that represents the subject which logically completes the sentence.

Table 9.5
continued

> Part 4d. When students are presented with a printed sentence read by the teacher with one word missing in either the subject, verb, or object position (e.g., "the _____ hit the ball"; the boy _____ the ball"; "the boy hit the _____ ") and three object or action pictures, they will touch the one picture that represents the subject, verb, or object which logically completes the sentence.
>
> Part 5. When students are presented with a printed sentence read by the teacher with one word missing in the subject, verb, or object position (e.g., "the _____ hit the ball"; "the boy _____ the ball"; "the boy hit the _____ ") and three printed words, they will touch the one word that logically completes the sentence.
>
> Part 6. When students are presented with a worksheet containing sentences composed of words they can label but which are missing one word in the subject, verb, or object position (e.g., "the _____ hit the ball"; the boy _____ the ball"; "the boy hit the _____ ") and three printed words above each sentence, they will mark the one word that logically completes each sentence.

PHASE III. The use of pictures, initial consonant sounds, and context to read unknown words.

> Part 1. Teaching students to label object pictures and describe action pictures as they are presented on worksheets.
>
> Part 2. When students are presented with a worksheet containing sentences composed of words they can label with the exception of one underlined word in the subject, verb, or object position and four pictures above each sentence, they will determine the label of the underlined word by marking and labeling the one picture which represents the object of action (a) with the same initial consonant sound as the underlined word and (b) which logically completes the sentence.

Source: Adapted from "Teaching Trainable Level Multiply Handicapped Students to Use Picture Cues, Context Cues, and Initial Consonant Sounds to Determine the Labels of Unknown Words" by D. Entrikin, R. York, and L. Brown, 1977, *American Association for the Education of the Severely and Profoundly Handicapped Review, 2,* pp. 171–173. Reprinted by permission.

Folk and Campbell (1978) outlined a six-step program that includes developing sight vocabulary from first names to common Dolch words, reading simple sentences, and enhancing sight orientation with phonics skills such as initial consonants and short vowel sounds. This program is represented in Table 9.6. According to Folk and Campbell, these procedures added more than 100 words to students' sight vocabularies and helped them acquire phonics skills to facilitate further gains. Similarly, Nietupski, Williams, and York (1978) described an effective procedure for teaching *cvc* trigrams to readers who had moderate retardation, through letter-sound correspondences and sound-blending tasks.

Snell (1988) identified the following four factors that should be examined to determine what academic skills (if any) should become instructional targets for these students and which methodologies should be selected.

1. How much time does the student have left in school?
2. What is the student's past learning performance on similar tasks?
3. What are the parents' and the student's preferences regarding academic instruction?
4. How do academic skill needs compare with the student's other skill needs? (p. 306)

Table 9.6
Sequence for Teaching Functional Reading

1. Step one consisted of presenting each child with two nouns (the S's name and another student's name), printed in red felt pen on 4″ × 8″ index cards. The S was told, "This is your name. Say ⎯⎯⎯⎯ " (the S's name). This procedure was repeated with the second name. Both cards were placed on the table and the S was told, "Find your name. Find ⎯⎯⎯⎯ 's name." The subject was given a primary reinforcer for each correct response. If the S responded incorrectly, the teacher said, "No, this says ⎯⎯⎯⎯ ," and proceeded to the next question. This procedure was utilized until the S could read all of the children's names with 100 percent accuracy.

2. Step two consisted of introducing the word "boy" and "girl." The procedures described in Step 1 were again employed. In addition to the activities listed in Step 1, a worksheet which consisted of drawing a line from the word "boy" or "girl" to each class member's name was used.

3. From Step 3 on, the words used varied from subject to subject. Initially, words were taken from the individual student's repertoire to insure clear articulation and comprehension. Although the procedure remained the same, as their proficiency increased, more sophisticated work sheets and activities accompanied the original introductory exercise.

4. The S next proceeded from nouns to adjective-noun phrases to verbs and then to complete sentences. The S demonstrated his comprehension of the adjective-noun phrases by pointing to the correct picture of the object. Mastery of the verbs was evaluated by having the S produce a motoric response in conjunction with the presentation of the word card. (The only exception was the verb "is" which was used in many of the sentences. The correct pronunciation of the word, when presented with the word card, was considered sufficient). Sentences were printed on 4″ × 15″ strips of paper. At the end of the sentence three pictures were drawn. The S was required to point to the picture which correctly depicted the meaning of the sentence.

5. The students were next given words from the Dolch Reading List. As the words became increasingly complex, so did ways of evaluating comprehension. For example, how does one know whether or not a S understands the word, "buy"? Criterion for comprehension was considered met when the S could use the word correctly in a sentence or a phrase when asked, "What does ⎯⎯⎯⎯ mean?"

   At this point, the introductory phrase was extended in order to include a brief definition of the word by the instructor. Basic word-attack skills were introduced in conjunction with Step 5. The S's were first taught to imitate all of the consonant sounds, one at a time. Before learning a new sound, criterion had to have been reached on the previous sound. Criteria consisted of, when asked, "What sound does ⎯⎯⎯⎯ say?" responding:

   a. Correct sound

   b. Like in ⎯⎯⎯⎯ , i.e., a word which began with that sound.

   Further checks were made by presenting the S with a picture of a "new word" (meaning a word not found on his reading list), and asking, "What is this a picture of?" If the child did not answer correctly, he was simply told, "This is a ⎯⎯⎯⎯ . What sound does it begin with?" If he replied correctly, he was told, "Good. It starts with ⎯⎯⎯⎯ ."

   Secondly, he was asked, "What letter does the word ⎯⎯⎯⎯ begin with?" This procedure was repeated until the child could identify all initial consonant sounds in this manner. Activities such as worksheets, sorting pictures, finding pictures which begin with specific sounds and listening to tapes were used to supplement the phonetic program.

6. Vowel sounds are now being introduced to one S. Basically the same type of procedure is being followed.

Source: From "Teaching Functional Reading to the TMR" by M. C. Folk and J. Campbell, 1978, *Education and Training of the Mentally Retarded, 13*, pp. 324–325. Copyright 1978 by the Council for Exceptional Children. Reprinted with permission.

By carefully considering these factors and by relating them to the realities of the student's subsequent environment, a decision can be made about whether to emphasize reading instruction of specific skills or delay or forego it.

Finally, clear programming alternatives exist in selecting an instructional approach once the specific skills are deemed important for the individual. As Snell (1988) noted, these include *bypassing* the skill by performing it for the individual; using an *academic prosthesis* to reduce the need for reading ability (e.g., a menu with pictures); teaching *specific, limited academic skills* (e.g., relevant protection words); or teaching *generalized academic skills.*

COMMERCIAL WORD RECOGNITION PROGRAMS

The programs discussed here emphasize decoding or word recognition. Although some of them also may include comprehension, they are grouped for convenience and to reinforce their primary emphases.

Phonic Reading Lessons (Kirk, Kirk, & Minskoff, 1986) are a revision of the *Remedial Reading Drills* (Hegge, Kirk, & Kirk, 1977) first developed in the 1930s and designed for children who read below a fourth-grade level and needed to master phonetic blending. The 72 lessons take a visual, auditory, and kinesthetic approach to teach vowel sounds, consonant and vowel clusters, and common phonograms, and they follow a specific pattern that builds upon previous lessons. The words are read orally, and the child is required to sound out each phonetic element before blending into a word. Repetitive writing and reading of the sounds are recommended. The last lessons in the book contain additional exercises on plurals, possessives, affixes, compound words, and syllables. The drills are most appropriate when used as a supplement to ongoing instruction and, as such, are inexpensive.

Edmark Reading Program (Edmark Associates, 1972, 1984): Level 1 of the Edmark Program was designed to teach a 150-sight vocabulary to students with retardation. Its target population could include nonreaders who have mild through severe retardation, as well as students with learning disabilities. The program prerequisites include basic receptive vocabulary, verbal skills (e.g., can repeat the words), and an ability to make gestural or verbal responses. Level 2 of the programs, more recently developed, teaches 200 additional sight words. As with Level 1, words were selected from the Dolch list and from primary books. This level includes adolescent characters in the stories.

The instructional kit contains four types of lessons based on word recognition, picture/phrase matching, direction books, and storybooks. The principles of errorless discrimination and operant technology are central to the instructional processes. The program is based on the assumption that word analysis can be taught after a child develops a sight vocabulary. Research reported by Walsh and Lamberts (1979) and Vandever and Stubbs (1977) found that students with moderate or severe disabilities made progress with Level 1 of the Edmark Program.

The *Glass Analysis for Decoding Only* (Glass & Glass, 1978) program emphasizes teaching common letter clusters. The program essentially consists of packs of cards organized into 119 clusters ranging from the most common to the most difficult. Students are taught a specific sound cluster and then, through a series of fast-paced steps, learn new words formed by adding letters that modify the specific cluster pattern. Students are taught both to see and to hear sounds as letter clusters within whole words. This unique technique also has been used successfully to motivate adolescent students still in need of word analysis practice (Schewel, 1989).

The *Gillingham-Stillman Remedial Reading Manual* (Gillingham & Stillman, 1960) was developed in the 1940s for children with specific learning disabilities in reading, writing, and spelling. Based on the language research of Samuel Orton, the manual teaches reading and spelling by demonstrating the symbolic nature of the printed language and by identifying the relationships of sounds to words. The method is basically phonetic in nature, with multisensory emphases reflected in the exercises involving the visual, auditory, and kinesthetic channels. Phonetic spelling regularities are taught first, and then the words are practiced through reading, writing, and spelling drills. Rules for phonetic spelling of exceptions, syllabications, plurals, and affixes are then taught. The practice of handwriting to correct reversals is an important aspect of the program. Word cards for drill and stories in the manual are provided. Although the program requires teacher training and a clinical setting for successful implementation, the manual itself contains helpful teaching guides that instructors can modify.

The Phonovisual Method (Schoolfield & Timberlake, 1940, 1978) is a phonetic system developed through work with children with speech and hearing impairments. It does not purport to be a complete reading program, but it can supplement a sight reading approach if word attack skills are taught. The authors developed vowel and consonant charts organizing these sounds according to their interrelationships. Pictures and colors are used to provide clues and identify sound relationships for children. The consonant chart has 26 sounds, organized vertically by voiced, breath, nasal, and other consonant sounds. The vowel chart consists of 18 short- and long-vowel sounds, including variant long-vowel spelling patterns. Vowels and consonant blends are taught after students have mastered the initial and final consonant positions. Compound words, syllabication, affixes, and nonphonetic spelling are also introduced. The charts are the heart of the program, and teachers can obtain them separately to illustrate specific sounds in any phonetic analysis program.

Reading Mastery Program (Engelmann & Bruner, 1984). The Direct Instructional System for Teaching Arithmetic and Reading (DISTAR) was designed as a 3-year teaching program for preschool and primary-grade children (Engelmann & Bruner, 1974, 1975). The reading program, which evolved into *Reading Mastery,* is phonetically based and relies on auditory and sound-blending skills. The program presents a phonetic alphabet of 40 symbols, which are taught in a highly sequential manner before introducing letter names. In each daily lesson the teacher reads the material to a small group of students and asks individuals to respond orally when given certain designated symbols. Each child's behavior and responses are carefully monitored during this exercise. The program also contains reading materials using the special symbols, as well as seatwork activities including word analysis and comprehension drills.

Update

Constructivist, Whole-Language Instruction

Whole language is a way of educating young children that many teachers accept and understand. The philosophy of whole language instruction resulted from teachers, administrators, teacher educators, and researchers who were looking for an alternative to skills based instruction. This approach considers language as a whole, not something that is broken into numerous, often disconnected parts. The following points summarize some of the concepts underlining the whole language approach to teaching writing.

- Language, including speaking, listening, reading, and writing, develop interdependently as well as in a social context.
- Students learn to read using authentic books, not basal readers.
- Students learn to write by engaging in the writing process.
- Students in a whole-language class are allowed to learn at their own pace rather than being subjected to a schedule in a basal reading or writing series.
- Students are involved in daily writing activities that focus on real life situations and experiences.
- Teachers serve as mediators during the whole language process, providing support but not overly interfering with the learning process.
- Students become involved in writing that is connected to their own lives.
- Students should be immersed in an environment that is filled with language materials and activities, including high interest reading materials, and print that they have helped produce.
- Students must be encouraged and motivated to share their experiences through literature.

Whole language instruction can be used with students with a variety of disabilities and learning strengths. It is not just an instructional system that is effective with gifted students or students who do not have problems in the reading and writing process. This particular model provides opportunities for students to be successful, regardless of their ability levels. It is appropriate for use with students who have language disabilities and are struggling with reading and writing activities, but often will need to be combined with decoding instructions for beginning readers.

Source: Reid, D. K. & Kuykendall, M. (1996). In D. K. Reid, W. P. Hresko, & H. L. Swanson (Eds.). *Cognitive approaches to learning disabilities,* 3rd ed. Austin TX: Pro-Ed.

A sight vocabulary covers phonetically irregular words, and teachers can assess skill development throughout the program using the tests provided. Other materials in this series are teacher's guides, lesson plans, reading books, workbooks, spelling books, take-home readers, and cassettes with sound pronunciations. The DISTAR technology and specific programs were carefully reviewed by Haring and Bateman (1977), who reported a substantial amount of empirical support for this instructional approach.

SRA Corrective Reading Program (CRP) (Engelmann, Becker, Hanner, & Johnson, 1980), an outgrowth of DISTAR, was designed for fourth- to twelfth-grade children with poor decoding skills. Decoding skills are improved by a combination of drills, repetitious reading of phonetic- and sight-vocabulary words, and reinforcement of the behavioral system. A comprehension program is also available.

The Decoding program within CRP has been the most widely used and researched. It provides a carefully sequenced hierarchy of continuous skills; pupil progress monitoring through criterion-referenced tests; lessons of about 45 minutes, in which pupils make group and individual oral responses as well as individual written responses; and incorporates reinforcement of pupil improvement through positive verbal feedback and earning points.

Placement into one of the three levels of the reading program is determined by performance on an assessment measure. Level A is essentially for the nonreader; it deals with basic skills such as sound blending, rhyming, sounding-out, and word and sentence reading. Level B provides for instruction on critical letter and word discrimination, letter combinations, story-reading, and questions. Level C is designed for students who are ready to decode a wide variety of words and sentence constructions they will encounter in varied reading materials. It emphasizes advanced word-attack skills, affixes, vocabulary, story-reading with comprehension questions, and outside reading applications.

Corrective Reading is among the few programs that have demonstrated effectiveness with older students who have reading difficulties. Specifically, reports have indicated positive results in improving the academic performance of junior high school underachievers (Campbell, 1983, cited in Becker, 1984), maladjusted students (Thorne, 1978), and senior high school-aged disabled readers (Gregory, Hackney, & Gregory, 1982). In an investigation of the effectiveness of CRP with fourth, fifth, and sixth graders with learning disabilities, Lloyd and colleagues (Lloyd, Cullinan, Heins, & Epstein, 1980) reported that the students who received CRP evidenced significantly higher scores on measures of reading and language skills. Finally, Polloway, Epstein, Polloway, Patton, and Ball (1986) reported positive results with middle and high school students identified as having learning disabilities and mild retardations. Corrective Reading is under revision; the interim Series Guide (Johnson, 1988) can be consulted for further information.

COMPREHENSION

Even though comprehension is central to the task of reading, relevant curriculum materials and related research sources historically have been less plentiful than those

Update

Whole Language Strategies

Whole language approaches stress the importance of meaning in language. Often presented as a diametrically opposite approach to reading than instruction in decoding, holistic approaches can rather best be seen as complementary approaches that emphasize the essence of reading, deriving meaning from the printed word. Specific activities consistent with the whole language approach can include:

- discussions of short stories led by the teacher
- the sharing of literacy experiences derived by students through reading books and stories
- sustained silent reading
- specific silent reading periods after which students write their reactions and share them with other students and the teacher
- group story writing (e.g., language experience approach)
- individual student writing exercises with shared work and collaborative revisions
- use of reading and writing to develop themes within specific content areas of the curriculum

Source: Polloway, E. A., & Patton, J. R. (2001). *Strategies for teaching learners with special needs,* (7th Ed.). Columbus, OH: Merrill.

with a word-recognition emphasis (Hurley, 1975). In recent years, however, this dearth has been met both by research and by curricular efforts. Certainly those who teach children with reading problems must be ready to develop effective instructional strategies to build comprehension of individual words as well as sentences, paragraphs, and passages.

According to Lerner (1985), comprehension skills can be divided into four semi-distinct levels:

1. *Literal:* comprehending the stated points of a passage.
2. *Inferential:* comprehending the implied as well as direct meanings of a passage.
3. *Critical:* comprehending a passage beyond inferences to judgments and evaluations that hinge largely on the reader's interpretations.
4. *Creative:* refining comprehension to a level that produces new insights and thoughts that spin off the passage read.

Spache and Spache (1973) identified three factors that affect reading comprehension: the child, the material, and the process of reading. The first variable consists of *the child's* conceptual level, specific skills and interests, sociocultural setting, opinions, and biases that compose his or her experiential background. A key concern is the child's ability to "access prior knowledge and relevant background experiences and then to assess whether the prior knowledge or background experiences are of sufficient quality and quantity to serve as an aid to reading comprehension" (Barclay, 1990, p. 85). This ability was seen as a key trait that distinguishes the mature from the immature reader. Snider's (1989) research indicated that a student who can decode adequately but lacks prior knowledge will need attention to the acquisition of such background knowledge and related vocabulary to improve comprehension.

The *material* being read—in particular, the level of difficulty of the passage, the vocabulary demands on the reader, and the degree of concept density—determines how easily a child can achieve comprehension. For example, though beginning readers understand thousands of words they cannot yet recognize, by third or fourth grade the challenge shifts from word recognition to understanding meaning (Harris & Sipay, 1990).

Most teachers readily acknowledge the importance of the first two variables, but the third, the *process,* may be inadvertently overlooked. Graham and Johnson (1989a) stressed the importance of prereading activities, including setting goals, making predictions, activating prior knowledge, using advance organizers, previewing, and introducing new concepts and vocabulary. In addition, factors during and after reading, such as rate followed, cuing systems, and type of questioning, must be considered.

In general, strategies for facilitating comprehension can be classified as either *teacher-directed* or *student-directed.* The former involve exercises in which the teacher structures the reading and then poses questions. The latter represents more of a learning strategy-type approach. Several representative approaches are discussed below.

LANGUAGE-EXPERIENCE APPROACH (LEA)

LEA has been described as both a developmental and a remedial reading program. The basis for LEA is the child's own oral language, which the student and the teacher develop into stories for reading. As a core program, it has the advantages of being a relevant approach, with built-in motivation, that adopts a whole language philosophy and thus promotes the integration of speaking, listening, reading, and writing. Language experience also can be used as a supplementary technique to build sight recognition and strengthen word vocabulary comprehension. By capitalizing on its motivational benefits, the teacher can use the technique to present specific sight words to the child by embedding them within his or her stories and by providing a helpful context to assist the child in understanding meaning.

Dictated experience stories are the heart of the LEA. In the definitive text on LEA, Stauffer (1970, p. 22) noted that the key is to "show pupils that reading is no more than talk written down." Some topics of interest, such as a current event in students' lives, an object brought to class, or a forthcoming trip, can stimulate communication. Individually or in small groups, the students talk about their chosen topic while the teacher transcribes their remarks. When the story is complete, the teacher and children read it aloud. Connections to writing also can spin off from this project. Stauffer (1980) indicated that LEA could provide the foundation for a reading instructional program. Besides its built-in motivational element, the LEA has the advantage of linking oral and written language, allowing for teacher creativity, and providing substantial flexibility and latitude in teaching.

The primary concern with the program is the teacher's ability to work from a relatively structure-free foundation. As Heller (1988) cautioned, this can pose a significant problem in a remedial setting. She indicated in particular that by trying to remain true to the students' natural oral language, the teacher often is confronted with group-dictated stories that are simply a list of sentences recorded verbatim. This provides limited samples to teach story structure to the students. To remedy this dilemma, she suggested that instruction follow good practice in both reading comprehension and written expression to achieve improved story structures. To do this, she outlined steps that would bring LEA in line with the stages of writing (see chapter 12), thus achieving a more holistic approach to instruction. As summarized, her suggestions (Heller, 1988, pp. 133-134) are:

1. *Prewriting*
   a. The activity begins by discussing a concrete experience the students have decided upon. Experiences based upon student interest may produce more effective narratives, as writing (dictation) topics evolving from them will likely be close to the students' hearts.
   b. The experience is discussed by activating the students' prior knowledge of relevant topics, because a person's scheme, or structured knowledge of any subject, is functional to comprehending and composing.
   c. A student-teacher generated purpose for writing or dictating is decided upon. Together, the topic is limited.
   d. The audience for whom the prose is intended is discussed.
   e. The teacher reads a model language experience story that contains a clear purpose and an easily identifiable audience. While reading it, the teacher encourages the students to predict what will happen next in the story, how the characters might change as a result of action, and how they think the story will end.

  f. The teacher engages in metacognitive modeling by describing the strategies used to understand (or construct) narrative form while reading (or writing) the model story.

  g. Before dictation begins, the teacher asks the students to think about the story they are going to create and make some notes. They should refer to the notes during the composing process. The notes will activate their prior knowledge of the topic as well as their ideas for developing a narrative with setting, plot, conflict, and characters.

  h. The teacher defines and gives further examples of story elements (setting, character, plot, resolution) as needed, using the model experience story.

2. *Writing/rewriting*

  a. The students and teacher actively monitor the dictation, referring to story parts whenever necessary, frequently reflecting upon what individuals involved in the lesson have contributed.

  b. The students or the teacher may stop the dictation when story cohesion is interrupted—when comprehension and composition break down. The students or teacher articulate what may be necessary to make the story understandable.

  c. As the story unfolds, it is read, reread, and rewritten. Students begin to realize that dictating a narrative requires comprehension of the story in progress. The writer is the first reader of his or her own work and bears the responsibility of constructing something meaningful to the intended audience. Whenever necessary, the students add, delete, or substitute as the dictation progresses. Throughout the dictation, active involvement in the composing-comprehending process is emphasized.

3. *Editing*

  After the LEA is completed, editing procedures can be implemented, specifically to enhance grammar as needed.

The use of dictated stories can add an element of incentive and variation for teaching word recognition and building vocabulary, in addition to building comprehension. Teachers should consider their use in both developmental and remedial settings. LEA is a logical component of a comprehensive whole language approach, which can contribute to successful progress of students across language domains (Stice & Bertrand, 1990). As Stice and Bertrand noted, "As children use language, they learn language and . . . they use language to learn" (p. 4).

DIRECTED READING THINKING ACTIVITIES (DRTA)

The DRTA is the most common teacher-directed approach. Using this method, teachers develop reading expectations in learners before they read a passage. Specific questions and discussion give the student a purpose before starting to read and a means of anticipating events that may occur in the passage. This orientation to task prepares students for what will be read and enables them to comprehend and recall key features.

The steps employed in DRTA vary according to the students, the specific skills being taught, and the overall lesson goals the teacher establishes. Basically, however, the method entails the following procedure. First, teachers orient students to the story and stimulate their interest and enthusiasm by discussing aspects of the story to be read. The title, pictures, and first sentences are good places to begin.

Second, teachers tell students what method of reading to use. The students should understand the purpose for reading so they know whether to skim quickly or read carefully for details. Specific questions can help set the purpose, although teachers should be careful not to make them so self-limiting that comprehension is impeded. Teachers can cue possible problem words in these questions. For example: "Read the first paragraph to find out why the boy had to go to the *hospital*." Depending on the student's ability level, teachers may direct silent reading for a sentence, a paragraph, a page, or a full story.

Third, once the reading assignment is complete, the students should answer and discuss the questions. Topics related to the purpose of the assignment can be explored, and questions tapping skills at various comprehension levels should be among those asked. Finally, silent rereading for specific objectives or oral reading as reinforcement can be included in the lesson.

OTHER TEACHER QUESTIONING STRATEGIES

As noted earlier, questioning strategies are critical tools for helping children develop specific comprehension skills. Because students' comprehension needs vary widely, however, questions should be designed to achieve appropriate results.

Some authors (Belch, 1975; Guszak, 1969) reported that 70 percent of teachers' questions is literal, requesting factual recall and recognition. It probably would be safe to assume that questions of that nature strengthened these abilities to the exclusion of other skills.

Lindsey and Kerlin's (1979) review of reading research on secondary students with learning disabilities elaborated on the consequences of literal questioning. They stated that comprehension problems are the key reading difficulties adolescents face at this time and that an overemphasis on literal comprehension had fostered this state of affairs.

A review by the Appalachian Educational Laboratory (AEL) (1990) focused on instructional practices in the classroom vis-a-vis teacher questioning. The brief list that follows highlights these points:

1. Higher-order vs. recall questions
   - Students in classrooms where higher-order questions are asked achieve substantially more than students in classrooms where most of the questions are recall/knowledge.
   - Achievement rises when teachers ask questions that require students to apply, analyze, synthesize, and evaluate information in addition to simply recalling facts.
   - Student achievement . . . and ability to generalize are enhanced when teachers ask questions at a variety of levels.
   AND YET
   - Teachers generally ask recall/knowledge questions [75–80% of the time] . . . The vast majority of teachers do not plan questions at the higher levels. This discrepancy is

most apparent for low achievers, who are asked questions requiring nothing more complex than simple recall.

2. Wait Time

When teachers use Wait Time I (following their questions) and Wait Time II (following student responses) of 3–5 seconds, it leads to behavior changes in students and teachers:
- Students give longer, more spontaneous, more appropriate responses.
- Students exhibit more speculative thinking, make more inferences, and ask more questions.
- Lower achieving students contribute more.
- Teachers show more flexibility in accepting student responses.
- Teachers ask more probing questions and fewer closed or informational questions.
- Teachers expect higher levels of performance from lower achieving students.

AND YET
- The time that a teacher pauses after asking a question and taking further action to elicit a response is only one second.
- When a student responds, teachers wait, on the average, less than a second before reacting. (pp. 9–11)

Clearly, sound questioning techniques are needed to develop and reinforce a child's cognitive processes. The following suggestions include some of those offered by Belch (1975):

1. Ask questions that demand more than simple yes/no responses.
2. Allow sufficient response time to encourage thinking.
3. Rephrase questions that produce incorrect responses or no responses at all.
4. Pursue answers by challenging students to support their responses.
5. Use selective directional techniques to involve all students.
6. Pursue responses with other questions that force students to evaluate and analyze.
7. Encourage attentional skills by avoiding excessive repetition of questions.

RE-QUEST

A useful technique based on teacher, and ultimately student, questioning, *Re-Quest* (Manzo, 1969) allows teachers to demonstrate question-asking behavior that can facilitate students' ability to generate their own questions. Mandlebaum (1989, p. 310) succinctly described steps to follow with *Re-Quest*. These steps would relate to a lesson using a reading passage at the child's instructional level:

1. The teacher explains to the student that the purpose of the method is to improve the ability to remember and understand what is read.
2. Next the teacher and student look at the title or picture and discuss what the story might be about. The student is asked to explain why he or she gives an answer (e.g., You said this story was going to be about school. What is in this picture that makes you think it is going to be about school?).
3. The teacher and student silently read the first sentence. The teacher then closes the book while the student asks questions about the first sentence. For instance, "Jeff

ran to school" could lead to questions such as: Who is the story about? Where did Jeff go? How did he get to school? Do you think Jeff was in a hurry? Why?

4. When the student has run out of questions, he or she closes the book and the teacher asks questions. The teacher should try to model question-asking behavior by asking as many higher-order questions as possible (e.g., Why do you think Karen got mad?).

5. The reading-questioning format continues until reaching a point in the story where the end can be predicted. At that point the student predicts what might happen.

6. The student then reads the rest of the passage silently and discusses the end with the teacher.

SURVEY-QUESTION-READ-RECITE-REVIEW (SQ3R)

The SQ3R technique is closely related to the DRTA in general but was intended as a student-directed strategy when originally developed by Robinson (1946). It can also be modified for various teaching or learning situations. The five steps in SQ3R are: survey, question, read, recite, and review. *Survey* introduces a story by focusing on pictures, the title, and the first sentence. Then *questions* orient the student to each paragraph or series of paragraphs. Next, students *read* each section to find answers to the questions, then attempt to *recite* the responses without referring back to the text. After students complete the story, they *review* it by answering direct questions and reading selected sections aloud.

MULTIPASS

Multipass is a learning strategy that can aid in reading comprehension as well as serve its most common purpose as a study skill strategy. Developed at the Kansas Institute for Research on Learning Disabilities (Schumaker, Deshler, Allen, Warner, & Denton, 1982) as a derivative of SQ3R, it calls for a series of "passes" through a reading passage, typically a content chapter in a textbook. The three passes are, briefly:

- *Survey Pass:* seeks to familiarize the student with the main ideas and organization of the chapter.
- *Size-up Pass:* helps students learn specific information from the chapter without having to read it through.
- *Sort-out Pass:* provides a vehicle for students to assess themselves on the content presented in the chapter.

Specific procedures to follow with each of these passes is presented in Schumaker et al. (1982).

COMPREHENSION MONITORING

An increasingly popular and important approach to enhancing comprehension is through self-monitoring of comprehension. This approach initially was popularized with readers having learning disabilities by Wong (1979), who developed a system she referred to as meta-comprehension or comprehension monitoring. As Billingsley and Wildman (1988) noted, with this approach mature readers use their prior knowledge of a topic to assist them in monitoring their comprehension during the reading process. Snider (1989) wrote that metacognitive strategies are apt particularly when a student possesses decoding skills and requisite background knowledge but nevertheless has difficulty with comprehension.

Schewel (1989) provided an excellent review of comprehension monitoring approaches. According to her, to learn to read, children must actively participate in the learning process, taking responsibility for their own learning. This necessity presents a problem because students with disabilities frequently assume a passive role (Brown & Palinscar, 1982; Torgesen, 1982). Their related deficits in metacognitive skills (e.g., self-monitoring and predicting) may severely restrict their success in learning to read (Wong, 1982). Comprehension monitoring or self-questioning presents a promising approach to promote the development of metacognitive skills, thus leading to improvement in comprehension (Griffey, Zigmond, & Leinhardt, 1988). Chan and Cole's (1986) research on students with reading disabilities has well demonstrated the effectiveness of comprehension monitoring approaches.

A specific approach to comprehension monitoring via self-questioning was discussed by Schewel and Waddell (1986). Students are instructed to follow these steps, listed by Schewel (1989):

1. Identify the main idea of a paragraph and underline it.
2. Develop questions related to the main idea and write them where they can be referred to easily.
3. Check those questions with the teacher's models to be certain that they are correctly stated.
4. Read the passage, answer the questions, and learn the answers.
5. Continually look back over the questions and answers to note the accumulation of information. (p. 230)

Rosenshine (1989) made a useful further distinction about such self-instructional approaches. The term *comprehension monitoring,* he indicated, suggests that the reader is becoming actively aware of his or her reading, whereas *comprehension fostering* means actually doing something about it. Possible processes that may assist in fostering include summarizing, clarifying, questioning, and predicting.

Graham and Johnson (1989a) have provided an apt summary on the importance of student-directed activities in reading:

A broad variety of teacher-directed activities can have a powerful effect on pupil pursuits during learning. Consequently, a reasonable combination of activities should prove advantageous. Further, although teacher-directed activities are likely to produce immediate effects on student performance, they may have limited long-term effects. That is, once teacher cues or supports are withdrawn, student performance may not remain at the same level. Consequently, teachers must help students internalize the powerful components built into teacher-directed activities. (p. 29)

One model that is consistent with the benefits of enhancing teacher- and student-directed reading activities is referred to as *cognitive coaching*. Paris and Oka (1989) described five characteristics of the reading coach that have direct implications for fostering comprehension:

1. Coaches model and explain useful strategies. Good coaches analyze tasks and describe procedures explicitly so each step toward successful performance is clearly understood.
2. Coaches and students agree on the same performance objectives. Their goals for improvement and commitment to persistence are shared. They also discuss the emotions that accompany success and failure.
3. Assessment and instruction are interwoven. Good coaches measure students' progress and provide instruction at developmentally appropriate levels. Coaching is interactive and addresses specific weaknesses identified by participants.
4. Responsibility for learning is shifted to students. Effective coaching provides guidance that students can internalize for self-regulated learning.
5. Progress is evaluated according to personal standards. The challenge of mastering a task and achieving one's individual standard of performance is more important than competing with others. (p. 37)

SEMANTIC MAPPING

A useful technique that can assist in comprehending single words and reading passages (Kameenui, 1990) as well as studying content material, is called semantic mapping. Essentially, the student uses his or her prior knowledge of the topic to assist in developing a diagram of what is to be read. This procedure thus can focus on the introduction of words with unknown meaning as well as the association between key themes or concepts within the passage being read. Schewel (1989) identified the steps in a semantic mapping process as follows:

1. Teacher presents either a stimulus word or a specific core question.
2. Students generate words related to the stimulus word or predict answers to the questions, which the teacher lists on the board.
3. Students, with the teacher, then put related words or answers in groups, drawing connecting lines between topics, forming a semantic map.
4. After reading the selection, students and teacher discuss the categories, rearrange or add to the map developed prior to reading. (p. 232)

Rooney (1988) developed a systematic procedure for studying that derives from the concepts of semantic mapping. Referred to as "wheels for reading," it uses the wheel as the basis for organization and keeping track of main ideas as well as details via a visual format. Figure 9.9 illustrates a wheel based on a reading passage about the Loch Ness monster.

Semantic mapping is an excellent tool for developing vocabulary (Kameenui, 1990) as well as enhancing comprehension in general. According to Rupley and Blair (1989), mapping provides students a chance to learn new words by tying them to previously learned concepts and words, understanding relationships between words, and organizing the information they have been reading. Thus, it is an effective way to present new vocabulary words and also to relate words to story content.

Loch Ness Monster

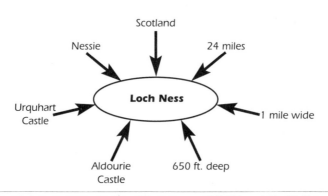

Source: From *Independent Strategies for Efficient Study* (p. 43) by K. Rooney, 1988, Richmond, VA: J.R. Enterprises. Reprinted by permission.

Figure 9.9
Wheels for Reading

VOCABULARY BUILDING

The several approaches to reading comprehension discussed above can facilitate acquisition of word meanings and sentence and passage comprehension. If students have difficulties with word meanings, however, direct instruction in vocabulary may be called for. Although vocabulary instruction was addressed in the discussion of sight vocabulary, we revisit it here to stress the importance of vocabulary building for comprehension as well.

Teaching words that have a common conceptual basis is an effective approach. Marzano et al. (1987) identified a *cluster approach* as one that teaches words in semantically related clusters; the words share some common basis even though they are not synonyms. Marzano (1984) reviewed words commonly found in elementary school textbooks and then organized the 7,300 words he found into 61 clusters. Of these, the first 15 clusters accounted for more than 50 percent of all the words found in these textbooks. Table 9.7 delineates these 15 clusters and the number of words in each. These words can be used to design instructional lessons and sequences in vocabulary.

After reviewing the literature on vocabulary instruction, McKeown and Beck (1988) concluded that two features characterize efforts that positively influence comprehension.

1. Students must be provided a high frequency of encounters with words and these exposures should be provided through a variety of instructional strategies and in multiple contexts.
2. Students need to actively think about the meaning of the words; relationships or clusters provide an effective strategy to achieve this objective.

Table 9.7
Vocabulary Clusters

Superclusters, Examples of Constituent Words, and Descriptions	Number of Words in Supercluster	Cumulative Number of Words
1. Occupations: career, manager, mayor, coach, businessman, printer, publisher	364	364
2. Types of motion: action, stillness, begin, end, chase, toss, pull, plunge, shrink	321	685
3. Size/quantity: tiny, large, amount, many, monstrous, one, two	310	995
4. Animals: pet, dog, snake, fish, spider, bird	289	1,284
5. Feelings/emotions: feeling, terror, shame, anger, sad, happy, love, excitement	282	1,566
6. Food types/meal types (names for various food types and situations involving eating): food, supper, meal, cookie, meat, vegetables, butter, cook	263	1,829
7. Time (names for various points and periods of time and words indicating various time relationships between ideas): lifetime, noon, season, month, today, earlier, now, afterward	251	2,080
8. Machines/engines/tools: equipment, engine, oven, hammer, axe, spoon	244	2,324
9. Types of people (names for various types or categories of people that are not job-related): person, woman, boy, neighbor, dweller, hero, enemy, mother, dad	237	2,561
10. Communication (names for various types of communications and actions involving communications): explain, talk, suggest, question, command, vow, complain	235	2,796
11. Transportation: car, plane, jeep, boat, bicycle, ship	205	3,001
12. Mental actions/thinking: wonder, plan, search, solve, teach, select, wisdom, belief	193	3,194
13. Nonemotional human traits (general, nonphysical traits of people): nice, lazy, sure, patient, stubborn, humorous, heroic	175	3,369
14. Location/direction: here, back, end, to, inside, on, under, close	172	3,541
15. Literature/writing: story, novel, poem, music, telegram, pen, write	171	3,712

Source: From "A Cluster Approach to Vocabulary Instruction: A New Direction from the Research Literature" by R. J. Marzano, 1984, *Reading Teacher, 38*, p. 170. Reprinted by permission of R. J. Marzano and the International Reading Association.

BIBLIOTHERAPY

Bibliotherapy, the use of books for therapeutic purposes, is an outgrowth of comprehension. It often has been recommended for students whose adjustment difficulties take the form of emotional or behavioral disorders in the classroom. As Schubert (1975) stated, "Bibliotherapy is helping students to help themselves solve their personal problems through reading (p. 497).

To implement a bibliotherapy program, teachers should match books and stories with the types of problems their students are having. In many cases, a child's concern and confusion about his or her learning problems may be ameliorated by reading about people who experienced similar difficulties. By identifying with a story character, a child may gain insight into the demands that the environment, friends, relatives, and self can make on one's life.

To facilitate the selection of reading materials, Schubert (1975) suggested that teachers ask students informal questions about their likes and dislikes, wishes, fears, and worries. They can select appropriate materials for direct instructional sessions or for independent reading.

This, and all of the techniques discussed previously, can help develop a child's comprehension skills. To implement a program of instruction, however, teachers must choose a series of reading passages appropriate to a student's level of interest and ability. Some teachers will find success through a language experience approach, an individualized reading program based on library selections, or a self-constructed set of stories. Supplementary commercial programs also can facilitate planning and instruction.

COMMERCIAL READING PROGRAMS

A variety of commercial curricular materials can serve as either core or supplemental programs in the development of reading comprehension skills. The commercial programs described earlier also may emphasize comprehension (e.g., Corrective Reading), but their emphasis on decoding resulted in their being placed in an earlier section. This section reviews a sample of materials that have been used successfully with learners who have special needs.

Teachers considering a commercial series should closely evaluate how well the program will meet the instructional needs of their students. Particular consideration should be given to the advantages and disadvantages of an individual program versus the core commercial program. Because reading is so complex, beginning teachers may be well advised to rely first on a basal program and then gradually shift to supplementary resources as increased pedagogical skills translate to less need for the crutch of a core program.

Basal Readers   A significant percentage of teachers choose basal readers from the variety of core programs available. These series have both distinct advantages and disadvantages. On the positive side, they contain inherent structure and sequence, controlled vocabulary, a wide variety of teaching activities, and preparation for the teacher. Weaknesses, on the other hand, include inappropriate pacing for an individual child, overconcern for certain skills to the exclusion of others, and encouragement of group instructional orientation. For the inexperienced teacher, however, these programs may represent an appropriate place to begin developing a responsive reading program. Numerous basals are available; those that have been advocated for students with disabilities are described briefly here.

Merrill Linguistic Reading Program (1975). The Merrill reading series is a highly structured program covering pre-primer to sixth-grade reading levels. The series can be used with all children but was designed specifically for students who need more structured and slower-paced material. The Merrill program follows a linguistic approach based upon the research of Charles C. Fries. Vocabulary is introduced through the three major spelling patterns (*cvc, cvcc, cvvc*) along with basic sight words. Minor spelling patterns and spelling irregularities are introduced at higher levels. Books at the lower levels are void of illustrations, to prevent interference with word attack and comprehension development.

The entire series emphasizes comprehension and word-attack skills. The teacher's manual provides detailed instruction for each lesson, including comprehension questions, spelling and writing exercises, and occasional games. The series contains placement and mastery occasional games. It also includes placement and mastery tests, skill books, word cards, reinforcement materials, and a literature appreciation kit.

Open Highways (Johnson, 1966, 1973, 1974). The *Open Highways* program is a remedial basal program with texts for all elementary school levels. It attempts to be both a diagnostic and a developmental series and was designed to prevent failure. Resource materials for adapting the program to individual needs include workbooks; spirit masters; picture, word and letter cards; and storybook boxes. This program represents the diversity of life with stories about people of many races from various locales, and it also blends selections that appeal to both genders. Many stories also touch on everyday experiences common to all children.

Stanwix House Reading Series (Stanwix House, 1970). The Stanwix House series was developed especially for children with disabilities who have a mental age of 5 years and up, and other children whose learning problems place their reading level below their chronological age. Although the design of this series resembles other reading programs, it introduces skills and vocabulary at a slower pace and gives children a greater opportunity to practice these skills. The materials start with prereading learning experiences and work toward independent reading through phonics and other word-analysis skills.

The carefully controlled cumulative vocabulary of more than 2,400 words includes words frequently used in reading as well as words of special significance to exceptional learners. Containing both fictional and factual information, the stories are targeted to developing social skills that all students need. Designed to be highly motivating, the stories are current and depict crosscultural children in both content and illustrations. Three different levels of parallel materials allow teachers to match stories to the needs of children with different functioning levels while their identical content allows group discussion.

Supplementary Resources   In addition to basal readers, a number of other sources are available to assist in the development of comprehension skills and to generally aid in effecting reading improvement. A representative sample is described here.

Barnell-Loft Specific Skills Series (Boning, 1976): The *Specific Skills Series* is a set of reusable paperback books for children with reading skills from first to twelfth grade. The eight different books for each grade level are entitled *Working with Sounds, Following Directions, Using the Context, Locating the Answer, Getting the Facts, Getting the Main Idea, Drawing Conclusions,* and *Detecting the Sequence.* Together, they provide an opportunity for intensive practice in each skill at each instructional level, with an emphasis on comprehension. The books have a controlled vocabulary and follow a consistent multiple-choice format throughout each skill area, facilitating independent work by the child. The reading material includes both fictional and factual information and can be highly motivating. A teacher's manual, with answers, worksheets, and placement tests, accompanies the series.

Learning Through Literature (Dodds & Goodfellow, 1990) provides an opportunity for students to interact with literature selections within a direct instruction teaching model. It contains lower-level units, story studies, for primary classes with students who are not mature independent readers, and upper-level units, novel studies, which are recognized children's literature selections or novels by award-winning authors. The latter units are intended for use with themes studied in grades three to six. The program is designed to be used as a vehicle for integrated study across curricular areas to supplement basals or provide a basis for individually developed reading programs.

High Interest-Low Vocabulary Materials   By definition, students with significant reading deficits operate at a level somewhat below their chronological age. Therefore, teachers have had to provide these students with interesting and relevant materials at levels of difficulty appropriate to their abilities. The 1970s and 1980s witnessed a significant increase in the number of high interest-low vocabulary series that can help solve this basic curricular problem.

Thypin (1979) outlined the various considerations related to selecting high interest-low vocabulary materials. Besides stressing the importance of appropriate readability levels, measured by sentence length and difficulty of vocabulary, she noted that these materials:

1. Should be relevant to the interests and needs of the target reader.
2. Should have level of content (conceptual) difficulty appropriate for the reader.
3. Should be within the grasp of the reader's cognitive skills.
4. Should have vocabulary consistent with the reader's oral language and phonetic skills.
5. Should make syntactic demands that parallel the reader's competence.
6. Should have an interesting appearance that appeals to the reader, especially in terms of the implied level of maturity.

Some sample high interest-low vocabulary programs are listed in Table 9.8, which is a summary derived from Polloway and Smith (1982) and Mercer and Mercer (1989). An excellent review of high interest-low vocabulary materials can be found in

Table 9.8
Selected High Interest-Low Vocabulary Materials

Series	Publisher	Focus	Reading Levels
Deep Sea Adventure	Harr Wagner	Boats, ocean, diving	1–5
Sailor Jack	Benefic Press, Westchester, IL	Adventures and amusing stories	pp*-3
Cowboy Sam	Benefic Press, Westchester, IL	Western	pp*-3
Skyline Books	Benefic Press, Westchester, IL	Space travel	1–3
Action Library	Scholastic Book Services, New York, NY	Romance, mysteries, and science fiction	2–5
Pal Paperback Kits	Xerox Education Publishers, Middletown, CT	Assorted interesting stories	1–5
Reading Skill Builders	Reader's Digest Services, Pleasantville, NY	Short stories on variant topics	1–4
Sports Mystery Stories	Benefic Press, Westchester, IL	Sports	2–4
Teen-Age Tales	D.C. Heath, Lexington, MA	Teenage situations	4–6
Space Age Books	Benefic Press, Westchester, IL	Space travel	1–6
Pacemaker Classics	Fearon-Pittman, Belmont, CA	Great works of literature	2.1–2.8
Hip Reader	Book-Lab, New York, NY	Inner city, varied ethnic groups	1–3
Dan Frontier	Benefic Press, Westchester, IL	Frontier life, American Indians	pp*-4
Jim Forest	Field Education Publishers, Chicago, IL	Wildlife, nature	p*-3
Americans All	Garrard Publishers, Champaign, IL	Biographies	4
Childhood of Famous Americans Series	Bobbs-Merrill, New York, NY	Biographies	4–5
Folklore of the World Books	Garrard Publishers, Champaign, IL	Global stories	2
Junior Science Books	Garrard Publishers, Champaign, IL	Science-oriented	4–5
Morgan Bay Mysteries	Field Education Publishers, Chicago, IL	Mysteries	2–4
Mystery Adventure Series	Benefic Press, Westchester, IL	Mysteries	2–6

*pre-primer
**primer

VanEtten and Watson (1978). In addition, attention should be given to motivating and relevant content available from other sources. For example, Hirshoren, Hunt, and Davis (1974) outlined an approach utilizing want-ads as a basis for reading instruction, and Mandlebaum (1990) discussed some examples of reading materials from children's and adolescent literature that have appeal for students of variant ages.

Patterned Language and Predictable Books   Materials that can expand overall reading opportunities for students include *patterned language books,* based on the regular repetition of a phrase. These books frequently repeat a phrase at the beginning or the end of a sequence or portion of a story or rhyme (Mandlebaum, 1989). A classic example is Maurice Sendak's *Chicken Soup with Rice* (Schewel, 1989).

Predictable books allow children to make a good guess about how a book will end or which words will continue to occur. Mandlebaum (1989) described one such book:

> An example of a story in which the reader can predict what will come next is *Teeny Tiny.* In this story, the "teeny tiny woman put on her teeny tiny *hat* and went out of her teeny tiny *house* to take a teeny tiny *walk.* Not only are the words "teeny tiny" repeated frequently in the sentence, but it is fairly easy to predict what the words would be if they were unknown. (p. 91)

As Schewel (1989) noted, sources such as these provide a way to stimulate fluent reading in children by setting up patterns and building in predictability. Thus, the stories provide semantic and syntactic cues to the readers, a particularly helpful type of assistance for those with disabilities. Finally, these resources represent access to some of the classic books of children's literature. A selected bibliography is presented at the end of the chapter.

SUMMARY

Reading instruction can be based on a variety of models of learning how to read. While some approaches emphasize a decoding orientation, others adopt a "top-down" approach that emphasizes the importance of meaning in reading. The Samuels' model provides a working hypothesis that illustrates the interaction between decoding and comprehension.

There are four key word recognition strategies that assist the reader. Sight word instruction emphasizes the development of automaticity as students learn to recognize an ever-increasing number of words immediately upon sight. Phonetic analysis provides a vehicle for teaching students to learn to use sound-symbol correspondences in analyzing unknown words. Contextual analysis bridges the gap between the analysis of words and the meaning of a passage and thus provides students with a symatic and semantic cuing system. Structural analysis provides the reader with the ability to attack words by considering affixes, contractions, compound words, and syllables. A variety of instructional programs have a primary emphasis on these word analysis strategies.

Comprehension is the essential goal in all reading instruction. Teachers can enhance students' comprehension by selecting instructional activities which include: varied teacher questioning strategies, promotion of student questioning before and after as well as during the reading of a passage, selections of interests that are consistent with students' ability, and opportunities that build on the individual's natural language.

PATTERNED LANGUAGE AND PREDICTABLE BOOKS

Adams, P. (1974). *This old man.* New York: Grossett & Dunlap.
Alain (1964). *One, two, three, going to sea.* New York: Scholastic Press.
Aliki (1962). *My five senses.* New York: Thomas Y. Crowell.
Aliki (1968). *Hush little baby.* Englewood Cliffs, NJ: Prentice-Hall.
Aliki (1974). *Go tell Aunt Rhody.* New York: Macmillan.
Antle, N. (1985). *The good bad cat.* Grand Haven, MI: School Zone Publishing Co.
Asch, P. (1977). *Monkey face.* New York: Parents' Magazine Press.
Ballan, L. (1972). *The animal.* Nashville: Abingdon Press.
Ballan, L. (1972). *Where in the world is Henry?* New York: Scholastic.
Barret, J. (1970). *Animals should definitely not wear clothes.* New York: Antheneum.
Barton, B. (1973). *Buzz, buzz, buzz.* New York: Scholastic Press.
Baskin, L. (1972). *Hosie's alphabet.* New York: Viking Press.
Battaglla, A. (1962). *Old Mother Hubbard.* New York: Golden Press.
Baum, A., & Baum, J. (1962). *One bright Monday morning.* New York: Random House.
Becker, J. (1973). *Seven little rabbits.* New York: Scholastic.
Beckman, K. (1969). *Lisa cannot sleep.* Danbury, CT: Franklin Watts.
Bellah, M. (1963). *A first book of sounds.* New York: Golden Press.
Bennett, J. (1986). *Teeny Tiny.* New York: G.P. Putnam's Sons.
Berenstein, S., & Berenstein, J. (1971). *The B book.* New York: Random House.
Bonne, R. (1961). *I know an old lady.* New York: Scholastic Press.
Brand, O. (1974). *When I first came to this land.* New York: G.P. Putman's Sons.
Brandenberg, F. (1970). *I once knew a man.* New York: Macmillan.
Brooke, L. (1968). *John Crow's garden.* New York: Frederick Warne & Co.
Brown, M.V. (1947). *Goodnight moon.* New York: Harper & Row.
Brown, M.W. (1949). *The important book.* New York: Harper & Row.
Brown, M.W. (1952). *Where have you been?* New York: Scholastic.
Brown, M.W. (1954). *The friendly book.* New York: Golden Press.
Brown, M.W. (1956). *Home for a bunny.* New York: Golden Press.
Brown, M.W. (1971). *The bus ride.* Glenview, IL: Scott Foresman.
Burningham, J. (1970). *Mr. Grumpy's outing.* New York: Scholastic Press.
Cameron, P. (1961). *I can't said the ant.* New York: Coward, McCann & Geoghegan.
Carle, E. (1975). *The mixed up cameleon.* New York: Thomas Y. Crowell.
Carle, E. (1977). *The grouchy ladybug.* New York: Thomas Y. Crowell.
Carle, E. (1981). *The very hungry caterpiller.* New York: Putnam Publishing Group.
Charlip, R. (1964). *What good luck, what bad luck.* New York: Scholastic Press.
Charlip, R. (1971). *Fortunately.* New York: Parents' Magazine Press.
Considine, K., & Schuler, R. (1965). *One, two, three, four.* New York: Holt, Rinehart & Winston.
Cook, B. (1962). *The little fish that got away.* New York: Scholastic.
deRegniers, B. (1961). *The little book.* New York: Henry Z. Walck.
deRegniers, B. (1972). *May I bring a friend?* New York: Atheneum.
Domanska, J. (1971). *If all the seas were one sea.* New York: Macmillan.
Duff, M. (1972). *Johnny and his drum.* New York: Henry Z. Walck.
Duff, M. (1978. *Rum pum pum.* New York: Macmillan
Einsel, W. (1962). *Did you ever see?* New York: Scholastic Press.
Emberly, B. (1967). *Drummer Hoff.* Englewood Cliffs, NJ: Prentice-Hall.

Emberly, B. (1969). *Simon's song*. Englewood Cliffs, NJ: Prentice-Hall.

Emberly, B. & Emberly, E. (1966). *One wide river to cross*. New York: Scholastic Press.

Emberly, E. (1974). *Klippity klop*. Boston: Little, Brown & Co.

Ets, M. (1955). *Play with me*. New York: Viking Press.

Ets, M. (1972). *Elephant in a wall*. New York: Viking Press.

Flack, M. (1932). *Ask Mr. Bear*. New York: Macmillan.

Galdon, P. (1973). *The three bears*. New York: Scholastic Press.

Galdon, P. (1981). *The three billy goats Gruff*. Boston: Houghton Mifflin.

Galdon, P. (1984). *Henny Penny*. Boston: Houghton Mifflin.

Galdon, P. (1984). *The three little pigs*. Boston: Houghton Mifflin.

Galdon, P. (1985). *The little red hen*. Boston: Houghton Mifflin.

Gelman, R. G. (1977). *Hey Kid!* New York: Avon.

Ginsburg, M. (1972). *The chick and the duckling*. New York: Macmillan.

Greenburg, P. (1968). *Oh Lord, I wish I was a buzzard*. New York: Macmillan.

Gregorich, B. (1984). *Jog, frog, jog*. Grand Haven, MI: School Zone Publishing Co.

Guilfolle, E. (1957). *Nobody listens to Andrew*. New York: Scholastic Press.

Guilfolle, E. (1962). *The house that Jack built*. New York: Holt, Rinehart & Winston.

Haban, T (1972). *Count and see*. New York: Macmillan.

Hoffman, H. (1968). *The green grass grows all around*. New York: Macmillan.

Hutchins, P. (1968). *Rosie's walk*. New York: Macmillan.

Hutchins, P. (1971). *Titch*. New York: Collier Books.

Hutchins, P. (1972). *Good night owl*. New York: Macmillan.

Joslin, S. (1968). *What do you say Dear?* New York: Scholastic Press.

Kalan, R. (1981). *Jump, frog, jump!* New York: Scholastic.

Keats, E. (1971). *Over in the meadow*. New York: Scholastic Press.

Kellogg, S. (1985). *Chicken Little*. New York: William Morrow & Co.

Kent, J. (1971). *The fat cat*. New York: Scholastic.

Klein, L. (1958). *Brave Daniel*. New York: Scholastic Press.

Krauss, R. (1948). *Bears*. New York: Scholastic Press.

Krauss, R. (1952). *A hole is to dig*. New York: Collier Books.

Krauss, R. (1970). *Whose mouse are you?* New York: Collier Books.

Krauss, R. (1971). *The lion's tail*. Glenview, IL: Scott Foresman.

Krauss, R, (1972). *Good night little abc*. New York: Scholastic Press.

Langstaff, J. (1971). *Gather my gold together: Four songs for four seasons*. New York: Doubleday.

Langstaff, J. (1974). *Oh, a-hunting we will go*. New York: Atheneum.

Laurence, L.E. (1969). *We're off to catch a dragon*. Nashville: Abingdon Press.

Lexau, J. (1969).*Crocodile and hen*. New York: Harper & Row

Lobel, A. (1975). *King Rooster, Queen Hen*. New York: Greenwillow.

Lobel, A. (1979). *A treeful of pigs*. New York: Greenwillow.

Mack, S. (1974). *10 bears in my bed*. New York: Pantheon.

Martin, B. (1967). *Brown bear, brown bear, what do you see?* New York: Holt, Rinehart & Winston.

Martin, B. (1967). *Spoiled tomatoes*. Oklahoma City: Bowmar.

Martin, B. (1970). *A ghost story*. New York: Holt, Rinehart & Winston.

Martin, B. (1970). *Monday, Monday, I like Monday*. New York: Holt, Rinehart & Winston.

Martin, B. (1970). *The haunted house*. New York: Holt, Rinehart & Winston.

Mayer, M. (1968). *If I had*. New York: Dial Press.

Mayer, M. (1975). *Just for you*. New York: Golden Press.

McGovern, A. (1967). *Too much noise*. New York: Scholastic.

Memling, C. (1961). *Ten little animals*. New York: Golden Press.

Memling, C. (1972). *Riddles, riddles from a to z*. New York: Golden Press.

Moffett, M. (1972). *A flower pot is not a hat*. New York: E.P. Dutton.
Nodest, J. (1963). *Who took the farmer's hat?* New York: Scholastic Press.
O'Neill, M. (1961). *Hailstones and halibut bones*. New York: Doubleday & Co.
Palmer, J. (1969). *Ten days of school*. New York: Macmillan.
Patrick, G. (1970). *A bug in a jar*. New York: Scholastic Press.
Peppe, R. (1970). *The house that Jack built*. New York: Delacorte.
Petersham, M., & Petersham, M. (1971). *The rooster crows: A book of American rhymes and jingles*. New York: Scholastic Press.
Polushkin, M. (1978) *Mother, Mother, I want another*. New York: Crown Publishers.
Quackenbush, R. (1965). *Poems for counting*. New York: Holt, Rinehart & Winston.
Quackenbush, R. (1973). *She'll be comin' around the mountain*. New York: J.B. Lippincott.
Quackenbush, R. (1975). *Skip to my Lou*. New York: J.B. Lippincott.
Rossetti, C. (1965). *What is pink?* New York: Holt, Rinehart & Winston.
Scheer, J., & Bileck, M. (1964). *Rain makes a difference*. New York: Holiday House.
Scheer, J., & Bileck, M. (1964). *Upside down day*. New York: Holiday House.
Sendak, M. (1962). *Chicken soup with rice*. New York: Scholastic Press.
Sendak, M. (1963). *Where the wild things are*. New York: Scholastic Press.
Dr. Seuss. (1963). *Dr. Seuss's abc*. New York: Random House.
Shaw, C. (1947). *It looked like spilt milk*. New York: Harper & Row.
Shulevitz, U. (1986). *One Monday morning*. New York: Macmillan.
Skaar, G. (1972). *What do the animals say?* New York: Scholastic.
Sonneborn, R. (1974). *Someone is eating the sun*. New York: Random House.
Spier, P. (1961). *The fox went out on a chilly night*. New York: Doubleday.
Tolstoy, A. (1968). *The great big enormous turnip*. Danbury, CT: Franklin Watts.
Watson, C. (1971). *Father Fox's pennyrhymes*. New York: Scholastic Press.
Welber, R. (1974). *Goodbye, hello*. New York: Pantheon.
Wildsmith, B. (1972). *The twelve days of Christmas*. Danbury, CT: Franklin Watts.
Wildsmith, B. (1982). *Cat on the mat*. Oxford: Oxford University Press.
Withers, C. (1967). *A rocket in my pocket*. New York: Scholastic Press.
Wolkstein, D. (1977). *The visit*. New York: Alfred A. Knopf.
Wondriska, W. (1970). *All the animals were angry*. New York: Holt, Rinehart & Winston.
Wright, H. (1965). *A maker of boxes*. New York: Holt, Rinehart & Winston.
Zemach, H. (1965). *The judge*. New York: Farrar, Straus & Giroux.
Zemach, M. (1965). *The teeny tiny woman*. New York: Scholastic.
Zemach, M. (1976). *Hush, little baby*. New York: E.P. Dutton.
Zolotow, C. (1958). *Do you know what I'll do?* New York: Harper & Row.

Source: Abridged from "Reading" by L. Mandlebaum in *Best Practices in Mild Retardation* (pp. 305–308) edited by G. A. Robinson, J. R. Patton, E. A. Polloway, & L. Sargent, 1989, Reston, VA: Council for Exceptional Children, Division on Mental Retardation.

REFERENCES

Allington, R. L. (1980). Word frequency and contextual richness effects word identification of educable mentally retarded children. *Education and Training of the Mentally Retarded, 15,* 118–120.
Appalachian Educational Laboratory (1990). *Designing instructional strategies: The prevention of academic learning problems*. Columbus, OH: Charles E. Merrill Publishing.
Bailey, E. J. (1975). *Academic activities for adolescents with learning disabilities*. Evergreen, CO: Learning Pathways.
Bamman, H., & Whitehead, R. (1968). *With American heroes*. Westchester, IL: Benefic Press.
Barclay, K. D. (1990). Constructing meaning: An integrated approach to teaching reading. *Interventions in School and Clinic, 26,* 84–91.
Bartel, N. R. (1986). Reading. In D. D. Hammill & N. R. Bartel (Eds.), *Teaching students with learning and behavior problems* (4th ed.) (pp. 23–89). Austin, TX: Pro-Ed.

Barudin, S. I., & Hourcade, J. J. (1990). Relative effectiveness of three methods of reading instruction in developing specific recall and transfer skills in learners with moderate and severe mental retardation. *Education and Training in Mental Retardation, 25,* 286–291.

Becker, W. (1984). Corrective reading program evaluated with secondary students in San Diego. *Association for Direct Instruction News, 3*(3) 1, 23.

Belch, P. (1975). The question of teachers' questions. *Teaching Exceptional Children, 2,* 46–50.

Billingsley, B. X., & Wildman, T. M. (1988). The effects of prereading activities on the comprehension monitoring of learning disabled adolescents. *Learning Disabilities Research, 4,* 36–44.

Boning, R. A. (1976). *Specific skills series.* Rockville Center, NY: Barnell-Loft.

Browder, D. M., & Snell, M. E. (1987). Functional academics. In M. E. Snell (Ed.), *Systematic instruction of persons with severe handicaps* (3rd ed.) (pp. 436–468). Columbus, OH: Charles E. Merrill Publishing.

Brown, A. L., & Palinscar, A. (1982). Inducing strategic learning from texts by means of self-informed, self-control, training. *Topics in Learning and Learning Disabilities, 2*(1), 1–17.

Camp, B. W. (1973). Psychometic tests and learning in severely disabled readers. *Journal of Learning Disabilities, 6,* 512–517.

Carbo, M. L. (1978). A word imprinting technique for children with severe memory disorders. *Teaching Exceptional Children, 11,* 35.

Carnine, D., & Silbert, J. (1979). *Direct instruction reading.* Columbus, OH: Merrill.

Chall, J. (1967). *Learning to read: The great debate.* New York: McGraw-Hill.

Chall, J. & Snow, C. E. (1988). *School influences on the reading development of low-income children.* (ERIC Digests Online Project.)

Chan, L. K. S., & Cole, P. G. (1986). The effects of comprehension monitoring training on the reading competence of learning disabled and regular class students. *Remedial and Special Education, 7*(4), 33–40.

Clymer, T. (1963). The utility of phonic generalizations in the primary grades. *Reading Teacher, 16,* 252–258.

Cohn, M., & Stricker, G. (1979). Reversal errors in strong, average, and weak letter namers. *Journal of Learning Disabilities, 12,* 533–537.

Crain, S. K. (1988). *The role of phonics in reading instruction.* ERIC Digests Online Project.

Deno, S. L., & Chiang, B. (1979). An experimental analysis of the nature of reversal errors in children with severe learning disabilities. *Learning Disability Quarterly, 2,* 40–45.

Dodds, T., & Goodfellow, F. (1990). *Learning through literature.* Chicago: SRA.

Dorry, G. W., & Zeaman, D. (1973). The use of a fading technique in paired-associate teaching of a reading vocabulary with retardates. *Mental Retardation, 11*(6), 3–6.

Dorry, G. W., & Zeaman, D. (1975). Teaching a simple reading vocabulary to retarded children: Effectiveness of fading and nonfading procedures. *American Journal of Mental Deficiency, 79,* 711–716.

Dulin, K. L. (1970). Using context clues in word recognition and comprehension. *Reading Teacher, 23,* 440–445; 469.

Dyck, N. J., Sankey, P., & Sundbye, N. W. (1983). *Survival words program.* Hingham, MA: Teaching Resources.

Edmark Associates (1972, 1984). *Edmark reading program.* Seattle: Edmark Associates.

Ekwall, E. E., & Shanker, J. L. (1988). Diagnosis and remediation of the disabled reader (3rd ed.). Boston: Allyn & Bacon.

Engelmann, S., Becker, W. C., Hanner, S., & Johnson, G. (1980). *SRA corrective reading program.* Chicago: Science Research Associates.

Engelmann, S., & Bruner, E. (1974, 1975). *DISTAR reading level I and II.* Chicago: Science Research Associates.

Engelmann, S., & Bruner, E. (1984). *Reading mastery program.* Chicago: Science Research Associates.

Entrikin, D., York, R., & Brown, L. (1977). Teaching trainable level multiply handicapped students to use picture cues, context cues, and initial consonants sounds to determine the labels of unknown words. *American Association for the Education of the Severely/Profoundly Handicapped Review, 2,* 169–190.

Fernald, G. M. (1943). *Remedial techniques in basic school subjects.* New York: McGraw-Hill.

Fernald, G. M. (1988). *Remedial techniques in basic school subjects: Methods for teaching dyslexics and other learning disabled persons* (L. Idol, Ed.). Austin, TX: Pro-Ed.

Fletcher, D., & Abood, D. (1988). An analysis of the readability of product warning labels: Implications for curriculum development for persons with moderate and severe mental retardation. *Education and Training in Mental Retardation, 23,* 224–227.

Folk, M. C. & Campbell, J. (1978). Teaching functional reading to the TMR. *Education and Training of the Mentally Retarded, 13,* 332–326.

Francis, W. N. (1958). *The structure of American English.* New York: Ronald Press.

Gaskins, I. W., Downer, M. A., Anderson, R. C., Cunningham, P. M., Gaskins, R. W., & Schommer, M. (1988). A metacognitive approach to phonics: Using what you know to decode what you don't know. *Remedial and Special Education, 9*(1), 36–41.

Gibson, E. (1963). Development of perception: Discrimination of depths compared with discrimination of graphic symbols. *Monographs of Society for Child Development, 28*(2, Serial No. 86).

Gillingham, A., & Stillman, B. (1960, 1968, 1970). *Remedial teaching for children with specific disability in reading, spelling, and penmanship.* Cambridge, MA: Educators Publishing Service.

Glass, E. W., & Glass, G. G. (1978). *Glass analysis for decoding only.* New York: Easier to Learn.

Goodman, K. S. (1973). Miscues: Windows on reading. In K. S. Goodman (Ed.), *Miscue analysis.* Urbana, IL: (ERIC Document Reproduction Number 2).

Graham, S., & Johnson, L. A. (1989a). Research-supported activities that influence the text reading of students with learning disabilities. *LD Forum, 15*(1), 27–30.

Graham, S., & Johnson, L. A. (1989b). Teaching reading to learning disabled students. *Focus on Exceptional Children, 21*(6), 1–12.

Gregory, R. P., Hackney, D., & Gregory, N. M. (1982). Corrective reading programme: An evaluation. British Journal of Educational Psychology, 52, 33–50.

Griffey, Q. L., Zigmond, N., & Leinhardt, G. (1988). The effects of self-questioning and story structure on the reading comprehension of poor readers. *Learning Disabilities Research, 4*, 45–51.

Guszak, F. J. (1969). Questioning strategies of elementary teachers in relation to comprehension. In L. A. Harris & C. B. Smith (Eds.), *Individualizing reading instruction: A reader.* New York: Holt, Rinehart and Winston.

Hargis, C. H. (1972). A comparison of retarded and non-retarded children on the ability to use context in reading. *American Journal of Mental Deficiency, 15*, 1–12.

Hargis, C. H. (1982). Word recognition development. *Focus on Exceptional Children, 15*, 1–12.

Haring, N. C., & Batemen, B. (1977). *Teaching the learning disabled child.* Englewood Cliffs, NJ: Prentice Hall.

Harris, A. J., & Sipay, E. R. (1990). *How to increase reading ability* (9th ed.). New York: Longman.

Hegge, T. G., Kirk, S. A., & Kirk, W. D. (1939, 1977). *Remedial reading drills.* Ann Arbor, MI: George Wahr Publishing.

Heilman, A., Blair, R., & Rupley, W. (1986). *Principles and practices of teaching reading.* Columbus, OH: Merrill.

Heller, M. F. (1988). Comprehending and composing through language experience. *Reading Teacher, 42*, 130–135.

Hendrickson, J., & Shores, R. E. (1978). Antecedent and contingent modeling to teach basic sight vocabulary to learning disabled children. *Journal of Learning Disabilities, 11*, 424–425.

Hirshoren, A., Hunt, J. T., & Davis, C. (1974). Classified ads as reading material for the educable retarded. *Exceptional Children, 41*, 45–46.

Hurley, O. L. (1975). Reading comprehension skills *vis-a-vis* the mentally retarded. *Education and Training of the Mentally Retarded, 10*, 10–14.

Johnson, G. (1988). *Corrective reading: Series guide.* Chicago: Science Research Associates.

Johnson, I. M., et al. (1966, 1973, 1974). *The new open highways.* Glenview, IL: Scott, Foresman.

Kameenui, E. J. (1990, October). *Instructional issues in the area of vocabulary learning.* Paper presented at Council for Learning Disabilities annual conference, Austin, TX.

Kameenui, E. J., & Simmons, D. C. (1990). *Designing instructional strategies: The prevention of academic learning problems.* Columbus, OH: Charles E. Merrill Publishing.

Kirk, S., Kirk, W., & Minskoff, E. (1986). *Phonic remedial reading lessons.* Novato, CA: Academic Therapy.

Lenz, B. K., & Hughes, C. A. (1990). A word identification strategy for adolescents with learning disabilities. *Journal of Learning Disabilities, 23*, 149–158, 163–164.

Lerner, J. (1985). *Learning disabilities: Theories, diagnosis and teaching strategies* (4th ed.). New York: Houghton Mifflin.

Lindsey, J. D., & Kerlin, M. A. (1979). A brief review of literature for secondary level LD. *Journal of Learning Disabilities, 12*, 408–414.

Lloyd, J. W., Cullinan, D., Heins, E., & Epstein, M. H. (1980). Direct instruction: Effects on oral and written comprehension. *Learning Disability Quarterly, 4*(3), 70–76.

Lorenz, L., & Yockell, E. (1979). Using the neurological impress method with learning disabled readers. *Journal of Learning Disabilities, 12*, 420–422.

Lyon, G. R. (May 1995). Research in learning disabilities supported by the National Institute of Child Health Human Development. Subcommittee on Disability Policy, Committee on Labor Human Resources, United States Senate. Unpublished manuscript.

Mandlebaum, L. (1989). Reading. In G. Robinson, J. R. Patton, E. A. Polloway, & L. Sargent, *Best prac-tices in mild mental retardation* (pp. 87–107). Reston, VA: Council for Exceptional Children, Divi-sion on Mental Retardation.

Mandlebaum, L. H. (1990). Lessons with literature. *LD Forum, 15*(4), 35–36.

Manzo, A. V. (1969). ReQuest procedure. *Journal of Reading, 13,* 123–126.

Marzano, R. J. (1984). A cluster approach to vocabulary instruction: A new direction from the research liter-ature. *Reading Teacher, 38,* 168–173.

Marzano, R. J., Hagerty, P. J., Valencia, S. W., & DiStefano, P. P. (1987). *Reading diagnosis and instruc-tion: Theory into practice.* Englewood Cliffs, NJ: Prentice Hall.

McClure, J., Kalk, M., & Keenan, V. (1980) Use of grammatical morphemes by beginning readers. *Journal of Learning Disabilities, 13,* 262–267.

McKeown, M. G., & Beck, I. L. (1988). Learning vocabulary: Different ways for different goals. *Remedial and Special Education, 9*(1), 42–46.

McMullen, D. (1975). Teaching protection words. *Teaching Exceptional Children, 7,* 74–77.

Mercer, C. D., & Mercer, A. R. (1989). *Teaching students with learning problems* (2nd ed.). Columbus, OH: Merrill.

Merrill linguistic reading program. (1975). Columbus, OH: Charles E. Merrill Publishing.

Miccinati, J. (1979). Fernald technique refinements. *Journal of Learning Disabilities, 12,* 139–142.

Moyer, S. B. (1982). Repeated reading. *Journal of Learning Disabilities, 15,* 619–624.

Moyer, S. B., & Newcomer, P. O. (1977). Reversals in reading: Diagnosis and remediation. *Exceptional Children, 43,* 424–429.

Nietupski, J., Williams, W., & York, R. (1978). Teaching selected phonic word analysis skills to TMR la-beled students. *Teaching Exceptional Children, 11,* 144–145.

O'Shea, L. J. (1990, Oct.) *Critique of whole language approaches to reading instruction for learners with mild handicaps.* Paper presented at Council for Learning Disabilities annual conference, Austin, TX.

O'Shea, L. J., Sindelar, P. T., & O'Shea, D. J. (1987). The effects of repeated readings and attentional cues on the reading fluency and comprehension of learning disabled readers. *Learning Disabilities Re-search, 2,* 103–109.

Paris, S. G., & Oka, E. R. (1989). Strategies for comprehending text and coping with reading difficulties. *Learning Disability Quarterly, 12,* 32–42.

Polloway, C. H., & Polloway, E. A. (1978). Expanding reading skills through syllabication. *Academic Therapy, 13,* 455–462.

Polloway, E. A., & Polloway, C. H. (1980). Remediating reversals through stimulus fading. *Academic Ther-apy, 15,* 539–543.

Polloway, E. A., Epstein, M. H., Polloway, C. H., Patton, J. R., & Ball, D. W. (1986). Corrective reading program: An analysis of effectiveness with learning disabled and mentally retarded children. *Reme-dial and Special Education, 7*(4), 41–47.

Polloway, E. A., Patton, J. R., Payne, J. S., and Payne, R. A. (1989). *Strategies for teaching learners with Special Needs.* Columbus, OH: Charles E. Merrill Publishing.

Polloway, E. A., Payne, J. S., Patton, J. R., & Payne, R. A. (1985). *Strategies for teaching retarded and spe-cial needs learners.* Columbus, OH: Charles E. Merrill Publishing.

Polloway, E. A., & Polloway, C. H. (1980). Remediating reversals through stimulus fading. *Academic Ther-apy, 15,* 539–543.

Polloway, E. A., & Smith, J. E. (1982). *Teaching language skills to exceptional learners.* Denver: Love.

Pope, L. (1967). *Guidelines to teaching remedial reading to the disadvantaged.* New York: Book-Lab.

Robinson, H. (1946.). *Why pupils fail in reading.* Chicago: University Chicago Press.

Robinson, G. A. (1986). *Essential vocabulary: Words and phrases found in community settings.* Des Moines: Iowa Department of Education.

Rooney, K. (1988). *Independent strategies for efficient study.* Richmond, VA: J. R. Enterprises.

Rosenshine, B. (October, 1989) Teaching explicit and implicit skills. Best practices in mental retardation conference, Davenport, IA.

Ross, A. D. (1976). *Psychological aspects of learning disabilities and reading disorders.* New York: Mc-Graw-Hill.

Rupley, W. H., & Blair, T. R. (1989). *Reading diagnosis and remediation* (3rd ed.). Columbus, OH: Charles E. Merrill Publishing.

Samuels, S. J. (1981). Some essentials of decoding. *Exceptional Education Quarterly, 1*(1), 11–26.

Schewel, R. (1989). Reading. In E. A. Polloway, J. R. Patton, J. S. Payne & R. A. Payne, *Strategies for teaching learners with special needs* (pp. 208–254). Columbus, OH: Charles E. Merrill Publishing.

Schewel, R. H., & Waddell, J. G. (1986). Metacognitive skills: Practical strategies. *Academic Therapy, 22*(1), 19–25.

Schilit, J., & Caldwell, M. L. (1980). A word list of essential career/vocational words for mentally retarded students. *Education and Training of the Mentally Retarded, 15*, 113–117.

Schoolfield, L. D., & Timberlake, J. B. (1940, 1960, 1978). *Phonovisual method book.* Rockville, MD: Phonovisual Products.

Schubert, D. G. (1975). The role of bibliotherapy in reading instruction. *Exceptional Children, 41*, 497–504.

Schumaker, J. B., Deshler, D. D., Allen, G. R., Warner, M. M., & Denton, P. H. (1982). Multipass: A learning strategy for improving reading comprehension. *Learning Disability Quarterly, 5*, 295–304.

Shepherd, M. (1980). *Phonetic and structural analysis: The Oakland way.* Boyd Tavern, VA: Oakland Farm School.

Simms, R. B., & Falcon, S. C. (1987). Teaching sight words. *Teaching Exceptional Children, 20*, 30–33.

Smith, F. (1973). *Psycholinguistics and reading.* New York: Holt, Rinehart and Winston.

Smith, D. D. (1979). Modeling effects on reading. *Journal of Learning Disabilities, 12*, 172–175.

Smith, D. D., & Lovitt, T. C. (1973). The educational diagnosis and remediation of written *b* and *d* reversal problems: A case study. Journal of Learning disabilities, 6, 356–363.

Snell, M. E. (1978) Functional reading. In M. E. Snell (Ed.), *Systematic instruction of the moderately and severely handicapped.* Columbus, OH: Charles E. Merrill Publishing.

Snell, M. E. (1988). Curriculum and methodology for individuals with severe disabilities. *Education and Training in Mental Retardation, 23*, 302–314.

Snider, V. E. (1989). Reading comprehension performance of adolescents with learning disabilities. *Learning Disability Quarterly, 12*, 87–96.

Spache, G. C., & Spache, E. B. (1973). *Reading in the elementary school.* Boston: Allyn & Bacon.

Staats, A. W., & Butterfield, W. H. (1965). Treatment of nonreading in a culturally deprived juvenile delinquent: An application of reinforcement principles. *Child Development, 36*, 925–942.

Staats, A. W., Finley, J. R., Minke, K. A., & Wolfe, M. (1964). Reinforcement variables in the control of unit reading responses. *Journal of Experimental Analysis of Behavior, 7*, 139–149.

Stanwix House. (1970). *Stanwix house reading series.* Pittsburgh: Author.

Stauffer, R. G. (1970, 1980). *The language-experience approach to the teaching of reading.* New York: Harper & Row.

Stice, C. F., & Bertrand, N. P. (1990). *Whole language and the emergent literacy of at-risk children: A two-year comparative study.* Charleston, WV: Appalachia Educational Laboratory.

Tarver, S. G., & Ellsworth, P. S. (1981). Written and oral language for verbal children. In J. M. Kauffman & D. P. Hallahan (Eds.), *Handbook of special education* (pp. 491–510). Englewood Cliffs, NJ: Prentice Hall.

Thorne, M. T. (1978). "Payment for reading": The use of the "Corrective Reading Scheme" with junior maladjusted boys. *Remedial Education, 13*(2), 87–90.

Thypin, M. (1979). Books for low reading level. *Journal of Learning Disabilities, 12*, 428–430.

Torgesen, J. K. (1982). The learning disabled child as an inactive learner: Educational implications. *Topics in Learning and Learning Disabilities, 2*(1), 45–51.

U.S. Department of Education. (1987). *What works: Research about teaching and learning* (2nd ed.). Washington, DC: Author.

Vandever, T. R., & Stubbs, J. C. (1977). Reading retention and transfer in TMR students. *American Journal of Mental Deficiency, 82*, 233–237.

VanEtten, C., & Watson, B. (1978). Reading comprehension: An overview of the concept and a review of materials. *Journal of Learning Disabilities, 11*, 30–39.

Wallach, M. A., & Wallach, L. (1976). *Teaching all children to read.* Chicago: University of Chicago Press.

Wallen, C. J. (1972). *Competency in teaching reading.* Chicago: Science Research Associates.

Walsh, B. F., & Lamberts, F. (1979). Errorless discrimination and picture fading as techniques for teaching sight words to TMR students. *American Journal of Mental Deficiency, 83*, 473–479.

Westman, J. D. (1990). *Handbook of learning disabilities: A multisystem approach.* Boston: Allyn & Bacon.

Wiederholt, J. L., & Bryant, B. (1987). Assessing reading. In D. D. Hammill (Ed.), *Assessing the abilities and instructional needs of the student* (pp. 161–340). Austin, TX: Pro-Ed.

Wong, B. Y. L. (1979). The role of theory in learning disabilities research: Part II. A selective review of current theories of learning and reading disabilities. *Journal of Learning Disabilities, 12*, 649–658.

Wong, B. Y. L. (1982). Understanding learning disabled students' reading problems: Contributions from cognitive psychology. *Topics in Learning and Learning Disabilities, 1*(4), 43–50.

10

Handwriting Instruction

A primary mode of communication in our society is through written language. Although more and more written communication is handled through typewriters, word processors, and computers, it is still a critical skill that individuals need to develop. Without legible handwriting, the best of compositions, notes, and correspondence may be ineffective. Without the ability to communicate through handwriting of a reasonable quality, individuals are at a major disadvantage in our rapidly changing society. What is reasonable "good handwriting is that which is easily written and easily read with the overall goal being legibility" (Wood, Webster, Gullickson, & Walker, 1987, p. 24).

Some professional educators and researchers believe that handwriting is no longer an important skill to teach to elementary school students (Luftig, 1989). They contend that in our highly and increasingly technological world, everyone eventually will be using computers and other technological devices that could make handwriting unimportant. Although the advances in technology have clearly impacted on the everyday use of handwriting for some people, competencies in this skill definitely remain important. Without the ability to communicate through handwriting, individuals will be unable to make notes, take down information quickly, and communicate with others in writing when technological devices are unavailable.

Stop and think how often during a given day you write down something. It could be a phone number, an address, a name, a grocery list, or some other essential piece of information. Therefore, "even in these days of self-correcting typewriters and magic word processors, handwriting is a necessary competency" (Hagin, 1983, p. 266). Although technology has given us new ways to utilize written communication, on numerous occasions people do not have typewriters, computers, or other aids available for written communication. People have to make notes about various things when all they have available are paper and pencil (Hagin, 1983).

Simply making notes is not sufficient either. How often have you made notes only to find out later that you could not read your own writing or determine exactly what you meant? If you have had difficulties with your own written communication, think what other teachers, supervisors, friends, and others must deal with when they try to read your writing.

Probably the one setting where handwriting is used most often is school. Students and teachers alike rely extensively on these skills every day (Herbert, 1987). The ability of students to use handwriting skills in note-taking, copying information from the board, and completing written work in a legible, understandable form "is of crucial value in their educational development and achievement" (Phelps, Stempel, & Speck, 1985, p. 46).

Teachers expect the majority of their students to complete academic assignments using handwriting. Students whose handwriting is illegible are at a significant disadvantage in school; their handwriting deficiencies can diminish their chances for success across all subject areas. Teachers develop impressions about a student based on a number of factors; legibility of the student's handwriting is one of them (Reis, 1989). "Legible writing is a tool for learning; poor writing is a barrier" (Hagin, 1983,

p. 266). Therefore, handwriting is an essential skill for young children that must be taught in our schools (Koenke, 1986).

Another setting in which handwriting can play a major role is in the workplace. Therefore, handwriting can be important in the transition from high school to adulthood and vocational success. Potential employers want their employees to be able to write legibly. Even completing a job application requires good handwriting skills, because individuals whose handwriting is barely readable may present a negative image to potential employers. Even though handwriting may be totally unrelated to the specific demands of a given job, the ability to complete a job application with neat, legible handwriting makes an impression on the employer. Adults also need legible handwriting to write personal letters, mail orders, complete forms such as those for income tax, and complete information for schools where children attend (Hagin, 1983).

TRENDS

Although continued fluency in handwriting is needed, the emphasis on handwriting instruction during the past several decades has been limited (Manning, 1986). The result has been a trend toward noticeable problems in illegibility, slowness, tension, and fatigue in the area of writing (Furner, 1983). The lack of emphasis could be a result of teachers' limited knowledge about instructing handwriting skills, or the general perception that handwriting instruction is unimportant (Manning, 1986). Regardless of the reasons why handwriting instruction has been somewhat neglected, the most recent trends in elementary curriculum development show some reemphasis in this area (Phelps & Stempel, 1989). Teachers should remember that students with normal gross and fine motor skills are capable of learning to write well; the only missing ingredient is effective instruction from teachers (Manning, 1986).

Because the importance of handwriting is being realized once again, many students are receiving appropriate instruction. Most students in elementary schools learn to use handwriting to express themselves and complete necessary forms. But some, too, have difficulties. As could be expected, many of the students who have problems in handwriting are those who receive special education services (Reis, 1989). Therefore, teachers working with students who have disabilities should be aware of the handwriting process, common handwriting deficiencies, approaches to assess handwriting problems, and strategies for implementing remedial programs focusing on handwriting deficiencies.

Handwriting skills can be taught in isolation or in context. Teaching handwriting skills in isolation requires teachers to teach specific steps involved in making letters and combining letters into words and sentences. These are mechanical skills taught using commercial materials or teacher-made activities. During the past several years, teaching handwriting skills in context with other language skills has become popular. Known as the whole language approach, this model fosters language arts skills by having students write their own compositions. Although this is an effective means of teaching handwriting to many students, this chapter describes how to teach specific skills related to the mechanics of writing.

Update

Handwriting's Cultural Context

Handwriting is now less often focused upon as a critical area given the increased emphasis on technology and, in particular, the increased use of keyboarding with computers. Nevertheless, handwriting retains its importance in our culture. Thornton (1996) recently published a book entitled *Handwriting in America: A Cultural History*. Thornton's work touches on, among other things, the traditional issue of conformity vs. uniqueness of style. Her work provides an interesting background for further consideration of handwriting instruction:

In the early 1900s . . . the Palmer method ruled. Mr. Palmer promised to deliver a tireless arm that could compete with the typewriter, but what really attracted educators were his handwriting drills. Any survivor of these drills will be happy to describe them to you. Sometimes they began with "preparatory calisthenics." Then, at the teacher's command, students executed row after row of ovals and "push-pulls." School officials were blunt about the value of these drills. The lessons they conveyed—conformity to standard models, obedience to authority—would reform juvenile delinquents, assimilate foreigners, and acclimate working-class children to their futures in the typing pool or on the factory line.

But, at that time, the rank and file in the penmanship army were . . . drawn to the message of graphology. Whatever they try to do to you in school, graphologists insisted, your handwriting will remain your own, indestructibly unique and, in the record of traits and talents that it provides, a guide to the singular life waiting for you. "Pick up the pen and stir the sleeping fire," intoned one graphologist. "You may have the potentialities of a Napoleon or a Paderewski. Your handwriting will tell you." It was these same would-be's who bared their souls in the many graphological-advice columns that appeared in the pulp magazines and tabloid papers of the 1920s and 1930s.

Here, then, was a run-in between the forces of conformity and those of individuality, an argument about the nature of the self. We often think of the self as an abstraction, something that philosophers or psychologists might ponder, but nothing you can put your finger on in the comings and goings of daily existence, the little events of the lives of ordinary people. Tracing the history of handwriting shows us that ideas do not float above us in some intellectual stratosphere. When people defined the self, they did so not as an abstract intellectual exercise but in the very real ways that they lived.

Source: Thornton, T. P. (1996, August 15) Handwriting as an act of self-definition. *The Chronicle of Higher Education,* p. 3–7.

NATURE OF HANDWRITING

As one moves away from oral language to the written form, various complexities emerge. Even a casual view of handwriting or penmanship reveals that this expressive act involves the integration and coordination of visual, motor, and memory skills. The complexity of the skill is such that, after careful consideration of the skills required, it is amazing that so many young children learn to express themselves in writing as easily as they do.

Handwriting is an extremely complex process. *Visual skills* are crucial to handwriting, because acuity, visual perception, and visual and sequential memory all enable the writer to see letters and words. Without the ability to see the forms constructed, individuals would not be able to perceive similarities and differences among them, or to remember what they saw. This combination of visual and motor skills comes into play as the individual attempts to produce letters and words. Try writing a long section of words with your eyes closed. Although you probably will be able to produce letters and words that are readable, the clarity of the production likely will be significantly less than it would be if you were to see the process.

Handwriting is a *perceptual-motor skill* that requires the individual to perceive a letter form, then translate the perceived form into a written symbol using motor skills. At the same time, the writer integrates previous perceptual images, through *memory*, and new visual images, including the working surface and the markings that have been made. Similar perceptual-motor acts are required to play games such as golf, baseball, ping-pong, or tennis. The integration of visual and motor abilities is a complex process that reaches its height in the demand of fine-motor activities such as writing.

Another characteristic that separates handwriting from speech or gestures is the amount of time required to produce an end product. Even with this time restriction, the permanence of written materials make these written language abilities critical in communication. The fact that written language is relatively permanent causes it to be scrutinized more frequently and closely than other language forms. Speed, accuracy, and neatness are important qualities in handwriting. Slow, tedious, and sloppy handwriting causes students to spend more time completing assignments, which makes the process tedious and may increase dissatisfaction with school assignments, and perhaps school itself. And, again, neatness of the writing may affect the teacher's attitude toward the student and influence grading procedures.

The development of handwriting skills begins even before children enter school and engage informal instruction. This early beginning of writing generally takes two forms: continuous curvy lines; or a series of circles or straight lines, or both. These early efforts have been grouped into five levels (Ferreiro & Teberosky, 1982). In these levels, children experiment and "write" as part of their literacy development.

Level I   Children use separate graphic characters that all look alike but children consider different.

Level II   Graphic forms are more defined and conventional letters have more similarities. There is a fixed number of forms.

Level III   Children assign a sound value to each of the forms; each form equates to a syllable.

Level IV   Children abandon the notion that each form equates to a sound and utilize more analysis of each form.

Level V   The code is broken and children realize that each form equates to a sound.

This early development of "writing" displays children's desires and willingness to learn written communication skills. Not only does it give children practice in fine-motor activities, but it also helps develop a motivation to learn how to communicate in writing.

SEQUENCE OF SKILLS

The sequence of skills in handwriting begins with a variety of prewriting exercises and ends with proper uses of punctuation in written expression. In general, the following sequence of skills must be achieved:

1. Grasping and using crayons and paint brushes.
2. Grasping and holding a pencil.
3. Moving the pencil in random patterns.
4. Reproducing patterns, such as line and wave patterns, letters, numbers, and words.
5. Copying letters and words.
6. Writing letters and words in manuscript.
7. Developing flowing movements required for cursive writing.
8. Copying cursive letters and words.
9. Writing cursive letters and words.
10. Writing sentences and paragraphs.

Although the sequence of skills seems to be simple and brief, most students take several years to become competent in all of these areas. Generally speaking, in kindergarten and first grade, students become comfortable with writing materials (crayons and pencils) and learn to copy and write using manuscript letters (Koenke, 1986). In the second grade, students refine their manuscript writing and may begin some cursive letters. Although some students still use manuscript letters in the fourth grade, by the end of this grade, most students rely totally on cursive writing. Beyond the fourth grade, emphasis typically is placed on written expression, not on the mechanics of handwriting, but individual students may continue to need assistance in the handwriting process, particularly those who have had a history of learning or motor difficulties.

ASSESSMENT OF HANDWRITING

Because writing problems are fairly common, comprehensive assessment of handwriting skills is an important component of educational planning and intervention.

Unlike the basic academic skills of reading and math, however, assessment of handwriting skills has not received a great deal of attention. In fact, it is an extremely unpopular activity (Luftig, 1989). Whereas numerous formal, standardized assessment instruments have been developed for domains such as reading, math, written expression, spelling, and general information, the number of formal tests for handwriting is extremely limited. Teachers' observations and informal assessment procedures are most often used to determine an individual student's handwriting skills, if any assessment is performed at all (Graham, Boyer-Shick, & Tippets, 1989).

Assessing handwriting skills varies a great deal from teacher to teacher, writing program to writing program, and formal assessment device to another. Even so, some general commonality can be found among assessment methods regarding the types of errors determined. These include letter formation, spacing, slant, line quality, letter size and alignment, and writing rate (Luftig, 1989). Most assessment instruments are informal. Formal assessment will be described first, followed by a discussion of informal, teacher-designed assessment.

FORMAL ASSESSMENT

Among the limited number of formal assessment tools available for handwriting are the Zaner-Bloser Evaluation Scale (1984), Test of Written Language–2 (TOWL–2) (Hammill & Larsen, 1988), Test of Legible Handwriting (Larsen & Hammill, 1989), and scales by Bezzi (1962) and by Freeman (1959). Also, some general achievement tests have sections that measure handwriting skills. For the most part, formal, commercial assessment instruments are limited in scope. First, only a small sample of handwriting is used to determine whether students can write or whether their written productions are adequate. Without extensive handwriting sampling, an individual student's strengths and weaknesses cannot be accurately determined. Second, many of the tests that determine handwriting skills also measure other academic areas. This could result in a poor handwriting sample.

General Limitations   Handwriting scales have been available since the early 1900s. These scales were the first attempt to systematically measure handwriting skills and take measurement error into consideration. Primarily, handwriting scales require students to write letters or words, either from a copy or from memory. The evaluator then attempts to match the student's writing to a set of graded samples that normally are arranged in a hierarchical format (Graham, 1986).

Although handwriting scales provide a controlled method of assessing handwriting skills, this type of assessment has some inherent problems. First, scales do not entail a broad enough sample of handwriting performances to cover the full repertoire of skills (Graham, 1986). Second, only a few samples are provided for comparison purposes. For example, the Test of Written Language–2 (TOWL–2) includes 10 graded samples, ranging from illegible (0) to highly legible (10) (Hammill & Larsen, 1988).

Another negative characteristic of handwriting scales is their lack of differentiation between the handwriting of males and females (Graham, 1986). Such differentiation in the evaluation of handwriting samples could add validity to the measures, because many studies suggest that, for whatever reason, girls have better handwriting than boys (Wood, Webster, Gullickson, & Walker, 1987).

In addition to these weaknesses regarding handwriting scales, Graham (1986) pointed out that they frequently do not report reliability, do not provide teachers with actual proficiency ratings, and do not help teachers individualize instruction or monitor the effectiveness of interventions. Therefore, though they may provide a general evaluation of a student's handwriting skills, they do not assist teachers in developing appropriate intervention strategies to improve handwriting.

Regardless of the weaknesses noted, handwriting scales can provide a great deal of valuable information for teachers who work with students with handwriting deficiencies. These scales can be used as a screening mechanism to determine which students need additional handwriting assessment and interventions. They also can help teachers develop and refine their informal assessment skills related to handwriting (Graham, 1986). Therefore, when used properly, handwriting scales can benefit teachers.

Specific Scales   One of the most popular instruments designed to formally assess handwriting is the Zaner-Bloser Evaluation Scale (1984). This is a group or individual instrument that allows teachers to determine the handwriting skills of students in grades one through twelve in approximately 15 minutes (Luftig, 1989).

The person administering the test writes designated words or phrases on the board for students to copy within 2 minutes. The resulting samples are then compared to a "standard" provided in the manual in the areas of letter formation, slant, alignment and proportion, and line quality. The scale yields an overall rating of excellent, satisfactory, fair, or poor. Figure 10.1 shows an example from the Zaner-Bloser Scales. Although the test provides an excellent method of determining overall handwriting skills, it does not provide diagnostic data that could help in developing an intervention plan (Luftig, 1989).

An instrument that can be used to determine handwriting readiness is the Writing subscale of the Basic School Skills Inventory–Diagnostic (Hammill & Leigh, 1983). The BSSI is designed for children ages 4 through 6 years and can be used as either a norm-referenced or a criterion-referenced instrument. Using this subscale, the teacher reads each item on the test and determines the answer based on familiarity with the student. The student is not actually "tested" in the sense that certain questions have to be answered, unless there is a question about a particular item (Hammill & Bartel, 1990). Table 10.1 includes some of these items found on the Writing subtest of the BSSI.

The Test of Legible Handwriting (Larsen & Hammill, 1989) can be used when a standard score related to handwriting ability is needed. Using a five-level scale, teachers rate samples of handwriting, which can be generated through the pictures in the Test of Written Language–2 (TOWL–2) or from some classroom activity. As with other formal handwriting assessment instruments, the Test of Legible Handwriting provides only a gross evaluation of handwriting abilities. Specific strengths and weaknesses that can be used to develop intervention programs are not derived from this test (Hammill & Bartel, 1990).

Another formal assessment instrument that can be used to determine hand-writing abilities is the Test of Written Language–2 (TOWL–2) (Hammill & Larsen,

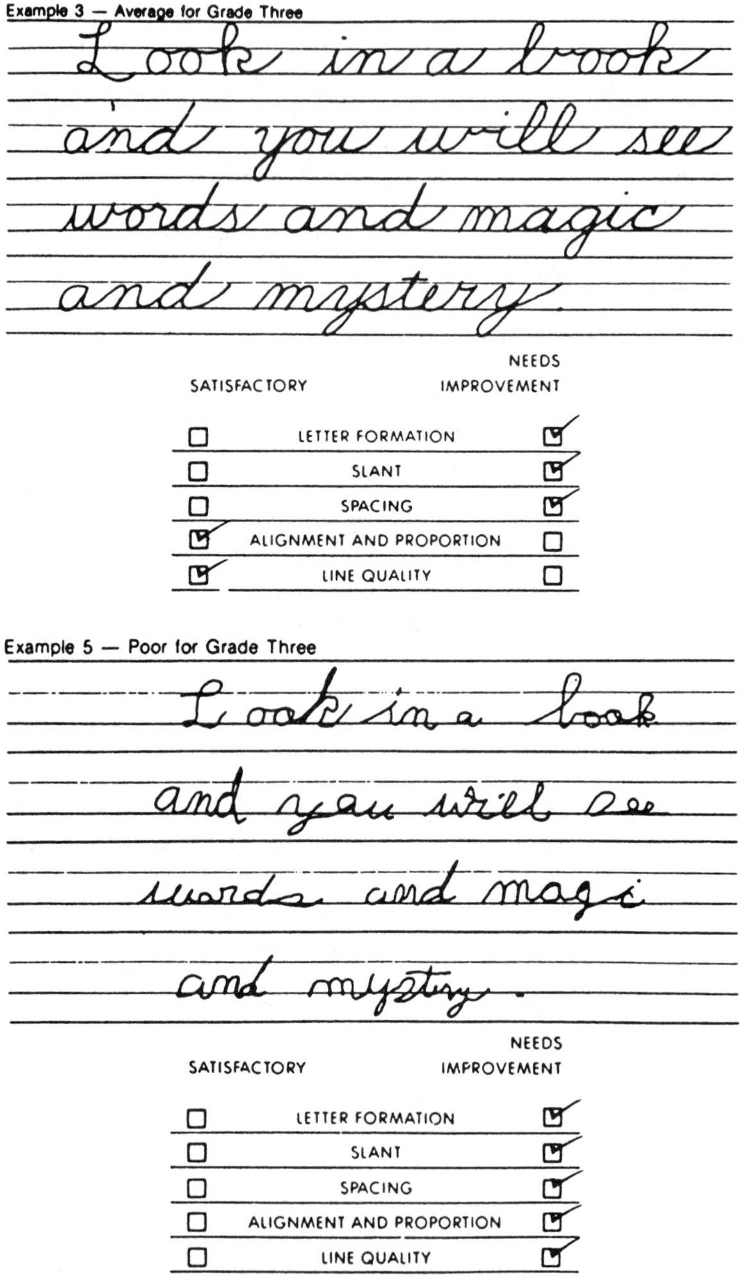

Example 3 — Average for Grade Three

*Look in a brook
and you will see
words and magic
and mystery.*

		NEEDS
SATISFACTORY		IMPROVEMENT
☐	LETTER FORMATION	☑
☐	SLANT	☑
☐	SPACING	☑
☑	ALIGNMENT AND PROPORTION	☐
☑	LINE QUALITY	☐

Example 5 — Poor for Grade Three

*Look in a book
and you will see
words and magic
and mystery.*

		NEEDS
SATISFACTORY		IMPROVEMENT
☐	LETTER FORMATION	☑
☐	SLANT	☑
☐	SPACING	☑
☐	ALIGNMENT AND PROPORTION	☑
☐	LINE QUALITY	☑

Source: From *Zaner-Bloser Evaluation Scale*, 1984, Zaner-Bloser, Inc., Columbus, OH. Copyright 1984. Reprinted by permission.

Figure 10.1
Example from Zaner-Bloser Evaluation Scale

Table 10.1
Examples of Questions from the Basic School Skills Inventory

1. Does the child write from left to right?
To earn a pass on this item, a child should demonstrate some consistent knowledge of left-right progression in writing. Letters or words may be illegible, poorly formed, misspelled, or otherwise inadequate and still be recorded as a pass if, in the execution of her written efforts, the child proceeds in a left-to-right sequence. This sequence does not even have to be on a straight line; diagonal writing is permissible, as long as it is basically left to right.

2. Can the child write his first name?
The intention of this item is to determine whether the child can write (manuscript or cursive) his first name on command. The letters do not have to be properly formed, nor does spelling have to be exactly correct. The result must, however, be recognizable as being the child's actual name. Writing one's name from a model is not acceptable here.

3. When given a common word on a card, can the child copy the word correctly on his own paper?
Place a card containing a common word with at least three letters on the child's desk. The pupil must copy the example correctly to receive credit for the item. The letters in the word must be recognizable and in proper order.

4. Can the child write her last name?
To receive credit for this item, a child should make a solid attempt at writing her last name. The name may be misspelled, and some of the letters may be reversed or poorly formed. The child receives credit for producing a recognizable version of her last name without copying from a model.

5. When writing, can the child stay on the line?
This is a relatively difficult task for many children. In scoring the item, you are concerned with the child's skill at organizing and spacing the letters squarely on the line, not with the legibility or quality of the letters themselves.

6. Can the child write simple sentences dictated by the teacher?
Create a simple sentence containing no more than four words that are in the child's vocabulary. Ask the child to write the sentence after you say it in a natural, conversational manner. Do not pause between words to enable the child to write each word after it is presented. You may repeat the sentence if the child does not appear to understand or remember it. To receive credit, the child must write each of the words in the correct sequence from left to right. Spelling, capitalization, punctuation, and penmanship should not be considered in scoring the item.

7. Can the child spell simple words correctly?
Ask the child to write each of the following words: **in, cat, make.** Say each word to the child, use the word in a simple sentence, and then repeat the word (for example, "**in**, the boy is **in** the house, **in**"). Although the quality of formation of letters is not important, the child must produce clearly recognizable letters in the correct sequences for all three words to pass the item.

Source: From *Basic School Skills Inventory-Diagnostic* by D. D. Hammill and J. Leigh, 1983, Austin, TX: PRO-ED, Inc. Reprinted by permission.

1988). The handwriting scale in the TOWL requires a sample of the student's handwriting taken from a spontaneous writing exercise. Graham et al. (1989) conducted a study to determine the validity of the handwriting scale of the TOWL. From a population of students with learning disabilities, the authors concluded that the scale was valid for measuring handwriting legibility.

Graham (1986) conducted a review of the TOWL, Zaner-Bloser, Freeman, and Bezzi scales. Table 10.2 summarizes this research and highlights the characteristics of these scales. Each of the scales is used at least occasionally in schools to determine handwriting proficiency. As mentioned, handwriting scales provide an excellent

Table 10.2
Characteristics of Handwriting Scales

Characteristics	Freeman (1959)	Bezzi (1962)	Zaner-Bloser (1979)	TOWL (Hammill & Larsen, 1983)[a]
1. Grade Levels	1–8	1–3	1–8	Approximately 3–12[b]
2. Style	Manuscript (1–2) Cursive (3–8)	Manuscript	Manuscript (1–2) Cursive (3–8)	Cursive
3. Handedness	Right and left	Right and left	Right and left	Right and left
4. Gender	Male and female	Male and female	Male and female	Male and female
5. General description	A series of eight 5-step scales	A series of three 5-step scales	A series of eight 5-step scales	A 10-step scale
6. Nature of scale	Ordinal	Ordinal	Ordinal	Not known[c]
7. Number of samples used in scale construction	135,491 samples from 162 cities	7,212 samples from all parts of the U.S.	Approximately 500 samples per grade level	Not reported
8. Criterion for scaling	General excellence	Quality and speed	General excellence	Legibility
9. Procedures for scaling	Median placement by judges	Quality and speed	Rank-ordered specimens and selected samples on the basis of letter form — slant, alignment, spacing, and line quality	Not reported
10. Nature of specimen obtained from student	Different specimens for each grade level	Different specimens for each grade level	Different specimens for each grade level	Single specimen
11. Directions for obtaining student specimen	Write from copy at usual speed	Copy at usual speed	Write from copy using their best handwriting	Write a story in response to three pictures
12. Method of scoring student specimen	Match student specimen to appropriate scale	Match student specimen to appropriate scale and determine speed of writing	Match student specimen to appropriate scale	Match student specimen to scale

[a]Handwriting subtest of the Test of Written Language.
[b]Normative scores are available for children ages 8–0 to 8–11.
[c]The nature of the scale could not be determined on the basis of the information authors provided.

Source: From "A Review of Handwriting Scales and Factors That Contribute to Variability in Handwriting Scores" by S. Graham, 1986, *Journal of School Psychology, 24*, p. 67. Copyright ©1986 Pergamon Press. Reprinted by permission.

screening mechanism for handwriting, but they do not provide information that facilitates remediation.

TEACHER-DESIGNED ASSESSMENTS

Commercial devices for assessing handwriting abilities are limited, and those that are available do not provide detailed information that can be used to develop and implement intervention programs. Therefore, teacher-designed assessments, as well as observations, may constitute the best method for evaluating specific strengths and weaknesses related to handwriting and for determining intervention strategies needed to remediate problems.

One method of determining handwriting skills is to ascertain which specific skills, along a hierarchy of skills, the student has mastered. Determining where skills are interrupted along the hierarchy will facilitate the teacher's conclusions about an intervention point. The following skills represent a hierarchy of handwriting skills:

1. Grasping the pencil. Proper pencil grip, according to Mendoze, Holt, and Jackson (1978), requires: (a) holding the pencil with the thumb, index finger, and middle finger, approximately an inch above the pencil point; (b) resting the pencil on the near side of the middle finger; (c) placing the thumb on the other side of the pencil, opposite the middle finger; (d) resting the index finger on the top surface of the pencil; and (e) resting the remaining portion of the pencil in the rounded space between the second joint of the thumb and index finger.
2. Holding the pencil at the proper slant.
3. Making random marks.
4. Making freeform (controlled) marks.
5. Imitating line and wave patterns and variant strokes.

6. Reproducing nonmeaningful patterns.

7. Reproducing meaningful patterns appropriate for manuscript or cursive writing.

8. Copying letters.
9. Writing letters.
10. Copying words.
11. Writing words.
12. Copying sentences.
13. Writing sentences.

In a classic study by Newland (1932), a team of 24 reviewers assessed the handwriting of more than 2,300 students. Results of the analysis revealed that the most common forms of illegibilities were found in the letters, *a*, *e*, *f*, and *t*. The study also showed that teachers tend to be most concerned about letter formation, spacing, and legibility (Otto, McMenemy, & Smith, 1973).

Letter formation has several problem areas. In manuscript writing, students must form letters at approximately a 90-degree angle to the horizontal line upon which they are written, keep straight lines straight, and form curved or circle portions of letters correctly. When learning cursive writing, students sometimes have difficulty forming letters at approximately a 45- to 90-degree angle to the horizontal line upon which they are written, creating the correct slant and curve, and producing letters of the proper size. Some students need to practice keeping lowercase letters proportionally smaller than uppercase letters.

Spacing involves leaving the correct amount of space between individual letters and words. It can be determined fairly objectively. Legibility creates a more difficult assessment problem.

Legibility is not a simple characteristic of handwriting but instead has many different elements including size, shape of letters, formation of letters, slant, alignment, neatness, and spacing (Wood et al., 1987).

Two questions that can be asked regarding assessment of legibility relate to the *criteria* used and the *accuracy of judgment* (Stowitschek & Stowitschek, 1979). Traditionally, legibility scales have been used to evaluate the legibility variable. These scales require subjective judgment to determine "how legible" the student's writing is. After reviewing legibility scales, Graham (1986) noted several disadvantages:

1. Scales do not contain sufficient samples of handwriting to cover the possible writing scales of any one group of children.
2. Handwriting scales are moderately reliable.
3. The utility of handwriting scales has not been demonstrated.
4. Most important, handwriting scales do not provide teachers with adequate evaluation information or information for individualizing instruction.

Despite these problems, handwriting scales still can provide beneficial information to teachers.

Although most traditional legibility scales have not been validated effectively, trained teachers and evaluators can use them to determine students' general writing legibility. Otto et al. (1973) indicated that once individuals are trained to use legibility scales, they are able to generally assess legibility without using any scale. Reliance on trained rating skills was a key facet in several of the investigations undertaken by Otto and his colleagues. They evaluated children's handwriting under three different conditions, using materials familiar to the student that contained all the letters of the alphabet. For example, using sample sentences (e.g., The quick brown fox jumped over the lazy dog), teachers instructed pupils to write the sentences in (1) their "best" handwriting; (2) their "usual" handwriting; and (3) their "fastest" handwriting. Students were given 5 minutes for the first two efforts. This procedure demonstrates whether a student can produce fluent and legible handwriting under the optimal condition and also in normal and speeded-up conditions.

Several researchers have tried to further objectify the assessment of writing legibility. Salzberg, Wheeler, Devar, and Hopkins (1971) used a printing assignment sheet on which students would be given a model for specific letters and asked to reproduce the letters on a separate sheet. Various criteria were used to evaluate the legibility of the responses. In another model of evaluating legibility, teachers utilize transparent overlays to determine the legibility of the student's writing (Helwig, Johns, Norman, & Cooper, 1976). By reducing the size of the standard, teachers can make the task more difficult and require more exact letter reproductions. Figure 10.2 depicts the transparency model.

Still another method of determining writing legibility is the teacher-made checklist. Checklists enable teachers to evaluate writing and keep a record for later

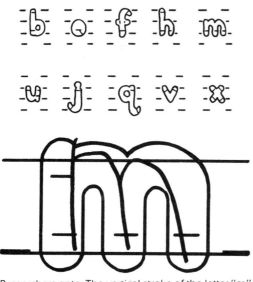

Researchers note: The vertical stroke of the letter "m" was not totally within the confines of the overlay; therefore it did not meet criteria for a correct response. The two-hump strokes meet all criteria of the behavior definition.

Source: From "The Measurement of Manuscript Letter Strokes" by J. J. Helwig, J. C. Johns, J. E. Norman, and J. C. Cooper, 1976, *Journal of Applied Behavior Analysis, 9*, p. 231. Copyright by the Society for the Experimental Analysis of Behavior, Inc. Reprinted by permission.

Figure 10.2
Evaluative Overlays for Assessment

evaluations and comparisons. Hammill and Bartel (1990) have suggested that checklists allow teachers to evaluate specific handwriting skills, such as letter formation. Table 10.3 gives an example of a checklist to help in evaluating letter formation.

REMEDIATING AND TEACHING HANDWRITING SKILLS

A great deal of information is available about how to teach reading and math, but the other "*R*," writing, has received little attention. In fact, it is not clear how most teachers even approach the teaching of handwriting (Bridge & Hiebert, 1985). For many teachers, handwriting instruction is an unpopular activity, but one that needs attention for some students. Therefore, teachers should address handwriting deficiencies to facilitate the success of their students.

The amount of time teachers spend on handwriting activities varies considerably from school to school and grade to grade. Bridge and Hiebert (1985) observed six classrooms in two schools to determine the quantity and nature of handwriting activities. Results indicated that the writing tasks used most often were practicing individual letter forms and words, filling in words in blank spaces, copying sentences,

Table 10.3
Sample Checklist for Evaluating Letter Formation

	Wrong	Right
1. a like o	*O*	*a*
2. a like u	*u*	*a*
3. a like ci	*ci*	*a*
4. b like li	*li*	*b*
5. d like cl	*cl*	*d*
6. e closed	*e*	*e*
7. h like li	*li*	*h*
8. i like e with no dot	*e*	*i*
9. m like w	*w*	*m*
10. n like u	*u*	*n*
11. o like a	*a*	*o*
12. r like i	*i*	*r*
13. r like n	*n*	*r*
14. t like l	*t*	*t*
15. t with cross above	*t̄*	*t*

Source: From *Teaching Students with Learning and Behavior Problems* (5th ed., p. 270) by D. D. Hammill and N. R. Bartel, 1990, Boston: Allyn & Bacon. Copyright ©1990 by Allyn & Bacon. Reprinted with permission.

and making a listing of spelling words. The study concluded that "children spend very little time in writing activities and that most of this time is spent in transcription activities that involve verbatim copying of other writers' texts" (p. 169).

The time that teachers do spend on handwriting instruction apparently is spent using commercial teaching programs. In a survey reported by Wood et al. (1987), 95 percent of the elementary schools surveyed used a commercial program. Although numerous programs are available, the majority of schools used one of three different programs: Palmer, Zaner-Bloser, or D'Nealian.

Palmer. The Palmer handwriting method is a traditional program that has been used for more than 100 years. Printing is taught before cursive, with an emphasis on five different strokes. Slant is not introduced until cursive, normally around the third grade. Materials are available for students and teachers, with suggested time frames for completing the lessons (Wood et al., 1987).

Zaner-Bloser. This handwriting program (Barbe, Lucas, Wasylyk, Hackney, & Braun, 1987) is similar to the Palmer method. It also is a well-established program, starting in 1913. The program uses six curved and straight line strokes. Slant is not introduced until cursive. Teaching materials are available (Wood et al., 1987). Figure 10.3 presents a sample page from the Zaner-Bloser handwriting program.

D'Nealian®. This is a relatively new program, first developed by Donald Thurber and published in 1978. This approach differs significantly from the Palmer and Zaner-Bloser programs in that the manuscript letters are not the traditional "stick and circle" strokes but resemble cursive letters. Slant is introduced from the very

Write the letters and words

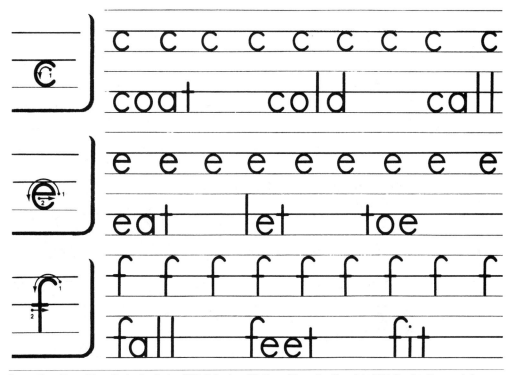

Source: From *Zaner-Bloser Evaluation Scales*, 1984, Columbus, OH: Zaner-Bloser, Inc. Copyright 1984. Reprinted by permission.

Figure 10.3
Sample page from Zaner-Bloser Handwriting Program

beginning of handwriting instruction (Wood et al., 1987). Figure 10.4 gives samples from a page in the D'Nealian workbook.

Wood et al. (1987) conducted a study to determine which of the three most popular handwriting programs was best. The investigators collected data on handwriting from 89 elementary schools, which yielded more than 3,000 individual handwriting samples. Schools in the survey used the Palmer or the Zaner-Bloser or the D'Nealian® Handwriting program. Results revealed that "comparable legibility resulted after receiving instruction in the three commercial handwriting programs" (p. 28). Therefore, the specific commercial program used in handwriting instruction may not have a major impact on students' handwriting skills.

Writing Cursive tT, iI, and uU

Cursive letters t, i, and u are like their manuscript forms. Add an uphill stroke to make each cursive letter. Write a row of each cursive letter.

Capital cursive letters may or may not be like their manuscript forms. Compare both forms of T, I, and U. Write a row of each cursive letter.

Source: From *D'Nealian® Handwriting, Book 4* by D. Thurber, 1987, Glenview, IL: Scott, Foresman and Co. Reprinted by permission.

Figure 10.4
Sample page from D'Nealian Handwriting® Program

HANDWRITING AND THE WHOLE LANGUAGE CURRICULUM

One means of teaching handwriting that has gained a great deal of popularity in some schools is to teach these skills through a whole language curriculum. Teaching handwriting skills with this approach may result in students' understanding the relationships among reading, writing, spelling, and comprehension. This holistic method of teaching handwriting allows teachers to provide instruction in the context of other language arts skills.

Teachers who use the whole language model to teach writing do not teach the mechanics of handwriting as an isolated skill. Rather, they teach handwriting skills in the context of students' compositions. In the whole language classroom, students receive encouragement and reinforcement for writing. With this practice, they generally improve their writing skills, including skills related to the mechanics of writing (Zemelman & Daniels, 1988).

MANUSCRIPT VERSUS CURSIVE WRITING

Currently, no standard accepted method exists for teaching beginners to write (Hagin, 1983). One argument that has been pervasive in handwriting instruction for decades is whether to teach manuscript or cursive first (Koenke, 1986). Even though various studies have tried to determine if one approach is superior to the other (Graham & Miller, 1980; Lovitt, 1973, cited in Kauffman, 1975), the matter continues to be debated. As in the past, most students currently learn both styles. Manuscript is taught first, and instruction in cursive begins in the second or third grade. Although the issue is debated for all learners, it is more critical for children with disabilities because learning two different styles and systems simply takes more time.

The traditional method of teaching manuscript first started in 1913, when Edward Johnson developed a simple manuscript alphabet for beginning writers. By the 1920s and 1930s, teaching manuscript first was the generally accepted method (Hagin, 1983).

Traditional arguments for teaching cursive or manuscript writing hinge on the alleged advantages one form has over the other. Advantages cited by proponents of manuscript writing are (Hagin, 1983, p. 267):

1. It is regarded as being easier to learn because the letter forms are simpler.
2. It resembles the print in books, so the child does not have to accommodate two graphic styles.
3. Beginning writing in manuscript is more legible than cursive.
4. It is required through life in applications and documents.
5. It promotes the independence of letters within words in teaching spelling.

Although most elementary school teachers focus on manuscript instruction first, during the past few years there has been a call for teaching cursive first. Advocates for cursive point out that cursive letters are hard to reverse, provide connections so students can see the "whole" word, and are faster to produce (Hagin, 1983). Among other reasons for teaching cursive first is to avoid the later transition from manuscript to cursive.

Graham and Miller (1980) reviewed the literature regarding manuscript versus cursive writing and found a lack of empirical support for many of the points that advocates cite for a particular approach. They indicated that the bulk of the evidence supports manuscript instruction, although the clear advantage of this form has not been conclusively demonstrated. The best course of action for many children is to begin instruction in manuscript writing, then make a subsequent determination about teaching cursive based on the anticipated ability of the student to master it. In some cases, the social value of cursive may be a primary rationale for providing instruction in this form.

ALTERNATIVES TO MANUSCRIPT AND CURSIVE

While the controversy regarding manuscript versus cursive continues, alternative handwriting instruction models have been developed. One alternative to both manuscript and cursive writing is the "model" or "mixed" script developed by Mullins, Joseph, Turner, Zawadski, and Saltzman (1972). Figure 10.5 provides a sample of the script and the guidelines for writing it. The script combines many advantages of both cursive and manuscript forms, including (a) making letters (especially uppercase) relatively similar to the printed word, (b) avoiding the difficult flourishes and loops of cursive, (c) achieving rhythm by linking lowercase letters, (d) being able to keep the pen on the paper, emphasizing directionality, and (e) possibly eliminating reversals. Although this form has not been used widely in the classroom, samples of adult handwriting anecdotally show that many people commonly use some modification of the mixed script.

Another alternative approach is the D'Nealian® Handwriting Program (Thurber & Jordan, 1978). This program, previously discussed as one of the most currently popular commercial programs (Wood et al., 1987), ties the manuscript forms closely to cursive forms by having the student produce each manuscript letter by making a continuous stroke without lifting the pencil while forming a letter. This system facilitates the transition to cursive because all printed letters except *f*, *r*, *a*, *v*, and *z* can become their cursive counterparts simply by adding "joining" strokes. Thurber (1975) has claimed that this system is a viable alternative to what he referred to as the illogical way children are taught to write—using the circles and sticks of manuscript print. Figure 10.6 depicts the D'Nealian® Handwriting alphabet.

Yet another alternative to handwriting instruction—one that is gaining popularity as a result of the personal computer (PC) explosion—is typing or, more specifically, keyboarding. This approach may be particularly beneficial for students with learning disabilities or physical impairments who have fine-motor coordination and control problems. Several methods have been developed to teach typing to young children (e.g., *Typing Keys* and *Typing Our Language*). Many computer programs currently on the market teach typing skills to children (e.g., *Kids on Keys*). Additional advantages accruing from typing skills include faster speed, highest degree of

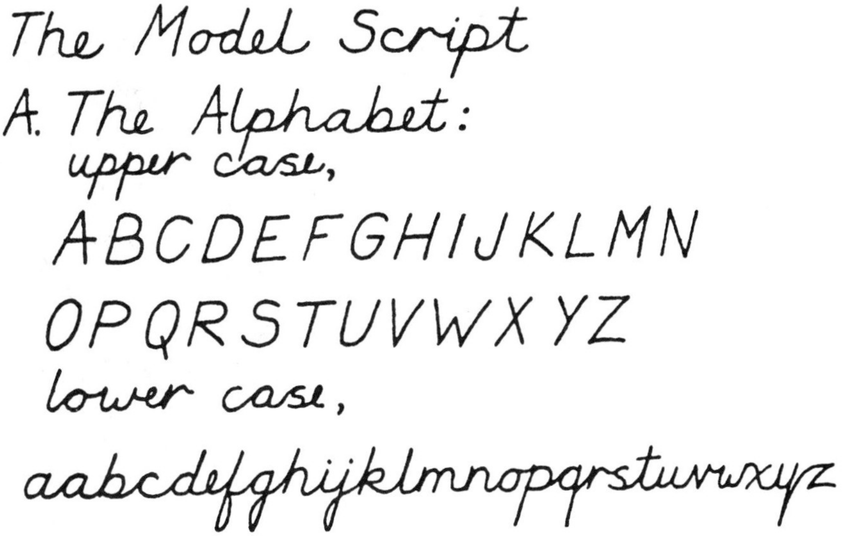

The Model Script
A. The Alphabet:
upper case,
ABCDEFGHIJKLMN
OPQRSTUVWXYZ
lower case,
aabcdefghijklmnopqrstuvwxyz

B. *Guidelines for writing:*
1. *Start words with a downstroke (an exception is the lower case "e").*
2. *Keep pen on paper until word is completed (an exception is a word beginning with a capital letter).*
3. *Give writing a slight slant.*
4. *Leave space between words.*
5. *Start at the left of the paper.*

Source: From "A Handwriting Model for Children with Learning Disabilities" by J. Mullins, F. Joseph, C. Turner, R. Zawadski, and L. Saltzman, 1972, *Journal of Learning Disabilities, 5*, p. 309. ©1972 by the Donald D. Hammill Foundation. Reprinted by permission.

Figure 10.5
Model Script

legibility, and inherent motivational advantages. Vacc (1987) studied the differences between correspondence written by adolescents with disabilities using handwriting and word processors. Results indicated that students who used the microcomputer spent more time on their letters, made more changes, and wrote longer letters than those who used handwriting.

Regardless of the teacher's personal position regarding manuscript, cursive, or alternative handwriting methods, several additional factors should be considered. These include readiness of the student, student's age, and student's previous writing history.

INSTRUCTIONAL ACTIVITIES

Handwriting instruction has been described as necessary to provide students with skills required for them to be successful in school and after they finish school. It also

Source: From *D'Nealian Manuscript* by D. Thurber, 1987, Glenview, IL: Scott, Foresman, and Co. Reprinted by permission.

Figure 10.6
D'Nealian® Alphabet and Numerals

has been pointed out that teachers do not tend to enjoy instructing in this area and most elementary school teachers rely on commercial materials in their handwriting programs.

Although there is no one best method to teach children how to write, some general guidelines are applicable. These are germane to instruction in this area whether the teacher uses a commercial program or teacher-made activities.

Readiness Skills   Various skills are necessary if students are to successfully learn to write, regardless of which form, manuscript or cursive, is taught first. These preparatory skills include:

1. Concepts of left to right, forward and backward, and start and stop.
2. Movement along guided line.
3. Movement in groove.
4. Movement with resistance.
5. Movement without solid guide.
6. Making figures without guide.
7. Making figures without a pattern.
8. Proper pencil grip.

In developing readiness skills, students achieve two basic prewriting goals: (a) enhanced coordination of visual and motor movements, and (b) development of handedness (identification of the preferred hand for later writing). Achieving the former goal leads directly into refinement of fine-motor skills; the latter helps the teacher emphasize the correct hand for writing.

Because visual-motor skills are the building blocks of good handwriting, readiness-level activities should focus upon these skills. Activities that effectively foster eye-hand coordination include tracing and coloring, cutting, and manipulating large and small objects. In each case, students should begin with large objects or designs and gradually move to smaller ones as their eye-motor coordination improves.

Initial tracing and coloring activities, for instance, should consist of giving students simple pictures of people, animals, houses, or vehicles and having them trace the outlines of these figures on tracing paper. After students learn to trace objects, they can develop finer motor skills by coloring in the pictures. During this period, teachers also should introduce specific geometric shapes, such as triangles, rectangles, and circles.

Cutting activities should follow the same process, starting students on large articles and gradually moving to smaller ones. Children might begin by drawing and cutting large seasonal symbols (Valentines, leaves, snowmen) for display, then moving to more refined tasks as their skills improve. More challenging tasks include cutting pictures from magazines for collages, and making small snowflakes.

Effective manipulative activities further develop coordination. Teachers should have students pick up small objects, make objects from play dough, and use nuts and bolts. Playing with jacks, Lincoln logs, Tinker Toys, and pick-up sticks also can help to refine manipulative skills.

Beginning to Write   Following the acquisition of readiness skills, students can begin actual writing exercises. A major concern at this point is the appropriate use of writing tools. Proper pencil grip is an important skill and has to be addressed before the child develops bad habits in this area. Teachers can help most students to develop the proper grip by having them grip the pencil one inch from the point between their thumb and first two fingers. To make this easier, teachers might use felt-tip markers, primary pencils, or pencils wrapped with tape. The "Hoyle Gripper," a three-sided plastic holder that comfortably forms the child's fingers into the correct position for gripping, is another effective option.

→ Keeps child from turning pencil around.

Templates — student traces from with in.

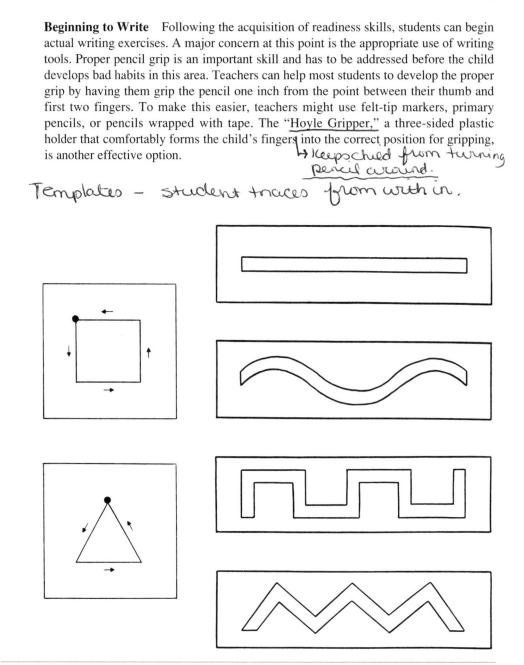

Source: From *Learning Disabilities: Educational Principles and Practices* (pp. 207–211) by D. J. Johnson and H. R. Myklebust, 1967, New York: Grune & Stratton. Reprinted by permission of Allyn & Bacon.

Figure 10.7
Sample Writing Templates and Stencils

Following attention to pencil grip, teachers should work on integrating the child's visual-motor abilities into prerequisite writing skills. Activities that facilitate integration can follow this kind of progression:

1. Encourage free scribbling so children get the feel of the pencil and build a foundation for later strokes.
2. Provide directionality exercises to teach the student a basic left-to-right orientation necessary for writing. Using templates and writing stencils, help students develop these skills. Figure 10.7 depicts some writing stencils and templates.
3. Develop the basic strokes necessary for writing by having children make circles, straight lines, curved lines, and diagonal lines.
4. Provide a logical progression of assistance by the modeling of procedures, physical prompts, nonverbal cues, forms to copy, and, finally, items to be written from memory.
5. Provide purposeful chalkboard exercises for young students as a transition to writing.

Manuscript Writing   After students acquire prehandwriting skills and proper pencil grip, teachers must teach or remedy manuscript writing skills. As mentioned previously, the vast majority of teachers use commercial programs. Therefore, a teacher working with children who have disabilities might modify commercial materials for instructional purposes, or possibly develop individualized programs. In manuscript writing, the student's first task is to master straight lines, curves, and circles. The teacher should introduce these strokes to the student gradually and systematically, using a progression designed especially for the individual student's needs. In the absence of a preferred sequence based on empirical data, the teacher can develop an instructional program by following these steps:

1. Be legible; speed is not as important.
2. Trace letters or words with the index finger and then with a writing instrument.
3. Trace letters on the chalkboard; ensure proper direction and sequence.
4. Connect dot letters.
5. Make letters in the air.
6. Complete letter fragments.
7. Copy letters from a written copy.
8. Write letters from memory (without copy).
9. Combine letters to form simple words.
10. Copy words from a written copy.
11. Write words from dictation (without copy).
12. Trace words on the chalkboard and on paper.
13. Write experience stories.

Cursive Writing   The instruction of traditional cursive letter forms or alternative cursivelike scripts can be based on many of the techniques noted in previous sections.

But because cursive letters are more complex and require a greater degree of skill to produce, teachers may have to provide additional opportunities for children to practice what they have learned and to copy both large and small letter sizes.

Cursive letters can be grouped into the same categories as manuscript letters, and teachers also can focus on letters that present the fewest problems for students. Applying these criteria, instructors would teach *i*, *e*, *s*, *l*, *t*, *m*, and *n* first. In this way, the student has an opportunity to enjoy successful experiences as he or she begins to acquire these skills.

In conclusion, teachers should observe the following guidelines for teaching cursive writing:

1. Be legible; speed is not as important.
2. Practice rhythm writing; trace and copy increasingly difficult rhythmic patterns.
3. Trace cursive letters on paper and on the chalkboard.
4. Write letters from copy and dictation.
5. Connect cursive letters to form words.
6. Trace words.
7. Connect dots to form written words.
8. Write words with and without copy.
9. Write experience stories.

In addition to these general guidelines, teachers should devise transitional activities to move students from manuscript to cursive writing, focusing special attention on: (a) joining or connecting letters, (b) letter slant, (c) dotted or crossed letters, and (d) positioning the paper. Table 10.4 describes certain actions related to each of these areas.

Table 10.4
Transitional Activities

Specific Area	Activities
1. Joining and connecting	• Connect manuscript letters • Connect letters to form words • Connect letters in name • Connect letters in words to form sentences
2. Letter slant	• Slant letters to right • Begin instruction with activities of connecting letters • Use models and guides
3. Dotted or crossed letters	• Cross letters after writing entire word • Dot letters after writing entire word • Practice a series of words
4. Positioning paper	• For cursive, position paper about 30 degrees to left for right-handed person • Slant paper to right for left-handed writer • Use desk guides for proper slant

Update

Maintenance and Fluency

While a substantial amount of attention has been given to the importance of the acquisition of handwriting skills, equally as important is the attention that should be given to the maintenance of skills and the enhancement of fluency. In order to achieve these related goals, the following strategies can be helpful:

- periodically evaluate the retention of specific strokes, letters, and words
- maintain checklists of specific skills of the students
- coordinate the reinforcement of skills between special education and general education teachers
- provide periodic writing sessions in which the primary emphasis is on practice
- display best handwriting work to reinforce performance and recognize achievement
- emphasize student's self-evaluation and correction
- acknowledge the importance of individuality while stressing the importance of legibility
- provide periodic opportunities for reinforcement contingent on accuracy in letter or word formation

Source: Adapted from Greenland, R. & Polloway, E. A. (1995) Handwriting: Fighting first impressions. ERIC Document Reproduction Service No. ED 378 754.

Remedial Programs   Although no one approach to teaching handwriting has been found to be superior, all effective instructional programs have some common characteristics. First, students should learn to verbalize rules about letter formation. This enables them to solidify their visual image of letters and reinforces rules about letter formation. Second, students should receive opportunities for self-evaluation and multiple forms of feedback. Also, copying letters appears to be more effective than tracing them (Wood et al., 1987).

Remediation is required for some students who are having difficulty with handwriting. Just as the number of programs to teach handwriting is limited, so are approaches to remediating handwriting skills. Therefore, teachers must individualize handwriting remediation based on the student's strengths and weaknesses. Hagin (1983) recommended the following when implementing handwriting remediation programs for students with disabilities:

1. The style of writing must be appropriate for the child's level of motor control.
2. Handwriting should be taught as a process involving body image, spatial orientation, awareness of kinesthetic feedback, and sequencing, not just a visual or motor activity.
3. Children must be given opportunities for visualizing letter forms.
4. Verbal cues from the teacher, slowly faded out, will assist students in learning skills.
5. Handwriting instruction should be direct and individualized.
6. Children must be taught to monitor their own handwriting.
7. Sufficient practice must be available for overlearning.
8. Handwriting must be viewed as a highly complex task.

Hagin (1983) developed a remedial writing program, *Write Right or Left*, based on the premise that "handwriting is a complex visual-motor-body image-kinesthetic-verbal skill that must be automatic to be effective" (p. 268). The program incorporates the principles listed above.

Left-Handedness   Left-handed writers have special needs and therefore may present special instructional challenges. Because left-handedness conflicts with the process of writing English from left-to-right, many young children have been urged or, in some cases, virtually forced to write with the right hand. As a result of this teaching error, legions of adolescents and adults cannot write legibly with either hand. Current thinking definitely opposes forcing children to write with the right hand when their natural preference is left-handedness (Hammill & Bartel, 1990; Lerner, 1988).

Left-handed writers do encounter some unique problems that teachers should address. Lerner (1988) has suggested the following general guidelines when teaching a left-handed person how to write:

1. The paper should be placed directly in front of the student for manuscript writing; for cursive, the paper should be slanted opposite to the slant for a right-handed student.

2. Pencil grip should be about one inch from the point, with the end directed over the left shoulder.

3. Hand position should be curved, not hooked, with the weight of the hand resting on the little finger.

In addition, pencils should be hard lead to help avoid smudging by the hand as it moves across the page; left-handed desks should be used when possible; and left-handed peer models who write well should be enlisted to assist other left-handed writers (see Figure 10.8)..

Even though left-handed individuals account for only about 10 percent of the population, the society and the school should make certain modifications for these individuals. This is even more important for left-handed students with disabilities. Teachers who instruct left-handed students can obtain further suggestions and assistance from materials designed especially for this group, such as the workbook available from Educational Publishing Company.

SUMMARY

This chapter began with a discussion about the importance of handwriting in our society. It was noted that school age children have to use handwriting on a regular basis to respond to the teacher's requests. Students respond to tests and other assignments using handwriting. For adults, handwriting is required to function in many job settings,

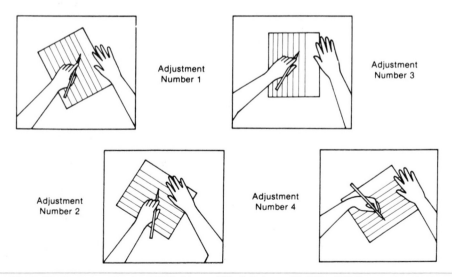

Source: From "Handwriting Research and Practice: A Unified Approach" by S. Graham and L. Miller, 1980, *Focus on Exceptional Children, 13*(2), p. 12. Reprinted with permission. ©1980 Love Publishing Company.

Figure 10.8
Approaches to Writing with the Left Hand

as well as in a variety of social and personal situations. Without an effective means of written expression, individuals are at a major disadvantage in our society.

The second section of the chapter dealt with the nature of handwriting. It was pointed out that handwriting is a very complex skill that requires hand-eye coordination, fine motor coordination, and visual perception. Deficits in any of these areas can result in problems. Formal and informal ways to assess handwriting were presented.

The final portion of the chapter focused on how to teach handwriting skills. Different commercial programs were described, as well as some teacher-made ways to help students develop good handwriting skills. A discussion was presented related to teaching manuscript or cursive first. It was concluded that for some students, one method may work better, but neither method always worked for all students. Finally, specific activities that teachers can use to teach handwriting were presented.

REFERENCES

Barbe, W. B., Lucas, V. H., Wasylyk, T. M., Hackney, C. S., & Braun, L. A. (1987). *Zaner-Bloser handwriting, basic skills and application book 1*. Columbus, OH: Zaner-Bloser.

Bridge, C. A., & Hiebert, E. H. (1985). A comparison of classroom writing practices, teachers' perceptions of their writing instruction, and textbook recommendations on writing practices. *Elementary School Journal, 86*, 155–172.

Bezzi, R. (1962). A standardized manuscript scale for grades 1, 2, and 3. *Journal of Educational Research, 55*, 339–340.

D'Nealian Handwriting, Book 4. (1987). Glenview, IL: Scott, Foresman.

Ferreiro, E., & Teberosky, A. (1982). *Literacy before schooling*. London: Heinemann Educational Books.

Freeman, F. (1959). A new handwriting scale. *Elementary School Journal, 59*, 218–221.

Furner, B. A. (1983). Developing handwriting ability: A perceptual learning process. *Topics in Learning and Learning Disabilities, 3*, 41–54.

Graham, S. (1986). A review of handwriting scales and factors that contribute to variability in handwriting scores. *Journal of School Psychology, 24*, 63–71.

Graham, S., Boyer-Shick, K., & Tippets, E. (1989). The validity of the handwriting scale from the test of written language. *Journal of Educational Research, 82*, 166–170.

Graham, S., & Miller, L. (1980). Handwriting research and practice: A unified approach. *Focus on Exceptional Children, 13*, 1–16.

Hagin, R. A. (1983). Write right—or left: A practical approach to handwriting. *Journal of Learning Disabilities, 16*, 266–271.

Hammill, D. D., & Bartel, N. R. (1990). *Teaching students with learning and behavior problems* (5th ed.). Boston: Allyn & Bacon.

Hammill, D. D., & Larsen, S. (1983). *Test of written language*. Austin, TX: Pro-Ed.

Hammill, D. D., & Larsen, S. (1988). *Test of written language–2*. Austin, TX: Pro-Ed.

Hammill, D. D., & Leigh, J. (1983). *Basic school skills inventory–Diagnostic*. Austin, TX: Pro-Ed.

Helwig, J. J., Johns, J. C., Norman, J. E., & Cooper, J. C. (1976). The measurement of manuscript letter stokes. *Journal of Applied Analysis, 9*, 231–236.

Herbert, M. (1987). Good handwriting: A continued priority for good teachers. *Business Education Forum, 41*, 34.

Johnson, D. J., & Myklebust, H. R. (1967). *Learning Disabilities: Educational Principles and Practices*. New York: Greene & Stratton.

Kauffman, J. M. (1975). Behavior modification. In W. M. Cruickshank & D. P. Hallahan (Eds.), *Perceptual and learning disabilities in children* (Vol. 2). Syracuse, NY: Syracuse University Press.

Koenke, K. (1986). Handwriting instruction: What do we know? *Reading Teacher, 40*, 214–216.

Larsen, S., & Hammill, D. D. (1989). *Test of legible handwriting*. Austin, TX: Pro-Ed.

Lerner, J. (1988). *Learning Disabilities* (5th ed.). Boston: Allyn & Bacon.

Luftig, R. L. (1989). *Assessment of learners with special needs*. Boston: Allyn & Bacon.

Manning, M. L. (1986). Responding to renewed emphasis on handwriting. *Clearing House, 59*, 211–213.

Mendoze, M. A., Holt, W. J., & Jackson, D. A. (1978). Circles and tape: An easy teacher-implemented way to teach fundamental writing skills. *Teaching Exceptional Children, 10*, 48–50.

Mullins, J., Joseph, F., Turner, C., Zawadzski, R., & Saltzman, L. (1972). A handwriting model for children with learning disabilities. *Journal of Learning Disabilities, 5*, 306–311.

Newland, T. E. (1932). An analytical study of the development of illegibilities in handwriting from the lower grades to adulthood. *Journal of Educational Research, 26*, 249–258.

Otto, W., McMenemy, R. A., & Smith, R. J. (1973). *Corrective and remedial teaching*. Boston: Houghton-Mifflin.

Phelps, J., & Stempel, L. (1989). Help for handwriting: Procedures at Texas Scottish Rite Hospital. *Education, 109*, 388–389.

Phelps, J., Stempel, L., & Speck, G. (1985). The children's handwriting scale: A new diagnostic tool. *Journal of Educational Research, 79*, 46–50.

Reis, E. M. (1989). Activities for improving the handwriting of learning disabled students. *Clearing House, 62*, 217–219.

Salzberg, B. H., Wheeler, A. J., Devar, L. T., & Hopkins, B. I. (1971). The effects on intermittent feedback and intermittent contingent access to play on printing of kindergarten children. *Journal of Applied Behavior Analysis, 4*, 163–171.

Stowitschek, C. E., & Stowitschek, J. J. (1979). Student help in evaluating handwriting performance. *Journal of Learning Disabilities, 12*, 203–206.

Thornton, T. P. (1996, August 15) Handwriting as an act of self-definition. *The Chronicle of Higher Education,* p. 3–7.

Thurber, D. N. (1975). *D'Nealian manuscript: A continuous stroke print*. Glenview, IL: Scott, Foresman. (ERIC Document Reproduction Service No. ED 169 533)

Thurber, D. N., & Jordan, D. R. (1978). *D'Nealian handwriting*. Glenview, IL: Scott, Foresman.

Vacc, N. N. (1987). Word processor versus handwriting: A comparative study of writing samples produced by mildly mentally handicapped students. *Exceptional Children, 54*, 156–165.

Wood, R. W., Webster, L., Gullickson, A., & Walker, J. (1987). Comparing handwriting legibility with three teaching methods for sex and grade differences. *Reading Improvement, 24*, 24–30.

Zaner-Bloser. (1984). *Zaner-Bloser evaluation scale*. Columbus, OH: Author.

Zemelman, S., & Daniels, H. (1988). *A community of writers*. Portsmouth, NH: Heinemann.

Spelling Instruction

Mary Beirne-Smith and Beverly H. Thompson

L earning to spell involves more than associating speech sounds with their graphic symbols. Spelling is a complex act that involves the recognition, recall, and production of correct letter sequences to form words (Graham & Miller, 1979). Society considers proficiency in spelling to be the mark of an intelligent, educated individual. According to Yule (1986), difficulties in spelling can interfere with educational achievement, employment opportunities, interpersonal relationships, and self-esteem. Competency in spelling, then, is a desirable educational outcome and, for most students, an attainable instructional goal. Students with mild learning disabilities, however, frequently have trouble learning to spell. The difficulties are often developmental in nature and seem to be related to a lack of understanding of the basic orthographic properties of our language.

ENGLISH ORTHOGRAPHY

Stubbs (1980) defined English orthography as a fundamentally alphabetic system in which speech sounds (phonemic units) are represented by letters or letter combinations (graphemes). In a perfect system, each phoneme would be represented by one grapheme and each grapheme would have only one sound. The English language, in this sense, is not perfect. It consists of 26 letters, variant and invariant sounds, silent letters, 300 different letter combinations for 17 vowel sounds, and words of foreign origin (Allred, 1977). Moreover, the spelling of any word is governed by its linguistic origin, its meaning, its grammatical function, and its derivation.

These apparent irregularities in our language have led some to question the predictability of sound-symbol associations and the advisability of teaching rule-based approaches to spelling. Proponents of whole word approaches to spelling argue that our written language is hardly a transcription of speech sounds. Horn (1960), for example, noted that children often have difficulty learning word attack skills, that most sounds have numerous spellings, that misspelled words are frequently phonetically correct, and that intensive instruction in phonics is not superior to methods that do not teach phonic skills.

In contrast, proponents of phonetic approaches to spelling argue that, though the sound-symbol association aspect of spelling is important, it is not all that must be considered in determining the regularity of our orthographic system. Other phonological factors, as well as morphological, semantic, syntactical, and frequency of use factors, are equally important. In a study of 17,000 words frequently used in children's writing, Hanna, Hanna, Hodges, and Rudorf (1966) found that when phonological factors such as syllabic stress, position in syllables, and internal constraints were taken into account, phoneme-grapheme associations were consistent 80 percent of the time. Similarly, Hall, Gerber, and Stricker (1989) concluded from their work in spelling that "[our] spelling system is not arbitrary—it only seems that way. Rather it contains a subtle but understandable order at the levels of phoneme representation, grapheme patterns, grammatical markings, and semantic relationships" (p. 349).

In practice, the two approaches are not necessarily mutually exclusive. When words conform to phonetic generalizations or when word patterns are readily apparent, a rule-based approach to spelling instruction is both sensible and productive. On the other hand, because spelling is not totally rule-driven, whole word approaches also have an appropriate place in the instructional program.

DIFFERENCES IN SPELLERS

Although few efforts have been made to determine prevalence, most experts believe that spelling disorders are widespread. Individuals who have difficulty in spelling tend to fall into two general categories: (a) those who demonstrate isolated deficits in specific spelling skills, and (b) those who exhibit a general pattern of academic and language-learning disabilities.

Knowledge of the order inherent in our orthographic system is one factor that distinguishes good spellers from poor spellers. Proficient spellers, although frequently unable to articulate the reasons for their ability to spell, seem to be able to analyze and manipulate the phonological, morphological, syntactical, and semantic properties of the orthographic system (Wong, 1986). Spellers who are proficient seem able to recall or revisualize the spelling of known or familiar words with little apparent effort. When faced with unknown or unfamiliar words, proficient spellers access, devise, or apply strategies to determine the correct spelling of the word. They use their knowledge of phonemic and morphemic rules to spell the word phonetically, generate several alternative spellings of the word, and then use revisualization to determine the correct spelling, or they consult an outside source such as the teacher, a peer, or the dictionary (Graham, 1985).

Less fluent spellers, on the other hand, seem to lack skills essential to producing correctly spelled words. Poor spellers have a limited core vocabulary of known spelling words, fail to use familiar word patterns to assist them in spelling unknown words (Graham & Miller, 1980), and are only fair judges of when they have spelled words correctly or incorrectly (Gerber & Hall, 1981).

Professionals who work with children and adolescents with difficulties in spelling note that spelling problems are often chronic and usually are difficult to remedy. Inadequate or inappropriate instruction, including poor selection of materials, overdependence on commercial materials (especially basal spelling series), failure to individualize instruction, failure to use appropriate instructional techniques, and inadequate allocation of instructional time are among the many factors that can jeopardize the ability of any student to learn to spell. Success in spelling for students with specific spelling skill deficits depends to a large extent on accurate diagnosis of the problem and implementation of an appropriate instructional program.

Disorders in spelling related to general academic or language-learning problems can be more difficult to remedy. Because spelling is an act of communication and primarily a written language skill, it cannot be considered apart from the total language arts curriculum. For this reason, some educators recently have begun to advocate a whole language approach to spelling instruction. Difficulties in language-related areas, such as articulation or mispronunciation, vocabulary development, handwriting, and reading, can interact with each other and with general problems in learning, such as lack of motivation, difficulty in understanding and following directions, lack of attention to task, and so forth, to make identification and remediation of spelling disorders problematic.

Obviously, the development of competence in spelling is a complex process. Recent research comparing spelling skills in students who are normally achieving and students with mild learning disabilities has contributed to our knowledge of how spelling develops and how to assess and remedy spelling problems. This research is discussed next.

DEVELOPMENT OF SPELLING SKILLS

Research on initial spelling attempts indicates that children develop spelling skills in much the same manner as they acquire language: hierarchically and sequentially. Children's strategies for spelling words develop in a broadly predictable sequence (Beers & Henderson, 1977; Gentry, 1984; Reed, 1975; Reed & Hodges, 1982), with closer approximations of the correct spelling of words reflecting the child's increasing linguistic awareness and knowledge of orthography.

These initial attempts at spelling (termed *invented spellings*) occur at a prephonetic or phonetic stage in which consonant or vowel sounds closest to the letter name they represent serve as the written word and, in competent spellers, progress to the point at which the speller spontaneously categorizes, compares, and contrasts words at a preconscious level of perception (referred to as *spelling by analogy*), and applies knowledge of the redundancies in words to learning to spell new words (Bailet, 1991). According to Templeton (1980), this phonological awareness develops at least through tenth grade and seems to be more related to experience with the written word than to experience with spoken language. Experience with the written word alone, however, does not ensure that the child will mature into a competent speller.

The progression in developing spelling skills requires increasingly complex cognitive knowledge. As children's linguistic awareness and knowledge of orthography increases, qualitative changes that result from their experiences with written language become apparent, and systematic and predictable changes in spelling patterns (i.e., error types) occur. Simply stated, as uncertainty about orthography is reduced, better quality spellings are observed.

Gentry (1984, pp. 15–16) has provided a five-stage system for identifying developmental spelling errors:

1. *Precommunicative spelling.* Spellers randomly string together letters of the alphabet without regard to letter-sound correspondence. Example: OPSOP = eagle; RTAT = eighty.
2. *Semiphonetic spelling.* Letters represent sound, but only some of the letters are represented. Example: E = eagle; A = eighty.
3. *Phonetic spelling.* Words are spelled like they sound. The speller represents all of the phonemes in a word, although the spelling may be unconventional. Example: EGL = eagle; ATE = eighty.
4. *Transitional spelling.* A visual memory of spelling patterns is apparent. Spellings exhibit conventions of English orthography; vowels in every syllable, e-marker and

vowel digraph patterns, correctly spelled inflectional endings, and frequent English letter sequences. Example: EGUL = eagle; EIGHTEE = eighty.

5. The word is spelled correctly.

Results of the studies on development of spelling skills indicate that children with mild learning disabilities who have difficulty learning to spell pass through the same developmental stages as their normally achieving peers, but at a slower rate (Gerber & Hall, 1982). In some instances, these students have been found to possess the orthographic knowledge needed to reduce response uncertainty, but they nevertheless fail to use it. Gerber and Hall noted that when faced with the task of spelling unknown or unfamiliar words, students with learning disabilities frequently reverted to less advanced levels of orthographic problem solving.

From the evidence on the development of spelling skills, Hodges (1981) concluded that:

1. Children make few, if any, random errors in spelling and, by observing and analyzing spelling errors, teachers can determine the child's scheme for spelling words.
2. Efficient spellers possess visual, morphophonemic, phonetic, and semantic information that they use to spell unknown words.
3. Learning to spell is constrained by the cognitive and linguistic factors inherent in the acquisition of language.
4. Learning to spell involves developing an understanding of the total framework of the orthographic properties of the English language. Therefore, children do not necessarily move sequentially from one aspect of orthography to another—from sounds and letters to syllables and words.

Hodges also recognized the unresolved issues about spelling instruction. Despite this concern, most authorities agree that recent perspectives on how spelling develops in children has substantially altered the way in which we view the assessment and remediation of spelling problems.

ASSESSMENT

Once the nature of the orthographic system and the general development of spelling skills are understood, the teacher's next task is to assess the specific skills of individual students. To assess a student's spelling skills, the teacher can select a number of formal and informal procedures.

FORMAL ASSESSMENT

The rationale for using formal tests to assess spelling skills depends on the purposes for which the test results will be used. In most educational settings, formal tests are used for administrative, identification, and placement purposes to detect or document a school performance problem. Formal tests provide a basis for pre- and post-testing as an unbiased measure of progress. They also may be used to compare proficiency in reading to proficiency in spelling to ascertain the scope and relative importance of the student's spelling skills. In such instances, formal tests are quite useful.

Using formal tests for educational planning, however, is quite another matter. Because the assessment of spelling skills seems relatively straightforward, teachers often are tempted to look only at the number of correct and incorrect responses. The practice of administering formal tests solely to obtain test scores must be viewed with caution. At best, test scores only inform the teacher of the student's standing relative to the norm group. Test scores provide little more than an estimated level of difficulty for choosing instructional programs and materials. More useful information can be obtained if the teacher analyzes students' errors and performance to identify the source of the problem.

Teachers, too, must be aware that the manner in which the spelling task is presented can affect the student's performance on the test. Some tests require the student to write the spelling word from dictation; others require the student to find the correctly spelled word in a series of words. Tasks of recall and tasks of recognition require different skills, and the implications for instruction, therefore, differ.

With these cautions in mind, diagnosticians can choose from a variety of formal instruments that assess spelling skills. Several broad-range achievement tests contain subtests with limited attention to this area. Some of these, such as the *Wide Range Achievement Test* (Jastak & Wilkinson, 1984) and the *Kaufman Test of Educational Achievement* (Kaufman & Kaufman, 1985), employ a traditional dictation format. Others, such as the *Peabody Individual Achievement Test–Revised* (Markwardt, 1989), require the student to recognize the correctly spelled word from a choice of words. The *Woodcock-Johnson Psycho-Educational Battery–Revised* (Woodcock & Johnson, 1989) tests both spelling recognition and recall on its Dictation and Proofing subtests.

Diagnosticians who are skilled in assessment might analyze individual responses on broad-range tests of achievement to locate the source of the student's problem; however, because the skills measured by these tests are limited by the number of items that test each skill, the tests do not provide a comprehensive assessment of the student's skill in spelling and thus are of limited value in instructional planning.

The Test of Written Spelling–2 (TWS–2) (Hammill & Larsen, 1986) provides a more comprehensive measure of spelling skills. The TWS–2 reflects the authors' theories that mastery of a certain number of spelling rules is necessary for independence in spelling and that words that do not conform to standard generalizations must be learned by rote memorization. The test is designed for students ages 6-6 to 18-5 and may be administered as either an individual or a group test. It uses a standard dictation format and consists of two subtests of 50 words each. Words for both subtests were selected because they frequently occur in 10 commonly used basal spelling series. Words on the predictable subtest conform to phonetic rules. Words on the unpredictable subtest are idiosyncratic in their spellings. The TWS–2 requires 15–25 minutes to administer and yields percentile ranks and standard scores for each subtest, as well as a total test score.

Reliability on the TWS–2 is satisfactory; however, the manual fails to report concurrent validity or whether students with handicapping conditions were included in the standardization sample. Despite these concerns, the TWS–2 is a useful tool in assessing spelling skills.

INFORMAL ASSESSMENT

Informal assessment of spelling skills entails gathering information from a wide variety of sources. Typically, spelling samples can be collected from dictated tests, free writing and compositions, responses to written questions in other content areas, and varied seatwork assignments. A complete list of sources for informal assessment information is provided in Table 11.1.

Table 11.1
Sources for Informal Assessment Information

A. Analysis of Written Work, Including Test Papers
   1. Legibility of handwriting
   2. Defects in letter forms, spacing, alignment, size
   3. Classification of errors in written work, letters, tests, etc.
   4. Range of vocabulary used
   5. Evidence of lack of knowledge of conventions and rules

B. Analysis of Oral Responses
   1. Comparison of errors in oral and written spelling
   2. Pronunciation of words spelled incorrectly
   3. Articulation and enunciation
   4. Dialectical and colloquial forms of speech
   5. Way of spelling words orally
      a. Spells words as units
      b. Spells letter by letter
      c. Spells by digraphs or syllables
   6. Rhythmic pattern in oral spelling
   7. Blending ability
   8. Quality and errors made in oral reading
   9. Giving letters for sounds or sounds for letters
  10. Oral responses on tests of word analysis
  11. Analysis of pupil comments as he states orally his thought processes while studying new words

C. Interview with Pupil
   1. Questioning pupil about methods of study
   2. Questioning pupil about spelling rules and errors in conventions
   3. Securing evidence as to attitude toward spelling

D. Questionnaire
   1. Applying check-list methods of study
   2. Having pupil rank spelling according to interest
   3. Surveying uses of written language

E. Free Observation in Course of Daily Work
   1. Evidence of improvement in the study of new words
   2. Observing extent of use of dictionary
   3. Extent of error in regular written work
   4. Study habits and methods of work
   5. Evidences of emotional and social maladjustment

Table 11.1
continued

F. Controlled Observation of Work on Set Tasks
   1. Looking up the meanings of given words in dictionary
   2. Giving pronunciation of words in dictionary
   3. Writing plural forms and derivatives of given words
   4. Observing responses on informal tests
   5. Observing methods of studying selected words
   6. Estimating pupil success when using a variety of methods of studying selected words

G. Analysis of Available Records
   1. Records of scores on tests in reading, spelling, language, handwriting
   2. School history
   3. Health data; physiological and sensory deficiencies and defects; and sociological data
   4. Anecdotal records

Source: From *The Diagnosis and Treatment of Learning Disabilities* (pp. 369–370) by L. J. Brueckner and G. L. Bond, 1955, Englewood Cliffs, NJ: Prentice Hall. Reprinted by permission of Prentice Hall, Inc.

Informal assessment has a number of advantages over formal assessment. By using a variety of sources, teachers have the opportunity to evaluate the student's ability to transfer skills, analyze trends both within and between content areas, avoid false positives resulting from limited samples that may indicate a problem but fail to differentiate carelessness from severe difficulties, and avoid false negatives created by a limited range of opportunities for spelling to be evaluated. Further, because informal assessment is often curriculum-based, it provides a more direct relationship between assessment and instruction. Information gathered can be easily translated into teaching strategies that meet the individual needs of students. Finally, testing can be accomplished in a relatively short time, so it is practical to use as a measure of continuous progress.

Error Analysis   Before the full value of informal assessment can be realized, the teacher must understand error analysis. Error analysis is a technique used to investigate the types of problems the student experiences, to discern trends in errors, and to determine the reasons for the problem. The procedure can be applied to any sample of student spelling.

Error analysis is based on the premises that students' production of words represent their best attempts at spelling and that spelling errors tend to be nonrandom and consistent. Recent research indicates that most of the errors students commit in spelling are consistent across dictated word lists (DeMaster, Crossland, & Hasselbring, 1986) and tend to be errors of omission and substitution or errors in vowels in midsyllables (Burns, 1980). Common spelling errors are (Spache, 1940):

1. Omission of a silent letter (e.g., *wether* for *weather, reman* for *remain, fin* for *fine*).
2. Omission of a sounded letter (e.g., *requst* for *request, plasure* for *pleasure, personl* for *personal, juge* for *judge*).

3. Omission of a doubled letter (e.g., *suden* for *sudden, adress* for *address, sed* for *seed*).

4. Doubling (e.g., *untill* for *until, frriend* for *friend, deegree* for *degree*).

5. Addition of a single letter (e.g., *darck* for *dark, nineth* for *ninth, refere* for *refer*).

6. Transposition or partial reversal (e.g., *was* for *saw, nickle* for *nickel, bron* for *born*).

7. Phonetic substitution for a vowel (e.g., *prisin* for *prison, injoy* for *enjoy*).

8. Phonetic substitution for a consonant (e.g. *prixon* for *prison, cecond* for *second, vakation* for *vacation*).

9. Phonetic substitution for a syllable (e.g., *purchest* for *purchased, financhel* for *financial, naborhood* for *neighborhood, stopt* for *stopped*).

10. Phonetic substitution for a word (e.g., *weary* for *very, colonial* for *colonel*).

11. Nonphonetic substitution for a vowel (e.g., *rad* for *red, reword* for *reward*).

12. Nonphonetic substitution for a consonant (e.g., *watching* for *washing, inportance* for *importance*).

Error analysis is a relatively simple procedure that can help the teacher determine where the student is within the developmental stages of spelling (DeMaster, Crossland, & Hasselbring, 1986). The procedure requires the teacher to gather a representative sample of the student's spelling performance, interview the student, and analyze the student's errors.

Once a sample of the student's work has been obtained, the teacher can decide on the type of analysis to apply and can analyze the words by error type and error tendency, as provided for in Figure 11.1. The teacher also might make notes on the strategies the student employed in spelling the words (e.g., sounding out, talking through, spelling from memory), and the student's speed of response. As shown in the figure, spelling errors can be analyzed as errors in whole words, in syllables, in sound clusters, or in letter sequences.

Analysis of whole words yields information only on the number of correct and incorrect responses. Although this approach is generally adequate with students who are not experiencing difficulties in spelling, it is insufficient for planning an instructional program for a student with a significant spelling disorder. For the student with significant problems in spelling, the teacher has to look more closely at errors in individual words. The teacher may, for example, count and record the number of correct syllables or sound clusters in the student's spelling attempt. In this approach, the student who spelled *sensible* as *sensable* would score 2 of 3 possible correct responses for syllables correct; the student who spelled *truck* as *trk* would score 1 of 3 possible correct responses for sound clusters correct.

When the problem is particularly persistent, counting the number of correct letter sequences provides the best instructional information. In this procedure, the student is awarded a point for each correct letter pair and for correctly beginning and ending the word. Carets are used to mark correct letter sequences and correct beginning and ending letters. An example of this procedure is:

Spelling 1	^^^^^^^^^^ p h o t o g r a p h	11 correct
Spelling 2	^^^^ ^ ^^ p h o t g r p h	7 correct
Spelling 3	^^^^^ f o t o g r a f	5 correct

Teachers who apply error analysis procedures to spelling assessment data are a step closer to designing an effective remedial spelling program.

Criterion-Referenced Tests   Unlike norm-referenced tests, which compare a student's performance in spelling to that of age- or grade-level peers, criterion-referenced tests (CRTs) are designed to compare the student's spelling performance to a specified level of mastery or achievement. The purposes of criterion-referenced tests are (a) to determine which skills the student has or has not mastered at a preset level of performance (e.g., 80%), and (b) to provide an objective measure of student progress on

Student_____   Date_____

Material/Level _____

Word List (   )   Paragraph (   )   Other

TYPE OF ANALYSIS
          Scoring: Word (   )   Syllables (   )   Clusters (   )   Letters (   )

PART OF WORD ERRED

		Regular	Predictable	Irregular	Comments
Type	Rules/Patterning				
	Consonants				
	Vowels				
Tendency	Order				
	Substitution				
	Insertion				
	Omission				

Beginning Time_____   Ending Time_____   Number minutes_____

Corrects_____   Errors_____

Source: Adapted from "Consistency of Learning Disabled Students" by V. DeMaster, C. Crossland, and T. S. Hasselbring, 1986, *Learning Disability Quarterly, 9*, pp. 89–96; and *A Microcomputer-based System for the Analysis of Student Spelling Errors* by T. S. Hasselbring and S. Owens, 1981, Nashville, TN: Peabody College of Vanderbilt. Reprinted by permission.

Figure 11.1
Spelling Error Analysis Chart

tasks of progressive levels of difficulty. Teachers can select from available published CRTs, or they can construct their own informal spelling inventories.

Published CRTs   Among the published CRTs from which the teacher can select to assess a student's spelling skills are two commonly used CRTs: the *Diagnostic Spelling Test* (Kottmeyer, 1970) and *Spellmaster* (Greenbaum, 1987).

Kottmeyer's *Diagnostic Spelling Test* is intended for use with students in grades 2 through 6. This test is presented in Table 11.2. The teacher administers the test using a standard dictation format. Responses are scored as correct or incorrect, tallied, and compared to grade-level criteria. Error type can be analyzed by consulting the Element Tested section of the test.

Greenbaum's *Spellmaster* system, designed for students in grades K–10, requires approximately 10 to 20 minutes to administer. Spellmaster consists of a series of inventories of words drawn from other diagnostic tests and is designed to assess the student's skill in spelling regular words, irregular words, and homophones. A scoresheet accompanying each inventory provides a means for the teacher to analyze student responses. This is shown in Figure 11.2

Informal Spelling Inventories   Teachers often find it desirable to construct their own assessment of students' spelling skills. Teacher constructed informal spelling inventories may be designed around specific skills or may be curriculum-based. In *specific skill assessment*, test items are designed to evaluate particular aspects of spelling. The test might be constructed to measure a single spelling skill (e.g., spelling of words with short vowel sounds) or a combination of skills (e.g., spelling of words with long and short vowel sounds and vowel diphthongs). After generating a list of rule exemplar words and administering the test, the teacher uses error analysis to determine which rules should be taught.

In *curriculum-based assessment*, the students are tested against the skills required by the school's curriculum or against skills described in objectives on their own individualized education program (IEP). Curriculum-based assessments may be designed by selecting a representative sample of words from the basal spelling series the school uses or from IEP objectives related to survival, high-utility, basic or content area vocabulary words. Mann and Suiter (1974) recommended that for the basal series test the teacher should randomly select 20 words from each grade level, begin testing two grade levels below the student's actual grade placement, and end testing at the level on which the student makes seven errors.

The purpose of assessing spelling skills is to facilitate the planning and implementation of an appropriate instructional program. Used individually, both formal and informal assessment procedures contribute to the teacher's knowledge of the student's present level of performance. In combination, the two procedures allow the teacher to more accurately identify specific areas of strengths and weaknesses. When error analysis is added to assessment procedures, the teacher has a powerful tool for formulating an instructional program that is effective in meeting the student's unique learning needs. In short, the best approach to assessment combines a variety of techniques for evaluating the student's skill in spelling and provides useful information for instructional decision making.

Table 11.2
Kottmeyer Diagnostic Spelling Test

Directions	
Give List 1 to second or third graders.	Grade Scoring, List 2:
Give List 2 to any pupil who is above third grade.	Below 9 correct: Below third grade
Grade Scoring, List 1:	9–19 correct: Third grade
Below 15 correct: Below second grade	20–25 correct: Fourth grade
15–22 correct: Second grade	26–29 correct: Fifth grade
23–29 correct: Third grade	Over 29 correct: Sixth grade or better
Give List 2 Test to pupils who score above 29.	Give List 1 Test to pupils who score below 9.

List 1		List 2	
Word	**Illustrative Sentence**	**Word**	**Illustrative Sentence**
1. not—He is **not** here.		1. flower—A rose is a **flower**.	
2. but—Mary is here, **but** Joe is not.		2. mouth—Open your **mouth**.	
3. get—**Get** the wagon, John.		3. shoot—John wants to **shoot** his new gun.	
4. sit—**Sit** down, please.		4. stood—We **stood** under the roof.	
5. man—Father is a tall **man**.		5. while—We sang **while** we marched.	
6. boat—We sailed our **boat** on the lake.		6. third—We are in the **third** grade.	
7. train—Tom has a new toy **train**.		7. each—**Each** child has a pencil.	
8. time—It is **time** to come home.		8. class—Our **class** is reading.	
9. like—We **like** ice cream.		9. jump—We like to **jump** rope.	
10. found—We **found** our lost ball.		10. jumps—Mary **jumps** rope.	
11. down—Do not fall **down**.		11. jumped—We **jumped** rope yesterday.	
12. soon—Our teacher will **soon** be here.		12. jumping—The girls are **jumping** rope now.	
13. good—He is a **good** boy.		13. hit—**Hit** the ball hard.	
14. very—We are **very** happy to be here.		14. hitting—John is **hitting** the ball.	
15. happy—Jane is a **happy** girl.		15. bite—Our dog does not **bite**.	
16. kept—We **kept** our shoes dry.		16. biting—The dog is **biting** on the bone.	
17. come—**Come** to our party.		17. study—**Study** your lesson.	
18. what—**What** is your name?		18. studies—He **studies** each day.	
19. those—**Those** are our toys.		19. dark—The sky is **dark** and cloudy.	
20. show—**Show** us the way.		20. darker—This color is **darker** than that one.	
21. much—I feel **much** better.		21. darkest—This color is **darkest** of the three.	
22. sing—We will **sing** a new song.		22. afternoon—We may play this **afternoon**.	
23. will—Who **will** help us?		23. grandmother—Our **grandmother** will visit us.	
24. doll—Make a dress for the **doll**.		24. can't—We **can't** go with you.	
25. after—We play **after** school.		25. doesn't—Mary **doesn't** like to play.	
26. sister—My **sister** is older than I.		26. night—We read to Mother last **night**.	
27. toy—I have a new **toy** train.		27. brought—Joe **brought** his lunch to school.	
28. say—**Say** your name clearly.		28. apple—An **apple** fell from the tree.	
29. little—Tom is a **little** boy.		29. again—We must come back **again**.	
30. one—I have only **one** book.		30. laugh—Do not **laugh** at other children.	
31. would—**Would** you come with us?		31. because—We cannot play **because** of the rain.	
32. pretty—She is a **pretty** girl.		32. through—We ran **through** the yard.	

Table 11.2
continued

List 1		List 2	
Word	**Element Tested**	**Word**	**Element Tested**
1. not 2. but 3. get 4. sit 5. man	Short vowels	1. flower 2. mouth	**ow-ou** spellings of **ou** sound, **er** ending, **th** spelling
6. boat 7. train	Two vowels together	3. shoot 4. stood	Long and short **oo, sh** spelling
8. time 9. like	Vowel-consonant -**e**	5. while	**wh** spelling vowel-consonant
10. found 11. down	**ow-ou** spelling of **ou** sound	6. third	**th** spelling, vowel before **r**
12. soon 13. good	Long and short **oo**	7. each	**ch** spelling, two vowels together
14. very 15. happy	Final **y** as short **i**	8. class	Double final consonant, **c** spelling of **k** sound
16. kept 17. come	**c** and **k** spellings of the **k** sound	9. jump 10. jumps 11. jumped 12. jumping	Addition of **s, ed, ing; j** spelling of soft **g** sound
18. what 19. those 20. show 21. much 22. sing	**wh, th, sh, ch,** and **ng** spellings and **ow** spelling of long **o**	13. hit 14. hitting	Doubling final consonant before adding **ing**
23. will 24. doll	Doubled final consonants	15. bite 16. biting	Dropped final **e** before **ing**
25. after 26. sister	**er** spelling	17. study 18. studies	Changing final **y** to **i** before ending
27. toy	**oy** spelling of **oi** sound	19. dark 20. darker 21. darkest	**er, est** endings
28. say	**ay** spelling of long **a** sound	22. afternoon 23. grandmother	Compound words
29. little	**le** ending	24. can't 25. doesn't	Contractions
30. one 31. would 32. pretty	Nonphonetic spellings	26. night 27. brought	Silent **gh**
		28. apple	**le** ending
		29. again 30. laugh 31. because 32. through	Nonphonetic spellings

Source: From *Teacher's Guide for Remedial Reading* by W. Kottmeyer, 1970, New York: McGraw-Hill. Reprinted by permission.

SPELLMASTER

REGULAR WORD TEST

1

Name:

Grade: Date:

Number Right: ☐

#	Beginning Consonants	Beginning Blends	Short vowels a	Short vowels e	Short vowels i	Short vowels o	Short vowels u	Ending Consonants	Ending Blends	Additions	Omissions
1	l		a					p			
2	r						u	g			
3	h				i			d			
4		fl				o		p			
5	v			e				t			
6	y		a					m			
7	g				i				ft		
8		dr					u	m			
9	v		a					n			
10	f					o			nd		
11	h			e				n			
12	d					o		t			
13		pl					u	g			

Figure 11.2
Spellmaster Error Analysis Scoresheet

INSTRUCTIONAL APPROACHES

The complex nature of our orthographic system and associated language-learning disabilities frequently interfere with the acquisition of spelling skills in students with mild learning disabilities. The importance of spelling to the education of these students is often not fully appreciated.

Competency in spelling is essential to the student's ability to function in other areas of the language arts curriculum. Competent spellers are less distracted by determining the correctness of the written word and more able to concentrate on other elements of written expression such as clarity, sequencing, and expressiveness. Fluency in spelling allows the speller to progress in related academic areas and to more ably communicate meaningful ideas to the reader. Better communication results in improved interpersonal relationships and increased self-esteem. As adults, spellers who are not conspicuous by their errors are more free to pursue a broad range of education and employment options.

PURPOSE OF SPELLING INSTRUCTION

The purpose of spelling instruction for students with mild learning disabilities, then, is to produce spellers who are competitive with individuals who do not demonstrate significant difficulties in spelling. To meet this aim, instructional programs must be effective and have clearly stated objectives. Cohen and Plaskon (1980, p. 328) delineated three basic objectives of spelling programs.

1. To accurately spell the most frequently used words that the student needs to write now and in the future.
2. To develop self-correction skills for adjusting spelling errors.
3. To develop the ability to locate the correct spelling of unfamiliar words.

Graham (1985) noted that effective spelling programs are comprehensive, student-oriented, varied, direct, individualized, and based on a solid foundation of empirical research. Hodges (1981) recommended that to be effective, instructional programs should:

1. Be incorporated in the general study of language to provide students with the opportunity to apply their knowledge of spelling and to examine the relationship between written and spoken language.
2. Employ a variety of materials and methods to accommodate differences in learning styles and rates.
3. Include regular writing activities that foster natural curiosity and encourage students to apply their increasing orthographic knowledge.
4. Include multiple opportunities for students to assess their attempts at spelling so they can learn from their mistakes.

Update

Best Practices for Spelling Instruction

Instruction in the area of spelling is an activity that occurs routinely in elementary schools. Common practice is for students to get a spelling list at the beginning of each week, review the list daily, often with sentence writing activities, and have a spelling test on Friday. In reviewing different approaches to spelling instruction over a fifteen year period for students with learning disabilities, Gordon, Vaughn, and Schumm (1993) found six primary areas of instructional practice. These include the following:

- Error imitation and modeling. This approach requires students to compare incorrectly spelled words with their correct spelling. Teachers copy the word, as it is misspelled, then point out ways that students can remember the proper spelling.
- Unit size. Many students have difficulty with long lists of spelling words. Having to remember the proper spelling for 10–20 words weekly may prove to be too much for some students, especially when the words are all presented at one time. Taking into consideration the unit size helps many students. Presenting only three words at a time, combined with effective instruction, is a good approach for many students.
- Modality. Students with learning problems often prefer practicing through different learning modes. Typing words at a computer, arranging and tracing letter shapes or three-dimensional letters, and simply writing the words all can be effective methods for teaching spelling. Teachers should use a variety of different strategies to enable students to use the method they most prefer.
- Computer-Assisted Instruction (CAI). Many students enjoy working at the computer. The drill and practice opportunities provided through CAI can be very beneficial in spelling instruction. There are also numerous software programs available that focus on spelling instruction and improvement.
- Peer Tutoring. Peer tutoring has become a valuable teaching tool for many teachers. Although teacher attention is needed at times, peer tutoring has been shown to be an effective means of instruction. Instruction in spelling can be effectively accomplished with peer tutoring arrangements.
- Study Techniques. Helping students with their study techniques can benefit them in all areas, including spelling. Many students simply do not know how to study. Therefore, some instruction in study techniques may have long term effects in many different areas of instruction.

Source: Gordon, J., Vaughn, S., & Schumm, J. (1993). Spelling interventions: A review of literature and implications for instruction for students with learning disabilities. *Learning Disabilities Research and Practice, 8,* 175–181.

Various instructional approaches have been developed to help students acquire spelling skills and ultimately develop an extensive written vocabulary. Some of these methods are better than others, but no single method has yet been determined to be the best way to teach spelling to students with difficulties in this area. We encourage teachers to carefully consider assessment information for the individual student when making goal-setting and programming decisions and to be flexible when selecting the most appropriate strategy. In many instances, the individual needs of a single student are best met by combining several instructional techniques in the total spelling program.

TRADITIONAL APPROACHES

Most educators are familiar with traditional patterns of spelling instruction in our schools. Instruction in spelling is assigned to a brief, isolated period in the daily school schedule. Commercial texts provide the basis for the program, and students progress through a series of daily activities designed to teach the spelling of linguistically similar words. A typical weekly schedule of spelling activities might be:

Monday:	Introduce new words.
Tuesday:	Write each word three times.
Wednesday:	Write each word in a sentence.
Thursday:	Take a practice test.
Friday:	Take a final test.

The persistence of this routine in our classrooms suggests that it is perceived to be an effective way to teach students to spell. Indeed, many students exposed to this type of instruction succeed in learning to spell. For students with difficulties in spelling, however, a simple pattern of this sort has not proven effective.

Unadapted, the whole group instructional approaches common to basal spelling programs are unsuccessful in meeting the needs of students with spelling disorders. Frequently, spelling series texts fail to provide for individualization, sufficient opportunity for word study, or adequate practice. Often, these series contain a large selection of inappropriate or ineffective activities, some of which actually may inhibit the student's ability to learn to spell (Cohen, 1969). Certainly, commercial spelling texts encourage teachers to view spelling as a product, not a process; the integration of skills related to spelling in the larger language arts curriculum is not encouraged.

Because commercial spelling series are readily available in schools, teachers often are reluctant to abandon basal spellers as an instructional option. Teachers who select these materials as the foundation of their instructional program should carefully consider how they can be adapted to meet their students' needs. Many of the procedures described in the sections on remedial approaches and specific instructional procedures can easily be adapted for use with commercial spelling programs.

REMEDIAL APPROACHES

Remedial approaches to spelling provide the teacher with ways to supplement traditional spelling programs or with viable instructional alternatives for students who have difficulty in learning to spell. Remedial instructional approaches emphasize individualization, a systematic method of word study, distributed repetitive practice, and performance feedback. Many remedial approaches provide for multisensory training. Graham and Voth (1990) have recommended the following curriculum modifications for implementing remedial spelling programs:

1. Instruction should be limited (at least initially) to high-frequency words and misspelled words from the student's own writing.
2. Words should be organized into small units (6-12 words) that emphasize a common structural element.
3. Distributed practice should be provided by introducing several words on successive days.
4. New and previously introduced words should be tested at the beginning and end of the daily spelling period; periodic maintenance checks should be conducted.
5. During daily tests, students should be encouraged to predict if they will and did spell words correctly. Students should correct the test with teacher supervision.
6. Students should use a systematic study procedure to study words missed on the daily pretest.
7. Students should practice missed words on succeeding days, using games and other interesting activities to improve fluency and accuracy.
8. The teacher should work to establish a strong link between instruction in spelling and the students' writing. Written products should be examined to determine if learned spellings are being generalized.
9. Students should be taught strategies or provided with resources to help them with their spelling while writing.

The remedial approaches described here are appropriate for individuals of all ages and for students with a variety of spelling problems. Teachers should select the approach that best fits their personal beliefs about teaching, their teaching style, and the individual needs of their students. When a combination of approaches is indicated, the teacher should ensure that the approaches selected are compatible; one method should enhance the effect of other method(s). Finally, the teacher should make an effort to determine which procedures are most efficient for the student.

Multisensory Approaches   Multisensory approaches to spelling involve the visual, auditory, and motor modalities. To spell a word, the student must be able to demonstrate auditory and visual discrimination of the sounds and letters in the word and possess the motor control necessary to write a word.

Although the efficacy of multisensory approaches is supported primarily by anecdotal reports, they are useful in providing the student with a systematic method of word study and repetitive practice. Table 11.3 lists several word study techniques that employ multisensory approaches to spelling.

Table 11.3
Word Study Techniques

Fitzgerald Method (Fitzgerald, 1951)
1. Look at the word carefully.
2. Say the word.
3. With eyes closed, visualize the word.
4. Cover the word and then write it.
5. Check the spelling.
6. If the word is misspelled, repeat steps 1–5.

Horn Method 1 (E. Horn, 1919)
1. Look at the word and say it to yourself.
2. Close your eyes and visualize the word.
3. Check to see if you were right. (If not, begin at step 1).
4. Cover the word and write it.
5. Check to see if you were right. (If not, begin at step 1).
6. Repeat steps 4 and 5 two more times.

Horn Method 2 (E. Horn, 1954)
1. Pronounce each word carefully.
2. Look carefully at each part of the word as you pronounce it.
3. Say the letters in sequence.
4. Attempt to recall how the word looks, then spell the word.
5. Check this attempt to recall.
6. Write the word.
7. Check this spelling attempt.
8. Repeat the above steps if necessary.

Visual-Vocal Method (Westerman, 1971)
1. Say word.
2. Spell word orally.
3. Say word again.
4. Spell word from memory four times correctly.

Gilstrap Method (Gilstrap, 1962)
1. Look at the word and say it softly. If it has more than one part, say it again, part by part, looking at each part as you say it.
2. Look at the letters and say each one. If the word has more than one part, say the letters part by part.
3. Write the word without looking at the book.

Fernald Method Modified
1. Make a model of the word with a crayon, grease pencil, or felt-tip pen, saying the word as you write it.
2. Check the accuracy of the model.
3. Trace over the model with your index finger, saying the word at the same time.
4. Repeat step 3 five times.
5. Copy the word three times correctly.
6. Copy the word three times from memory correctly.

Cover-and-Write Method
1. Look at word. Say it.
2. Write word two times.
3. Cover and write one time.
4. Check work.
5. Write word two times
6. Cover and write one time.
7. Check work.
8. Write word three times.
9. Cover and write one time.
10. Check work.

Source: From "Spelling Research and Practice: A Unified Approach" by S. Graham and L. Miller, 1979, *Focus on Exceptional Children*, *12*(2), p. 11. Reprinted by permission. ©1979 Love Publishing Company.

Linguistic Approaches   Linguistic approaches to spelling emphasize the regularity of sound-symbol associations in our language and their graphic representations in orthography. Linguistic approaches employ instructional methodologies that accent rules governing the phonological, morphological, and syntactical features of words. Words for instruction are selected on the basis of their appropriateness for teaching phonics generalizations, structural analysis, or linguistic patterns (Lerner, 1988).

As previously mentioned, some controversy exists over the advisability of teaching spelling generalizations, particularly to students who have disabilities. Some students who have mild disabilities will experience difficulty in learning any rules, some may succeed in learning and applying only a few rules, and others will learn the rule but be unable to apply it in their written language. Because the English language can provide "productive relationships" (Hodges, 1966, p. 332) between sounds and symbols, however, instruction in rules can be an important mediating influence in spelling.

Students with mild learning disabilities can profit from rule-based instruction in spelling if the teacher guides the development of useful conventions by presenting a limited number of important and functional rules. Although dated, the suggestions Brueckner and Bond (1955) provided for teaching spelling rules still generally apply:

1. Select a rule to be taught. Teach a single rule at a time.
2. Secure a list of words exemplifying the rule. Develop the rule through the study of words it covers.
3. Lead the pupils to discover the underlying generalization by discussing with them the characteristics for the words in the list. If possible, have the pupils actually formulate the rule. Help them to sharpen and clarify it.
4. Have the pupils use and apply the rule immediately.
5. If necessary, show how the rule, in some cases, does not apply, but stress its positive values.
6. Review the rule systematically on succeeding days. Emphasize its use, and do not require pupils to memorize a formalized statement. (p. 374)

We caution teachers that students with mild learning disabilities frequently have difficulty with discovery approaches to learning. For these students, direct teacher instruction is more likely to be successful than the inductive approach (see #3) Brueckner and Bond suggested. In addition, Mercer and Mercer (1989) stated that, to be functional, a rule should apply more than 75 percent of the time. Howell and Morehead (1987) acknowledged that not all rules are useful, but they designated high utility rules as ones that apply more than half the time. Rules that Howell and Morehead consider to be high utility are:

1. Double the letters *f*, *l*, *s*, or *z* in most one-syllable words when preceded by a short vowel. Examples are *cliff, sniff, bluff, whiff, cuff, puff, fell, tell, swell, ball, spill, fill, spell, brass, press, cross, miss, fuss, pass, buzz, fizz, jazz*. Exceptions are *bus* and *gas*.
2. The silent *e* at the end of a word makes a short vowel long. Examples are *pin* and *pine*, *dim* and *dime*, *hat* and *hate*, *mat* and *mate*, *rat* and *rate*, *cub* and *cube*, *plan* and *plane*, *cap* and *cape*, *at* and *ate*, *mad* and *made*, *mop* and *mope*, *kit* and *kite*, *rod* and *rode*, *hid* and *hide*, *rip* and *ripe*, *fad* and *fade*, *cut* and *cute*, *tub* and *tube*, *can* and *cane*, *hop* and *hope*, *not* and *note*, and *fin* and *fine*.
3. When you hear *k* after a short vowel, spell it *ck*; when you hear *k* after a long vowel or consonant, spell it *k*. Examples are *neck, dusk, flank, track, hunk, slack, stuck, deck, rink, milk, check, tuck, task, fleck, lack, coke, make, rock, knock,* and *stink*. Use *c* at the end of polysyllabic words when you hear *ik*. Examples are *attic, plastic, metric, cosmic, classic, Atlantic, optic, frantic*.
4. When you hear *j* after a short vowel, you usually spell it *dge*. After a long vowel or consonant, you use *ge*. Examples are *age, gadget, lodge, huge, strange, cage, nudge, stage, page, bridge, change, hinge, edge*.
5. When you hear *ch* after a short vowel, use *tch*. When you hear *ch* after a long vowel or consonant, you use *ch*. *Ch* is always used at the beginning of a word. Examples are *chop, bench, batch, pinch, church, witch, blotch, pitch, porch, crutch, lunch, sketch, fetch, patch*. Exceptions are *rich, which, much, such, sandwich*.

6. When you have a one-syllable word with a consonant at the end of a word that is preceded by a *short* vowel and the suffix begins with one vowel, double the consonant. If any one of these conditions is not met, don't double. Examples are *ship* and *shipper*, *ship* and *shipping*, *hot* and *hottest*, *slop* and *sloppy*, *mad* and *madder*, *rob* and *robber*, *star* and *starry*, *fat* and *fatter*, *fog* and *foggy*, *wit* and *witness*, *grin* and *grinning*, *mad* and *madly*, *cold* and *colder*, *farm* and *farming*, *dust* and *dusty*, *rant* and *ranted*, *boat* and *boating*, *weed* and *weeding*, *blot* and *blotter*, *grim* and *grimmest*, *rest* and *restless*, *flat* and *flatly*, *slim* and *slimmer*, *feed* and *feeding*, and *win* and *winning*.

7. A word ending in a silent *e* drops the *e* before a suffix beginning with a vowel, but does not change before an ending beginning with a consonant. Examples are *hope* and *hoping*, *dive* and *diving*, *write* and *writing*, *tune* and *tuneful*, *shine* and *shiny*, *time* and *timer*, *hope* and *hopeless*, *take* and *taking*, *sore* and *soreness*, *flame* and *flaming*, *fame* and *famous*, *care* and *caring*, *hide* and *hiding*, *hope* and *hoped*, *lone* and *lonely*, *use* and *useful*, *sure* and *surely*, *close* and *closely*, *make* and *making*, *life* and *lifeless*, *like* and *likeness*, *shade* and *shady*, *noise* and *noiseless*, and *tire* and *tiresome*.

8. Double the consonant when adding a suffix after a short vowel. Examples are *capped, caper, capping, moping, mopping, mapped, filling, filed, filing, filled, taping, tapping, taped, tapped, tapper, hopped, hoped, hopping, hoping*.

9. In words ending in *y* preceded by a consonant, the *y* changes to *i* before any ending except *-ing* or *-ist*. In words ending in *y* preceded by a vowel, keep the *y*. Examples are *cry* and *crying*, *rely* and *reliance*, *pray* and *prayer*, *worry* and *worrying*, *joy* and *joyful*, *enjoy* and *enjoyment*, *say* and *saying*, *sleepy* and *sleepiness*, *glory* and *glorious*, *delay* and *delayed*, *merry* and *merriest*, *study* and *studying*, *lonely* and *loneliness*, *pay* and *payable*, *carry* and *carried*, *stray* and *strayed*, *fly* and *flier*, *supply* and *supplied*, *healthy* and *healthier*, *spy* and *spying*, *funny* and *funniest*, *tiny* and *tiniest*, *injury* and *injurious*.

10. When adding *ble, dle, fle* to a word, consider the initial vowel sound. A long vowel or consonant simply needs *ble, dle, fle*. A short vowel continues to need all the help it can get. Examples are *buckle, freckle, puddle, ruffle, stable, rifle, stifle, staple*.

11. While most nouns form the plural by adding *s* to the singular, nouns ending in *s, x, sh,* and *ch* form the plural by adding *es*. A noun ending in *y* preceded by a consonant forms the plural by changing the *y* to *i* and adding *es*. Examples are *cats, dogs, kisses, boxes, fishes, churches,* and *candies*.

12. An apostrophe is used to show the omission of a letter or letters in a contraction. The possessive of a singular noun is formed by adding an apostrophe and *s*. The possessive of a plural noun ending in *s* is formed by adding an apostrophe. Examples are *cannot* and *can't*, *will not* and *won't*. *I had* and *I'd*, *I will* and *I'll*, *had not* and *hadn't*, *Jim's car*, *the dog's bone*, *the groups' scores*.

Source: From *Curriculum-Based Education for Special and Remedial Education* (Table 13.4, p. 314) by K. W. Howell and M. K. Morehead, 1987, Columbus, OH: Merrill. Copyright © 1987 by Merrill Publishing Company. Reprinted with permission of Merrill, an imprint of Macmillan Publishing Company.

Whole Language Approaches   Unlike linguistic approaches that employ a skill-sequence or "bottom-up" approach to learning, whole language approaches favor a "top-down" or holistic approach to spelling instruction. Whole language approaches to learning reject, in theory at least, the rule-based techniques that define linguistic approaches to spelling instruction. The focus in whole language approaches is on immersing the student in written language experiences that facilitate discoveries about the way words are represented in print and allow the student to communicate meaningful ideas.

Update

Invented Spellings

An educational innovation of the 1990s has been the use of invented or creative spellings. The approach is often a component of whole language instruction (see Chapter 9). The general assumption is that students should be able to express themselves without having to be concerned with accuracy and spelling. A further assumption is that the use of invented spelling will have a positive effect on writing fluency and creativity.

The efficacy of invented spelling used with students with special needs is essentially an unexplored topic. While general agreement exists that spelling should be considered always as a post-writing concern (i.e., students should focus on accuracy only after writing rather than in the middle of writing a composition), there certainly remains significant disagreement as to whether acceptance or essentially encouragement to create new spellings ultimately will have a positive effect on the writing of students.

Teachers are encouraged to consider approaches such as invented spelling as experimental methods of teaching. In other words, if they are being used, it becomes incumbent upon the teacher to evaluate the effectiveness of the approach and continue it only if it is having positive results. With students with special needs, resolution of whether to consider this approach will likely be determined by the inclusive classroom setting in which a given student spends a portion or all of their instructional day. How is spelling taught in that class? How will transfer be achieved between a pull-out program and the general education classroom? Which approach best promotes acceptance into the inclusive setting?

Teachers who employ whole language approaches begin by engaging the student in meaningful written language experiences such as letter writing or keeping a daily journal or diary. The student's own ideas and interests should determine the form of the written language experiences and these, in turn, direct the type of instruction the teacher delivers. In this approach, students are encouraged to experiment with spelling according to their stage of spelling development. The teacher acts as a nonjudgmental evaluator whose purpose is to facilitate the refinement of spelling skills. Orthographic principles are introduced only when the student demonstrates a need to learn a specific rule. Norris (1989, pp. 99-101) set forth five principles for applying whole language approaches to spelling instruction:

1. *Language learning begins with contextual language.* By contextualizing spelling instruction, children simultaneously discover properties of word structure while attaching meaning and use to the process of spelling.
2. *Writing is a communication process in which experience is shared.* Rather than being viewed as a task to complete for purposes of demonstrating mastery, spelling is viewed as a means of sharing meaning with an interested listener/reader.
3. *Instruction begins with the child's level of spelling knowledge.* Spelling progresses through predictable stages as children acquire increasing experience with and knowledge of written language.
4. *Instruction is discovery-based.* The teacher's impact is designed to facilitate refinement rather than to demand correctness and accuracy.
5. *The goal of instruction is to facilitate a developmental change in the strategies a child uses to represent words* rather than in the child's mastery of the correct words.

Implementing a whole language approach requires instructional techniques different from those teachers typically employ in spelling instruction. Teachers who use these approaches must be organized, creative, and, to a certain extent, intuitive in determining when and in what areas to introduce instruction related to the orthographic properties of language. The advantage of whole language approaches is that the student has greater opportunity to use knowledge about spelling in context. We know, however, that students with mild learning disabilities frequently have difficulty generalizing skills and concepts learned. Thus, a potential disadvantage of this approach is that, by introducing skills only when the need arises, students may fail to learn spelling principles that teach the relationships between words. Finally, teachers who plan to implement whole language approaches to spelling instruction should be aware that empirical research supporting these approaches is, at this time, extremely limited.

Word Lists   Teachers of students with mild learning disabilities often elect to teach spelling from word lists. Depending on the student's individual needs, the teacher may decide to use high-frequency word lists such as Horn's (1960) *Words Most Commonly Used in Writing*, 100 of which are given in Table 11.4; various functional word lists such as such as survival words and phrases (see Chapter 8, Tables 8.1 and 8.2); spelling demons, as listed in Table 11.5; or lists compiled by the teacher from content area texts or mistakes in the student's own writing.

Table 11.4
Words Most Commonly Used in Writing

1. I	21. at	41. do	61. up	81. think
2. the	22. this	42. been	62. day	82. say
3. and	23. with	43. letter	63. much	83. please
4. to	24. but	44. can	64. out	84. him
5. a	25. on	45. would	65. her	85. his
6. you	26. if	46. she	66. order	86. got
7. of	27. all	47. when	67. yours	87. over
8. in	28. so	48. about	68. now	88. make
9. we	29. me	49. they	69. well	89. may
10. for	30. was	50. any	70. an	90. received
11. it	31. very	51. which	71. here	91. before
12. that	32. my	52. some	72. them	92. two
13. is	33. had	53. has	73. see	93. send
14. your	34. our	54. or	74. go	94. after
15. have	35. from	55. there	75. what	95. work
16. will	36. am	56. us	76. come	96. could
17. be	37. one	57. good	77. were	97. dear
18. are	38. time	58. know	78. no	98. made
19. not	39. he	59. just	79. how	99. glad
20. as	40. get	60. by	80. did	100. like

Source: From *A Basic Writing Vocabulary: 10,000 Words Most Commonly Used in Writing* by E. Horn, 1926, Iowa City: University of Iowa Monographs in Education, First Series, No. 4.

Word lists can be categorized in two ways: (a) fixed lists, or (b) flow lists. On *fixed lists*, a new set of words is assigned each week. The student engages in a series of activities designed to teach the spelling of the words on the list, and a test is given at the end of the week. Follow-up on missed words is generally not provided, and words on the new list may bear little or no resemblance to words on the previous list. On *flow lists*, the number of words initially presented is limited. Once the student masters a word, it is dropped from the list and a new word is added. The advantage of flow lists is that students do not waste valuable time practicing known words. Most authorities agree that flow lists are more beneficial than fixed lists in teaching spelling to students with mild learning disabilities, especially when routine review of previously mastered words is included in the teaching procedures.

Cognitive Approaches   Cognitive approaches to spelling instruction are based on recent research on the developmental model of the acquisition of spelling skills. According to this perspective, spelling is a complex, high-order cognitive skill. Children develop spelling skills in a series of predictable stages related to their specific knowledge of the orthographic properties of language and their general problem-solving skills. Students with mild learning disabilities who experience difficulty in learning to spell pass through the same stages as their normally achieving peers, but at a slower rate. These students possess but fail to use the orthographic problem-solving behaviors nec-

Table 11.5
Spelling Demons

ache	course	its	perfectly	sense
afraid	double	it's	piano	separate
against	easier	kitchen	picnic	shining
all right	eighth	knives	picture	silence
although	either	language	piece	since
angry	enemy	lettuce	pitcher	soldier
answered	families	listening	pleasant	squirrel
asks	fasten	lose	potato	stepped
beautiful	fault	marriage	practice	straight
because	February	meant	prettiest	studying
beginning	forgotten	minute	pumpkin	success
boy's	friendly	neighbor	purpose	taught
buried	good-bye	neither	quietly	their
busily	guessed	nickel	rapidly	there's
carrying	happened	niece	receive	through
certain	happily	ninety	rotten	valentine
choose	here's	ninth	safety	whose
Christmas	holiday	onion	said	worst
clothes	hungry	passed	sandwich	writing
climbed	husband	peaceful	scratch	yours

Source: From *Spelling in Language Arts 6* by A. Kuska, E. J. D. Webster, and G. Elford, 1964, Ontario, Canada: Thomas Nelson & Sons Ltd. Reprinted by permission.

essary to produce correctly spelled words; their difficulties in spelling result from their inefficient organization and retrieval of orthographic information (Gerber, 1984; Gerber & Hall, 1989; Wong, 1986).

According to Wong (1986), effective spelling instruction addresses the phonological or linguistic structure of the language, called *domain-specific knowledge*, and teaches learning strategies for spelling, such as self-questioning or self-monitoring. Wong (p. 172) provided the following self-questioning strategy:

1. Do I know the word?
2. How many syllables do I hear in the word (write down the number).
3. I'll spell out the word.
4. Do I have the right number of syllables down?
5. If yes, is there any part of the word I'm not sure of spelling? I'll underline that part and try spelling the word again.
6. Now, does it look right to me? If it does, I'll leave it alone. If it still doesn't look right, I'll underline the part I'm not sure of the spelling and try again. (If the word I spelled does not have the right number of syllables, let me hear the word in my head again and find the missing syllable. Then I'll go back to steps 5 and 6).
7. When I finish spelling, I'll tell myself I'm a good worker. I've tried hard at spelling.

Update

Cover, Copy, and Compare

For many years, the learning strategy of cover, copy, and compare has been used effectively to promote student learning of specific skills including spelling. In particular, it offers an approach in which students can independently engage in word study, such as in preparation for a spelling test. McLaughlin and Skinner (1996) suggest the following considerations for using cover, copy, and compare. With this method, the student is taught to:

- Look at a specific written word
- Cover the word
- Write the word from memory
- Uncover the word for review
- Assess the accuracy of the response by comparing it to the original word

As McLaughlin and Skinner note, the cover, copy, and compare strategy requires little instructional time. It can be taught directly by modeling the steps within the strategy, verbalizing each component step and then monitoring the students as they follow the steps in the procedure. They recommend that after a student has spelled a word correctly for three days that it be dropped from the spelling list and a new word be added.

Source: McLaughlin, T. F. & Skinner, C. H. (1996) Improving academic performance through self-management: Cover, copy and compare. *Intervention in School and Clinic, 32,* 113–118.

SPECIFIC INSTRUCTIONAL STRATEGIES

In addition to the more general approaches for spelling instruction, teachers should investigate a host of specific strategies to ensure a flexible and responsive educational program. In this section we discuss some instructional considerations that might prove useful in building such a plan.

CORRECTED-TEST METHOD

In their review of research on spelling, Graham and Miller (1980) reported that the corrected-test technique resulted in the greatest spelling improvement. Under the teacher's direction, students correct specific spelling errors immediately after being tested. The authors noted that this procedure enables students to observe which words are particularly difficult, to identify the part of the word creating the difficulty, and to correct the error under supervision.

STUDY-TEST VERSUS TEST-STUDY-TEST

In the test-study-test procedure, the student is first administered a pretest and then studies only the unknown words. A posttest is administered at the end of the unit of study to determine the student's level of mastery. Progress is charted, and words missed on the posttest are added to the word study list for the following week.

The study-test procedure differs from the test-study-test procedure in the absence of a pretest. The pretest is omitted to avoid frustration from poor performance and, therefore, the development of a failure set toward certain words. Petty (1966) and Stevens, Hartman, and Lucas (1982), however, determined that the test-study-test method was superior to the study-test method.

INSTRUCTIONAL CUES

The prompting or cuing of instructional stimuli can highlight the correct spelling of individual words. The purpose of this technique is to simplify the student's task in producing correct responses, and thus reduce or eliminate errors.

To implement a cuing response, the teacher first must identify the student's specific spelling difficulties. Specific vowel sounds, certain serial positions in words, or nonphonetic elements, for example, may prove troublesome for the student. *Color-coding* can be used to cue certain letters or combinations of letters. For older students who might be offended by the primary-grade implications of the color-coding approach, *underlining* the trouble spots often works.

Configuration (using ascending and descending letters to outline the shape of the word) also may be useful in helping the student to learn difficult-to-spell words. In configuration, the teacher blocks the shape of the words and the student selects the word that fits each configurational pattern. The teacher should be aware that configuration loses its utility when words have similar configurational patterns (e.g., *look, hook, book*). Also, to our knowledge, configuration as a method for teaching spelling has no empirical support.

MNEMONIC DEVICES

Mnemonic devices have been found useful in teaching students memory tasks in reading and when lists of information must be learned in content areas. The task of learning a series of mnemonic devices, however, can place as much strain on the student's memory as the memory task itself. Therefore, the teacher is advised to limit the use of mnemonic devices in spelling to those the student can associate with previous learning and easily remember. Examples of spelling mnemonics are illustrated in Table 11.6.

MOTIVATIONAL TECHNIQUES

Because the task of learning to spell is difficult for many students with mild learning disabilities, teachers should be aware of activities and teaching techniques that increase motivation. Games, peer tutoring, computer and other media activities can offer an incentive for students to learn. When using these activities and techniques, teachers have to carefully avoid those that highlight a student's weakness. With a little ingenuity, most activities and procedures can be modified to avoid this problem. Fostering a positive attitude toward spelling can be accomplished by emphasizing student progress, encouraging pride in correctly spelled papers, using a variety of teaching approaches, designing tasks so students can achieve, and showing the student the role of spelling in practical and social situations (Graham, 1985).

Table 11.6
Mnemonic Devices for Spelling Demons

1. <u>Stationery</u> is paper.
2. Is old age a <u>tragedy</u>?
3. A <u>professor</u> is a prof.
4. Bad <u>grammar</u> may mar your writing.
5. The I's are <u>parallel</u> in this word.
6. <u>Principle</u> is a synonym for rule.
7. A <u>principal</u> is a pal.
8. A good <u>secretary</u> can keep a secret.
9. Three e's are buried in <u>cemetery</u>.
10. There is no word in English ending in "full" except the word <u>full</u> when it stands alone; e.g., thankful, spoonful, helpful, etc.
11. There is no word in English beginning with "recco." <u>Recommend</u> means to re (again) commend.
12. <u>All</u> <u>right</u> is the same as all wrong.

Source: From *Corrective and Remedial Teaching* (2nd ed., p. 272) by W. Otto, R. A. McMenemy, and R. J. Smith, 1973, Boston: Houghton Mifflin. Reprinted by permission.

STUDY SKILLS

In the absence of direct teacher instruction, study skills allow the student to acquire, use, and refine knowledge. Students who have study skills are able to more actively participate in their own learning and thus become more independent learners. Although our knowledge of teaching study skills to students with mild learning disabilities does not directly address spelling instruction, we believe that the general principles of efficient study techniques apply to all areas of the school curriculum, including spelling. Hoover (1989, pp. 473–474) developed the following guidelines for teaching study skills:

1. Introduce simple variations of study skills in the early grades.
2. Gradually increase to more complex elements associated with each study skill as students progress through the grades.
3. Identify specific goals and objectives for a study skills program prior to program implementation.
4. Let students' individual strengths and weaknesses guide decision making concerning what study skills to emphasize at any particular time.
5. Know what motivates students to use different study skills, and emphasize these motivations in program implementations.
6. Explain and demonstrate proper use of each study skill.
7. Expect students to use different study skills appropriately through guided practice and planned learning experiences.
8. Provide opportunities for practicing study skill usage to assist students in acquiring and maintaining mastery of the skills.
9. Facilitate the use of study skills in natural classroom settings and on a regular basis as the need arises in different subject areas and learning activities.
10. Assist students in generalizing skills acquired through an emphasis on more complex uses of the skills once initial mastery of the basic study skills has been achieved.

COMPUTER-ASSISTED INSTRUCTION

Computer-based approaches represent a relatively new innovation in spelling instruction. Many students find the novelty of computer-based instruction to be a motivating influence. Computer-assisted instruction has the additional advantage of allowing students to independently practice spelling skills, receive immediate feedback and reinforcement, chart their performance, and keep records of progress over time.

As with any material, the quality of software programs for spelling varies. Teachers are advised to evaluate the software in terms of the objectives of the instructional program and the ease with which the student is able to use the program. Teachers should be aware, too, that the computer keyboard may present special problems for students who do not have typing skills. Varnhagen and Gerber (1984) found that the task of locating letters on the keyboard interfered with the student's performance on the spelling task.

ERROR DETECTION AND CORRECTION

To teach the long-term goal of competency in spelling, students with mild learning disabilities must be able to detect and correct errors in their written language. Proficiency in spelling requires that the student proofread written assignments for errors and learn when a dictionary is needed and how to use the information it contains. Graham and Miller (1980) suggested a variety of activities for teaching proofreading skills. Among them:

1. Provide a short list of words that include misspelled words to be found.
2. Provide a short passage with errors ranging from ones that are apparent to spelling demons.
3. List the total number of words purposely misspelled in a written composition, and have the students locate them.
4. Have the student select the correctly spelled words from a series of alternative forms.
5. Provide a passage with the words that may be incorrect, and have students use study skills to determine their accuracy.

The specific dictionary skills the student should learn include: (a) the application of alphabetizing skills to estimate the location of a word; (b) the use of individual page guide words; (c) the use of syllabic markings; and (d) the identification of various diacritical markings.

SUMMARY

Spelling is a complex act that requires the speller to have knowledge of our orthographic system, the ability to recall or revisualize previously learned words, and the ability to devise, use, or apply strategies for determining the correct spelling of words. Individuals who experience difficulty in spelling generally demonstrate isolated deficits in specific spelling skills or a pattern of academic and language-related disabilities. Spelling develops in individuals in a predictable and hierarchical sequence. Students with mild learning disabilities who experience difficulty in learning to spell pass through the developmental sequence in the same order, but at a lower rate, than students who do not experience difficulty in spelling. Both formal and informal assessment procedures are useful in determining factors related to the student's spelling disability; however, informal procedures, particularly curriculum-based measures and error analysis procedures, are more useful in planning an educational program for the student with spelling disabilities. A number of instructional procedures have been developed to assist in teaching students to spell. The most effective of these approaches are empirically based, teach spelling as an integral part of the language arts and school curriculum, employ a variety of materials and methods to accommodate individual differences and provide students with direct, explicit instruction, sufficient practice and review, and strategies for locating and correcting spelling errors.

REFERENCES

Allred, R. A. (1977). *Spelling: The application of research findings.* Washington, DC: National Educational Association.

Bailet, L. L. (1991). Development of disorders of spelling in the beginning school years. In A. M. Bain, L. L. Bailet, & L. C. Moats (Eds.), *Written language disorders: Theory into practice* (pp. 1–24). Austin, TX: Pro-Ed

Beers, J. W., & Henderson, E. (1977). A study of developing orthographic concepts among first graders. *Research in the Teaching of English, 11,* 133–148.

Brueckner, L. J., & Bond, G. L. (1955). Diagnosis and treatment of learning disabilities. In E. C. Frierson & W. B. Barbe (Eds.), *Educating children with learning disabilities.* New York: Appleton-Century-Crofts.

Burns, P. C. (1980). *Assessment and correction of language arts difficulties.* Columbus, OH: Charles E. Merrill Publishing.

Cohen, L. (1969). *Evaluating structural analysis methods used in spelling books.* Unpublished doctoral dissertation, Boston University.

Cohen, S. B., & Plaskon, S. P. (1980). *Language arts for the mildly handicapped.* Columbus, OH: Charles E. Merrill Publishing.

DeMaster, V., Crossland, C., & Hasselbring, T. S. (1986). Consistency of learning disabled students' spelling performance. *Learning Disability Quarterly, 9,* 89–96.

Fitzgerald, J. (1951). *The teaching of spelling.* Milwaukee: Bruce Publishing Co.

Gentry, J. R. (1984). Developmental aspects of learning to spell. *Academic Therapy, 20*(1), 11–19.

Gerber, M. M. (1984). Ortho problem-solving ability of learning disabled and normally achieving students. *Learning Disability Quarterly, 7,* 157–164.

Gerber, M. M. & Hall, R. J. (1989). Cognitive-behavioral training in spelling for learning handicapped students. *Learning Disability Quarterly, 12,* 159–171.

Gerber, M. M., & Hall, R. J. (1981). *Development of orthographic problem-solving strategies in learning disabled children* (Research Report NO. 37). Charlottesville, VA: University of Virginia Learning Disabilities Research Institute.

Gerber, M. M., & Hall, R. J. (1982). *Development of spelling in learning disabled and normally achieving children.* Unpublished monograph, University of California, Santa Barbara.

Gilstrap, R. (1962). Development of independent spelling skills in the intermediate grades. *Elementary English, 39,* 481–483.

Gordon, J., Vaughn, S., & Schumm, J. (1993). Spelling interventions: A review of literature and implications for instruction for students with learning disabilities. *Learning Disabilities Research and Practice, 8,* 175–181.

Graham, S. (1985). Teaching basic academic skills to learning disabled students: A model of the teaching/learning process. *Journal of Learning Disabilities, 18,* 528–534.

Graham, S., & Miller, L. (1979). Spelling research and practice: A unified approach. *Focus on Exceptional Children, 12*(2), 1–16.

Graham, S., & Miller, L. (1980). Handwriting research and practice: A unified approach. *Focus on Exceptional Children, 13*(2), 1–16.

Graham, S., & Voth, V. P. (1990). Spelling instruction: Making modifications for students with learning disabilities. *Academic Therapy, 25,* 447–457.

Greenbaum, C. R. (1987). *Spellmaster assessment and teaching system.* Austin, TX: Pro-Ed.

Hall, R. J., Gerber, M. M., & Stricker, A. (1989). Cognitive training: Implications for spelling instruction. In J. N. Hughes & R. J. Hall (Eds.), *Cognitive-behavioral psychology in the schools* (pp. 347–388). New York: Guilford Press.

Hammill, D. D., & Larsen, S. C. (1986). *Test of Written Spelling–2.* Austin, TX: Pro-Ed.

Hanna, P. R., Hanna, J., Hodges, R. E., & Rudorf, E. H. (1966). *Phoneme-grapheme correspondences as cues to spelling improvement* (USOE Publication No. OE-32008). Washington, DC: U.S. Government Printing Office.

Hodges, R. E. (1966). The case for teaching sound-to-letter correspondences in spelling. *The Elementary School Journal, 66,* 327–336.

Hodges, R. (1981). *Learning to spell: Theory and research into practice*. Urbana, IL: National Council of Teachers of English.

Hoover, J. J. (1989). Implementing a study skills program in the classroom. *Academic Therapy, 24*, 471–478.

Horn, E. (1954). *Teaching spelling*. Washington DC, American Educational Research Association.

Horn, E. (1960). Spelling. *Encyclopedia of educational research*. New York: Macmillan.

Howell, K. W., & Morehead, M. K. (1987). *Curriculum-based evaluation for special and remedial instruction*. Columbus, OH: Charles E. Merrill Publishing.

Jastak, S., & Wilkinson, G. S. (1984). *Wide range achievement test*. Wilmington, DE: Jastak Associates.

Kaufman, A. S., & Kaufman, N. L. (1985). *Kaufman assessment battery for children*. Circle Pines, MN: American Guidance Service.

Kottmeyer, W. (1970). *Teacher's guide for remedial reading*. New York: Webster/McGraw Hill.

Kuska, A., Webster, E. J. D., & Elford, G. (1964). *Spelling in Language Arts 6*. Ontario, Canada: Thomas Nelsons & Sons Ltd.

Lerner, J. (1988). *Learning disabilities: Theories, diagnosis, and teaching strategies* (5th ed.). Boston: Houghton Mifflin.

Mann, P. H., & Suiter, P. (1974). *Handbook in diagnostic teaching: A learning disabilities approach*. Boston: Allyn & Bacon.

Markwardt, F. C. (1989). *Peabody individual achievement test–Revised*. Circle Pines, MN: American Guidance Service.

McLaughlin, T. F. & Skinner, C. H. (1996) Improving academic performance through self-management: Cover, copy and compare. *Intervention in School and Clinic, 32*, 113–118.

Mercer, C. D., & Mercer, A. R. (1989). *Teaching students with learning problems* (3rd ed.). Columbus, OH: Charles E. Merrill Publishing.

Norris, J. A. (1989). Facilitating developmental changes in spelling. *Academic Therapy, 25*, 97–107.

Otto, W., McMenemy, R. A., & Smith, R. J. (1973). *Corrective and remedial teaching*. Boston: Houghton Mifflin.

Petty, W. T. (1966). Handwriting and spelling: Their current status in the language arts curriculum. In T. D. Horn (Ed.), *Research on handwriting and spelling*. Champaign, IL: National Council of Teachers of English.

Reed, C. (1975). *Children's categorization of speech sounds in English* (Research Report No. 17). Urbana, IL: National Council of Teachers of English.

Reed, C., & Hodges, R. E. (1982). Spelling. *Encyclopedia of educational research*. New York: Macmillan.

Spache, D. E. (1940). Characteristic errors of good and poor spellers. *Journal of Educational Research, 34*, 182–189.

Stevens, T. M., Hartman, A. C., & Lucas, V. H. (1982). *Teaching children basic skills: A curriculum handbook* (2nd ed.). Columbus, OH: Charles E. Merrill Publishing.

Stubbs, M. (1980) *Language and literacy: The sociology of reading and writing*. London: Routledge & Kegan Paul.

Templeton, S. (1980). Spelling, phonology, and the older speller. In E. H. Henderson & J. W. Beers (Eds.), *Developmental and cognitive aspects of learning to spell: A reflection on word knowledge* (pp. 85–96). Newark, DE: International Reading Association.

Varnhagen, S., & Gerber, M. (1984). Use of microcomputers for spelling assessment: Reasons to be cautious. *Learning Disability Quarterly, 7*, 266–270.

Westerman, G. (1971). *Spelling and writing*. San Rafael: Dimensions.

Wong, B. Y. L. (1986). A cognitive approach to teaching spelling. *Exceptional Children, 53*, 169–173.

Woodcock, R. W., & Johnson, M. B. (1989). *Woodcock-Johnson Psycho-Educational Battery–Revised*. Allen, TX: DLM Teaching Resources.

Yule, V. (1986). The design of spelling to match needs and abilities. *Harvard Educational Review, 56*, 278–297.

T he ability to communicate in written form has been called the highest achievement in language for people in modern cultures. Effective written communication requires the application of conceptual and organizational skills in situations ranging from the concrete to the abstract. To produce excellence, writing demands a psychological rather than a mechanical commitment (Polloway, Patton, & Cohen, 1981).

Written communication builds upon the language skills of speaking, listening, and reading. Though considered an honored and respected ability, however, it paradoxically was often overlooked as an important curricular domain. Riemer (1969) emphasized the significance of writing for higher education, business, and various professions and decried the American educational system for failures in the pedagogy of writing. He stated:

> American adults don't write, because they are the victims of a system intensely determined to make them readers, not writers, and because there is no true and proper curriculum designed to develop writing. (p. 43)

The lack of attention to written expression in the curriculum has reflected to some extent the paucity of research in this area. Recently, however, written language has been ascending, with significant increases in research activities and programming, including the development of practical instructional techniques that have begun to influence practice in both regular and special education.

Advances in research and programming in written language come at an opportune time, as indicated by a 1986 media report from the federal government. According to this report document, 80 percent of all high school students write inadequately, over half do not like the process of writing, and approximately four fifths cannot write well enough to ensure that they will always accomplish their purpose. Just as these findings suggest major problems in writing for the general student population, one can deduce that the stresses and disabilities of students in special education programs accentuate the same problems (Polloway & Decker, 1988).

What is written expression? Certainly it is a broad instructional area that ranges from writing a simple sentence to organizing research reports or term papers. Johnson and Myklebust (1967) suggested that conceptual writing includes two basic facets: formulation and syntax. *Formulation* refers to the generation of ideas and the creative writing that stem from an intention to communicate. *Syntax* focuses on mechanics and deals with the grammatical structure of written efforts.

Specialized instruction in written communication is essential for all students who have acquired prerequisite skills in reading and oral language. For many exceptional children, composition will be a logical extension of other language skills. Others may encounter their first language problems in composition. For a small, yet significant, group of exceptional children, disorders in this area may be "pure" in the sense that they do not seem to be related to or consistent with abilities in reading or oral language. Gregg (1991) noted that problems in written expression could be attributable to an underlying cognitive processing problem, poor instruction, a lack of appropriate experience in manipulating language structures (difficulty in integrating subject, text, and reader in order to write coherently), as well as other specific disorders, such as attention deficit and poor self-concept.

Among the number of considerations in writing instruction, five general ones, identified by Decker and Polloway (1989), are introduced here.

1. Writing draws on previous linguistic experiences. Prior problems, such as in listening, speaking, and reading, may be reflected, and perhaps magnified, in the area of writing.
2. Writing must be viewed as both *process* and *product*. Products typically have been the primary objectives, and educators have had to ensure that students reach that goal. But, for instance, some students may mistakenly believe that textbooks are written by obscure scholars who simply transcribed their thoughts directly to a finished product. It would be helpful for these children to understand the process behind the development of the product, such as by pointing out the concept of the "rough draft."
3. Because writing is a form of communication, it requires an identifiable audience to facilitate the setting of purpose. Writers do not have the luxury of presenting unclear ideas that can be clarified in further exchanges, as in oral communication. As students learn to write, they need to keep in mind who will read their products.
4. Writing must be tied to cognition. Prior to writing, students should be given ample opportunity to discuss what they intend to write, so they are appropriately prepared.
5. Writing provides a unique opportunity for personal expression. In this sense, it is not simply a goal but also a vehicle. Writing can provide opportunities to express feelings, attitudes, and concepts. Writing can and should become both end and means (Dehouske, 1979; Rich & Nedboy, 1977).

A MODEL FOR WRITTEN LANGUAGE

Although aspects of the writing process may be automatic, or at least semiautomatic, for mature writers, students with difficulties in writing may have problems at a more conscious, functional level. Hall (1981) identified three stages of the writing task as *prewriting, writing,* and *postwriting.* These are incorporated within Figure 12.1, a conceptual model of the written language process. The model was developed from the perspective of the learner/writer and therefore is concerned with input to the student, task demands on the student, and output by the student. As discussed by Polloway, Patton, and Cohen (1981, 1983), major components of the model have direct implications for basic instructional principles and remediation.

PREWRITING

The prewriting stage is essentially a *planning* stage. During this time, the writer focuses on developing and elaborating on ideas, setting the purpose, organizing ideas in logical

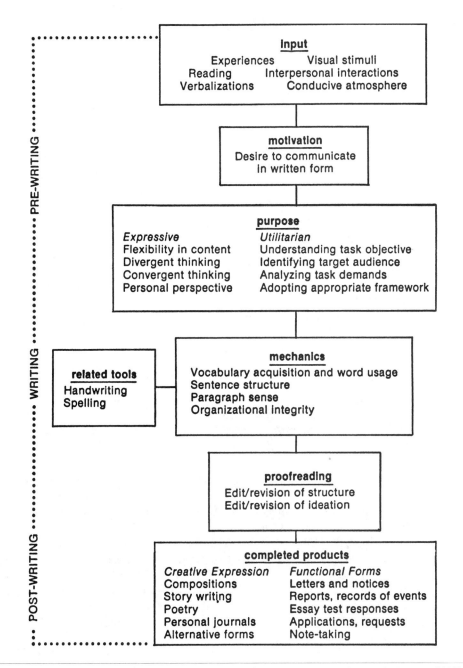

Source: From "Written Language" by E. A. Polloway, J. R. Patton, and S. A. Cohen in *Promising Practices for Exceptional Children: Curriculum Implications* (p. 298), edited by E. L. Meyen, G. A. Vergason, and R. J. Whelan, 1983, Denver: Love Publishing.

Figure 12.1
Model for Written Language

fashion, and assessing the reading audience. As noted in Figure 12.1, prewriting incorporates the three interrelated aspects of input, motivation, and purpose.

Input   Input refers to the source of stimulation to the student. It summarizes the ways in which the educational and home environments can be manipulated to influence the would-be writer. The basis for its consideration is simply, as Petty and Bowen (1967) stated, "input must precede outgo." Without stimulation we cannot anticipate response. Through the verbalizations of others, opportunities to experience the environment through diverse means (e.g., field trips, athletics, classroom activities), encounters with reading, verbal and nonverbal interpersonal interactions, and continuous and varied auditory/visual stimuli (e.g., multimedia, television, films, photographs), the student can develop an interest in a given topic and the degree of familiarity necessary for effective communication.

Motivation   Motivation stems directly from the various forms of input. Students have to develop the felt need to communicate, because attitude toward writing is among the most important instructional considerations (Alley & Deshler, 1979; Mercer & Mercer, 1989; Smith, 1974). In addition to antecedent events, motivation can be achieved through consequences such as increased personal interaction and positive feedback.

Purpose   As the basis for organizing writing, purpose creates an awareness of writing as a natural process of communication (Golden, 1980). For learners who have disabilities, two general purposes for writing are *expressive* and *utilitarian*. These represent variant forms of writing that are separated in our model to highlight their different objectives. Expressive or creative writing emphasizes the personal communication of experiences and thoughts in an original way; utilitarian or functional writing conveys information in a more structured form, as with letters and reports (Mercer & Mercer, 1989).

Despite this oversimplified distinction, the two purposes need not be oppositional. The two forms can be teamed to facilitate the acquisition of abilities (Cohen & Plaskon, 1980). In addition, as noted by Petty and Bowen (1967), utilitarian writing can become more creative as it becomes more individualistic, novel, and unusual. Thus, although the instructor initially should differentiate between the two forms in assisting students with disabilities to set purpose, the relationship between them ultimately may become less disparate.

By helping the writer set and refine purpose, the teacher is encouraging students to be more attentive to the demands of the topic, to be more reflective of ways to achieve goals, and to become actively involved in each of the writing stages necessary to produce an acceptable product. These concerns—attention, reflection, and active learning—frequently have been identified as major deficiencies in the learning repertoire of students who have mild disabilities (see, for example, Epstein, Hallahan, & Kauffman, 1975; Ross, 1976; Torgeson, 1977; Wong, 1979).

In expressive writing, the specification of purpose entails several critical features. First, the writer must appreciate the inherent *flexibility* in selecting and developing content for the theme. Next, the writer must be able to tap *divergent thinking* to explore the specific ideas of interest within the parameters of the assignment. *Convergent thinking* provides the vehicle for organization by narrowing the scope and allowing for the selection of relevant information. Finally, the constant input of a *personal perspective* ensures a unique and original product.

In utilitarian writing, the shift in focus dictates a parallel change in the writer's consideration of purpose. *Understanding the task objective* is requisite. Second, the writer must identify the *target audience* so appropriateness of form can be matched to the reader's characteristics. Although the audience is also a concern in creative expression, it is far more critical in functional writing.

WRITING

The writing stage is essentially the *drafting* or transcribing process. According to Vogel and Konrad (in press), this stage encompasses use of appropriate grammatical conventions, clear expression of ideas, specific word choices, diversity in vocabulary, appropriate forms of varied sentence structures, and appropriate transition reflective of a logical ideational progression. It also includes attention to the tool subjects of handwriting and spelling.

The specific items outlined in Figure 12.1 summarize the basic mechanics common to semantically, syntactically, and organizationally sound written products. Each of these categories subsumes subskills related to the development of writing competence.

Vocabulary acquisition and *word usage* are the basic semantic foundations for writing. Two instructional goals predominate: (a) to encourage students to make use of the variety of words they already possess (in their oral receptive and expressive lexicon), and (b) to help students learn and use new words, particularly as they aid in the written discussion of a given topic.

Word usage is concerned with the appropriate construction of meaningful phrases and sentences based on selections from a student's vocabulary. Key instructional objectives include curtailing the redundant use of common words, increasing the use of descriptive words, alternating synonyms for common thoughts, selecting words that most precisely fit meaning, avoiding awkward combinations, and maintaining consistency with the purpose of the writing task and the intended audience.

Sentence structure is used here as a generic term referring to the range of major syntactical concerns within sentences, including appropriate verb tense, noun-verb agreement, noun-pronoun agreement, correct forms for other morphological structures, capitalization, and punctuation. In addition, the need for variety in the sentence forms and functions used should be emphasized.

Paragraph sense means the transition in writing from syntactically accurate sentences to well written compositions or reports. It taps the student's ability to organize thoughts in a coherent fashion that conveys a central message to the reader. In a developmental sense, four sequential abilities have to be learned:

1. Paragraphs must express a single concept or main idea.
2. Initial topical sentences should provide a lead-in for the reader.
3. Subsequent sentences should provide further support to the concept being discussed.
4. Final sentences in longer paragraphs should serve a summary or transitional function.

Organizational integrity is concerned with the overall product. The focus is on how the mechanics and the writing style manage to achieve the identified purposes. Students must be alert to how they sequence ideas, consistency between the discussion and the conclusions, clarity of the message communicated, retention of personal style (when appropriate), and relevance of detail to the stated purpose.

POSTWRITING

The postwriting stage consists of rewriting through revision and editing. The major concern should be to improve the skills and the ideas of the writing task.

Classified in the conceptual model as an essential aspect of the postwriting stage, *proofreading* basically entails the process of editing and revising for both content and structure. Frequently, the importance of proofreading may not be apparent to learners who have disabilities, because of an emphasis on task completion. In other cases, problem learners may associate editing with failure, as a result of overcorrection of previous writing assignments. Lovitt (1975) noted that many writers consider revision as simply changing punctuation marks and misspellings. To move beyond this limited concept of proofreading, students must be taught specific steps to follow in reviewing their own written work samples.

Proofreading should offer far grater advantages to the writer than a repetitive completion of worksheets. As Poplin, Gray, Larsen, Banikowski, & Mehring (1980) indicated, the benefits include the more meaningful nature of the exercise because of students' greater familiarity with the words and ideas they created and the increased potential for generalization of skills.

The three stages of writing have been considered separately because this distinction enables instruction to focus on the specific tasks facing the would-be writer. In practice, however, the three phases are certainly not perfectly discrete. For example, planning continues to take place during the postwriting stage, and some revising takes place during the writing stage. This process of *recursion* (Scarmadalia & Bereiter, 1986) is certainly a common occurrence. Nevertheless an initial focus on the stages of writing provides a process-type approach for students, assisting them in enhancing their thinking and in developing an "inner voice" by thinking about what they are to do (Thomas, Englert, & Gregg, 1987). To illustrate the writing process as related to skilled and unskilled writers, Isaacson (1987) analyzed the unique characteristics of these two groups of writers across the three stages, which he called planning, transcribing, and revising. Table 12.1 provides a summary.

ASSESSMENT

The assessment of compositional skills is a complex process. A variety of conceptualizations have been developed to determine what should be evaluated and how the evaluation should be accomplished. Although no set sequence of skills is readily available, the use of prescriptive teaching procedures and the need for initial and ongoing analysis are as important here as they are in other curricular skill areas. Also, teachers must

Table 12.1
The Writing Process of Skilled and Unskilled Writers

Stage	Unskilled Writer	Skilled Writer
Planning	Does not participate in prewriting discussions.	Explores and discusses topics.
	Spends little time thinking about topic before beginning composition.	Spends time considering what will be written and how it will be expressed.
	Makes no plans or notes.	Jots notes; draws diagrams or pictures.
Transcribing	Writes informally in imitation of speech.	Writes in style learned from models of composition.
	Is preoccupied with technical matters of spelling and punctuation.	Keeps audience in mind while writing.
	Stops only briefly and infrequently.	Stops frequently to reread. Takes long thought pauses.
Revising	Does not review or rewrite.	Reviews frequently.
	Looks only for surface errors (spelling, punctuation).	Makes content revisions, as well as spelling and punctuation corrections.
	Rewrites only to make a neat copy in ink.	Keeps audience in mind while rewriting.

Source: From "Effective Instruction in Written Language" by S. L. Isaacson, 1987, *Focus on Exceptional Children, 19*(6), p. 4.

consider not just skills but the overall communicative effectiveness of a writing sample as well (Bailet, 1991).

Moran (1987) outlined the selections available to teachers with regard to the emphases of assessment. Briefly these include:

1. Assessment of *composition* (the creation of written discourse to communicate with the audience) versus *transcription* (the mechanics or conventions of writing).
2. Assessment by *indirect* (evaluation of contrived samples to determine knowledge of standard English) versus *direct* (evaluation of actual writing samples) measures.
3. Assessment of *process* (the strategies involved in writing) versus *product* (the completed writing samples gathered from students' work).
4. Assessment via *holistic rating* (overall evaluation of writing based on an established rating scale tied to anchor papers) versus *analytic scoring* (attention to specific subskills).

Both formal and informal approaches can be used to assess written language. In terms of formal assessment, achievement-oriented tests and diagnostic tests are available with subtests related to the area of written language. Achievement tests only rarely provide useful information for teaching. Polloway et al. (1983) provide a list of achievement tests along with a brief description of the features that relate to writing. Table 12.2 summarizes the relevant features of representative diagnostic tests. Bailet (1991) contains critiques of written language instruments.

Various informal writing assessments also have been developed. Table 12.3 presents commonly used informal techniques, and the following discussion highlights specific informal techniques to assess fluency and vocabulary, structure and organization of sentences and paragraphs, and ideation.

FLUENCY AND VOCABULARY

Once students begin to write, teachers should start assessing fluency and vocabulary. The term *fluency* refers to the quantity of writing a child produces (Cartwright, 1969) and contains a related instructional goal of increasing the length and the complexity of the sentences a child writes. Assessment, therefore, begins by focusing on the number of words used per sentence, and later on the variety of sentence styles a child writes.

The words-per-sentence figure is computed simply by dividing the number of words in a passage by the number of sentences in that passage. In Figure 12.2 the average length of sentences has been computed for a passage taken from a 9-year-old child. Naturally, the longer the sentence length, the more mature style it typically represents. With students who show consistent interest in successive writing lessons, this measure can evaluate positive changes in written fluency that can be tied to annual goals or short-term objectives. Although the actual number of words used per sentence does not measure the quality of writing, it can indicate increased facility.

Besides evaluating fluency, teachers should observe the types of sentences students use. Basically, sentences are of four types related to *form* and four types related

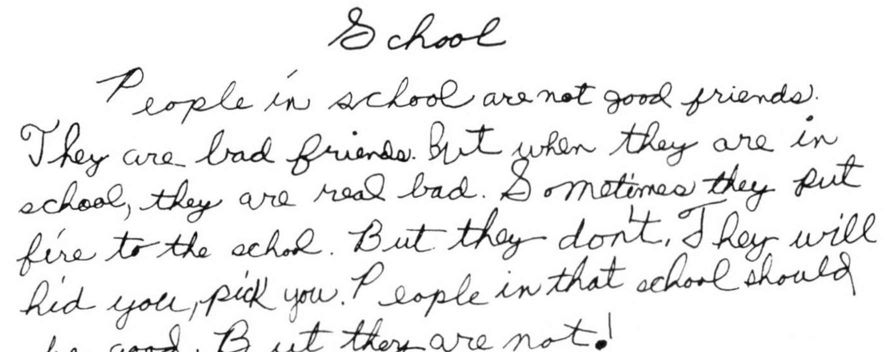

School

People in school are not good friends. They are bad friends. But when they are in school, they are real bad. Sometimes they put fire to the school. But they don't. They will hid you, pick you. People in that school should be good. But they are not!

Determining Words Per Sentence		
No. of sentences	=	8
No. of words	=	48
Words per sentence	=	6

Figure 12.2
Assessing Fluency

Table 12.2
Representative Diagnostic Tests

Test	Age/Grade Appropriateness	Type of Administration	Norm- or Criterion-Referenced	Subtests	Type of Derived Scores	Features
Picture Story Language Test (PSLT) (Myklebust, 1965)	(A) 7 to 17	Individual or Group	Norm	(3 scoring areas) 1. Productivity Scale 2. Syntax Scale 3. Abstract-Concrete Scale (Semantics)	1. Age-Equivalent 2. Percentile Ranks 3. Standard Scores	Student is shown a picture and then asked to write a story about what is seen.
Test of Written Language (TOWL–2) (Hammill & Larsen, 1988)	(A) 8-6 to 14-5	Individual	Norm	**Principal Subtests** 1. Vocabulary 2. Thematic Maturity 3. Spelling 4. Word Usage 5. Style **Supplemental Subtests** 1. Thought Units 2. Handwriting	1. Grade-Equivalent 2. Standard Scores 3. Written Language Quotient	Student is shown a series of three pictures and then asked to write a story based on these pictures. The sample obtained is used to determine scores for Vocabulary, Thematic Maturity, Thought Units, and Handwriting. The other subtests are presented separately.
Brigance Diagnostic Inventory of Basic Skills (Brigance, 1982)	(G) Pre K–9	Individual, Group	Criterion	1. Capitalization 2. Punctuation 3. Parts of Speech	None	This instrument is used most effectively when a student's responses can be analyzed in greater depth and used for educational planning; no normative data are available.

Source: Adapted from "Written Language" by E. A. Polloway, J. R. Patton, and S. A. Cohen in *Promising Practices for Exceptional Children: Curriculum Implications* (p. 298), edited by E. L. Meyen, G. A. Vergason, and R. J. Whelan, 1983, Denver: Love Publishing.

Table 12.3
Representative Informal Procedures for Assessing Written Expression

Technique	Description	Methodology	Example	Comment
1. Type-Token Ratio	Measure of the variety of words used (types) in relation to overall number of words used (token)	$\dfrac{\text{Different words used}}{\text{Total words used}}$	type = 28 token = 50 ratio = $\dfrac{28}{50}$ = .56	Greater diversity of usage implies a more mature writing style
2. Index of Diversification	Measure of diversity of word usage	$\dfrac{\text{Total number of words used}}{\text{Number of occurrences of the most frequently used word}}$	total words = 72 number of times the word **the** appeared = 12 index = 6	An increase in the index value implies a broader vocabulary base.
3. Average Sentence Length	Measure of sentence usage (number of words per sentence)	$\dfrac{\text{Total Number of words used}}{\text{Total number of sentences}}$	total words = 54 total sentences = 9 words per sentence = 6	Longer length of sentences implies more mature writing ability.
4. Error Analysis	Measure of word and sentence usage	Compare errors found in a writing sample with list of common errors		Teacher can determine error patterns and can prioritize concerns.

5. T-Unit Length (Hunt, 1965)	Measure of writing maturity	1. Determine the number of discrete thought units (T-units)
		2. Determine average length of T-unit:
		$\dfrac{\text{Total words}}{\text{Total number of T-units}}$
		3. Analyze quantitative variables:
		  a. no. of sentences used;
		  b. no. of T-units
		  c. no. of words per T-unit
		Note: Use the following convention for summarizing this information (no. of sentences; no. of T-units; no. of words per T-unit.
		4. Analyze qualitative nature of sentences
			"The summer was almost over and the children were ready to go back to school."
			Quantitative:
			(1; 2; 5 + 10)
			Qualitative:
			1. compound sentence
			2. adverbs:
			  of degree — "almost"
			  of place — "back"
			3. adjective — "ready"
			4. infinitive — "to go"
			5. prepositional phrase
			  adverbial of place —
			  "to school"
				This technique gives the teacher information in relation to productivity and maturity of writing skills.

Source: From "Written Language" by E. A. Polloway, J. R. Patton, and S. A. Cohen in *Promising Practices for Exceptional Children: Curriculum Implications* (pp. 300–301), edited by E. L. Meyen, G. A. Vergason, and R. J. Whelan, 1983. Denver: Love Publishing.

to *function.* Teachers should recognize these types to determine whether a student's writing shows a variety in style. The four sentence forms, and examples of each, are:

1. *Fragment:* Wherever the girl wanted to go.
2. *Simple:* The quick brown fox jumped over the lazy dog.
3. *Compound:* The girls were unable to attend the party, and the boys were very disappointed.
4. *Complex:* After the rain had subsided, the game was able to continue.

When assessing sentence form, teachers should be concerned primarily with the frequency of fragments and the varied use of the other three alternatives.

The four functions result in these types of sentences:

1. *Declarative:* Bryant has a good jump shot from the corner.
2. *Interrogative:* Does the weatherman think it will snow tonight?
3. *Imperative:* Line up immediately.
4. *Exclamatory:* What a beautiful day it is!

When assessing function, a teacher looks for the varied use of the four options in appropriate situations.

As fluency increases, students also need to develop a broader written *vocabulary.* With a larger number of words in the writer's repertoire, he or she can avoid redundancy and begin developing a more specific, descriptive, and fluid style. Two basic approaches to assessing vocabulary are: (a) determining type-token ratios, and (b) documenting the use of unusual words (Cartwright, 1969).

Type-Token Ratio   A type-token ratio measures the variety of words the writer uses (types) against the overall number of words used (tokens), providing a percentage of different words in a given passage. Thus, a ratio of 1.0 indicates no redundancy; a ratio of .5 suggests frequent repetition. Figure 12.3 shows the computation of the type-token ratio for a writing sample by a 12-year-old child.

Computation of the ratio can be used for comparative purposes (as with IEP goals) as long as the length of the passage being analyzed is held constant. Generally, a passage length of 50 to 100 words is the most valuable in determining the ratio. Based on the use of type-token ratios, an instructional objective might, for example, call for an increase in ratio from .60 to .70. The assumption is that this increase would reflect a significant improvement in the strength of written vocabulary.

Unusual Words   Analyzing the number of unusual words in a passage can supplement the type-token ratio. Here, the teacher identifies the words in a writing sample that the student did not use in previous efforts. For beginning writers, teachers might focus on words that do not appear on frequency-of-use lists. For more advanced writers, judgments may have to be subjective.

Although this form of assessment is less objective than other measures, it can form the basis for a running list of new words the student is using. Additions to the list

> I would like to help needy children. And I would like to get married + have children of my own. I would like to adopt children + bring them up as my own. I would like to be a helper to join Vistas + teach children how to get a education like I am. Or teach them about God's Word.

Type-Token Ratio		
No. of tokens (total words)	=	60
No. of types (different words)	=	34
Type-token ratio = 34/60	=	58%

Figure 12.3
Assessing Vocabulary: Type-Token Ratio

then could be tied to reinforcement strategies. Figure 12.4 shows a sample writing passage that a teacher subjectively assessed for unusual words. In light of the student's past efforts, the teacher identified the five words given below the sample as unusual for this child. An alternative is to involve students in the process through a self-assessment scheme.

STRUCTURAL AND ORGANIZATIONAL ANALYSIS

To assess a child's proficiency at writing correct sentences and organizing them into clear paragraphs, teachers can use structural and organizational analysis. *Structural analysis* refers to the grammatical aspects of sentences, and *organizational analysis* measures form beyond the sentence, such as paragraphing and compositional style.

The evaluation of structural skills stems directly from the use of error analysis. The teacher should determine what grammatical components have priority for an individual child and then assess whether these skills are or are not part of the child's writing repertoire. Teachers can record when the skill was first taught and acquired, when evidence showed that the child had maintained and applied the skill in compositions, and when subsequent follow-up checks were made. Figure 12.5 presents a sample form that might be used for this purpose.

Based on a profile of a child's structural problems, the teacher can look for trends in error patterns, which then become priorities for remediation. Figure 12.6 presents a language sample, written by an 11-year-old boy, from which the teacher devel-

I was thinking one day about my future in my bedroom one day. that I was going to be a state police. I alway wanted to drive a police car. the reason why I wont to be a state police because they go fast and the other reason is to control the siren and flasher on the roof.

Unusual Words/Subjectively Selected	
police	flasher
control	reason
siren	

Figure 12.4
Assessing Vocabulary: Unusual Words

oped a tentative analysis of priority concerns. Subsequent writing samples would help the teacher clarify instructional objectives.

Error analysis does have limitations. Most important, children frequently use only the grammatical forms they have mastered; therefore, error analysis procedures should be broadened by having the students identify specific errors in unfamiliar sentences (Hammill & Poplin, 1978).

Error analysis also may focus on a student's weaknesses and produce a failure set toward writing. To overcome this problem and make error analysis a motivator, teachers should involve children in instructional planning aimed at acquiring new skills instead of correcting mistakes. As Weiner (1979) noted, teachers also can help children understand the distinction between mistakes that are errors in execution and mistakes that are the result of problems in processing, logical thinking, and expression.

Organizational analysis focuses on children's ability to clearly deliver their ideas. For students who are beginning to write, teachers should judge whether the composition is or is not generally sequential and easy to follow and whether it does or does not convey a message consistent with the writer's original intent. At an advanced level, evaluation also assesses specific paragraphing skills, and teachers should watch for the use of topical sentences, the establishment of one major or central idea, and the presence of transitional words within sentences and transitional sentences between paragraphs. Figure 12.7 presents a paragraph written by a 10-year-old student along with an analysis of its organization.

Specific Skills	Acquisition	Maintenance	Follow-up
1. Punctuation			
a. period			
1. sentence			
2. abbreviations			
b. question mark			
c. comma			
d. apostrophe			
1. possession			
2. contractions			
e. colon			
f. hyphen			
g. exclamation mark			
h. semicolon			
2. Capitalization			
a. first word in sentence			
b. proper nouns			
c. I			
d. titles			
e. abbreviations			
3. Verb Usage			
a. subject agreement			
b. tense			
c. use of auxiliaries (is, etc.)			
4. Pronoun Usage			
a. subject v. object			
b. unclear antecedents			
5. Other Word Usage			
a. unneeded words added			
b. omissions			
c. inappropriate plurals			
d. incorrect adjectives			
e. incorrect adverbs			
f. nonstandard English patterns			
6. Sentence Sense			
a. run-on sentences			
b. choppy sentences			
c. overuse of "and"			
d. inappropriate use of fragments			

Figure 12.5
Written Structural Analysis: Sample Form

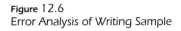

I are going to get a good job. Have a nice house. And I'll have a motorbike and a chevrolet car, Have a girl friend, But never get married.

my job will an artest. So I can quit when ever I want to and rest,

> **Preliminary Error Analysis**
> 1. Absence of subject pronoun (I)
> 2. Verb forms of to be
> 3. Verb forms for have
> 4. Use of sentence fragments
> 5. Use of choppy sentences

Figure 12.6
Error Analysis of Writing Sample

IDEATION

Ideation deals with content and is the most subjective of the assessment techniques discussed here. Nevertheless, ideation is the cornerstone of true expression and therefore should be viewed as critical to the evaluation process.

The assessment of subject matter should be separated from the evaluation of structural difficulties. Lerner (1985) has encouraged teachers to consider using dual grades for writing (if grading is being used) so that students can be evaluated separately on the two aspects of writing represented by (a) subject matter and (b) structure.

When assessing ideation, the teacher should consider the following questions;

1. Is the composition *relevant* to the topic assigned or selected and consistent with stated objectives?
2. Do the ideas in the composition represent *original* thinking on the child's part?
3. Does the composition demonstrate expression of *personal perspectives* on the topic rather than relying on comments by others?
4. Do the ideas expressed show a *clarity of thought*, presenting the major facets of a topic in appropriate sequence?
5. Does the composition reflect a *basic interest* in the topic, and thus a *motivation* to commit ideas to the written form?

Considering these evaluative questions can be essential, particularly when choosing the proper means for teaching an individual child.

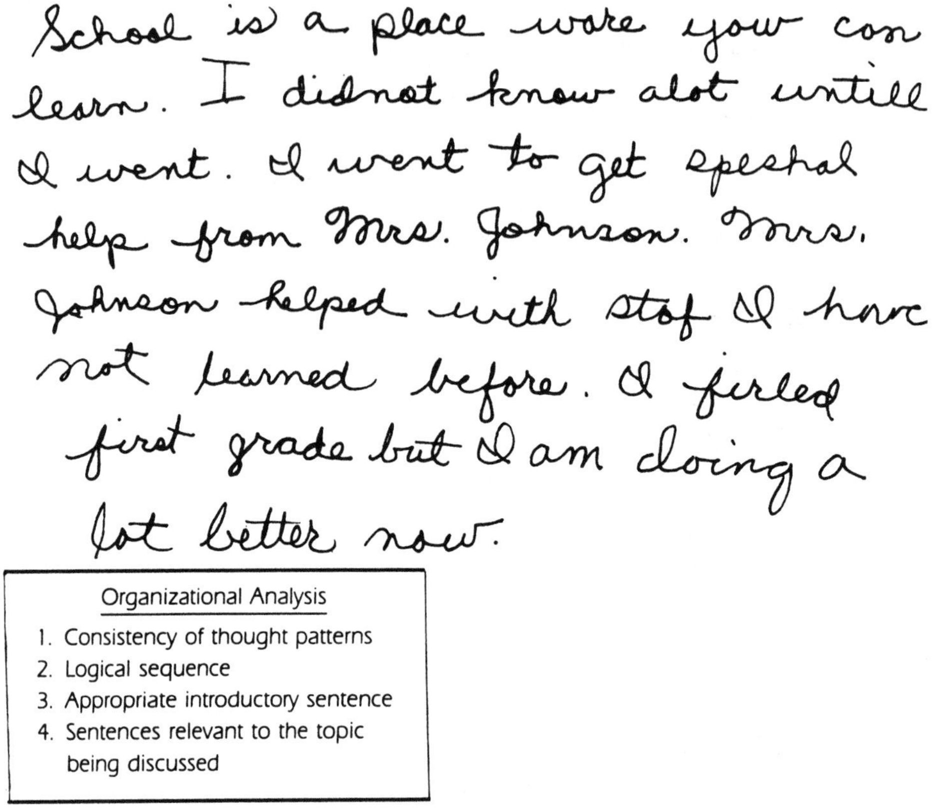

School is a place ware you can learn. I didnot know alot untill I went. I went to get speshal help from Mrs. Johnson. Mrs. Johnson helped with stof I have not learned before. I firled first grade but I am doing a lot better now.

Organizational Analysis

1. Consistency of thought patterns
2. Logical sequence
3. Appropriate introductory sentence
4. Sentences relevant to the topic being discussed

Figure 12.7
Assessing Organization Skills

ADDITIONAL ASSESSMENT AREAS

In addition to the above-described areas of informal assessment, the following items developed by Polloway et al. (1983, pp. 297, 302–304) may prove helpful.

Input

1. Students' educational backgrounds.
2. How students spend their free time.
3. What books students have read.
4. What students talk about when they are at home with peers.
5. An individual student's learning style or how he or she learns more efficiently.

Motivation

1. The value of importance of writing as students perceive it.
2. Students' interests, as ascertained by administering interest inventories that explore educational, extracurricular, and community interests, as well as preferences in hobbies, books, movies, and the like.

3. Career goals.
4. Reinforcement preferences.

Expressive Purpose
1. Can students establish a purpose when they write?
2. Are they able to brainstorm (use divergent thinking)?
3. Can they progressively narrow down the scope of a topic (use convergent thinking)?
4. Can they generate written samples that reflect their own thinking?

Utilitarian Purpose
1. Can students understand *why* they are writing something?
2. Do they realize *to whom* they are writing?
3. Do they recognize the *major components* of their task?

Mechanics   As previously discussed, both formal and informal techniques are useful in assessing students' written expressive ability in the areas of vocabulary acquisition, word usage, and sentence structure. Student-produced writing samples are preferable to contrived samples.

More directive efforts may be required to assess students' abilities in paragraph sense and organizational integrity. To assess paragraph sense, a teacher might survey writing samples and look for the following in the student's paragraphs:

1. One main idea.
2. A topic sentence that focuses attention on the main idea.
3. Supporting sentences that detail information relevant to the topic.
4. A summary or transitional sentence when appropriate.
5. Indentation and a new line for beginning a new paragraph.

With regard to organizational integrity of the total product, the following are important considerations:

1. Logical sequencing of ideas throughout the composition, essay, or letter.
2. Internal consistency (Do conclusions follow from the discussion? Do specific points made relate to the general topic?).
3. Clarity of thought.
4. Continuity of movement rather than abrupt changes.

Proofreading   To a great extent, many of the formal assessment devices available actually require proofreading skills. They often are restricted, however, to the skill of editing for structural errors rather than editing for content. To determine if students are able to effectively use proofreading and editing skills, evaluation could focus on the following questions:

1. Can students identify specific mechanical errors within a sentence or a paragraph?
2. Can they identify organizational and ideational problems within a composition?
3. Can they effectively use strategies for proofreading (e.g., a sequential list of self-check statements)?

4. Can they evaluate whether the objectives or purposes of the completed written draft have been met?
5. Can they transfer these skills from contrived exercises to actual written assignments?

The successful blend of information from informal and formal techniques within a structured conceptualization of written language will enable the teacher to overcome some of the inherent problems in assessment noted earlier. The result should be a clear profile of an individual's strengths and difficulties, which then can assist in designing appropriate instructional programs.

INSTRUCTIONAL STRATEGIES

A written language methodology and curriculum designed distinctly for students with handicaps is not being proposed in this discussion. Rather, teachers should organize their curriculum around regular class language activities to the extent that students participate in general education programs. Regardless of the situation, methods of teaching written expression more often reflect close ties to, and adaptations of, general curriculum than in any other language area (Kirk & Johnson, 1951; Langone, 1990; Wallace & McLoughlin, 1988). Therefore, the teacher's task is to begin from a foundation of sound instructional strategies for written communication and make modifications that will be effective for individual needs of learners who have disabilities.

PREWRITING

The basis for beginning writing and written language instruction is *stimulation*. Students must receive input that fosters the formulation of their own ideas. Teachers should capitalize on the other language domains to enhance this process. For example, opportunities to talk about personal experiences and listen to others' encounters can provide a basis for writing purpose and content. Reading interesting stories can develop the student's desire to communicate feelings about the ideas the author expresses. Dawson and Zollinger (1957) outlined an instructional language experience-type approach that provides a means of integrating the various language arts.

Petty and Bowen (1967) have emphasized the importance of ensuring an appropriate climate for writing. They noted several aspects of such a climate that would provide an atmosphere conducive for writing: the teacher's attitudes and personality (characterized by an open and friendly rather than a rigid demeanor), establishment of frequent opportunities for writing, and students' awareness of the potential outlet for their work. Students who have disabilities need to develop a sense that writing is an enjoyable rather than a punitive activity. An emphasis on stimulation through oral language does not ensure improvement in specific task skills (Phelps-Gunn & Phelps-Terasaki, 1982); however, it does provide the requisite orientation and cognitive focus necessary to begin the writing task.

A preeminent concern is for the development of intention to communicate, the desire to share one's thoughts with a given readership. Without attention to motivation, an individual's writing likely will reflect only minimal personal perspective and creativity and will fail to realize the basic goals of functional writing tasks.

Ideally, motivation should be a function of one's own internal needs to communicate and to express feelings, ideas, and needs. As Tway (1975) noted in reference to children without disabilities: "No one can really motivate anyone else to write; motivation must come from within. Teachers can only stimulate" (p. 193). Tway also suggested that motivation could best be developed by showing basic respect for a student's expression, by establishing real purpose in writing, by endowing writing with a special sense of importance and enjoyment, and by ensuring the writer that a specific goal is in sight.

In the case of exceptional learners, however, motivational problems often are intensified because of the failure set that many students have acquired through previous writing experiences. Alley and Deshler (1979) emphasized this point by noting that students' feelings toward writing should be their teachers' first consideration. As Lerner (1981) stated, children who have experienced a dearth of success:

> . . . soon learn to beat the game by limiting their writing vocabulary to words they know how to spell, by keeping their sentences simple, by avoiding complex and creative ideas, and by keeping their compositions short. (p. 344)

Given this general tendency of some writers, Brigham, Graubard, and Stans (1972) questioned the basic assumption that "writing flows from the writer" (p. 442) and that primary emphasis must be placed in building motivation solely through stimulation. The option they proposed was to identify a series of objective aspects of writing, place reinforcement contingencies on them, and thus improve compositional skills through the sequential reinforcement of specific skills. The ABA methodology and results of this study and related ones are further discussed in succeeding sections.

Based on the valid identification of students' interests, anchoring a writing program to these interests seems desirable, keeping in mind that what appeals to some students may not appeal to all their classmates. If teachers truly are concerned about individualizing their students' programs, capitalizing on students' interests makes good pedagogical sense.

Initial instruction with beginning writers should focus on helping them set purpose and complete instructional exercises designed to emphasize task objectives. Short, specific assignments are valuable for sharply defining the student's task and, therefore, enabling a clear focus on the purpose of the assignment. For example, exercises with a creative purpose could include writing a paragraph on the descriptive properties of an interesting classroom object, on the qualities of friendship, on one's favorite time of the day, or on a scene from a favorite movie. Utilitarian exercises could include composing an invitation to a party, an announcement of a school movie, a covert note to a friend, a brief article for the school newspaper, or a postcard to be sent to a relative.

Setting purpose continues to have importance for advanced writers as well. For expressive writing, students should be encouraged to ask themselves these types of questions:

- What interests me most about this topic?
- What information do I know about this topic?

- What else do I need to learn about it?
- How can I relate this information?
- How can I best organize it?
- What are my personal opinions about the subject?
- How can I convey my personal feelings in my writing?

For utilitarian writing, students should consider these questions:

- What is my objective in this task?
- To whom am I writing? What do they know about this topic?
- What do they want to know?
- How can I make sure I convey the necessary and correct information?
- Do I need to do research on the topic to be familiar with it?
- How should I arrange and organize my writing to be most effective in meeting my objective?

To facilitate the prewriting or planning stage, teachers can introduce their students to a variety of formats that assist in the planning process. Figure 12.8 illustrates four alternative formats that may prove useful.

DRAFTING

Of the three components within this writing model, the writing or drafting stage is the broadest. Isaacson (1987) clearly contrasts the writing products of skilled and unskilled writers, providing a good overview of the types of difficulties common during this stage. Key questions in writing instruction are: How are skills most effectively learned? How are they most effectively taught?

The distinctions made by Smith (1982), as discussed by Isaacson (1987, 1989), illustrate variant writer responsibilities. Two roles inherent in the writing process are the author and the secretary. The *author* role revolves around formulating and organizing ideas, and selecting words and phrases to express those ideas. The *secretarial* role emphasizes the physical and mechanical concerns of writing, such as legibility, spelling, punctuation, and grammatical rules. Both roles are critical to the writer's success, so orientations toward both are important in an instructional program (Gould, 1991; Isaacson, 1989).

Teach-Write Approach   Sink (1975) distinguished between a focus on teach-write versus write-teach. The former corresponds reasonably well with the secretarial role of writing and may be considered a product approach. This approach emphasizes formal grammar instruction, an emphasis on structure, skill exercises, perhaps diagramming of sentences, and often a reliance on worksheets and workbook pages. The teach-write approach is extremely common in classrooms; however, its traditional usage is not indicative of its proven effectiveness.

After extensively reviewing 50 years of research on this topic, Sherwin (1969) found little evidence of its success with learners in general; there is even less reason to expect that the approach would be effective for individuals with disabilities. Sherwin (1969) concluded that this type of instruction "is an inefficient and ineffective way to

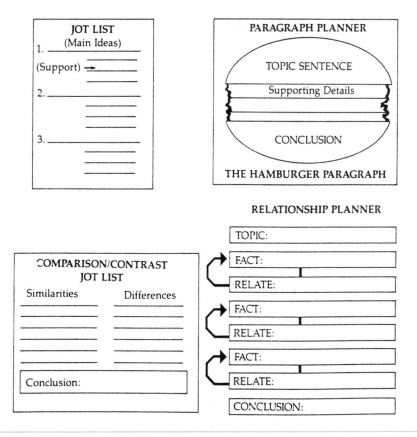

Source: From "Strategies for Teaching Composition Skills to Students with Learning Disabilities" by A. Vallecorsa, R. R. Ledford, and G. G. Parnell, 1991, *Teaching Exceptional Children, 23*(2), p. 53. Copyright 1991 by the Council for Exceptional Children. Reprinted by permission.

Figure 12.8
Formats for Various Types of Student Writing

help students achieve proficiency in writing" (p. 135). He cited a 1962 dissertation by Harris, deemed to be the most methodologically sound of the research reviewed, which concluded that the approach may have a relatively harmful effect on the correctness of children's writing. Although Sherwin (1969) also concluded that writing alone does not teach writing, he summarized his review by noting that the most important features of instruction are "motivation, selective criticism, discussion, practical explanation, and revision" (p. 168).

The key concern with a teach-write approach is that instructional activities can be completed without opportunity for true writing. At the same time, the activities carry the threat of possible damage to motivation, overwhelming students and leading them to respond with fear and avoidance (Gould, 1991), and serving as a reminder that they "can't" write (Lynch & Jones, 1989). Additionally, it requires a major commitment to time, something that special education programs may already have in limited supply for writing instruction (Christenson, Thurlow, Ysseldyke, & McVicar, 1989; Silverman, Zigmond, Zimmerman, & Vallecorsa, 1981; Zigmond, Vallecorsa, & Leinhardt, 1980).

Write-Teach Approach   The alternative is the write-teach focus, a process orientation to writing, initially stressing the primacy of the author role. This focus emphasizes ideation over form honoring ideas and later establishing structure. The write-teach approach also capitalizes on the desire to write and avoids stifling the writing effort. Structure is then emphasized within the context of actual writing opportunities. This approach is more holistic, because students learn to write through the process of writing (Gould, 1991).

Graves (1985) stated the case for this approach:

> Most teaching of writing is pointed toward the eradication of error, the mastery of minute, meaningless components that make little sense to the child. Small wonder. Most language arts texts, workbooks, computer software, and reams of behavioral objectives are directed toward the "easy" control of components that will show more specific growth. Although some growth may be evident on components, rarely does it result in the child's use of writing as a tool for learning and enjoyment. Make no mistake, component skills are important; if children do not learn to spell or use a pencil to get words on paper, they won't use writing for learning any more than the other children drilled on component skills. The writing-processing approach simply stresses meaning first, and then skills in the context of meaning. (p. 43)

Even though research with students who are progressing normally supports the proposition that they learn to write by writing, no research conclusively supports this presumption for students with mild disabilities (Lynch & Jones, 1989). Nevertheless, the write-teach process-type approach receives more widespread support. Cohen and Plaskon (1980) encouraged the use of spontaneous daily written expression opportunities as a basis for instruction in conventional skills. Poplin et al. (1980) concluded:

> Until otherwise proven, meaningful experiences with immediate, reasonable, and knowledgeable feedback still seem to offer the most effective method of improving mechanical, conventional knowledge of the writing process without interfering with and stifling the all-important ability to "get across" in writing what the student intends to communicate. (p. 52)

The write-teach option has several implications for instruction. Most significant is that for writing to improve, students need to write regularly. Graves (1985) recommended that students write at least four days per week; irregular instruction merely reminds students of their inability to write. In addition, the amount of time for writing must be increased; Christenson et al. (1989) reported an average of only 15 minutes per day for written language (composition) instruction for students with mild disabilities. Providing these opportunities to write in a positive, supportive atmosphere is a logical supplement; and journal writing is an approach that has been used effectively for this purpose.

Given the opportunity to write, developmental skills can be handled through *selective feedback* on a limited number of skills. Students will profit most from feedback specific to their own text and specific to the skills of importance to them. Selective feedback is preferred to the extremes of inordinate corrections on papers and generalized, meaningless comments about "good work" or the like (Polloway & Decker, 1988).

One way to accomplish the selective feedback goal is through a *teacher conferencing approach* (Barenbaum, 1983). With this orientation, the teacher proofreads written assignments and provides feedback directly to students, most often in an oral conference. This approach provides an opportunity to introduce and reinforce specific skills and conventions. A conferencing approach is quite consistent with the process orientation to writing. It helps to promote writing as a thinking act versus a mechanical act. It is a more holistic approach, in which grammar and spelling, for example, can be emphasized within the context of the composing process (Vallecorsa, Ledford, & Parnell, 1991).

Developing Initial Writing Skills   Most writers would probably agree that getting started is the most difficult part of writing. Teachers can help students over this obstacle in several ways.

First, teachers should *provide an atmosphere conducive to expression* by creating a relaxed time in which students view writing as enjoyable rather than punitive. This atmosphere can be fostered by stressing the importance of personal expression and playing down the need to adhere rigidly to prescribed forms. This emphasis should be effective in deterring failure as a part of the student's experiences in writing.

Second, teachers should *tie writing to the child's spoken language*. The language experience approach, developed by Dawson and Zollinger (1957), is closely related to this orientation. Their instructional program proceeds through the following sequence:

1. The child first composes a story and dictates it to the teacher.
2. Then the child copies the story from the teacher's transcription in order to develop technical writing skills.
3. The teacher dictates a story to the child to write.
4. The child completes an unfinished story as dictated to the teacher.
5. The child rewrites the story independently.
6. The teacher designs practice activities that capitalize on specific skills related to written passages.

Teachers also should help beginning writers with functional writing related to specific, defined purposes, as discussed earlier. Assignments might be letters, notes to friends, invitations, directions, announcements, signs, filling out forms, brief biographies, speeches, and news items for school newspapers. These assignments can help the student see the value and relevance of written communication and increase his or her intention to write. By keeping the assignments sharply defined, students can more easily focus their thoughts. As Lovitt (1975) noted, teachers should stress functional skills tied to specific purposes rather than jumping from one objective to another.

Teachers also should keep initial assignments reasonably short. Long assignments or extended writing periods may cause children to link writing with boredom, general disinterest, and perhaps failure. A brief period of 15 to 30 minutes should be enough time for beginning writers to formulate and communicate their ideas.

Developing Vocabulary   As noted earlier, the goal here is to increase the size of students' writing vocabulary and to increase the frequency with which the students use new words. The basis for instruction is to expose students to varied verbal forms and assist them in incorporating the words into their compositions. Specific objectives should include acquiring a store of synonyms for commonly used words, becoming familiar with a variety of descriptive words. and using unusual words and original phrases as alternatives to more typical lexical options.

Teachers should be aware that many otherwise capable students tend to avoid using words they cannot spell, thus reducing the quality of their writing. Only when they can be convinced to not worry about spelling and concentrate on ideas can a true appreciation of their abilities be obtained (Johnson & Myklebust, 1967). Similarly, when working with students for whom English is a second language, the primary concern should be with qualitative aspects rather than with correct spelling.

Cohen and Plaskon (1980) stressed that students who have mild disabilities should develop a vocabulary they can use accurately: "Although the objective is to expand the child's facility with words, it must not be gained at the expense of writing fluency. A functional goal of providing [them] with word skills which allow them to successfully manipulate a limited core of words is advisable" (p. 295). Those authors therefore suggested teaching word clusters that can center on topical themes, including words for naming and describing common actions, personal attributes, and time, as well as facility with prefixes, suffixes, synonyms, and common idiomatic expressions.

Various instructional exercises can be developed to assist in building vocabulary. Van Allen (1976) suggested the use of a *word wall*, which can be devoted to lists of words that might be helpful to students in writing. The list could include high-frequency words, common descriptors, words pertaining to the senses, and specialized words tied to holidays or to specific units being studied. It also could be modified and individualized by developing a notebook of words for each student.

For individual writing assignments, the entire class initially could generate a list of key words to be written on the board. In this way, the conceptual break required to select and revisualize specific words could be avoided, and at the same time students would be provided practice in using these words.

Bailey (1975) suggested two other teaching ideas that can help students build a store of written labels within categories. In *adjective brainstorming*, teachers present a word to the students and have them generate specific descriptors that might apply (e.g., summer: hot, humid, sunny, fun). And in the instructional exercise *functions*, the children list examples of objects or things that serve a specific function (e.g., car repairs: wrench, screwdriver, rubber hammer, lubricating oil).

Several studies have supported the value of *reinforcement contingencies* on vocabulary development. Maloney and Hopkins (1973) reported that points awarded to students in grades four through six, contingent on the number of different adjectives and action verbs used and the variant ways to begin sentences, enhanced these three aspects of composition and also resulted in more creative papers. Glover and Gary (1976) suggested that students' writing could be improved by developing vocabulary usage through the identification of "unusual uses" for a variety of nouns. Four measures of creativity (fluency, flexibility, elaboration, and originality) improved as a result of applying this technique. Kraetsch (1981) reported data indicating that oral instructions to a student to write "as many words and ideas as you can" had a significant effect on written output as measured by the quantity and diversification of words and the quantity of sentences produced. In each study, vocabulary was shown to improve, along with other aspects of writing, through reinforcement strategies.

Developing Sentences   The most important focus within the mechanics of written language should be the sentence. By stressing well developed sentences, teachers wil be training students to think clearly and to express themselves in complete thoughts Many students who have difficulty writing may rely on simple, repetitive, "safe" sen tence structures, resulting in less fluent writing products. Others may experiment un successfully with variety and produce awkward constructions (Hall, 1981). For either of these two subgroups of poor writers, the instructional focus must be on teaching students to expand sentences within acceptable structural patterns. Several approaches to sentence expansion have been developed.

An appropriate beginning point is to balance encouragement for "real writing" with use of *patterned sentence guides* and structures (Isaacson, 1987). Using guides relieves content demands and structural ambiguities and can assist students in concentrating on effective communication.

The simplest form of patterned guide is labeling a picture set into a proscribed sentence pattern. For example, one could have the student label simple objects with a sentence such as, "This boy is tall."

After this beginning, several alternatives are available. A relatively straightforward technique for teaching sentence structure, developed by Giordano (1982) is called the *CATS approach*. A CATS exercise encompasses the four stages of *C*opy, *A*lter (i.e., substitute a word), *T*ransform (i.e., change a tense, a number, the gender, negation, an interrogative), and *S*upply a response (to a teacher-generated question). This approach provides a simple transition from initial writing to the subsequent use of appropriate sentence structures. Students are encouraged to actually write and move from initial copying to generating their own responses.

Fennimore (1980) reported on instructional activities developed to facilitate sentence understanding and variety. She referred to these as *sentence extension activities*, because the basic premise of the instruction is to enhance students' oral, and then written, sentences by enlarging the repertoire of words and forms available to them. For example, the sentence, "The boy ran" was extended by having the class identify lists of alternatives to *boy* and *ran*, adverb and adjective modifiers for the subject, modifiers of the verb, prepositional phrases to indicate where the boy ran, and so forth. This type of exercise then can become incorporated into compositional efforts that may stem from the original brief sentence form.

Sentence expansion is the basis for the *Phelps Sentence Guide Program* (Phelps-Terasaki & Phelps, 1980). This systematic program involves a structured questioning process to which students respond in complete sentences. Logical extensions include instruction on nouns (e.g., *Who* did it?), verbs (e.g., *What* was done?), descriptors (e.g., *What kind?*), and objects (e.g., *To what? For what?*). By combining oral and written language, these subskills and other related ones can be taught within the context of sentence meaning in lieu of being presented as specific semi-isolated items in a grammar instructional sequence.

A revision of this popular program is *Teaching Competence in Written Language* (Phelps-Terasaki & Phelps-Gunn, 1988). The authors have indicated that the program is based upon three elements: (a) a modification of the Fitzgerald Key (generally similar to the Sentence Guide; see Figure 12.9), (b) the use of an interactive teacher-student structure, and (c) an emphasis on social and contextual (pragmatic) uses of written language. The program contains 44 lessons ranging from introduction to the subject of a sentence to persuasive paragraphs.

A subsequent logical step toward the extension of sentences can come through *sentence combining*. This involves expanding simple sentences into more complex ones. Research indicates that it is an effective way to improve the overall quality of writing and can assist in increasing syntactic maturity (Isaacson, 1987; Scarmadalia & Bereiter, 1986).

In Strong's (1983) program of sentence combining, the student has the task of combining clusters of sentences; he or she is informed that this can be accomplished in a variety of ways and that no single specific response is indicated. Below is a cluster that appears early in the program; students are to combine the respective pairs of sentences into a single sentence.

2.1. Cowboys swagger around.	2.2. They get their gear together.
3.1. Clowns roll out their barrels.	3.2. The barrels are battered.
4.1. Bulls stand in their pens.	4.2. The bulls are huge.
5.1. The sun beats down.	5.2. The announcer introduces the first entry.
6.1. People lean forward in the bleachers.	6.2. They strain to see the chute.
7.1. A shout goes up.	7.2. The bull comes charging out.
8.1. He is a giant animal.	8.2. He has a tornado's energy.
9.1. His eyes are fierce.	9.2. His horns are wicked.
10.1. The cowboy is tossed to one side.	10.2. He tumbles end over end. (p. 5)

Although Strong's program does not begin with true writing, because students are working from what is already written, it encourages them to expand and develop their own creation. Individual tasks finish with an *invitation* to finish the story, which requires students to generate their own ideas.

Strong's program provides a prototype for instruction in this area, but it is limited with students who have disabilities because the lessons are not extensive enough to provide the amount of necessary practice. Therefore, if teachers use the sentence combining approach, they have to also generate their own clusters. One practical example of how that can be done was presented by Reutzel (1986).

Developing Paragraphs   Once children have acquired a working knowledge of sentence structure and grammatical forms, the emphasis can shift to overall organization of paragraphs and short stories. Burns (1974) said that children need to learn these rules before they can understand paragraph sense:

1. A paragraph should deal with a single topic.
2. A paragraph typically has a topic sentence.

CONNECTORS	WHO/WHAT?	DOING WHAT?	DETAILS
And First Second Next Then Last	Which? What kind of? How much? How many?		Why? (because, since, so that) What? When? Where? How?

Source: From *Teaching Competence in Written Language: A Systematic Program for Developing Writing Skills* by D. Phelps-Terasaki and T. Phelps-Gunn, 1988, Austin, TX: PRO-ED, p. 6. Copyright 1988 by PRO-ED, Inc. Reprinted by permission.

Figure 12.9
Sentence Guide

3. A paragraph typically develops a topic.
4. Sentences in a paragraph are related to each other.
5. A long, self-contained, expository paragraph should be concluded or summarized with a general sentence related to the topic or beginning sentence. The last sentence of one paragraph may lead into the next paragraph. (p. 96)

Otto, McMenemy, and Smith (1973) suggested that "the most important concept for students to attain relative to paragraph development is that written communication is essentially a matter of making assertions and elaborating upon them" (p. 394). Consistent with this statement, specific teaching techniques should help students state their basic premises and expand their thoughts.

Buchan (1979) developed a technique for teaching organization based on the need to assert and elaborate. She called this technique the *why and because* method, because the student is first encouraged to question a statement and then specify reasons to support that opinion. For example, students can be asked why "good friends are the most important thing in the world." Their answers ("because . . .") then serve as topical sentences for a paragraph or a series of paragraphs on the subject.

Brief, functional tasks provide an excellent opportunity for initially teaching the concept of paragraphs. For instance, writing a letter to purchase an item fits this format very well. The topical sentence can identify the item to be purchased. The additional sentences then provide a description of the item, a discussion of the form of payments, and the address to which it should be sent (Polloway & Decker, 1988). Practice such as this can help to reinforce the concept of expressing only one main idea in a paragraph.

Letter writing also can be used to illustrate how paragraphs are related and frame an overall successful communication. For example, a friendly letter can be shown to (prototypically) include three paragraphs: news about oneself, questions about the friend to whom you are writing, and answers to questions that may be been posed in a previous letter. Phelps-Terasaki and Phelps-Gunn's (1988) program provides a series of lessons for teaching students how to write more well developed paragraphs as a way to furthering their skills in composition.

POSTWRITING

Revising and editing are critical skills upon which the quality of a finished product hinges, particularly when teachers are using the write-teach approach. To expect that most students will automatically revise and edit their work would be naive. As noted earlier, many students may come to view proofreading as an aversive rather than a positive process. Even those who are willing to revise and edit must develop that ability; they must be shown *how* to proofread (Hillerich, 1979). The teacher's role, therefore, is one of modeling the specific techniques inherent in the revision and editing process and delineating its advantages to the finished product.

For revision to become acceptable to students, they must be sold on the concept of the working draft. To present this concept, the writing stage should be discussed as simply the initial effort to get on paper the information to be shared, and the postwriting stage as an alternative to the conceptual breaks that might occur within the task. The postwriting stage must evolve toward a positive association for students; it has to shift beyond the association of rewriting as punitive action.

The instructional goal is to have students learn the basic steps necessary to revise their writing and to later apply the steps independently. The questions listed below, incorporating suggestions by Dankowski (1966), Burns (1980), and Polloway et al. (1983), provide an outline of self-evaluation procedures for writers to follow:

1. Does each sentence make sense?
2. Is every word spelled correctly?
3. Are punctuation marks used correctly? Are any needed marks omitted?
4. Are words capitalized that should be?
5. Have I used descriptive words and phrases?
6. Are any of the points vague and in need of clarification?
7. Can anything be said more clearly?
8. Overall, is the paper organized in a way to make the reader's job an easy one?
9. Have I met the objectives?

The entire proofreading process may be too involved for students with writing difficulties to tackle at one time. Therefore, although complete evaluation would require consideration of all aspects, one or two should be selected for given assignments until students refine both their writing and editing skills.

Update

Story Grammar Strategies

The use of story grammar strategies has become a popular way to enhance the writing and reading skills of students and, in particular, students with special needs. Hagood (1997) outlines a series of strategies that provide ways to enhance learning for students. These strategies include:

- Teach students to use self-questioning techniques to increase their comprehension of a narrative text (i.e., Who is the story about? Where does it take place? What is the problem in the story? How is the problem solved? How does the main character feel about the solution?).
- Teach students to use story maps to organize a story's components (i.e., use visual organizers to enable students to enhance their understanding).
- Teach students to use story grammar to increase their writing skills (i.e., use explicit instruction to assist students in organizing their ideas in order to write for an audience).
- Develop group narrative dramatizations through the use of visual, auditory, and kinesthetic learning channels (e.g., use multisensory activities to enhance students' involvement with understanding and communicating stories).
- Teach students to analyze and critically compare the story elements of two similar stories (e.g., use graphic organizers to discuss similarities and differences between specific stories).
- Teach students to manipulate and analyze the components of story grammar (e.g., rewrite stories by changing, for example, the setting of a story and modifying other elements that necessarily change when the setting does).

Source: Adapted from: Hagood, B. F. (1997) Reading and writing with help from story grammar. *Teaching Exceptional Children, 29*(4), 10–14.

Organizing proofreading instructional exercises in the classroom can be done in a variety of ways. One effective technique to develop an initial orientation toward proofreading is to have students practice verbalizing the various steps. Consistent with this approach, Hansen (1978) suggested that students work on the editing process by reading their stories aloud to the teacher during individual conferences to learn to listen for inconsistencies. Gould (1991) indicated that revision also can be facilitated in group conferences in which peers provide feedback on an individual's work, asking questions about things that are unclear and discussing possible changes.

One helpful approach to organize proofreading activities is *error monitoring*, a learning strategy represented by the acronym *COPS* (Schumaker et al., 1981):

C   Have I *capitalized* the first word and proper nouns?
O   What is the *overall* appearance? Have I made any handwriting, margin, messy, or spacing errors?
P   Have I used end *punctuation*, commas, and semicolons correctly?
S   Do the words look like they are *spelled* right? Can I sound them out, or should I use the dictionary?

COPS is intended to be introduced one step at a time. Once students have learned a given skill, they can be introduced to the process of proofreading for that skill. After they have been trained to proofread for each of the components separately, they can be directed to use all four of them at the same time. COPS subsequently can serve as a way to review completed compositions or essays and search for specific errors as indicated.

Obviously the process of proofreading has far more to it than simply checking for capitalization, overall appearance, punctuation, and spelling. If students acquire these skills, instruction should begin to focus on higher levels of editing, with special attention to content and organization. Figure 12.10 provides an evaluation guide that Vallecorsa et al. (1991) have suggested would be particularly apt for self-questioning efforts by more mature writers.

SPECIAL CONSIDERATIONS

STRATEGY TRAINING

Implicit in much of the discussion in this chapter is the need for students to be actively involved in the process of writing. Thus, they should be encouraged to think about the process of writing. As noted earlier, a key to successful writing is for the student to develop an "inner voice"—that is, to think about what he or she is doing (Thomas et al., 1987). A key way to promote this is through *strategy training*. We mentioned some specific strategies (e.g., COPS) earlier, and revisit the concept here in a more global sense.

Graham, Harris, and Sawyer (1987) advocated the use of *self-instructional strategy training* to facilitate writing development. Based on cognitive behavior modification, self-control training, and learning strategies instruction, it has seven steps (p. 4): pretraining; review of current performance level; description of strategy; modeling of

Update

DEFENDS

Successful composition writing requires students to develop appropriate strategies for learning steps in writing and having a basis for recalling these necessary steps when completing an assignment. The DEFENDS strategy was developed by Ellis (see Lenz, Ellis, & Scanlon, 1997) to assist students in learning how to express a point of view in compositions. It can also be used for writing book reports, essay exam questions, and other assignments. The steps of the strategy are as follows:

Decide on the audience, goals, and position.
Estimate main ideas and details.
Figure the best order of main idea and details.
Express the position in the opening.
Note each main idea and supporting points.
Drive home the message in the last sentence.
Search for errors and correct.

Source: Lenz, B. K., Ellis, E. S., & Scanlon, D. (1997). *Teaching learning strategies to adolescents and adults with learning disabilities.* Austin, TX: Pro-Ed.

I. Organization of Ideas
_____A. Topic sentences
_____B. Supporting details
_____C. Order of ideas
_____D. Use of transition words

II. Style ____
_____A. Vocabulary
_____B. Sentence structure
_____C. Grammar

III. Spelling
_____A. Spelling demons
_____B. Personal trouble words

IV. Handwriting
_____A. Clarity
_____B. Spacing
_____C. Neatness

V. Conventions of print
_____A. Format
_____B. Capitalization
_____C. Punctuation

Source: From "Strategies for Teaching Composition Skills to Students with Learning Disabilities" by A. Vallecorsa, R. R. Ledford, and G. G. Parnell, 1991, *Teaching Exceptional Children, 23*(2), p. 53. Copyright 1991 by the Council for Exceptional Children. Reprinted by permission.

Figure 12.10
Evaluation Guide

strategy and self-instructions; mastery of strategy; controlled practice; and independent performance.

Graham et al. described four strategies: increasing vocabulary diversity, generating content for writing, engaging in advanced planning, and revising and editing compositions. They concluded that training of this nature would complement remedial instruction in writing and could be used to enhance students' ability at the level of using basic skills to get started and also with advanced compositional efforts.

ENHANCING IDEATION AND CREATIVITY

The final goal of instruction in written language is to develop the creative talents of students. At this point, the student moves beyond the basic functions and mechanics of writing to an emphasis on developing, crystalizing, and expressing ideas.

Stressing creative expression in writing deemphasizes overcorrection regarding mechanical aspects. Creative writing favors the content over the craft. Tiedt (1975) encouraged teachers to appreciate the ideas writers express reasonably coherently rather than to focus on omissions, misspellings, poor handwriting, or missing punctuation marks. She underlined the need to concentrate on the positive aspects of students' writing. If students learn that *how* they write is more valued than *what* they write, the result will likely interfere with the expressive and communicative processes (Golden, 1980).

Johnson and Myklebust (1967) provided an excellent outline of a progression of ideation reflected in the varying content of students' products. Basically, their idea sequence follows the concrete to the abstract. The first stage, *concrete-descriptive*, involves the use of a simple descriptive sentence or a series of sentences about common things in the child's environment (e.g., The girl is running to the store). The second stage, *concrete-imaginative*, includes inferences from some stimulus or experience. In this stage, students are encouraged to draw generalizations, to imagine what is happening, and to then respond accordingly.

The other two stages in the Johnson and Myklebust progression are characterized by a shift in emphasis to abstractions. The third level, *abstract-descriptive*, places greater stress on the concepts of time and sequence, and students are urged to write stories with logical order, appropriate transitions, and the development of plot and characters. The final level, *abstract-imaginative*, is based on open-ended types of questions and propositions upon which students base their perceptions. Stylistic improvements such as figures of speech can be incorporated at this stage.

To promote development in this area, teachers should make available a variety of topics appropriate for compositions, to instill interest and stimulate thinking. Books by Carlson (1970) and Petty and Bowen (1967) and Table 12.4 offer suggestions. The value of contingencies placed on writing (as noted earlier) to yield creativity also should be considered. The following methods for introducing a composition are noteworthy:

1. Providing a lead-in sentence to the writer, to serve as the beginning line of a story, often helps students overcome writer's block and begin to work.
2. Creating a hypothetical situation tends to stimulate students' thinking and encourage them to speculate on possible occurrences (What if . . .).
3. Using invented circumstances can stimulate students' creativity.
4. Ending a short story in the middle of a sentence and prior to a crucial event lets students continue the story with minimal difficulty.

Many other vehicles are available to the teacher for encouraging students' expression. Examples include story-writing, poetry, and developing diaries or journals as independent writing activities.

Story writing can take on a variety of forms as a tool to motivate composition writing. An interesting approach called "class-mating" was developed to increase writing motivation in secondary level students by having them develop stories to be read by elementary-aged children (Collins, 1980). According to Collins, this strategy provides an audience for writing and enables teachers to point out the need for grammatical accuracy in standard English for "published" work.

Teachers often shy away from teaching *poetry*, because of their students' language limitations. In discussing the creations of young adolescents, Rich and Nedboy (1977) noted that the question is not whether the writing is truly poetry, because the mark of success is not in the creation of a literary product ". . . but in the use of poetry writing as a vehicle for reaching a variety of other goals" (p. 94). Similarly, Nathanson, Cynamon, and Lehman (1976) commented:

> Teaching poetry to exceptional children of any chronological age, of any intellectual level, or of any handicapping condition enables the classroom teacher to expand his or her own potential beyond the purely functional approach to curriculum development. (p. 90)

Update

Teaching Details

For many students who have difficulty in writing, a particular challenge is developing compositions that provide sufficient detail to make a story interesting and more comprehensive. Working with adolescents with special needs in a detention facility, Tomlin (1998) developed the two simple strategies outlined below as a way to remind students of areas they should consider when they are developing their stories.

1. STOP

Specific details

Time of day or time of year

Other relevant information

Place or location

2. RAPP

Relevant information to the focus of the story

Age of the characters

Physical characteristics

Personality traits

Source: Tomlin, D. (1998). Learning strategies for use with adolescents with learning and behavior problems. Unpublished manuscript, Lynchburg College, Lynchburg, VA.

Personal diaries or *journals* have been a popular instructional adjunct ever since the report by Fader and McNeill (1968) trumpeted the value of this approach. The technique is based on having the student write for a designated length of time or a designated number of pages without teacher evaluation. The student selects the topics, which range from simply copying exercises to truly creative expression.

In a related vein, Tsimbos (1980) described how journals could be used with children for whom English is a second language. In this program, students are required to write a minimum number of words per day without regard for correctness. The teacher then reads these and gives responses limited to specific English vocabulary words or ideas that will assist the student in better expression. Essentially, the program provides a basis for communication in English between student and teacher.

Students can be given 15 to 20 minutes each day to write in a personal journal on any topic of interest. Teachers should not correct these journals but rather use them to help the writers develop ideation rather than structure. If the writing takes the form of a diary, teachers may agree to read these only when the student gives his or her approval.

Journal writing also can be tied to reinforcement strategies based on the length of time a student spends in writing or the number of words or pages written. Brigham, Graubard, and Stans (1972) reported that reinforcement improved the length and quality of writing, the variety of words used, and the ideas expressed. In this program, students earn points for the number of words they write or the different or new words they use.

THERAPEUTIC USE OF WRITING

The therapeutic quality of writing has been documented frequently and was well illustrated by Dehouske (1979) in her work with adolescents. She used written expression to help students reveal personal feelings that otherwise might have remained unspoken. The following story (Dehouske, 1979) clearly shows how students learned to use writing as a vehicle for self-expression:

> Once, a while back there was a little deformed line in the midst of all the straight lines. He felt all out of place and all the straight lines laughed at him. One day he decided to have an operation to straighten himself out. While he was out of town having his operation, someone stepped on something and bent all of the straight lines in town, and everyone laughed at him.
> Moral: You can't win. (p. 68)

This form of writing is an initial means for having students share their ideas and perceptions and thus provides a foundation for possible therapeutic benefits.

In a similar vein, Rich and Nedboy (1977) developed a poetry-writing program for inner-city students. First, students are to read the works of other students, in books such as Koch's (1970) anthology, then contribute their ideas to a group poetry project, each student adding successive lines to a poem. The following verses stemmed from an initial effort reported by Rich and Nedboy:

Table 12.4
Themes for Written Compositions

What if I had a million dollars . . .
My favorite television show is . . .
"My Family"
My favorite toy is my _____ .
The most interesting person I know
What if I could be in any fairy tale I wanted
The day I joined the circus
What TV character would I like to be
What I plan to do after I graduate from high school
It happened at the junior prom
What is my favorite movie
My favorite sports hero
The day I went to outer space
The secret clubhouse in the woods
The championship Little League game
My trip aboard a Martian aircraft
My discovery of an Egyptian tomb
The Wild West character I would most like to be like
How I choose my friends
Who would you like to be for one day if you could be anybody in the world?
I wish I could spend my summer vacation in . . .
My best friend is . . .
Why colors remind me of moods
The most disgusting T.V. commercial I've ever seen
Spending the day with my favorite rock group
Going steady
If you could change your past, what would you change?
My hobbies
My favorite song
My first job
The project my service club does
The day I got my license to drive
What is the first thing you want to do when you turn 18 and why?
If you could go anywhere in the world, where would you go and by what means?
My dog learns to talk
What if . . . I was a seed
The truth about the haunted house
20 years from now
My trip to the ACC tournament
How could I ever explain it to my parents?
The night was dark and the moon was yellow . . .
Faster! Faster! I have to get there as soon as I can or else . . .
What if . . . the sun never came up
You have just invented a special type of chemical potion . . .
My life at age three
The day I became a butterfly
Then it happened! Wahoo! I heard the crowd yell.
I love my jeans

Trains an' Stuff

A train feels he don't like to get stepped on no more
A train feels burned
A train hates to be pushed
We feel great but the train feels bad
The train gets mad
Once in a blue moon they clean it
The train wishes he was a human being. (p. 93)

The objective of this type of exercise is to give students a chance to use their language skills and their life experiences. The key concern is that students become comfortable with written language as a mode of expression, not the quality of the poetry. In this way, writing can help students develop and refine their ideas and emotions.

D'Alelio (1976) likewise found that creative writing could help children with disabilities. He reported that students could be motivated toward writing tasks by first discussing them in a group setting. One activity that he found valuable for the transitional stage from oral discussion to writing was to have students identify specific descriptor words for story characters, which then were listed on the board. This exercise became the basis for further efforts at individual writing. D'Alelio concluded that one aspect of teaching creative writing is most important:

> Behind all of the resistance which you may face initially when you institute creative writing as part of your curriculum, the children *want* to be able to express themselves. The pupils want to be able to write and when they find they can trust you to help them do it, you and your class will be starting on one of the most exciting and mutually rewarding experiences you can share. (p. 262)

In the area of written expression, as with the other language domains, the benefits that accrue to the learner can clearly outdistance the acquisition of specific skills. Development and refinement of communication skills can have a profound influence on personal and social development as well.

DEVELOPING FUNCTIONAL WRITING

Utilitarian writing dictates greater concern for structure than does creative expression, but it nevertheless should provide an opportunity for a personalized form of communication. The most common types of functional writing include letters, notices, invitations, reports, and applications; these were discussed earlier.

Two other areas of functional writing warrant special attention because of their particular importance to adolescents with writing difficulties: note-taking and essay exam writing. These skills become more important as students enter higher grades. Although both areas relate more closely to study skills than to written expression, they demand attention because they typically are neglected in formal instruction.

Note-Taking   Consider how you developed your own personal note-taking skills—whether you created your own system, received formal instruction, or viewed someone else's format and adopted it. Regardless of which of these apply, all students at some time must become "note-takers." School failure or success may depend in part on whether a student becomes efficient at this task (Polloway et al., 1983).

Note-taking skills become necessary, for example, when listening to a speaker, watching a film, or reading a textbook. Alley and Deshler (1979) categorized note-taking into three specific skill areas:

1. Outlining—the sequential arrangement of main features of a book, a subject, or a lecture.
2. Formal note-taking—the concise but comprehensive statement of essential matter read or heard.
3. Informal note-taking—the brief, spontaneous recording of material to assist the memory or for subsequent reference or development. (p. 129)

The value of these skills is in their great assistance to students organizationally, an important concern for many students with mild disabilities. The following list developed by Patton (in Polloway et al., 1983) offers a few ideas for teachers in helping students become better note-takers:

1. Preparation
   a. Make sure all necessary materials are ready. This may include specially prepared paper (e.g., with a specific note-taking format).
   b. If available, obtain ahead of time from the instructor a skeletal outline of the lecture.
2. Instruction
   a. Give practice at taking notes.
   b. Provide feedback on the quality and quantity of notes.
   c. Teach the use of various shorthand conventions, abbreviations, or personal codes (e.g., *s* for without, *c* for with).
   d. Emphasize that students are *not* to write down every word.
   e. Provide training in how to recognize instructors' key words (e.g., "most important") or key behaviors (e.g., writing a phrase on the board) of instructors.
3. Aids
   a. Have students use small, pocket-size notebooks for a variety of reasons (e.g., "things to do today," assignments, questions to ask the instructor).
   b. Encourage the taping of lectures to augment poor in-class note-taking skills.
   c. Have students check their notes with those of others. (p. 316)

Essay Test-Taking   Although techniques are available for maximizing students' performance on various types of tests, our attention is directed here to essay situations that require written expressive skills. To students with problems in written language, the essay test can be devastating. The conventions of writing already discussed still supply, but a few additional suggestions from Patton (in Polloway et al., 1983) are offered:

1. Nurture a positive, success-oriented attitude toward the impending test situation.
2. Encourage students to use their time effectively, both when preparing prior to the test and during the test itself.
3. Have students respond first to the essay questions to which they know the answers, and postpone the more difficult ones.

4. Instruct students on how to recognize and understand certain "task-demand" clue words such as *compare, contrast, describe, elaborate,* and *list.*
5. Encourage students to outline the answer to each essay question before writing down any response.
6. Incorporate the use of mnemonic aids (for example, the taxonomic breakdown of King-dom, Phylum, Class, Order, Genus, Species may be remembered more readily through the mnemonic phrase, "King Peter Comes of Good Stock").
7. Use alternative means of evaluation with students who encounter great difficulty with written form, because their performance may not accurately reflect their competence or knowledge. (pp. 316–317)

SUMMARY

Written language represents the highest achievement within the language domains. Since it builds on prerequisite knowledge and abilities in oral language, reading, spelling, and handwriting, there are not surprisingly a number of individuals who struggle achieving competency in this domain.

There are three stages in the writing process. The prewriting, or planning, stage requires consideration of stimulus input, motivation to write, and the setting of pur-pose. It places demands on the writer to become actively involved in thinking about communicative intent and adapting it to the audience for whom it is intended.

The writing or transcribing stage involves both craft and content. The former en-tails the mechanical skills associated with the secretarial function in writing while the latter involves the author role. Particular instructional foci in a writing program in-clude vocabulary and sentence development, paragraphing skills, and compositional writing.

The postwriting stage involves the dual processes of revising and editing. Revis-ing typically refers to necessary changes made in the content while editing focuses on mechanical aspects of writing.

Attention to the three stages of writing enables students to develop a variety of writing products. Comprehensive writing programs include attention to both func-tional and creative writing opportunities.

Note Portions of this chapter include some material adapted from Polloway, Patton, and Cohen (1983) and from Polloway and Decker (1988).

REFERENCES

Alley, G. R., & Deshler, D. D. (1979). *Teaching the learning disabled adolescent: Strategies and methods.* Denver: Love Publishing.

Bailet, L. L. (1991). Written language test reviews. In A. M. Bain, L. L. Bailet, & L. C. Moats (Eds.), *Writ-ten language disorders: Theory into practice* (pp. 165–188). Austin, TX: Pro-Ed.

Bailey, E. J. (1975). *Academic activities for adolescents with learning disabilities.* Evergreen, CO: Learning Pathways.

Barenbaum, E. M. (1983). Writing in the special class. *Topics in Learning and Learning Disabilities, 3*(3), 12–20.

Brigance, A. H. (1982). *Brigance diagnostic comprehensive inventory of basic skills.* North Billerica, MA: Curriculum Associates.

Brigham, T., Graubard, P., & Stans, D. (1972). Analysis of the effects of sequential reinforcement contingencies on aspects of composition. *Journal of Applied Behavior Analysis, 5*, 421–429.

Buchan, V. (1979, September-October). By using the why and because method. *Today's Education*, pp. 32-34.

Burns, P. C. (1974). *Diagnostic teaching of language arts.* Itasca, IL: F. E. Peacock Publishers.

Burns, P. C. (1980). *Assessment and correction of language arts difficulties.* Columbus, OH: Charles E. Merrill Publishing.

Carlson, R. K. (1970). *Writing aids through the grades.* New York: Teachers College Press.

Cartwright, G. P. (1969). Written expression and spelling. In R. M. Smith (Ed.), *Teacher diagnosis of educational difficulties.* Columbus, OH: Charles E. Merrill Publishing.

Christenson, S. L., Thurlow, M. L., Ysseldyke, J. E., & McVicar, R. (1989). Written language instruction for students with mild handicaps: Is there enough quantity to ensure quality? *Learning Disability Quarterly, 12*, 219–229.

Cohen, S. B., & Plaskon, S. P. (1980). *Language arts for the mildly handicapped.* Columbus, OH: Charles E. Merrill Publishing.

Collins, J. L. (1980). Class-mating: A strategy for teaching writing in urban schools. In G. Stanford (Ed.), *Reading with differences.* Urbana, IL: National Council of Teachers of English.

D'Alelio, W. A. (1976). A strategy for teaching remedial language arts: Creative writing. In J. J. Long, W. C. Morse, & R. G. Newman (Eds.), *Conflict in the classroom* (3rd ed.). Belmont, CA: Wadsworth Publishing.

Dankowski, C. E. (1966). Each pupil has his own editor. *Elementary School Journal, 66*, 249–253.

Dawson, M. A., & Zollinger, M. (1957).*Guidance language learning.* Yonkers-on-Hudson, NY: World Book Co.

Decker, T. W., & Polloway, E. A. (1989). Written language. In G. R. Robinson, J. R. Patton, E. A. Polloway, & L. Sargent (Eds.), *Best practices in mild mental retardation* (pp. 109–131). Reston, VA: Council for Exceptional Children, Division on Mental Retardation.

Dehouske, E. J. (1979). Original writing: A therapeutic tool in working with disturbed adolescents. *Teaching Exceptional Children, 11*, 66–70.

Epstein, M. H., Hallahan, D. P., & Kauffman, J. M. (1975). Implications of the reflectivity-impulsivity dimension for special education. *Journal of Special Education, 9*, 11–25.

Fader, D. N., & McNeill, E. B. (1968). *Hooked on books: Program and proof.* New York: Berkeley Publishing.

Fennimore, F. (1980). Attaining sentence verve with sentence extension. In G. Stanford (Ed.), *Dealing with differences.* Urbana, IL: National Council of Teachers of English.

Giordano, G. (1982). CATS exercises: Teaching disabled writers to communicate. *Academic Therapy, 18*, 233–237.

Glover, J., & Gary, A. L. (1976). Procedures to increase some aspects of creativity. *Journal of Applied Behavior Analysis, 8*, 79–84.

Golden, J. M. (1980). The writer's side: Writing for a purpose and an audience. *Language Arts, 57*, 756–762.

Gould, B. W. (1991). Curricular strategies for written expression. In A. M. Bain, L. L. Bailet, & L. C. Moats (Eds.), *Written language disorders: Theory into practice* (pp. 129–164). Austin, TX: Pro-Ed.

Graham, S., Harris, K., & Sawyer, R. (1987). Composition instruction with learning disabled students. *Focus on Exceptional Children, 20*(4), 1–11.

Graves, D. H. (1985). All children can write. *Learning Disabilities Focus, 1*(1), 36–43.

Gregg, N. (1991). Disorders of written expression. In A. M. Bain, L. L. Bailet, & L. C. Moats (Eds.), *Written language disorders: Theory into practice* (pp. 65–97). Austin, TX: Pro-Ed.

Hagood, B. F. (1997) Reading and writing with help from story grammar. *Teaching Exceptional Children, 29*(4), 10–14.

Hall, J. K. (1981). *Evaluating and improving written expression: A practical guide for teachers.* Boston: Allyn & Bacon.

Hammill, D. D., & Larsen, S. C. (1988). *Test of written language–2.* Austin, TX: Pro-Ed.

Hammill, D. D., & Poplin, M. (1978). Problems in writing. In D. D. Hammill & N. Bartel (Eds.), *Teaching children with learning and behavior problems.* Boston: Allyn & Bacon.

Hansen, C. L. (1978). Writing skills. In N. G. Haring, T. C. Lovitt, M. D. Eaton, & C. L. Hansen (Eds.), *The fourth R: Research in the classroom.* Columbus, OH: Charles E. Merrill.

Hillerich, R. L. (1979). Developing written expression: How to raise—not raze—writers. *Language Arts, 56,* 769–777.

Hunt, K. W. (1965). *Grammatical structures written at three grade levels* (Research Report No. 3). Champaign, IL: National Council of Teachers of English.

Isaacson, S. L. (1987). Effective instruction in written language. *Focus on Exceptional Children, 19*(6), 1–12.

Isaacson, S. L. (1989). Role of secretary vs. author in resolving the conflict in writing instruction. *Learning Disability Quarterly, 12,* 200–217.

Johnson, D. J., & Myklebust, H. R. (1967). *Learning disabilities: Educational principles and practices.* New York: Grune & Stratton.

Kirk, S. A., & Johnson, G. O. (1951). *Educating the retarded child.* Cambridge, MA: Houghton-Mifflin.

Koch, K. (1970). *Wishes, lies, and dreams.* New York: Random House.

Kraetsch, G. A. (1981). The effects of oral instructions and training on the expansion of written language. *Learning Disability Quarterly, 4,* 83–90.

Langone, J. (1990). *Teaching students with mild and moderate learning problems.* Boston: Allyn & Bacon.

Lenz, B. K., Ellis, E. S., & Scanlon, D. (1997). *Teaching learning strategies to adolescents and adults with learning disabilities.* Austin, TX: Pro-Ed.

Lerner, J. W. (1985). *Learning disabilities: Theories, diagnosis, and teaching strategies* (4th ed.). Boston: Houghton-Mifflin.

Lovitt, T. C. (1975). Applied behavior analysis and learning disabilities: Part II. *Journal of Learning Disabilities, 8,* 504–518.

Lynch, E. M., & Jones, S. D. (1989). Process and product: A review of the research on LD children's writing skills. *Learning Disability Quarterly, 12,* 74–86.

Maloney, K. B., & Hopkins, B. L. (1973). The modification of structure and its relationship to subjective judgments of creative writing. *Journal of Applied Behavior Analysis, 6,* 425–433.

Mercer, C. D., & Mercer, A. R. (1989). *Teaching students with learning problems.* Columbus, OH: Charles E. Merrill Publishing..

Moran, M. R. (1987). Options for written language assessment. *Focus on Exceptional Children, 19*(5), 1–12.

Myklebust, H. (1965). *Picture story language test.* Los Angeles: Western Psychological Services.

Nathanson, D., Cynamon, A., & Lehman, K. (1976). Miami: Snow poets creative writing for exceptional children. *Teaching Exceptional Children, 8,* 87–91.

Otto, W., McMenemy, R. A., & Smith, R. J. (1973). *Corrective and remedial teaching.* Boston: Houghton-Mifflin.

Petty, W. T., & Bowen, M. E. (1967). *Slithery snakes and other aids to children's writing.* New York: Appleton-Century-Crofts.

Phelps-Terasaki, D., & Phelps, T. (1980). *Teaching written expression: The Phelps sentence guide program.* Novato, CA: Academic Therapy.

Phelps-Gunn, T., & Phelps-Terasaki, D. (1982). *Written language instruction: Theory and remediation.* Rockville, MD: Aspen Systems.

Phelps-Terasaki, D., & Phelps-Gunn, T. (1988). *Teaching competence in written language: A systematic program for developing writing skills.* Austin, TX: Pro-Ed.

Polloway, E. A., & Decker, T. W. (1988). Written language. In G. R. Robinson, J. R. Patton, E. A. Polloway, & L. Sargent (Eds.), *Best practice in mild mental disabilities* (pp. 453–479). Des Moines, IA: State Department of Education.

Polloway, E. A., Patton, J. R., & Cohen, S. B. (1981). Written language for the mildly handicapped. *Focus on Exceptional Children, 14*(3), 1–16.

Polloway, E. A., Patton, J. R., & Cohen, S. A. (1983). Written language. In E. L. Meyen, G. A. Vergason, & R. J. Whelan (Eds.), *Promising practices for exceptional children: Curriculum implications* (pp. 285–320). Denver: Love Publishing.

Poplin, M., Gray, R., Larsen, S., Banikowski, A., & Mehring, T. (1980). Comparison of components of written expression abilities in learning disabled and non-learning disabled children at three grade levels. *Learning Disability Quarterly, 3,* 46–53.

Reutzel, D. R. (1986). The reading basal: A sentence combining composing book. *Reading Teacher, 39,* 194–199.

Rich, A., & Nedboy, R. (1977). Hey man . . . We're writing a poem: Creating writing for inner city children. *Teaching Exceptional Children, 9,* 92–94.

Riemer, G. (1969). *How they murdered the second R.* Toronto, Ontario: W. W. Norton.

Ross, A. O. (1976). *Psychological aspects of learning disabilities and reading disorders.* New York: McGraw-Hill.

Scarmadalia, M., & Bereiter, C. (1986). Research on written composition. In M. C. Wittrock (Ed.), *Handbook of research on teaching* (3rd ed.) (pp. 778–803). New York: Macmillan.

Schumaker, J. B., Deshler, D. D., Nolan, S., Clark, F. L., Alley, G. R., & Warner, M. M. (1981). Error monitoring: A learning strategy for improving academic performance of LD adolescents (Research Report No. 32). Lawrence, KS: University of Kansas Institute on Learning Disabilities.

Sherwin, J. S. (1969). *Four programs in teaching English: A critique of research.* Scranton, PA: International Textbook (for National Council of Teachers of English).

Silverman, R., Zigmond, N., Zimmerman, J. M., & Vallecorsa, A. (1981). Improving written expression in learning disabled students. *Topics in Language Disorders, 1*(2), 91–99.

Sink, D. M. (1975). Tech-write/Write-teach. *Elementary English, 52,* 175–177.

Smith, F. (1982). *Writing and the writer.* New York: Holt, Rinehart and Winston.

Smith, R. M. (1974). *Clinical teaching: Methods of instruction for the retarded.* New York: McGraw-Hill.

Strong, W. (1983). *Sentence combining: A composing book* (2nd ed.). New York: Random House.

Thomas, C. C., Englert, C. S., & Gregg, S. (1987). An analysis of errors and strategies in the expository writing of learning disabled students. *Remedial and Special Education, 8*(1), 21–30.

Tiedt, I. M. (1975). Input. *Elementary English, 52,* 163–164.

Tomlin, D. (1998). Learning strategies for use with adolescents with learning and behavior problems. Unpublished manuscript, Lynchburg College, Lynchburg, VA.

Torgeson, J. K. (1977). The role of nonspecific factors in the task performance of learning disabled children: A theoretical assessment. *Journal of Learning Disabilities, 10,* 27–34.

Tsimbos, L. (1980). Journal of writing for non-native speakers of English. In G. Stanford (Ed.), *Dealing with differences.* Urbana, IL: National Council of Teachers of English.

Tway, E. (1975). Creative writing: From gimmick to goal. *Elementary English, 52,* 173–174.

Vallecorsa, A., Ledford, R. R., & Parnell, G. G. (1991). Strategies for teaching composition skills to students with learning disabilities. *Teaching Exceptional Children, 23*(2), 52–55.

Van Allen, R. (1976). *Language experiences in communication.* Boston: Houghton-Mifflin.

Vogel, S. A., & Konrad, D. (in press). Characteristic written expressive language deficits of the learning disabled: Some general and specific intervention strategies. *Journal of Reading and Learning Disabilities International.*

Wallace, G., & McLoughlin, J. (1976). *Learning disabilities: Concepts and characteristics.* Columbus, OH: Charles E. Merrill Publishing.

Weiner, E. S. (1979). Improvement in reading through writing. *Academic Therapy, 14,* 589–595.

Wong, B. (1979). Research and educational implications of some recent conceptualizations in learning disabilities. *Learning Disability Quarterly, 2*(3), 63–68.

Zigmond, N., Vallecorsa, A., & Leinhardt, G. (1980). Reading instruction for students with learning disabilities. *Topics in Language Disorders, 1*(1), 89–98.

13

Adolescents and Language Disabilities

L|ike many other handicapping conditions, disabilities in various language do-
mains do not simply disappear when children reach the magical era of puberty.
Language disorders may continue beyond childhood into adolescence, and often through adolescence into adulthood. Problems related to language create many difficulties for adolescents. For one thing, social acceptance is critical during this developmental period; peer approval is vastly more important than parental approval for
many adolescents. Language disorders can impact on this approval. Problems in language can result in peer rejection and lowered self-concepts that might have longlast-
ing effects on the adolescent. Language skills are directly related to school success
(Shea & Bauer, 1991).

Language problems in adolescents not only affect their social status among
peers but also impact negatively on their academic success. Receptive oral language skills, including reading and listening, are crucial to completing many high
school courses. Deficiencies in these areas make it difficult for them to acquire
information.

High-school students also need to have competence in expressive language.
Because a great deal of written work is required of students in secondary classes, students with deficiencies in writing skills are at a major disadvantage in completing
written assignments. Likewise, the ability to respond orally to questions and to enter
into discussions is important for secondary students. Problems in these areas may result in school failure. Although some middle-school and secondary-school teachers
might be willing to make accommodations for students with oral and written language
problems, others are not. Many teachers simply expect students to perform at a certain
level, and students who are incapable of performing at that level receive failing grades.
These problems might be compounded for students who pursue postsecondary educational opportunities.

Many of the language problems adolescents experience are similar to those of
elementary-aged students. The purpose of this chapter is not to show the differences
between language disorders of elementary-school children and adolescents but, rather,
to provide an overview of adolescence and the problems facing all children during this
often turbulent developmental period. Language problems may compound adolescents' problems, and the nature of adolescence can impact on the importance of language. This chapter provides a basis for understanding adolescents and the effects of
language problems on this population.

NATURE OF ADOLESCENCE

Adolescence is a distinct developmental stage in most cultures. It is that period between childhood and adulthood. Its exact nature varies among cultures. In some cultures, where children have to grow up quickly to carry out certain responsibilities, adolescence barely exists. In other cultures, such as ours, adolescence often continues for
many years.

DEFINITION OF ADOLESCENCE

Adolescence has been defined in various ways. This period of development has been described as "(1) the transitional period between childhood and adulthood, (2) the period during which an emotionally immature person reaches the final stages of physical and mental development, and (3) the period of the attainment of maturity" (Smith, Price, & Marsh, 1986, p. 212). It often is thought of as a period of crisis, when major changes occur in a person's life and cause confusion and turmoil. If students have disabilities, the problems often are magnified (Dossetor & Nicol, 1989).

Whereas the beginning of adolescence usually is marked by puberty, when the body changes and becomes sexually active and capable of reproduction, the ending of adolescence is less definite. Some authorities say that adolescence ends when the individual reaches a certain chronological age. Others accept the idea that adolescence ends when the individual achieves economic independence. When using age as the upper limit, the question is: What age? Mercer (1987) suggested that adolescence ends after the age of 22. Others present the age limit of 18 or 21. No agreement exists about the age limitation, and even less agreement is apparent when economic independence is the criterion for the end of adolescence.

The period of adolescence is marked by major physiological and emotional changes, and teenagers mature in many different ways. Because this developmental period involves such major changes, some professionals divide adolescence into subcategories to further describe it. These might include early adolescence, from approximately ages 12 to 15; middle adolescence, 15 to 18, and late adolescence, 18 to 22 (Mercer, 1987). Regardless of the method of classification, adolescence remains a period of significant transition from childhood to adulthood.

During adolescence, many changes occur that result in the need for adolescents to perform a series of significant tasks. These tasks, which have remained fairly constant since they were first recognized in the literature in the 1950s, include the following (Smith et al., 1986):

1. Creation of a sense of sexuality as part of a personal identity.
2. Development of confidence in social interactions.
3. Infusion of social values into a personal code of behavior.
4. Acceptance of biological changes.
5. Attainment of a sense of emotional independence.
6. Contemplation of vocational interests.
7. Identification of personal talents and interests.
8. Awareness of personal weaknesses and strengths.
9. Development of sexual interests with non-family members.
10. Development of peer relationships.
11. Completion of formal educational activities.
12. Preparation for marriage, parenting, and adult relationships. (p. 212)

Everyone going through adolescence must endure these tasks, but the presence of a disability may significantly affect their accomplishment. For example, students with various disabilities, including language deficits, may have difficulties establishing favorable peer relationships. Table 13.1 summarizes some of the problems that can occur with these tasks as a result of the presence of a disability.

CHARACTERISTICS OF ADOLESCENTS

Although there is a wide variability among adolescents, some general characteristics can be associated with most students during the ages of 12 to 22. For one thing, adolescents develop physically into their adult stature and appearance (Mercer, 1987). Usually this physical development does not occur slowly and gradually but, rather, with a rapid growth spurt.

Among the major physical changes that transpire during the rapid growth of adolescents are significant increases in height, strength, and stamina; boys develop wider shoulders, and girls develop wider hips (Scarr, Weinberg, & Levine, 1986). Onset of the growth spurt varies between boys and girls, Typically, girls begin their growth spurt before boys, usually between ages 10 and 11. The rapid growing period is about 3 years. For boys, the rapid growth period begins at about age 12 or 13 and continues for approximately 5 or 6 years (Woolfolk, 1990). Figure 13.1 depicts the adolescent growth rates for boys and girls.

Modern phenomena include the earlier beginning of puberty and the increasing size of people in our society. The average age for girls to experience their first menstrual period has dropped from about 14 or 15 to 11 or 12 years of age. Also, boys and girls are growing bigger and stronger than their parents. The armor adult male soldiers used in medieval Europe would be the right size for 10-year-old boys today (Scarr et al., 1986).

Early onset of puberty and increased growth may be the result of two factors: (a) better nutrition and sanitation, and (b) genetic mixing. Improved nutrition and sanitation effects are easily understood. Our society simply has been fortunate to produce enough food to eat, and to produce even better, more nutritious foods. Genetic mixing

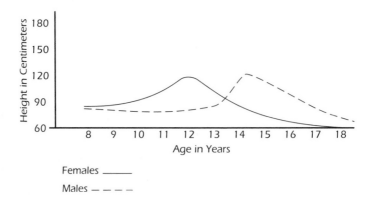

Source: Adapted from *Readings from Scientific American: Biological Anthropology* (p. 39) by J. M. Tanner, 1974, San Francisco: W. H. Freeman. Reproduced by permission.

Figure 13.1
Adolescent Growth Spurt

Table 13.1
Developmental Tasks and Resultant Questions

Developmental Tasks	Questions to Consider
1. Creation of a sense of sexuality as part of a personal identity	• How is this affected by the presence of a physical handicap? • Does poor school performance and low social status impact this?
2. Development of confidence in social interactions	• Do negative classroom experiences play a role? • Do others assume social inadequacy is an automatic result of being handicapped?
3. Infusion of social values into a personal code of behavior	• Do adults protect students with handicaps to such a degree that they do not have experiences that allow them to develop a sense of what social values exist? • Does the handicap or others' reaction to it prevent experimentation with social behavior?
4. Acceptance of biological changes	• Are students with handicaps denied accurate information about their own bodies and sexual maturity? • Do students with lower intellectual performance sometimes have difficulty gleaning information by osmosis or comprehending information?
5. Attainment of a sense of emotional independence	• Are students with handicaps given the same opportunity as other adolescents to make their own decisions? • Do adolescents with handicaps have more difficulty dealing with emotion?
6. Contemplation of vocational interests	• Are students with handicaps limited in vocational choices because of preconceived notions of their ability? • Are vocational training options too tightly tied to labels and not to true individual ability?
7. Identification of personal talents and interests	• Do students with handicaps have more difficulty identifying positive traits with themselves as a result of the negative events they experience?
8. Awareness of personal weaknesses and strengths	• Do students focus more on their limitations than strengths? • Do students with handicaps have an inaccurate self-concept?
9. Development of sexual interests with non-family members	• If the individual has disabilities, is it more difficult to develop heterosexual contacts? • Do public prejudices serve as barriers to the development of sexual interests?
10. Development of peer relationships	• Do adolescents with handicaps have fewer opportunities to develop peer relationships? • Are some students isolated socially by the limitations of their label more than by the actual effects of the condition?
11. Completion of formal educational activities	• Has PL 94-142 increased the likelihood of this? • Should students with handicaps receive special diplomas that identify them as handicapped.
12. Preparation for marriage, parenting, and adult relationships	• Do students with handicaps receive information concerning family responsibilities? • Do some community attitudes operate against adolescents so that adult relationships are difficult to achieve?

means less promulgation within families. Many years ago, incestuous relationships were much more common and acceptable than they are today. Both of these factors seem to have accelerated the onset of puberty and enhanced physical development (Scarr et al., 1986).

Concomitant with the physical growth spurt is the sexual maturation of individuals during adolescence. Boys and girls become men and women from a sexual perspective. Just as girls' physical growth spurt occurs before boys', girls also develop sexually before boys do. The onset of sexual maturity for girls, termed *menarche*, is the beginning of the monthly menstrual cycle, which will occur until menopause, approximately 35–40 years later. The age of menarche varies from approximately 9.5 years to 14.5 years; the average age is 12.8 years (Kerr, Nelson, & Lambert, 1987). Boys reach sexual maturity on the average 1–3 years after girls. Their sexual maturity, which results in their capacity to develop and ejaculate sperm, occurs at a mean age of 13.5 years (Kerr et al., 1987). Physical changes in the bodies of girls and boys, accompanying sexual maturity, include breast development in girls and lowering of the voice in boys.

In addition to physical and sexual development, moral development occurs during adolescence. The development of morality, which begins in childhood, continues through adolescence. The morality of adolescents may be reflected in their attitudes toward cheating on schoolwork, aggression toward other persons or property, stealing, and engaging in illegal activities. Adolescents commonly experiment with moral issues during this period. They may shoplift or commit acts of vandalism just to do it.

Part of the reason the development of morality is important for adolescents is the increased emphasis they place on peer approval. As a result, morality as defined by their parents may be replaced by their own thinking as well as the thinking of their age peers. This can result in a moral code significantly different from their parents.

PROBLEMS CREATED BY RAPID GROWTH AND SEXUAL MATURATION

The rapid physical growth and sexual maturation of adolescents often causes problems for students. Adolescents have to get used to their new bodies and the physiological changes that occur simultaneously. Adjustments must be made to the rapid physical growth and the development of sexual maturity. Many adolescents go through a time when they do not like themselves. They do not like the way they look, the way they act, or the way they feel. Normal skin problems in the form of acne may cause an adolescent to literally withdraw from contact with peers.

Adolescents must deal not only with their physically and sexually changing bodies but also with their emotions. Adolescence can be an emotionally difficult time. Acceptance of their changing bodies, the importance of peer acceptance, doubts about self-concept, and often growing tensions with parents create difficulties. Frequently the end result is a feeling of being "mixed up"; they may cry easily, snap at their parents, and behave in ways that they themselves do not understand.

As noted, a common characteristic of individuals during the adolescent years is the strong influence of peers (Mercer, 1987). For many adolescents, peer group membership and peer approval both take precedence over parental influence. In fact, "Peers form a social environment that often antagonistically confronts the family and the adult society at large" (Sebald, 1989, p. 33). The rise in importance of peers is concomitant with the declining influence of the family (Larson, Kubey, & Colletti, 1989). This in itself can result in problems.

Although the increased influence of peers is difficult for many parents to accept, it is simply a reality that must be considered in parental and adolescent relationships. The influence of teachers over adolescents also lessens during this period. Teachers, like parents, must understand the important role of peer relationships and work within those relationships. Attempting to sabotage peer relationships will likely backfire, actually making it more difficult for parents and teachers to establish a relationship with the adolescent.

A characteristic of adolescence related to academic work is the development of formal or abstract reasoning abilities. Although intellectual levels remain fairly constant throughout a person's life, specific mental abilities change, as Piaget noted in his research. Adolescents develop the ability to manipulate hypothetical situations and to assimilate information from a variety of sources. These abilities enable them to engage in philosophical and scientific thinking and to plan for their futures (Mercer, 1987).

Other characteristics of adolescents may include their (a) growing mobility, (b) long attention span, (c) limited patience for boredom, (d) self-motivation, and (e) high levels of interaction with their surroundings. As Mercer (1987) noted, adolescents do not lack motivation, attention, and interaction as long as they are dealing with something in which they are interested. The key is to focus these attributes in specific directions. This is the challenge for parents and teachers.

CHARACTERISTICS OF ADOLESCENTS WITH DISABILITIES

In addition to the characteristics common to all adolescents, those with disabilities are likely to have other traits. These include academic deficits, problems with social skills, motivational problems, and problems with behavior. These characteristics typically have a negative impact on school performance and the relationships between these students and students who do not have disabilities. They also may create problems between adolescents and their parents.

ACADEMIC DEFICITS

Students with disabilities, by definition, have academic deficits. Definitions applied to determine the eligibility of students for special education programs include criteria that the disability must adversely affect the student's educational performance (Hallahan & Kauffman, 1991). Therefore, by definition, adolescents with mental retardation, learning disabilities, and behavioral disorders exhibit academic problems.

For students with mental retardation, these academic deficits are widespread. They likely include below average performance in all academic areas, poor memory and problem-solving skills, deficient thinking skills, and delayed or limited use of language (Polloway, Patton, Payne, & Payne, 1989). The level of manifestation of these deficits is related to the students' intellectual functioning.

Students with learning disabilities also have significant academic problems. In fact for these students, academic deficits are the primary problem (Mercer, 1987). Adolescents with learning disabilities differ from those with mental retardation in that they might experience academic problems in only a few, specific subject areas. For example, an adolescent with learning disabilities may have reading problems but do very well in math. Or, a student may be an excellent reader but have significant difficulties with written expression (Gearheart & Gearheart, 1989).

For students with behavior disorders, academic problems are linked to the inability to maintain appropriate behaviors. As a result of these students' frequent inappropriate behaviors, they usually are below average in academic achievement. As Kauffman (1989) stated, "Although some disturbed students work at grade level and a very few are academically advanced, most function a year or more below grade level in most academic areas" (p. 185).

SOCIAL SKILL DEFICITS

Another area in which most adolescents with mild disabilities have problems is social skills. These students often lack necessary social skills, display inappropriate behaviors, and have difficulties with interpersonal relationships (Sabornie & Beard, 1990). Problems of this kind will likely affect interrelationships with age peers, parents, and teachers.

In one study, teachers were asked to rate the social status of students with mild mental retardation. Results indicated that more than 20 percent of the older students in the sample were rejected by their peers (Polloway, Epstein, Patton, Cullinan, & Luebke, 1986). Sabornie and Kauffman (1987) confirmed these results in their finding that students with mild mental retardation held more negative perceptions about their peers than nondisabled students and were more rejected than nondisabled peers.

MOTIVATION PROBLEMS

Motivation and learning are interrelated. Without motivation, students at the secondary level may limit the effort they put forth toward any learning task. Motivation can be enhanced by positive reinforcement (Woolfolk, 1990). This reinforcement can be teacher-designed, or it can be a natural reinforcer for the student. For example, in language training, the adolescent may be motivated to improve oral language skills because of an upcoming job interview that requires certain oral language competencies. This would be a natural reinforcer.

Studies have revealed that students classified as having mental retardation, learning disabilities, and behavior disorders all have frequent problems in motivation (Epstein, Polloway, Patton, & Foley, 1989; Kauffman, 1989; Masters & Mori, 1986). By the time students with these disabilities reach adolescence, they have experienced several years of failure and frustration. As a result, they may have withdrawn from exerting any effort in academic tasks for fear of failure. This lack of motivation can lead to limited efforts in writing and other language skill development (Meyer, Pisha, & Rose, 1991).

Several factors can affect motivation. Some of these, which frequently are noted as characteristics of students with disabilities, are (a) anxiety, (b) self-concept problems, and (c) low expectations of teachers (Mehring & Colson, 1990). Masters and Mori (1986) suggested that one way to improve motivation is for teachers to spend more time focusing on the goals of their students.

BEHAVIOR PROBLEMS

Behavior problems among adolescents with disabilities is a fairly common characteristic. For students classified as emotionally disturbed, problem behaviors are widespread (Kauffman, 1989). Even though adolescents with mental retardation and learning disabilities may not exhibit the severity or frequency of behavior problems as students identified as behavior disordered do, they frequently have problems that are likely to be, at least in part, the result of frustration and low self-esteem.

PSYCHOLOGICAL PROBLEMS

Many adolescents with disabilities have a variety of psychological problems. Examples include feelings of anger, incompetence, inadequacy, and frustration; behaviors of impulsivity and boldness; and a lack of motivation, excessive dependency, and shyness (Ness & Price, 1990). These behaviors, which may be the consequence of years of failure, can create many problems for students.

GENERAL PROBLEMS FACING ADOLESCENTS

Most adolescents face a host of challenges that simply reflect the developmental period. These include alcohol and drug abuse, pregnancy, suicide, and self-esteem problems. Because the nature of adolescence is transition and turmoil, there is little surprise that many problems occur during this developmental period. Although not all adolescents experience these problems, they are prevalent enough to pose a potential problem for all teenagers. If students have disabilities, these concerns can become even more problematic.

SUICIDE

Suicide has become a leading problem among adolescents in this country (Smith, 1990). In fact, "Suicide and self-harm have reached epidemic proportions among adolescents" (Ritter, 1990, p. 83). Suicide is now the second leading cause of death for adolescents.

Students with disabilities are even more likely to be at risk for suicide than their nondisabled peers. Adolescents with learning and behavior problems are likely to develop frustration and depression, which can lead to suicidal behaviors. Poor social skills, which are found frequently in students with disabilities, have been found to be related to depression (Spirito, Hart, Overholser, & Halverson, 1990). Stress, low self-esteem, and depression are all related to suicidal behavior. Because these are common characteristics of adolescents with disabilities, the risk factor for suicide for this group is great (Guetzloe, 1988).

In response to the high rates of suicide among adolescents, some schools have developed suicide education programs (Norton, Durlak, & Richards, 1989). These programs are aimed at all students in secondary schools. Special education teachers must make sure that students in their programs are also involved in the suicide education programs.

DRUG AND ALCOHOL ABUSE

Adolescents are likely candidates for drug and alcohol abuse. Because of peer pressure, the need for recognition, and an escape from the problems of adolescence, alcohol and drug abuse becomes a coping mechanism for many adolescents. In one study, 48 percent of the boys in the sample reported having been drunk by the age of 14 years, 5 months; and 11 percent reported having been drunk at least 10 times by that age (Anderson and Magnusson, 1990). Hammer and Vaglum (1990) studied the drinking habits of men and women in several age groups. Their findings indicate that "alcohol consumption varies according to changes in the life situation; the highest consumption of alcohol was found among both men and women during the transition period between adolescence and young adulthood" (p. 139).

In addition to alcohol, adolescents frequently become involved with other drugs. Watts and Wright (1990) studied several groups of adolescents to determine the extent of their drug use. The findings revealed that students who were adjudicated as delinquent had a much greater likelihood of using drugs than other high school students. Among White students, 48.6 percent of youth who were delinquent reported using marijuana, compared to 10.5 percent of the high school students overall.

Adolescents with disabilities may be particularly at risk for developing alcohol and drug abuse. Johnson (1988) listed the following characteristics of drug and alcohol abusers:

- Stress.
- Problems with social experiences.
- Problems with moral and character development.
- Depression.
- Low self-esteem.

Students in secondary special education programs frequently experience these kinds of problems, thereby making special education adolescents possible candidates for developing alcohol and drug abuse.

PREGNANCY

Unplanned pregnancies among teenagers in the United States are often the result of the troubled period of adolescence (Romig & Bakken, 1990). In this era of sex education,

Update

Solutions to Homework Problems

As indicated in an earlier box, homework presents unique challenges to students with special learning needs and particularly adolescents. Recent research in the area of homework has identified a variety of successful strategies. As outlined by Bryan and Sullivan-Burstein (1997), these include the following:

1. Examine current practices
- jot down how long you think an assignment should take your students to complete
- ask students to indicate on their work how long it actually did take to complete
- have students select a smiling, frowning, or neutral face to indicate their feelings about an assignment
- discuss with other teachers homework assignments and attempt to reach consensus about length and frequency

2. Develop innovative homework assignments
- work with other teachers to adopt similar practices and standard styles
- use games and fun activities as assignments
- relate assignments to the student's life outside of the classroom to add relevance.
- provide awards for homework completion.

3. Use a homework planner
- use a planner to help students acquire organizational skills (e.g., short-hand notations on a calendar)
- use the planner to communicate with parents and ask them to sign it when assignments have been completed
- teach students how to graph their completion rates in the planner

4. Teach study skills
- assist students in identifying a time and place for doing homework, having the necessary materials available, remembering to bring it to school, and reducing homework distractions
- monitor the effects of television viewing and other distractions
- teach students strategies to take notes, to increase reading comprehension, and to use mnemonic strategies

Source: Adapted from Bryan, T., & Sullivan-Burstein, K. (1997) Homework how-to's. *Teaching Exceptional Children, 29,* 32–37.

fear of AIDS, and the general impression that teenagers know and understand about preventing pregnancies, the number of unplanned pregnancies is surprising. Despite all the hoopla about sex education, many adolescents still engage in sexual activity without the use of contraceptives or other protection (Arnett, 1990). For students with disabilities, this again may harbor special problems that require a curricular response.

LOW SELF-ESTEEM

The self-esteem of adolescents is related to peer acceptance and group membership. Adolescents who feel rejected by their peers are likely to suffer from low self-esteem. Kennedy (1990) found a relationship between the peer social status of adolescents and their physical appearance. Self-esteem also has been linked to stress. A study of self-esteem and stress among high school students in North Dakota found that stress results in a lowered self-esteem, and further determined that the number of negative events was correlated with the level of self-esteem (Young, Rathge, Mullis, & Mullis, 1990). Unfortunately, adolescents with disabilities experience numerous negative events in their lives.

Other factors also are linked with self-esteem. For example, the way parents interact with their children directly impacts on their self-esteem (Scarr et al., 1986). Children who are constantly berated by their parents, told they are "dumb," or accused of not trying are likely to develop feelings of inferiority and lowered self-esteem.

SCHOOL DEMANDS PLACED ON ADOLESCENTS

Not only do adolescents face the demands of rapid physical and physiological changes in their bodies and the growing need for peer approval, but schools also place many demands on them, which can lead to problems, including the demands to (Mercer, 1987):

— attend to lectures and take comprehensive notes.
— develop a high level of competence in written expression.
— complete a comprehensive high school curriculum that requires many different kinds of skills.
— read and comprehend a variety of different kinds of materials.

Other demands of secondary schools include: (a) the high reading levels of textbooks, (b) having to work independently, (c) the need for listening and note-taking skills, and (d) having to participate orally in classroom activities (Buttrill, Niizawa, Biemer, Takahashi, & Hearn, 1989). These demands tied to academic activities are in addition to the social demands required for peer and adult approval. Most students in secondary schools meet these demands without any major problems, but if students have language deficits, unsuccessfully dealing with these requirements frequently leads to failure.

Many of the demands described require competence in oral language. Students have to attend to lectures, understand spoken language, and summarize the content of the information in the form of notes. They have to be able to properly decode language through reading. Finally, they have to participate in oral expressive activities. For students with language disabilities or disorders, these activities often are impossible to accomplish successfully. The end result may be general failure across all subject areas. Language competence, a key element in academic success, is especially critical in secondary schools.

LANGUAGE PROBLEMS AND INTERVENTION WITH ADOLESCENTS

Language problems of children in elementary schools frequently carry over into adolescence. A study by Algozzine, O'Shea, Stoddard, and Crews (1988) revealed that adolescents without disabilities demonstrate a significantly higher level of communication competence than their peers with learning disabilities. Problems in receptive and expressive language may create monumental problems for students in secondary classes. Therefore, secondary special education teachers and speech/language therapists must be prepared to identify language problems and develop appropriate intervention programs. The discussion that follows is intended to complement the previous chapters' attention to instructional programs by focusing specifically on concerns surrounding adolescents.

PROBLEMS IN RECEPTIVE LANGUAGE

As previously mentioned, students with problems in receptive language are at a major disadvantage in academic settings. Difficulties in receiving language through hearing or reading often result in academic failures. Although deficits in receptive language present problems for all students, the problems are actually more acute for students in secondary programs, with their emphasis on competency in content areas. Students are expected to learn facts about subjects such as history, science, and literature, and these facts must be learned through reading and listening. Deficits in receptive language deter the development of competence in these areas.

Reading   One of the most important skills for adolescents is reading. During their secondary education, students must read if they are to be successful in regular classrooms. Although some accommodations, such as tape-recorded materials, will lessen the impact of reading deficits, secondary students who are unable to read and comprehend written materials in content courses are at a major disadvantage.

Reading involves the ability to decode words and comprehend the content. The reading process can be described as (a) understanding written language, (b) a complex mental process, and (c) thinking (Roe, Stoodt, & Burns, 1987). The Report of the Commission on Reading defined reading as constructing meaning from written materials (Anderson, Hiebert, Scott, & Wilkinson, 1985). Too often, students with language problems have reading deficits that have a direct, negative impact on their success in other academic areas (Wallace, McLoughlin, 1988).

Secondary special education teachers have to provide assistance to students with reading problems.

Whereas teaching reading is an assumed task for teachers at the elementary level, confusion concerning reading instruction may abound at the secondary level.

Roe et al. (1987) described some faulty assumptions that frequently are voiced about reading instruction at the secondary level. Among the misconceptions are:

1. Teaching reading is only a concern at the elementary level.
2. Teaching reading in the content areas is separate and distinct from teaching subject matter.
3. Reading needs in the secondary school can be met through remedial work alone.
4. A reading specialist or an English teacher should be responsible for the teaching of reading.
5. The teaching of reading and the teaching of literature are one and the same. (pp. 7–8).

In reality, teaching reading should be a major concern of all teachers at the secondary level. Although classroom teachers are unlikely to have reading groups and use basal reading series, they nevertheless should engage in improving the reading skills of adolescents. Only about a third of the middle schools surveyed in a recent study employed a reading resource teacher (Irvin & Connors, 1989). Therefore, reading instruction in secondary schools is the responsibility of all teachers in all subject areas. Reading obviously is important in English and literature, but it is not less important in history and biology.

Although the bulk of remedial reading programs are designed for elementary students, several programs target adolescents. Teachers need to think through remedial reading intervention with adolescents to ensure that they are not wasting the student's time. For instance, if a particular program has not been effective with the student for three previous years, it probably will not result in positive benefits now. Before deciding to use a specific program, the following questions should be considered (Masters and Mori, 1986):

1. Does the instructional method/material offer an approach that hasn't been used under good instructional conditions before? Has the student been exposed to the program and experienced little or no success using good teaching practices?
2. How is the instructional method/material significantly different from what has been attempted before?
3. Is there adequate instructional time available in the student's day and week to accommodate the program?
4. Will the instructional method/material offend and/or bore the student? In this case the material would appear to have been developed for the elementary student and/or demands a routine so regimented that the instructional task is tedious and uninteresting.
5. Does the method/material offer instruction that allows the student to process the information in ways that the student has not experienced?
6. Is there evidence that the instructional method/material is effective? It is important to know that the skills the student has learned can be applied to the academic demands of the classroom. (pp. 157–158)

Students' reading vocabulary is critical for their overall academic success. Not knowing words they come across in reading assignments will likely result in their not understanding the reading assignment, leading to failure in the subject area. It also can result in such tedious, slow reading that students will quickly get bored with the whole reading process. Therefore, teaching vocabulary is a key component of reading instruction for secondary students.

Consistent with the discussion in chapter 9, vocabulary and word recognition can be taught in several ways in secondary schools: (a) sight word approach, (b) context clues, (c) structural analysis, (d) compare/contrast strategy, and (e) phonics (Roe et al., 1987). No one approach is always effective with most secondary students. Therefore, teachers must take advantage of whichever method works best with a given child. Special education teachers and reading specialists are available to help determine this approach and to assist other teachers in its implementation. Table 13.2 describes some activities that are useful with each of these approaches.

Schwartz (1988) suggested a method of teaching vocabulary in content area textbooks. The method, called "concept of definition," or CD, "helps students to (1) select and evaluate sources of information for determining the meaning of a new term, (2) combine and organize new information with their prior knowledge about the concept, (3) test their understanding, and (4) recall vocabulary concepts" (p. 109). Regular classroom teachers can easily implement this model in content courses.

In addition to word recognition and vocabulary, specific skills required for comprehension are critical for academic success of adolescents in content classes. Subjects such as social studies and biology have their own vocabularies; therefore, students need to understand the vocabulary unique to several disciplines. Woodward and Peters (1983) suggested that the following skills are important for secondary students' comprehension in specific subject areas:

Table 13.2
Approaches to Teach Vocabulary

Approach	Activities
Sight Word	• Use flash cards • Use mechanical devices such as tachistoscope displaying one word at a time • Play games such as word bingo
Structural Analysis	• Divide words into structural components • Use worksheets for practice with two lists of words that, when combined, form a compound word • Divide words into syllables
Compare/Contrast Strategy	• Have students compare unknown parts of words with any known parts
Phonics	• Have students pronounce words from phonetic spellings and diacritical marks
Using the Dictionary, Glossary, and Thesaurus	• Teach students to use pronunciation key and abbreviations in the dictionary • Have students complete dictionary assignments such as, "Look up the word 'hemisphere.' What are the two guide words on the page?"

Source: Adapted from *The Content Areas* (3rd ed., pp. 29–37) by B. D. Roe, B. D. Stoodt, and P. C. Burns, 1987, Boston: Houghton-Mifflin. Copyright ©1987 by Houghton Mifflin Company. Adapted with permission.

Social Studies
- learn a new technical vocabulary
- locate facts
- translate abstract ideas into meaningful concepts
- organize material; identify, distinguish, and translate relationships and interrelationships of ideas
- recognize, interpret, and distinguish concepts of time, space, and chronological order

Math
- translate numerical symbols into verbal symbols
- translate formulas into significant relationships
- read very slowly

Science
- locate the stated problem
- list the facts that related to this problem
- analyze these facts
- predict outcomes from these facts
- verify the outcomes with the facts distinguished and analyzed. (pp. 234–235)

In comprehending reading materials in content areas, students must understand certain frequently used terms. Table 13.3 summarizes words from various subject areas that secondary students need to be able to read and understand.

Adolescents with reading problems might benefit from instruction in how to read for comprehension. An example is the SQ3R method, discussed in chapter 9. SQ3R stands for survey, question, read, recite, and review. This method (a) is supported by cognitive theory, (b) can be found in almost all secondary study skills books, (c) has been used for more than 40 years, and (d) is highly structured and relatively easy to learn (Jacobowitz, 1988).

The SQ3R method has been around for a long time. It is only one way of helping students with their reading vocabulary and comprehension. Teachers have taken this method, modified it, and implemented it in a variety of ways. The key is that students have a systematic method to increase their comprehension.

Listening and Attention   In addition to reading for content, adolescents acquire a great deal of information through listening. The ability to attend to someone who is talking, and to comprehend the information received, is vital for students in secondary classrooms. Although many different instructional approaches are used in secondary programs, lecturing remains the primary mode of instruction for many teachers (Smith, 1990; Michel & Weaver, 1984; Wagenaar, 1981). This only serves to reveal the criticality of good listening skills for adolescents.

Some students are simply good listeners. They "tune in" to the person speaking and are able to comprehend a large portion of the information. But other students with disabilities have problems with listening. Teachers must develop programs that will enhance these students' listening and auditory comprehension skills (Forster & Doyle, 1989). Without competence in these areas, students probably will not be able to learn by sitting in lectures and taking notes.

A model presented by Forster and Doyle (1989) provides a way to focus attention during listening activities. This model requires students to listen to a simulated

Table 13.3
Important Words for Specific Purposes

Words Used in Cause and Effect Patterns

why	as a result of	reasons	so that
if	the effect of	since	hence
so	on account of	therefore	thus
cause	due to	consequently	
because	outcome	this led to that	

Words Used in Sequence Patterns

first	next	later	in 1943	secondly
second	then	still later	in 1958	thirdly
third	finally	later on	after that	eventually
yesterday	tomorrow	last	to begin	to sum up
today	steps	lastly	procedure	
in conclusion		at last	plans	

Words Used in Listing Patterns

several	kind(s)	way(s)	one	number words: one, two, three
many	type(s)	varieties	another	types
series	style(s)	in addition	still another	third kind
few	couple	some	an example	

Words Used in Comparison/Contrast Patterns

different	but	compare
different from	on one hand	both
similar	on the other hand	as well as
same	however	not only
alike	contrast	but also
not alike	although	either . . . so
while	than	unless
yet	equally important	on the contrary
in spite of		

Source: From *The Learning Disabled Adolescent* (pp. 47–49) by D. M. Woodward and D. J. Peters, 1983, Austin, TX: PRO-ED. Copyright 1983 by PRO-ED, Inc. Reprinted by permission.

newscast and later summarize its contents. Students use an outline to avoid distractibility during the exercise. Outlines, advance organizers, and other means of facilitating attention to auditory input may enable students to attend to a lecture or other verbal discourse long enough to acquire information.

Masters and Mori (1986) have suggested several activities that students can use to help with their listening skills. Noting that maintaining close attention during a long lecture is often difficult, they recommend that students do the following:

- Take notes.
- Draw small, simple pictures that provide a general explanation of the content that is presented.

- Try to anticipate what will be said next.
- Actively employ memory strategies during the presentation.
- Restate the main ideas to yourself during the presentation, and try to tie in the related or supporting points.
- Formulate questions and ask them either during or immediately after the presentation. (p. 130)

Many students use these types of skills spontaneously, but students with receptive language disorders may need actual instruction in their use. Therefore, teachers might want to give actual lessons on how to develop listening skills such as those noted here.

PROBLEMS IN EXPRESSIVE LANGUAGE

Just as adolescents have problems with receptive language, some have difficulty expressing themselves orally and in writing. Inability to perform in these areas can create major academic problems for students at the secondary level. Students in secondary schools are expected to express themselves in writing and orally. In fact, just about all the information teachers receive from students is either written or oral. Students complete written assignments, take written tests, engage in oral discussions, and respond to oral questions. Limited competence in these areas can easily result in academic failure.

Written Expression   Written expression can be described as the expression of thoughts in written format through expressive language. It is a complex, cognitive process that does not develop without instruction (Gould, 1991). Gregg (1991) underlined the complexity of written expression by stating that it "requires that the writer simultaneously deal with a subject, text, and reader" (p. 66). It is not a simple skill that can be developed easily; writing must be practiced over a period of time (Manion, 1988). For adolescents with mild disabilities, abilities in written expression can greatly facilitate successful integration into regular classes (Minner, Prater, Sullavan, & Gwaltney, 1989).

The ability to express thoughts in writing depends on a number of skills, including speaking, reading, handwriting, spelling, capitalization, punctuation, word usage, and grammar (Wallace & McLoughlin, 1988). To this list Gould (1991) added (a) background knowledge, (b) semantics, (c) syntax, and (d) graphosymbolics (Gould, 1991). Students might have problems in any one or more of these areas and require intervention.

Intervention programs for students with problems in written expression can use an isolated skill approach or a holistic approach. The *isolated skill approach* focuses on teaching specific skills involved in written expression, such as handwriting, spelling, and syntax. A drawback with this method is that integration of these skills may not occur. Following a successful remedial program in isolation, a student may have a thorough understanding of the rules of grammar but may not be able to apply these skills in spontaneous writing. Another disadvantage is that teachers have a tendency to criticize discrete errors rather than to judge the entire writing effort when taught in isolation (Gould, 1991).

The *holistic approach* to remediation in written expression is the opposite of the isolated skills method. Using this method, students actually learn writing skills by writing. The overall writing process is judged, not only the skills related to handwriting, spelling, and syntax (Gould, 1991). The holistic approach is allied with the whole language model that many schools are adopting to teach reading and writing together.

Oberlin and Shugarman (1988) recommended three activities to improve adolescents' written expression. The first focuses on the relationship between prewriting and prereading activities, and the second activity provides a method for previewing unfamiliar reading materials. The third activity enables students to connect prior knowledge to information in a text. Table 13.4 describes each of these activities.

Another activity that can be used to enhance the written expression of adolescents is a writing workshop. The workshop for secondary students proposed by Manion (1988) would focus on the process of writing as well as the end product. Components of the training include:

- prewriting—determining topic and general outline.
- writing—completing a draft.
- responding—reacting to conferences with the teacher.
- revising—making revisions based on content conferences.
- editing—making final changes in content and style.
- publishing—working with the teacher to finalize the product.

Table 13.4
Activities to Improve Written Expression

Activity	Steps
Relate prewriting and prereading	1. Brainstorm with students. List steps author goes through before writing a text. 2. Transform list of prewriting activities into prereading questions such as, "What is the specific topic?"
Preview unfamiliar texts	1. Read one to three sentences to students. 2. Discuss unfamiliar terms. 3. Reread passage and have students write it. 4. Display passage and ask students to compare it with their copy. 5. Have students edit their writing. 6. Discuss writer's style, word meanings.
Connect prior knowledge to text information	1. Have students survey a reading passage. 2. Select one key concept from passage and develop an essay question. 3. Have students write response to essay question. 4. Share responses. Note any misconceptions. 5. Guide reading of text. 6. Ask students to respond in writing once again to the essay test. 7. Repeat essay question on final test.

Source: Adapted from "Purposeful Writing Activities for Students in Middle School" by K. J. Oberlin and S. L. Shugarman, 1988, *Journal of Reading, 31,* pp. 720–723. Reprinted with permission of Kelly Oberlin and the International Reading Association.

Spelling   One component of written expression is spelling. Although spelling, along with the use of proper grammar, may not be emphasized during the beginning of a program to teach written expression, it should be considered after initial interest in writing is secured. At the secondary level, spelling instruction should be integrated into the total language arts curriculum rather than dealt with in isolation (Woodward, 1981).

When remediating spelling for adolescents, teachers should consider the following guidelines (Masters & Mori, 1986):

1. Spelling should be linked to practical tasks. Since spelling tasks in "real life" seldom if ever require the oral spelling of single words in list form, the remedial program must prepare students for the tasks they currently and ultimately will be required to do.
2. Since spelling commonly requires a written or typed response using many "automatic" words, the program should work jointly on spelling and cursive handwriting.
3. Because approximately 120 to 150 basic words make up the bulk of our writing, time should be spent on practice exercises that make the spelling of these words almost automatic.
4. The alphabet as well as phonetic principles should be stressed, allowing students to speak the letters and/or sounds as they practice.
5. Since the multisensory approach appears to be quite effective with mildly handicapped adolescents, it should be incorporated into spelling instruction.
6. Remediation should utilize one of the most successful instructional approaches available: direct instruction.
7. Instruction should provide as many visual concrete images from which to associate auditory sounds as possible.
8. The materials should be readily available, inexpensive, and easy to follow. (p. 170)

A spelling approach described by Dangel (1987) should appeal to adolescents. The model, which uses the game of football as a basis for the program, is called "the coach's spelling approach." It has three steps: scouting, practicing, and keeping stats. Table 13.5 describes the actions that occur in each step.

Handwriting Problems   Still another component of written expression is handwriting. As discussed in chapter 10, on handwriting skills, the ability to communicate in

Table 13.5
Remedial Spelling Approach: The Coach's Spelling Approach

Activities	Description
Scouting the week's spelling words	1. Learn to recognize words 2. Identify tendencies of words 3. Identify difficult words that will require more practice time
Practice words	1. Select a practice approach 2. Practice until mastery
Keep statistics	1. Keep records of success 2. Adjust practice based on performance statistics

Source: From "The Coach's Spelling Approach" by H. L. Dangel, 1987, *Teaching Exceptional Children, 19,* pp. 21–22. Copyright 1987 by the Council for Exceptional Children. Reprinted with permission.

writing is critical for many students. For those with disabilities, these skills are even more important.

Handwriting instruction at the secondary level must be integrated into other parts of the curriculum. Just as reading instruction is the responsibility of all teachers, so is handwriting. Though teachers in content courses should be most concerned with the acquisition of competencies related to the content of the course, they also should be interested in the student's ability to write legibly.

In the following ways, secondary teachers can implement instruction in handwriting while primarily teaching subject matter:

- Require written work.
- Require written work to be neat and legible.
- Give extra or bonus points for written work that is neat and legible.
- Give students the opportunity to rewrite work that is poorly written.
- Develop activities for students to write letters to various people and groups (such as letters to the editor, U.S. troops overseas, etc.) that hopefully will encourage pride in written work.

Oral Expression   Some adolescents have problems with oral expression. This creates difficulties in their presenting information orally as well as responding orally to teachers and peers. Participating in class discussions—a common teaching technique in secondary schools (Smith, 1990)—is also hampered by oral expression problems. Woodward (1981) has suggested the following general guidelines in implementing oral language programs for adolescents.

1. Oral communication instruction should address the needs of students in everyday situations.
2. The classroom should be used as a learning situation.
3. Instruction should emphasize the interactive nature of speaking and listening.
4. The program goal should be that of enhancing the student's repertoire and use of effective speaking behaviors.
5. Oral communication skills can be enhanced by using parents, supportive staff, and appropriate instructional technology.
6. Communication instruction should be a clearly identifiable facet of the curriculum.
7. The program should be based on a school-wide assessment of the speaking and listening needs of students.
8. Program effectiveness is increased through in-service training of all curriculum area teachers on the development of effective communication environments in their classrooms.
9. Program emphasis should focus on specific behaviors that the student is able to change.
10. Local communications programs should be integrated at the state level to establish a resource network. (pp. 85–86).

Expressive Vocabulary   Students must have a sufficient vocabulary to be able to express themselves effectively. Though many students develop a good vocabulary through reading and exposure to new words in their language environment, some students do not have ample opportunities to develop their vocabularies. For these students, teachers must develop and implement vocabulary-building activities. As examples:

1. Have students choose one new word each day, make up a sentence, and state the sentence to the teacher at a designated time during the day.
2. Choose two sides for teams and have each side take a turn in properly using a word the teacher gives in a sentence.
3. Have students listen to the newscast each evening and make a list of unknown words; the student is to use words properly in a sentence during a particular time of the day.

Developing activities for teaching expressive vocabulary requires only creativity on the teacher's part. The key is to encourage students to use their oral expressive skills, and to positively reinforce their use.

Pragmatics   Pragmatics, or the functional use of language, is a primary area of concern for adolescents. If students are unable to express themselves in a functional manner, making their wishes, needs, feelings, and responses understood, their oral language efforts may be wasted. The importance of pragmatics, especially for adolescents, cannot be overemphasized (Mandell & Gold, 1984).

Chapter 1 contains a description of some activities for teaching language skills to adolescents. Practicing functional use of language is the best method for students to learn the proper use of language. Modeling, prompting, immediate reinforcement, and self-correction activities often are used in teaching pragmatics to adolescents.

A major part of teaching pragmatics to adolescents is gaining their confidence and trust, and helping them feel good about their ability to use oral language. Structuring the classroom environment to support students in their use of oral language is critical. Additional instructional activities that focus on pragmatics are provided elsewhere in this text. Teachers need to remember the importance of pragmatics for adolescents with language deficiencies and facilitate appropriate language usage among this population.

GENERAL INSTRUCTIONAL CONSIDERATIONS WITH ADOLESCENTS

Teaching adolescents with language problems requires specific intervention techniques. Individual student strengths and weaknesses, determined through a comprehensive assessment, will determine the specific nature of the program. Several general intervention strategies, however, should be considered with any program.

STUDENT MOTIVATION

Prior to achieving success with any intervention program, the student must be motivated to participate and put forth effort. A key element in motivating adolescents is to get their involvement. Larson and McKinley (1985) have suggested that student involvement begin before initiating the assessment process: "Prior to assessment, the student should be informed of what behaviors are going to be assessed (e.g., listening, speaking, and thinking skills) and how they are going to be assessed (e.g., informally by the clinician and student talking and interacting with each other and more formally through some specific tests)" (p. 72). Student involvement leads to a sense of ownership in the program that is implemented. Students have a real stake in the program's success.

COUNSELING

Another general intervention strategy described by Larson and McKinley (1985) is counseling. Counseling is the process whereby teachers communicate with students about their language disabilities. Teacher and student share information, and the teacher provides support for the student's feelings and emotional needs. Although teachers are not trained counselors, they still may find some general practices useful.

Group sessions are often an excellent vehicle for providing intervention to adolescents with language problems. Among the advantages of group sessions (Larson & McKinley, 1985):

- Students learn they are not the only ones with language problems.
- Students receive emotional support from each other.
- Students participate in an ongoing language evaluation of each other.
- Groups facilitate oral interactions.

This topic is discussed in somewhat greater detail in Polloway, Patton, Payne, & Payne (1989).

SPECIFIC INSTRUCTIONAL APPROACHES

In addition to the general instructional concepts just discussed, some specific concerns and activities relate to language disorders among adolescents.

CURRICULAR OPTIONS

One factor that could impact on language intervention programs for adolescents is the secondary curriculum. At the secondary level the curriculum generally is arranged into three areas: college preparatory, general academic, and vocational. Students choose among these curricular areas based on their long-range plans and current abilities. Factors involved in this decision might include teachers' recommendations, parental desires, students' ambitions, an understanding of capabilities and demands, and peer approval.

Curriculum choices are important at all grade levels, K through 12, but curriculum is most important at the secondary level (Polloway, Patton, Epstein, & Smith, 1989). The curriculum at the secondary level offers students choices that will critically impact on their futures. Regardless of the reasons why students choose various curricular paths, the choices are critical to adult success.

Update

Acquisition and Generalization of Learning Strategies

Teaching adolescents requires an emphasis on the development of independence. A particularly fruitful approach is to teach learning strategies so that students learn how to learn. Deshler, Ellis, and Lenz (1996) provided a comprehensive discussion on how to teach adolescents to learn to use learning strategies. Their recommendations for instruction included the following:

1. Pretest and make commitments
    A. Orientation and pretest
    B. Awareness and commitment
2. Describe the strategy
    A. Orientation and overview
    B. Current strategy and remembering system
3. Model the strategy
    A. Orientation
    B. Presentation
    C. Student enlistment
4. Verbal elaboration and rehearsal
    A. Verbal elaboration
    B. Verbal rehearsal
5. Controlled practice and feedback
    A. Orientation and overview
    B. Guided practice
    C. Independent practice
6. Advanced practice and feedback
    A. Orientation and overview
    B. Guided practice
    C. Independent practice
7. Confirm acquisition and make generalization commitments
    A. Confirm and celebrate
    B. Forecast and commit to generalization
8. Generalization
    A. Orientation
    B. Activation
    C. Adaptation
    D. Maintenance

Source: Adapted from Deshler, D. D., Ellis, E. S., & Lenz, B. K. (1996). *Teaching adolescents with learning disabilities: Strategies and methods* (2nd ed.), p. 36. Denver: Love Publishing: (reprinted with permission).

For students with mild disabilities, three alternative curricular orientations are generally available: (a) remediation, (b) maintenance, and (c) functionality (Polloway, Patton, Epstein, & Smith, 1989). Remediation covers both academic remediation and social skills remediation. The maintenance option offers students the supports necessary for success in regular classroom programs; it includes tutoring and instruction in learning strategies. The functionality curriculum deals with skills necessary for success as an adult .

All secondary school students fit somewhere in these curricular areas. For those without disabilities, the options of college preparatory, general academic, and vocational are available. These three basic options are also available to students with disabilities, but they also have the assistance provided by remediation, maintenance, or functionality. Within this framework will come language intervention for students with these types of disorders. Because language intervention is most successful when implemented in natural settings through spontaneous language exchanges, it could occur in any of the curricular options discussed.

STUDY SKILLS

Of particular interest to many secondary students with disabilities is their success in integrated, regular classrooms. One intervention model that can facilitate success is study skills. Even though the development of appropriate study skills should begin during the elementary school years, the application of study skills has particular relevance for adolescents in secondary school programs (Hoover, 1989a).

Study skills can be defined as those skills that enable a student to acquire information, store and retrieve information, and express information adequately for success in academic and social environments. Examples of study skills are listening, note-taking and outlining, report writing, time management, and self-management of behavior (Hoover, 1989b). Many of these study skills relate directly to language problems. As already stated, listening is a key to success in secondary classes. If students have a weakness in this area, learning how to listen, or how to maximize listening skills, is critical (Mandlebaum & Wilson, 1989).

Study skills can be effective in enhancing receptive language and expressive language. For example, listening, note-taking, and reading skills facilitate receptive language abilities, and providing assistance in oral expression and organizing materials for written output improve expressive language (Smith & Dowdy, 1989; Smith & Tompkins, 1988). Hoover (1988, 1989a, 1989b) provides additional information on instructional approaches to teach study skills.

ACCOMMODATIONS

Accommodations are similar to study skills in that they facilitate the success of students with disabilities in integrated, regular classrooms. The difference is that accommodations are efforts by the teacher to modify the environment and curriculum in such a way that students with disabilities can achieve success, whereas study skills are strategies students can use to facilitate their own success. Teachers can make numerous accommodations to increase the likelihood of success for adolescents with language problems.

Accommodations include a variety of changes in materials and methods. They include outlines, study guides, advance organizers, audiovisual aids, variations in instructional strategies, seating arrangements, and tape recordings (Smith et al., 1986). Still other accommodations focus on the alteration of materials, such as reducing the content of textbooks (Ellis & Lenz, 1990), alternative methods of testing students, and changes in requirements. Table 13.6 summarizes some of these accommodative strategies that can be used with adolescents who have language problems.

GENERAL SCHOOL SURVIVAL SKILLS

In addition to general and specific language intervention strategies, school personnel who work with secondary students with language disorders should provide instruction in general survival skills. During implementation of the intervention strategies that hopefully will lessen the impact of the language problem, adolescents still face survival in their regular courses. One of the key roles of special education teachers is to facilitate the success of students in their integrated, mainstream classes. For many of these students, including those with language problems, this includes teaching survival skills.

Table 13.6
Examples of Accommodative Strategies

Strategy	Description
Outlines	Simple course outlines assist pupils in organizing notes and information.
Study Guides	Expanded outlines. Provide specific information such as assignments and evaluation criteria.
Advance Organizers	A set of questions or other guides indicating the most important parts of reading assignments.
Audio-Visual Aids	Overhead projectors, films, film strips, and chalkboard are examples. Reinforce auditory information and enable students with auditory deficits to access information.
Varying Instructional Strategies	Alternative teaching strategies enable students to utilize their most efficient learning style.
Seating Arrangement	Place students in locations that minimize problems. Examples: close to front of class for children with auditory and visual problems; away from other children for students with behavior problems; away from windows and doors for those with distractibility problems.
Tape Recorders	Using tape recorders can greatly benefit children with visual problems, memory problems, reading problems, etc. Taped textbooks, tests, and lectures can facilitate learning.

Although many secondary special education teachers focus strictly on remediating academic deficits, students often fail in mainstream classes because they lack certain survival skills (Schaeffer, Zigmond, Kerr, & Heidi, 1990). These skills also have been called "teacher-pleasing behaviors" because they can result in positive interactions between student and teacher. School survival skills have been defined as "those skills that enable students to meet the demands of the regular curriculum, or regular educators, and of large-group instruction" (Kerr, Nelson, & Lambert, 1987, p. 86). These skills greatly enhance the likelihood that students with language disabilities will be successful in the classroom.

Schaeffer et al. (1990) described six different survival skills that some secondary students need to develop to achieve success:

1. Attending class.
2. Arriving promptly.
3. Going to class prepared.
4. Meeting assignment deadlines.
5. Talking to teachers appropriately.
6. Reading and following directions.

Although these may seem obvious, many students simply do not adhere to these principles.

Students who do not have disabilities may be able to get by without these skills. For students with problems, however, pleasing teachers may be a critical component for success. Therefore, teaching teacher-pleasing behaviors should be taught to many students. Table 13.7 outlines some activities that can be used to teach school survival skills.

SUMMARY

This chapter has presented information about adolescents and unique language problems experienced by this group. The first part of the chapter discussed the nature of adolescence. Definitions and different ways to look at adolescence were presented. The conclusion was that adolescence, at least in our society, is a period of transition, frequently associated with turbulence. The various physical changes that occur during the adolescent period were also presented.

The next section dealt with characteristics found in adolescents with disabilities. It was pointed out that these students frequently experience academic, social, and emotional problems. While many problems are found among all adolescents, those with disabilities have a tendency to exhibit them more severely. Unique language problems experienced by adolescents with disabilities were also presented.

Ways to provide instruction to adolescents with language problems were provided. These included strategies to help students with reading problems, as well as ways to provide effective intervention for problems in content areas, such as history and science.

Table 13.7
Activities to Teach School Survival Skills

Survival Skill	Activity
Attending Class and Punctuality	<ul><li>Use hall monitors in the school</li><li>Require written passes; have assigned seats</li><li>Relate attendance and punctuality to real-life jobs, such as airport security and traffic police officers</li></ul>
Class Preparedness	<ul><li>Require students to bring materials to class</li><li>Establish clear expectations</li><li>Use peers to ask questions related to class preparedness</li></ul>
Meeting Assignment Deadlines	<ul><li>Establish clear assignments and deadlines</li><li>Develop self-monitoring of assignments</li><li>Ask questions daily to require self-monitoring</li><li>Use peers to ask questions related to meeting assignments</li><li>Require some assignments each day</li></ul>

Source: Adapted from *Helping Adolescents with Learning and Behavior Problems* (pp. 90–104) by M. M. Kerr, C. M. Nelson, and D. L. Lambert, 1987, Columbus, OH: Charles E. Merrill Publishing. Copyright ©1987 by Merrill Publishing Company. Adapted with permission of Merrill, an imprint of Macmillan Publishing Company.

The final section of the chapter provided information about instructional techniques for adolescents with disabilities. Strategies discussed included motivation and counseling. The final portion of this section dealt with specific instructional techniques for adolescents.

REFERENCES

Algozzine, B., O'Shea, D. J., Stoddard, K., & Crews, W. B. (1988). Reading and writing competencies of adolescents with learning disabilities. *Journal of Learning Disabilities, 21*, 154–160.

Anderson, R. C., Hiebert, E. H., Scott, J. A., & Wilkinson, I. A. G. (1985). *Becoming a Nation of Readers: The report of the Commission on Reading.* Washington, DC: National Institute of Education.

Anderson, T., & Magnusson, D. (1990). Biological maturation in adolescence and the development of drinking habits and alcohol abuse among young males: A prospective longitudinal study. *Journal of Youth and Adolescence, 19*, 33–44.

Arnett, J. (1990). Contraceptive use, sensation seeking, and adolescent egocentrism. *Journal of Youth and Adolescence, 19*, 171–180.

Bryan, T., & Sullivan-Burstein, K. (1997) Homework how-to's. *Teaching Exceptional Children, 29*, 32–37.

Buttrill, J., Niizawa, J., Biemer, C., Takahashi, C., & Hearn, S. (1989). Serving the language learning disabled adolescent: A strategies-based model. *Language, Speech, and Hearing Services in Schools, 20*, 170–184.

Dangel, H. L. (1987). The coach's spelling approach. *Teaching Exceptional Children, 19*, 21–22.

Deshler, D. D., Ellis, E. S., & Lenz, B. K. (1996). *Teaching adolescents with learning disabilities: Strategies and methods* (2nd ed.), p. 36. Denver: Love Publishing: (reprinted with permission).

Dossetor, D. R., & Nicol, A. R. (1989). Dilemmas of adolescents with developmental retardation: A review. *Journal of Adolescence, 12*, 167–185.

Ellis, E. S., & Lenz, B. K. (1990). Techniques for mediating content-area learning: Issues and research. *Focus on Exceptional Children, 22*, 1–16.

Epstein, M. H., Polloway, E. A., Patton, J. R., & Foley, R. (1989). Mild retardation: Student characteristics and services. *Education and Training in Mental Retardation, 24*, 7–16.

Forster, R., & Doyle, B. A. (1989). Teaching listening skills to students with attention deficit disorders. *Teaching Exceptional Children, 21*, 20–23.

Gearheart, B. R., & Gearheart, C. J. (1989). *Learning* Disabilities (5th ed.). Columbus, OH: Merrill.

Gould, B. W. (1991). Curricular strategies for written expression. In A. M. Bain, L. L. Bailet, & L. C. Moats (Eds.), *Written Language Disorders*. Austin, TX: Pro-Ed.

Gregg, N. (1991). Disorders of written expression. In A. M. Bain, L. L. Bailet, & L. C. Moats (Eds.), *Written Language Disorders*. Austin, TX: Pro-Ed.

Guetzloe, E. (1988). Suicide and depression: Special education's responsibility. *Teaching Exceptional Children, 20*, 25–28.

Hallahan, D. P., & Kauffman, J. M. (1991). *Exceptional Children* (5th ed.). Englewood Cliffs, NJ: Prentice-Hall.

Hammer, T., & Vaglum, P. (1990). Use of alcohol and drugs in the transitional phase from adolescence to young adulthood. *Journal of Adolescence, 13*, 129–142.

Hoover, J. J. (1988). *Teaching handicapped students study skills* (2nd ed.). Lindale, TX: Hamilton Publications.

Hoover, J. J. (1989a). Implementing a study skills program in the classroom. *Academic Therapy, 24*, 471–478.

Hoover, J. J. (1989b). Study skills. In E. A. Polloway, J. R. Patton, J. S. Payne, & R. A. Payne (Eds.), *Strategies for teaching learners with special needs* (4th ed.). Columbus, OH: Charles E. Merrill.

Irvin, J. L., & Connors, N. A. (1989). Reading instruction in middle level schools: Results of a U.S. survey. *Journal of Reading, 32*, 306–311.

Jacobowitz, T. (1988). Using theory to modify practice: An illustration with SQ3R. *Journal of Reading, 32*, 126–131.

Johnson, J. L. (1988). The challenge of substance abuse. *Teaching Exceptional Children, 20*, 29–31.

Kauffman, J. M. (1989). *Characteristics of behavior disorders of children and youth* (4th ed.). Columbus, OH: Charles E. Merrill Publishing.

Kennedy, J. H. (1990). Determinants of peer social status: Contributions of physical appearance, reputation, and behavior. *Journal of Youth and Adolescence, 19*, 233–244.

Kerr, M. M., Nelson, C. M., & Lambert, D. L. (1987). *Helping adolescents with learning and behavior problems*. Columbus, OH: Charles E. Merrill Publishing.

Larson, R., Kubey, R., & Colletti, J. (1989). Changing channels: Early adolescent media choices and shifting investments in family and friends. *Journal of Youth and Adolescence, 18*, 583–599.

Larson, V. L., & McKinley, N. L. (1985). General intervention principles with language impaired adolescents. *Topics in Language Disorders, 5*, 70–77.

Mandell, C. J., & Gold, V. (1984). *Teaching handicapped students*. St. Paul: West Publishing.

Mandlebaum, L. H., & Wilson, R. (1989). Teaching listening skills in the special education classroom. *Academic Therapy, 24*, 449–460.

Manion, B. B. (1988). Writing workshop in junior high school: It's worth the time. *Journal of Reading, 32*, 154–157.

Masters, A. A., & Mori, L. F. (1986). *Teaching secondary students with mild learning and behavioral problems*. Rockville, MD: Aspen Publications.

Mehring, T. A., & Colson, S. E. (1990). Motivation and mildly handicapped learners. *Focus on Exceptional Children, 22*, 1–12.

Mercer, C. D. (1987). *Students with learning disabilities* (3rd ed.). Columbus, OH: Charles E. Merrill.

Meyer, A., Pisha, B., & Rose, D. (1991). Process and product in writing: Computer as enabler. In A. M. Bain, L. L. Bailet, & L. C. Moats (Eds.), *Written Language Disorders*. Austin, TX: Pro-Ed.

Michel, T. A., & Weaver, R. L. (1984). Lecturing: Means for improvement. *Clearing House, 57*, 389–391.

Minner, S., Prater, G., Sullavan, C., & Gwaltney, W. (1989). Informal assessment of written expression. *Teaching Exceptional Children, 21*, 76–79.

Ness, J., & Price, L. A. (1990). Meeting the psychosocial needs of adolescents and adults with LD. *Intervention, 26*, 16–21.

Norton, E. M., Durlak, J. A., & Richards, M. H. (1989). Peer knowledge of and reactions to adolescent suicide. *Journal of Youth and Adolescence, 18*, 427–438.

Oberlin, K. J., & Shugarman, S. L. (1988). Purposeful writing activities for students in middle school. *Journal of Reading, 31*, 720–723.

Polloway, E. A., Epstein, M. H., Patton, J. R., Cullinan, D., & Luebke, J. (1986). Demographic, social, and behavioral characteristics of students with educable mental retardation. *Education and Training of the Mentally Retarded, 21*, 27–34.

Polloway, E. A., Patton, J. R., Epstein, M. H., & Smith, T. E. C. (1989). Comprehensive curriculum for students with mild handicaps. *Focus on Exceptional Children, 21*, 1–12.

Polloway, E. A., Patton, J. R., Payne, J. S., & Payne, R. A. (1989). *Strategies for teaching learners with special needs*, 4th ed. Columbus, OH: Charles E. Merrill Publishing.

Ritter, D. R. (1990). Adolescent suicide: Social competence and problem behavior of youth at high risk and low risk for suicide. *School Psychology Review, 19*, 83–95.

Roe, B. D., Stoodt, B. D., & Burns, P. C. (1987). *The content areas*, 3rd ed. Boston: Houghton-Mifflin.

Romig, C. A. & Bakken, L. (1990). Teens at risk for pregnancy: The role of ego development and family processes. *Journal of Adolescence, 13*, 195–199.

Sabornie, E. J., & Beard, G. H. (1990). Teaching social skills to students with mild handicaps. *Teaching Exceptional Children, 23*, 35–38.

Sabornie, E. J., & Kauffman, J. M. (1987). Assigned, received, and reciprocal social status of adolescents with and without mild mental retardation. *Education and Training in Mental Retardation, 22*, 139–149.

Scarr, S., Weinberg, R. A., & Levine, A. (1986). *Understanding Development*. New York: Harcourt Brace Jovanovich, Publishers.

Schaeffer, A. L., Zigmond, N., Kerr, M. M., & Heidi, E. F. (1990). Helping teenagers develop school survival skills. *Teaching Exceptional Children, 23*, 6–9.

Schwartz, R. M. (1988). Learning to learn vocabulary in content area textbooks. *Journal of Reading, 32*, 108–118.

Sebald, H. (1989). Adolescents' peer orientation: Changes in the support system during the past three decades. *Adolescence, 24*, 32–41.

Shea, T. M., & Bauer, A. M. (1991). *Parents and teachers of children with exceptionalities* (2nd ed.). Boston: Allyn & Bacon.

Smith, K. (1990). Suicidal behavior in school aged youth. *School Psychology Review, 19*, 186–195.

Smith, P. L., & Tompkins, G. E. (1988). Structured notetaking: A new strategy for content area readers. *Journal of Reading, 32*, 46–53.

Smith, T. E. C., Price, B. J., & Marsh, G. E. (1986). *Mildly handicapped children and adults*. St. Paul: West Publishing.

Smith, T. E. C. (1990). *Introduction to education* (2nd ed.). St. Paul: West Publishing.

Smith, T. E. C., & Dowdy, C. A. (1989). The role of study skills in the secondary curriculum. *Academic Therapy, 24*, 479–490.

Spirito, A., Hart, K., Overholser, J., & Halverson, J. (1990). Social skills and depression in adolescent suicide attempters. *Adolescence, 25*, 543–552.

Tanner, J. M. (1974). Variability of growth and maturity in newborn infants. In M. Lewis & L. A. Rosenblum (Eds.), *The effect of the infant on its caregiver* (pp. 77–103). New York: Wiley.

Wagenaar, T. C. (1981). High school seniors' views of themselves and their schools: A trend analysis. *Phi Delta Kappan, 63*, 29–32.

Wallace, G., & McLoughlin, J. A. (1988). *Learning disabilities: Concepts and characteristics*, 3rd ed. Columbus, OH: Charles E. Merrill Publishing.

Watts, W. D., & Wright, L. S. (1990). The relationship of alcohol, tobacco, marijuana, and other illegal drug use to delinquency among Mexican-American, Black, and White adolescent males. *Adolescence, 25*, 171–181.

Woodward, D. M. (1981). *Mainstreaming the learning disabled adolescent*. Rockville, MD: Aspen Publishers.

Woodward, D. M., & Peters, D. J. (1983). *The learning disabled adolescent*. Austin, TX: Pro-Ed.

Woolfolk, A. E. (1990). *Educational psychology*, 4th ed. Englewood Cliffs, NJ: Prentice-Hall.

Young, G. A., Rathge, R., Mullis, R., & Mullis, A. (1990). Adolescent stress and self-esteem. *Adolescence, 25*, 333–341.

Author Index

A

Abbeduto, L., 43, 203
Abbot, T., 194
Abood, D., 294
Adams, G., 161, 163
Adams, P., 335
Adler, S., 68
Alain, 335
Alberto, P., 136, 145, 153, 154
Aldridge, J., 34, 55
Algozzine, B., 194, 459
Aliki, 335
Allaire, J., 193
Allen, D. A., 34, 51, 207, 216, 219, 234
Allen, G. R., 325
Allen, J. E., Jr., 240
Allen, R. R., 231
Alley, G. R., 408, 423, 442
Allington, R. L., 307
Allred, R. A., 373
Altman, R., 48, 156
Amster, J. B., 106
Amster, W. M., 106
Anderson, D., 121, 277
Anderson, R., 153, 175
Anderson, R. C., 459
Anderson, T., 456
Anderson, T. H., 259
Anthony, D., 194
Antle, N., 335
Applalachian Educational
   Laboratory, 323
Aram, D. M., 40
Armbruster, B. B., 259
Arnett, J., 458
Aronson, A. E., 41
Asch, P., 335
Audet, L. R.,
Azrin, N. H., 48

B

Baca, L., 69
Baer, D. M., 122, 162, 163, 175, 224
Bagnato, S. J., 101, 102
Bailet, L. L., 58, 375, 411
Bailey, D. B., 100
Bailey, E. J., 309, 428
Bain, A. M., 60
Baker, B., 188
Bakken, L., 456

Baldwin, M., 172
Balian, L.,
Ball, D. W., 318
Balla, D. A., 47
Ballan, L., 335
Balthazar, E. E., 47
Bamman, H.,
Banikowski, A., 410
Bankson, N. W.,
Bankston, N. W., 231
Barbe, W. B., 357
Barclay, K. D., 261, 320
Barenbaum, E. M., 427
Barney, L., 172
Barret, J., 335
Bartel, N. R., 107, 126, 127, 204, 205, 206, 207, 210, 225, 243, 275, 284, 349, 355, 368
Barton, B., 335
Barudin, S. I., 244, 293, 311
Baskin, L., 335
Bateman, B., 119, 318
Bates, M., 275
Battaglla, A., 335
Bauer, A. M., 448
Baum, A., 335
Baum, J., 335
Bausell, R. B., 122, 278
Bean, R. M., 102, 269
Beard, G. H., 454
Beck, I. L., 328
Becker, J., 335
Becker, W. C., 318
Beckman, K., 335
Beers, J. W., 375
Belch, P., 323, 324
Bellah, M., 335
Bennett, J., 335
Bereiter, C., 74, 410, 430
Berenstein, J., 335
Berenstein, S., 335
Berko, F., 196
Berko, J., 11
Berkowitz, S., 194
Berlin, L.,
Bernstein, B., 72, 73, 74, 84
Bernstein, D. K., 7, 14, 15, 22, 60
Bernthal, J. E., 231
Bertrand, N. P., 122, 322
Bezzi, R., 348, 351
Biberdorf, J. R., 124
Biel, C. D., 69, 84
Biemer, C., 458

Bierne-Smith, M., 34, 203
Bigler-Burke, L, 46
Bileck, M.,
Billingsley, B. X.,
Binet,
Blachowicz, C. L. Z., 226
Blackstone, E., 188
Blair, R., 297
Blair, T. R., 248, 294
Blank, M., 327
Blau, A. F., 215, 216
Bliss, C., 184, 188
Bliss, L.,
Bloom, L., 5, 13, 26, 34, 51, 58, 138, 212
Blum, I. *125*
Bohannon, J. N., 15, 17, 18, 19, 21, 22, 23
Bolton, S., 177
Bond, G. L., 391
Boning, R. A. 332
Bonne, R., 335
Bonner, G., 141
Boorstein, H., 193
Boose, J., 225
Borkowski, J. G., 122
Borstein, H., 194
Bos, 27
Bowen, M. E., 408, 422, 437
Bowerman, M. F., 13
Boyer-Shick, K., 348
Brady, P. M., 86
Brand, O., 335
Brandenberg, F., 335
Braun, L. A., 357
Bray, C., 224
Bricker, D. A., 20, 136, 174
Bricker, W. A., 20, 134, 135
Bridge, C. A., 355
Brigance, A. H., 413
Briggs, T., 136
Brigham, T., 423, 439
Brimer, R., 135, 136, 140, 173, 177, 183
Brink, J.,
Brooke, L., 335
Brooks, P., 43, 203
Brophy, 101
Browder, D. M., 244, 292, 311
Brown, A. L., 326
Brown, K. L., 231
Brown, L., 124, 173, 311
Brown, M. V., 335

Brown, M. W., 335
Brown, V.,
Brown, V. L., 104
Brown, W., 191
Brueckner, L. J. 391
Bruner, E., 316
Bruner, J., 136, 139
Bryan, T., 14, 276, 457
Bryant, B., 241, 261, 264, 284
Bryen, D., 175, 193, 203
Buchan, V., 431
Budd, C., 193
Buhr, J. C., 202
Buium, N., 46
Bullis, M., 136
Bunce, B. H., 226
Burberry, J., 194
Burke, C., 270
Burke, G. M.,
Burkhart, L.,
Burningham, J., 335
Burns, J. M., 204, 208, 212
Burns, P. C., 379, 430, 432, 459
Burton, T., 134
Busch, R., 248
Butterfield, W. H., 292
Buttrill, J., 458
Byrne, K., 43
Bzoch, K. R., 24, 28

C

Calculator, S., 43
Caldwell, M. L., 294
Camereon, P., 335
Camp, B. W., 292
Campbell, B., 50
Campbell, J., 244, 311, 313, 318
Cantrell, J., 194
Capabianco, R. F., 43
Carbo, M. L.,
Carle, E., 335
Carlisle, M.,
Carlson, L., 136
Carlson, R. K., 437
Carnine, D., 260, 284
Carpenter, R.,
Carr, E., 180, 184
Carrier, J., 154, 183, 191, 192
Carrow, E., 104
Carrow-Woolfolk, E., 139, 175
Carter, J. L., 43
Cartwright, G. P., 412, 415

Case, J. L., 231
Catterson, J., 263
Cavanaugh, J. C., 122
Cermak, C., 207, 220
Chalfant, J. C., 55
Chall, J., 247, 248, 255, 258, 277, 284, 294, 297, 298
Chan, L. K., S., 326
Chandler, B., 122, 278
Chapman, R., 176, 179
Charles I of England,
Charlip, R., 335
Cheseldine, S., 46
Chiang, B., 287
Chinn, P. C., 68
Chisholm, R. W., 43
Chomsky, N., 8, 12, 17, 18, 19, 134, 138, 173
Christenson, S. L., 426
Cimorell Strong, J. M., 224
Cipani, E.,
Clark C., 191
Clark, C. R., 223
Clark, F. L.,
Clary, D. L., 214, 232
Cleland, C. C., 50, 134
Clymer, T., 298
Coggins, T.,
Cohen, B. H., 81
Cohen, L., 388
Cohen, M., 195
Cohen, S. A., 406, 443
Cohen, S. B., 386, 405, 406, 408, 426, 428
Cohn, M., 217
Cohrs, M., 141
Cole, J., 173
Cole, L., 140
Cole, M., 173
Cole, P. A., 58, 78
Cole, P. G., 326
Coles, G., 40
Colletti, J., 453
Collins, J. L., 437
Colson, S. E., 455
Commins, N. L., 81
Compton, C., 134, 140, 141
Connors, N. A., 460
Considine, K., 335
Cook, B., 335
Cooke, N. L., 123
Coon, C., 193
Cooper, E. B., 60, 203
Cooper, H. M., 121, 277
Cooper, J., 151, 354
Cooper, J. D., 56
Coughran, L., 223
Cowin, E., 202
Crain, S. K., 250, 297
Crais, E. R., 149, 152
Crews, W. B., 459
Crist, K., 145
Croll, P., 278
Cronin, M. E., 124

Crossland, C., 379, 380, 381
Crowe, T. A., 78, 79
Cullinan, D., 318, 454
Culp, D.,
Cummins, J., 86, 88. 90
Cunningham, P. M.,
Cynamon, A., 437

D

Dale, P. S., 18
D'Alelio, W. A., 441
Dangel, H. L., 466
Daniels, H., 359
Dankowski, C. E., 432
Dashiell, S., 177
David, L. E., 50
Davies, C., 191
Davis, B. X., 225
Davis, C., 175, 334
Davis, T., 153, 175
Dawson, M. A., 427
Dawson, M. M., 275
Decker, T. W., 405, 406, 427, 432, 443
Dehouske, E. J., 406, 434
deLabry, J., 154
DeMaster, V., 379, 380, 381
Denison, L., 161
Deno, S. L., 102, 267, 269, 275, 287
Denton, P. H., 325
de Regniers, B., 335
De Serres, B., 226
Deshler, D. D., 325, 408, 423, 442, 470
Detamore, K., 188, 195
Devar, L. T., 354
de Villiers, J. G., 8, 24, 25, 43, 46, 159
de Villiers, P. A., 8, 24, 25, 43, 46, 159
DiLorenzo, T. M., 124
Dinkmeyer, D., 223
Di Simone, F.,
DiStefano, P. P., 277, 278, 288
Divoky, D., 69
D'Nealian Handwriting, Book 4, 356, 357, 358
Dobrich, W., 202
Dodds, J., 141
Dodds, T., 332
Dollard, J., 48
Domanska, J., 335
Doob, L. W., 48
Dorry, G. W., 292, 293
Dosderor, D. R., 449
Dowdy, C. A., 37, 471
Downer, M. A.,
Doyle, B. A., 227, 462
Drew, C., 39, 140
Dudley-Marling, C., 61, 232
Duff, M., 335
Dulin, K. L., 310

Dunn, L., 225
Dunn, L. M., 103, 262
Dunst, C., 151
Durlak, J. A., 456
Durrell, D. D., 263
Dyck, N. J., 244, 293
Dyer, K., 155

E

Eble, K. E., 14
Edly, L.,
Edmark Associates, 315
Edmonds, M. H., 21, 23
Edwards, S., 214, 232
Egan, M. W., 39
Egan, W., 140
Eimas, P. D., 25
Einsel, W., 335
Eisenson, J., 41, 54, 58, 60, 202
Ekwall, E. E., 265, 288, 291
Elder, P., 175
Elford, G., 396
Elium, M. D., 124
Ellis, E. S., 271, 272, 435, 470, 472
Ellsworth, P. S., 284
Emberly, B., 335, 336
Emberly, E., 336
Emihovich, C., 69
Engelmann, S., 74, 316, 318
Engleman, S., 223
Englert, C. S., 410
Entrikin, D., 311
Epstein, M. H., 86, 102, 114, 121, 203, 269, 277, 318, 408, 454, 469, 471
Erickson, L. M., 124
Esveldt-Dawson, K., 124
Ets, M., 336
Evans, J., 91
Evans, S., 145
Evans, W., 145
Eyde, D., 156

F

Faas, L. A., 55
Fader, D. N., 439
Falcon, S. C., 289
Falvey, M., 145
Fandal, A., 141
Fant, C. G., 8
Farrar, M., 46
Favell, J. E., 124
Feldman, C. F., 14
Fennimore, F., 429
Fernald, G. M., 291
Ferreiro, E., 346
Ferrell, K., 124
Fey, M. E., 219
Figueroa, R.,
Fillmore, C., 138
Finch-Williams, A., 44, 45

Fink, W. T., 124
Finley, J. R., 292
Finn, D. F., 37
First, J. M., 69
Fischer, R. M., 234
Fitzgerald, J.,
Fitzgerald, M. T., 234
Flack, M.,
Flanders, 101
Flavell, J. H., 21, 44
Fletcher, D., 294
Fodor, J., 138
Fokes, J., 224
Foley, R. M., 86, 114, 121, 203, 277, 454
Folk, M. C., 244, 311, 313
Forbes, C. R., 278
Ford, A., 124
Forness, 5, 125
Forster, P. 227
Foster, R., 140, 462
Foushee, D. R., 43, 203
Fox, B.,
Foxx, R. M., 48
Francis, W. N., 297
Frankenberg, W., 141
Freagon, S., 175
Fredricks, H., 164
Freeman, F., 348, 351
Fristoe, M., 193
Fuchs, D., 102, 267
Fuchs, L. S., 102, 267, 269
Fullerton, P.,
Furner, B. A., 344

G

Galdon, P., 336
Galofaro, B., 223
Galton,
Garber, N. B., 50
Garcia, 85
Gardner, B. T., 2, 183
Gardner, M.,
Gardner, R. A., 2, 183
Garman, D.,
Garrett, E., 136
Gary, A. L., 428
Gaskins, I. W., 296
Gaskins, R. W.,
Gearheart, B. R., 40, 56, 145, 454
Gearheart, C. J., 40, 56, 145, 454
Gelman, R. G., 336
Gentry, D., 43
Gentry, J. R., 375
Gerber, M. M., 373, 374, 376, 396, 400
Germann, G., 102
Gersten, R., 260
Gibbs, D. P., 60, 203
Gibson, E., 286
Gickling, E. E., 102, 269
Gillette, Y., 174, 176, 180
Gillingham, A., 316

Gilstrap, R.,
Ginsburg, H., 73
Ginsburg, M., 336
Giordano, G., 429
Glaser, A. J., 225
Glass, E. W., 315
Glass, G. G., 315
Glazzard, P., 234
Gleason, J. B., 2, 14, 15
Glover, J., 428
Goetz, L., 172
Goin, L., 119
Gold, M., 145
Gold, V., 28, 468
Golden, J. M., 408, 436
Goldenberg, D., 98
Goldman, R., 218, 220
Goldsmith, S. C., 53, 55
Gonzales, E., 84
Goodfellow, F., 332
Goodman, K. S., 269, 270, 284
Goodman, L., 193, 194
Goodman, Y., 75, 81, 270
Gordon, J., 387
Gorrell, J., 151
Gould, B. W., 56, 424, 425, 426, 434, 464, 465
Graden, J., 277
Graham, S., 274, 294, 320, 326, 348, 349, 351, 354, 359, 360, 369, 373, 374, 386, 389, 390, 398, 399, 401, 434
Graubard, P., 439
Graves, D. H., 426
Graves, S., 34, 55
Gray, B. B., 224
Gray, R., 410
Green, J., 191
Greenbaum, C. R., 382, 385
Greenburg, P., 336
Greer, J., 153, 175
Gregg, N., 405, 464
Gregg, S., 410
Gregorich, B., 336
Gregory, N. M., 318
Gregory, R. P., 318
Grice, 14
Griffey, Q. L., 188, 326
Griffin, W. J., 225
Grilley, K., 186
Grinnell, M., 195
Grossman, H. J., 50, 100
Grove, D., 164
Grove, R., 50
Guerin, G. R., 208, 214, 215
Guess, D., 162, 163, 172, 175, 224
Guetzloe, E., 456
Guevara, A. E., 91
Guilfolle, E., 336
Gullickson, A., 343, 349
Guralnick, M., 174
Gustason, G., 194, 195
Guszak, F. J., 323
Gutman, A. J., 46

Gwaltney, W., 464

H

Haban, T., 336
Hackney, C. S., 357
Hackney, D., 318
Hagerty, P. J., 277, 278, 288
Hagin, R. A., 343, 344, 359, 368
Hagood, B. F., 433
Hall, J. K., 406, 429
Hall, M., 180
Hall, R. J., 373, 374, 376, 396
Hall, S., 48
Hallahan, D. P., 12, 40, 41, 121, 140, 408, 453
Halle, J., 173, 174, 194
Halle, M., 8
Halliday, M. A. K., 15, 25, 203
Halverson, J., 455
Hamilton, L., 194
Hammer, S. E., 114
Hammer, T., 456
Hammill, D. D., 53, 55, 104, 126, 127, 204, 205, 206, 207, 210, 225, 275, 348, 349, 355, 368, 377, 413, 417
Hamre-Nietupski, S., 179, 181, 184, 193
Handleman, J. S., 124
Hanlon, R. C., 207, 220
Hanna, J., 373
Hanna, P. R., 373
Hanna, R.,
Hanner, S., 318
Hansen, C. L., 434
Harbin, G. L., 100
Hardman, M. L., 39, 40, 43, 140
Hargis, C. H., 54, 55, 289, 307, 309
Haring, N. C., 119, 140, 145, 318
Harris, A. J., 247, 248, 256, 286, 288, 294, 320
Harris, K., 434
Harris, K. C., 275
Harris, S. L., 124
Harris-Schmidt, G. P., 4
Harris-Vanderheiden, D., 176, 191
Hart, K., 455
Hart, B., 16
Hart, M., 195
Hartman, A. C., 398
Harvey, J., 110, 114
Hasbrouck, J., 202
Hasselbring, T., 119, 379, 380, 381
Haught, P., 145
Hearn, S., 458
Hedrick, D., 222
Hegge, T. G., 315
Heidi, E. F.,
Heilman, A. W., 248, 275, 277, 297, 300, 303, 308
Heins, E., 318

Heller, H. W., 121, 297
Heller, M. F., 321
Helm-Estabrooks, N., 224
Helmick, R., 48
Helwig, J. J., 354
Henderson, E., 375
Henderson, R. W., 69
Hendrickson, J., 290
Henning, D., 101
Herbert, M., 343
Heron, T. E., 123, 151, 155, 275
Hess, R. D., 72
Heward, W., 123, 151
Hiebert, E. H., 355, 459
Hill, C., 180, 181
Hillerich, R. L., 432
Hilliard, A. G., 82
Hirshoren, A., 134, 334
Hixon, T. J., 34
Hodges, R. E., 373, 375, 376, 386, 391
Hodgkinson, H. L., 69
Hoff-Ginsberg, E., 46
Hoffman, H., 336
Hoffnung, A., 150
Hofmeister, A. M., 275
Holdgrafer, G., 139
Hollis, J., 183
Holmes, M., 278
Holt, W. J., 353
Holtz, K.,
Hoover, J. J., 400, 471
Hopkins, B. I., 354
Hopkins, B. L., 428
Hopper, C., 48
Hopper, R., 20
Horn, E., 373, 394, 395
Horner, R., 193
Horner, V. M., 81
Horstmeier, D., 143, 163
Horton, K., 225
Hoskins, B., 223
Hourcade, J. J., 244, 293, 311
Howell, K., 145, 391, 392
Hresko, W. P., 53, 104
Huer, M.,
Hughes, C. A., 260, 311
Hummel, L. J.,
Hunt, J., 44, 150, 157
Hunt, J. T., 334
Hunt, K. W.,
Hurlbut, B., 191
Hurley, O. L., 320
Hurvitz, J. A., 226
Hutchins, P., 336

I

Iacono, T., 172, 193
Idol, L., 269, 275
Ingram, D., 5
Irvin, J. L., 460
Isaacson, S. L., 410, 424, 429, 430
Isaacson, W., 234

Itard, J. M. G.,
Iwata, B., 191

J

Jackson, D. A., 353
Jacobowitz, T., 462
Jago, A., 195
Jago, J., 195
Jakobson, R., 8
James, S. L., 2, 7, 10, 24, 25
James VI of Scotland, 15
Jastak, J. F., 262
Jastak, S., 377
Jenkins, J. M., 124
Jenkins, J. R., 124
John, V. P., 81
Johns, J. C., 354
Johnson, D. D., 250, 251
Johnson, D. J., 405, 428, 436
Johnson, G., 318, 422
Johnson, I. M., 331
Johnson, J., 188
Johnson, J. L., 456
Johnson, L. A., 294, 320, 326
Johnson, M. B., 377
Johnston, E. B., 225
Johnston, J. R., 43
Jones, S. D., 426
Jones, T., 183
Jordan, D. R., 360
Joseph, S., 360
Joslin, S., 336
Joyce, D., 175, 193
Jungebut, A., 240

K

Kaczmarek, L., 158, 180
Kahn, J. V., 44, 195
Kaiser, A., 135, 137, 139, 172, 173, 174, 175
Kalan, R., 336
Kalk, M., 302
Kameenui, E. J., 294, 308, 327
Kamii, C., 157
Kampwirth, T. J., 275
Kaplan, J., 145, 154
Kaplan, S. J., 48
Karlan, G., 136, 179
Karlin, R., 226
Karnes, M. B., 224
Kataoka, J. C., 123
Katayama, K. M., 43, 203
Kates, B., 191
Katz, J., 138
Kauffman, J. M., 12, 39, 40, 41, 48, 49, 107, 121, 140, 159, 267, 359, 408, 453, 454, 455
Kaufman, A. S., 377
Kaufman, N. I., 377
Kavale, K., 125
Kayser, H., 80, 86

Kazdin, A. E., 124
Kazuk, E., 141
Keats, E., 336
Keenan, V., 302
Keith, T. Z., 121, 277
Kellogg, J. B., 69
Kellogg, S., 336
Kellogg, W., 183
Kemp, J. C., 222
Kennedy, J. H., 458
Kent, J., 336
Kent, L., 160
Keogh, W., 136
Kerlin, M. A., 323
Kerr, M. M., 452, 473
Kirk, S. A., 243, 248, 250, 315, 422
Kirk, W., 315
Kirsch, I. S., 240
Kirschner, A., 194
Klein, L., 336
Klein, M., 180
Kleppe, S. A., 43, 203
Kliebhan, J. M., 248
Knoblock, P., 48
Knox, M., 174, 179
Knutson, N., 102
Koch, K., 439
Koegel, R. L., 124, 158
Koenig, L. A., 69, 84
Koenke, K., 344, 346, 359
Kologinsky, E., 180, 184
Kolstoe, O. P., 122
Konrad, D., 409
Kottmeyer, W., 382, 384
Kraetsch, G. A., 429
Krappman, V. F., 121
Krassowski, E. B., 224
Krauss, J. W., 46
Krauss, R., 336
Kubey, R., 453
Kumin, L., 57
Kuska, A., 396
Kymissis, E., 175
Kysela, G., 139

L

Labov, W., 75, 76, 77, 78, 79
Lahey, M., 34, 51, 58, 137, 140, 175, 212, 215
Lambert, D. L., 452, 473
Lambert, H., 193
Lambert, N., 140
Lamberts, F., 315
Landers, M. F., 122, 278
Landis, C., 172
Lane, S., 102, 269
Langone, J., 122, 244, 247, 422
Langstaff, J., 336
Lapointe, C., 53
Larsen, S. C., 104, 348, 349, 377, 410, 413
Larson, R., 453
Larson, V., 468, 469
Laurence, L. E., 336

League, R., 24, 28
Ledford, R. R., 427
Lee, L. L., 18
Lee, V., 138
Leff, R.,
Lehman, K., 437
Leigh, J., 349
Leinhardt, G., 326, 426
Leland, H., 140
Lenneberg, E. H., 19, 20, 24, 26, 40, 138
Lenz, B. K., 260, 311, 435, 470, 472
Leonard, L. B., 35, 36, 37, 51
Lepre-Clark, C., 46
Leri, S. M., 47
Lerner, J., 4, 53, 55, 60, 248, 320, 368, 390, 419, 423
Leverentz, F.,
Levine, A., 39, 450
Levine, L., 224
Lewis, J., 219
Lewis, R., 140, 141
Lewis, R. B., 187
Lexau, J., 336
Liberman, I., Y., 55
Liberty, S., 193
Liles, B. V., 223
Lindsey, J. D., 323
Lippert, E.,
Lippke, B., 188, 195
Lloyd, J. W., 121, 125, 318
Lloyd, L., 173, 193, 194
Lobel, A., 336
Lombardino, L., 150
Lorenz, L., 290
Lou, S.,
Lovaas, O., I., 49, 158
Love, H. D., 50
Lovitt, T. C., 153, 277, 287, 359, 410, 427
Lucas, E. V., 21
Lucas, V. H., 357, 398
Luckasson, R., 100
Luebke, J., 79, 454
Luftig, R., 143, 343, 348, 349
Lynch, E. M., 426
Lyon, R., 242, 295

M

MacDonald, E. T., 190
MacDonald, J. D., 39, 56, 139, 143, 150, 157, 163, 174, 176, 180
Mack, S., 336
MacKenzie, P., 191
MacMillan, D. L., 86
MacWhinney, B., 23
Magee, P. A., 53
Magnusson, D., 267, 456
Maher, S. R.,
Mahoney, G., 139, 174, 195
Maier, A. S., 208, 214, 215
Mainord, J. C., 50

Maloney, K. B., 428
Mandell, C. J., 28, 468
Mandlebaum, L., 324, 334, 471
Manion, B. B., 464, 465
Mann, P. H. 382
Mann, V. A., 202, 203
Manni, J. L., 86
Manning, M. L., 344
Manzo, A. V., 324
Marcus, S., 156
Mardell-Czudnowski, C., 98
Markwardt, F. C., 262, 377
Marquis, I., 188
Marsh, G. E., 37, 68, 203, 205, 449
Marston, D., 267
Martin, B., 336
Martin, F. N., 54
Marzano, R. J., 277, 278, 288, 328
Masters, A. A., 454, 460, 463, 466
Matson, J. L., 124
Maurer, S., 134
Mayer, M., 336
Mayhall, W. F., 124
McCardle, P., 78, 79
McCarthy, C., 139
McCarver, R. B., 124
McClennen, S.,
McClure, J., 302
McConkey, R., 46
McCormick, L., 2, 3, 13, 15, 23, 24, 39, 43, 46, 49, 60, 61, 86, 140, 175, 205, 218, 220, 221, 234
McDade, H. L., 234
McDonnell, J., 164
McGimsey, J. F., 124
McGiver, A.,
McGovern, A., 336
McGuffey Informal Reading Inventory,
McKeown, M. G., 328
McKinley, N. L., 468, 469
McLaughlin, B., 69, 70
McLaughlin, T. F., 121, 397
McLean, J. E., 13, 21, 22, 138, 150, 155, 163
McLean, J. R., 44
McLoughlin, J., 140, 141, 459, 464
McMenemy, R. A., 353, 431
McMullen, D., 293
McNaughton, S., 191, 192
McNeill, D., 19
McNeill, E. B., 439
McNerney, C. D., 46, 172, 181
McNutt, G., 127
McNutt, J. C., 47
McVicar, R., 426
Mecham, M., 141
Mehring, T. A., 410, 455
Meichenbaum, D., 121
Meisel, J. M., 90, 91
Memling, C., 336
Mendoze, M. A., 353
Menyuk, P., 40, 43, 44
Merbler, J. B., Jr., 118

Mercer, A. R., 263, 332, 391, 408
Mercer, C. D., 145, 263, 332, 391, 408, 449, 450, 452, 453, 454, 458
Merrill Linguistic Reading Program,
Meyer, A., 455
Meyers, A., 124
Miccinati, J., 291
Michaelis, C., 174
Michel, T. A., 462
Miller, G. A., 18
Miller, J., 174, 179, 193
Miller, L., 60, 219, 235, 359, 360, 369, 373, 374, 390, 398, 401
Miller, N. E., 48
Miller, T., 175, 176
Milling, L., 141
Mimms, A., 121, 277
Minke, K. A., 292
Minner, S., 464
Minskoff, E., 315
Miramontes, O. B., 81
Mire, S. P., 43
Mirenda, P., 172, 193
Mithaug, D., 193
Mix, B., 141
Moerk, E., 172
Moffett, M., 337
Molt, L., 143, 173, 179, 184, 186, 188, 193, 194
Momeier, G.,
Moores, D. F., 223
Moran, M. R., 212, 214, 235, 411
Morehead, M. K., 391, 392
Mori, L. F., 454, 455, 460, 463, 466
Morley, J., 202
Morris, R. C., 225
Morris, WSKE II,
Mowrer, O. H., 48
Moyer, S. B., 287, 289, 290
Mullins, J., 360
Mullis, A., 458
Mullis, R., 458
Muma, J. R., 231
Musselwhite, C., 138, 173, 184, 186
Myers, J., 134, 172
Myers, P. I., 53, 55
Myers, S., 180
Myklebust, H. R., 405, 413, 428, 436
Myles, B. S., 189

N

Naremore, R. C., 20, 81
Nathanson, D., 437
National Commission on Excellence in Education,
Naylor, D., 50
Nedboy, R., 406, 437, 439
Neisworth, J. T., 101, 102
Nelson, C. M., 452, 473

Nelson, K., 21, 26
Nemeth, M., 202
Ness, J., 455
Nevin, A., 269, 275
Newcomer, P. L., 53
Newcomer, P. O., 287
Newland, T. E., 353
Newport, E., 139
Nicol, A. R., 449
Nietupski, J., 179, 181
Nihira, K., 140
Niizawa, J., 458
Nissen, H., 183
Nodest, J., 337
Nolan, S.,
Norman, J. E., 354
Norris, J. A., 394
Norton, E. M., 456
Nowacek, J., 230

O

Oberlin, K. J., 465
O'Connell, C., 145
O'Donnell, R. C., 225
Oka, E. R., 327
Oleksiuk-Velez, A., 215
Oliver, P. R., 124
Oller, D. K., 41, 54, 180
Olsen, L., 69
Olson, J., 43
Olswang, L.,
O'Malley, M. H., 12, 13, 20
O'Neill, M., 337
Opticommunicator,
Orelove, F. P., 124
O'Rourke, T., 193
Ortiz, A. A., 75, 80, 90
Ortiz, L., 84
Osborn, J., 223
Osborn, L. R.,
O'Shea, D. J., 290, 459
O'Shea, L. J., 284, 290
Otis-Wilborn, A., 202
Otto, W., 353, 354, 431
Overholser, J., 455
Owens, R. W., 46, 47, 136, 137, 138, 139, 162, 183
Owens, S., 381

P

Palinscar, A., 326
Palmer, J., 337, 356, 357, 358
Paluszny, M. J., 50
Paolucci-Whitcomb, P., 269, 275
PARC v. Pennsylvania, 134
Paris, S. G., 327
Parker, F., 11
Parnell, G. G., 427
Paschal, R. A., 121
Pate, J., 184
Patrick, G., 337

Patton, J. R., 34, 39, 48, 60, 71, 86, 102, 110, 114, 119, 121, 123, 124, 203, 234, 244, 269, 274, 277, 310, 318, 405, 406, 443, 454, 469, 471
Paul-Brown, D., 156, 157
Payne, J. S., 15, 34, 110, 203, 234, 274, 311, 454, 469
Payne, R. A., 34, 110, 234, 274, 311, 454, 469
Peak, T., 191
Pear, J. J., 124
Pearson, D. P., 261
Peckins, I., 223
Pecyna, P., 184
Pegnatore, L., 180, 181
Peppe, R., 337
Perkins, W. H., 232
Peschka, C. M., 124
Peters, D. J., 461
Petersham, M., 337
Peterson, G., 150
Peterson, G. A., 46
Peterson, N. L., 34, 37, 51, 55
Petty, W. T., 398, 408, 422, 437
Pfetzing, D., 194, 195
Phelps, J., 343, 344
Phelps, T., 429
Phelps-Gunn, T., 225, 422, 430, 432
Phelps-Terasaki, D., 225, 422, 429, 430, 432
Phillips, J. L., 47
Piaget, J., 4
Pickert, S. M., 226
Pisha, B., 455
Plaskon, S. P., 386, 408, 426, 428
Plourde, L.,
Podemski, R. S., 68, 69, 71, 91
Polloway, C. H., 244, 245, 246, 257, 258, 259, 287, 288, 303, 305, 318
Polloway, E. A., 34, 39, 47, 53, 71, 86, 102, 110, 114, 119, 121, 122, 123, 124, 126, 127, 203, 234, 244, 245, 246, 265, 269, 274, 277, 287, 288, 303, 305, 310, 318, 332, 367, 405, 406, 411, 420, 427, 432, 442, 443, 454, 469, 471
Polushkin, M., 337
Pond, R.,
Pope, L., 241
Poplin, M., 410, 417, 426
Poulson, C., 175
Prater, G., 464
Prater, R., 223
Prather, E.,
PRC Light Talker,
PRC Touch Talker,
Premack, D., 2, 136, 183, 191
Price, B. J., 37, 68, 203, 205, 449
Price, L. A., 455
Prizant, B. M., 43, 235
Proctor, W., 122, 278

Q

Quackenbush, R., 337

R

Rago, W. V., 48, 134
Ranieri, L., 124
Rather, T., 179, 184
Rathge, R., 458
Reed, C., 375
Reed, M. T., 54
Reetz, L. J., 226, 227
Regan, R. R., 100
Reich, P., 232
Reich, R., 195
Reichle, J., 136, 179
Reid, D. K., 53, 104
Reid, K.,
Reinen, S., 191
Reis, E. M., 343, 344
Reschly, D. J., 86
Reutzel, D. R., 430
Reynolds, M. C., 126
Rice, M., 139, 173, 202
Rich, A., 406, 437, 439
Richards, M. H., 456
Richgels, D. J., 204, 208, 212
Rieff, M.,
Rieke, J. A., 219
Riekehof, L., 193
Riemer, G., 405
Rilla, D. C., 226
Rincover, A., 124
Risley, R., 16
Rittenhouse, R., 134, 172
Ritter, D. R., 455
Robbins, A. M., 41, 54
Roberts, J. E., 149, 152
Robinett, J., 188
Robinson, G., 244, 293
Robinson, H. B., 47, 137, 325
Robinson, N. M., 47, 136
Robinson, S. M., 29, 217, 229
Roderique, T., 244
Roe, B. D., 459, 460, 461
Rogers-Warren, A., 139, 163
Romig, C. A., 456
Romski, M., 184
Rondal, J. A., 46
Rooney, K., 121, 327
Rose, D., 455
Rose, S.,
Rosenberg, J.,
Rosenberger, P. B., 40
Rosenfield, S., 102
Rosenshine, B., 124, 326
Ross, A. D., 274, 297
Ross, A. O., 408
Rossetti, C., 337
Rotatori, A., 175
Rotholz, D., 194
Rowland, C., 136
Ruder, C. C., 226
Ruder, K., 135, 161, 226

Rudorf, E. H., 373
Rupley, W. H., 248, 294, 297, 327
Ryan, B. P., 224
Ryan-Flottum, M.,
Rynders, J., 46

S

Sabornie, E. J., 454
Sachs, J., 24
Sacks, S.,
Sailor, W., 141, 162, 163, 172, 173, 175, 224
Salend, S. J., 222
Salisbury, C., 158
Saltzman, L., 360
Salvia, J., 86, 148
Salzberg, B. H., 354
Samuels, S. J., 54, 56, 256, 284, 289, 308
Sandall, S. R., 124
Sankey, P., 293
Santos, O. B., 202
Sapir, S., 41
Saulnier, K., 194
Sawyer, R., 434
Saxman, J. H., 34
Scanlon, D., 435
Scarborough, H. W., 202
Scarmadalia, M., 410, 430
Scarr, S., 39, 43, 450, 452, 458
Schaeffer, A. L., 473
Scheer, J., 337
Scheffelin, M. A., 55
Scheibel, G., 191
Schewel, R., 273, 274, 316, 326, 327, 334
Schiefelbusch, R. L., 2, 3, 13, 15, 23, 43, 49, 135, 137, 145, 173, 183, 205
Schilit, J., 294
Schlesinger, L. M., 13
Schoenbrodt, L., 57
Schoenheimer, J., 202
Schommer, M.,
Schoolfield, L. D., 316
Schreibman, L., 158
Schubert, D. G., 330
Schuler, A., 172
Schuler, R.,
Schumacher, G.,
Schumaker, J. B., 434
Schumm, J., 387
Schwartz, R. M., 461
Schweigert, P., 136
Scott, J. A., 459
Searle, D., 61, 232
Sears, R. R., 48
Sebald, H., 453
Secord, W.,
Seely, P., 139
Seibert, J., 180
Seidenberg, P. L., 60
Seitz, S., 156
Seltzer, M. M., 46

Semel, E. M., 53, 104, 214, 215, 217, 232
Sendak, M., 337
Dr. Seuss, 337
Sevick, R., 184
Shames, G. H., 47, 232
Shane, H.,
Shanker, J. L., 288, 291
Shankweiler, D., 55
Shapero, S., 278
Sharpton, W., 145, 153, 154
Shaw, C., 337
Shea, T. M., 448
Shellhaas, M., 140
Shepherd, M., 303
Sherrod, K. B., 46, 150
Sherwin, J. S., 424, 425
Shinn, M. R., 102
Shipley, K. G., 43, 203
Shipman, D. A., 56
Shipman, V. C., 72
Shores, R. E., 290
Shriberg, L. D., 34
Shugarman, S. L., 465
Shulevitz, U., 337
Siegel, G., 138
Siegel-Causey, E., 172, 173
Silberberg, M. C., 261
Silberberg, N. E., 261
Silbert, J., 284
Silvaroli, N. J., 265, 266
Silverman, F., 186
Silverman, R., 426
Simmons, D. C., 308
Simmons, E., 277
Simms, R. B., 289
Simon, C.,
Simon, C. S., 223
Simpson, R. L., 189
Sinclair, H., 139
Sindelar, P. T., 290
Sink, D. M., 424
Sipay, E. R., 247, 248, 256, 286, 288, 294, 320
Skaar, G., 337
Skinner, B. F., 15, 17, 153, 173
Skinner, C. H., 397
Sloan, J. M., 57
Slosson, R. L., 262
Smith, D.,
Smith, D. D., 287, 290
Smith, F., 18, 284, 424
Smith, J., 153
Smith, J. D., 47, 244, 265
Smith, J. E., 332
Smith, J. O., 225
Smith, K., 455
Smith, L., 180
Smith, M., 124, 136
Smith, P. L., 471
Smith, R. J., 353, 431
Smith, R. M., 408
Smith, S., 189
Smith, S. W., 114

Smith, T. E. C., 34, 37, 55, 59, 68, 69, 80, 86, 202, 203, 205, 234, 449, 462, 467, 469, 471, 472
Smolin, L.,
Snell, M. E., 39, 48, 49, 140, 153, 155, 157, 159, 180, 186, 193, 203, 244, 292, 311, 313
Snider, V. E., 256, 258, 260, 320, 326
Snow, C. E., 248, 258, 277, 284, 294
Snyder, L. K., 153, 154, 155
Snyder-McLean, L. K., 13, 21, 22, 44, 46, 138, 150, 163
Sommers, R. K.,
Sonneborn, R., 337
Spache, D. E., 379
Spache, E. B., 320
Spache, G., 263, 320
Speck, G., 343
Speece, D. L., 275
Spier, P., 337
Spinelli, F. M., 219, 234
Spirito, A., 455
Spooner, F., 121, 277
Spradlin, J., 138
Sprague, M., 188
Squires, E. L., 226, 227
Staats, A. W., 17, 292
Staats, C. K., 17
Stainback, S., 134
Stainback, W., 134
Stans, D., 423, 439
Stanwix House, 331
Stauffer, R. G., 321
Stefanakos, K., 223
Steiner, V.,
Stemmer, N., 138, 173
Stempel, L., 343, 344
Sternberg, L., 140, 161, 163, 172, 177, 180, 181
Stevens, R., 124
Stevens, T. M., 398
Stevenson, H. W., 4
Stewart, T., 139
Stice, C. F., 122, 322
Stillman, B., 316
Stillman, R., 173
St. Louis, K., 138, 173, 184, 186
Stoddard, K., 459
Stoel-Gammon, C., 54
Stokes, F., 122
Stoll, A.,
Stoller, L., 121
Stoodt, B. D., 459
Storm, R. H.,
Stowitschek, C. E., 354
Stowitschek, J. J., 354
Stremel, K., 154
Stremel-Campbell, K., 136, 139, 194, 195, 223
Stricker, A., 373
Stricker, G., 287
Strickland, B., 114

Strong, W., 430
Strother, D. B., 121
Stubbs, J. C., 311, 315
Stubbs, M., 373
Sugarman, S., 136
Suiter, P., 382
Sullavan, C., 464
Sullivan-Burstein, K., 276, 457
Sundbye, N. W., 293
Swanson, H. L., 96, 101, 102
Swenson, K., 124
Switzky, H., 175

T

Taenzer, S. F., 207, 220
Takahashi, C., 458
Talkington, I. W., 48
Tanner, J. M.,
Tarver, S. G., 275, 284
Taylor, O. L., 58, 78
Taylor, R., 140, 141, 151
Taylor, W. H., 87
Teberosky, A., 346
Templeton, S., 375
Terhaar-Yonkers, M., 54
Terrace, H., 183
Terrell, B. Y., 219, 234
Tharinger, D., 140
Theodore, G.,
Thomas, C. C., 410, 434
Thompson, V. P., 102, 269
Thorne, M. T., 318
Thornton, T. P., 345
Thurber, D. N., 360
Thurlow, M. L., 277, 426
Thurman, S., 138
Thypin, M., 332
Tiedt, I. M., 69, 70, 78, 82, 83, 436
Tiedt, P. L., 69, 70, 78, 82, 83
Tiegerman, E., 15
Tikofsky, R., 12, 13, 20
Timberlake, J. B., 316
Tindal, G., 102, 202
Tippets, E., 348
Tobin,. A.,
Tolstoy, A., 337
Tomasello, M., 46
Tomlin, D., 438
Tompkins, G. E., 471
Topper, S., 193
Torgeson, J. K., 326, 408
Tsimbos, L., 439
Turnbull, A. P., 114
Turnbull, H. R.,
Turner, C., 360
Turnure, J., 46, 139
Turvey, J. S., 121
Tway, E., 423

U

Umberger, F., 136
U. S. Department of Education, 240, 277, 297

Utley, B., 172
Uzgiris, I. C., 44, 136, 150

V

Vacc, N. N., 361
Vaglum, P., 456
Valencia, S. W., 261, 277, 278, 288
Vallecorsa, A., 426, 427, 434
Valletutti, P., 180
Van Allen, R., 428
Vanderheiden, D., 191
Vanderheiden, G., 176, 186, 188
Vandever, T. R., 311, 315
Van Dijk, J., 181
VanEtten, C., 334
Van Hattum, R., 228
Varnedoe, D. R., 234
Varnhagen, S., 400
Vaughn, 27
Vaughn, S., 387
Vender, B.,
Vincent, L., 124, 161
Vinograd-Bausell, C. R., 122, 278
Virginia Department of Education, 22
Vogel, S. A., 409
von Tetzchner, S., 180
Voth, V. P., 389
Vygotsky, L., 41, 139

W

Waddell, J. G., 326
Wade, S. E., 55
Wagenaar, T. C., 462
Wagner, K., 137
Walberg, H. J., 121, 126
Waldo, L., 180
Walker, C. M., 141, 250, 255
Walker, J., 343, 349
Wallace, C., 75, 81
Wallace, G., 107, 121, 267, 459, 464
Wallace, T., 229
Wallach, G. P., 53, 55
Wallach, L., 286
Wallach, M. A., 286
Wallen, C. J., 289
Walls, R., 145
Walmbold, C., 158
Walsh, B. F., 315
Walter, O., 158
Walton, J. H., 78, 79
Wang, M. C., 126
Warncke, E. W., 56
Warner, M. M., 325
Warren, S., 135, 137, 139, 163, 172, 173, 174, 175
Warren-Leubecker, A., 15, 17, 18, 20, 21, 22, 23
Waryas, C. L., 154, 223
Wasylyk, T. M., 357
Watson, B. L., 96, 101, 102, 334

Watson, C., 337
Watts, W. D., 456
Weaver, R. L., 462
Webber, M. S., 28
Webster, E. J. D., 396
Webster, L., 343, 349
Webster, N., 2
Weinberg, R. A., 39, 450
Weiner, E. S., 417
Weinrich, B. D., 225
Weinstein, T., 121
Weishahn, M. W., 56
Welber, R., 337
Weller, C., 58
Weller, E., 195
Welsh, J. M., 121
Wendt, E., 188
Wesson, C., 202, 205, 216, 218
West, J. F., 275
Westerman, G.,
Westling, D. L., 122, 124
Westman, J. C., 243
Westman, J. D., 296
Wheat, M. J., 100
Wheeler, A. J., 354
White, O., 145
Whitehead, R.,

Whorf, B. L., 3
Widerstrom, A., 138
Wiederholt, J. L., 104, 127, 241, 261, 264, 284
Wiig, E. H., 6, 47, 53, 58, 104, 207, 214, 217, 224, 232
Wilcox, B., 173
Wildman, T. M., 326
Wildsmith, B., 337
Wilkinson, F., 262
Wilkinson, G. S., 377
Wilkinson, I. A. G., 459
Will, M. C., 126
Willette, R., 223
Williams, F. L., 79
Williams, P. C., 54
Williams, W., 313
Willis, J. H.,
Wilson, B. E., 78, 79
Wilson, C. L., 115
Wilson, J., 126, 127
Wilson, M.,
Wilson, M. S., 225
Wilson, P., 193
Wilson, R., 471
Windmiller, M., 140
Winnikur, D. W., 86

Withers, C., 337
Witt, B., 225
Wolf, B., 39, 140
Wolfe, M., 292
Wolkstein, D., 337
Woltosz, G., 176, 177, 186, 192
Woltosz, W., 176, 177, 186, 192
Wondriska, W., 337
Wong, B. Y. L., 326, 374, 396, 408
Wood, B. S., 15, 24, 26, 223
Wood, R. W., 343, 349, 354, 356, 357, 358, 360, 368
Woodcock, R. W., 191, 263, 377
Woodward, D. M., 461, 466, 467
Woolfolk, A. E., 450, 454
Workman, A. E., 121
Wright, H., 337
Wright, L. S., 456
Wulz, S., 180
Wyatt v. Stickney, 134

Y

Yerkes, R., 183
Yockell, E., 290
Yoder, D. E., 43, 174

York, R., 311, 313
Young, G. A., 458
Younginger, K., 143, 173, 179, 184, 186, 188, 193, 194
Ysseldyke, J. E., 86, 100, 148, 277, 426
Yule, V., 373

Z

Zaner-Bloser Evaluation Scale, 351, 356, 357, 358
Zawadzski, R., 360
Zawolkow, E., 194, 195
Zeaman, D., 292, 293
Zegar, M.,
Zemach, H., 337
Zemach, M., 337
Zemelman, S., 359
Zigler, E., 47, 154
Zigmond, N. K., 55, 326, 426, 473
Zimmerman, I.,
Zimmerman, J. M., 426
Zollinger, M., 422, 427
Zolotow, C., 337

Subject Index

ABA methodology, 423
Acuity, 54
Adaptive behavior scales, 140
ADHD, 47
Adolescence, 448
  definition of, 449
  drug and alcohol abuse, 456
  peer influence during, 452-453
  pregnant, 456, 459
  social skills in, 454
  suicide in, 455-456
Advanced organizers, 229, 274,
  463, 472
Alcohol abuse by adolescents, 456
Alternative communication
  systems, 177, 179
American Association on Mental
  Deficiency, Adaptive
  Behavior Scale, 140
American Indian languages, 82
American sign language (Ameslan
  or ASL), 193, 194
Analysis
  configurational, 288
  contexual, 272, 288, 302,
    307-310
  organizational, 416, 417
  phonetic, 288, 291, 296-298,
    300, 302, 310
  structural, 288, 302-307, 390,
    416-417
  word, 256, 258, 291, 308
Applied behavior analysis, 267
Apraxia, 60
Acquisition learning, 119, 121
Articulation difficulties, 231
Assessment, 97, 99-100
  cognitive, 150-151
  communication, 176
  construct model of, 96
  curriculum-based (CBA), 101,
    102, 211, 267, 269, 382
  ecological, 101-102
  of handwriting, 348-352
  instruments (for initial
    language), 141, 143
  language, of students with
    severe disabilities, 139
  of minority culture students,
    86-87
  of oral language, 205, 207, 208,
    216
  principles, 100-101
  procedures for, 105-107, 109
  of reading, 261-271
  social, 150
  of spelling, 376-382
  standardized, 86
  steps in, 97
  teacher interactions during, 149
Assessment in Infancy checklist,
  150-151

Attentional
  deficits/problems, 47-48, 54,
    406
  in adolescents, 462
  reading, 284
Auditory
  attention span, 249
  comprehension, 462
  discrimination, 10, 55, 249
  readiness for reading, 286
  skills, 226-227, 241
Augmentative communication
  devices/systems, 39, 177
  nonoral, 184, 186, 187, 188,
    191-192
Autism, 49, 50, 184, 189, 193
Automatic expressive processing,
  60
Automatic receptive processing,
  55-56

Babbling, 25, 54, 173
Barnell-Loft Specific Skills Series,
  332
Basal
  readers, 330-331
  spelling series, 377-388
Basic School Skills Inventory
  (BSSI), 349
Behavior(s)
  approach to reading, 291-292
  competing, 136
  disorders/problems in
    adolescents, 453, 454
  extralinguistic, 136
  interactive, 150
  modification, 125
  prelinguistic, 136
  self-abuse, 49
  self-stimulatory, 48
  Skinner's theory of, 137-138,
    173
  theories of language delay, 135
Bereiter, Carl, 74
Bibliotherapy 330
Bilingual(ism)
  and bilingual education, 71,
    80-81, 84, 88
  Binary contrasts, 8
  Black
    dialect/English, 75-79, 80
    linguistic differences, 72
    definition of, 80
  Hispanic, 81-82
  immersion programs, 88, 90
  intervention/education
    materials, 91, 203
Blissymbols, 188, 191, 192
Bloom's semantic/cognitive
  theory, 138
Brain pathology, and language
  disorders, 39-41

Brainstorming, adjective (activity),
  428
Case grammar approach, 215
CATS approach, 429
Charles I of England, 15
Chomsky, Noam, 12-13, 15,
  17-18, 138, 173
Classroom Reading Inventory,
  266-267
Clinical Evaluation of Language
  Functions, 104
Cloze procedure, 267, 303, 308-
  309
Cluster approach, 328
Coaching, language, 222
Code switching, 90
Cognition
  definition of, 43
  and written expression, 406
Cognitive
  approaches to spelling
    instruction, 395-396
  assessment, 150-151
  basis for language
    development, 21-22
  basis for spelling, 375
  behavior modification, 121,
    125, 434
  coaching, 327
  development, 44, 138-139, 174
  discrimination, 137
  maturation, 21
  processes, 4, 5, 7, 28, 97
  readiness, 21, 135
  reading strategies, assessing,
    271
  skill deficits, 287-288
  theories (Piagetian), 135
Color-coding, 398
Commission on Reading, 459
Communication, 172-173, 441
  abstract systems of, 191-193
  adult-to-child, 139
  alternative, 177, 179, 183-184
  augmentative systems, 184, 186
  for children with severe
    disabilities, 136
  definition of, 172
  development, 138
  disabilities, 57
  disorders, 56
  facilitated, 189
  functional, 161-162, 207, 221
  intent(ion), 56, 422, 427
  interpersonal, 4, 222
  language as, 2, 14, 39
  nonoral/nonverbal, 136, 173,
    181, 183, 184
  with parents, 115
  prelanguage/preverbal, 150,
    180-181

problems, 34, 43, 51, 216
severe disabilities and, 48, 136
skills, 22
spontaneous, 226
in students' language, 84
symbolic, 173
transactional model of, 46
unit, 139
verbal/oral, 6, 114, 136, 137,
  235
written, 6, 343, 346-347, 405,
  422, 427
written expression as, 406
Communication board, 186, 191
Communication Programming
  Inventory, 177
Competing behaviors, 48-50
Composition, 409. See also
  Written expression
  assessment of, 410-412
Comprehension, 13, 22, 25, 28,
  54, 55, 56, 137, 203
  assessing, 104
  instruction, 298
  language, 286
  listening, 229, 231
  monitoring, 325-327
  reading, 58, 125, 256, 258,
    259-260, 271, 284, 288,
    290, 291, 294, 295, 303,
    308, 318, 320, 325, 330,
    461, 462
  vocabulary, 321
  word, 302
Computer-assisted instruction
  (CAI), in spelling, 387, 400
Configuration, in spelling
  instruction, 398-399
Consonants, 9, 19, 25, 250, 255,
  286, 298, 300, 302
Construct model of assessment, 96
Content, language, 7, 13-14
Contextual
  analysis, 256, 258, 272, 288,
    307-310
  cues/clues, 304, 305, 310, 311,
    461
Contingency management,
  154-155
Contractions, 303
Conversation, 27, 28, 57, 163
  rules of, 14
Cooing, 25
Cooperation, with parents, 275,
  277, 278
Coordination (motor), 363
COPS, 434
Corrected-test method of spelling
  instruction, 398
Counseling adolescents, 469
Cover, copy, compare strategy for
  spelling, 397

Creativity, in writing, 429, 436-437
CRP (Corrective Reading Program), 318
Criterion-referenced assessment/testing, 102, 104
Cues, 153-154, 307-308, 334, 368
  in spelling instruction, 398
Culture(al)
  differences in, 68-69, 82, 84
  language and, 4
  minorities, 81, 88
  pluralism, 69, 75, 80
Curriculum
  -based assessment, 101, 102, 211, 267, 269
  -based measurement, 211
  criteria for selecting, 126-127
  integrated, 123
  LAP, 160
  whole-language, 221, 284, 317, 319, 321, 344, 359

Decoding, 2, 5, 22, 54, 55, 250, 271
  in reading, 284, 295, 296, 300, 303, 305, 315, 318, 330, 458, 459
DEFENDS strategy, 435
Denver Developmental Screening Test-Revised (DDST), 141
Depression, in adolescents, 455-456
Diagnosis
  educational, 96, 139, 143
  reading, 261
Diagnostic-prescriptive instruction/teaching, 96, 102, 110
Dialects, 7, 70-71
  Black, 75-79, 80
Dictionary skills, 401
Directed Reading Thinking Activities (DRTA), 322-323
Disability(ies). See also Mild disabilities; Severe disabilities
  in adolescents, 449, 453
  and communication, 136
  federal definitions of, 59
  group teaching for students with, 126
  and homework, 121
  minority students with, 68
Discovery approaches, 391, 394
Discrimination, language, 17, 136, 137, 151, 173, 233
  auditory, 249, 300, 302
  errorless, 293, 315
  in infancy, 24-25
  letter, 286-287
  in reading, 241
Discrimination, cultural/racial, 100
DISSECT, 311
DISTAR program, 164, 316, 318

Diversity/differences
  crosscultural behavioral, 86
  cultural, 68-69, 82, 84
  language/linguistic, 70, 71
D'Nealian handwriting program, 357-358, 362
Dolch word list, 250, 313
Down syndrome, and language, 46
Drafting component of writing, 424
Drug abuse, 456
Durrell Analysis of Reading Difficulty, 263
Dysarthria, 60
Dysgraphia, 60
Dysfluency, speech, 231
Dysnomia, 58

Echolalia, 25, 49-50
Edmark Reading Program, 315
Education for All Handicapped Children Act, 97, 234. See also IDEA; Public Law 94-142
Electronic communication aids, 188
Eligibility for special education, 97, 98, 99
Encoding, 2, 5, 6, 56, 204
Engelmann, Siegfried, 74
English orthography, 373-374, 375, 394, 395
Environment
  language-enriching, 252
  natural, 155-158, 214, 219, 220-221, 222, 235, 400
Environmental Language Intervention Program (ELIP), 143, 150
Environmental Language Inventory (ELI), 143, 150
Environmental Pre-language Battery (EPD), 143, 150
Error analysis, 211
  spelling, 379-381, 382
  in written expression, 416-417
Error detection and correction, 401
ESL (English as a second language), 85, 439
Essay test-taking, 442-443
Evaluation, 98, 110. See also Assessment
Eye-motor coordination, 363, 365

Fading, 123, 154, 159
  in reading, 287, 293
FAPE, 59, 109
Feedback, 119, 123, 221, 400
  in handwriting, 368
  in reading, 318
  in spelling, 389
  in written expression, 408, 426-427
Fernald approach, 290-291
Fingerspelling, 193, 194, 195

Fitzgerald Key, 430
Fluency
  handwriting, 367
  oral, 119, 121
  reading, 248, 256, 290
  spelling, 386, 389, 393
  in written expression, 412, 415, 428, 429
Formulation, in written expression, 405
Functional Speech and Language Training Program, 162-163

Generalization(s), 158-159, 218, 219, 222, 394, 410, 470
  of learning, 122-123, 161, 235, 400
  phonic/phonetic, 298, 302, 373
  of reading skills, 246, 255, 303
Gesture(al)
  communication, 173
  as communication system, 193
  prompts, 153
Giant word units, 74
Gifted and talented, 86
Gillingham-Stillman Remedial Reading Manual, 316
Glass Analysis for Decoding Only, 315-316
Grammar, 11, 202
  development of, 28
  transformational, 12-13, 18, 19
Graphemes, 10, 250, 373
Gray Oral Reading Test-Revised, 264-270
Group instruction, 124, 126
Grouping, 123-124, 126

Handwriting, 6, 343-344, 374
  assessment of, 347-348
  cursive, 365-366
  D'Nealian method, 357-358, 360
  fluency, 393
  formal assessment of, 348-349, 351-352
  handedness and, 363, 368-369
  informal assessment of, 348
  instruction in, 344, 355-358, 361, 363-366, 368-369, 466-467
  keyboarding, 360
  legibility of, 353-354, 358, 361, 366, 367, 467
  manuscript, 365
  manuscript versus cursive, 359-360
  Palmer method of, 345, 358
  readiness, 349, 363
  remediation, 368
  script, 360
  sequence of skills in, 347
  skills, 353, 355
  teacher-designed assessment of, 352-355

Zaner-Bloser scale, 348, 349, 357
Hearing loss/impairment, 195
  and language disability, 41, 43, 51, 54, 184
  and reading, 316
Hispanic bilingualism, 81-82
Holistic approach(es). See also Whole language
Holophrases, 26
Homework, 121, 276, 277, 457

IDEA provisions, 42, 47, 59, 100, 109, 110
  of IEP, 112
  for IFSPs, 152
  for fair assessment, 86
  for minority students, 68
  for special education placement, 89
Ideation, 419, 426, 436-437, 439
Illiteracy, 240
Imitation, 22. See also Modeling
Individualized education programs (IEPs), 37, 59, 89, 98-99, 102, 109, 112, 114, 382
  annual goals, 111-112, 113-114
  justification for, 110
  levels of performance, 11, 112
  short-term objectives, 114
Individualized family service plans (IFSPs), 99, 152
Individualized instruction/ individualization, 84, 123, 222
  in spelling, 388, 389
Informal Reading Inventory (IRI), 264-266
Innate theory of language development, 18-20
Institutionalization, 46-47, 58
  and generalization, 158
Instruction(al)
  child-directed, 157
  control, 151
  in creative writing, 436-437
  direct, 157, 235, 332, 391
  group, 124
  in handwriting, 344, 355-358, 361, 363-366, 368-369
  individual, 123-124, 235
  mand model of, 157
  language, 157
  objectives, 107
  for reading, 243, 274-275, 277-278
  in spelling, 386-388, 396, 398-401
  time-delay model of, 157
  top-down, 284, 334
  in written expression, 406
Intention (to communicate), 56, 422, 427
Interactionist perspectives of language acquisition, 20-23, 139, 174

Intervention, early, 219-220
  with adolescents with
    disabilities, 464-465
  language, 220-221
Intervention Strategy Program,
  161
Isolated skill approach, 464

Journals/diaries, writing, 439

Kansas Institute for Research on
  Learning Disabilities, 325
Kaufman Test of Educational
  Achievement, 377
Keyboarding, 360-361
Knowledge
  cognitive, 13
  domain-specific, 396
Kottmeyer's Diagnostic Spelling
  Test, 382, 383-384

Labeling, 87, 103
Language, 2, 3, 135. *See also*
  Assessment; Nonverbal
  language; Oral language
  acquisition, theories of, 15,
    17-23, 137, 173
  comprehension, 286
  content, 7, 13-14
  contextual, 394
  deficit view of, 71-75, 79, 84
  definition of, 2, 38, 172-173
  differences position, 75-76
  diversity, 70
  dominant, 88
  elaborated, 72
  expressive, 5, 11, 25, 27, 28,
    41, 44, 160, 222, 448, 471
  figurative, 14
  form, 7
  formal codes of, 69-70, 79
  functional, 145, 219, 468
  functions of, 4
  inner, 4
  instruction, 157
  literal, 13
  patterned, 334
  patterns, 70, 106
  programs, commercial,
    221-222
  public, code of, 169
  readiness, 44, 150
  receptive, 5, 25, 27, 28, 153,
    160, 176, 188, 216, 218,
    222, 226, 241, 459
  repetitions, 49
  restricted, 72-74
  rules of, 18
  social basis of, 44, 46
  standard, 69, 76
  stimulation, 222, 226
  teaching/instruction/training,
    137, 163, 175, 220
  use, 7, 14

written, *See* Composition;
  Handwriting; Written
  expression

Language acquisition device
  (LAD), 18, 138
Language Acquisition Program
  (LAP), 160-161
Language delay, 35, 37, 40, 51,
  56, 134, 136, 138, 160, 175,
  177
Language development
  in adolescence, 28-29
  in childhood, 25-28
  formal assessment of, 140-143
  and generalization/
    maintenance, 158
  in infancy, 24-25
  research on, 134, 137
  sequence of, 24-26, 28-29
  theories of, 137
Language disabilities, 34, 57
  in acquisition, 37
  in adolescence, 448, 459
  classifying, 34-35, 37-38
  hearing loss and, 41, 43
  mild-moderate, 51-52
  severe, 38-39, 40, 41, 43, 44,
    47, 48-51, 139
  in written expression, 464-465
Language experience approach
  (LEA), 289, 320-322, 330,
  427
Language probes, 145-146, 211,
  214
Language sample, 106, 146, 148,
  150, 215-216
Learned theory of language
  development, 15, 17, 20
Learning
  acquisition, 119, 121
  generalization, 122-123
  maintenance, 123
  and motivation, 454
  parent role in, 234
  stages, 119, 121-123
  strategies, 396, 434
  time, academic, 277, 278
Learning disabilities, 40, 51, 57,
  203
  adolescents with, 453, 454, 455
  keyboarding and, 360-361
  in reading, 242, 287, 290, 315,
    316, 318, 323, 326
  and spelling, 376, 387
Learning strategies, 470, 471
Learning Through Literature, 332
Left-handedness, 368-369
Legibility (of handwriting),
  353-354, 358, 361, 366,
  367, 467
Letter
  formation, 353, 355, 368
  reversals, 287-288
Letter writing, 432

Linguistic(s), 17
  approaches to spelling,
    390-392
  assessment, 151
  awareness, 375
  competence, 7, 26, 47
  functioning, 157
  performance, 7
  prerequisites to reading, 249
  processing, 53
  rules, 138
  training, 134
Listening, 6, 27, 54, 180, 204,
  205, 219, 248, 249, 405
  in adolescence, 448, 458, 462,
    463-464, 471
  assessment of, 208, 212, 214
  attention, 229, 462
  comprehension, 229, 231
  critical, 231
  developing, 226-227, 229
  formal tests for, 209-210
  to parents, 115
  problems in, 217-218
Literacy, 240-241, 245-246, 247,
  346

Maintenance, 158, 159
  curricular option, 471
  of handwriting skills, 367
Manually coded English, 194
Mapping, 57
Mean length of utterance (MLU),
  11-12, 216
Meaning, 7, 11, 12-13, 14, 18, 19,
  22, 55, 56, 138, 192, 204,
  231
  constructing, 459
  reading for, 249, 284, 294, 297,
    303, 310, 319, 328
Memory, 241, 346, 453
Mental retardation, 205
  adolescents with, 453, 454, 455
  and language disorders, 43, 44,
    46-47, 49, 50, 51, 203
  language program for, 164
  and reading, 244, 311, 313
Merrill Linguistic Reading
  Program, 331
Metacognition, 271, 322, 326
Metacommunication, 207
Metathesis, 35
Mild disabilities
  adolescents with, 454
  and handwriting, 368
  and reading instruction,
    310-311
  and spelling, 375, 386, 391,
    394, 395, 399, 400
  and written expression, 408,
    426, 428, 441, 442, 464
Milieu language training, 155
Minority cultures
  and immersion programs, 90
  language problems in, 88

and special education, 68
  teaching strategies with, 91-92
Miscue analysis, 269-271
Mixing language systems, 91
Mnemonic strategies/devices, 125,
  399, 443
Modeling, 27, 119, 153, 218, 222,
  230
  handwriting, 365
  pragmatics, 468
  reading strategies, 290, 322
  writing, 432
Monolingual immersion, 88
Morality, 452
Morphemes, 11, 231, 256, 302,
  303
Morphology, 11-12, 58
Morse code, 192
Motivation, 139
  in adolescents, 454-455,
    468-469
  to communicate, 176, 408, 423
  language as, 27
  in reading, 274
  in spelling, 399
  in written expression, 420-421,
    437
Motor skills, 346, 363
Multipass, 325
Multiple oral readings, (MOR),
  289-290
Multisensory approaches to
  spelling, 389
Mutism, 49, 50

Nasality, 10
National Assessment of
  Educational Progress
  (NAEP), 121, 240
National Committee of Reading,
  247
Native American languages, 82
Nativist theory of language
  acquisition, 18
Neurological Impress Method
  (NIM), 290
Nonoral programming, 184
Non-SLIP, 191-192
Nonverbal language, 172
Note-taking, 441-442, 458, 471

Objectives
  instructional, 107
  short-term, 118
Object permanence, 21, 44
Open highways, 331
Operant conditioning, 17, 20, 138,
  173
Operants, 17, 155, 159, 291, 315
Oral language, 26, 58, 202. *See
  also* Speech
  assessing, 208, 211, 212,
    214-216
  commercial programs, 221-222,
    223-225

expressive, 204, 232, 234
fluency, 248
functions of, 203
hearing loss and, 41
instructional activities, 222, 226, 467-468
parent involvement in, 234
as a process, 52-53
programs, 218-220
receptive, 204, 232, 448
samples, 106
and severe disabilities, 172
Oral language assessment, 99, 100, 140
formal, 208, 209-210
goals of, 207
informal, 208, 211, 212, 213, 214, 216
Organizational integrity, 410
Otitis media, 54

Palmer method of handwriting, 345, 358
PALS program, 161-163
Paralanguage, 2
Paragraph sense/paragraphing, 409, 416, 421, 430-431
Parallel talk, 27, 230
Parent(s) participation
in assessment, 100
in IEP, 112
in language intervention, 234-236
in skill maintenance, 158-159
and cooperation with, 275, 277, 278
Peabody Individual Achievement Test-Revised (PIAT), 262, 377
Peabody Picture Vocabulary Test-Revised, 103-104
Peer
influence in adolescence, 448, 452-453, 456, 458
tutoring in spelling, 387
Perception, 44
Perceptual-motor skills, 346
Phelps Sentence Guide Program, 429
Phonemes, 7, 11, 19, 250, 286, 295, 298, 373
classifying, 8-10
and graphemes, 10
Phonic(s), 19, 25
and phonetic analysis, 250, 288, 291, 296-298, 300, 302, 310
teaching, 298, 300, 302, 311, 313, 461
in teaching spelling, 390
Phonic Reading Lessons, 315
Phonological awareness, 295, 375
Phonology, 7-10, 54-55
Phonovisual method, 316

Piaget, Jean, 15, 20, 21, 44, 135, 136, 150
Poetry writing, 437, 439, 441
Portfolio assessment, 211
Poverty, effects of, on language, 74
Pragmatic(s), 14, 15, 56, 212
approach to language acquisition, 22-23, 139
instruction in secondary school, 468
Prelinguistic, 172
Prewriting, 406, 408-409
activities, 321-322
instruction, 422-424
Probes
academic, 211
language, 145-146, 214
Production, 56, 58, 60
phonological, 60
Proficiency, 119, 121, 123
Prompts, 151, 153-154, 222, 398, 468
Proofreading, 410, 421-422, 432, 434
Psycholinguistic(s), 17
theory of language acquisition, 15, 138, 139, 296
use of miscue analysis, 269-271
Public Law 94-142, 111, 114.
See also Education for All Handicapped Children Act; IDEA; IEP

Questioning strategies, 323
self-, 326, 396, 433

Readability
analysis, 294
level of textbooks, 259, 260
Readiness
handwriting, 349, 363
reading, 241, 248-249, 286-288
Reading, 6, 28, 54, 55, 203, 226, 240-241
adolescents and, 459-462
attention, 284
comprehension, 58, 125, 241, 246, 258, 259-260, 288, 295, 318, 320, 325
development, 247-248, 250
diagnosis, 261
difficulties, 241, 243, 298, 318, 320
disabilities, 240, 274, 291, 326
fluency, 248, 256
functional, 244, 245-246
learning disabilities in, 242
linguistic prerequisites to, 249
literacy, 245-246
oral, 277
parent involvement in, 275, 277, 278
program, developing, 274-275, 276-277

rapid, 256
readiness, 241, 248-249, 286-288
remedial, 240, 320, 331, 460
at secondary level, 448, 460
silent, 277, 292, 319
for survival, 243-244, 245, 246
vocabulary, 311, 462
wide, 258-260
and written expression, 405
Reading assessment, 261
survey tests, 261-262
Reading Mastery Program, 316, 318
Ready-Set-Go: Talk to Me, 163
Rebus symbols, 191, 309
Reception, 54-56
Referents, 136
Regular education initiative, 126
Reinforcement, 17, 119, 121, 123, 136, 153, 154-155, 159, 173, 219, 400, 454
of handwriting, 367
language, 232
natural, 221, 454
in pragmatics, 468
in reading, 274, 318
in written expression, 423, 428, 429, 439
Remedial
logic, 175
programs, 471
Re-Quest, 324-325
Retardation. See Mental retardation
Role models, 46
Role playing, 222
Rote memorization, 377

Screening, 97, 98, 103
instruments, language, 141
of language functioning, 207
Scripting, 222
Section 504, 59
Self-
correction, 468
esteem in adolescents, 458
evaluation of writing, 432
questioning, 326, 396, 433
talk, 27, 230
Semantic(s), 13, 21, 55, 56, 58, 138, 192, 231
organizers, 57
Semantic mapping, 327
Sendak, Maurice, 334
Sensorimotor experience, 21, 44, 48
Sentence
combining, 430
development, 429
structure, 409
Severe disabilities
assessing language in children with, 139-143, 151

and facilitated communication, 189
and language learning/ programming, 172, 174, 175-176, 180, 184
language programming for, 154, 161, 163
in reading, 244, 311, 313, 315
teaching language to children with, 134-135, 137, 139
Shaping, 155
Sight
vocabulary, 298, 300, 311, 313, 315
words, 288, 289-294
Sign language, 56, 193, 195
Skinner, B. F., 15, 17, 136-137, 153, 173
Slosson Oral Reading Test (SORT), 262
SMART approach to reading, 291-292
Social/pragmatic approach to language development, 22-23
assessment, 150
basis of language, 44, 174
development, 22-23
skills in adolescents, 454
Socialization, 139, 150
Sociolinguists, 139
Social skills, 331
in adolescents, 453, 455
Sound-symbol correspondence/ association, 10, 248, 296, 297, 302, 304, 373, 390
SRA Corrective Reading Program, 318
Spache Diagnostic Reading Scales, 263-264
Spanish language, 71
educational materials, 91
Speaking, 204, 219, 405
formal tests for, 208-210
problems in, 216
Special education. See also Individualized education program
in adolescence, 453, 456, 459
and CBA, 269
eligibility for, 97, 98, 99, 103
and handwriting, 344
interventions, 60-61
language and, 2, 35, 37, 39
minorities in, 68, 86, 87, 89
oral language programs and, 235
and Public Law 94-142, 97, 110
and reading, 275
Section 504 and, 59
skills, 6
teacher, 218
and written expression, 405, 426

Speech, 56, 173
  acquisition, 19
  definition of, 3
  development, 17
  disorders/impairment, 51, 60,
    184
  dysfluencies, 231
  hearing loss and, 41
  lack of. See Mutism
  nonverbal, 56
  patterns, 58
  sounds, 11, 60. See also
    Morphology
  teaching, 136, 232
  severe disabilities and, 163
  telegraphic, 26
Speech-language pathologist
  (SLP), 60-61, 219, 231,
  235-236, 459
Spelling, 6, 331, 373
  assessment
    formal, 376-377
    informal, 378-380, 382
  demons, 396
  development of, 373-376, 380
  disorders/problems, 374, 388,
    389, 396
  errors, developmental, 375
  fluency, 386
  instruction, 386-388, 396,
    398-401, 466
  invented, 375, 393
  phonetic, 316, 373, 375
  remediation, 389-392
  rules, 377, 391
  in secondary school, 466
  whole word approaches to,
    373
Spellmaster, 382, 385
SQ3R, 325, 462
Standard English, 69, 76, 78, 79,
  88, 203, 214
Stanwix House Reading Series,
  331
Stereotypy, 48
Stimulus
  control, 151
  generalization, 158
  prompts, 153-154, 398
Strategy training, 434
Story
  grammar, 433
  maps, 433
  writing, 437
Stress, 458
Structural analysis, 288, 302-307,
  390, 416-317, 461
Study skills, 400, 457, 471
Study-test procedure, 398
Submersion programs, 88
Suicide, 455-456
Survey tests, 261-262

Survival
  skills, 472-473
  vocabulary/words, 311, 394
Survival Words Program, 293
Syllabication, 303-304
Symbols, language, 21, 25, 38,
  137, 172, 174, 184
  systems of, 184, 187, 188, 191
Syntax, 11, 12-13, 55, 58, 192,
  231, 310, 405

TARC (Topeka Association for
  Retarded Citizens)
  Assessment System, 141
Task analysis, 107, 114, 145
Teacher
  competencies in bilingual
    education, 84, 86
  role in oral language
    intervention, 235
Teacher conferencing approach,
  427
Teaching. See also Instruction
  handwriting, 344, 355-358
  one-on-one, 124, 126
  prescriptive, 107, 109
  reading, 284
Teaching Competence in Written
  Language, 430
Teach-write approach, 424-426
Teenagers. See Adolescence
Tests/testing, 96. See also
  Assessment
  achievement, 411
  criterion-referenced, 103, 208
  diagnostic, 263-264
  formal, 103-104, 106
  informal, 104-105, 145, 268
  of listening, 208, 209-210
  norm-referenced, 103, 208
  standardized, 208, 216
  survey, 261-262
  for written expression, 413-414
Test for Auditory Comprehension
  of Language, 104
Test of Early Language
  Development, 104
Test of Language Development-2
  (TOLD), 141, 143
Test of Legible Handwriting, 348
Test of Written Adolescent
  Language-Revised, 104
Test of Written Language-2
  (TOWL-2), 104, 348, 349,
  351
Test of Written Spelling-2, 377
Test-study-test procedure, 398
Thinking
  convergent, 408-409
  divergent, 408
  logical, 44
Time-delay model, 157

Total communication, 195
Tracing (as reading strategy), 291
Transactional model of
  communication, 46
TRIELP program, 164
Type-token ratio, 415
Typing skills, 360-361

Unit planning, 122
U. S. Department of Education,
  240
Utah Test of Language
  Development-3, 141

Van Dijk program, 181
Verbal
  approximations, 17
  language acquisition, 160
  mediation, 4, 197
  prompts, 153
Verbal language instruction for
  children with severe
  disabilities, 135, 137
Visual
  discrimination, 248
  -motor skills, 363, 365
  readiness for reading, 286
  skills, 346
Vocabulary, 55, 202
  acquisition, 409, 421
  building, 328, 428, 468
  child's, 26
  comprehension, 321
  deficiencies, 56
  development, 57, 226, 294,
    296, 310, 374, 428
  expressive, 467-468
  functional, 175
  high interest-low vocabulary,
    332
  protection, 243
  readiness, 286
  reading, 311, 460, 462
  receptive, 160
  sight, 250, 294, 304, 311, 313,
    318, 328
  survival, 311
  teaching, 460-461
  written, 415, 428
Voice disorders, 231
Vowels, 9, 10, 19, 25, 250, 286,
  300, 302, 304
Vygotsky, Lev, 44

Webster, Noah, 2, 250
Werner, Heinz, 44
Whole language approach, 100,
  122, 221, 284, 465
  in handwriting, 344, 359
  in reading, 317, 319, 321
  in spelling, 374, 392, 394

Whole word approach, 289, 297,
  373, 374
"Why and because" method, 431
Wide Range Achievement Test-
  Revised (WRAT), 262, 377
Wide reading, 258-260
Woodcock-Johnson Psycho-
  Educational Battery-
  Revised, 377
Woodcock Reading Mastery Test,
  263
Word(s)
  analysis, 256, 258, 291, 308
  attack, 250, 256, 296, 310, 373
  banks, 289
  comprehension, 302
  compound, 303
  identification strategy, 311
  imprinting, 291
  lists, 394-395
  recognition, 259, 288, 290,
    296, 302, 303, 310, 311,
    315, 320, 461
  sight, 288, 289-294
  survival, 292-294
  units, giant, 74
  unusual, 415-416
  usage, 409
  wall, 428
Words Most Commonly Used in
  Writing, 394, 395
Write-teach approach, 426-427,
  432
Writing, 6, 56, 58. See also
  Handwriting
  in adolescence, 448
  creative, 436-437
  samples, 421
Written expression, 6
  adolescents', 465
  assessment of, 410-412
  creative, 408
  developing, 427
  diagnostic tests for, 413
  holistic approach with, 465
  informal procedures for
    assessing, 414
  instruction in, 406
  postwriting stage of, 410, 432,
    434
  prewriting stage of, 406-409,
    424
  problems with, in adolescents,
    464-465
  therapeutic uses of, 439, 441
  utilitarian/functional, 408, 409,
    421, 423, 424, 427,
    441-443
  writing stage of, 409-410, 424

Zaner-Bloser Evaluation Scale,
  348, 349, 357